Jewellery in Britain
1066 – 1837

Frontispiece
Great George paved in diamonds and with ruby, sapphire and
amethyst details, from the insignia of George III.
Royal Collection.

Jewellery in Britain
1066 – 1837

A DOCUMENTARY, SOCIAL, LITERARY
AND ARTISTIC SURVEY

DIANA SCARISBRICK

MICHAEL RUSSELL

First published in Great Britain 1994
by Michael Russell (Publishing) Ltd.
Wilby Hall, Wilby, Norwich NR16 2JP

Designed by Humphrey Stone

Typeset in Linotron Ehrhardt
at The Spartan Press Ltd, Lymington, Hants
Printed and bound in Great Britain
by Biddles Ltd, Guildford and King's Lynn
Colour sections printed
by Balding and Mansell, Wisbech, Cambs

ISBN 0 85955 190 3

To Martin Norton

Contents

Line Illustrations in the Text

Colour Plates

Monochrome Plates

Foreword

Few nations have evolved without leaving an elaborate legacy surrounding both the making and the wearing of jewellery for ceremonial and personal use. The British were no exception.

The different ways in which jewels were regarded and worn in Britain during the eight hundred years following the Norman Conquest reflect the powerful processes of change that kept transforming the structure of society – a society that thereafter never lost its political and economic independence, however receptive it might be to foreign influences, especially of a technical or cultural kind. By the time this survey opens, jewellery had become more than an item of personal adornment for the enhancement of the wearer's beauty or, because of its supposedly efficacious amuletic properties, the wearer's protection and well-being. Jewellery had long been established as a vehicle for expressing man's place in society – his rank and his wealth. Britain, like the rest of medieval Europe, had developed a strictly hierarchical society, in which the distinctions between the classes were sharply drawn – even down to such superficial details as the clothes they might be permitted to wear and the jewellery they might display on their person. Later, when the enforcement of these sumptuary laws gradually became less effective towards the end of the Middle Ages, the ceremonial function of jewellery both at court and in the wealthier circles of society was in no way diminished – indeed, because of Renaissance Europe's vastly increased wealth, the trend was towards even greater displays of costly jewellery to emphasise the fixed order of society. However, from the advent of baroque fashion after the mid seventeenth century to the beginning of the Victorian era, the role of jewellery was far more subtle and varied – though none the less instructive for the historian of the British social scene.

Indeed, almost as much can be learnt about the role of jewellery in Britain from the documents, the designs and the pictorial evidence as from the small percentage of old jewellery that has survived. Not only have wars, financial crises, thieves and accidental losses taken their toll, but the dictates of fashion have ensured that many a splendid item of jewellery should be melted down and reworked while its precious stones were being recut before re-emerging – almost unrecognisable – in their new settings. The recycling of jewellery has been a large-scale phenomenon that becomes the more difficult to chart the further back in time the study attempts to probe.

For these reasons, the surviving specimens from earlier times have become the corpus of tangible evidence that uniquely serves to illuminate the technical skills of the craftsmen and the artistic merits of the designers, so rarely – and so inadequately – recorded in the archives. They put the 'flesh' on the dry bones of historical record and, indeed, often provide the clue as to how best to interpret the written sources. No survey of the subject can hope to be complete when, patently, neither the documentary sources nor the jewellery itself can provide a comprehensive picture but, in the last seventy years, so much new detailed information has been extruded from both sets of material that a fresh appraisal is both justified and, perhaps, overdue.

The last – and only – time that a book devoted to this subject appeared in print was in 1921, when the late Dr Joan Evans, a former President of the Society of Antiquaries, wrote a youthful account of *English Jewellery from the Fifth Century A.D. to 1800*. Succeeding generations have approached the material in very different ways, using new scientific methods, new photographic archives and new critical criteria to analyse and evaluate the evidence. The story of jewellery in Britain since the Conquest is now a richer – and more objectively observed – heritage in which the part played by foreign artists and craftsmen is more clearly understood. European jewellery, as worn by the top echelons of society, has probably always been international, with certain centres taking the lead at different periods as the quality of patronage and talent fluctuated. To have Diana Scarisbrick's detailed over-view of the complex history of jewellery in Britain is essential if its international contribution is to be accurately assessed. As a prosperous colonial power with territories around the globe, many rich in deposits of gem-stones, gold and silver, Britain began to play a major role in expanding the world's trade in jewellery – but the way in which that story developed belongs to another, and rather different, book. Here, in this survey, which ends before the Victorian era of mass-production, the author has presented the tangible evidence – much of it still in private ownership and, therefore, not easily accessible for study – within the context of the written sources, and, in the process, helps us to understand why, despite the dramatic changes in society, jewels have yet to be outmoded. Jewellery may be the oldest of the decorative arts but it shows no sign of losing its mysterious appeal.

HUGH TAIT

Acknowledgements

I must first acknowledge my debt of gratitude to three former Keepers of the Metalwork Department of the Victoria and Albert Museum: Charles Oman, with whom I discussed the arrangement of the material in this book, Claude Blair, who has given me so much encouragement, and Ronald Lightbown, who drew my attention to the wealth of unexplored documents now housed in the County Record Offices. Their successors in the Department have also been kind: both Marian Campbell and Philippa Glanville have given me useful references, and Dr Richard Edgcumbe has commented on the Georgian section, given me access to the museum's collection of jewellery and obtained illustrations. Thanks are also due to Edwin Wallace of the Photographic Library, Francesca Hyman of the Department of Ceramics, Robert Skelton of the Indian Department and Lucy Cullen of the Department of Architecture and Sculpture.

In the British Museum I have received valuable advice from Antony Griffiths of the Department of Prints and Drawings and from John Cherry, who has read the medieval section. His colleague in the Department of Medieval and Later Antiquities, Hugh Tait, not only read the chapters covering the sixteenth and seventeenth centuries and advised on the choice of illustrations but has very kindly written the foreword. I am profoundly grateful to him.

The staff of other museums who have answered my enquiries efficiently include Alan Jobbins of the Science Museum; Brian Spencer, Rosemary Weinstein and Amanda Herries of the Museum of London; Ian Lowe and Arthur MacGregor of the Ashmolean Museum; Julia Poole and Graham Pollard of the Fitzwilliam Museum; Mary Cra'ster of the Museum of Archaeology and Anthropology, Cambridge; Pamela Wood of the Castle Museum, Nottingham; Glenys Wilde of the City Museum and Art Gallery, Birmingham; Lindsay Allason Jones of the Museum of Antiquities, Newcastle upon Tyne; Evelyn Newby of the Paul Mellon Institute for British Art; Simon Cottle of the Glasgow Museum and Art Gallery; David Caldwell and George Dalgleish of the National Museum of Scotland; and Rosalind Marshall of the Scottish National Portrait Gallery.

I also appreciate help from colleagues abroad: Dr Herta Lepie of the Domschatzkammer, Aachen; Dr Lorenz Seelig of the Bayerisches Museum, Munich; Richard Randall Jnr of the Walters Art Gallery, Baltimore; and Julia Kagan of the Hermitage Museum, Leningrad. I must express my gratitude to Her Majesty The Queen for graciously permitting me to use the Royal Archives at Windsor, to quote from them and to reproduce a painting from the Royal Collection.

I would like to thank Miss Jane Langton CVO and Miss Elizabeth Cuthbert LVO of the Royal Archives. Other archivists and librarians whom I have consulted include the staff of the Westminster Public Library Archives and the Guildhall Archives; and those in the County Record Offices of Berkshire, Clywd, Cumbria, Essex, Devon, Durham, the Isle of Wight, Lancashire, Leicestershire, Norfolk, North Riding, Northumberland, Somerset, and East and West Sussex, as well as those at the National Trust properties of Uppark and Sudbury Hall. I owe a very special debt to Susan Hare of the Goldsmiths' Hall; to Bernard Nurse, Adrian James and John Hopkins of the Society of Antiquaries; and to Colin Stephenson and all the staff of the London Library.

The friends in the sale rooms who have helped me particularly are James Miller, Amanda Stücklin, Peter Hinks and Alexandra Rhodes of Sotheby's, and, from Christie's, Jeremy Rex-Parkes, Peter Cochrane, Katherine Curtis, Juliet Foy, Susan Adams and also Rupert Neelands of the South Kensington branch, who contributed references from eighteenth-century literature. The antique jewellery consultant at Christie's, Mary Feilden, has opened so many doors for me that I would like to record my gratitude for her great kindness. The dealers who have assisted my research include Edward Green of Garrard and Co., who gave permission for me to examine the Garrard ledgers; Edward Donohoe of Donohoe Antiques; David Lavender; Brian Norman of Harvey and Gore; Robert Parsons of Wartski; Michael Bell and Roy de Rosa of S. J. Phillips; Richard Digby; and Diana Foley.

The following kindly answered appeals for information: the Rev. Philip Caraman, S.J., the Rev. Mark Elvins, Rosemary Rendel, the late Owen Parsons, and the Librarian of Emmanuel College, Cambridge, Frank Stubbins. Over the years I have received help from Peter Day, Keeper of the Collections at Chatsworth; from Dr Aileen Ribeiro and Christopher Gatiss, both of the Courtauld Institute; and from Dr Martin Henig, Dick Lyon, Michael Dillon, Dr John Hayward, Gerald Burdon, the Hon. Georgina Stonor, Joe Friedman, John Watts, Rosalind Mazzawi, Benjamin Zucker and Barbara Scott. I have been most fortunate to have had the assistance of my dedicated editor, Paul Chipchase, who undertook the great labour of preparing the text for publication. The book has benefited from his exemplary professional skills and wide learning. I must record too my indebtedness to Humphrey Stone, the designer, for his excellent taste, and to John Goodall, who helped with research, typed the manuscript and compiled the index.

Special thanks are due to the late Denys Sutton, who introduced me to my publisher, Michael Russell; and to John Cornforth of the Fitch Foundation, which has provided financial support. Since the book has been sponsored by S. J. Phillips, from whom I have learnt much, it is gratefully dedicated to the beloved chairman, Martin Norton. Lastly, I must thank my husband, Peter: we discovered antique jewellery together and he has shared the problems and pleasures of writing about it.

Author's Note

Not all the jewellery worn by the men and women of the British Isles over the period from the Norman Conquest to the accession of Queen Victoria was 'made in Britain' by indigenous craftsmen in a distinctively national style. The story is more complicated than that, for much was imported, and from the earliest times foreign goldsmiths and jewellers established themselves in London and the provinces. But whatever their origin, all the jewels discussed and illustrated here have a British provenance or were excavated on British soil. Since they represent only a fraction of the vast quantities that have vanished, the narrative has been based on documentary sources, particularly the family papers now housed in the national libraries of Edinburgh and London and in the County Record Offices. Further evidence has been drawn from portraits, contemporary literature, design books, the records of the Goldsmiths' Company and auction sale catalogues, particularly those of Christie's. Every so often it has been possible to distinguish between continental and British fashions in jewellery; British work can usually be recognised by the use of local materials, patriotic motifs and techniques peculiar to the London trade. There is no doubt that British jewellery, like all the decorative arts, has been much influenced by changes in social customs and style. Its history, built up from fragments of personal detail found in so many diverse sources, brings us closer to the private concerns and familiar emotions of the men and women of the past than any other artistic achievement of these islands.

I

The social context of medieval jewellery 1066 – 1509

The Conquest of 1066 was followed by a great programme of church building which fully established in English art the Romanesque and early Gothic styles that originated in France. The patrons – king, nobility and higher clergy – had, too, a sense of personal grandeur, lived luxuriously, and wore valuable jewellery to assert their rank. In the 1377 version of his poem, *The Vision concerning Piers the Plowman*, William Langland was perhaps recalling the appearance of Alice Perrers, mistress of Edward III, in his description of Lady Mede (Reward):

> I loked on my left half · as the Lady me taughte,
> And was war of a womman · wortheli yclothed,
> Purfiled with pelure · the finest upon erthe,
> Y-crounede with a corone · the kyng hath non better.
> Fetislich hir fyngres · were fretted with golde wyre,
> And there-on red rubyes · as red as any glede,
> And diamantz of derrest pris · and double manere saffres,
> Orientales and ewages · envenymes to destroye.
> Hire robe was ful riche · of red scarlet engreyned,
> With ribanes of red golde · and of riche stones;
> Hire arraye me ravysshed · suche ricchesse saw I nevere.[1]

During the later Middle Ages, when the growing wealth of the towns made it possible for the citizens to display their riches in the same ostentatious fashion, sumptuary laws, such as that of 1363, were enacted to regulate the dress of all, from knight to yeomen, craftsmen and merchants.[2] The futility of such legislation is demonstrated by the quantity of jewellery in wills and inventories, and by Chaucer's descriptions of burghers wearing the luxuries legally reserved for knights and their ladies. Similar laws passed by Edward IV proved equally ineffective,[3] and rich clothing and jewels continued to be worn by all with the means to do so, irrespective of rank.

Inventories and wills, from those of members of the royal family down to those of the rich merchants of London, reveal the wealth of fine jewels which existed in Britain in the Middle Ages. A few items of the first rank have been handed down in treasuries, and others, not necessarily typical, have been found in hoards or on their own. As a result of the great increase in urban archaeology during recent years, it is now possible to examine a much wider range of medieval jewellery, much of it from datable levels and with precise provenances, ranging from the products of master goldsmiths down to the cheaper imitations in gilt bronze set with pastes and even lead alloys with cast replicas of gem-stones and pearls. While some patterns are found across Europe, others seem to have had a very local vogue for short periods. It is, therefore, possible for the first time to examine a much wider range of jewellery than has hitherto been available.

ROYALTY

Although it is ostensibly the story of King Arthur and his predecessors, Geoffrey of Monmouth's *Historia Regum Britanniae* (*c.* 1130) actually describes the splendour of Norman court life. The furs, silk robes, plate and jewels which Henry II bought for himself indicate a decided taste for the fine and rare.[4] Rich dress and jewels are depicted on the tomb effigies of his wife, Eleanor of Aquitaine († 1204), and their daughter-in-law, Berengaria († 1230) at Fontevrault and Le Mans.[5] The importance of King John's collection is confirmed by the number of items he lodged with the Knights Templars in 1204,[6] and by Roger of Wendover's assumption that the king's death had been caused in part by the loss of his treasure in the Wash:

> There befell him so great a grief of mind on account of the things swallowed up by the waves that he was seized by a sharp fever and began to be grievously sick.[7]

According to Matthew Paris the preparations for the marriage of King John's daughter, Princess Isabella, to the Emperor Frederick II in 1235 exceeded all previous royal or even imperial expenditure and display.[8] Roger of Wendover described jewels made for the occasion: a crown 'of most cunning work and from the finest gold and most precious gems, in which were carved four English kings, martyrs and confessors . . . rings likewise and gold brooches ornamented properly with precious gems'.[9] Both Henry III and his wife, Eleanor of Provence, whom he married in 1236, were immensely attentive to details of dress, decoration and ceremonial and set the standard for the court. The climax of royal ostentation was reached in the fourteenth century by Edward III, the Black Prince and Richard II. Richard's magnificent appearance could well have inspired the portrait of Youth in the *Parlement of the Thre Ages*:

> He ne hade no hode ne no hatte bot his here one –
> A chaplet one his chefe-lere, chosen for the nones,
> Raylede alle with rede rose, richeste of floures,
> With trayfoyles and trewloves of full tried perles,
> With a chefe charebocle chosen in the myddes.
> He was gerede alle in grene, alle with golde by wevede,
> Embroddirde alle with besanttes and beralles full riche;
> His colere with calsydoynnes clustrede full thikke,
> With many dyamandes full dere dighte one his sleves.
> The semys with saphirs sett were full many,

With emeraudes and amatistes appon iche syde
With full riche rubyes raylede by the hemmes.[10]

In the fifteenth century Sir John Fortescue, tutor to Henry VI's son, declared that a show of splendour not only bolstered royal authority but was an essential attribute of kingship itself:

It shall need be that the King have such treasure as he may make new buildings when he will for his pleasure and magnificence, and as he may buy him rich clothes, rich stones, and other jewels and ornaments convenient to his state royal. And often times he will buy rich hangings and other apparel for his houses and do other such noble and great costs as besitteth his royal majesty. For if a King did not do so, he lived then not like his estate, but rather in misery and more in subjection than doth a private person.[11]

The necessity for such conspicuous expenditure, which was recognised not only by Edward IV but also by Henry VII, was clearly set forth in the Act of Resumption passed in the first Parliament of the latter. King Henry dressed to impress his foreign visitors, as the Milanese ambassador, Raimondo de' Raimondi, reported to Lodovico Sforza after an audience in 1497:

His Majesty in addition to his wonderful presence was adorned with a most rich collar full of great pearls and many other jewels, in four rows, and in his bonnet he had a pear-shaped pearl, which seemed to me most rich.[12]

The king spent £16,000 in 1503 on jewels for himself and his daughter, Queen Margaret of Scotland, and on 31 March 1504 purchased 'diverse precious stones and other Juells that com from beyonde the see' for £30,000.[3]

COURTIERS

High living, lavish hospitality, expensive clothes and jewels were not limited to the royal family. Among the goods returned to the executors of Maurice, Lord of Berkeley, in 1327 were:

Divers pearls, Emerauds, Rubies, and Saphires, A pair of paternosters of great pearls, two crosses of Gold.[14]

In 1355 Sir Baldwin de Fryville owned a collection of pearls, jewelled circlets, a crown, nouches, two gem-set rings, two jet paternosters with ruby and pearl gauds and five botoners (strips of cloth with buttons for garments) of different designs.[15] Jewels stolen from the Earl of Huntingdon in 1377 included a girdle with pendant and toret, gold and pearl eagles, one of which was set in a large pearl chaplet, an emerald, pearl and sapphire clasp enclosing a figure of St George under a cover plate, rings, brooches, the garnishing for a coronet, and his seal and signets.[16] Another courtier whose taste mirrored that of his royal master was Sir Thomas Percy, K.G., created Earl of

Worcester in 1397. He was beheaded after joining his nephew's rebellion in 1403 and his jewels were seized by Henry IV: a richly jewelled gold circlet (with separate sections loose), several ouches (one with two eagles and another with Richard II's device of the white hart), a girdle, rings, seals, etc.[17] In 1439 Isabel, Countess of Warwick, bequeathed her 'grete sharpe' (perhaps a baldric) to be made into a chalice for the Lady Chapel at Tewkesbury, and her gold chain to be made into a crown for our Lady of Caversham, set with stones taken from her tablets of St Catherine and St George; another tablet, 'With the Image of oure lady with a glasse to-fore it', was to be offered to the shrine of Our Lady of Walsingham; ouches with 'my grete diamond' and 'my Baleys' (spinel ruby) were willed to her son, and pearls and other unspecified jewels were to be sold to fund individual money bequests.[18] Royal favourites flaunted their jewels in public. Piers Gaveston, whose collection was subsequently confiscated, was so decked out at the coronation of Edward II that he 'more resembled the god Mars than an ordinary mortal'.[19] Alice Perrers presided over the Smithfield Joust of 1375 as Lady of the Sun, resplendent in jewels given her by Edward III. But after Edward's death she was obliged to return some of the more important pieces to the Crown.[20]

BURGHERS AND GENTRY

This taste for jewellery was emulated by the tradesmen and burghers. Ralph de Berri, cordwainer of London, bequeathed to his widow, Amice, in 1313 'the moiety of all our chamber as in jewels, gold, silver, and clothes of wool and linen';[21] and the city draper, John Botiller, left in his will of 1361 'all my jewels, viz. rings, brooches and paternosters'.[22] The visionary, Margery Kempe (*c.* 1373 – after 1438), married to one of the wealthiest merchants of Lynn in Norfolk, confessed that she 'wold not leevyn hir pride ne hir pompows aray . . . for sche weryd gold pypys on hir hevyd';[23] and to finance her desire to outshine her friends she started a brewery and a corn-mill. The Paston letters describe the fashion-conscious women of the country gentry, to whom outward signs of status were of the greatest importance. Margaret Paston wrote to her husband after Queen Margaret visited Norwich in 1453:

> I borowd my coseyn Elysabeth Cleris devys [necklace], for I durst not for shame go with my beds among so many fresch [gaily attired] jantylwomen.[24]

In the same mood, her daughter-in-law, Margery, asked John Paston for a new girdle in 1477:

> I ham waxse so fetys [neat] that I be not gyrte in no barre of no gurdyl that I have but of one.[25]

The jewels of a prosperous country lady, Elizabeth Lewkenor, are listed in her inventory of 1465: ten rings (four of them set with diamonds), a chain with an enamelled gold crucifix, girdle, brooches, pearls, head ornaments and paternosters.[26]

ECCLESIASTICAL JEWELLERY

Certain jewels – the ring, the precious mitre and the crozier – were prescribed by Canon Law; and others, such as the rationale, were adopted by local custom. Festal vestments might be worked with gems and pearls, and in 1195 Bishop Hugh Pudsey of Durham owned 'nine chasubles of which the first [was] of red samite nobly embroidered with plates of gold and bezants and many great pearls and precious stones'.[27] Orphreys garnished with pearls and stones in settings were ordered for the Chapel Royal in 1321.[28]

In the twelfth and thirteenth centuries some bishops further adorned the necks of their chasubles with the rationale, a plaque set with precious stones or coloured glass, apparently in imitation of the Aaronic breastplate of the Jewish High Priests; at least one has survived.[29] They can be seen on several episcopal effigies – among them that of Walter de Cantelupe († 1266) in Worcester Cathedral, who also had a precious mitre with recesses for setting 'jewels', gloves and an episcopal ring.[30]

There were also the substantial morses which fastened heavy copes, such as that bought by the Treasurer of the Household to Edward III, wrought of silver-gilt and enamel.[31] Decorative pins attached the pallium to the chasuble; those found in the tomb of Archbishop Hubert Walter († 1205) in Canterbury Cathedral have flattened heads engraved with daisies.[32] Others are depicted on the effigy of Archbishop John Stratford († 1348), also at Canterbury, who wears the later form of mitre, the peaks edged with goldsmith's work, and his apparels and maniple ornamented with pearls and metal appliqué flowers and quatrefoils.[33]

The many episcopal rings from the twelfth century onwards which have been recovered from tombs correspond to descriptions in the Wardrobe records and inventories. Most prelates owned several: John de Sandale, Bishop of Winchester († 1319), left sixty-four rings, two brooches, two girdles, and five loose sapphires.[34] Otherwise, little survives except for the crozier, mitre garnishings and girdle belonging to William of Wykeham, Bishop of Winchester and Chancellor of England († 1404), which are still at New College, Oxford.[35] The parish clergy owned jewels too: in 1432 thieves stole from John Bredhill, of King's Swinford in Staffordshire, his six paternosters of coral, jet and amber, six brooches and six rings.[36] As patrons, the English kings presented the nuns of Amesbury with their gold profession rings; and Edward I also gave his sister, a nun of that house, 'a gold brooch with six emeralds price 20 marks' as a New Year's gift.[37] While this may have been intended for her to offer at a shrine when she travelled with the court, the evidence of Chaucer's Prioress demonstrates that nuns did wear jewellery:

Of smal coral aboute hir arm she bar
A peire of bedes, gauded al with grene,
And theron heng a brooch of gold ful sheene,
On which ther was first write a crowned A,
And after *Amor vincit omnia*.[38]

A late-fourteenth-century poem, *The Complaint of the Ploughman*, upbraided those monks who rode:

. . . on a courser as a knight
With hauke and hounds eke
With brooches or ouches on his hood.[39]

SOCIAL AND ECONOMIC USE OF JEWELLERY

As jewels, like plate, because of their intrinsic value formed a financial reserve in addition to their role as personal ornaments, national laws and local guild regulations from the thirteenth century were designed to prevent fraud.[40] Jewels were pawned to raise money, and from the reign of John there were many such transactions by the English kings.[41] Henry V and Henry VI frequently pledged certain items from the royal collection as security for loans from their kinsmen, Richard, Duke of York, and Henry Beaufort, Bishop of Winchester (the richest prelate in the realm), to be repaid when the taxes granted by Parliament were received.[42] Similar use of jewels as a capital resource by the nobility and gentry is recorded in the Paston letters.[43]

According to the Wardrobe records, it was customary to give jewels to courtiers on festivals and at marriage,[44] and Queen Eleanor, wife of Henry III, bought 322 rings, 143 clasps and 71 girdles in 1242 for this purpose.[45] They were also occasionally awarded as tournament prizes,[46] and given as presents to other monarchs and their representatives; and in the later Middle Ages livery collars were often so used (see below).

Shrines received gifts of jewels from pilgrims and by bequest. Offerings made to the shrine of St Alban were recorded, in part with drawings, by Matthew Paris in the thirteenth century; and again in the late-fourteenth- and fifteenth-century Benefactor's Book.[47] Thomas Carr of York, to take one example, left money to buy gold chains for the statue of the Virgin and Child on the altar of York Minster in 1444,[48] and the Countess of Warwick's bequests in 1439 to the shrines at Caversham and Walsingham have been cited above (p. 4). Leo of Rozmital, an aristocratic visitor from Bohemia, was struck by the wealth of the shrine of St Thomas at Canterbury, which he said was 'so richly adorned with pearls and precious stones that one would think there is no richer shrine in all Christendom'.[49]

LIVERIES AND ORDERS

The first surviving secular Order of Knighthood, the Garter, with membership limited to the Sovereign, the Prince of Wales and twenty-four Knights, was established by Edward III in 1348. After the first nominations by Edward, subsequent vacancies were to be filled by election at the annual feast held at Windsor on the festival of St George; and from the late fourteenth century emperors and kings, initially relatives of the Sovereign, were among the select fellowship.[50] Until the end of the fifteenth century the insignia consisted of a buckled Garter, sometimes with the motto set with jewels or embroidered with pearls, worn below the knee; and robes worn at the Windsor ceremonies. Following the example of the Golden Fleece, Henry VII added a collar and neck-badges to the insignia, but the statutes were not amended until later.[51]

As the tournament evolved at the end of the thirteenth century, many of the knights taking part did so in retinues organised under the banners of great lords.[52] According to the *Register of the Black Prince* his knights were given identical jewels for a tournament held in 1352: 'seven ouches worked with eagles . . . Sixty buckles, sixty girdle-tips and a hundred and twenty bars' were bought 'for the knights of the prince's companionship for the tournament at Windsor'.[53] From such devices stemmed the livery collars and badges which were so prominent in the faction-ridden world of the later Middle Ages. They were not only bestowed on vassals, but given to foreign visitors to the court and exchanged with other sovereigns.[54] In the Wilton Diptych (*c.* 1390–9) Richard II wears the livery collar of the King of France and his own device of the white hart enamelled *en ronde bosse* (Plate 1). The white hart is also worn as a badge by the angels attending the Virgin and Child to whom he is being presented.[55]

HERALDRY

Ownership might be indicated by the use of the arms either in full or in part, showing only the principal charge. The earliest example of a coat-of-arms forming the design for an English jewel is the Folkingham brooch, which dates from the mid twelfth century (Plate 19); thereafter heraldry developed rapidly as a decorative theme. From the mid thirteenth century the right to use arms was no longer the exclusive preserve of knights and the nobility but was claimed by merchants, especially the London aldermen, who had the same status as barons.[56]

CHOICE OF JEWELS

The relative popularity of the gem-stones chosen for setting in jewels varied from time to time, and the combination most favoured – emerald, ruby and sapphire – has its counterpart in the stained glass of the age.[57] Prized for their beauty, jewels and gem-stones also had symbolic meanings ascribed to them. In a letter to King John in 1205 Pope Innocent III explained the symbolism of his gift of four rings: their roundness signified eternity; their number 'constancy of mind' and the 'four principal virtues . . . Justice, Fortitude, Prudence and Temperance'; and the stones Faith (the greenness of the emerald), Hope (the serenity of the sapphire), Charity (the red of the garnet) and Good Works (the clarity of the topaz). This detailed explanation suggests that not all of the associations intended were common knowledge.[58] Gem-stones were also valued on account of their 'virtue' or magical powers: John de Sandale, Bishop of Winchester († 1319), owned a 'great ring . . . with a good sapphire for credit of virtu'.[59] The magical properties were part of the lore of gem-stones inherited from antiquity and elaborated by later Christian writers.[60] From the mid eleventh century, translations of the Latin lapidaries were available, and Chaucer alluded to their use:

> And they were set as thik of nouchis
> Ful of the fynest stones faire,
> That men rede in the Lapidaire.[61]

ENGRAVED GEMS

As there is no evidence that gem-engravers existed in England until the sixteenth century, cameos and intaglios set in medieval jewels and plate must have come either from Romano-British sites or from abroad. A school of glyptics flourished in Constantinople from at least the ninth century and, since the Imperial Roman collections had been transferred there, the city was also a source of ancient gems, some of which were removed by the Crusaders after the Sack of 1204.[62] Byzantine artists may have been recruited then for the workshop established in the Hohenstaufen kingdom in Southern Italy and Sicily by the Emperor Frederick II; after his death in 1250 some may have moved on to Paris, as a guild of gem-engravers was recorded there in 1268.[63]

Cameos and intaglios might be found on Roman sites such as Verulamium near St Albans, which is known to have been explored in the eleventh century by abbots wishing to clear the ruins.[64] Other finds could be made during ploughing or building works in London and elsewhere.

Although the original significance of the subjects engraved on the ancient cameos and intaglios was either forgotten or only partially understood, in medieval compilations concerning gem-stones and mythology it was generally believed that such devices added significantly to the inherent 'virtue' of the material.[65] A cameo of an emperor in the character of Aesculapius which Ethelred the Unready gave to the shrine of St Alban was hired out for confinements, since it was reputed to secure an easy delivery.[66] A Gnostic gem, a bloodstone intaglio of Abrasax, chief deity of the Basilidian system, depicted with a cock's head, human body and serpents for legs, bearing a shield and wielding a mace, set in a gold ring, was buried with Bishop Sefrried of Chichester († 1151), who was presumably unaware of its heretical antecedents.[67] Another, also Gnostic and set in a ring, comes from the coffin of Archbishop Hubert Walter († 1205) at Canterbury Cathedral. A plasma intaglio of a lion-headed, rayed serpent, identified by a blundered Greek inscription as Chnoubis, it was believed to be beneficial to the stomach.[68]

The magical properties of some of the devices were explained in a thirteenth-century lapidary, *De Sculpturis Lapidum*:[69] a jacinth cameo of a siren guaranteed invisibility, Pegasus or Bellerophon conferred speed or courage (I.i) and Andromeda reconciled quarrelling couples (I.ii). Social success attended those wearing silver rings set with pyrites engraved with a dove and an olive branch: 'everybody will invite you to be his guest and will feast you much and frequently' (III.ii). These magical powers were further enhanced if the stones were discovered by chance in the ground, which imparted the aura of good luck.[70]

The seventy-three cameos and intaglios pawned with other jewels by Henry III in 1267 provide a conspectus of the materials and iconography of engraved gems in a mid-thirteenth-century English royal collection.[71]. With the exception of crystal and sapphire intaglios and some mother-of-pearl cameos, they are all onyxes and sardonyxes, and there were thirty-three portraits, single, double or triple,. Most were probably ancient, but some, such as the two scenes from the Old Testament – 'a cameo with the sons of Jacob' and 'Moses and the Serpent' – the Majesty (or Christ enthroned) and the Virgin, compare with the surviving medieval gem-stones.[72] Another group – of lions, dogs, eagles and a charioteer – might be contemporary Hohenstaufen interpretations of ancient gems. The majority were set in plain gold collets, but sometimes more elaborate settings are mentioned, such as the ruby- and emerald-studded frame of the Sons of Jacob cameo.[73]

Although no later English medieval collections could compare with this, engraved gems continued to play a role in jewellery. Edward I owned gold rings, ouches and a pendant all set with cameos,[74] and there were others in Piers Gaveston's inventory.[75] They are rarer after the reign of Edward II, and the 'oriental sapphire set in gold with one image of the Virgin Mary' and 'one cameo placed in gold with one image of St John' in the posthumous inventory of Queen Isabella in 1357 are unusual.[76]

Engraved gems were also used by the nobility and higher ecclesiastics. In 1237 Henry III ordered that two onyx cameos with pearls be fixed to a chasuble,[77] and in 1332–3 a 'morse of gold for one choir cope, of diverse stones and pearls, enamelled, with one great cameo in the middle, of two men's heads', valued at £13 6*s* 8*d*, was listed in the Wardrobe.[78] The brooch of gold set with three emeralds and three cameos, given to Lady de Montibus, widow of a Constable of Stirling Castle, by Edward II in 1316–17,[79] could be the counterpart of that found at Oxwich Castle in Wales (Plate 13). Cameos were also set in rings, exemplified by the plasma bust of a woman found at

Witney.[80] Inscriptions occasionally identify the owner: a plasma intaglio of Minerva holding a branch framed in a gold rim inscribed as S RICHARD RE[G?) has been associated with King Richard I;[81] and a jasper intaglio of a man in a pointed hood, a contemporary portrait, inscribed S. CHRISTINE ALMARICI, was the personal signet of Christine Almaricus.[82] A sapphire intaglio of a veiled head, also contemporary, set in a ring from Hereford, is framed in gold with the message TECTA : LEGE : LECTA : TEGE (Read what is hidden, hide what is read) often found on privy seals.[83] There are also love mottoes: AMOR VINCIT FORTITUDINEM is inscribed on a silver pendant set with an ancient cornelian intaglio of two fauns, one removing a thorn from the other's foot; and EN VEIE DE AMI on the bezel of a ring set with a medieval intaglio of a lion passant.[84] The Earl of March († 1380) bequeathed 'a ruby engraved as a signet',[85] and surviving from that time is a fine ring, probably Italian, set with a ruby intaglio head and with an invocation to St George round the sides of the bezel. On account of its quality and this allusion to the patron saint of England and the Order of the Garter, the ring has been associated with the Black Prince.[86] Another ruby intaglio, which is set in a fifteenth-century ring believed to be English, is engraved with a facing crowned head resembling that on the coins of Charles V of France (1364–80) and, like the others, probably came from a late-fourteenth-century Parisian workshop. The inscription declares TEL IL NECT (There is nothing like it).[87]

MATERIALS

Until the sixteenth century, when the resources of the New World became available, the supply of precious metals and gem-stones was limited to what was sporadically mined in England and Wales and the recycled materials of unfashionable and damaged pieces. The work of refiners was, therefore, of particular interest to the Goldsmiths' Company which made regulations for them from 1438.[88]

Jet came from Yorkshire, and white, golden, dark red and blue-black amber from the North Sea coast and the Baltic. The Wardrobe accounts of Edward II differentiate between pearls from the Scottish rivers and the better-quality imports from the Orient: 'one gold crown with ten fleurons in which the large pearls are of Scotland and the clusters are of Oriental pearls'.[89] Coral and other gems, both precious and semi-precious, came from abroad, and Pegolotti's treatise on Asian trade outlines the sources and cost for some items *c.* 1340.[90]

Almost all precious gem-stones and the best pearls were therefore imported, many of them already set in jewels, and the term 'Parisian work' often occurs in royal inventories and accounts.[91] As early as *c.* 1125 William of Malmesbury commented on the quantity of luxury goods brought into London via Germany.[92] In the thirteenth century, purchases were made from merchants who had travelled from Piacenza, Venice and Paris.[93] Edward I's queen, Eleanor, bought jewels from Parisian and Florentine merchants, either directly or through Adam, the royal goldsmith.[94] The intricacies of the fourteenth-century international jewellery trade were recorded in the account books of Francesco Datini, the merchant of Prato, who dealt in jewellery from Avignon and Spain along with luxury items from Florence and elsewhere.[95] His partner, Baldassare degli Ubriachi, planned to visit Ireland while Richard II was there in the hope of selling him jewels; and he wrote to Datini that there was no market in England for cheap stones, adding that the best time for business there was at New Year and at royal weddings, when the demand for jewels, not only for the bride but also as gifts to those attending, sent prices up.[96] After the deposition of Richard II, the Tuscan merchant Deo Ambroghi in Paris immediately speculated on the chances of the remarriage of Henry IV and predicted: 'whomever he may wed there will be great feasting in England and silken clothing and jewels will go up in price . . . wherefore I would advise . . . any who have fine jewels to send them there'.[97]

While London, because of the presence of the court, was the major centre for the trade, other towns were involved in it too. The Venetian and Genoese merchant communities at Southampton dealt in jewels, plate and other luxuries, and the port books record the re-export of unsold items.[98]

GOLDSMITHS

Whether as members of a merchant guild or organised in a separate guild or company, the goldsmiths, being rich, played a leading role in their communities and were responsible for the mints and the standard of the currency. Their names have been preserved in only a few places and little information is available about the craft activities.

In London the goldsmiths were organised in an adulterine (unlicensed) guild by 1179–80; this must have been in existence for some years, as their alderman could be fined 45 marks – £30 in the sterling of the day, a very large sum by modern standards.[99] Although they did not receive their first royal charter until 1327, the king had charged the goldsmiths to enforce standards for gold and silver in 1238 and 1241, and extended this power to the whole kingdom by a statute of 1300.[100] The system of marking was further refined in 1363 when each goldsmith was obliged to stamp his products with a personal mark;[101] and in London and York the local ordinances provided that this should only be done if 'the jewel is such that it may be touched without spoiling the shape'.[102]

Another statute, authorising the setting up of provincial assay offices in York, Newcastle upon Tyne, Lincoln, Norwich, Bristol and Coventry in 1423, was not always acted on at the time.[103]

For most of the Middle Ages one or more goldsmiths would have been active in the major towns and they are known to have been in Leicester from the thirteenth century.[104] The unusually complete freedom records for York list the names of eight goldsmiths admitted between 1272 and 1327, thirty-one between 1327 and 1377 and the same number between 1377 and 1399. From 1400 to 1420 there were twenty-seven goldsmiths admitted, from 1421 to 1460 forty-six goldsmiths and four jewellers, and from 1461 to 1509 thirty-seven goldsmiths and one jeweller.[105] Significantly this expansion of activity coincides with the increase in the production of gold in Europe.[106]

Not all the goldsmiths were English. The foreign merchants who imported jewels for sale (see p. 10 above) were far outnumbered by the alien craftsmen who settled here. They were not always welcomed by their English colleagues and as early as 1370 the London Goldsmiths issued ordinances to control the 'stranger' workmen as well as the quality of jewels brought into the country. The four wardens of the craft examined imported jewels to ensure that they were 'good and true', and false stones were to be crushed.[107] The German goldsmith, John of Cologne, was admitted to the freedom of York in 1367–8 and a Fleming, Warmebolt de Arleham (or van Haarlem), in 1385–6.[108]

From 1334 the Warden's Minute Books of the London Goldsmiths' Company provide information about the misdeeds of members and others from the provinces whose goods, on sale in their shops or at the great fairs, had been found wanting by the Company's officials. Counterfeit gems made of glass, and substandard alloys or the excessive use of solder or lead filling to increase weight, were the commonest misdemeanours. Although they do not give a complete survey of the items made at any one time, the charters, ordinances and royal statutes together indicate the types of product which were then open to abuse. The 1327 charter drew attention to the making of 'counterfeit articles of gold and silver such as coronals [coronets], brooches, rings and other jewels in which they set glass of different colours to imitate the true stones';[109] and the statute of 1423 cited base-metal 'brooches, rings, beads [paternosters or rosaries] . . . gipser rings [purse fittings] . . .'[110] The charter of 1505 ordered 'wares of jewels, stones of pearl, coral and of other jewel stones whatsoever, countefeited in gold or silver, as in necklaces, seals, rings or girdles, or otherwise to be suppressed'.[111]

The Girdlers' Company of London received a charter at the same time as the Goldsmiths, Skinners and Tailors, with similarly extensive powers of search. Their ordinance of 1344 laid down that 'no man of the trade shall garnish or cause to be garnished, girdles or garters with any but pure metal, such as latten, or else with iron or steel'.[112] Later the York Girdlers were known to be making small latten fittings such as 'dagger chapes, purse knoppes . . . girdilles or any other maner gere or harness of laton stele or yren'.[113] Gold or silver fittings had to be made by the goldsmiths. It would therefore seem probable that, besides base-metal girdle and purse fittings, the girdlers produced large quantities of latten rings and brooches. They too were present in all major towns and, in York, were far more numerous than the goldsmiths.

DESIGNS

Designs, which reflect the principal artistic styles of the period, were also determined by the degree of skill available. At first the patterns were formed by irregularly shaped gem-stones set over the surface;[114] then, with the establishment of the lapidaries' shops in Paris, the later medieval jewellers could have stones cut precisely to the required shapes set closely together.

Religious motifs were popular on account of their devotional and apotropaic significance. Both these elements are combined in the eleventh-century reliquary from Sandford-on-Thames which has a figure of Christ in Majesty and an inscription confirming the amuletic character of the contents.[115] The Crucifixion, Holy Trinity, Virgin and saints all occur on later pendants and jewels;[116] and the large group of iconographic rings depicting popular saints and the Five Wounds seem to be exclusive to England and Scotland (see Plate 25 and pp. 61–2 below).

Nature was a continuing inspiration, and some motifs were derived from the imagined world of the bestiary: harpies, dragons alone or fighting with human beings, and other creatures.[117] In the thirteenth century the stiff-leaf foliage on the shoulders of rings, and the stylised quatrefoils which fill the central band of a hexafoil brooch, compare with architectural ornament.[118] The more naturalistic treatment of plant forms characteristic of sculpture during the reigns of the first two Edwards was also adopted for jewellery, represented by the open pods on bosses between the collets of a jewelled ring brooch *c.* 1300.[119]

Throughout the period, inscriptions – religious invocations, magical formulae and love mottoes – played an important role. Some jewels were made in the form of Lombardic capitals, the most important of which is the fourteenth-century M ouch preserved at New College, Oxford (Plate V).

Heraldic motifs were also used, especially the badges or devices, not only in rings and brooches but also in bracelets, such as that owned by Henry V: 'a gold bracelet with two antelopes of the same garnished with a ruby'.[120]

TECHNIQUES

The twelfth-century treatise of Theophilus, *On Divers Arts*, provides the only description of the methods of the early-medieval goldsmith, though it is concerned primarily with the making of church plate rather than jewels.[121] The methods were hammering, engraving and chasing for working plates of gold and silver, wire-drawing for chains or filigree, and either lost-wax or piece-mould casting for more substantial parts; and moulds survive for items of jewellery.[122] The spangles and 'bezants' which adorned garments from the fourteenth century were made by hammering thin sheets into engraved moulds, exemplified by one that has survived from the 1330s.[123] By the fifteenth century this had become a specialised occupation within the craft.[124] Base-metal jewellery was cast rather than assembled.

Enamelling was widely employed, at first by the cloisonné or champlevé methods; then, from the early fourteenth century, translucent *basse taille*; and finally the *en ronde bosse* was employed. The jewel might be enamelled in one piece or separate enamels could be made and set into the jewel like the gems themselves. While opaque enamel could be applied to some base metals, the translucent colours could only be successful on gold or silver-gilt. Niello, a black filling which made engraved decoration stand out clearly against the metal ground, was also popular, though little has survived in good condition.[125]

Early-medieval gem-stones were polished *en cabochon*, retaining their original shapes. Although some were pyramidal, as in the rings from the tombs of Bishop Ranulf Flambard († 1128) and Bishop William of Ste Barbe († 1152) in Durham Cathedral, most were rounded.[126] Because few diamonds form a perfect octahedron, most were shaped to make a regular pyramid, or point-cut, and from this technique the more elaborate cuts developed. By the end of the fourteenth century even diamonds were being worked to precise shapes such as square or quarré, and faceted or *de taille*.[127] Gems were usually mounted in box collets or held by claws, and by the end of the fourteenth century they could be clustered in 'troches' for crowns and other large jewels.[128] The colour of the stone could be enhanced by lining the inside of the collet with a foil, and thus glass or crystal might pass undetected.[129] Despite the regulations, counterfeit stone were widely used, even by royalty; the main technique was flashing – mingling fine layers of colourless and coloured glass – which produced a glass that held light like a ruby or sapphire.[130] According to the Port Book of Southampton, 1435–6, imports from Italy included glass for jewellery as well as for the table.[131] Box collets also facilitated the use of doublets, thin slivers of a gem-stone, backed by thicker glass or crystal; these too occur in royal jewels.[132] Pearls might be set in collets or on gold pins with the points carefully burred to secure them.

Base-metal jewellery, particularly rings and brooches, were usually made from the copper alloy, latten, which could be gilt. Softer metals like lead, tin and pewter were made into pilgrim signs and cheap copies of livery devices. The ornament worked by chasing, engraving or filigree in gold and silver jewellery was simulated by cast details. Base metal might also be used to strengthen gold and silver pieces, but the practice was not approved by the wardens since it could not always be detected at their searches, and added to the weight and therefore the value of the piece.[133]

DRESS

Of the many changes in medieval dress the most momentous was the introduction of tailoring in the mid fourteenth century. Before this the basic outer costume of upper-class men and women consisted of a tunic or gown, a mantle and, especially for women, a variety of head coverings. At first the tunic worn by nobles was often short, showing cross-gartered hose, and covered by a mantle clasped on the right shoulder, thus leaving the sword-arm free.[134] In the twelfth century the tunic worn at court usually reached the ankles, and monuments show that at least two could be worn together – one of fine linen and an outer garment of silk with orphreys and embroidery.[135] For ceremonial use the mantle might be fastened in front by a large clasp similar to the ecclesiastical morse.

Women's dress did not differ greatly from that worn by men in the twelfth and thirteenth centuries, although two outer gowns are sometimes shown, with the uppermost slit or cut away at the sides to reveal the girdle. The head was covered by a kerchief and by a wimple which framed the face and covered both neck and ears. The mantle was worn draped loosely on the shoulders or fastened by chain or tasselled silk cords passing through clasps and held by a slide. Occasionally a single large clasp was worn at the throat.[136]

Coronets were worn by both men and women,[137] as were ring brooches which fastened the tunic or chemise at the neck.[138] Since the coronet and mantle clasps were the most important items, they are usually more valuable than the other jewellery recorded in the inventories.

The short tunics closely fitted to the body with tailored sleeves which revolutionised dress between 1340 and 1360 popularised the new invention of the button, which first appeared on women's gowns at the beginning of the century.[139] Women's dress remained ankle-length, but the bodice now revealed the figure, scandalising preachers and chroniclers.[140] The houppelande, a full-length robe of rich material with a high collar and wide sleeves, is depicted in the Wilton Diptych and other paintings around 1400, when it was the usual garment for both men and women at court.[141] Deep necklines, perhaps following the fashion set in France by Agnes Sorel, were filled by necklaces, carcanets and collars in the fifteenth century.[142] The sequence of rapidly changing fashions can be followed in the monuments and paintings of the period.[143]

2

The categories of medieval jewellery 1066 – 1509

JEWELS FOR THE HEAD

Crowns, circlets, demi-circlets, chaplets and coronals, attires and cauls with orles swathed like turbans were worn by the upper ranks of society. Besides denoting status, they emphasised the forehead, chief point of feminine beauty. Coronets, which in modern times are the prerogative of peers and their wives, were worn at court, especially at weddings; and it was not until the sixteenth and seventeenth centuries that the heralds formulated the rules laying down the design proper for each rank of the peerage.

CROWNS

Although crowns are now regarded as part of the regalia,[1] in the Middle Ages they were worn more frequently and were closer in design to those worn by the nobility. The English kings owned several crowns besides that of St Edward, which was used at coronations.[2] Those on the royal tombs at Fontevrault, Espan, Worcester and Westminster represent the plain and solid early style. A rare survival is the crown of Richard, Earl of Cornwall and King of the Romans, since 1272 in the Treasury at Aachen and described in his deed of gift as 'a gold crown most beautifully adorned with rubies, emeralds, sapphires, pearls and other costly stones', these last including fine ancient cameos.[3] During the fourteenth century, fleurons became more naturalistic, developing into slender pinnacles like those on the crown of Princess Blanche in the Residenz at Munich[4] (Plate I). It may have belonged to Queen Anne of Bohemia († 1394) and is possibly that described in the inventories of 1397 and 1399 as

> a crown of 11 works garnished with 11 sapphires, 33 balais and 132 pearls, 33 diamonds (of which 8 are counterfeit). Item 6 fleurons each of a balais, 5 sapphires, each of 9 pearls (of which 7 pearls in all are missing). Item 6 lesser fleurons each of a sapphire, 4 small balais, 1 emerald (of which an emerald is missing), and 2 small pearls.[5]

Whether made in Prague,[6] Paris or London, as one of the three surviving crowns or coronets asssociated with English medieval royalty it exemplifies those in the Wardrobe records and those described in literature. Richard II appears in the poem *Mum and the Sothsegger* (also called *Richard the Redeless*) wearing his coronation crown:

Crouned with a croune / that kyng under hevene
Might not a better / have boghte, as I trowe
So full was it filled / with vertus stones,
With perlis of pris / to punnysshe the wrongis,
With rubis rede / the righth for to deme
With gemmes and juellis / joyned to-gedir,
And pees amonge the peple / for peyne of thi lawes
It was full goodeliche ygrave / with gold al aboughte;
The braunchis above / boren grett charge;
With diamauntis derve / y-douutid of all . . .
And sapheris swete / that soughte all wrongis,
Ypowdride wyth pete / ther it be oughte,
And traylid with trouthe / and treste al aboute;
For ony cristen kynge / a croune well ymaked.[7]

This description is close to the 'Great Crown' pawned by Richard II in 1379[8] and to that depicted on the effigy of Henry IV at Canterbury.[9] The third surviving English royal crown is that of Margaret of York, Duchess of Burgundy, in the Aachen Cathedral Treasury (Plate II). Her name is inscribed on the circlet, which, like the fleurons above, is ornamented with jewelled white roses of the House of York.[10]

CORONETS, CHAPLETS, ORLES AND CAULS

A narrow gold fillet with finely wrought running scrolls found in the ruins of Iona[11] (Fig. 1) corresponds to the simple design on a monument to an unknown lady of *c.* 1300 at Stevenage, Herts.[12] As with the crowns, the fleurons on the more elaborate coronets varied from stylised to more naturalistic designs, such as the four-petalled flowers set on a fillet *c.* 1350 at Ledbury, Herefordshire,[13] and which remained in fashion well into the fifteenth century. They were jewelled versions of the garlands of fresh flowers worn on the head. The character Idleness, in the Chaucerian translation of the *Roman de la Rose*, is described as being richly and exquisitely dressed:

. . . of fyn orfrays hadde she eke
A chapelet; so semly oon
Ne werede never mayde upon.
And faire above that chaplet
A rose gerland had she sett.[14]

An inventory of 1338–9 includes a chaplet with 'enamelled birds with doublets',[15] and birds hold letters on the headdress of Isabel Cockayne († 1447) at Polesworth,

Fig. 1 Gold fillet with filigree trails of leafy scrolls: early twelfth century. National Museum of Scotland. Drawn by Marion O'Neil.

Warwickshire.[16] Inscriptions on chaplets depicted on tombs are usually religious; the Lombardic letters M for Mary on the fillet of the widow of Sir John Wilington († 1378), now at Atherington, Devon,[17] and the IHC MERCI, repeated thrice, on that John Gower († 1408) at Southwark Cathedral[18] illustrate the practice.

The more elaborate, taller designs, like the 'sercle of golde with x. pynacles garnysed with cviii saphirs garnades & emerawdes and clxvj perles' pledged against a loan of 1438,[19] are shown on fifteenth-century monuments. Beatrice, Countess of Arundel (*c.* 1415), at Arundel, Sussex,[20] wears a similar circlet of clusters and lozenges, while Alice, Duchess of Suffolk († 1475), at Ewelme, Oxon.,[21] and Isabel, Countess of Essex († 1483), Little Easton, Essex (MS II), wear circlets crested with fleurs-de-lis; Joyce Baroness Tiptoft (*c.* 1475) at Enfield, Middx. (MS I), has fleurons. The coronets of William, Earl of Arundel († 1487), and his wife Joan are decorated with a continuous row of oak leaves, alluding to a Fitzalan badge; hers is shaped behind to the curve of the head, a style seen on other fifteenth-century monuments and paintings, both here and on the continent.[22]

From the early fifteenth century, a turban-like orle, derived from those worn by knights round the basinet, was an alternative to the circlet; there is one on the effigy of Lady Thorpe († 1417) at Ashwelthorpe, Norfolk.[23] It is ornamented with trailing foliage and ouches, that in the centre being an eagle or falcon – both royal badges. The eagle device also appears on the effigies of Margaret Greene († 1417) at Lowick, Northants.,[24] and of Lady Wilcote († 1442) at Northleigh, Oxon. – where it alludes to the Wilcote arms.[25]

Cauls, or jewelled and embroidered nets enclosing the hair, replaced the wimple and veil in the second half of the fourteenth century, for married ladies other than widows. Lady Beauchamp (*c.* 1388) at Worcester Cathedral[26] wears a jewelled caul kept in place by a bandeau of small clusters and lozenges in the style described by Chaucer:

> A fret of goold she hadde next hyre her
> And upon that a white corone she ber
> With many floures, and I shal nat lye;
> For al the worlde, ryght as the dayesye
> Ycorouned is with white leves lite,
> Swiche were the floures of hire coroune white.
> For a perle fyn and oryental
> Hyre white coroun was ymaked al.[27]

At the turn of the century the netted caul developed into jewelled boxes enclosing the ears; this style is illustrated by the two wives of Ralph, Earl of Westmorland (*c.* 1425), in their effigies at Staindrop church, Durham.[28] By mid century the caul was further expanded into extravagant shapes with a marked vertical emphasis, exemplified by the tall mitre-like headdress of Lady Vernon (*c.* 1451) at Tong, Salop,[29] by the heart-shaped form worn by Agnes Staunton († 1458) at Castle Donington, Leicestershire

(MS I), and by the butterfly headdress of Lady Say († 1473) at Broxbourne, Herts. (MS II). The caul which is depicted in the portrait of Queen Margaret of Scotland by Hugo van der Goes in 1476 is particularly splendid. Edged with a border of pearl clusters rising to a peak at the back of the head, it is composed of a network of pearl lozenges within open quatrefoils with drop pearls. More pearls fringe the lower end of the coronet, which is curved to the back of the head and has a wide jewelled bandeau centred on a brooch crested with leafy sprays.[30] It compares with that worn by the Countess of Arundel (*c.* 1487), as does her open-sided surcoat, and both could depict them as brides – unlike the more common style, with the ladies in their widow's weeds.

In many respects men's head ornaments are similar to those of women. Fourteenth-century knights wore fillets round their basinets, as does John of Eltham († 1336) at Westminster Abbey, with lozenge-shaped settings in a jewelled band crested with fleurs-de-lis.[31] John de Stonor, appointed Lord Chief Justice of the Common Pleas in 1329 († 1354), at Dorchester Abbey, Oxon., wears a circlet embellished with rosettes.[32] Roses alternate with clusters of the circlet about the basinet of John, Lord Willoughby De Eresby (*c.* 1396), on his effigy at Spilsby, Lincs.[33] Richard II owned several circlets, all were richly jewelled, one with white roses.[34]

Circlets were awarded as prizes at tournaments and, in one case, to a knight – Eustace de Ribemont – who had distinguished himself in battle against Edward III. At the dinner afterwards, according to Froissart, Edward wore 'a chapelet of fyne perles' and, after praising the captured knight for his prowess, 'toke the chapelet that was upon his heed, beyng both fayre, goodly and ryche, and sayd, Sir Eustace, I gyve you this chapelet for the best doar in armes in this journey past of eyther party; and I desyre you to bere it this yere for the love of me . . . and I quyte you your prison and ransome.'[35]

Like the brooch (see p. 36) below), the chaplet was adopted as an heraldic charge and, as such, was borne by the families of Fitzralph, Fitzwilliam and Hilton.[36]

CHAINS, NECKLACES, COLLARS AND ORDERS

The sumptuary law of 1363, which forbade yeomen and craftsmen to wear gold or silver collars or chains with other kinds of neck ornament, demonstrates their widespread use and – in the eyes of king and magnates – abuse by those not of the rank entitled to such display.[37] At the end of the century the author of *Mum and the Sothsegger* singled out chains as an example of conspicuous expenditure by courtiers:

> For they kepeth no coyne that cometh to here hondis
> But chaungyth it for cheynes that in chepe hangith.[38]

The fashion for chains, which spread across central and northern Europe from Austria to the British Isles, developed with the rise of the livery collar.[39]

Value was related to weight. Thus the gold chain which Henry IV while Earl of

Derby took from Sir John Dalyngrygg was only valued at £6 13*s* 4*d*,[40] but Richard II owned a 'gold collar all full of gold feathers of which x. have an ouche garnished of a square balace and viij large pearls, weighing ii, lb.' valued at £700, and another jewelled collar with the French device of the broom cod valued at £1266 13*s* 4*d*.[41] Chaucer emphasised the weight of the gold chains worn by Zenobia at Aurelian's triumph;[42] and the particularly massive collar of the Lord High Admiral, John, Earl of Oxford, in 1513 was composed of one-hundred-and-sixty-one links with a sailor's whistle attached.[43]

The effigies at Arundel of Thomas, Earl of Arundel († 1415), his wife show him wearing his collar of Esses, and with a tablet hanging from a fine chain.[44] There is a larger chain or necklace with a loop and pendant jewel touching the neckline of the gown on a contemporary effigy now at Atherington, Devon.[45] Most effigies, particularly brasses, used conventions for many details like chains well into the sixteenth century. Hence rectangular links engraved like a double row of bricks appear on the brass to Helen Hardy († 1486) at Lyddington, Rutland (MS I). Round links are depicted as closely fitting in brasses of 1490 at Charwelton, Northants. (MS I), and at Harley, Salop (MS I). Others, such as that of Lionel, Lord Welles († 1461), at Metheley, Yorks., have large, more openly spaced links similar to those in German portraiture.[46] Margaret Paston's description of the future husband of Kateryn Walsom in 1448 as 'the galaunte with the grete chene' implies that chains were not so common among the country gentry, and therefore stood out.[47] They were worn by both men and women and, before 1466, Margaret Paston asked her son to return the 'chene and the litill chene' she had lent to him.[48]

Occasionally wills specified designs, such as the 'cheyne that i was wonte to were that is to say the grete lynkes' mentioned in 1504 and the 'litell flate chayne of golde' bequeathed in 1509.[49] The variety of links is demonstrated by surviving examples: broad, double, single, flat, twisted, oval, round and rectangular. There are two from the Fishpool Hoard, *c.* 1460: one short and heavy, composed of twin circles joined together in figures of eight, the other longer and lighter, of intersecting ovals.[50] The Clare cross hangs from a double-stranded chain of twisted ovals, and the crown of the Dunstable Swan jewel (Plate 20) has a chain of plain oval links.[51] More elaborately decorated types are known from records: 'a cheyne of gold made of letters and crownes',[52] one of waterflowers,[53] and a 'cheyne of golde with vii knottes'.[54]

Lora de St Quintin († 1369 and engraved *c.* 1397) at Brandesburton, Yorks. (MS II), wears her beads round her neck with a ring brooch attached to them; and an anonymous lady (*c.* 1410) at South Ormsby, Lincs. (MS I), wears them in a double row. The custom is mentioned in a list of jewels given to Sir John Howard's wife in 1467: 'my master gaff her a peyr of bedes for a gentylwomannes nekke gaweid with viij. gawdeid of goolde and viij. perles'.[55]

Women's necklaces which appear in the fifteenth century rapidly develop into complex carcanets, some built up on corses of silk or velvet. In 1467 Sir John Howard gave his wife 'a devyse of goolde with xiiij. lynkes and the ton halffe of the lynkes enamyled set with iiij. Rubyis iij. dyamawntes and vij. perles'.[56] In 1473 'a colar of gold set upon blak velwet with stones and perles wayng iij. oz. di. or ther aboute, the weche colar is garnassid with xij perles gret and small and viij rubyes' was pledged for a loan.[57] Such necklaces are shown on brasses. Eden Barre (*c.* 1474) at Clehonger, Herefordshire (MS I), wears a choker composed of clusters framed in roundels, as well as a long chain and pendant. Stock workshop patterns similar to the necklace worn by Maria Hoose, wife to Jan de Witte, in 1473 and to that in the *Salome* by Hans Memling,[58] composed of long drops with pearls or smaller stones round the edges, are depicted on several brasses: Agnes Yelverton (*c.* 1472) at Rougham, Norfolk (MS I), Joyce Tiptoft (*c.* 1475) at Enfield, Middx. (MS I), both Peyton wives (*c.* 1484) at Isleham, Cambs. (MS III), Elizabeth Clere (*c.* 1488) at Stokesby, Norfolk (MS II), and Joan Cromwell (*c.* 1490) at Tattershall, Lincs. (MS IV). The last has the drops alternating with trefoils. Similarly, in the restored stained-glass group portrait at Canterbury Cathedral, each of the daughters of Edward IV wears an identical carcanet.[59] Other portraits of fifteenth-century royalty depict wide bands studded with coloured stones alternating with pearls.[60]

Lady Urswyck (*c.* 1479) at Dagenham, Essex (MS I), wears another style, the pearls being threaded into trellis patterns with festoons terminating in jewelled clusters to each side of a large diamond-shaped pendant. Naturalistic motifs were also used: Frances Windham (*c.* 1480) at Felbrigg, Norfolk (MS IV), has a single leaf pendant to her necklace, and Mary de Grey (*c.* 1495) at Merton, Norfolk (MS III), a fringe of oak leaves. The collar worn by Richard III in one of his portraits had pairs of leafy branches enclosing the square-cut stones[61] and compares with the wreath of leaves curving upwards to the settings on the collar of Elizabeth Say (†. 1473) at Broxbourne, Herts. (MS II).

Jet scallop shells of St James are often mentioned in wills and fringe the necklace of John Bradbourne's wife (*c.* 1483) at Ashbourne, Derbyshire.[62]

LIVERY COLLARS

The idea inherited from antiquity that only knights should wear golden collars was honoured in fifteenth-century usage relating to livery collars, for esquires wore silver. Livery collars were bestowed by kings and magnates alike. In some cases the recipients had the right to distribute a specified number of collars on their own account. Richard II had two collars with the livery of his first wife, Anne of Bohemia: one composed of pearl branches of rosemary, the other with a white ostrich with a blue leg standing beneath a tree in a green field.[63] In the Wilton Diptych he wears the collar of his father-in-law, Charles VI of France (Plate 1) – possibly the gold collar of broom cods set with spinels, sapphires and pearls listed in his inventory.[64] The Duchesses of Lancaster and Gloucester, the Countess of Huntingdon and John of Gaunt's daughter,

1 Richard II wearing a jewelled collar of broom cods and a badge of the chained white hart. Detail from the Wilton Diptych, National Gallery, London.

Joan, were given collars at the King's second wedding in 1396.[65] Magnates, like the king, owned several collars and exchanged them as tokens of friendship, as well as distributing them to their followers. In 1426 John, Duke of Bedford and Regent of France, sent to Paolo Guingi of Lucca 'two little gold collars of the device of the Duke of Bedford of England'.[66] It used his badge of the Racine (tree root) and his beast, the yale. A collar with a hart lodged within park palings is worn by Sir Thomas Markenfield (late fourteenth century) at Ripon, Yorks.,[67] and by Ralph Neville, Earl of Westmorland, and his sons in a miniature in the Neville Book of Hours[68] (Plate 2) – perhaps for his livery. Thomas, Lord Berkeley († 1417), at Wotton-under-Edge, Glos. (MS 1), wears a collar with his family device, a mermaid.

The Pisan, an ornamental collar bought by Henry IV which his son and grandson, Henry V and Henry VI, pledged as a security for loans, is described in detail in 1415.

> a pusan of gold called the *rich coler* conteynyng xvi. culpons or peces upon the which are viii. antelops garnised with xxti. greet peerles. And upon the same coler are v. baleys wherof iiii. are of entaille square and the vthe is vi. quartred. and upon the same coler are ii. greet peerles joynyng untoo the baleys. Also upon the same coler are viii corones of gold ech of hem anameled wyth a resoun of *une sanz pluis*, and upon oon of the same corones are ii. grete diamandes square and poynted. Also upon the same coler are x. owches eche of hem wyth double floures of gold garnysed, and on eche of the same owches is a grete baleys and vi greete peerles of which baleys vii are of entaille square and iii of hem are rounde and ragged. Also upon the same coler is an oother litel owche, wythe double floures of gold garnysed with a balays of entaille square. and v. peerles.[69]

The antelope derives from the first wife of Henry IV, Mary Bohun; it was a Bohun beast.

2 Ralph Neville (1364–1425) and his sons, wearing collars with a hart lodged within park palings. From the Neville Book of Hours, Bibliothèque Nationale, Paris.

LANCASTRIAN LIVERY COLLARS

The will of John of Gaunt does not mention the collar of Esses, but in 1394, in reply to the Earl of Arundel, Richard II told the Lords in Parliament that he had assumed his uncle's collar in 1389 on his return from Spain, as a token of his love, and that he would allow his retainers to wear it also.[70] The earliest documentary references are in the accounts of Henry IV, who in 1391–2, as Earl of Derby, bought 'one collar of gold with seventeen letters of S after the manner of feathers with scrolls and scriptures in the same and a swan in the tiret'; in 1393–4 there occurs a 'collar made with rolled esses and given to Robert Waterton because the lord had given the collar of the same Robert to another esquire'; and in 1396–7 'a collar made together with Esses, of flowers of "soveigne vous de moy" hanging and enamelled'.[71] As king, Henry IV bought from Christopher Tildesley a gold collar 'with twenty-four letters of S pounced with "souverain", and four bars, two pendants, and a tiret with a nouche garnished with a balas and six large pearls'.[72] Another magnificent collar was commissioned by Henry IV from the same goldsmith in 1406–7. Made of gold, it was

> worked with this word 'souveignez' and letters of S, and x enamels and garnished with xii. great pearls, twelve great dyamds [*sic*], viij Baleys, viij Sapphires together with one large nouche in the fashion of a triangle with one large ruby fixed in the same and garnished with iv large pearls.[73]

The Esses may allude to the motto [MA] SOUVERAYNE, which was on his seal as Duke of Lancaster in 1399 and was painted on the tester of his tomb at Canterbury Cathedral.[74] He had bought many collars, some gilt, whilst travelling as Earl of Derby, and some of these may have been given to foreigners.[75] Henry V had twenty-four gold collars sent to him at Rouen in 1419,[76] while in 1430 Henry VI sent six gold and twenty-four silver-gilt collars and others of silver to the Emperor Sigismund to be distributed 'among the dwellers in Basyle [Basle] and other knights and esquires, after the advice and discretion of the said Emperor and the King's ambassador' – three of them being depicted on monuments.[77] A similar grant of fifty collars to the Marquis of Gonzaga in 1436 specified that they were to be given to persons of noble blood.[78]

The collar is first depicted on the effigies of Sir John Swynford († 1371) at Spratton, Northants., and Robert le Marmion († 1387) at West Tanfield, Yorks.[79] On her effigy at Canterbury, Joan of Navarre wears the collar Henry IV ordered at the time of their marriage in 1403;[80] and it is worn by other ladies, probably after having held office at court. Henry VI's New Year's gift to Grisell Bellknap in 1428 was 'One coller of silver gilt, of his livery, Price xii.s.'[81] Both the poet John Gower († 1402) at Southwark Cathedral,[82] who changed his allegiance from Richard II to become court orator to Henry IV, and Thomas, Earl of Arundel († 1415), at Arundel, Sussex,[83] wear the Lancastrian collar as a badge of political partisanship.

3 Silver Lancastrian livery collar terminating in a tiret with a spirally fluted ring. Museum of London.

The varying numbers of letters made of gold, silver-gilt or silver were either joined together with links to make a chain or sewn on a corse between borders, with a tiret or buckle joining the ends. Later collars added ornamental spacers or knots; and a pendant, a royal beast or cross, could be added. An inventory of jewels in the royal collection *c.* 1399–1410 included 'viii letters of S for a collar each of xv. perles'.[84] In the late-fifteenth-century portrait at Windsor, Henry VI's collar consists of golden Esses alternating with square-cut gems; and in 1426 he combined the S with the broom cods of Charles VI to underline his claim to the thrones of England and France.[85] The cross worn with the collar in the Windsor portrait[86] is unusual, although there does not seem to have been any consistent use of pendants with the Lancastrian collar. In some monuments none is visible because the hands cover the area where the pendant should hang. A corbel head in the south aisle of Southwell Minster wears the collar like a strap, with Esses applied to it, buckled round the throat with the end hanging straight down behind the buckle, like the Garter. Tirets, or trefoil ornaments, were most common and were used on the best-preserved collar, found in the Thames by Kennet Wharf and now in the Museum of London.[87] It compares with that held in the fingers of Edward Grimston, the ambassador to Burgundy, in his portrait by Petrus Christus.[88] A spirally fluted ring hangs from the tiret to which a further pendant may have been attached (Plate 3).

Jewelled pendants, like those described in the royal inventories, hang from the collars of Sir John Routh (*c.* 1420) at Routh, Yorks. (MS I), and Robert, Lord Hungerford († 1439), at Salisbury Cathedral,[89] but heraldic beasts were more usual. The Bohun swan, a device inherited from Henry IV's first wife, hangs from the collar of John Gower, modelled in relief on a medallion.[90] After the accession of Henry VII, who revived the collar for members of his household, the Tudor rose and the Beaufort portcullis badges were adopted as pendants. Worn by Nicholas Kniveton († 1495) at Mugginton, Derbyshire (MS I), the portcullis thereafter appears in the portraits of heralds, legal dignitaries, and the Lord Mayors of London.

YORKIST LIVERY COLLARS

Edward IV adopted a new livery collar composed of two of his badges, the sun and the rose, which were worn with a third badge, the white lion of March, as a pendant. The rose had been the device of Edmund of Langley, Duke of York (1362–1402), and the sun was assumed in consequence of the three suns which were seen joining into one before the Battle of Mortimer's Cross in 1461 and interpreted as an omen of victory. As a mark of friendship, Leo of Rozmital, brother of the Queen of Bohemia, and members of his suite were admitted by Edward IV to his 'fellowship' on a visit in 1465–7 and were given 'gold and silver badges which he himself hung about our necks', and some of the party were knighted.[91] Lion pendants hang from the collars of Sir Robert Harcourt († 1471) at Stanton Harcourt, Oxon.,[92] and of another Harcourt at Aston church, Warwick.[93] In the latter the suns and roses are linked by a double row of long rectangular links, but, like the Esses, they could be applied to a corse. In the triptych by Hans Memling, both Sir John and Lady Donne wear the collar with the lion pendants[94] (Plate 4). The collar is also worn by the Countess of Arundel (*c.* 1487) like a choker, and it has the Fitzalan oak leaves between the suns and roses. Doubtless this was a present, like that given by Sir John Howard to his wife in 1467.[95]

Richard III redesigned the Yorkist collar, substituting roses in sunbeams for the alternate suns and roses, and his own badge of the boar for the lion of March. An

4 Lady Donne wearing a Yorkist collar of suns and roses with pendant lion. Detail from the triptych by Hans Memling, *c.* 1468. National Gallery, London.

example of this collar is worn by Richard Neville, while his wife has the older form, on their effigies *c.* 1484 at Brancepeth, Durham.[96]

Yorkist emblems were combined with Tudor roses in the reign of Henry VII. Prince Arthur wears a collar of tasselled knots filled with three pearls and double roses with gems in the centre in a portrait *c.* 1500 and in the royal collection.[97] This type is also listed in the inventory of his brother, Prince Henry: 'a collar of golde with rede roses & white enameld with paunceis with wyres of pynnes', and 'a fair rose of rubeis sett in a rose white & grene with iii. fayr perles'.[98]

WAITS COLLARS

Owing to the poor preservation of civic records we only have information about the silver collars worn by the town minstrels, or Waits, in eleven cities. The earliest seems to be Coventry in 1423, followed by Norwich in 1426–7. In 1475 the London Waits were given collars of Esses with shields of the city arms, while at Exeter *c.* 1500 the surviving collars combined the city arms with roundels inscribed with X and R. The links of silver castles and gilt leopards at Norwich *c.* 1550, and of dragon's heads with crosses at King's Lynn *c.* 1550 and 1594, also derived from the arms of the towns.[99]

GARTER INSIGNIA

Soon after the establishment of the Order of the Garter by his father Edward III, the Black Prince bought 'two garters garnished with gold' and a 'garter enameled blue'.[100] Richard II had an even more elaborate Garter: 'the fabric blue with buckle and pendant of gold garnished of 9 pearls of one kind and 40 pearls of another kind; which pendant contains a sapphire in the middle and 4 diamonds; with 11 gold bars'.[101] In the fifteenth century, designs varied from the gilt Garter, ornamented with pearls and flowers, made by Matthew Phelip the London goldsmith for the King of Portugal,[102] to the magnificent jewel which Edward IV sent his brother-in-law, the Duke of Burgundy. The motto of the Order was spelt out in hog-back diamonds interspersed with rubies, and the buckle and pendant were studded with rubies, diamonds and four pearls.[103]

Relatively few monuments show the insignia of the Order. Richard, Earl of Warwick († 1439), at Warwick wears the Garter at the knee over his armour,[104] while both John, Earl of Shrewsbury († 1453), at Whitchurch, Salop, and Sir Robert Harcourt († 1471) at Stanton Harcourt[105] wear the mantle with the scutcheon of St George. The wives of the Knights Companion were also given the mantle and the Garter, which was worn on the arm, a practice illustrated by Alice, Duchess of Suffolk († 1475), at Ewelme, Oxon.[106]

PENDANTS

Pendants with suspension loops to hang at the neck from chains, collars and necklaces, or from the beads worn at the girdle, could be either secular or devotional in design. John Metford bequeathed in 1487 'a Cheyn of golde conteyning in length 2 yardes with an Ocche [i.e., ouche] therto sett with 6 perles and a Diamond in the Middes . . . a Cheyn of gold with a gold Crosse of saint Antonye hanging thereby'.[107] A larger selection was bequeathed to her son by Dame Margaret Capel, widow of a Mayor of London, in 1516:

> his faders [Sir William Capel's] cheyne which was the young kyng Edward Vth . . . a cheyne of gold with a paunes flower set with a rose of Diamondes and three perlys weying 6 unces 1 quarter Demi . . . a cheyne of fyne gold with a long cross sett with a rubye . . . a flatt cheyne of workyng gold with a cross of fyne golde garnished with a rubie harte wise and three little diamondes weying 4 ounces 3 quarters and a penny weight . . . my less flat cheyne of workyng gold with an agnes [i.e., Agnus Dei] of fyne golde with the Trinitie on the one side and our Lady Assumpcion on the other side weying an ounce 3 quarters 2 pennyweight a cheyne of base gold of 27 long lynkes which I bought of one Rydley my Lord of Kentes servant.[108]

JEWELLED PENDANTS

Matthew Paris illustrated three jewelled pendants given to the Abbey of St Alban before 1259: two were set with cabochon sapphires, the plain gold mounts being shaped to the irregular outline of the stones; and a peridot, presented by John, Bishop of Ardfert († 1245), and believed to cure spasms, was pierced to receive a small sapphire in a gold collet. The edge of one of the sapphire pendants was 'most subtly' engraved with an inscription and the back nielloed with a Crucifixion by the donor, Nicholas the Goldsmith of St Albans, who had received it from Robert, brother of St Edmund Rich, Archbiship of Canterbury († 1240).[109] A like combination of jewel and devotional representation was the 'great Scottish pearl with pentacol in which it has an image of Our Lady enamelled behind' which was recorded in 1338.[110] Earlier, Edward I owned a valuable sapphire pendant,[111] and Edward II 'a gold pentacol with 1 pearl, emeralds and rubies' and another with 'a cameo, rubies and pearls'.[112]

Later roundels appear as stock designs on several brasses: both Joan Skirne (*c.* 1437) at Kingston upon Thames, Surrey (MS I), and Lady Daubeny (*c.* 1430) at South Petherton, Somerset (MS I), wear round pendants with pearls framing a cruciform motif in a plain-rimmed border. Edward IV in several portraits has rows of circular pendants hanging from chains across his breast.[113]

Pendants were given as love tokens. The small gold padlock in the Fishpool Hoard (Plate 8) is inscribed DE TOUT MON CUER amidst floral sprays;[114] it recalls the 'cheyne of goolde with a lokke of goolde gernyshed with a rubye' which Sir John Howard gave to his wife in 1467.[115] The effigy of Isabel, second wife of Sir John Cockayne († 1447), at Polesworth, Warwick,[116] shows a similar padlock worn as the centrepiece of a chain, fastening it in front. Even more symbolic is the heart-shaped gold pendant found at Rocklea Sands in Poole harbour inscribed TRISTES EN PLAISIR and engraved with an ivy leaf and tears[117] (Fig. 2), recalling those shed on the jewel which Chaucer's Troilus gave to Cressida 'with teres wete . . . as for a remembraunce'.[118]

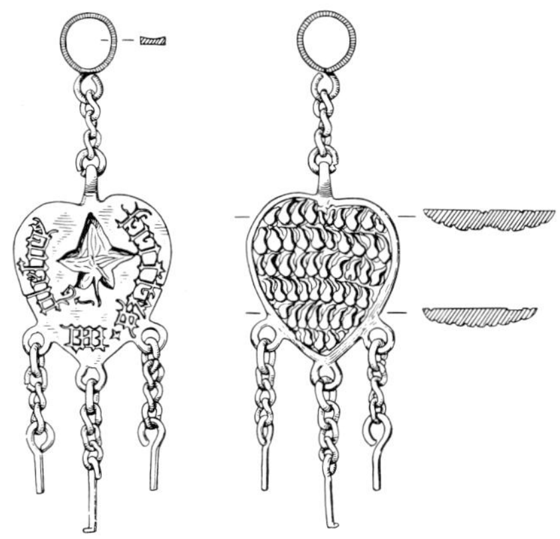

Fig. 2 Heart-shaped gold pendant: fifteenth century. British Museum

RELIQUARIES

An early gold reliquary pendant containing relics of St Thomas of Canterbury was given by Reginald FitzJocelin, Bishop of Bath (1174–91), to Queen Margaret of Sicily († 1183) who had appealed to the Pope on behalf of his father, Jocelin, Bishop of Salisbury, excommunicated for his opposition to Becket's policy as archbishop. It is rectangular, with a dragon's head suspension loop, and the frame is inscribed, identifying the (now missing) relics, which would have been covered with a piece of horn or crystal. On the back, figures depict Bishop Reginald blessing the queen with a Latin inscription 'Bishop Reginald hands this over to Queen Margaret of Sicily'.[119] A piece of the True Cross and relics of SS. Andrew, Fergus, Margaret, Ninian and Norbert are concealed beneath a plain wooden cross and pearls under a domed rock-crystal cover in a twelfth-century circular pendant. It is associated with a bishop of Galloway, the cathedral belonging to the Premonstratensian Canons founded by St Norbert, where the other saints were venerated.[120] Splinters from the True Cross were usually enclosed in cruciform reliquaries, such as that which Thomas, Duke of Gloucester, gave to St Albans in the fourteenth century.[121] Tiny fragments of wood and granite (perhaps from the True Cross and Rock of Calvary) are inside the fifteenth-century gold cross from Clare Castle, Suffolk. The front is engraved with the Crucified Lord, with traces of red enamel on the ground and the usual INRI label, and on the back, flowers, with four pearls at the intersection of the arms.[122]

The 'cace of silver gild and enameld with Relikes therin, with a crucifix, a Mare and John on the lidde, and an Image of our lady on that other syde with two men knelyng' which was among Brother Randolf's jewels[123] and Dame Isabel Morley's 'tablett of gold garneshid with perle conteyning certeyn Reliks within a berall in the same tablet with two images one of the Resurrection and another of Our Lady'[124] compare with two jewels in the British Museum. One, a pendant found on Reculver beach, is made from two round plaques of St John the Baptist and St Catherine, each framed in a twisted-cable border with relics in the space between.[125] The other, a square case with triple-arched top and projecting semicircular bosses at the sides, from Devizes, is engraved on the back with St John the Baptist and on the front with an archbishop, perhaps St Thomas of Canterbury, each flanked by white flowers (Plate 5). The inscription A MON DERRYNE (At the last moment of my earthly life) and tears (originally enamelled) on the sides complete the design and invoke the intercession of both saints at the moment of death.[126] The same saints appear on either side of the crucifix on the front of a reliquary in the shape of a Tau cross from Matlaske in Norfolk, now in the Norwich Museum[127] (Plate 6). An important lozenge-shaped reliquary was found at Middleham Castle, Yorkshire, in 1985 (Plate 7). The front is set with a square cabochon sapphire in a beaded collet and is engraved with the Trinity on the ground of branches; it is bordered with the inscription ECCE AGNUS DEI QUI TOLLIS PECCATA MUNDI

5 Enamelled gold reliquary pendant, showing an archbishop – possibly St Thomas of Canterbury – engraved on the front. Fifteenth century. British Museum.

6 Enamelled gold Tau cross reliquary pendant with St John the Baptist and St Thomas of Canterbury standing beside Christ Crucified. Fifteenth century. St Peter Hungate Museum, Norwich.

7 Enamelled gold lozenge-shaped reliquary pendant. Front: the Holy Trinity within a border inscribed ECCE AGNUS DEI QUI TOLLIS PECCATA MUNDI TETRAGRAMMATON ANANYZAPTA and set with a large cabochon sapphire. Back: the Nativity, watched by God the Father above, and with the Holy Lamb below, within a border of fifteen saints. Fifteenth century. Sotheby's.

TETRAGRAMMATON ANANYZAPTA. On the back, an engraving of the Nativity is framed by a border with fifteen standing figures of saints, all but one identifiable by their attributes as Peter and Paul, Augustine of Canterbury(?), Jerome, Anne, Our Lady, John the Baptist, Barbara, Margaret, Catherine, John the Evangelist, Mary Magdalene, George and Bartholomew.[128] The number and some of the names recall the group of Fourteen Holy Helpers in Need, devotion to whom as a group was widespread at this time.

CROSSES

As a token of baptism, the cross was worn daily and cherished. Eleanor, Duchess of Gloucester, in 1399 bequeathed her 'gold cross hanging by a chain with an image of the Crucifix, and 4 pearls about it . . . as thing of mine that I most love'.[129] While some were small and plain, worn inside the dress, others like the foregoing were intended for display. An example of the simple baptismal cross, with equal arms and five slightly larger squares in the centre and at the end of each limb, engraved with quatrefoils set saltirewise, has been found on a house site in Northampton. It dates from the twelfth or early thirteenth century. Similar crosses are in the Aylesbury Museum and have also been found in early medieval levels at Novgorod the Great in Russia.[130] Gem-stones or pearls could be set at the intersection of the arms or, like the Countess of Gloucester's 'little gold cross with a sapphire in the middle', on the surface.[131] This jewelled style is exemplified by Henry V's 'Cross with 1 Crucifix of gold, garnished of 4 small Baleis, and of many small pearls',[132] and that 'cross with four great pearls and one ruby in the midst' bequeathed by Maud, Countess of Cambridge († 1446), the number of jewels alluding to the Five Wounds.[133] The style is also represented by the cross from the Fishpool Hoard with the front set with four rectangular amethysts in the arms and an empty collet at the centre, and pins for pearls at the intersection. The symbolic number is repeated on the back by a ruby in a claw setting and four dog-flowers in squares on each arm[134] (Plate 8).

Crosses were also engraved with images; William Boston, of Boston, a Merchant of the Staple, in 1508 bequeathed a 'crosse of gold with the picture of Our Lord which I wear daily',[135] and in the 1465 inventory of Elizabeth Lewkenor of Sussex was a crucifix 'off golde & oure lady with oure lorde yn her armys y-nameled hangyng on A small cheyne off gold' – an ancient combination.[136]

Inscriptions were devotional or talismanic. Inscribed on a gold cross floretty seized from Brother John Randolf in 1419 was the motto AMER ET SERVIER,[137] and IHC for Jesus is on the back of a jet cross from Kirkcudbright.[138] Nielloed on the back of a fourteenth-century silver cross from Dumfriesshire is the magical word AGLA[139] (Plate 9), and the 'crosse of gold with a crappot [toadstone] in the same' bequeathed to his son Walter in 1506 by Sir William Calverley is in this apotropaic category.[140]

Various shapes of cross were used in addition to the simple Greek type (equal-

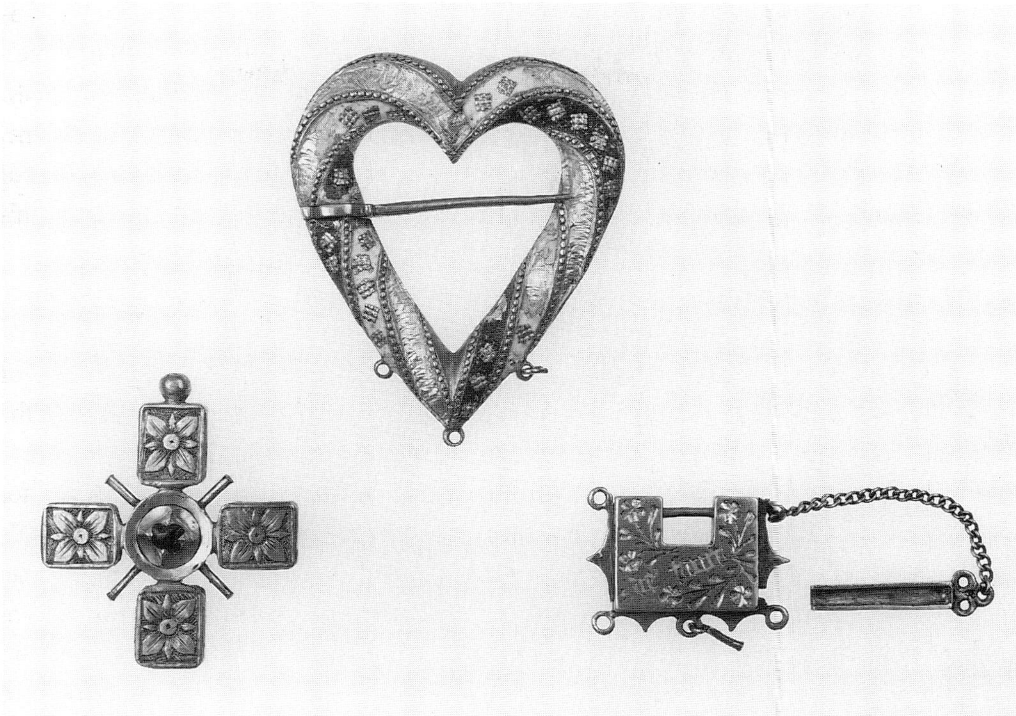

8 Gold jewels from the Fishpool Hoard. Cross set with a ruby between the arms. Heart-shaped ring brooch with inscription at the back. Padlock inscribed MON CHER amidst foliage on the front and DE TOUT on the back. Fifteenth century. British Museum.

9 Nielloed silver cross. Front: arms engraved in ladder-like lines around a central disk. Back: central disk inscribed AGLA. Fourteenth century. National Museum of Scotland.

armed) and the Latin type (with the lower arm longer). Cecily, Duchess of York, bequeathed to the Queen in 1495 a 'crosse croslette of diamantes';[141] and a 'crosse of golde ragged, which was my father's accustomably worn abowte my necke' – that is, a cross with the lopped end of branches on the arms, the heraldic cross ragully – is mentioned in the will of the Countess of Oxford in 1537.[142] Crosses shaped like the Greek letter T, the Tau cross, were associated with St Anthony and with the prophecy of Ezekiel that the elect would be recognised by the sign of the Tau on their brows. A London draper, Thomas Salle, in 1468 left his wife 'an Antony crosse of golde to hang on hir bedis' and 'an Anthony crosse of golde with iij dyamondes a ruby and a pearle

10 Gold Tau cross with St Anthony ringing his bell. Fifteenth century. Roman Baths Museum, Bath City Council.

fixed in the same'.[143] Besides the Matlaske reliquary, whose broad shape has the arms of a Tau cross projecting from it, three other examples have survived: one from Bridlington engraved with the Annunciation,[144] another from a grave on the site of St James's church, Bath, with St Anthony[145] (Plate 10), and the third from Winteringham, South Humberside.[146]

TABLETS

Tableaux of religious subjects or figures of God and the saints were represented on single panels, diptychs or triptychs, sometimes covered with crystal or glass, and worn as pendants. The images or 'histories' might be engraved or enamelled or worked in low relief in gold, silver, mother-of-pearl, ivory or boxwood, and embellished with gems and pearls. An inventory of the goods of Humphrey, Earl of Essex, in 1322 included a 'small tablet with one Crucifix and one "Mariole" of Our Lady enamelled';[147] this compares with a small early- fourteenth-century lozenge-shaped gold pendant in the

British Museum with the same subjects[148] (Plate 11). Such tablets became more elaborate, and those made by John Palyng for Queen Isabella's New Year's gifts in 1397 were intricately wrought and set with rubies and sapphires.[149] Some images appear regularly: the Virgin and Child; the Virgin's Coronation and Annunciation; the Holy Trinity; the three Magi; and St Katherine, St John the Baptist and St George.[150] Henry VI's New Year's gift to Humphrey, Duke of Gloucester in 1445 was 'A Tabulet of Gold with an Ymage of the Pite of our Lord, Garnished with Stones and Perle, Bought of Mathew Phelip'.[151] Devotion to the Christ of Pity, which started in Italy, became very popular in the north and prayers before the images were granted indulgences.[152]

11 Gold lozenge-shaped pendant showing front with the Virgin amidst flowers, formerly enamelled. Early fourteenth century. British Museum.

AGNUS DEI

Wax roundels made from the remains of the Paschal candles, impressed with the Agnus Dei and blessed by the Pope on the Thursday in Easter week in the first and every seventh year of his pontificate, were highly valued relics and are listed in a 1338 Wardrobe inventory.[153] There were four in the posthumous inventory of Edward II's widow in 1358 – cased in silver-gilt, gold, and enamelled.[154] Some were also studded with gem-stones and pearls, like one bequeathed by Nicholas Alwyn, alderman of London, in 1505: 'an Agnus dei of gold with a ruby and iv oryent perles with spangles pendaunt';[155] or that in the will of Elizabeth Browne, a London widow, in 1497: 'an Agnus with a baleys, 3 saphires, 3 perles, with an Image of saint Antony a pon it';[156] and other cases were enamelled or nielloed on both sides with images of the Virgin, the Crucifixion, the Christ of Pity, the Annunciation or Assumption, and various saints. Others were mounted in mother-of-pearl carved in relief, like that bequeathed by

Thomas Salle in 1468: 'an Agnus Dei of gold with the ymage of seint George graven in the moder of perle in the same . . . an Agnus Dei of gold with the figure of our lord God in the sepulchre gravenne in the moder of perle in the same'.[157] In 1496 Sir Robert Radcliffe bequeathed to Our Lady of Walsingham his 'Agnus Dei with the Vernacle on the one side and the holy Lambe on that other side with all the Reliques that be therin'.[158] So many were pledged to the Goldsmiths' Company for misdemeanours that they were clearly in great demand and every jeweller probably had some in stock.[159]

BROOCHES AND BUCKLES

Before the introduction of buttons in the fourteenth century, brooches made of precious or base metals or even of wood, in various sizes, were the all-purpose fasteners of clothing.[160] They were also pinned to hats, attached to beads and worn as ornaments linked together in pairs (Plate III). The guide to the French language written *c.* 1415, *Femina*, ascribed

> . . . to the ladyes fayre Iewelez
> Cotez of soy, brochys of gold.[161]

RING BROOCHES (FERMAIL, FIRMACULUM)

The commonest type of medieval brooch consisted of a pin attached to an open circle, left plain or decorated with figures, inscriptions, punched or nielloed ornament and gem-stones. These ring brooches, the heraldic fermail, appear in family and other arms. Three such brooches, each of a different design, are on the non-armorial seal of Robert St John, *c.* 1200.[162] The ring brooch is first found in the twelfth century, and a number can be dated approximately by the associated coins in hoards ranging from *c.* 1180 to *c.* 1320. While surviving examples show that they continued to be made throughout the fourteenth and fifteenth centuries, none has been found in the later medieval hoards.[163] From the fifteenth century they are part of the arms of the Goldsmiths' Company and, in 1448, a drawing of a shield with 'three buckles of silver made on the wyse as in here with flowers of silver on the buckles made of iiij like a trewlove' was sent to John Paston[164] (Fig. 3).

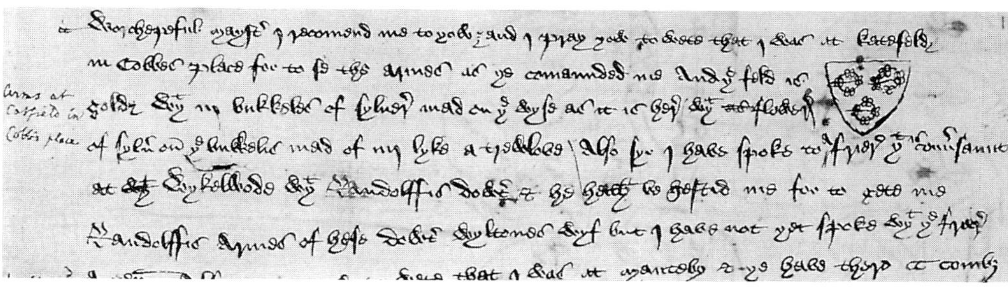

Fig. 3 Shield charged with three 'truelove' ring brooches: from a manuscript of the Paston Letters, 1448. British Library.

12 Gold ring brooch set with garnets and sapphires in high collets between fruit pods. Late thirteenth/early fourteenth century. Manchester City Art Galleries.

13 Gold ring brooch set with onyx cameo heads alternating with rubies (one missing). *c.* 1320–40, cameos perhaps earlier. National Museum of Wales, Cardiff, from Oxwich.

Ring brooches of the simplest character have been found in England and Scotland[165] made of gold, silver or silver-gilt (Plate IV), and bronze: round, oval, square or polygonal and decorated with small flowers. A square brooch with flowers at each corner was found at Billingsgate, London,[166] and the Wardrobe accounts describe more elaborate designs. A small fourteenth-century brooch found in London has the ring set with rubies and sapphires between punched gold sections like a miniature crown; and a larger brooch at Manchester has a gem set in the middle of the pin and eight garnets and sapphires in high collets between bosses with pods[167] (Plate 12). Such brooches in bronze have been found at Winchester from the late-thirteenth- and fourteenth-century levels.[168] Two bronze brooches in the Norwich Castle Museum have birds in high relief between the collets and were cast from different moulds. The better modelled of the two is a fragment from Caistor by Norwich and, since they are so unusual and two versions of the design have been found in Norfolk, it is safe to assume that they represent a local fourteenth-century type.[169] The most important survival is the Oxwich brooch *c.* 1320–40, named after the castle in West Glamorgan where it was discovered in 1968.[170] The ring is set with three cameo heads and as many cabochon rubies (one lost) in collets with beaded edges (Plate 13). In the opinion of Hans Wenzel the cameos were engraved *c.* 1250, but since similar coiffed heads of craftsmen are seen in the enamels of the silver altar of St James at Pistoia Cathedral *c.* 1316, they could also be contemporary.[171] Since they do not fit the collets perfectly, they must be replacements for the original stones. A ring brooch with cast heads was found in the Münster Hoard of *c.* 1340 in Westphalia;[172] and the beaded edges to the collets compare with those on jewels from the Colmar treasure which was dated by coins to *c.* 1342–53 or a little later.

A recent discovery from Boxley, Kent, is a fourteenth-century bronze ring brooch, with traces of rust from an iron pin. Cast in an open mould (the back shows traces of the filing needed), the face was subsequently engraved with lines. Allowing the space for the pin, there are six forked and cusped projections round the circumference and it seems to be a unique design. A smaller lead alloy oval brooch from an old collection in King's Lynn has also lost its fitting. Cast with cabochon 'gems' separated by pellets for pearls on hatching, the profile of the ring rises in a curve from the outer edge to the inner, no doubt for greater strength. Probably found locally in the river, it is not a type recovered so far in London.[173]

Inscriptions, nielloed or enamelled, were a popular decoration. Some are straightforward claims to wonder-working powers, as on a ring brooch in the British Museum with CELELI VVS AVEZ ENCLOS VVS SALV EV MER NE LA OS (This which you have fastened on saves you by sea or in battle).[174] Others invoke the protection of the Christian religion, such as the black-letter + AVE DE + MOY MERCIE + PITE MON COER EN + VOUS REPOCE on a brooch found near Doune Castle, Scotland, written on the smooth sections of the twisted ring beginning to the right of the pin[175] (Plate 14).

14 Gold ring brooch with twisted scroll inscribed in black letter + AVE DE + MOY MERCIE + PITE MON COER EN + VOUS REPOCE. Early fifteenth century. National Museum of Scotland.

The name of Christ, according to the *Revelation of the Monk of Evesham* was considered

> a remedye against sudden death: Trewly and verily and the crysten peple wolde wryte dayly on her forhedys and about the placys of her herte wyth her fyngur of [?or] in any other wyse these ij wordys that conteynyth the mysterye of the helthe and salvacyon of mankynde, that ys to wytte and to saye Ihesus Nazarenus.[176]

It was used in this way on brooches. 'A gold brooch of the old manner, and the name of

15 Gold ring brooch formed from two pairs of cuffed sleeves terminating in clasped hands, inscribed AND TO THEE MARY HIS MODER BRIGHT. Fifteenth century. Museum of Antiquities, Newcastle upon Tyne.

God written in each part' had been given to John of Gaunt by his mother, Queen Philippa, who 'commanded that I keep it with her blessing', and he in turn bequeathed it to his son, Henry IV.[177] It occurs with the names of two of the Magi on the Kames brooch *c.* 1300 – IESUS NAZARENUS REX IUDEORUM JASPAR MELPCHIOR – and that of one of the Fates, ATROPA. The ring is figurative, with the bodies of six dragons, each biting the tail of the one in front, making a full circle.[178] All three of the Magi are named on two brooches from the Thames water-front[179] and on the Glenlyon brooch, which combines them with the last word of Christ on the cross, CONSUMATUM. On this last, an heirloom of the Campbells, the front of the flat ring is set with pearls in tall cone-shaped turrets alternating with crystals and amethysts.[180] Some inscriptions invoke the protection of the Virgin or St John the Baptist, and a clay mould for brooches, found at Ashill in Norfolk, bears the Angelic salutation AVE MARIA GRATIA PLEN[A].[181] A ring brooch made in the form of clasped hands (a motif found on rings from the reign of Henry II,[182] although not so far on brooches of that period) has a double inscription in English: on the front TO THEE IHCU MY TROUGHT I PLIGHT and on the back AND TO THEE MARY HIS MODER BRIGHT[183] (Plate 15). Ring brooches with pairs of clasped hands were found in the Münster Hoard of *c.* 1340, and similar brooches have been reported from Austria to Scandinavia.[184] In these the pairs of hands follow the line of the ring but another type has a single pair projecting from the circumference. A thirteenth-century gold example is in the British Museum and another from Felixstowe, Suffolk, is made of bronze and can be seen in the Norwich Castle Museum collections.[185] There were hands holding a diamond in a blue enamelled brooch bequeathed by Philippa, Countess of March, to her son Edmund in 1378;[186] it compares with a fourteenth-century brooch in the British Museum inscribed + AVE MARIA G.D. with the projecting hands holding an opal.[187]

Heart-shaped ring brooches were inscribed with appropriately loving mottoes: 'j broche of golde shapyn like an harte, writen therinne "in thy heart is my heart a vous me lie"' and another with 'a ma vie de coer entier'.[188] Two are so alike that they might come from the same maker. That from the Fishpool Hoard has the face decorated with beading in blue and white enamel and on the back, in black letter, JE SUY VOSTRE SANS DE PARTIER amidst flowers and leaves; the other has the front imbricated and the back inscribed NOSTRE ET TOUT DITZ A VOSTRE [D]ESEIR.[189]

The posy, reason or motto 'sans de partier', with its promise of fidelity, is inscribed – variously spelt – on at least seven brooches and six rings. Equally affectionate is the inscription IO SUI ICI EN LIU DAMI: AMO (I am here in place of a friend: love) on the back of another thirteenth-century ring brooch with front studded alternately with rubies and sapphires (Plate 16); it could have been a lover's gift.[140] The same theme occurs on two other brooches, one of plain gold with the ring inscribed with the rather proprietorial declaration: (front) + IEO : SUI : FERMAIL : PUR : GAP [*sic*] : DER : SEIN; (back) + KE : NU : SUILEIN : NIMITTE : MEIN (I am a brooch to guard the breast, that no rascal may put his hand thereon).[191] The other, a square silver-gilt brooch recovered recently from Thames Street, London, EC4, has the letters + I / O:A I.E. / N.C. / LO / S[ ] / RA / NI (I hold closed . . .) between garnets on the front only.[192] The love motto and charm 'Amor omnia vincit' – the words that Chaucer's Prioress had on the brooch hanging from her beads – occurs on a brooch at Shakespeare's Birthplace Museum, Stratford-upon-Avon.[193] A bronze ring brooch is ornamented with the figures of two lovers with raised hands clasped overhead and the pin extending from his waist to hers[194] (Plate 17).

Two silver ring brooches *c.* 1250 echo the dragon theme of the Kames brooch, with dragons fighting with men, or in pairs facing each other with tails entwined.[195]

16 Gold ring brooch. Front: inscribed IEIO VH EMI between rubies and sapphires. Back: inscribed to: IO SUI ICI EN LIU DAMI: AMO. Thirteenth century. British Museum.

17 Bronze ring brooch formed from a pair of lovers clasping hands. Fourteenth century. University Museum of Archaeology and Anthropology, Cambridge.

LETTER BROOCHES

Two brooches with the letter A for Amor had their meaning reinforced with inscriptions. One, 'An old flat brass fibula, flat serrated on the outside, inscribed LOVE LEDIT TO MI LEMEN, and on the other side, JOLIE ET QUI ME PORTE in old English characters', was found at Calne, Wiltshire.[196] The other, also from that county, is studded with coloured stones and on the face AGLA (the abbreviation of the talismanic formula 'Atha gebri leilan Adonai', Thou art mighty for ever O Lord), and on the back IO FAS AMER E DOZ DE AMER (I am love and the gift of love)[197] (Plate 18). The most magnificent surviving English letter brooch was bequeathed to New College by Peter Hylle in 1455 (Plate V). It is a silver-gilt crowned Lombardic letter M with beaded edges, enclosing the Archangel and the Virgin of the Annunciation, and combines miniature sculpture, enamel, a diamond, carbochon rubies, emeralds and pearls. The figures stand on bases similar to those made for statues, and the remains of the hinge for

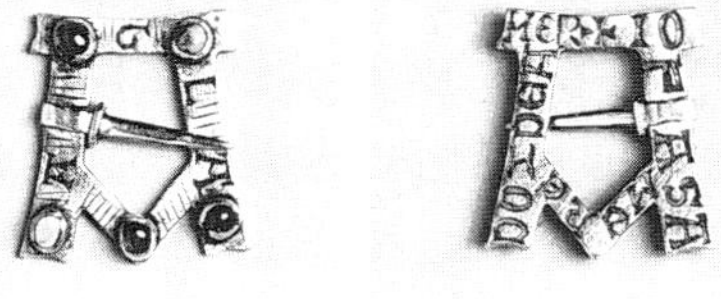

18 Gold letter A brooch. Front: studded with coloured stones and inscribed AGLA. Back: inscribed IO FAS AMER E DOZ DE AMER. Thirteenth century. Walters Art Gallery, Baltimore, USA.

the pin can be seen on the back.[198] The type of design was also used by glaziers[199] and a like brooch, with St Denis and a kneeling monk in the arches of an M, in the Treasury of St Denis, Paris, may have been made in the same, presumably Parisian, workshop.[200]

DISK BROOCHES (MONILE)

Next in importance after the ring brooch and its derivatives was the disk type: a circular plate of metal, engraved, filled with gem-stones or otherwise ornamented. The gift of a monile, which in classical Latin means a necklace or torque, was illustrated by a disk brooch in the Benefactor's Book at St Alban's Abbey; and a Yorkshire will of 1440 clearly states that the English for monile was nouche.[201] An early example is copied from a coin of Henry I *c.* 1110–12, with the inscription round the edge + GOTPINE [*sic*] : ON : GLOECI (+ Godwine (moneyer) at Gloucester), but with the letters engraved instead of being made with punches as on the coins. A piece of wire is soldered on the back to make both catch and pin.[202]

In the disk type, coloured stones and pearls were clustered around a large central stone radiating outwards like the points of a star. An early example, set with a large sapphire encircled by three (of four) pearls in round collets in a filigree octofoil, was found in 1774 with coins of the eleventh century near the church of St Mary-at-Hill in London.[203]

A variant of this type was the wheel brooch, which derives its name from the ribs linking the centre with the outer border. Some inexpensive examples of silver-gilt set with pastes survive, having been sewn on to a mitre, and a large gilt-bronze hexafoil brooch was found at Topler's Hill, Edworth, Bedfordshire.[204] Now in the University Museum of Archaeology, Cambridge, it is set with crystals, amethysts, emerald-coloured pastes and pearls in collets round the circumference and at the inter-section of the arms, and with small star-like troches on the cusps. The Lochbuy brooch, with a domed crystal centre encircled by eight obelisks standing on the rim, each set with a river pearl, is a late representative of this type.[205]

Few details apart from the type of stone and the value were recorded for the many brooches given by monarchs and their families to religious houses and courtiers. Only one of Piers Gaveston's brooches was adequately described: 'a brooch of gold with two emeralds two rubies four pearls and a sapphire in the middle'.[206] The role of enamel is mentioned in connexion with an important brooch belonging to the Black Prince: 'a gold brooch enamelled, with an Eastern ruby in the middle and five diamonds and twelve great stones'.[207] Not all were round. The mantle of Lady Montacute († 1354) on her effigy at Christchurch, Oxford, is clasped with a lozenge-shaped leafy brooch set with a large cabochon stone;[208] and Queen Isabella owned one with a cruciform design: 'one great brooch of gold with pearls and other stones in fashion of one cross'.[209] In 1378 Sir John Foxle bequeathed 'a gold brooch [monile] with a letter S carved and enamelled'.[210] The hexafoil brooch on the mantle of Queen Anne († 1394) at

Westminster Abbey is set with a central gem in a high collet with large pearls between triple clusters at the tips of the incurved sides.[211]

PILGRIM SIGNS

The secular brooches in base metal that have survived, including crowned initials and livery badges, are far outnumbered by those bought at places of pilgrimage at home or abroad, and usually found in the rivers at London and Paris. Most were made of lead or pewter, though some were of precious metal like 'my blake bonet with a double toff a bruche of sylver of Our Lady of Walsingham' bequeathed by Henry Roper in 1517.[212] Moulds for casting them are in the British Museum, the King's Lynn Museum and the Museum of London,[213] and there was a forge for working metal at the Walsingham shrine.

Writing *c.* 1200, Giraldus Cambrensis recalled a visit with his friends to the Bishop of Winchester at his palace in Southwark, when the bishop said that he knew they had just come from Canterbury by the signs hanging round their necks.[214] In the decades that followed, such signs were worn in the hat, secured either by a stud or sewn on loops. Both English signs – identifiable by their iconography and by their pierced openwork techniques – and signs from continental shrines are represented in finds and collections.[215] After the translation of the body of St Thomas to a new shrine in 1220, the Canterbury pilgrimage surpassed all others in popularity in England and many of the signs were connected with it. They include the initial of the saint, his mitred bust beneath a Gothic canopy, his voyage on board ship after his exile in France, his triumphal ride to Canterbury, the sword and scabbard of his martyrdom, and the shrine and holy water ampullae.[216] Other badges represented the cults of Our Lady of Walsingham, St Alban, St Edmund, the uncanonised Thomas, Earl of Lancaster, and many others, often of very local importance.[217]

ICONOGRAPHIC BROOCHES

Some examples of religious and secular iconographies have already been mentioned and others are recorded, like the 'brooch of gold and a large sapphire and environed of large pearls and 1 image of St George within the brooch, when a man wishes to see it man can open it' stolen from the Earl of Huntingdon in 1377.[218] Other saints were visible, not hidden. There was the silver-gilt St Christopher on the breast of Chaucer's Yeoman,[219] and a gold ring brooch is engraved with figures of St Christopher and St George, with interlaced ornament on the back.[220] Secular motifs were also used, such as the 'broche with a jintylle woman' recorded in 1473 as a pledge.[221]

HERALDIC EMBLEMS

Heraldic charges were made into brooches of eagles, lions, fleurs-de-lis and crowns.[222] The earliest example, a gold brooch in the form of a kite-shaped shield with a rounded

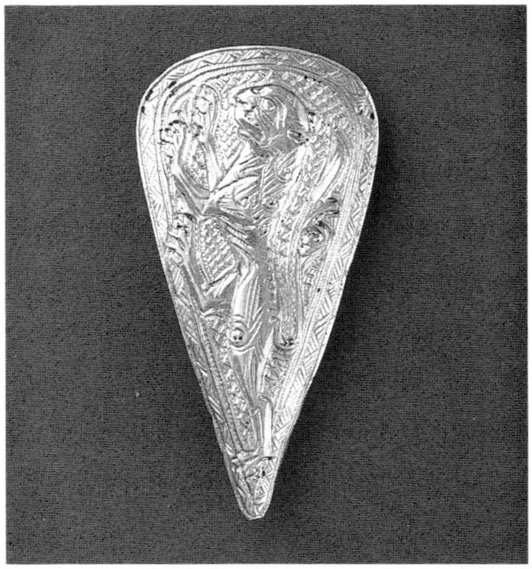

19 Gold shield brooch bearing charge of a lion rampant. Twelfth century. Private collection, from Folkingham; on loan to the British Museum.

top (a type which disappeared after *c.* 1180), is engraved with a lion rampant on a cross-hatched field with a broad plain rim (Plate 19) like those on the shields of the Bayeux Tapestry. It was found at Folkingham Castle, Lincs., which was held by Simon de St Liz, Earl of Northampton, in the right of his wife, Alice – by one or other of whom it was probably lost.[223] A favourite heraldic charge, it recalls the shield borne in the *Gesta Romanorum* by the strongest of three knights because it was 'kyng of bestes, and all bestes drede the lyon'.[224] The upper face of an early-fourteenth-century ring brooch on loan to the Ashmolean Museum (Fig. 4) is enamelled with banners of the arms of France, England, Evreux (?), Henry of Lancaster, Bohun, Despencer, Warenne and Beauchamp, and must have been made early in Edward II's reign. Edward's sister Eleanor, widow of Henry III, Count of Bar, married John de Warenne, Earl of Surrey, in 1306 and all the families represented were connected by marriage with descendants of Henry III of England.[225]

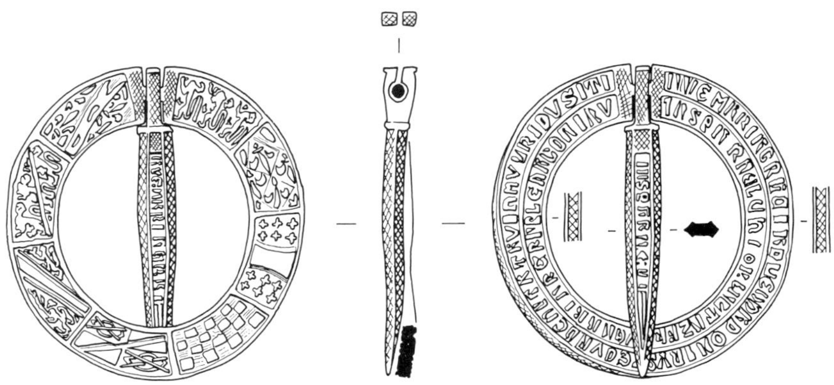

Fig. 4 Heraldic enamelled bronze ring brooch: early fourteenth century. Chaddesley Corbett Loan, Ashmolean Museum, Oxford. Drawn by Nick Griffiths.

20 The Dunstable swan, enamelled white on gold, and chained *c.* 1400. British Museum.

The Bohun swan, like the antelope, was a device of Mary, first wife of Henry IV; an example of *c.* 1400, richly enamelled *en ronde bosse* with thick white opaque enamel ruffled feathers and black eyes and feet, shown in the act of strutting ashore, was found at Dunstable with the original pin and catch intact, and the fine chain hanging from the crown about its neck (Plate 20). It is comparable to the white hart badges depicted in the Wilton Diptych,[226] and a similar brooch is worn by Joan Peryent († 1415) at Digswell, Herts. (MS I), on the down-turned collar of her houppelaunde – recalling in position, if not size or type, that worn by the carpenter's wife, Alison, in the *Canterbury Tales*:

> A brooch she baar upon hir lowe coler,
> As brood as is the boos of a bokeler.[227]

A silver brooch of a Saracen's head, bequeathed by a fourteenth-century clerk to the Virgin in the chapel of Rouncesvalles near Charing Cross, may also have had an heraldic significance; it was the crest of the Lords Cobham of Sterborough, among others.[228]

The badges of the great magnates were worn as brooches by their retainers. A silver crescent badge survives, with a P and smaller crescents engraved on it, for the Percy family; and just such a badge was bequeathed by William Stowe of Ripon in 1430: 'my livery of silver Englished "cressaunt" and my livery Englished "coller"' to the shrine of St Wilfrid.[229] Others were made of lead or even cloth, like the 13,000 cognisances of the boar ordered by Richard III in 1483.[230] In his portraits Richard II is shown wearing what may be a rose jewel in his hat.[231]

CLOAK CLASPS

Velvet, silk or cloth-of-gold mantles and cloaks lined with fur were dignified ceremonial attire as well as a protection against the cold. Some were fastened, like choir copes, with a large brooch at the neck or – for men – on the right shoulder,[232] but most effigies show a tasselled cord passing through ornamental clasps and fitted with a slide to draw the garment more tightly across the breast.[233] From the fourteenth century, buttons were used for shoulder fastenings.[234]

Clasps had to be heavy enough to take the weight of yards of material, and designs are relatively uniform; many of the popular ones must be stock workshop patterns. The clasps are, however, seldom identified in inventories or wills, although the inventory for Humphrey, Earl of Hereford, *c.* 1319 listed '2 silver brooches for [a] mantle in a little ivory case'.[235] The rosette occurs frequently: it is on the early-fourteenth-century effigy of a lady of the Ryther family at Ryther, Yorks.,[236] and, framed in a round border, in the brass of Elizabeth Cobham († 1375) at Lingfield, Surrey (MS I). In the fifteenth century the border is elaborated into jewelled polylobes, as in the brasses of an unknown lady (*c.* 1410) at South Ormsby, Lincs. (MS I), and of Joan Skirne (*c.* 1437) at Kingston upon Thames, Surrey (MS I).

Blanche of the Tower (*c.* 1376) on her effigy at Westminster Abbey has a stock pattern of rosettes in lozenges.[237] The thick straight-sided lozenge clasps with cruciform patterns worn by a lady of the Dinham family (*c.* 1400) at Kingskerswell, Devon,[238] are almost identical with the pair depicted on an early-fifteenth-century lady at Broughton, Oxon.[239] Clasps of this design worn by Henry IV on his effigy (*c.* 1420) at Canterbury Cathedral[240] are linked by a jewelled band. The lozenge-shaped clasps on the mantle of his wife, Joan of Navarre, on the same tomb are shown as set with cabochon gems or pearls. Similar jewels decorate the roundel clasps with pearled crosses worn by Thomas, Earl of Arundel († 1415), at Arundel.[241] Lady Waterton (*c.* 1424) at Methley, Yorks.,[242] has a round domed form; and another unusual style of roundels (now empty) in squares, *en suite* with the buttons of her gown, is worn by Myfanwy, wife of Sir Goronwy ap Tudor (*c.* 1385), at Penmyndd, Anglesey.[243]

Personal choice and detailed instructions must account for the occasional use of royal badges or coats-of-arms on cloak clasps. A pair of lion's masks clasp the mantle of an unknown lady (*c.* 1350) at Staindrop church, Durham,[244] and the eagles facing in different directions which match the ouche in the torse worn by Sir Edmund Thorpe's wife (*c.* 1417) at Ashwellthorpe, Norfolk,[245] may be royal badges. The shields of arms of Bonville, and possibly Damarell quartering Bonville, make the clasps of an unknown woman on a brass (*c.* 1440) at Luppitt, Devon (MS I).

Occasionally naturalistic motifs are used. A Fitzalan lady (*c.* 1306) at Bedale church, Yorks.,[246] wears a pair of leaf-shaped clasps; and Christine Phelip († 1470), wife of the royal jeweller Matthew, at Herne, Kent (MS IV), has a design of open flowers. There are double roses on the clasps of the Countess of Essex (*c.* 1483) on her brass at Little Easton, Essex (MS II); and, as befits the widow of a former Treasurer, Joan, Lady Cromwell († 1479, engraved *c.* 1490), at Tattershall, Lincs. (MS IV), is resplendent in multi-petalled clasps, each with a large stone in a scalloped setting.

SLIDES

The slides to hold the mantle cords could be given ornamental features. The brass of Christine Phelip at Herne has an elaborate sphere with two grooved bands between a narrow cable-twist spiral ribbon; and Joyce Tiptoft (*c.* 1470) at Enfield, Middx. (MS I), a small double circle of beads like a coronet.

OUCHES

The middle English ouch or nouche derived from an old Germanic, or perhaps Celtic, term for a buckle or clasp. This is confirmed by the fifteenth-century Anglo-Latin wordlists and a Yorkshire will of 1440 listing 'unum monile Anglice nouche auri cum uno saphiro in medio et j dyamond de super et circumpositum cum perelis et emeraudes'.[247] It was also used for parts of larger jewels such as coronets, and Henry IV's 'Pisan' collar had

x. owches eche of hem wyth double floures of gold garnysed, and on eche of the same owches is a grete baleys and vi greete peerles of whych baleys vii are of entaille squ are and iii of hem are rounde and ragged.[248]

They were among the customary gifts made by the English royal family to their courtiers and to shrines, such as that given to St Thomas of Canterbury in 1316.[249]

Few details are recorded of Piers Gaveston's ouches, which were enamelled and set with gems.[250] Some were geometrical: 'a square gold ouch with one topaz and other stones' was offered to Our Lady of Caversham in 1316–17,[251] and there was 'one ouch in fashion of a lozenge with iii emeraldes and iii oriental pearls with i baleis in the middle' in the royal collection, 1343–4.[252] There were also naturalistic designs – a 'gold ouch in the fashion of leaves' in the same inventory – while some of the fine gems of the Black Prince were mounted in designs inspired by the trefoils and pinnacles of Gothic architecture.[253] Rich bright gems contrasted with white pearls in Richard II's large 'gold nouche garnished with seven balays six sapphires four emeralds and twelve clusters of pearls, in each cluster a diamond', and in 1445 Henry VI bought similar ouches from Matthew Phelip.[254] They long remained in fasion; Margaret Capel (1516) bequeathed:

an ouche of gold sett with a great balas and with a great safure and two perles and a litill emerod in the myddes . . . the ouch of gold she weryth upon her best crosse garnisshed with a great garnet and with 6 perles . . . [and] an owche of gold sett with a balas and saffure and with 6 perles.[255]

Many ouches were heraldic. Humphrey, Earl of Hereford († 1322), owned a 'gold nouch cut like one shield with an eagle of sapphires, rubies, pearls, and a ruby pendant in its beak';[256] and Edward III gave a 'great nouche with an eagle and a great diamond in the breast, and garnished with rubies, diamonds and pearls' as a wedding present in 1359.[257] Eagle badges were distributed by the Black Prince to his tournament companions (see above, p. 7). Of the eagles on badges in Richard II's collection, one gripped pearls in its claws, another seized a deer, a third with white feathers was in a round frame, and a fourth with black feathers was on a grassy mound.[258] Interestingly, his friend Thomas, Earl of Worcester, had an ouch bearing two eagles, and another with a 'stag in the midst', both garnished with gems and clusters of pearls.[259] Sir Edmund Thorpe († 1417) and his wife wear this royal badge on their effigies at Ashwellthorpe, Norfolk[260] – he on the right shoulder and she as mantle clasps and in the centre of her torse. John, Earl of Oxford and Lord High Chamberlain (†1513), had a fine gold and gem-studded eagle displayed which he gave to Our Lady of Walsingham.[261]

The eagle was only one of many devices associated with the English crown. Among the ouches listed in the 1397 inventory of Richard II were 'nouches each with a Griffon garnished', a device of his grandfather, Edward III; a 'gold greyhound enamelled white with i sapphire and i pearl about the neck'; a 'great nouche with i white falcon seated on i perch'; and also his own device: 'i nouche of gold enamelled with i white hart under i castle' and another with 'a Damsel with i white hart lying on i terrace under i tree'. The great English families were also represented in the king's collection: the Bohun swan, Mortimer's lion, the Arundel horse, all richly jewelled.[262] In the fifteenth century the Duke of York pledged an ouche of his badge 'with a greet poynted diamand sette upon a roose enameled white' to Sir John Fastolf.[263]

Not all ouches were heraldic. An 'ouche of gold garnished of precious stones with two images in the fashion of a king and queen' was recorded in 1356,[264] and another of Edward III's ouches had a 'small castle'.[265] Some presented elaborate tableaux; Richard II had one with a child riding a leopard, and others with women sitting on a sun and with a unicorn.[266] Thomas, Earl of Worcester's 'moorhen being on a green terrace' was in the same style.[267] Matthew Phelip supplied several figurative ouches in 1445: 'in the manner of a Gentilwoman' or a 'Parc'.[268] The favourite motif of lovers appeared on an ouche pledged by the Duke of York: 'in facion of a ragged staf with ij ymages of a man and woman garnysshed with a ruby, a diamande, and a greet peerle'.[269]

Ouches with religious imagery seem to have been rarer, but Edward III owned a 'gold ouch of St Eustace' and another of Our Lady below a letter K. Another such letter jewel, Y for her initial, came from Queen Isabella, as did the M ouche worn attached to the crucifix on her beads and given to her by her daughter Joan, Queen of Scotland.[270]

MILITARY AND CIVILIAN BELTS, LADIES' GIRDLES AND APPENDAGES

Swords, daggers, purses, beads and other items hung from the belt or girdle, which was an essential part of the dress of the Middle Ages. While lesser folk wore belts and girdles of plain leather or cloth harnessed with bronze, those worn by the upper classes were very rich, usually of silk and harnessed with gold or silver-gilt, enamels and jewels. King John owned at least forty belts of red leather or silk, variously ornamented with silver and gold fittings set with gem-stones.[271] Martin of Holy Cross, Master of Sherborn Hospital, Durham (1254), left his 'great girdle of black silk with gold harnessed of silver' and two more girdles 'of silk with gold with harnessing of silver gilt'.[272] Except for those of base metal, the fittings were made by goldsmiths, although some were imported. In 1324 the royal collection included 'a girdle of the old fashion with letters of pearls of which the buckle and the tag are enamelled of scutcheons of the arms of England and others' and a 'girdle of Paris work with lozenges of white pearls, and between the lozenges plates enamelled with images' and another 'for a sword in the fashion of Genoa garnished with enamels of the arms of Lancaster'.[273] Equally, English work was to be found abroad. In 1408 an inventory of the Duke and Duchess of Orléans listed a 'gold girdle in the English fashion, richly jewelled with the buckle having a sun in the middle and on the same sun a collet without a stone encircled by small pearls' and other gem-stones.[274]

The belt was one of the items which Edward III tried to control by his sumptuary law (see above, p. 1). According to Chaucer, Langland and the wills, most citizens and parish clergy took no notice of this and subsequent laws, and went on showing off their silver-mounted girdles and purses. By the fifteenth century, many styles of decoration were available and belts made acceptable wedding presents; many people owned several.[275]

MILITARY BELTS

The *cingulum militis* worn round the hips with the sword was first made of bands of leather or other stiff material, strengthened and adorned by bars and studs, with the buckle as the focus of the decoration. This type remained popular throughout the thirteenth and and fourteenth centuries and is exemplified by the wide belt of William de Valence († 1296) at Westminster Abbey,[276] which has vertical bars between paired rosettes. Rectangular panels with 'Jill in the Green' heads, double eagles, etc., ornamented the belt on the oak effigy of Sir Robert de Bois († 1334) at Fersfield, Norfolk;[277] and there are large cruciform studs on the sword-belt of John of Eltham († 1336) in Westminster Abbey.[278] He wears an ogival buckle, but that on the contemporary effigy of John, Earl of Hereford, at Hereford Cathedral is rectangular with trefoils, matching tag, and bars with large roses closely set together.[279] Other motifs were more personal: Catherine-wheels, perhaps alluding to a patron saint; initials or badges, like the crosses moline taken from his arms, on the belt of John, Lord Willoughby (*c.* 1396), at Spilsby, Lincs.,[280] or the lion masks alternating with rosettes of Sir John Lyons (?1349) at Warkworth, Northants.[281] The Black Prince bought a belt mounted with enamelled silver-gilt fittings for £15,[282] and the belt on his effigy is adorned with the lions of England.[283]

A more elaborate version of the military belt, consisting of hinged plaques with one rather larger to mask the buckle, appeared in the second half of the fourteenth century. The centres of the plaques could be filled with stones, rosettes, lozenges, leaves, quatrefoils or small shields of arms.[284] The large 'jewels' filling the centre of some were represented on effigies by glass inlays, like that of Sir William Pembridge, K.G. († 1375), at Hereford Cathedral.[285] Examples of heraldic buckles can be seen on the effigies of Thomas, Earl of Warwick († 1401), at St Mary's, Warwick (MS I), and Robert, Lord Hungerford († 1455), at Salisbury Cathedral.[286] Others may have had royal connexions: Sir Richard Redman († 1427) at Harewood, Yorks.,[287] has an eagle. The belt of William of Aldeburgh († 1368) at Aldborough, Yorks. (MS I), was made of plaques representing castles, an architectural theme repeated on the buckle like a fortified gateway worn by Sir Nicholas Longford († 1402) at Longford, Derbyshire.[288] Later in the fifteenth century the belt had either been dispensed with, or was very plain and functional.

CIVILIAN BELTS AND GIRDLES

Women's girdles were usually narrower than those worn by men and the end with its tag could reach to the hem of the gown. The girdle was often harnessed like the military belts described above. Two of the earliest examples are seen on the effigies of Queen Eleanor of Aquitaine and her daughters-in-law, Berengaria and Isabella of Angoulême.[289] The foundation corse of silk, velvet or damask was often black, but bright reds, greens and blues, either plain or mixed with white, are known. The gold or silver bars, studs, buckles and tags showed up well against these colours, and were further embellished with niello, enamels, pearls and real or imitation gem-stones.[290]

Girdles were one of the customary English court gifts, and were often distributed as well at marriages – both to the couple and to their attendants. In 1296 Edward I gave his daughter Elizabeth, Countess of Holland, 'a girdle with pearls and a purse of the king's arms'.[291] His granddaughter, another Elizabeth, Countess of Guelders, gave away belts to her attendants in 1332,[292] and for the marriage of Blanche of Lancaster in 1359, her grandfather, Edward III, purchased belts of enamelled gold studded with gem-stones and pearls.[293]

There is a long girdle with a large buckle and plain pendant on the effigy of Anne of Bohemia († 1394) at Westminster Abbey,[294] and a similar narrow corse closely set with rosettes is worn by Joan of Navarre († 1420) at Canterbury.[295] For much of the period the girdle was partly hidden under the cote, which may account for their simpler style of decoration compared with those worn by men. William of Hatfield (*c.* 1376) at York Minster[296] wears the fashionable court dress with a belt of large square plaques, and his brother, William of Windsor, of the same date at Westminster Abbey has a similar belt, whereas the girdle of their sister, Blanche of the Tower, has only plain square studs.[297] Most pairs of effigies show a like contrast. Four hinged roundels of gilt bronze enamelled with the arms of England and Old France alternately must come from a belt made either for Edward III or for one of his daughters.[298] Effigies of men in civilian dress are less common than those in armour, but a narrow belt with a plain buckle and long pendant is seen on an anonymous mid-thirteenth-century man at St James's, Bristol,[299] while another at Sandwich, Kent (*c.* 1360), wears the knightly belt with plaques.[300]

Girdles and belts were also worn by ecclesiastics such as Geoffrey le Scrope, Canon of Lincoln (1382), who owned a 'girdle (certum) of velvet with pearls'.[301] The fragment of a belt, traditionally associated with William of Wykeham, and made *c.* 1350–1400, is a rare survival. The plaques are set with green and white pastes, crystals and translucent enamels of monkeys (some winding horns), hares etc., hinged and with beaded edges to the settings.[302]

Several kinds of decoration could be used together. Religion and heraldry combine on the belt of Sir Richard Willoughby († 1362) at Willoughby, Notts., with his cross moline, the Sacred Monogram IHC and St Christopher on the tag.[303] Another figure of St Christopher, who gave protection from sudden death, was on a 'gurdill of Blake sylke lyned with rede lether with a golde bokyll & a pendaunt and in the same pendaunt an ymage of seynt Christofre: in the gurdill bey xlvj stodys of selver' bequeathed by Thomas Bath of Bristol in 1420.[304] The Rod of Jesse,[305] scallop shells[306] and the Three Kings of Cologne[307] ornament other belts, as do invocations such as LAUS DEO or secular hortations such as LOVE ME BUNT FASTE.[308] Single letters on buckles, etc., can stand for the name of the wearer, and are exemplified by the R on the silver buckle of Robert Chamberlain, Esquire, a benefactor of St Alban's Abbey,[309] and the T on the tag of a Gloucestershire wool merchant at Northleach, *c.* 1400 (MS I). In 1400 John Sandford of Tickhill gave his 'second best girdell harnest with an S';[310] and there are long inscriptions on the belts worn by Millicent Meryng († 1419) at East Markham, Notts. (MS I), and an anonymous woman at Northop, Flint.[311]

At the end of the fourteenth century, more motifs are drawn from nature: blue borage flowers, red and white roses, columbines and golden ivy leaves. Cecily, Duchess of York, bequeathed in 1495 her 'dymysent [i.e., demiceint] of gold with a collumbine and a diamont in the same', and since the columbine occurs on other items in her jewellery, it may have been her device.[312] Some of the motifs are common to several effigies and may represent workshop patterns: the triple rose, cornflowers and oak sprigs with acorns, the last ending in tassels, appear on a small group of brasses from London, from Clehanger, Hereford (MS I), from Oulton, Suffolk (MS I), and from Crowan, Cornwall (MS II), *c.* 1474–90.

Heraldic devices played a role in the belts of Richard II – one having 'stag's heads and little pearls', another the ostrich plumes which were the livery of his first wife, Anne of Bohemia.[313] Perhaps the miniature chairs studding the belt of John, Earl of Oxford, were the badge of his office as Chamberlain.[314]

Buckles were most often round but there were also square designs, like the large one on the effigy of Lady Gascoigne (*c.* 1419) at Harewood, Yorks.,[315] and a design of small neat squares that could be decorated with leaves, etc., and enamelled. As an alternative the demiceint, decorated only at the front, was linked by two or three large motifs such as open rings, disks, roses, etc., sometimes with a pendant finial or tassel. This style is seen in the figures of Edward IV's daughters in the royal window at Canterbury Cathedral, each having paired white roses with pear-shaped pendants, perhaps pomanders.[316]

APPENDAGES

Purses of velvet and silk with gold and silver or latten mounts matched the belts, and were their almost invariable companion. In 1332 Eleanor, sister of Edward III, bought one from Antolino Bache of 'gold silk embroidered with pearls'.[317] Richard II had purses of Damascus silk with gold frames, and in the fifteenth century they were large and elaborate in design. John Browne († 1442, engraved *c.* 1465) at All Saints, Stamford, Lincs. (MS I), has one with an elaborate frame, and that of Thomas Andrewes († 1490) at Charwelton, Northants. MS I), has a Tau cross on the mount. The less wealthy, such as the carpenter's wife in Chaucer's *Canterbury Tales*, used the less expensive metals:

> And by hir girdel heeng a purs of lether
> Tasseled with silk, and perled with latoun.[318]

Daggers, knives, penners and inkhorns, paternosters and pomanders all hung from belts. Elizabeth, Countess of Oxford, bequeathed 'my pomaunder of golde like a pere, used to be worne att my gurdle'.[319] Decorative pendants hung from the girdle which the wife of the Green Knight gave to Sir Gawain as a protective charm:

> For pryde of the pendauntez thagh polyst they were,
> And thagh they glyterede golde glent upon endez.[320]

Richard II's ostrich-plume belt was hung with little bells ('sonettez') and in 1407 Alice, wife of the Canterbury brazier John Barbour, bequeathed 'a green girdle apparelled with bells'.[321] They can also be seen in manuscripts and on monuments abroad.

PATERNOSTERS

In 1322 Humphrey, Earl of Hereford, owned two 'pair of Paternosters the one of coral, the other of jet with gilt gaudes'.[322] The practice of counting prayers on beads was well established by then, but there was no set formula, so that the number of beads varied. To judge from the monuments, men seem to have favoured a string of larger beads, ten or eleven in number, as in the set bequeathed by Roger Flower in 1420: 'my pair of bedys that i use myself and with the x aves of silvere, and a paternoster over-gilt, preying him to have mynde of me sumtime when he seithe our lady sawter on hem'.[323] Women favoured smaller beads in longer sets making a loop, such as John Elveden's 'one pair of beads of jet containing 180 jet stones gauded with gold',[324] rather more than the 150 required to match the number of Psalms. These could be hung about the neck, looped round the arm or worn at the girdle. The former fashion is illustrated by the effigy *c.* 1382 at Northop,[325] and by Sir John Howard's gift in 1467 of 'a peyr of bedes for a gentylwomannes nekke with viij gawdeid of goolde and viij perles'.[326] Beads hang from the girdles of Lady Curzon (*c.* 1490) at Kedleston, Derbyshire,[327] and of Sir William Laken († 1375) at Bray, Berks. (MS IV). John Sandford bequeathed his 'best girdell harnest with a pare of lambre bedes'.[328] Chaucer's Prioress wore hers like a bracelet:

> Of smal coral aboute hire arm she bar
> A peire of bedes, gauded al with grene,
> And theron heng a brooch of gold ful sheene.[329]

This practice of attaching jewels to the paternoster, perhaps a parallel to the jewels offered to venerated images, is also found in wills. A pair of beads given to Richard II by the Abbot of Waltham had a tablet with a crucifix and the Coronation of Our Lady in it.[330] A lady in a monument in Bangor Cathedral has five brooches attached to her beads,[331] and in 1493 Robert Hunt bequeathed beads of coral and silver-gilt with a gold heart, while the Countess of Oxford left to her sister 'my image of our lady of Pitie to hange at her bedes to pray for my soule'.[332] Some devotional adjuncts, like Maud Baker's 'peyr of blak bedys with v woundys of golde' in 1503, were probably so supplied by the maker.[333]

The paternosters of the later Middle Ages, then, displayed wealth as much as devotion, and as early as 1381 a London goldsmith stocked them in a variety of precious materials.[334] There was a variety of designs available to suit the tastes of those like Lady Zouche, who wrote to a friend in 1402 asking her to find 'a pair of beads of gold for the lady my mother with the quaintest Paternoster that you can find whatever they cost'.[335] The Earl of Salisbury gave Richard II beads with 'seven gauds with two children in each gaud', and Richard owned others in 1397 'of gold garnished with pearls and the buttons enamelled green', and a pair in the fashion of 'coklez' with gauds of 'cokill' (mother-of-pearl), enamelled white on gold with two balases and small pearls, a gift from the Abbot of Westminster.[336]

Not only the kings owned several paternosters. In 1451 Sir Thomas Cumberworth could bequeath beads to the Cardinal Archbishop of York, the Bishop of St Asaph, Lord Cromwell, his friends, relations, retainers and nuns, which were made of jet, coral, gold, bone, wood and his 'gret bedes of laumber [i.e., amber] with a ryng of unicorn horne by them'.[337] The appearance of the beads was also enhanced by the coloured silks used to string them. Lady Anne Scrope in 1498 bequeathed her 'grete bede of goold lassed with sylke crymmesyn and goold, with a grete botton of goold, and tassllyld with the same'.[338]

Such a set was rare; most had only the gauds made of precious metals, which is one reason why the English rosary which descended in the Langdale family of Houghton Hall in Yorkshire is so remarkable (Plate 21). It consists of fifty double-sided oval beads with six larger gauds having bevelled faces, ending in a large four-sided knop, engraved with two figures on each bead identified by black-letter texts. One decade is devoted to English saints and others are found in the third and fourth decades.[339]

BUTTONS

The buttons on the sleeves of an early-fourteenth-century woman's effigy at Stevenage, Herts.,[340] are one of the earliest instances of ornamental dress fastenings which became general with the adoption of tightly fitting clothes at the mid century. In 1353 the Black Prince bought three sets of buttons: 'twenty-four round buttons, silver-gilt and enamelled' at £12; 'one button set worked with stones and pearls' at £5; 'twelve silver-gilt buttons' for 24*s*; and he bought others from Bernard Lumbard in 1361, while John de la Mare received £200 for 'a set of buttons for the princess'.[341] Not all his buttons were so costly; a bronze button with his arms impaling those of his wife is in the Museum of London.[342] Unfortunately, there are no details of the buttons which the London jeweller Pynchoun made for Richard II in 1384.[343]

Clusters from the neck to below the waist button the dress of Elizabeth, Lady Montacute († 1354), at Oxford Cathedral,[344] and other ways of wearing buttons are shown on the eight weepers around her tomb chest. Two of the daughters' gowns are trimmed with small buttons on the front; a third has a pair fastening her mantle at the neck and six more trim the opening at the hem. The short tunic worn by one of the sons is buttoned down the front and from elbow to wrist. There are four large buttons at the neck of another son, with four more fastening the mantle at the shoulder – a style also adopted on the effigy of William of Hatfield († 1349?) at York Minster.[345] The long robe of Sir Richard Willoughby († 1362) at Willoughby, Notts.,[346] is fastened in front with twenty small buttons which, with those on his sleeves, recall contemporary verses:

21 The Langdale rosary. Gold, with beads, gauds and knop engraved with saints and scenes from the Gospel, identified by black letter inscriptions. Late fifteenth century. Victoria and Albert Museum.

> Botones azur'd wor ilke ane
> From his elboth to his hand;[347]

and the innumerable buttons in *The Romance of Sir Degrevant*:

> To telle hir botouns were dure
> They were namelde with asure.[348]

The effigies depict several designs – plain bosses, squares, cinquefoils, hexafoils and clusters – and coloured stones or glass may have been set in some of them, as in the long set of stepped squares enclosing lozenges worn by Lady Willington (late fourteenth century) at Atherington, Devon,[349] or the round disks with beaded borders of Amice, wife of William, Lord Fitzwarine (*c.* 1361), at Wantage, Berks.[350]

Figurative elements occur in the large round pearl buttons with animals in the centre worn by Lady Mohun (*c.* 1360–70) at Canterbury Cathedral[351] and the 'botoner de wode-woses' priced at 100*s* in the 1355 inventory of Sir Baldwin de Fryville.[352] He also owned buttons of rose and star design, and one of 'muge' or musk, a type described in greater detail in the 1378 will of Sir John Foxle: 'one gold button ornamented with good large pearls, with musk contained in the said button'.[353]

DRESS PINS

Reference has been made to the decorative pins used to fasten the pallium to the chasuble (p. 5 above), and a number of pins for fastening dress have been found in the Winchester excavations.[354] Cast with globular, polyhedral or flat heads, or set with a glass bead for the terminal, they came from many dates from A.D. 650 to the fifteenth century. Some had the heads made in two parts, doubtless to reduce the weight of the solid cast versions. Made in both silver and bronze, they must have been a more common dress accessory in the Middle Ages than the relatively few instances in paintings and sculpture would suggest.

POINTS OR TAGS

Metal ends to prevent ribbons and cords used for fastening dress from fraying were used from at least the eleventh century, some of that age having been found at the Assize Court site at Winchester. During the fourteenth and fifteenth centuries, a black gloss finish was often given to them, and from about 1400 a standard pattern was being used.[355]

BRACELETS AND ARM RINGS

The bracelet enhanced feminine beauty, and the woman whose looks were praised in a poem by Geoffrey de Vinsauf *c.* 1210 had arms 'rich in bracelets'.[356] Thereafter they seem to disappear until the 1397 inventory of Richard II: '2 bracelets (armell) all of gold garnished about . . . with 14 Emeralds, & 12 garnets & the small pearls'.[357] His arm ring with sapphire, diamonds and pearls, a New Year's gift to the Duke of Lancaster from the Treasurer of England, had pendant broom cods and a jewelled ring.[358] Antelopes, another heraldic motif, occur on a bracelet of Henry V.[359] During the fifteenth century, bracelets in royal inventories were richly studded with gems, as was the 'bracelet with one great diamond and one baleys garnished with great pearls' valued at £50,[360] sometimes set in designs of flowers,[361] hunting-horns[362] and figures such as Queen Margaret's

> bracelet of gold made of 2 ladies enamelled white, each holding in her hand a flour of 4 diamonds with 1 ouche about their heads garnished of a ruby, 1 large diamond pointed & 3 great pearls, and under the feet of the said ladies are sitting 2 sapphires.[363]

Such jewels were not worn only by the royal family. Sir Thomas Dalton bequeathed two gold bracelets studded with precious stones and pearls in 1415[364] and Richard Dixton, an esquire, in 1438 left a gold bracelet to Jane Greyndour.[365] Similar bequests continued into the sixteenth century, as exemplified by Dame Margaret Capell's 'brasselet of gold sett with perles and stones' in 1516.[366]

FINGER RINGS

It is rare for more than the value and type of gem-stone to be recorded in medieval descriptions of rings, but this is outweighed by the number which have survived – far exceeding any other category of jewel. Those from the tombs of known bishops and those found in hoards with coins can be dated. Worn by men and women of all classes, rings were made of gold, silver or gilt bronze. It was fashionable to wear several, sometimes more than one to a finger, on both upper and lower joints.[367] The two major categories were decorative rings set with gem-stones and functional signets.

GEM-SET RINGS

Rings set with gems were prized for their intrinsic value, their beauty and the virtues or magical powers imputed to them by popular lore. Hubert de Burgh was accused of bestowing upon Llewellyn of Wales a ring from Henry III's treasury which made the wearer invincible, and stories of other wonder-working rings can be read in the romances.[368] In the mid fifteenth century Sir John Cumberworth bequeathed 'a ryng of unicorn horn' for testing food for poison and a 'ryng with the grene stone for the crampe'.[369]

The simplest design, a stirrup-shaped hoop rising to an apex at the bezel, was claw-set with a coloured stone *en cabochon*. Size and weight varied considerably, most being rather small stones, and an elaborate version came from the tomb of Geoffrey of

22 The Lark Hill Hoard of six finger rings, illustrating various bezel designs. Viking style with twin wires plaited; three rectangular bezels, set with a crystal foiled red, a yellow paste and an amethyst; nielloed in cross pattern; and clasped hands. Twelfth century. British Museum.

Ludham († 1265) at York Minster.[370] Two others set with sapphires, illustrated by Matthew Paris, were given to St Albans, inscribed with the nielloed initials of the owner or donor. One had belonged to Prior Roger de Norton (Abbot in 1260) and was a gift from Archdeacon John de Wymondham; the other was from Richard Animal, a fellow pupil with Eleanor of Aquitaine, who had given him the ring, perhaps before 1140.[371] A most splendid sapphire ring with fleur-de-lis claws was found in the grave of Bishop Henry Woodlock († 1316) at Winchester Cathedral.[372]

An alternative to the stirrup ring was one with a 'pie-dish' bezel, enclosing the stone in a wider setting, joined to a plain hoop which could have decorated shoulders.[373] Three less expensive rings of this type are among the six found with coins of the reign of Henry II in the Lark Hill Hoard at Worcester; they are set with an amethyst, a crystal (formerly foiled with red) and a yellow paste[374] (Plate 22).

Another group of gold rings, their bezels set with irregularly shaped sapphires, have the shoulders in the form of dragons similar to those in Romanesque carvings and manuscripts. One, from Cannington in Somerset, has the sides of the bezel pierced with eagles and the hoop is engraved with the Angelic Salutation: AVE MARIA GRA / TIA PLENA DMI[375] (Plate 23). Three large pontifical rings set with showy mixtures of coloured gems and pearls, similar to disk brooches, were illustrated by Matthew Paris. One hoop was inscribed with the name of the donor, Henry of Blois, Bishop of

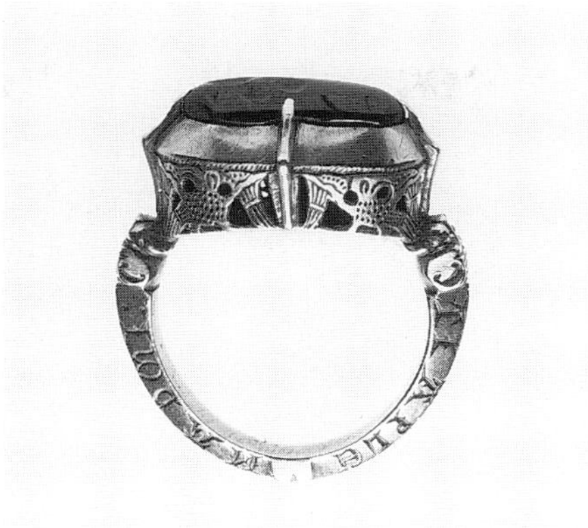

23 Gold ring set with a sapphire, the pierced sides of the bezel with birds, the hoop terminating in animal heads and inscribed AVE MARIA GRA/TIA PLENA DMI. Late twelfth/early thirteenth century. British Museum, from Cannington, Somerset.

Winchester († 1171), a well-known collector.[376] Another, slightly later in date, had on the back of the bezel a verse referring to John de Crundale, chaplain to Archbishop Stephen Langton (who may have been the original owner). The bezel was set diagonally across the hoop, with four pearls, four sapphires and two emeralds amidst filigree scrolls.[377] This design is very similar to an early-thirteenth-century French ring.[378] A simpler design is used for a gold ring from the tomb of Archbishop Walter de Grey of York († 1255), which is set with a large sapphire in an oblong bezel with incurved sides set alternately with emeralds and garnets. These small stones enhance the importance of the sapphire.[379] John de Sandale, Bishop of Winchester, in 1319 owned 'one pontifical ring with a great sapphire surrounded by twelve small emeralds, price 106*s* 8*d*' and 'one great ring of crystal with a good sapphire for credit of virtu, surrounded by small rubies and emeralds enclosed in a certain upper box, price 26*s* 8*d*'.[380]

Gimmel rings with twin hoops occur, symbolic of lovers or the married state; they are recorded in an account *c.* 1224–5 – 'one gemel ring with two stones'[381] – and in 1241, when Henry III gave 'a gimmel ring with a ruby and two emeralds worth 100*s*' to a visiting count, which he had purchased through his clerk Edward, son of Odo, from Peter Lemaire of Paris.[382]

Mixed gem-stones might be set in the hoop, either all round the circumference or just at one point, as in a thirteenth-century ring with a London provenance, set with a sapphire and an amethyst flanked by two smaller turquoises.[383] The contrast of coloured stones with pearls became more frequent. Margaret Brown, widow of a London poulterer, bequeathed in 1361 'one ring with a sapphire and pearls'.[384]

King John owned diamond rings,[385] and in the fourteenth century these stones could be purchased, not only by the Black Prince, but also by citizens such as Margaret Brown.[386] These would have been point-cut but by 1400 new cuts had been developed, and in 1496 Sir Robert Radcliffe could bequeath a ring 'set with a tabull diamond'.[387]

Richly set rings were worn as evidence of status, and Lady Mede, the personification of Reward in Langland's *Piers Plowman*, is singled out in all versions of the poem for her many rings (see above, p. 1). Philippa, Countess of March (1378), left a ruby ring with the border enamelled 'russet',[388] and brightly enamelled sprays of leaves and flowers embellished the shoulders of rings from the second half of the fourteenth century. This naturalistic ornament appears on the shoulders of the sapphire ring inscribed with the name of WYLLMS WYTLESEY for William Whittlesey († 1374), Archbishop of Canterbury.[389] Cusped collets with claws remained the most usual form of setting for gem-stones well into the fifteenth century, varied by quatrefoils and cinquefoils. The standard of work was not always reliable, and in 1476 Dame Elizabeth Stonor appealed to her husband:

> Sir, I pray you send me no more ryngis with stonys ffore the ryng that you sent me by Henry Blakhall, the stone is ffllyn owght be the way and loste: wherefore I ame sorry.[390]

SIGNETS

Seals were required for business and legal transactions, and in the later Middle Ages signet rings were often used, and could be handed down in families. By the fourteenth century, ownership might be more easily ascertained as heraldry replaced the engraved gems of the earlier period. Some just bore a shield, suitable for use as a secret seal, but others were inscribed with the name. As Earl of Derby, Henry IV paid a goldsmith of Calais 28*s* in 1390 'for 1 gold signet . . . with the making of the same signet and to "engrave" with 1 "plume" and 1 "coler" '.[391] The ostrich feather was one of his badges, like the bear and ragged staff of the Earls of Warwick, the Percy (?) lion and the boar of Richard III, all of which survive on signets.[392] Sometimes the devices chosen indicated the user's occupation or office; a ring found in the Thames with a fortified gateway might have belonged to a sheriff and the silver ring with scissors inscribed GRACE to a tailor of that name; the latter is paralleled in stained glass at York.[393] Merchants had their own distinctive marks with a cross and flag, perhaps with initials, and these too were engraved on rings. An excellent example is that of Henry Smale and illustrates the high quality of workmanship employed for them.[394] Other non-armorial signets bear a rebus: a ship and wine barrel for Shipton, or the inscription Edmund and a hart for Edmund Hart.[395] Some devices, like the branch of Dame Mawte Courtenay,[396] or the cockatrice of John Bondy, a London skinner (1479), had a personal significance which has been lost.[397] One with a cockatrice's head and leg, both erased, and inscribed YN TO WODE, from a stone coffin at Heigham, is now in the Norwich Castle Museum.[398] The barley sheaf of Thomas Goodale (1499), a hurer or maker of caps, alluded to his name,[399] and a hawk's lure amidst flowers, fleurs-de-lis and the initial T, presumably expressing the sporting instincts of the owner, forms part of the Fishpool Hoard.[400] Initials were the commonest signet device, crowned and sometimes flanked by palm fronds.[401] In most cases the bezel was fixed, but some could be turned over for a second device. 'My grete turning signet of golde' is mentioned in Thomas Butside's will (1497), and a contemporary example with a bell (for the owner's name?) and the Vernicle is in the British Museum.[402]

DEVOTIONAL RINGS

The bezel of the ring found in the grave of John Grandison, Bishop of Exeter 1327–69, is engraved with the Virgin and Child on a ground of blue enamel.[403] A goldsmith in 1378 delivered 'against Christmas, twelve rings of Christophers',[404] and such rings were common in the fifteenth century. William Gunwardby, Bishop of Dunkeld and Suffragan to Lincoln and Ely *c.* 1431–54, bequeathed a 'ring of gold with the picture of Blessed Margaret enamelled in it',[405] and in 1477 Margaret Paston asked her husband John to 'wer the ring with the emage of seynte margrete that I sent you for a remembraunce tyl ye come home'.[406] These rings with saints or small religious scenes appear to have been limited to England and Scotland, and were called 'iconographic rings' by the Victorian collectors. As many are inscribed EN BON AN it seems that they were given as New Year's gifts. The principal themes found on them are the Crucifixion, the Trinity, the Annunciation, the Virgin and Child, and SS. John, Catherine and George. Some of these also appear on the shoulders of gem rings and signets.[407]

Rings were also used as private reliquaries. Elizabeth, Lady Fitzhugh, bequeathed one with a relic of St Peter's finger in 1427,[408] and the most magnificent surviving example of such a ring comes from the Thame Hoard (Plate 24). The enamelled

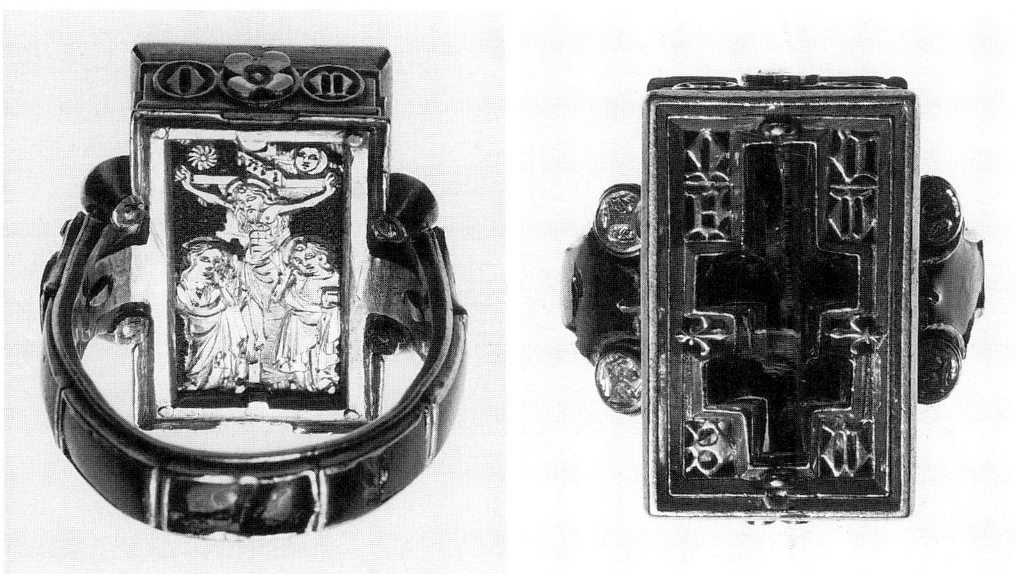

24 Gold ring with reliquary bezel set with an amethyst cut in the form of a double cross, inscribed in Lombardic letters MEMANTO MEI DOMINE. Back: the Crucifixion, engraved. *c.* 1380. Visitors of the Ashmolean Museum, Oxford, from Thame.

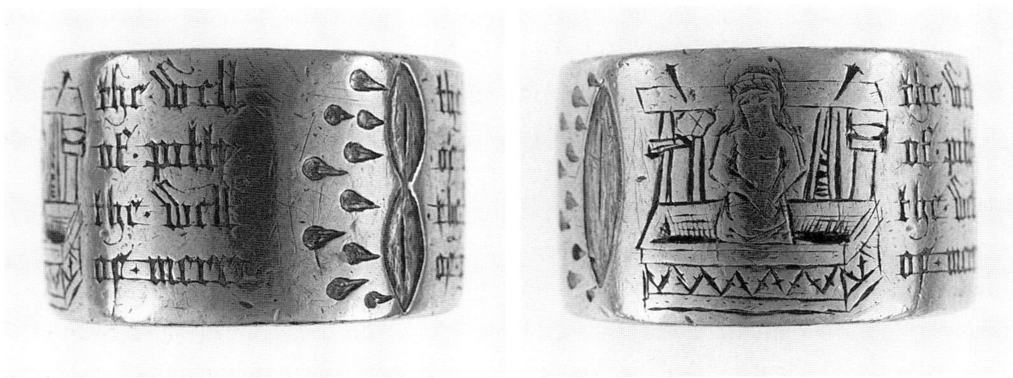

25 Gold ring with broad hoop engraved with the Five Wounds, identified by black letter inscriptions. Centre: Christ in the Tomb, with Instruments of His Passion. Fifteenth century. British Museum.

gold bezel once contained a relic of the True Cross under a double-barred cross of amethyst. The back is engraved with the Crucifixion and the openwork sides have the text MEMANTO MEI DOMINE in Lombardic letters.[409]

A group of late-fifteenth-century rings expressed devotion to the Five Wounds of Christ (Plate 25). Sir Robert Radcliffe bequeathed one in 1496 and in the next year Sir Edmund Shaa, a former Mayor of London, bequeathed sixteen 'graven with the welle of pite, the welle of mercy and the welle of everlasting life, and with all other images llike as John Shaa and Rauf lathum understanden right wele . . . concerning the same'.[410] A like ring is engraved inside and out and the will shows how as early as this some craftsmen specialised in particular lines.

Some rings with devotional subjects were engraved deeply enough to be used as signets. Sir John Howard gave his wife in 1457 a 'gret sygnnet of golde with the vernycle'.[411] Thomas Apulton (1508) of Little Waldingfield in Essex bequeathed a 'signett of gold graven with Seynt John's hedde'.[412]

Other rings had ten bosses on the hoop, and the bezel engraved with a saint or the Sacred Monogram IHC, and served as a substitute for the beads.[413]

Religious and magical inscriptions, such as Robert Hunt's 'ryng of gold with Christus passus est written thereupon'[414] or Sir John Foxle's 'great gold ring with one sapphire inset and the names of the Three Kings engraved in the one ring',[415] compare with those on the ring brooches. They follow the same sequence, with Lombardic letters being replaced by black letter in the later fourteenth century.

LOVE AND MARRIAGE RINGS

A gold ring is an integral part of the marriage ceremony described in the Middle English romance *King Horn*.[416] Some were plain bands, but others were made 'riche e bel' with gem-stones. According to the Anglo-Norman *L'Art d'Aimer* a diamond was particularly appropriate,[417] but in practice the stones varied considerably, rubies being the choice of the Earl of Richmond in 1359.[418] Queen Isabella was married to Richard II with a 'ring of a sapphire garnished of gold with one ruby' valued at £100, presumably on account of the size of the stones;[419] and Dame Edith Scott (1474) left a 'ring of gold with a safyour that was my wedding ring'.[420] The motif of clasped hands, the *fede* signifying trust, which appeared on a silver ring dating from the reign of Henry II,[421] never went out of fashion. In a fifteenth-century version the clasped hands issue from buttoned cuffs and at the base of the hoop is another symbol of love, the heart with a forget-me-not blooming from it.[422] Clasped hands could be placed opposite the bezel in gem rings, their message emphasised by a love motto or posy inscribed within the hoop. The type is exemplified by a thirteenth-century gold ring with sapphire flanked by dragon's heads, inscribed IE · SUI · DE · DRUE · SI · NE · ME · DO · NEI · MIE (I am a love token do not give me away).[423] Most posies in the fifteenth century were inscribed on hoop rings, with spacers of flowers or leaves, either enamelled or nielloed. Two rings of unusual character were inscribed on the inside only. One resembling a wreath of branches, found in the Thames, bears the message: WHEN YE LOKE ON THIS THYNK ON THEM [THA]T GAVE YOU THYS; the other, a wide hoop engraved with the Virgin and Child, the Trinity and a saint, amidst trailing flowers and leaves, was a token given before a journey: MOST IN MYND AND YN MYN HERT / LOTHEST FROM YOU FERTO DEPART[424] (Plate 26). Many iconographic rings are inscribed with love posies and were probably used for weddings, as with the bequest by William Rede of Boston (1508) of his 'moders wedding ring with two images and enamelled'.[425]

26 Gold ring engraved with flowers and foliage between three lozenge-shaped panels framing the Trinity, the Virgin and a saint. There is a lover's inscription inside the hoop. Fifteenth century. British Museum.

3

The social context of Renaissance jewellery 1509 – 1625

The redistribution of wealth in the sixteenth century brought to the forefront of society new families who indulged in a display of affluence not equalled again in British jewellery history until the reign of George IV.

As early as 1514 Henry VIII enacted a new sumptuary law to try and restrict the use of certain types of jewellery and materials to particular classes:

> And that noman from henceforth undre the degre of the Son of a Duke Marques or Erle or the degre of a Baron use in his apparell of his body . . . any cloth of Gold or cloth of Sylver . . . with any gold or silver . . . or goldsmythe work . . . and that noman undre the degre of a Knight were any cheyne of gold or gilte or colour [i.e., collar] of Gold or any gold aboute his neke or enbracelettes of gold . . . and that no man undre the degre of a Gentilman were any silk poynted or were any poyntes with aglettes of Gold or silver or silver gilte or any button or broches of Gold or silver or gilte or any goldsmyth werke.[1]

The passion for luxury continued and another attempt to regulate it in 1532[2] was also disregarded; in 1585 Philip Stubbes complained that the universal 'pride of apparel' made it impossible to know 'who is noble, who is worshipful, who is gentleman and who is not'.[3]

ROYALTY

Jewels were an essential part of the image of Henry VIII, and no English king after him wore so many. His commanding presence was made even more impressive by the richness of gold-embroidered clothing clasped with jewels, magnificent hat brooches and collars of rubies the size of walnuts. An innate sense of theatre ensured that he always stood out, whether presiding at court revels, as a warrior in the tilting-yard, as bridegroom at each of his six marriages, and even at sea when, as pilot of a great galley, he wore a sailor's coat and trousers of cloth-of-gold and a gold chain worked with his motto DIEU ET MON DROIT with a gold whistle which he blew as loud as a trumpet.[4]

Year after year he added to the collection of jewels which had created such a stir at the Field of Cloth of Gold in 1520. He went on to spend the enormous sum of £10,801 8*s* 9*d* on jewellery in the three years prior to 1532, when he met Francis I again at Calais.[5] Only in 1537 was there a decline in interest, when a French jeweller was dismissed on the ground that 'he has no more money, and that it has cost him a great deal to make war'.[6] The large numbers of jewels coming from the dissolved monasteries may also have had a role at this time in lessening the need for purchases from abroad. In 1546 he refused to take a great diamond as part of a loan agreement, and his agent in Flanders wrote that 'the time is unmeet to pester the king with jewels, who already has more than most of the princes of Christendom'.[7] However, there was one great jewel which he could not resist, and which he was negotiating to buy at the time of his death in 1547. This was the Three Brothers: three perfectly matched balas rubies set without foil around a high-point diamond, with three round pearls between the rubies and a fourth pendant.[8] Taken from Charles the Bold, Duke of Burgundy, after his death at Grandson in 1477, it had come into the hands of the banking house of Fugger. Edward VI completed the transaction in 1551 and the jewel was described in an appendix to the inventory of Henry VIII, and in those of Mary I and Elizabeth I.[9]

Gifts of jewels were received from courtiers at New Year and some are recorded in the Gift Rolls for 1532 and 1534.[10] The king was also given jewels as prizes at tournaments at home and abroad, including an eagle pendant and a diamond rose brooch.[11] After the fall of Cardinal Wolsey in 1530 his collection was appropriated by the king, and further huge additions followed the suppression of the monasteries. In April 1536 Cardinal Pole declared that 'all the treasures (*donaria*) of the churches in England have been taken to the King at London'.[12]

Each of Henry's six queens wore jewels suited to her rank. During their early married life Katherine of Aragon was richly dressed, often in her native Spanish style, and wore jewels with her badges of the castle, the pomegranate and arrows and the rose. Supplanted by Anne Boleyn, she resisted the king's demand for the return of her jewels and, when forced to give in, did so with great dignity.[13] Very little remained at her death apart from a reliquary of the True Cross and a gold collar from Spain.[14]

Every stage of the courtship of Anne Boleyn was marked by the gift of a jewel. The king informed her admirer, Sir Thomas Wyatt, of his own interest over a game of bowls by pointing to a ring which he had removed from her finger and always wore, while Sir Thomas used the chain of a jewelled tablet which had been hers to measure the distance between the bowls.[15] The jewels Henry and Anne gave each other are mentioned in their love-letters. The king wrote to her:

> seeing I cannot be present in person with you I send you the nearest thing to that possible, that is, my picture set in bracelets, with the whole device, which you know already, wishing myself in their place when it shall please you.

In reply she sent him a jewel symbolic of her own difficult situation, representing a ship tossed about on a stormy sea with a lonely damsel on board.[16] Cornelius Hayes brought her a collection of jewels and, closely supervised by the king, altered others, some perhaps returned by Katherine of Aragon.[17] Ennobled as Marchioness of Pembroke,

Anne accompanied the king to Calais in 1532 for a meeting to affirm the Anglo-French alliance, and in recognition of her importance the French king gave her a great diamond.[18] Some of her jewels in the records recall her brief reign as queen: buttons with the initial A, a brooch with a crowned HA and another with RA in diamonds.[19]

According to George Vertue, Anne Boleyn first suspected the king's infidelity when she noticed Jane Seymour wearing his miniature in a pendant at her neck.[20] Queen Jane's jewels were recorded, and they include the cipher of the initials H and I.[21] Some of them are depicted in her portrait by Holbein: a gabled hood bordered with a band of pearls and gem-stones, with matching necklace and edge to the neck of the gown; a pendant of stones in a foliate setting; a diamond jewel of the Sacred Monogram; a jewelled girdle and massive rings.[22]

After their amicable separation, Henry's fourth wife, Anne of Cleves, continued to reside in England. In her will of 1557 she left her best jewels, which may have been gifts at the time of her marriage, to Queen Mary I and the Princess Elizabeth 'for a remembraunce'.[23] She had also kept her wedding ring, inscribed with the posy GOD SEND ME WEL TO KEPE, and instructed that it should be 'broke in pieces as a thing which she knew of no force or value'.[24]

The next marriage – with Katherine Howard in 1541 – was celebrated with the acquisition of jewels, and her inventory provides an exceptionally full account of the collection of an English Renaissance queen, with classical motifs and the ciphers H and HK.[25] Disgraced after a short reign of eighteen months, she too was stripped of all these splendours and beheaded.

Similarly Katherine Parr, who married the king in 1543, received the jewels proper to her rank. Her queenly appearance was described in 1544 by the Secretary of the Spanish Duke of Najera: a kirtle of brocade and an open robe of cloth-of-gold, the sleeves lined with crimson satin trimmed with three-piled crimson velvet; a train more than two yards long. Suspended from the neck were two crosses, and a jewel of very rich diamonds; in her headdress, also, were many rich and beautiful ones. Her girdle was of gold, with very large pendants.[26] On her marriage with Thomas Seymour after the king's death, she was ordered to return her jewels, and complained bitterly about this.[27]

In his portraits the future king, Edward VI, wears hat brooches and aglets (Plate 27) but his governess, Lady Margaret Bryan, told Cromwell in 1538 that 'He hath never a good jewel to set in his cap'.[28] More came his way as he grew older; he wrote in 1546 thanking Queen Katherine for his New Year's present, a jewel with miniatures of herself and the king.[29] This may be the 'brouche conteyninge the Image of Kinge Henry theight with the Quene having a crowne of Diamountes over them and a rose of diamountes undre them and on eche side a man of Diamountes' listed among the jewels of Mary I.[30] The dynastic tablet with on 'thone side H and K a rose and E all of Diamountes with Oistrich fethers and fyve small rubies and on thother side a faire diamounte holden by an Image with four other diamountes' may have been a gift to him,

27 The Prince of Wales, later King Edward VI, wearing a hat badge with classical nude in relief, aglets clasping slashed sleeves and in hat. Portrait by a follower of Holbein, *c.* 1545. Sotheby's.

since it alludes directly to his place in the succession.[31] Edward VI, who liked rich clothes and jewels just as much as his father, completed the purchase of the Three Brothers and also bought a diamond ring from the Fugger.[32] It was in his reign that the final inventory of the jewels and plate of Henry VIII was compiled, recording a treasure never to be surpassed by another English monarch.[33]

Mary I (the 'Miladi Prinsis' of Holbein's designs for jewels), who was bastardised and excluded from court at the time of her parents' divorce, was better treated after Katherine Parr became queen.[34] Her name reappears in the lists of New Year's gifts for 1543[35] and, on the wedding day, her stepmother, Queen Katherine, gave her a pair of ruby bracelets. Her accounts as princess include gifts of jewels for her half-sister, Princess Elizabeth, and her cousins, Lady Jane and Lady Catherine Grey.[36] When she became queen, diplomats noticed how she

> seems to delight above all in arraying herself elegantly and magnificently . . . She also makes great use of jewels, wearing them both on her chaperon and round her neck, and as trimming her gowns in which jewels she delights greatly, and although she has plenty of them left by her predecessors, yet were she better supplied with money than she is, she would doubtless buy many more.[37]

Her husband, Philip II of Spain, sent Jacopo da Trezzo to England with gifts of jewels,[38] and the collar of gold set with nine diamonds, which, in her will, she says the king gave her at Epiphany after the wedding, may be the 'rich collar of eighteen pieces, wherof nine with ciphers of the letters P: and M:, nine of diamonds, 8 of them pointed and one a table, every piece having a pearl pende' which survived into the reign of James I.[39]

Although Queen Mary's will directed that all the jewels which her husband had given her should be returned to him, Philip gave to Queen Elizabeth, 'anything she wanted . . . as a good brother should'.[40] The Peregrina pearl, and the great diamond jewel which Mary I wears on her breast in portraits, did go to Spain, but most remained here. In 1584 Leopold von Wedel noticed at Whitehall a large box, covered with red velvet and filled with the precious stones, collars and other jewels which Mary had been given by her husband.[41]

According to Wedel, Queen Elizabeth dressed 'like goddesses are wont to be painted', and jewels were an integral part of her dazzling image. The Venetian ambassador met her in 1559, 'dressed entirely in purple velvet, with so much gold and so many pearls and jewels that it added much to her beauty'.[42] Like her father, brother and sister, 'she was a true lover of jewels and pearls, all sorts of precious stones',[43] and she made it known that gifts of jewels were always welcome.

The New Year Gift Rolls record jewels given to Elizabeth I and the collection was inventoried in 1587, when Mrs Blanche Parry, who had been in charge since 1558, handed it over to Mrs Mary Radcliffe.[44] Further lists were made in 1600, when out-of-date and damaged items were dispersed.[45] Jewels came from various other sources: her share of the plunder of the Spanish treasure ships[46] and by shrewd purchases. When the famous pearls of Mary, Queen of Scots, a wedding gift from Catherine de' Medici, consisting of six ropes and twenty individual pearls each the size of a nutmeg, were offered for sale, Queen Elizabeth was able to buy them at a very good price.[47] Another bargain was the Portugal diamond.[48] Besides these and her hereditary jewels, which were of great value, she liked the emblems and esoteric figurative designs which symbolised her virtuous life and care for her kingdom; they were often shown in the more important portraits.[49] They became part of the legend of her reign and in 1626 Sir John Eliot referred to them nostalgically: 'O, those jewels! The pride and glory of this kingdom! Which have made it so far shining above all others!'[50]

Eliot's speech lamented the dispersal of the collection inherited by James VI of Scotland and I of England, who succeeded in 1603. He and his wife, Anne of Denmark, did indeed part with quantities of jewels, but they also acquired others to express their vision of the Divine Right of Kings, which James explained to Parliament in 1605: 'Kings were God's vice-gerents on earth and so adorned and furnished with some

28 Queen Anne of Denmark. Portrait after Paul van Somer, *c.* 1617. National Portrait Gallery.

sparks of Divinitie'.[51] This politically desirable display (Plate 28) began with the purchase of the 53.8 carat Sancy diamond for his coronation in 1604. In 1608 the Venetian ambassador described a masque: 'what beggared all else and possibly exceeded the public expectation was the wealth of pearls and jewels that adorned the Queen and her ladies, so abundant and splendid that in every one's opinion no other court could have displayed such pomp and riches'.[52] The climax of this princely magnificence came in 1613 when, at the marriage of the Princess Royal with the Elector Palatine, the king estimated that the jewels worn by himself, the queen, the bride and Prince Charles, were worth nearly one million sterling.[53]

As jewels were such an essential part of the panoply of the state, on his accession James I set aside certain jewels as inalienable Crown property, separate from the personal jewellery of the royal family.[54] The inventory of the queen's personal jewellery was made in 1606 and notes were added until 1612; it shows what had been inherited from the time of Henry VIII and the date of their removal for reuse, often in making plate.[55] The accounts of her jeweller, George Heriot, who was in London from 1605 to 1615, also supply details.[56] Many of Queen Anne's jewels were given away after her death in 1619, but some were sent to Spain as gifts, valued at £600,000, for the Infanta and the court when Prince Charles was negotiating for his proposed marriage in Madrid; but when these plans came to nothing, the Spaniards returned them.[57]

COURTIERS

The wills of Elizabeth, Countess of Oxford, and George, Earl of Shrewsbury, record the jewels owned by courtiers in the first half of the sixteenth century who shared the same ideal of magnificence.[58] The *Lisle Letters* show the attention paid to jewellery by Honour, Viscountess Lisle, and the members of her family, and the care taken to get the desired designs executed.

In 1539 Viscountess Lisle bought a chain and border from Guillaume le Metais, a French court jeweller busy with orders from the Duchess of Etampes, mistress of Francis I.[59] Her silver girdles and aglets also came from Paris, and some of her jewels were broken up there to make two new brooches. She was charged 20 sous for the designs sent for her approval: one was secular – a person seated under a cloth of estate – and the other religious, with the Assumption of the Virgin, which she decided to have set with diamonds.[60] Much thought was given to the setting of stones, and in 1535 the agent at Bruges wrote sending to 'your ladyship . . . a pattern of the goldsmith's doing and the xx with spots be the places where the diamonds should stand. In case your ladyship like it not you must send him the pattern of your mind'.[61] Once it was agreed, the order could be executed within three weeks. Old favourites, the worse for wear, were not always broken up: an Annunciation was re-enamelled, and a gillyflower jewel strengthened with gold taken from a cross.[62] By such means she was able to obtain, even from afar, jewels to her own specifications from the best Parisian and Flemish makers.

The higher clergy maintained the great state of their predecessors. Cardinal Wolsey, who also held the most important secular office after the king – that of Lord Chancellor – accumulated a vast treasure which was listed after his fall and death in 1530.[63] This tradition of clerical splendour was also maintained by Archbishop Warham of Canterbury († 1532), who left his best mitre to Henry VIII – perhaps the precious mitre depicted in his portrait by Holbein.[64]

As a consequence of the simplification of ritual at the Reformation the use of such vestments was questioned, and the abolition of the images and shrines of saints stopped the gifts and bequests of jewels to adorn them. Unlike Warham, Archbishop Cranmer was painted in 1546 in the plain convocation robes, and the prominent armorial signet on his finger alluded rather to his administrative duties than to his spiritual office.[65] The intaglio of Vulcan's Forge, which Archbishop Parker gave to Queen Elizabeth I, could also be significant, for the iconography is classical, not Christian.[66] James Montagu, Bishop of Winchester and Prelate of the Order of the Garter († 1618), bequeathed a Garter ring to his friend James Riseley which, like the expensive diamond rings which he left to his family and friends (including George Villiers, the future Duke of Buckingham), was secular in character.[67]

At Elizabeth I's state entry into London for her coronation in 1559, her court 'so sparkled with jewels and gold collars that they cleared the air, though it snowed a little'.[68] The most important courtiers, like the Earl and Countess of Pembroke,[69] the Earl of Sussex[70] and the queen's favourite, the Earl of Leicester,[71] all had large collections of jewels, some being especially rich in Garter insignia. Sir Henry Lee (1530–1611), the Queen's Champion for the Accession Day Tilts until 1590, owned several jewels variously listed in the papers of a Chancery suit after his death. They included a diamond-set gold cross; two tablets, one with the picture of Elizabeth and the other of his mistress; an agate cameo; a picture of him tilting with the Earl of Essex; jewels called 'the Gloabe . . . Robyn redbrest . . . Lynnett . . . Raven . . . Butterflye'; and a diamond ring.[72]

Many jewels are listed in the will of Anne, Duchess of Somerset, widow of the Protector of Edward VI who was executed in 1552. The best – a pearl and gold bead chain, diamond jewel and large pearl – were inherited in 1587 by her son, the Earl of Hertford, whose wife received 'a fayre tablet to weare with antique work of one syde and a row of diamondes on the other syde' and a watch.[73] Bess of Hardwick (1518–1608), Countess of Shrewsbury and ancestress of the Dukes of Devonshire, Kingston and Portland, is perhaps the best-known Elizabethan lady after the queen. She became rich through her four marriages, and accumulated much jewellery, some of which was inventoried in 1567. During the sixteen years that she and her last husband, Shrewsbury, had Mary, Queen of Scots, in their charge, they received many gifts from her: a gold collar set with cameos, pomander bracelets and pendants, all recorded in her own hand. There is also a list of the jewels which the earl gave her in 1568 after their marriage, and which she refused to return when they quarrelled. Her choicest jewels were intended for her granddaughter, Arabella Stuart, who was descended on her father's side from Henry VIII's eldest sister, Margaret. This royal connexion placed Arabella in the possible line of succession, and the countess hoped that she might become queen when Elizabeth I died. Unfortunately Arabella became involved in intrigues and, so disappointed was her grandmother, that her bequest was annulled.[74] In 1607, however, Arabella received 'jeweles, chaines, pearle rings, and other things' from her uncle, Sir William Cavendish, first Earl of Devonshire (1618), beginning with a 'Riche Sable, the head and clawes of Goldsmith worke, enamelled and set with diamonds and rubies'.[75]

The Jacobean courtiers likewise patronised the royal jewellers and spent heavily on jewels, particularly for special occasions, as did Lord Montagu at the wedding of the Princess Royal in 1613.[76] Lionel Cranfield, Lord Treasurer (1621–4) and Earl of Middlesex (1622), agreed with Peter Van Lore, within a year of taking office, to pay £2,000 for 'one chain of diamonds valued at £500 and one faire jewel with a great diamond and pearl hanging at it valued at £1,200'. During his term as Treasurer he bought other jewels from Van Lore on a hire-purchase system, assigning the dividends from a sugar plantation two years in advance to pay for them, and by this means acquired a fine collection.[77]

The will and inventory of Henry, Earl of Northampton, in 1614 shows the kind of jewellery owned by a nobleman of the period. He bequeathed his 'best George' to Prince Charles; and to his nephew, the Earl of Suffolk, a fine 'Jewel of three stones, one of them being that Ruby which his excellent Majestie sent me out of Scotland as his first token', as well as a diamond cross inherited from his mother, the third Duchess of Norfolk.[78] A gold tablet with the miniature of the Earl of Essex, and a diamond ring which the Elector Palatine had given him at the time of his wedding in 1613, must also have been valued for their associations; he had too a 'Ringe sett with 15 Diamondes in a true lovers' knotte with the wordes *Nec astu nec ense*' (Neither by cunning nor by the sword).[79]

Ambassadors such as the Earl of Hertford spent heavily on jewels for presents as well as display. Sent on a mission to Brussels in 1605, he bought a great diamond and also twelve diamond buttons from Peter Van Lore, costing £3,450 payable in five instalments from June 1605 to May 1607.[80] The dashing appearance of the Duke of Buckingham made a great impression on his contemporaries:

> it was common with him at any ordinary dancing to have his cloaks trimmed with diamond buttons, to have diamond hat-bands, cockades and earrings, to be yoked with manifold knots of pearl, in short to be manacled, fettered and imprisoned with jewels.[81]

Another nobleman, William, Lord Compton (1567–1630), created Earl of Northampton in 1618, derived his great wealth from his father-in-law, Sir John Spencer, a

London cloth merchant. Soon after her father's death in 1610 Lady Compton asked her husband for £6,000 to spend on jewels and £4,000 for a pearl chain to appear suitably attired at court.[82]

Not all jewels were the property of the wearers: many hired extra items for special occasions. The steward of Robert, Earl of Leicester, reported that

> When the late Queene [Anne] made a maske att Whitehall, wherin the maskers came in like Moores . . . I borrowed of Mr. Hanbury and Michael Gouldsmiths, and of Sir John Spilman, as many jewells as were worth 10,000*li*; out of which jewells there were two dyamonds lost – The loane of which jewels and the dyamonds which were lost cosst yor Honor 040*li*.[83]

CITIZENS AND SQUIRES

At a muster of the City of London in 1539

> The aldermen were in coats of black velvet, a horse back, with great chains of gold . . . and the aldermen's deputies with coats and frocks of white damask satin taffeta, and some of velvet, with chains and ouches, with other gold works upon their headpieces, sallets and skulls. And all the constables and divers other honest men of 'haviour and reputation, citizens, were clothed all in white silk . . . with chains and goldsmiths' work, very rich and sumptuous.[84]

Such a show of prosperity was not limited to the rich citizens of London. Thomasine Bussey, widow of a Lincolnshire gentleman, bequeathed a large quantity of jewellery in 1545: three gem-set rings, three girdles, four crosses (all but one gem-set) including a 'Sancte Andros cross' (saltire) and a 'Sancte Anthonys [Tau] cross of golde with a bell', a bejewelled flower and pomander, a 'litle cheyne of golde' and a pair of aglets.[85] A smaller collection belonged to Jane, widow of Sir Thomas Dacre of Lanercost, who died in 1574, bequeathing massive gold chains (one valued at £65 5*s*), a black and white biliment, two gold rings, a signet carved with a rose, two pairs of bracelets (one of pomander, the other of flagon chain) and an enamelled gold pansy set with pearls and rubies.[86] The inventory of Sir Thomas Ramsey († 1590), Lord Mayor of London in 1577, included 'a great chaine of golde' valued at £110 14*s* 4*d*; 'a girdell of golde' worth £81 4*s* 6*d*; 'a booke of golde' at £7 4*s*; seven rings and 'j golde ringe of Sir Thomas Ramsey's armes' at £6 6*s* and 51*s*; with 'silver spectacles', this totalled £208 15*s* 11*d* – less than a third of the value of his plate.[87]

The new men of the Tudor age acquired jewellery along with land and town properties. John Gostwyke (1480–1545), who was Comptroller of Cardinal Wolsey's household and then one of Cromwell's Commissioners, profited greatly from the Dissolution of the Monasteries. He bought ex-monastic lands in Bedfordshire and Hertfordshire, and on his death owned 15,000 acres. Only a few of the jewels are specified in his will, but he directed that the least valuable of his best three table diamonds should be given to James Goldsmythe, a London fishmonger, and that Mrs Goldsmythe should have a gold chain which had cost him £13 6*s* 8*d*.[88]

Another of Cromwell's agents who had become rich through the Dissolution was Thomas Burgoyn († 1546), Auditor of the Duchy of Lancaster, who lived at Dutton in Bedfordshire and had other properties in London and elsewhere. He left to his wife, Anne, rings, jewels, ornaments and a silver parcel-gilt casting-bottle with their initials T and A; and to those cousins living on the day of his burial, a mourning ring each worth 10*s*.[89]

Pride of possession was strong and in some families jewels were designated heirlooms in wills. Thus in 1550 John Sayer of Worsall left to his son, William, a chain, cross, flower and signet, all of gold, as 'Arelomes perteyning ye sone & hier'.[90]

LESSER FOLK

After ten years' travel abroad, Fynes Moryson observed that the English were even more sumptuous than the Persians 'because they affect all extreamities', the rich flaunting their silks, velvets, rings and chains of gold, and all the others – farmers, artisans and peasants – following the train of fashion as far as they could afford it.[91]

The play of the *Four PP* – palmer, pardoner, 'poticary and pedlar – about 1540 cited the types of cheap jewellery sold to country-women by the pedlar: 'Broches, rynges and all manner of bedes'.[92] Autolycus in Shakespeare's *The Winter's Tale* was another pedlar whose stock consisted of amber necklaces, bugle bracelets, brooches, rings and pomanders set with counterfeit stones.[93] The custom of children wearing 'saffron guilt brooches and groats with hoales in 'hem' is mentioned by Jonson in *Eastward Ho* in 1605; he compared it with the rubies and diamonds worn in the caps of the Indian children in Virginia (*sic*).[94]

None of this 'trumpery' was of permanent value and so the wills of those who wore it do not convey more than an austere picture of their appearance, only mentioning the few items of gold or silver. Some are recorded in probate inventories for Oxfordshire from 1550 to 1590. There was Anne Dartes (*c.* 1573), who owned two silver rings, belt fittings, silver hooks and four pairs of beads (two of red coral and silver, one enamelled gilt, and two with crucifixes); and a shoemaker, Richard West († 1577), had two small rings (one gold, the other silver) worth 3*s*.[95] Mary, widow of Richard Paris of Dagenham, left in her will of 1582

> 3 silver pins, a pair of silver hooks, a silver ring, and a silver whistle . . . a silver ring . . . a little silver jewel . . . a silver jewel.[96]

Some had richer collections, and were probably of a higher degree, like Elizabeth Barton of Shoreditch († 1543), servant to Lady Mary Seymour, who owned 'a riband of crane colour sylk with 2 golden buttons . . . a paire of black bedes and a black gyrdyll of stolework . . .'; to her inventory she added 'a ryng of silver and gylte 8*d*, A golde jemmowe 8*d*', and 'A pere off silver howkes 20*d*'.[97] Margaret Boweman, who died in the same year, left a

pere of hokes gilt and a pere of bedis with dobbull gawdys of silvir gilte . . . a Kyrdyll of stoleworke with the demesent gilt . . . a pomandur of silvir . . . a ryng of golde with the 5 wondys . . . mi best ryng with a medas . . . the second ryng with a amedas . . . a ring with a jassyng . . . a ryng with a sparke turkes.[98]

By the turn of the century the beads and crosses have disappeared from these wills. A yeoman, Rowland Rayner of Cowley in Middlesex, left in 1603 'one chest standing in my bedchamber which was my mother's with all that therein is vide: two rings of gold, two silver pinnes, two Hockes and one braselet of silver and gould'.[99] John Blanely, servant to Robert Tatton, however, had only two rings, 'a jemall ringe of silver' and a little 'hoope ringe of gold'.[100]

SOCIAL AND ECONOMIC USE OF JEWELLERY

The role of jewellery in the sixteenth and early seventeenth centuries was not limited to giving pleasure and displaying status: it was also a negotiable asset. Banking houses dealt in jewels as well as money, and loans were often conditional on the purchase of over-valued jewels or plate. The haggling involved comes alive in the correspondence of Stephen Vaughan, Henry VIII's agent in Flanders. When required to raise money for the defence of Boulogne in 1546, the Antwerp merchants would advance only half in cash, insisting that the balance be taken in jewels – on which interest also had to be paid.[101] The same practice was followed by the Fuggers of Augsburg, first sending lead copies or drawings of the jewels proposed; and the large sums paid to the Florentine bankers Francesco dei Bardi and John Cavalcanti were probably the means by which Stephen Vaughan established relations with an alternative supply of money.[102]

Because the banking system was not fully developed, and the flow of currency unreliable, jewellery continued to be pledged as security for loans. Henry VIII lent money to the Emperor Maximilian and the Archduke Charles of Austria on this basis, and a fleur-de-lis of great value was deposited with him as a pledge for the sum advanced.[103] The loan made by Elizabeth I to the Emperor Rudolph II in 1578 was secured by 300 items of jewellery and plate.[104] Her successors frequently resorted to pawning jewels for loans from their goldsmiths, and the directions given by Anne of Denmark to Sir John Spillman in 1615 were only one instance of many transactions.[105] In 1617 money was so short that the £10,000 needed for a royal journey to Scotland could only be obtained in this way.

Private individuals did likewise. Henry VIII paid £20 to redeem a jewel which Anne Boleyn had pledged with her sister, Mary.[106] In 1607 Sir Arthur Gorges was forced to pawn good jewels to buy his house, and complained that although his pearls and diamond ring were worth £1,100 he could only raise £500 on them, and he asked the

Earl of Salisbury to 'set these prisoners at liberty' and buy them outright.[107] In 1623 Endymion Porter sent two jewels to his wife from Madrid, telling her to wear the prettiest as a reminder of him, and to pawn the other if she needed money.[108]

Great events were marked by gifts of jewels and at their leave-taking at the Field of the Cloth of Gold in 1520 Francis I and Henry VIII exchanged splendid pieces 'for a remembraunce'. Perhaps the 'faire tablet of golde on eche side of the same a rose of Dyamondes and within the same tablet a figure of the frensh kyng with a faire Dyamonde on his brest lozenged'[109] entered Henry's collection at that time. It was also customary to present ambassadors and their suites with diamond rings, chains and medals of honour, and similar gifts could be given to other visitors. The lutenist John Dowland recalled in 1595 that 'When I came to the Duke of Brunswick he used me kindly and gave me a rich chain of gold . . . From thence I went to the Lantgrave of Hessen, who sent a ring into England to my wife.'[110] Exceptionally, Sir Henry Wotton (1568–1639), who served the Queen of Bohemia, did not keep the diamond jewel given to him by her enemy the Emperor, but bestowed it on his landlady in Vienna.[111] Queen Elizabeth I's diplomatic gifts were modest in comparison with the extravagant gestures of James I and Anne.[112] To mark the peace treaty with Spain in 1604 they gave the Constable of Castile 'a tablet of diamonds with a great pendant pearl hanging at it, having in it the pictures of the King and Queen's Majesties' bought from Spillman for £1,000.[113] While on a mission to Brussels in 1605, the Earl of Hertford gave away gold chains and pearls, as well as money, to the officers and servants of the Archduke's household and to the two ladies with whom he had danced.[114] During the seventeenth century the standard gift to ambassadors was a diamond ring, and the Venetian ambassador reported 'a singular act of grace on the part of her Majesty to my son by giving him a diamond brooch for his hat'.[115]

The course of royal marriage negotiations was smoothed by gifts of jewels. Eric XIV of Sweden's ambassador wrote from London in 1559:

> I cannot conceal from Y:r Maj:ty that the ladies and maidens who are daily with the Queen are not pleased with me because they do not get any great gifts from Y:r Maj:ty, that is the Marchioness, Miladi Cobban [Cobham] . . . and others who say they can do much to forward the cause and do very much favour Y:r Maj:ty, and also some of the Gentlemen.[116]

The Duke of Alençon gave jewels not only to Elizabeth but also to courtiers through whose influence he hoped to further his suit. A flower 'set with Mounseures Diamondes', presumably a gift to her husband, was owned by the Countess of Sussex, and the Earl bequeathed 'by legacie to remaine as an heirloome to the house of Sussex for ever five precious stones which were given by the Emperor in a rapier, valued at £2000'.[117] Writing from Madrid in 1623, both Prince Charles and the Duke of Buckingham begged James to send more jewels for the prince to cut a better figure and to reward those supporting his courtship of the Infanta.[118]

Jewels expressed the loyalty of courtiers in an individual way. Some of the most imaginative, and expensive, were given to Elizabeth I by her favourites, the Earl of Leicester and Sir Christopher Hatton, who both owed their advancement to her; those given by Sir Henry Lee have been published.[119] When in January 1580 the queen appeared wearing one of his presents, the Earl of Hertford was delighted:

> at night when twelve of Her Majesty's musicians were in concert, she came out and passing by saluted me, and thanked me for my new year's gift . . . three or four times calling me to hear the music as she sat, saying I had judgement, she showed me last year's new year's gift hanging at her girdle. I told her she did me very great honour in the wearing and that she was worthy of a better favour. Within a few days I should have a jewel for her. She said that Frances Howard had told her of one she saw and I answered it was even the same.[120]

Such presents became less frequent in the next reign, as James I preferred to receive money.

The progresses, when the monarch travelled to different parts of the kingdom to see and be seen, were another occasion for the gift of jewels. A former servant of Lord Burghley explained the custom in Elizabeth I's reign thus:

> she was very rich in Jewells, which had been given her by her subjects; for in times of Progress there was no person who entertained her in his house but (besides his extraordinary charge in feasting her and her train) he bestowed a Jewel on her; a custom in former times begun by her special favourites that (having in great measure tasted of her bounty) did give her only of her own; though, otherwise, that kind of giving was not so pleasing to gentlemen of meaner quality.[121]

The last such entertainment enjoyed by the queen was at Harefield in 1602, when she was given on arrival 'jewels in the shape of a rake and fork', and at the house a 'diamond heart'; on leaving, she was given a 'jewel in the form of an anchor' signifying that 'where ever you shall arrive, you may anchor safely, as you do . . . in the harts of my Owners'.[122] Similar gifts were made to Queen Anne at Althorp in Northamptonshire, at the masque which greeted her on her way to London from Scotland in 1603.[123]

Courtiers also bequeathed jewels to Elizabeth I. The Earl of Leicester († 1588) gave her a jewel ablaze with emeralds and diamonds attached to a rope of 600 white pearls as 'a token of a humble faythfull harte as the last that ever I can send her'.[124] From Lady Dacres († 1595) came a jewel worth £300 'in dutiful remembrance', and in 1601 Lord Willoughby de Eresby left either a cup or jewel to the value of £100 as a pendant to his request to her about the wardship of his children, 'as may best content her and best represent the loyalty of his heart'.[125]

Monarchs too made presents of jewels, either at New Year or at other times, as occasion required. Henry VIII gave Sir Nicholas Carew some of Katherine of Aragon's jewels when he was in favour; when he was imprisoned in the Tower in 1539, the Imperial ambassador thought Lady Carew might have to return them.[126] Mary I gave

29 The Phoenix jewel, enamelled gold with silhouette bust of Queen Elizabeth framed in a wreath of Tudor roses. Back: her device of the phoenix in flames beneath the royal cipher. 1570–80. British Museum.

many jewels to her ladies-in-waiting and godchildren, and at their marriage in 1554 Philip II distributed others.[127] On New Year's day 1574 Queen Elizabeth gave the Earl of Leicester a pear pearl, which he kept all his life in the original wrapping.[128] The Phoenix jewel (Plate 29) and the Armada jewel, which combined devices with her portrait medal, had a political purpose. The English equivalent of the German *Gnadenpfennig*, they were probably given as a reward for outstanding service to her.[129] The most usual mark of favour from James I and his queen was a miniature in a jewelled case or a diamond ring, such as that given to Sir Edward Coke for discovering the murderers of Sir Thomas Overbury.[130]

Good relations might also be restored after a period of coldness by the gift of a jewel or token. When Cardinal Wolsey was taken ill, the king showed his sympathy by sending his ruby ring engraved with his portrait and, at his request, Anne Boleyn added the gold tablet from her girdle.[131] In 1535, when Viscount Lisle was declared innocent after two years in prison, Henry VIII's secretary, Sir Thomas Wriothesley, brought a diamond ring to him 'for a token to him, and to tell him to be of good cheer'.[132]

The *Lisle Letters* describe also the exchange of small pieces of jewellery between friends, to be worn for friendship and affection or to recall a promise made or a favour requested. As a special mark of esteem the Countess of Sussex sent Viscountess Lisle a ring which the Queen of Hungary had given to a friend, and then worried about its return.[133] Such rings did not always fit and were attached to black thread wound round the wrist or hung from the neck (see below, p. 150). From Caernarvon in September 1623 Jane Awbry sent a tablet to her cousin, Owen Wynn, asking him to 'wear it when you ar with your sw[ee]ttehartes and when you see them then you will remember mee'.[134]

The feast of St Valentine on 14 February was marked by the exchange of gifts, which might be jewels, between men and women. In 1530 Henry VIII had five Valentines of goldsmiths' work;[135] and, when Sir Anthony Browne drew Princess Mary as his Valentine in 1543, she sent him a brooch set with a cameo of the Sacrifice of Isaac.[136] The custom continued: among the jewels which Philip II left for Queen Elizabeth I was his Valentine from the Countess of Arundel: 'a small necklace with thirteen roses, a garter and thirteen knots, as well as a small St George'.[137] There was a gold rosemary branch among Elizabeth I's jewels described as a Valentine.[138] In the next reign the Valentines given by the Duke of Buckingham were much more extravagant. In 1618 he spent £2,000 on gifts for various ladies, including the unmarried daughter of Sir James Crofts, who received a carcanet valued at £800.[139]

SOURCES OF GEM-STONES AND PEARLS

The poet Michael Drayton in 1597 compared the beauty of Jane Shore with the jewels in the shop of her husband, a London goldsmith, saying how futile it was for foreign merchants like the Portuguese to import stones from India

> When happie SHORE can bring them forth a Girle,
> Whose Lips be Rubies and her Teeth be Pearle.
> How silly is the *Polander* and *Dane*,
> To bring us Crystall from the frozen Maine?
> When thy cleare Skins transparence doth surpasse
> Their Crystall, as the Diamond doth Glasse.[140]

India had been the principal source of diamonds for more than two thousand years and Portuguese involvement in the gem trade, which resulted in Lisbon becoming an important centre, began when Vasco da Gama sailed directly to India via the Cape of Good Hope. Stones were supplied from Lisbon to the cutters at Antwerp and, through the Fugger agents, to jewellers at Augsburg and Nuremberg. In 1609 the Dutch East India Company sought the exclusive right to ship diamonds from Borneo, but these mines yielded less than those of India.[141]

The great market at Bellergan, where Golconda diamonds, rubies, sapphires and other stones were sold, was described by Ralph Fitch, who was there in 1585. He also visited the other centres of the trade: Goa, established by the Portuguese as their principal centre, and the ports of the coast of Kalinga, the Gulf of Cambray and Gujurat, as well as the diamond-producing areas of Bihar and Oudh in the Ganges plain.[142]

Rubies came from Burma, as did spinels, although Afghanistan was an important source for the latter, as also for lapis lazuli. Turquoises, Turkish stones, came from Nishapur in Persia and from the Sinai peninsula. Sapphires were mined in Ceylon (Sri Lanka), as were garnets, which were also found in Bohemia. Opals, which are increasingly a feature of English jewellery, came from mines at Czerwenitza, then in Hungary and now part of Czechoslovakia. Chalcedony and its many coloured varieties – cornelian, sard, chrysoprase and plasma – with onyx, sardonyx, bloodstone and moss agate, all came from Europe.[143]

As in the Middle Ages, oriental pearls were the most prized and were supplemented by those found in Scottish rivers.[144] The coast of Venezuela was another source of supply but the richest pearl fisheries were in the Persian Gulf and in the Indian Ocean round Sri Lanka. Fitch visited two famous pearl fisheries, the Islands of Baharim and Ormus, and recorded his impressions of the glorious pearls which he saw there, large, round and lustrous.[145]

Gold and silver continued to be mined in Europe and, to a very small extent, in the British Isles, but the discovery of the mines of the New World brought vastly increased supplies of both metals, as well as emeralds (from 1588) and topazes. For the ships laden with their treasure, the journey to Spain, despite the use of a convoy system, was hazardous – especially when to shipwreck was added the danger of piracy by the Elizabethan sea dogs. When the *Golden Hind* returned to Plymouth in 1580 after a three-year voyage round the world, the hold was crammed with treasure taken from intercepted Spanish ships.[146]

Notwithstanding the competition from Lisbon, Venice remained an important centre for the eastern trade throughout the period. Writing from there in 1539 the young Richard Shelley observed: 'the Venetians and Araguses [Ragusans] make themselves rich by fetching our kerseys to sell in Turkey and bringing pearls and stones to all Christendom'.[147] Paul Pindar (1565–1650) took advantage of the opportunities offered by the Venetian market. Sent there at eighteen as factor to a London merchant, he stayed for fifteen years, trading on commission, and became very rich. From 1609 to 1611 he was Consul for the English merchants at Aleppo, and then ambassador in Turkey for nine years, always actively trading. Knighted in 1620, he returned to London. The carved oak façade of his splendid house in Bishopsgate has been preserved.[148] The diamonds he brought home were highly prized, and the king, Prince Charles and the Duke of Buckingham all bought them.[149]

Others tried to make their fortune by trading in gem-stones, Sir Walter Ralegh and Sir Robert Shirley among them. The latter wrote from Persia in 1607 to urge his father to invest as much as he could afford: 'If your fortune or credit were sufficient to send hither a reasonable sum to employ upon precious stones and other rich merchandise, it would bring you infinite profit, without expense or hazard.'[150]

SUBSTITUTES

Although Fynes Moryson observed that in England 'jewels must be oriental and precious, it being disgraceful to wear any that are counterfeit',[151] imitation coloured stones, foiled glass and doublets are specified in inventories and could be mixed with genuine gems, despite the Goldsmiths' regulations.

The production of these inferior wares and imitation jewellery was aided by the privilege of sanctuary enjoyed by craftsmen living in London at St Martin le Grand. Exempt from the control of the City Companies and their rules about the employment of alien workers, they flourished.

At first the glass used was imported but after 1570 high-quality glass was being produced in the Wealden centres under Venetian masters. Katherine Howard's beads of green glass[152] and the pair of shell-shaped earrings of the same material belonging to Mary, Queen of Scots,[153] were probably imported. Counterfeit sapphires were set in a girdle knot of the Countess of Pembroke and in a pair of Anne of Denmark's bracelets.[154] Pursalayn, artificial cameo, was used for beads, as in those which belonged to Lady Jane Grey and later to Mary I – a 'pair of beads of white purslyn with eight gawdes of gold'.[155] From 1608 there were extensive imports of glass and porcelain beads from France.[156] At home Mansell obtained the patent authorising him to make glass, including bugles.[157] Colourless topaz from Germany, zircons from Sri Lanka, and rock crystal from Bristol (as in the 'ring with a sapphire stone and thirtie little Bristowe stones'), Cornwall and Scotland or even Scandinavia, provided cheap alternatives to diamonds.[158]

THE SPOILS OF THE CHURCH

Thomas Cromwell, who designed and masterminded the Dissolution of the Monasteries, had been Keeper of the Jewel House since 1532. He saw to it that the accumulated treasure of both lesser and greater houses was acquired by the Crown. Bequests of jewels to churches had continued until this time; in 1535 a Lincolnshire priest, Robert Awbray, bequeathed to St Hugh of Lincoln 'a ringe of golde to be nayled upon his myter' and a 'crosse of golde to be nayled upon the altar beside the image of our Lady to the honour of her'.[159] The richest shrine in the kingdom was that of St Thomas of Canterbury, where the sheets of gold covering the reliquary were almost wholly paved with precious stones and jewels, and at its destruction the spoils 'in gold and precious stones filled two great chests such as six or seven strong men could no more convey one of them out of the church'.[160]

Of the estimated 289,786 ounces of plate and jewels so plundered, it is estimated that nearly one-sixth went to the Jewel House for remaking and the rest to the Mint for coining. Some of the ecclesiastical ornaments were still in the Jewel House in 1600.[161]

Sequestration of the lesser wealth of the chantries followed under Edward VI, and even Mary I permitted confiscation of the great gold head of St George from the chapel at Windsor; parts of it were made into cramp rings and chains by her goldsmith Robert Raynes.[162]

ENGRAVED GEMS

The revival of gem-engraving, which came with the Renaissance, was reflected in England by an increased use of both cameos and intaglios for adorning plate and jewels. Engraved gems (both ancient and medieval) came from the monastic treasuries, and others were imported;[163] others still were made here, either by foreign craftsmen who had settled in London, or more rarely by Englishmen.[164]

There are two characteristic themes in Tudor glyptic art: the royal portrait and St George. The earliest portraits depict Henry VIII, alone and with his son, and Edward as Prince of Wales.[165] They are cameos carved in three-layered sardonyx in the *intaglio rilevato* technique in which the relief carving does not rise above the border of the stone and with the image repeated on the back in incuse. Although apparently by the same hand, they cannot be attributed to any of the gem-cutters recorded, such as Richard Astyll, Michael Berger and John Mayne.[166] Henry's portrait was also engraved on a ruby in a ring given him by Cardinal Wolsey, to whom Henry returned it when the cardinal was taken ill,[167] and on a chalcedony signet ring owned in 1576 by Dorothy Abington of Hindlip, whose husband had been Cofferer to the Royal Household.[168]

Portraits of Mary I are rare, perhaps because they may have been reworked for Elizabeth I.[169] Numerous cameo portraits of Queen Elizabeth set in brooches, rings and pendants are known, not only from documents and pictures, but from the many examples that survive. They were made in various sizes, using sardonyx, garnet, sapphire and turquoise. They may have been the speciality of one workshop and acquired by other jewellers for commissions or stock.[170] One of the earliest instances comes from 1586, when the Earl of Rutland paid £80 to Peter Van Lore for 'a brooch of her Majestie's picture in an aggatt, set with 53 diamondes'.[171] Some of the portraits seem to copy medals, and although each uses the same type, with small differences in detail, the queen is always in left profile, idealised, with her dress and jewels meticulously rendered.[172] They use the same technique as the Henrician cameos and are again anonymous, although Nicholas Hilliard may have been involved as the artist responsible for the miniature portraits of the queen, and some may have been made by the French engraver Julien de Fontenay.[173] Made in the latter part of the reign to be worn as badges of loyalty, they have a political character which is emphasised in a sardonyx cameo at Chatsworth. Depicting the queen and her predecessors, it encapsulates the Tudor succession.[174] The cameo portraits of James I are rarer and are based on a portrait by Vanson, *c.* 1595.[175]

Medallions of St George were used for the Lesser George, part of the Garter insignia, and smaller versions were set in rings and other jewels without implying membership of the Order. Three cameos for the Lesser George are mentioned in Henry VIII's inventory, one described as 'a tablet of Agathe of Seynt George' and another as made with a white stone.[176] In some of her cameo portraits, Elizabeth I has a cameo of St George at her neck. The Garter knights often owned several such cameos. Thomas, Earl of Sussex, had one of cornelian and the Earl of Northampton three – two of agate framed in diamonds and one of lapis lazuli with a figure of Christ and a dragon on the back, set in a gold enamelled frame.[177]

The appeal of engraved gems lay not only in their craftsmanship, which was rooted in antiquity, but also in their subject matter, which reflected religious belief and cultural interests. Intaglios were principally set in rings, and Shakespeare in *Romeo and Juliet* described the diminutive Queen Mab as

> In shape no bigger than an agate-stone
> On the forefinger of an alderman.[178]

Henry VIII's gold ring 'with a seal in it and a head graven in cornelyn' corresponds with several surviving examples of signets depicting classical heads.[179] Armorial seal engraving, which flourished at the same time, is best represented by the rings given to his friends by Sir Thomas Gresham. Each had the arms engraved on crystal with the tinctures painted on foil behind and the Gresham grasshopper crest engraved at the back of the bezel[180] (Plate VI). Intaglios were only rarely set in other jewels, but Henry VIII had a 'tablet of gold with a sapphire inwardly graven',[181] and a ruby with an orb is at the centre of the Drake Star.[182]

The contrasting layers of sardonyx were skilfully exploited for their pictorial value, and though sardonyx was also set in rings, it was used with greater effect in other jewels, such as Henry VIII's 'capp of blacke vellat . . . having theryn a Brouche of an Agathe hedde . . .',[183] which might be compared with that worn on the headdress of Lady Godsalve in the Holbein portrait.[184] The Earl of Leicester in a portrait by Van der Meulen has a cameo depicting the Devotion of Curtius set in the brooch pinning the plume of heron feathers to his cap.[185]

Other portraits depict cameo-set tablets and pendants: a daughter of St Thomas More wears one from a black ribbon at her neck, and Eleanor Berlowes holds a tablet with a head of Mars on her girdle.[186] Still in their original settings are the Gatacre pendant, with a late antique amethyst cameo of Medusa, a double portrait in a pendant enamelled with the arms of Langford, and the onyx bust of a woman in contemporary dress in an enamelled filigree setting found near Fotheringham Castle in Suffolk[187] (Plate 30). This is a coarse version of the type of an idealised illustrious lady, sometimes called Mary, Queen of Scots, produced in the second half of the sixteenth century, and may be English.

30 The Fotheringham pendant, enamelled gold. Front: onyx cameo portrait of an illustrious lady in contemporary dress, in scrolled frame. Back: cruciform and scrollwork design, formerly enamelled. Late sixteenth century. British Museum.

The 'great carcanet set with nine camewes' in the stock of Nicholas Herrick can be compared with a necklace depicted in a portrait in the Devonshire collection which is composed of enamelled gold links set alternately with busts of Roman emperors and Cleopatras or Lucretias.[188] Similar iconographic series were made up into chains. John Mabbe had one in his stock comprising 40 agates, 960 pearls and 161 gold pipes.[189] Lady Jane Dudley (1537–54) wore another, perhaps a rosary, hanging from her girdle,[190] and in 1576 the Countess of Lincoln gave Queen Elizabeth I a gold girdle with sixteen agate heads and fifteen pearl 'troches'.[191] There were also pairs of bracelets of cornelian and agate heads, similarly spaced with pearls or other stones, in the royal collection.[192] These groups of cameos of uniform size and related subjects made luxurious buttons, and Thomas, Earl of Sussex, bequeathed a set of one hundred and sixteen, each mounted with an agate.[193]

Cameos were also combined with enamelled gold and precious stones in fine and elaborate *commessi*. Edward VI lent his 'faire tablet of gold, to open in the back, made like a castle, garnished with xxvij diamonds, eight rubies, and four sapphires, cut lozenge-wise, with a picture of a woman and an agate holding a small diamond in her hand, like a glass' for the wedding of Sir Andrew Dudley and Lady Clifford.[194] This *commesso* was an allegory of Prudence who, according to Valeriano, 'not only examines present things but meditates on the past and looks out as if from a mirror'[195] (Plate 31).

Christian iconography was well represented among the gems of Henry VIII and Mary I: the Virgin and Child, the Nativity, the Crucifixion, the Deposition, the

31 A lady of the Wentworth family with a *commesso* of Prudence hanging on a ribbon from her girdle and a jewelled pendant at her breast. Details of both jewels. Portrait by Hans Eworth. Tate Gallery.

Resurrection and Old Testament scenes like the Judgement of Solomon.[196] There were also the tablet 'with a picture of Our Lady of Piti in a blewe stone' owned by Lady Jane Grey, and a garnet engraved with the Virgin in the stock of Robert Amadas.[197] Only one of John Mabbe's large stock of engraved gems was religious, a garnet head of the Virgin.[198]

Although Henry VIII had a cameo of two birds back-to-back inscribed VOLUCRES CELI – birds of heaven – and another of a phoenix,[199] such subjects from nature were rare and portrait busts were by far the most common. Besides Roman emperors and empresses, youths and children, there were exotic Turks, bearded and wearing turbans. The contrasting layers of onyxes and sardonyxes were utilised for the busts of Moors and Mooresses, as in the cameo set in the Gresley jewel in which the dark skin of the Negress is enhanced by the white veil on her head and compares with the 'agate of a woman morens hedde with a white Launde upoon the hedde' in the 1561 Pembroke inventory.[200] A Negro and a white woman with a classical profile are juxtaposed in the sardonyx cameo set in the cover of a locket with her miniature portrait which Queen Elizabeth I gave to Sir Francis Drake (Plate IX); they are perhaps personifications of Europe and Africa.[201]

The cameos owned by John Mabbe in 1576 depicted the heroes of classical mythology and history who appealed most to the Elizabethans: Hercules, Vulcan, Mutius Scaevola and Julius Caesar.[202] Not all were engraved in hardstones, and the more easily carved shells and mother-of-pearl were also set in jewels of quality.[203]

GOLDSMITHS

London continued to be the major centre for the manufacture of all kinds of jewellery, with larger or smaller numbers of craftsmen in the bigger provincial towns and cities. Foreign influence, already strong in London and York in the fifteenth century, was further aided by the availability of engraved pattern books from the continent and by large-scale immigration due to the persecution of Protestant minorities in France and the Low Countries. The records of these immigrants, made for the government, provide us with far more detailed information about them than the Goldsmiths' records gave in the medieval period. A new feature, documented but not yet fully explained, is the rise in importance of the provincial goldsmiths attested by the establishment of local Assay Offices at Chester (1554), Norwich (1565) and, for a short time, Exeter (1573).[204]

Foreign jewellers and merchants continued to come and offer their wares to the king and the court. Import and export licences were now a legal requirement. Henry VIII reserved for himself the first sight of all jewels and plate brought into the country, and levied a duty on sales made elsewhere.[205] According to the chronicler Halle, the visit of a French embassy in 1518 gave opportunity for 'rascals pedlers and juellers who brought over devers merchandise' to take advantage of the immunities granted to ambassadorial suites.[206] A few, like Peter van der Wale of Antwerp, seem to have been given some status as 'king's jeweller' and provided Henry VIII with large quantities of jewellery.[207] The king's agents abroad also acted as intermediaries; a letter from Stephen Vaughan at Antwerp in 1546 was accompanied by a watercolour of an 'owche' then on offer.[208] Royal patronage continued under Edward VI, though to a lesser extent, and revived on a large scale under Elizabeth I, who used her ambassador in Paris both to buy items for her and to encourage French goldsmiths to 'come hither with furniture of aglets, chains, bracelets, &c: to be bought both by herself and by the Ladies to be gay in this Court towards the progress'.[209] Not all were fortunate in their enterprises. Some were turned down for financial reasons, and others had items stolen or lost; a French merchant at the court of Henry VIII in 1547 'while geving his attendaunce there in the vain hope of laying out his jewels before a generous patron of his craft had five brooches robbed out of the pocket of his cote'; another, at the court of Elizabeth, had a jewelled fan valued at 'xv or xvi C crowns' stolen in 1561.[210] The patronage of James I and Anne of Denmark was directed more to the acquisition of fine stones and pearls than to the intricately wrought Mannerist jewels favoured by Elizabeth I. The change was gradual: in 1604 licence was granted to import 'a golden shield set with diamonds and precious stones of great value, to sell for his profit where he shall choose', and in 1613 Sir John Throckmorton gave safe conduct to a Flushing merchant, Jacob Marens, 'for bringing over of certain jewels, some to be sold and some to be given away'.[211]

Important as the items acquired from such visitors may have been, the alien goldsmiths resident in England, and the court artists like Holbein the Younger who made designs for others to carry out, had a more pervasive influence.[212] Letters of denization and naturalisation identify many of these craftsmen and their original homes, but the most useful records are the returns of 'Strangers in London' made in 1571, 1593 and 1635 which do not merely give the strangers' names but also state how long they had been here and the number of servants they maintained.[213] The returns of 1571 and 1593 list 138 persons described as goldsmiths (88), jewellers (7, including one who was also a stone-cutter), button-workers (25), lapidaries including agate, diamond and stone-cutters (19). Most are described as Dutch, a term which included the subjects of the Emperor in Germany and those of the King of Spain in modern Belgium, and smaller numbers of French, Spanish and uncertain nationalities. It is clear that many had been settled in London for long periods, in some cases up to forty years. There are certain patterns discernible in the places of their origin: all but three of the lapidaries came from the Low Countries, three more specifically from Antwerp and one from Amsterdam, while about half of the button-makers came from France.[214]

Where these aliens had extensive dealings with the court, much can be found out about them in the State Papers Domestic. Hans of Antwerp settled in London *c.* 1513, married an Englishwoman, and worked for both Henry VIII and the Princess Mary. A friend of Holbein, some of whose designs may have been made for his use, he was admitted to the Goldsmiths' Company in 1537 on the recommendation of Thomas Cromwell, Keeper of the Jewel House since 1532.[215] A recent study of two gold and enamel girdle book covers with inscriptions taken from the Bishop's Bible of 1539 points out that the design for one cover is based on that used by Hieronymus Mamacher of Antwerp for a commission from Abbot Arnold van Dyest of Tongerlo.[216] John Spilman, who appears to have been in London from 1582, was described as the queen's 'Jueller and Goldsmith' there in 1589, and continued to work for James I, who knighted him in 1605.[217] He was one of the most successful of the foreign goldsmiths and jewellers who tried to make a career at the English court. His contemporary Arnold Lulls was also patronised by James I, and a book of his designs has been published.[218] His relative, Sir Peter Van Lore, was even more prominent at court: he was knighted in 1621 for his part in advancing £30,000 needed to support the Count Palatine and Elizabeth of Bohemia's claim to the Bohemian throne.[219] Nicasius Russell was another goldsmith who was also a designer; he did a great deal of work for James I and Anne of Denmark and is known to have been active in London from *c* 1585[220] (Fig. 5).

Fig. 5 Blackwork design by Nicasius Russell for miniature case, lockets and rings: *c.* 1610. Victoria and Albert Museum.

Native-born goldsmiths were not neglected. Robert Adamas (1470–1532) married a granddaughter of Hugh Bryce, another royal goldsmith, and ended his successful career as Master of the Jewel House. As with Hans of Antwerp, some surviving jewels may be associated with his workshop, including the fine Tudor collar of Esses bequeathed by Sir John Allen in 1545 to his successors as Mayors of London.[221] In the reign of Elizabeth I the fortunate survival of two inventories provides us with a survey of the goods held by two goldsmiths. In 1576 John Mabbe had licence for the sale of certain itemised jewels, notwithstanding his earlier difficulties over infringements of the standards, doubtless as an insurance policy against further intervention by the Wardens of the Company.[222] Nicholas Herrick died in 1592; the posthumous inventory of his house and shop lists the contents of a goldsmith's stock valued at £2136 13*s* 10½*d*. It is interesting in showing that gold was used in eleven degrees of fineness, varying in price from 3*s* to £3 6*s* 8*d* the ounce.[223] A younger brother, William, was apprenticed to Nicholas in 1574, and died in 1652, having served as jeweller to both Elizabeth I and James I. The miniaturist Nicholas Hilliard (1537–1619) was the son of an Exeter goldsmith; he was apprenticed to the same craft, and was made a freeman of the London Company in 1569. He is known to have worked on a jewel for the Earl of Hertford and to have designed a Great Seal for Elizabeth I, but his part in the design or making of the Phoenix and Armada jewels or the Barbour and Drake pendants has not been documented.[224]

James I and Anne of Denmark had patronised jewellers in Edinburgh before 1603 and the most celebrated of them, George Heriot, followed the court to London and continued to work for the king and queen until shortly before his death in 1623.[225]

Despite the continued patronage of English or Scots goldsmiths, the Company still felt strongly that the foreign competitors not only took away their business but indulged in fraudulent practices to increase their profits. In 1622 they laid a complaint, naming seventy resident alien goldsmiths, alleging that their activities did 'take away a great part of the living and maintenance of the free goldsmiths of this city', but it had little effect in reducing the numbers of the quality of their competitors.[226]

Prior to the Elizabethan period, there seems to be little evidence for English participation in the international jewellery trade but in 1561 one John Dimock went to Sweden to sell jewels to the king,[227] and in 1585 Ralph Fitch recorded that he had left William Leedes, jeweller, in the service of the 'King of Zalabodim Echebar in Fatepore' by whom he had been given a house, slaves and money.[228]

TECHNIQUES, DESIGNS AND MOTIFS

Bright enamels, shimmering pearls and burnished metal enlivened by engraving or chasing combine harmoniously with gem-stones in the jewellery of the Renaissance. Although sometimes 'set to the sken',[229] most jewels were foiled to enhance their colour and sparkle, a practice to which Marlowe referred: 'What sparkle does it [the diamond] give without a foil?'[230] Diamond cutting evolved from the early point, table and hog-back (used for letter and monogram jewels) to the rose cut illustrated in the drawing of diamonds pledged with Sir John Spillman in 1615 (Fig.6).

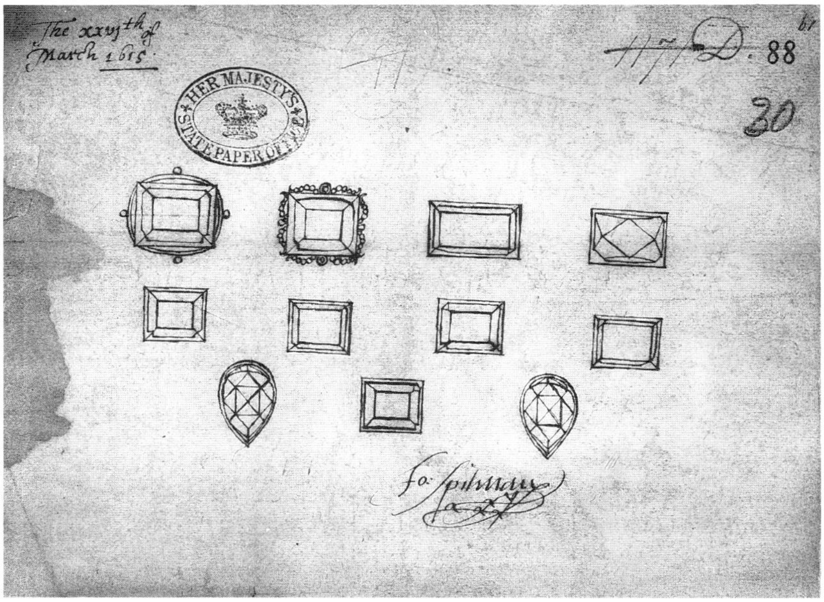

Fig. 6 Drawing of diamonds offered to Sir John Spillman by Queen Anne as security for a loan: 1615. Public Record Office.

The medieval bowl collets with troughs impressed round the sides evolved into the trefoil, quatrefoil and polyfoil settings, with the shield-like recesses divided by double arches. Settings were plain and flat until 1540; thereafter enamel and chased ornament was applied to the lower half, with strap-work based on the engravings of Virgil Solis and others.[231] The importance of these rich settings was explained in the comparison made by Drayton, when he likened Jane Shore, first seen in her husband's shop, to

> . . . an un-cut Diamond in Lead,
> Ere it be set in some high-prized Ring,
> Or garnished with rich enamelling;
> We see the beautie of the Stone is spilt,
> Wanting the gracious Ornament of Gilt.[232]

This emphasis on goldsmith's work gave way in the seventeenth century to a different style of jewellery, in which the settings were subordinated to the stones. Massive chased collets were replaced by narrow fillets of metal grouped together much more unobtrusively to form a skeleton to secure the gems. Enamel was used to a lesser extent, on the backs of settings, while bright colours were replaced by monochrome black or white. The transitional style is exemplified by the designs attributed to Arnold Lulls.[233]

Some terms occur so often in inventories that they must refer to easily recognised common techniques: open goldsmith's work (perhaps filigree), Spanish work (a style of heavy enamelled gold with scrollwork in reserve), and Paris work. The London goldsmith Morgan Wolf supplied brooches and chains in this style to Henry VIII and Elizabeth I also owned jewels in these styles.[234]

Apart from the increased sophistication in stone-cutting, it is not so much in technique that Renaissance jewellery differs from medieval as in the inspiration of the designs and the way in which materials and techniques were used. Holbein's designs illustrate the beginning of a Renaissance style in English jewellery[235] (Fig. 7). It drew on the classical heritage which was being rediscovered in Italy and on the new styles of drawing and composition for figure subjects. The arabesque – elegant interlaced ornament derived from Arabic sources – was used by Holbein in his designs,[236] while the northern style of this ornament was popularised in 1548 by Thomas Geminus's book, *Moryse and Damashin renewed and encreased very profitably for Goldesmythes and Embroderers*.

Fig. 7 Drawing by Hans Holbein of a hat badge for a lover, with Cupid striking the hour; inscribed ASPETTO LA HORA: 1530–5. Trustees of the Chatsworth Estates.

As in medieval jewellery, knots formed the links for necklaces and collars, joined the initials in monogram jewels, and formed independent ornaments. There were the elaborately tasselled knots of the Garter collar and the simpler type imitating the knot on the cord girdle worn by friars. In 1529 Dame Maud Parr bequeathed 'eighteen diamonds sett with fryers knottes', and girdles and tablets in Princess Mary's wardrobe were similarly ornamented.[237] True-lovers' knots appealed because of their symbolism 'which naught but death shall loose',[238] and bracelets with this motif were given to Elizabeth I by Sir Christopher Hatton, who said that it was 'the knot she most loves, and she thinks cannot be undone'.[239]

Queen Anne of Denmark had several jewels with knots, including 'A Chaine of open goldsmithes worke in knottes of severall greatnes & fashion, conteining fower score & sixe peeces linked together', set with pearls, rubies and diamonds, that was later given to 'Lady Anne Liviston'.[240] The knot could be used alone, as in her 'Jewell of gold in forme of a knotte, enameled blewe on ye backside', set with a ruby, diamonds and pearls.[241] Others used the heraldic knot badges; her 'faire Chaine of three sortes of

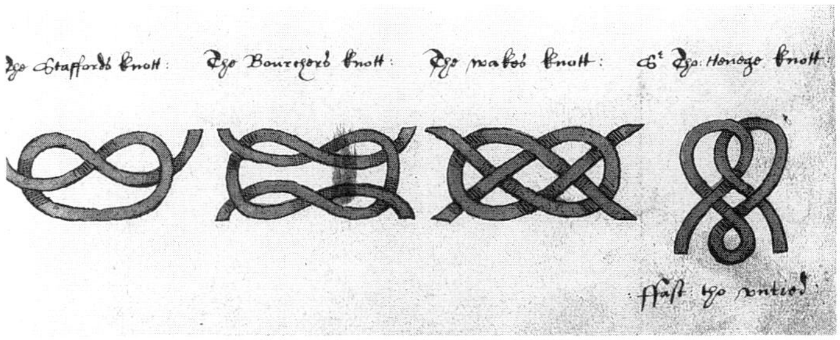

Fig. 8 The Stafford, Bourchier, Maltravers and Heneage knots. British Library.

knottes, conteining xlviij knottes', was probably that given to Queen Elizabeth I by the Earl of Leicester in 1584 with 'xxiiij knotts, like Bouser knotts, xij Matreves knotts, xij lytle Senckfoyles', using the devices of the Bourchier and Maltravers families.[242] (Fig. 8). The Queen of Bohemia was painted by Van Mierevelt wearing a chain of this type, which could well be the same one, venerated as an heirloom, which she begged her son Charles to acquire from her creditors and to preserve in his family[243] (Plate 32). Two surviving knot jewels also use the heraldic forms: the miniature case with the Heneage knot and motto, and the Stafford knots linking a necklace of double crescents and jewelled clusters[244] (Plate 33).

32 Queen Elizabeth of Bohemia wearing a chain of diamond knots and a crowned heart jewel. Portrait by M. van Miereveld. Private collection.

33 Gold, pearl and ruby necklace of double crescent, clusters and Stafford knots with crowned anchor pendant. *c.* 1600. Collection of Baron Hans Heinrich Thyssen-Bornemisza de Kaszon.

Heraldry is a recurring theme in Tudor and Jacobean jewellery. Henry VIII had jewels, like his plate, decorated with the Tudor rose and portcullis badges and with the badges of his first wife, Katherine of Aragon; one was later owned by Anne of Denmark: 'A Jewell of gold with a square Emerald supported by a dragon & and grayhound on ye backside, the halfe Rose & ye halfe Pomegranate'[245] The roses of Lancaster and York may also have been used separately, as Elizabeth I had a 'flowere of golde with a white rose sett with rubies and a red rose of diamonds three sparks of rubies and a table sapphire and two ragged pearls',[246] and other jewels with them were made for James I and Anne. Several of the jewels given to Elizabeth I by the Earl of Leicester were worked with the ragged staff or bear and ragged staff badges he had inherited from the old Earls of Warwick.[247]

The most common heraldic jewel continued to be the signet ring, but arms were also used on the covers of girdle books and tablets or miniature cases, and on the backs of pendants.[248] The Seton family crest, a griffin, was made into a ruby and sapphire jewel for Alexander, Earl of Dunfermline,[249] and the phoenix badge of the Seymours was worn as a magnificent jewel by Dame Elizabeth Knightley, daughter of the Duke of Somerset[250] (Plate 34).

The *fede* motif of clasped hands continued to be popular and sometimes the hands held a heart or a jewel between them.[251] Jewelled hearts were also made for Anne Boleyn,[252] and for her daughter, Elizabeth I, who is depicted wearing such a jewel.[253] Some of the heart jewels which Anne of Denmark bought from George Heriot were not only held in loving hands but crowned, or wounded by an arrow or dart – devices illustrated in the emblem books of Whitney and Wither.[254]

Other emblematic jewels alluded to the sea, ships and anchors, to military life and to the chase.[255] More common were devices drawn from nature. Princess Mary had a gold tablet ornamented with honeysuckle and woodbine, and similar motifs – eglantine, pansy, peasecods, marygolds, roses, etc. – were used on many of Elizabeth I's jewels.[256] She also liked birds, and had examples of a dove, a cock, a pelican, a peacock, an ostrich and an owl, besides other creatures like crabs and crayfish, a snail, a tortoise and even a homely haddock's head.[257]

Individual identity could also be asserted by the use of initials and monograms or ciphers. Henry VIII had a chain of gold Hs linked by pillars, and Anne Boleyn wore a gold B with three hanging pearls as a pendant.[258] Whereas Holbein's designs for such jewels were only sparsely set with gems, later examples, like the diamond E ring for Elizabeth I or the A brooch worn in his hat by James I in a portrait attributed to Vanson, are closely set with stones.[259] Longer inscriptions were also used; they might be Biblical and classical quotations or mottoes. Katherine Howard had a brooch with figures and 'scriptures over their heads, with the King's word under the said brooch',[260] and this last, DIEU ET MON DROIT, was also found on jewels belonging to Mary I.[261] Queen Elizabeth used the motto SEMPER EADEM and this – with another, HINC SPES – is

34 Phoenix jewel, badge of the Seymours, worn on chains below the ruff. Detail from the portrait of Lady Elizabeth Knightley by Marcus Gheeraerts, 1591. Yale Center for British Art, Paul Mellon collection, New Haven, USA.

found on her jewels.[262] Longer inscriptions include the name of her suitor, the Duke of Alençon – FRANCOS DE VALOS – spelt out in diamond letters on a bracelet, while other, complimentary mottoes – CARUM QUOD RARUM and GEMMA PRECIOSIOR INTUS – are found on jewels owned both by her and Anne.[263] The latter also liked cipher and inscribed jewels, and ordered bracelets with both Greek and Latin letters from George Heriot.[264]

After 1600, chased ornament was replaced by flatter surfaces which were enamelled and resembled peas in a pod. This pea-pod style was widely used on rings, pendants, watches and miniature cases; early examples are found on the Barbour jewel and a drawing in the Lulls album with snakes and leafy trails[265] (Fig. 9).

Fig. 9 Drawing of an emerald pendant by Arnold Lulls. Victoria and Albert Museum.

Several of the designs characteristic of the Lulls drawings had already appeared under Elizabeth I. In 1561 the Earl of Pembroke owned a 'great ballise with pearl pendant set with snakes green enamelled' and the queen had a chain of snake links.[266] The Earl of Leicester's diamond star was probably worn in his hat with a feather,[267] while Lady Cheke gave the queen a 'jewell of gold lyke a starre, garnished with sparkes of dyamons of sondry cuttes, and one small pearle pendante'.[268] The sun was used on the back of some of Elizabeth's star jewels, and her 'sun of a rubie graven the beams garnished with sparks of diamonds and rubies' may have been similar to that which she gave to Sir Francis Drake.[269] Crescents and 'moones on the wane' occur in the Lulls drawings, in Anne of Denmark's inventory and in portraits of Elizabeth I as Diana.[270]

CLASSICAL INFLUENCE

The most notable departure from medieval design came from classical art as reinterpreted in Italy. The rounded arches, the orders and pediments of classical architecture replaced Gothic forms, while new motifs from sculpture, from engraved gems and from the grotesques discovered in the ruins of Nero's Golden House in Rome were also used as models.

Acanthus leaves, terms rising from foliage rather than a pedestal, putti, satyrs and masks, cornucopiae, etc., were all used and called 'antiques'. A tablet with an 'antike face' was given to Henry VIII in 1534, and the next year a 'gold chain enamelled with black, and a great tablet hanging thereto with an antique chased on it' was delivered to him at Windsor.[271] Katherine Howard had a white enamel brooch with a border of 'antique boys' – putti[272] – and Elizabeth I had a jewel with gems set in 'antiques',[273] while Spenser mentions jewelled buskins decorated with knots and 'entayled with curious antickes and full fayre aumayled'.[274]

Holbein's historiated designs often drew on classical imagery: Diana and Actaeon, Cupid stung by bees, and the Fall of Icarus.[275] Henry VIII owned a 'goodly table of Hercules' and another tablet with Venus and Cupid.[276] Those of Elizabeth I are sometimes identified in the inventories: Ixion on the wheel, Cupid, Cleopatra,[277] Bacchus on a tun[278] is listed among others in Anne of Denmark's collection. Her own taste, however, favoured the new styles and jewels which expressed her family associations by ciphers or miniatures.

DEVOTIONAL JEWELLERY

With the Reformation, the character of devotional jewellery changed radically; beginning in the latter part of Henry VIII's reign after his break with Rome, the change accelerated under Edward VI, reversed under Mary I, and returned in a modified form under Elizabeth I. It can be documented in wills and probate inventories, although some items, especially the paternosters or prayer beads, lingered on for some years after 1558. In 1571 a statute attempted to do away with the traditional aids to Catholic devotion and enacted that a range of ornaments 'called or named by the Name of Agnus Dei, or any Crosses Pyctures Beades or such lyke vayne and superstitious Thynges from the Bysshop or Sea of Rome' were prohibited and those found guilty of possessing them were subject to outlawry and forfeiture of lands and goods.[279] James I in 1605–6 empowered the Justices of the Peace to search Recusant households:

> And that if any Altar Pix Beades Pictures or suche like Popish Reliques . . . in the opinion of the saide Justices . . . shall be thought unmeete for such Recusant as aforesaid to have or use, the same shall be presently defaced.[280]

This was not universally observed. Away from London, in the splendid isolation of Naworth Castle in Cumbria, members of the recusant Howard family could dress like continental Catholics. There is a portrait *c.* 1610 by an unknown artist depicting a Howard lady arrayed like a nun about to be professed, probably to commemorate her initiation into a sodality or third Order, resplendent in court dress pinned with rosettes in the red and white Howard livery colours. She holds a processional crucifix in one hand and a tall lighted candle in the other, both garlanded with leaves and flowers. These symbols are echoed in her jewellery: the cruciform medallion with the winged lion of St Mark, the crystal reliquary hanging below it, and the gold crucifix on the sleeve by the shoulder (Plate XV).

Paternosters or pairs of beads (the name rosary only slowly came into use after 1547) remained popular in the first part of the period and took many decorative forms. In 1535 Lady Ryngeley thanked Viscountess Lisle for 'your bedes of coral, with a heart of gold, which was to me a great comfort, I knowing that you loved them so well, for you were wont to wear them about your arm'.[281] Katherine Howard owned twenty-three of different designs and materials, the gauds usually differentiated from the beads.[282] Dame Maud Parr had 'a paayre of beades of jacentes with white scriptures and beades of gold betwixt them' – such inscriptions being unusual.[283] Others had figured beads, such as that with 'white and green faces garnished with a pillar at the end and set with garnets and rubies' which belonged to Henry VIII.[284] Representations of the Five Wounds were also used for some gauds[285] but others seem to have been purely decorative. Henry VIII gave Princess Mary a pair of beads of crystal with gold gauds and a decorative tassel of pearls and goldsmith's work at the end; she also owned a rosary of agate eggs, each enclosing a scene from the Gospels in enamel.[286] She always carried a pair of beads and when she rode in procession through London in 1551 her escort of knights, ladies and gentlemen all had 'a payre of beads of black'.[287]

Under Elizabeth, their use – and mention in wills or inventories – gradually declined, especially after the 1571 act. Recusants imported them illicitly, and wooden rosaries were made at Little Oakley, Northants., and perhaps at other centres of the old faith.[288] Decade or paternoster rings (with the Sacred Monogram, cross and nails on the bezel) continued to be made until well into the eighteenth century – perhaps a more discreet substitute.[289] For generations the Every family of Egginton Hall, Derbyshire, owned a pendant with gold relief of the Virgin and Child behind an amethyst in an octagonal rayed frame inscribed with its history:

> When Spanneshe fleet fled home for feare
> This golden piktur then was found
> Fast fexsed unto Spanniards eare
> Who drowned laye on Irishe grounde.
> Anno 1588[290]

AGNUS DEI

In 1538 Elizabeth, widow of Sir Bartholomew Read, a former Mayor of London, bequeathed a 'tablet of Agnus Dei of gold garnished with balaces and pearls'.[291] Being consecrated by the Popes, the Agnus Dei was regularly singled out for attention in post-Reformation laws against Catholic practices. The consignment received by Mary I in 1556 included 'a little book in Italian, declaring the ceremonies used in making them, and at the end of it their virtue, which is great'.[292]

RELIQUARIES

At the Field of the Cloth of Gold, Cardinal Wolsey gave Madame Louise of Savoy a relic of the True Cross enclosed in a jewelled cross. He himself always wore a cross of this kind, declaring that, in prosperity, he would not part with it for £1,000.[293] Katherine of Aragon kept one until she died, when it was delivered by Thomas Cromwell on the king's order to the Princess Mary.[294] Other reliquaries are mentioned in wills, like that owned by Dame Maud Parr or the Countess of Oxford's 'little crosse of gold having closed in the same a piece of the Holy Cross which I dayly wear about my neck'.[295]

A circular reliquary of enamelled gold, believed to have belonged to Sir Thomas More and probably of German origin, had on one side the figure of St George and on the other Christ as the Man of Sorrows with the Instruments of the Passion and other

35 St Thomas More reliquary. Enamelled gold, the back with relief of Christ as Man of Sorrows with Instruments of His Passion, and busts of Judas, Pontius Pilate, St Peter and the woman servant, within a wreath of flowers. Relief, *c.* 1535; frame later. Trustees of Stonyhurst College.

actors therein (Plate 35). The side is inscribed with a quotation from the *Aeneid* (I.99); it reputedly holds a miniature which is in poor condition.[296] A reliquary cross said to have belonged to him has also been preserved. The Greek inscription on the back identified the contents as 'a relic of St Thomas the Apostle'.[297]

After 1571 direct allusion to such items in wills became rare, but in 1623 Viscount Montague directed that he should be buried in a Capuchin friar's habit and that his son Francis should have 'the crosse of gould which I usually were about my necke having in it a piece of the holy Cross'.[298]

PROTESTANT JEWELS

The increase in the use of Old Testament subjects for jewels seen towards the end of Henry VIII's reign does not necessarily reflect the new religious ideas, as such jewels were also acquired by the Princess Mary.[299] Only one jewel in the royal inventories examined seems to express the propaganda of the reformers. A tablet belonging to Katherine Howard had on one side 'the pycture of the busshop of Rome ronnyng away Lamentyng and divers other persones one settyng his fote upon the busshop overthrown'.[300]

Elizabeth I inherited her father's collection of crosses and many other old devotional jewels, and others were given to her, like the 'smale juell of golde, with the holy lambe of mother of perle, garnished with two very smale perles and two very smale dyamondes, and three mene perles pendaunt' listed in 1579.[301] Although some of the emblematic jewels in her portraits, like the pelican and the phoenix, had a religious significance,[302] her preferred emblem of things spiritual was the armillary sphere. Worn as an earring in the Ditchley portrait, used as links in a chain, or hung as a pendant on her sleeve,[303] its religious significance for her is explained by a drawing in a Psalter which she gave an unknown friend. The sphere is shown above the open pages of a Bible inscribed 'Verbum Domini'; below is an Italian motto meaning 'Unfortunate is he who places his trust in mortal things.'[304] Armillary spheres are incorporated into bracelets depicted in a portrait of an unknown lady in the royal collection.[305]

ICONOGRAPHIC JEWELS

Historiated jewels retained their popularity throughout the sixteenth century and their subject matter is widened by the inclusion of more scenes from the Old Testament, some of which reflected the traditional choice of typological subjects: the Fall of Man,[306] Joseph and his Brethren (Plate 36) and, on a German pendant *c.* 1570 in the Burghley House collection, the ascent of the Prophet Elijah into heaven and Jonah in the whale. The latter subject also occurred on a jewel owned by Robert Johnstone, George Heriot's executor: 'a medal of gold representing Jonah in the whale's belly'.[307] New subjects included Hagar and Ishmael and Lot's wife being turned into the pillar of salt (seen also in a portrait).[308] The Old Testament jewels acquired by Princess Mary belonged to the traditional series: Abraham and Isaac, Jacob's ladder, Moses and the

36 Enamelled gold pendant. Front: Joseph abandoned in the well by his brothers. Back: a bird pecking at fruit beneath a baldachino. 1550–60. British Museum.

37 Enamelled gold hat badge with relief of Christ and the Woman of Samaria at Jacob's Well, inscribed + OF A TREWTHE + THOW ART THE TREW MESSIAS. *c.* 1540. British Museum.

38 Lady Vaux wearing a Virgin and Child jewel. Copy after the portrait by Hans Holbein the Younger, *c.* 1535. Collection of H.M. Queen Elizabeth II.

Temple of Solomon.[309] Elizabeth I, who had fewer jewels in this category, used them for political purposes, especially the theme of the Flood. This occurs in a pendant of a rainbow and dove, and on the back of the Armada Jewel where the Ark, tossed on the sea, inscribed SAEVAS TRANQUILLA PER UNDAS (Peaceful through the stormy waves), refers to the queen's safe guidance of the English Church.[310]

The designs for historiated jewels among those made by Holbein the Younger include New Testament subjects; these can be found listed in inventories and depicted in portraits.[311] As with the Old Testament scenes, new subjects are found, like the marriage at Cana and the Samaritan woman at Jacob's well, which has the English text + OF A TREWTHE + THOW ART THE TREW MESSIAS proclaiming its origin[312] (Plate 37). Henry VIII had several jewels depicting the Virgin and Child, similar to the one worn by Lady Vaux in her portrait by Holbein[313] (Plate 38); a tablet Viscountess Lisle ordered from Paris in 1536 had the Assumption and also St Catherine on it.[314]

A portrait of Mary I attributed to Hans Eworth shows her wearing a round tablet at the girdle with the Evangelists seated around a diamond cross crosslet potent.[315] After 1558 such jewels become rarer, and those with the Annunciation and the 'Romane A of diamondes under a cloude, with the figure of Christ & our Lady crowned' owned by Anne of Denmark were probably heirlooms.[316] Equally unusual are the gold tablet of Our Lady owned by Henry Howard, Earl of Northampton, and another that belonged to the first Earl of Dunfermline († 1622); but the former affirmed his Catholic faith at his death in 1619 and the latter, although he became a Protestant in 1585, was a godson of Mary, Queen of Scots.[317]

JESUS JEWELS

The Sacred Monogram, the abbreviated form of the Greek name of Jesus normally written as IHS, was a popular subject. A large black-letter jewel is worn on her bodice by Jane Seymour in a Holbein portrait and others are listed in the royal inventories.[318] The portrait of Anne of Denmark by Van Somer shows such a jewel pinned to her standing lace collar, and one from her collection was sent to Prince Charles in Spain.[319] The Countess of Arundel wears a black-letter diamond IHS jewel in her portraits – by Marcus Gheeraerts (Plate 39), by Daniel Mytens (Plate 39) and finally by Van Dyck.[320] There is a similar design among those in the Arnold Lulls album: the letters are bordered by his characteristic broken scrollwork[321] (Fig. 10). A group of mid-sixteenth-century brasses depict ladies with the IHS monogram on their tablets, and Ann Fermer *c.* 1552 at Easton Neston, Northants. (MS I), has Roman capitals for the monogram, although the Cave brass of Chicheley, Bucks., *c.* 1558 (MS I) retains the black letter.

39 The Countess of Arundel with diamond Sacred Monogram jewel pinned to her neckline. Portrait by Marcus Gheeraerts, *c.* 1620. Collection of the Duke of Norfolk, Arundel Castle.

Fig. 10 Drawing of Sacred Monogram by Arnold Lulls. Victoria and Albert Museum.

HEARTS

Some heart jewels were given a religious significance by being combined with figures of saints: St Peter of Milan in a heart of 'Spanish work' studded with diamonds; SS. George, Anthony and Sebastian engraved on gold; and St Anne on the back with the Five Wounds on the front.[322] The latter motif is on the heart tablet at the girdle of Jane Foxe *c.* 1554 at Ludford, Herefordshire (MS 1). The lily, emblem of the Virgin, ornamented a heart owned by Sir Matthew Cradocke in 1529,[323] while the monogram M and I could make a plain heart into a badge of faith.[324]

MEMENTO MORI

The *memento mori* theme was expressed by skulls and other symbols of mortality, with appropriate Latin or English texts. In 1537 Richard Rychardin sealed a letter to Thomas Cromwell with the device of a 'death's head with the motto Morieris'.[325] Another motto, NOSCE TEIPSUM, used on the bezel of the great gold *memento mori* ring of Sir Richard Gresham (1485–1549), implied that self-knowledge was the best preparation for death.[326] A ring with a white skull worn by Edward Goodman is inscribed BEHOLD THE ENDE, and others of this type with different texts have survived, one being a turning bezel with the other side engraved with the arms of Harman of Suffolk as a signet.[327] In his will of 1591, Gyles Blofeld of Bedford left a ring with a skull, flanked by ragged staves presumably for decoration rather than as a badge.[328]

Some of these jewels were associated with dramatic events. Lady Catherine Grey, imprisoned in the Tower of London, sensing she was about to die, sent her husband a ring which, she said, bore her portrait. Inscribed WHYLE I LIVE YOURS, the depiction was a death's head; and within hours she had died.[329]

Not all *memento mori* jewels were rings, and an important survival was found in the ruins of Tor Abbey in Devon. It is a coffin-shaped pendant which opens to show a skeleton, the outside enamelled with moresques in the style of Thomas Geminus and inscribed THROUGH · THE · RESURRTION · OF · CHRISTE · WE · BE · ALL · SANCTIFIED[330] (Plate 40). Since another skeleton of identical size exists, the jewel cannot have been unique. Some death's heads were richly jewelled: two in John Mabbe's stock were framed in rubies and pearls, and in 1579 another was incorporated in a gem-encrusted tablet of the Sacrifice of Isaac.[331]

During the sixteenth century, bequests of mourning rings, to be worn in memory of the deceased, became more common. Usually their value is stated, or coins bequeathed to be made into a ring, but the design is seldom specified in detail. An exception is the will of Anne Newdigate, which expressed her 'will and desire . . . to have a few plain gold Rings made of ten or twelve shillings price with a pansy being my father's Crest,

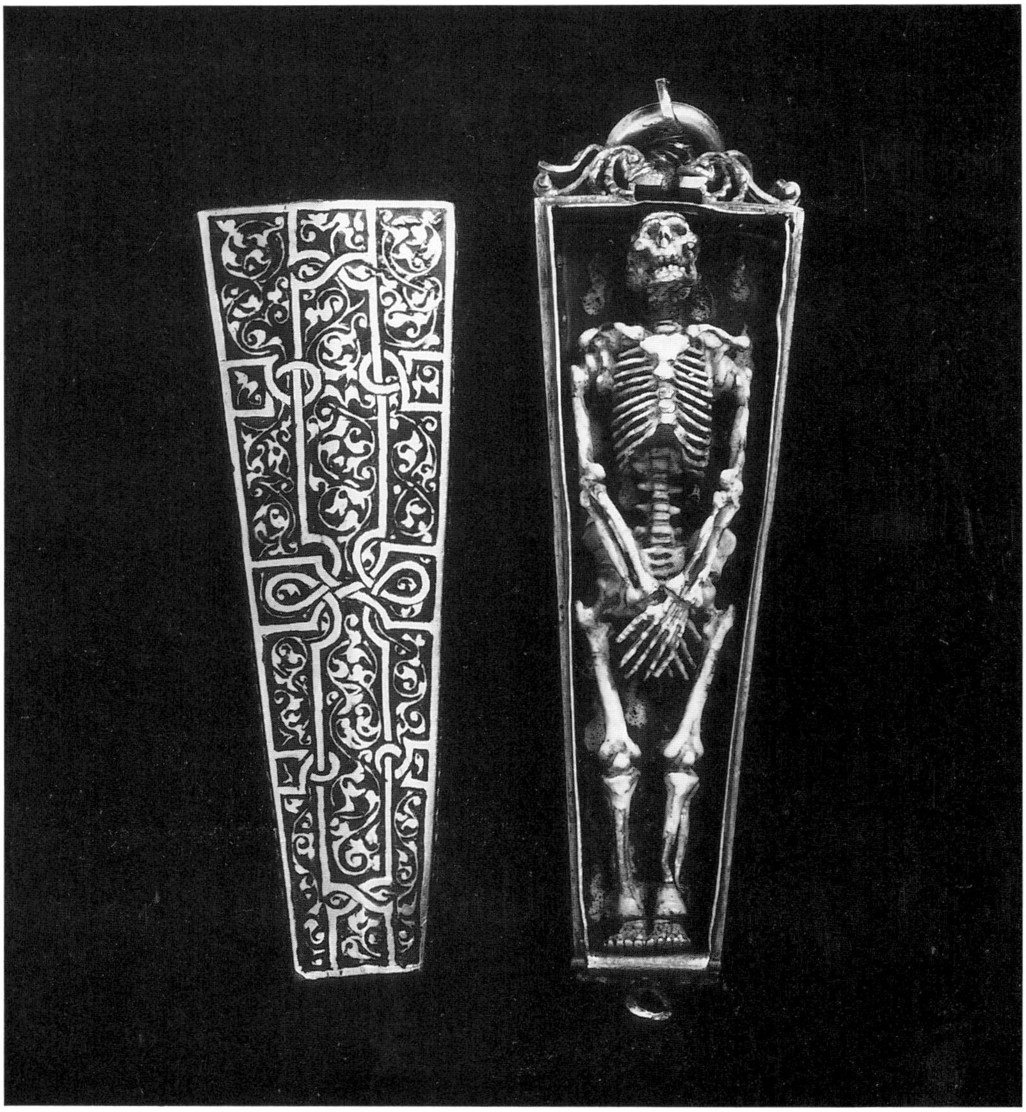

40 Enamelled gold coffin pendant enclosing skeleton. *c.* 1540. Victoria and Albert Museum, from the ruins of Tor Abbey.

engraven on the outside and two letters for my name enamelled with black on either side the pansy and an inscription within to be in latin, these words following: Death is the beginninge of life'.[332]

MAGICAL JEWELLERY

Neither the Renaissance nor the Reformation shook popular belief in the medicinal and magical properties of precious and semi-precious stones, and new books like that by Anselm de Boodt, physician to Rudolph II, brought the traditional lore up to date.[333]

After her imprisonment Katherine Howard was forced to return a ring of small intrinsic value to Henry VIII 'unless the stone, as is said, has some virtue against spasms'.[334] Mary, Queen of Scots, owned an amethyst 'contre la melancholie',[335] and Robert Burton attributed similar powers in 1621 to the carbuncle and coral which 'drive away childish fears, overcome sorrow, and hung about the neck repress troublesome dreams'.[336]

Stones were thought to be more efficacious if worn close to the skin, and a pendant set with a large peridot, a hessonite garnet and a tear-shaped sapphire drop was left open at the back for this purpose[337] (Plate 41). Their properties were enhanced by the old talismanic formulae engraved on the back of the gold frame: + IHS + MARIA + DETRAGRAMMATA ANNANISAPTA + DEI (see above, p. 32). Reginald Scot in his *Discoverie of Witchcraft* (1584) explained:

> Ananizapta strikes death while it death seeks to harm
> Evil death is captured when Ananizapta is said
> Ananizapta of God now have pity on me.[338]

An even more esoteric charm was nielloed on the silver bracelet which the magician, Dr John Dee, gave to Queen Elizabeth I. She may have believed in its powers, for she gave her favourite, Robert, Earl of Essex, a ring inscribed with the words IESUS AUTEM (Luke 4.30) to protect him from highway robbers and the dangers of travel.[339]

41 Enamelled gold pendant set with a hessonite garnet and peridot, in acanthus foliate frame, and hung with a sapphire drop. Back: inscribed with a magical charm. Mid sixteenth century. Victoria and Albert Museum.

Some animal products were believed to act as antidotes to, or detectors of, poison. Chief among them was the unicorn's horn, the tusk of the narwhal, in accordance with the bestiary tale of the unicorn purifying the water with its horn before the animals drank.[340] The dramatist George Chapman refers to the eagerness with which this horn was sought by jewellers:

> I once did see,
> In my yong travels through Armenia,
> An angry Unicorne in his full career
> Charge with too quick an *eie* a jeweller
> That watcht him for the Treasure of his browe,
> And ere he could get shelter of a tree,
> Naile him with his rich Antler to the Earth.[341]

It was of great value. Small pieces would be set in jewels, and one of Viscountess Lisle's French correspondents wrote to ask her help in having a 'piece of unicorn's horn' set.[342] The Danny jewel, a boat-shaped pendant enamelled with moresques (Plate 42), has such a piece, and another, stocked by Nicholas Herrick in 1592, was studded with a sapphire, diamonds and rubies.[343] Sir Peter Carew wears one at the base of a jewel crowned by two 'antique boys' with masks of a woman and a lion (Plates 43). Two more

42 The Campion of Danny jewel. Enamelled gold pendant incorporating a segment of 'unicorn's horn' (narwhal tusk). *c.* 1550. Victoria and Albert Museum.

43 Sir Peter Carew with unicorn horn mounted in a jewel with 'antique boys' and the masks of a woman and a lion, hanging from a ribbon. Details from a portrait by Gerlach Flicke, 1549. Collection of the Earl of Yarborough.

like jewels were owned by Elizabeth I: 'a Tablett of Unicornes horne havinge in it a whistle and a woman sittinge upon it' and another 'litle pece of Unicorne' kept in a jewelled tablet set with an agate cameo of the queen.[344] She also owned a 'Besore [Bezoar] stone sett in golde hanging at a litle Bracelett of a flagon Cheyne. The most parte of this stone spent', presumably from use; it was a concretion from the intestines of a ruminant, most often a Persian goat.[345]

Ben Jonson mentions a toadstone set in a jewel, and these palatal teeth from fossil fish were also believed to be antidotes to poison.[346] Gyles Blofeld in 1591 bequeathed a 'rynge of gold which is set with a lardge toadestone', and some were set in double bezels.[347]

44 Heart-shaped gold pendant containing a charm inscribed with the name and birthday of John Monson. 1597. Victoria and Albert Museum.

Another strange charm was the gold heart-shaped locket inscribed JOHN MONSON BORN THE TENTH OF SEPTEMBER AT 12 OF THE CLOK AT NIGHT 1597[348] (Plate 44). He had been born with the caul, part of the membrane enclosing the foetus, wrapped about his head, and since this was considered lucky and gave protection from drowning, it was mounted for him to wear.

DRESS

Renaissance dress in England continued the late-fifteenth-century styles, especially for men, and changed slowly over the years according to the dictates of fashion.[349] Henry VIII's sense of his importance in international affairs, and the spur of rivalry with the French court, helped to maintain a degree of magnificence seldom equalled since.

Tunic or doublet and hose, with a girdle or sword-belt, remained the basic items of male attire throughout the period, whatever changes occurred in profile and cut. In the first half of the century the gown worn over them was long and furred for greater dignity, with sleeves hanging down to the hem from which the arms emerged through slits at the elbow.[350] It continued to be worn by civic and other officials, by Privy Councillors and by the legal and learned professions.[351] Fashion introduced for the younger courtiers a short waist-length cloak, often with a standing collar, worn elegantly draped over the left shoulder.[352] The soft low cap could be richly adorned with jewels: aglets, buttons and brooches or badges; it was replaced towards the end of the period by a variety of hats with tall crowns less extravagantly adorned.

As in the fifteenth century, gold chains continued to be worn as a sign of status. The livery collars gradually became restricted to certain offices, although well into the reign of Henry VIII it was still regarded as a sign of allegiance. The Garter collar introduced by Henry VII was worn not just at the Order's feast in April but also at the principal courts of the year. At the Elizabethan court fashionable gallants might wear a single earring, bracelets, rings and a miniature case with the queen's or their mistress's portrait under the jewelled lid.

Ladies' dress changed more, and after 1558 it followed the fashions set by the queen, with some foreign influences.[353] The long gowns of the early years of the century were replaced by bodices and skirts spread over frames or bolsters about the hips, and the collar of the chemise was enlarged to make the ruff and the standing collars of the last phase which framed the face. Wired for support, these collars had jewels pinned to them; others were fixed in the piled-up hair[354] (Plate XI). These styles supplanted the early Tudor gabled hood and the later Paris headdress, although the latter continued for mourning dress. Whereas the portraits of Mary I show that she preferred the earlier style of gown, merely adopting the new headdress, those of Elizabeth I show a much more lavish use of jewels. They were often designed to express conceits or emblems, perhaps requested by the person who commissioned the painting, for very few can be positively identified in the royal inventories.[355]

Children were dressed and bejewelled as miniature versions of their parents.

45 Alice, Countess of Derby, wearing ropes of pearls, a diamond necklace with pearl fringe, pear pearl earrings, and crown with pearl spikes between fleurs-de-lis, diamond star in the centre. Portrait by an unknown artist, *c.* 1590. Private collection.

4
The categories of Renaissance jewellery, 1509 – 1625

JEWELS FOR THE HEAD

CROWNS AND CORONETS

Although the inventories show that the number of crowns and coronets owned by the king and the higher nobility were fewer than in the Middle Ages, they had not declined in splendour and contributed enormously to the grandeur of the court ceremonies, which were unrivalled.[1]

Henry VIII's elaborate Imperial crown was described minutely in his posthumous inventory. The 'border' was richly jewelled and the crosses and fleurs-de-lis upon it were set with larger stones and the fleurs-de-lis also bore three images of kings, of St George and Our Lady. The number of the arches is not specified but the 'Dyademe above' was also set with diamonds, and it weighed 98 ounces.[2] An equally splendid crown made for Mary I, which she wore over a jewelled caul, was so heavy that she had to hold up her head in her hands.[3] A portrait of Elizabeth I in her coronation robes no doubt depicts the same crown with the jewelled circlet, alternating crosses and fleurs-de-lis, and four arches supporting an orb and cross, although other portraits show only two arches.[4] The three great courts – at Christmas, Easter and Pentecost – continued to be marked by the sovereign wearing a crown. At New Year in 1581 Queen Elizabeth wore a new crown set (among the other gem-stones) with five enormous emeralds, two of them round and three as long as her little finger, presented to her by Sir Francis Drake.[5]

In the next reign Queen Anne presided over the spectacular masques which were such an important feature of early Stuart court festivities, wearing the circlet made specially for her coronation in London. Although the king had ordered it to be kept with the other crowns in the Secret Jewel House at the Tower of London, he was persuaded to let her remove it.[6]

The higher nobility, above the rank of baron, continued to wear coronets at coronations, and a description of that of Elizabeth I mentions them being worn in the procession to Westminster Abbey, when she was followed by duchesses, marchionesses, countesses, etc. dragging their trains after them, going two by two, and being exquisitely dressed, with their coronets on their heads, and so handsome and beautiful it was a marvellous sight.[7]

During the sixteeth century, the design of coronet proper to the degree of the wearer was established; unlike the later custom, they could still be jewelled, as was the ducal coronet delivered to Lady Jane Grey.[8] Elizabeth, Countess of Oxford († 1537), at Wivenhoe, Essex (MS III), and Thomas Boleyn, Earl of Wiltshire († 1539), at Hever, Kent (MS IV), have similar coronets. A jewelled band supports a row of pearls – in the former example set on spikes, more like a viscount's coronet. The modern pattern is seen in a portrait of Alice, fifth Countess of Derby, with diamond-set fleurons and tall spikes with pearls rising from the jewelled rim, combined with a fringe of pendants and a diamond star in the centre showing below it.[9] (Plate 45).

CAP AND HAT JEWELS

A velvet or satin cap with a feather was as much part of the dress of an English gentleman as the gold chain about his neck, and in 1513 the Venetian ambassador remarked that most had 'one or two ornaments' on them.[10] These could be aglets or buttons and brooches pinned or sewn to the fabric.

Like the medieval pilgrim signs, which continued to be used until the Reformation, these brooches expressed religious and other sentiments. Christian and classical themes could be represented, not only in cameos and *commessi*, but also in enamelled gold medallions. Lady Jane Grey had a 'fair brooch with a little square table ruby, and divers pictures enamelled with red, black, and green'.[11] A group of such medallions illustrating Old and New Testament subjects, with stylistic and technical features in common, has been identified as English, since one was inscribed in that language.[12]

In the second half of the century the historiated medallions were replaced by decorative compositions of gem-stones. The new fashion is introduced by Elizabeth I's 'jewel of gold like a starr of sparckes of Diamondes sett upon a capp',[13] which must have resembled the ruby, opal and diamond star which she gave to Sir Francis Drake.[14]

James Wright was robbed in 1597 of a 'jewel, in fashion of a feather of gold set with diamonds and rubies',[15] and feathers, like the similar aigrettes, remained in fashion throughout the reign of James I. The 'fayre jewell, like a feather of gould, conteyning a fayre table-diamond in the middest and fyve-and-twenty diamondes of divers forms made of sondrous other jewels' in the royal schedule of 1606 is pinned to the upturned brim of the hat worn by James I in a portrait by John de Critz.[16] In 1622 he ordered old jewels in the Tower to be broken up to make others in a new style 'of the targett fashion for hats'.[17] He hung the Sancy diamond as a pendant to another splendid hat jewel, the Mirror of Great Britain, which can be seen in another portrait by De Critz (Plate 46). He also reserved for his hat the rubies called the Three Brothers (Plate 47). Anxious that Prince Charles should cut a regal figure in Madrid in 1623 he sent him

46 King James I, his hat brim pinned with the Mirror of Great Britain jewel with Sancy diamond pendant. Portrait by John de Critz. Private Collection.

47 King James I with the Three Brothers jewel pinned to his hat. Gripsholm, Sweden.

the Three Brethren that you knowe full well, but newlie sette and the Mirroure of Fraunce, the fellowe of the Portugall dyamont quich I wode wishe you to wear alone in your hatte with a little blakke feather.[18]

The king thought also of the Duke of Buckingham, who was with the prince, and included a table diamond for his hat.[19]

Emblematic and naturalistic motifs also appeared in Jacobean hat jewels. There was the 'diamond bay leaf for the hat' which Queen Anne bought from George Heriot[20] and the diamond anchor which the Duke of Buckingham wore as Lord High Admiral[21] (Fig. 11).

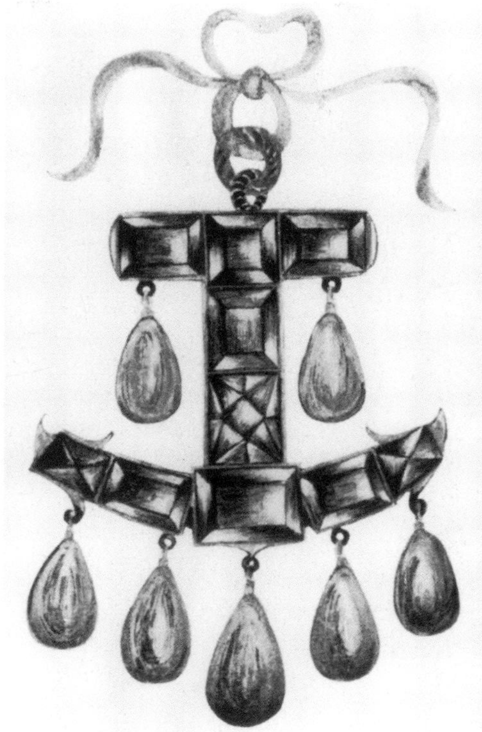

Fig. 11 Drawing of the Duke of Buckingham's diamond and pearl anchor by Thomas Cletscher: *c.* 1642. Museum Boymans Van Beuningen, Rotterdam

Portraits of Prince Henry († 1613) depict jewels alluding to his enthusiasm for learning, and maritime and military exploits. One of the three large diamond brooches in the hat in his 1604 Garter portrait is crowned with a ship, and another has an armillary sphere at the base.[22] He is unsheathing his sword in the portrait sent to the Duke of Savoy between 1604 and 1610, and this soldierly stance is emphasised by the plumed diamond helmet pinned to his hat brim.[23] The ostrich feathers in the high-crowned hat beside him in a portrait by Robert Peake are fastened by a brooch with his coroneted monogram H P, and the hat band too is jewelled.[24] Such ornaments are also listed in the inventory of the Earl of Somerset in 1617: 'a hat band of black velvet having 20 peeces with diamonts' and the '12 barrs of a hat-band, each having 10 small diamants'.[25]

BILIMENTS AND BODKINS

According to Fynes Moryson, 'The graver sort of married women used to cover their head with a Frenchhood of Velvet, set with a border of gold buttons and pearles.'[26] At the court of Henry VIII these borders, sometimes called biliments, were worn with the gabled headdress, and had to be rich. Anne Basset was anxious to acquire more than 120 seed pearls for hers, as she could not appear 'in the Queen's service unless they might be set full'.[27] From mid century, when the new style of hood was introduced, the biliment was divided into two parts, as illustrated in George Gower's portrait of Mrs Denton.[28] Lady Pembroke could choose from an 'upper border of golde conteyning xxiii peces the large peces being enamelled white blacke grene and blewe and the rounder pieces with white knobbes' and her 'upper border black enamelled . . . conteyning xxiii pieces' and an 'undre bordre of gold sutelike to the same conteyning xxix peces'.[29] The twelve 'habilliaments' in the 1587 inventory of Queen Elizabeth are all in this style with jewelled settings, one in forty-three pieces 'like katherine Wheles', sometimes alternating with single pearls or clusters.[30]

In 1584 Sir Christopher Hatton gave Elizabeth I

> an attire for the hedd, conteyning VII peeces of golde, three of them being crownes imperiall, garnished with smale diamonds, rubyes, perles, and ophals, on thone side, and on thother IV peces, being victoryes, garnished with diamonds, rubyes, perles and ophalles.[31]

Fixed to a wire frame and crowning the tall padded hair, these superseded the biliment in the next reign. The queen and the richest of the court ladies, like the Countess of Bedford, wore attires of pear-shaped pearls standing up like a halo, but less expensive designs were made from seed pearls, and a base-metal wire frame for an attire has been found in the Thames.[32]

Another way of decorating the hair was with jewelled bodkins. Two Elizabethan portraits depict their use. Elizabeth Long (1568–1611), who married William Russell in 1583, has three: a pearl cross over the brow flanked by a rosette and a wounded heart; and the Maid of Honour Elizabeth Brydges (1589) also has three with a biliment, one being a cipher of H W.[33] Many of Elizabeth I's sixty-six bodkins had figurative designs: a tortoise, an elephant, a frog, a woman on horseback, and a deer enclosed in a hunter's horn.[34] Anne of Denmark wore more bodkins than any other jewellery and the most important, set with the Portugal diamond, may be the one with a large table-cut stone pinned to a tuft of feathers with a pendant pearl and ruby drop which she wears in a portrait by Van Somer.[35] Rare stones of perfect quality, such as the diamond bought for £1,330 15*s* from the Earl of Pembroke,[36] were set *à jour* in claws, but most were set in box collets enamelled black and framed by scrolls.

Coloured stones – amethysts, garnets, emeralds and cabochon and table-cut rubies – were similarly set in bodkins, the larger as solitaires, the smaller as clusters or in geometric patterns, sometimes with pearl drops.[37] Queen Anne pinned some of her best pear pearls in her hair for the wedding of the Princess Royal to the Elector Palatine in 1613, and so impressed the Venetian ambassador, Foscarini, that he wrote that they were the 'largest and most beautiful there are in the world'.[38] More personal devices were her diamond crossbow reflecting her passion for hunting, and the crowned cipher C4, also diamond-set, given her by her brother, Christian IV of Denmark, which she also wore as a brooch on her ruff.[39] The most impressive of the aigrettes in the Arnold Lulls album is rich enough for a royal patron. It was set with a large table ruby framed

Fig. 12 Drawing of an aigrette by Arnold Lulls. Victoria and Albert Museum.

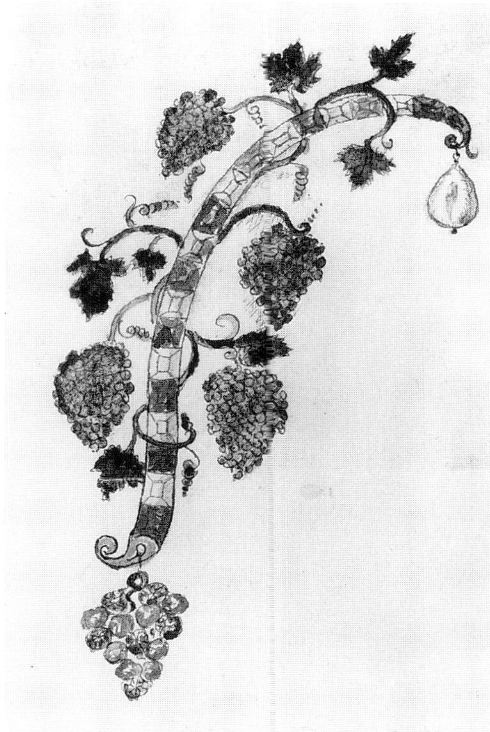

Fig. 13 Drawing of a branch of vine leaves with carved amethyst grapes by Arnold Lulls. Victoria and Albert Museum.

with table diamonds and enclosed in a diamond crescent within a cartouche with scrolled edges and tipped by a pearl[40] (Fig. 12).

Other designs in the book are a branch of vine leaves with carved grapes (Fig. 13) and variants on the feather, with continuous rows of gem-stones pointing upwards like a tuft of feathers and joined at the base by a sun-burst or crescent moon.[41]

A similar jewel is worn on the side of the head in a portrait of the Countess of Mar and Kellie, the plumes clasped by a C-scroll enclosing diamonds of different cuts and sizes.[42]

EARRINGS

As long as the ears were covered by the hood there was no place for earrings, and in 1542 Andrew Borde remarked on the strange custom in Spain, where 'the women have silver ringes in theyr eres'.[43] By 1575 the custom had spread to England and Lady Paget Carey gave Elizabeth I 'two emeraldes pendante peice fassion, for eare rings, hanged in golde'.[44] Although in most of her portraits the queen wears large pear pearls in her ears, there are exceptions: the armillary sphere worn in the Ditchley portrait, and a tiered composition of three table-cut diamonds above a lozenge-shaped diamond between two pearls, with three ruby drops and a large pear pearl pendant, in the Rainbow portrait. Her adoption of the armillary sphere was no doubt prompted by the use made of it by Sir Henry Lee, her host at Ditchley in 1592.[45]

As earrings had to hang next to the face, the quality of the stones and pearls was of the first importance, as is demonstrated in the dialogue between Fulvia and her servant Gallia in Ben Jonson's play, *Catiline*:

FULVIA. Look
Within, i' my blue cabinet, for the pearl
I'd sent me last, and bring it . . .
GALLIA. Is this it, madam?
FULVIA. Yes, help to hang it in mine ear.
GALLIA. Believe me,
It is a rich one, madam.
FULVIA. I hope so:
It should not be worn there else . . .[46]

Since pear-shaped pearls were so well suited for use as pendants, and matched the fashionable pearl necklaces, they became a favourite choice for earrings, eclipsing

48 Sir Gilbert Houghton wearing an earring with a jewelled S hung with a wounded heart. Portrait by Paul van Somer. Collection of Mr Archibald Stirling of Keir.

gem-stones. Anne of Denmark had many pearls in her collection, both pear and round, that were no doubt used in this way.[47] Pearls might also be combined with diamonds, while the latter, mounted in small chain loops, sometimes mixed with opals and rubies, were themselves used as earrings.[48] The queen also bought figurative and naturalistic subjects from George Heriot: diamond Negro heads, lizards, pairs of globes, and hands holding snakes.[49] There was already a snake earring with a diamond head in her collection[50] and the theme was used by Lulls for the top of an earring above a crescent hung with one or three pearl or emerald drops.[51] Additional emphasis was given to the ears by the black ear-strings looped and tied in bows from the turn of the century and depicted in the Van Somer portrait of the Countess of Mar and Kellie.[52]

In 1583 Stubbes criticised 'dissolute minions . . . not ashamed to make holes in their ears whereat they hang ringes and other jewels of gold and precious stones', a fashion James I disapproved of.[53] Nevertheless some of the courtiers wore them, as did Sir Walter Ralegh, most often with a single or double pearl pendant in one ear.[54] Some were more elaborate, like the jewelled hoop with pendant S and wounded heart worn by Sir Gilbert Houghton in his portrait by Van Somer[55] (Plate 48).

JEWELS FOR THE NECK

COLLARS

Henry VIII wore great gold collars across his shoulders, set with very large gems, and took a close interest in their design.[56] One massive collar weighed 88 ounces and was

> of Spanish work wherin be 16 faire balasses six gret pointed diamontes square lozinged on another table long dyamont six square one other table diamond hart facioned one table diamond six squared a great triangle diamond one long lozinged diamount and the great Myrrour[57]

Another collar is shown in the portrait at Rome; it is set with huge spinels, some square, some oval, in petalled mounts alternating with large pearls in foliate links.[58]

The rich collars that indicated noble rank are described in inventories.[59] The design of the collar on the effigy of Thomas, Duke of Norfolk († 1554) at Framlingham, Suffolk, has letters spelling out the motto GRACIA DEI SUM QUOD SUM (By the Grace of God I am what I am), alluding to his providential deliverance from death in 1547, when Henry VIII died the day before that set for his execution.[60] Collars with mottoes and emblems belonging to Elizabeth I were owned by Anne of Denmark. Two had HINC SPES, one with ragged staves and the other with a hand coming out of cloud to rescue a ship in distress; the phoenix was the centrepiece for a collar with SEMPER EADEM, and the Greek letters Alpha and Omega appeared in the midst of the flattering inscription GEMMA PRECIOSIOR INTUS.[61] They remained in fashion, and in 1622 James I gave a jewelled collar of thirty-nine links with letters and set with table diamonds, rubies and pearls, to the Duchess of Lennox, his cousin's wife, at New Year.[62] In the following year he sent 'a collar of gold conteyning thirty pieces whereof fifteen are roses in each a great pointed diamond and fifteen crowned ciphers of the King and Queen's names having in each of them a table diamond' to Prince Charles in Spain.[63]

The range of designs used in collars was very wide. Queen Elizabeth I had 'a riche Coller of golde contayning x faier table diamondes, and one pointed diamonde in the middest and xii peeces of goldsmithes worke wrought like friers knottes and set with pearles with a flower of golde'.[64] The spectacular collar which the Earl of Leicester gave to the queen in 1577 consisted of thirteen great emeralds with spacers, each of five large pearls framed in rubies.[65] Such 'cinques' of pearl appear as the main elements, with smaller jewelled and enamelled pieces and three (perhaps four) large multi-layered Tudor roses and a Phoenix pendant, in the portrait of Elizabeth I called after this jewel.[66] Another collar combined links with pearls, singly or in twos, and 'eleven peeces with Imagery of men and beastes'.[67]

Other collars with figurative elements were given to the queen at New Year, like that given by Lady Walsingham in 1576 'being two serpents, the hedds being ophall, a peramyt [pyramid] of sparckes dyamondes, in the top therof a strawbury with a rocke rubye' or the one with scallop shells and fishes given by Sir Christopher Hatton in 1589.[68] Other collars were mounted on a corse to show the design to greater advantage, like the

> Coller of two sortes of peeces of openworke like buttons conteining xix peeces, whereof x set with twoes of pearle, viij with one small table diamond, and one in the middle with one table Diamond and iiij triangles, vpon a double yellowe silke Lace.[69]

The continuing importance of the collar is seen in new commissions from James I and his queen, one of which emphasised their continuity with the Tudors by having the roses of Lancaster and York made by George Heriot.[70] After the death of Anne, James I gave it to the Duchess of Lennox, who wears it in her portrait by William Larkin (Plate 49); she bequeathed it to her nephew, telling how it had been given by the king.[71]

CARCANETS AND NECKLACES

Carcanets and necklaces were worn close to the neck, and some could be divided to use as bracelets or else placed on the head as an edging to the hood. The earlier designs were composed of button-like links with jewels and pearls, as in Katherine Howard's 'carcane for the neck, of goldsmith's work, wherin is set in gold vj. very faire table diamonds and v. very faire rubies, and betwixt every of the same stones is two fair pearls containing in the whole xxiiij'.[72] The quality and size of the pearls varied. Nicholas Herrick had in his stock a carcanet of thirteen links set with forty rubies and 430 diamonds, with 'certain flatt pearl in each'.[73] Dame Elizabeth Willoughby of Wollaton

49 The Duchess of Lennox wearing a jewelled collar of roses of York and Lancaster, a pearl and diamond coronet, aigrette, brooch and girdle, with a crowned heart pendant hanging from a pearl necklace. Detail from the portrait by William Larkin, *c.* 1620. Collection of Lord Tollemache, Helmingham.

had a necklace of 'two sorts of little pearl, laced with rubys or garnetts, and a diamond hanging down through the boots' (*sic*: French *bout* = end).[74] In her portrait by George Gower, however, she wears a large collar instead of this necklace.[75] A portait of Ralph Sheldon's wife *c.* 1593–5 depicts her wearing a necklace of three strands of small pearls with black beads, perhaps of glass or jet, between every three pearls, and a large gold and diamond pendant[76] – a simpler style which was to become more popular later.

Carcanets were more elaborate in design, and used the same motifs as the chains or collars: knots of pearl,[77] gold friar's knots,[78] and ciphers or inscriptions. Henry VIII owned several of the latter, with the letters E, H and K, sometimes combined with hearts or hearts held by hands.[79] In 1583 the Earl of Leicester gave Elizabeth I a carcanet of 'xx peeces, being letters and a sipher in the midest . . . and at the sipher a pendant', while two years later the Countess of Suffolk gave one which spelt out the word DURABO.[80]

Some of the carcanets were richly jewelled, like one given at New Year 1577 by the Earl of Leicester:

> a carcanett of golde enamuled, 9 peeces whearof are garnished with sparcks of dyamondes and rubyes, and every one of them a pendante of golde enamuled, garnished with smale sparcks of rubyes, and an ophal in the middes. Ten other peeces of golde lykewise enamuled, every of them garnished with very smale dyamondes, two large raged pearles set with a rose of sparcks of rubyes, and every of the two lesser pearls pendant, and a pendant of golde, in every peece a lozengye dyamonde and a smale rubye, and in the middes a large pendant of golde garnished with meane rubyes, an ophall, and a meane perle pendant.[81]

Other carcanets used heraldic or symbolic motifs in their design, like Sir Christopher Hatton's gift in 1579 of a carcanet with 'VII redd roses of golde, in every of them very smale diamonds, and in the topp a garnet and eight troches of meane perles, four in every troche, and XIV perles pendante, being lose'.[82] Ruby and pearl mullets, the donor's heraldic difference, hung from a carcanet given by the Earl of Nottingham in 1599–1600,[83] and were combined with 'half moones' or crescents in another from the Earl of Northumberland.[84] Here there is probably an allusion to the Percy badge but, in an earlier gift by Lord Howard of Effingham (later Earl of Nottingham) in 1587, the inclusion of crescents in the links would relate to their use in Elizabeth I's iconography.[85]

When necklaces became much simplified in design in the next century, and these elaborate carcanets were broken up for reuse.[86] Queen Anne's preference was for pearls, which she wore in chokers and in necklaces with fringes of diamonds in gold collets, a taste shared by most ladies of the day.[87] With less complicated designs, necklaces could be restrung at home, and in 1616 the Countess of Dorset 'did string the pearls and diamonds left me by my mother into a necklace'.[88]

CHAINS

The Venetian ambassador remarked that at the Field of the Cloth of Gold the English 'had many gold chains which were not so usual in France'.[89] At the joust commemorating the translation of the relics of St Thomas of Canterbury on 7 July 1516, Sir Edward Guildford wore a chain of great weight and value, and his retinue of forty gentlemen each had a good chain of five fingers' breadth about their necks, with links of H and K in compliment to the king and queen.[90] Henry VIII had a number of such chains with letters or inscriptions, among the latter one with SPES MEA DEUS.[91] Before proceeding to Guines and Calais in 1527–8 Cardinal Wolsey's suite wore gold chains as an essential part of their attire.[92] They were also given to brides at their marriage, and in 1521 Sir Humphrey Baumaster bequeathed to his daughter Mary 'towards hir marriage a chayne of golde to be made by my wife for hir'.[93] Even some schoolboys were given them, as was the thirteen-year-old Philip Sidney in 1567, whose two gold chains cost £42 12*s*.[94] The wealthy owned several, variously described as best, greater, great and small, to be worn baldric-wise over one shoulder or about the neck in one or more rows. Used as diplomatic gifts, their weight and value were graded according to the importance of the recipient.[95] The gift of a chain could also be a mark of royal favour, as with the gift of a chain by Elizabeth I to Sir Martin Frobisher before his third voyage to seek the North-West Passage to Asia in 1578.[96] Although they appear to have been unfashionable for men in the early seventeenth century, when Fynes Moryson commented that men now 'seldome or never' wore 'any chaines', they continued to be given to diplomats, and women went on wearing them.[97]

Many designs were used for chains. Nicholas Herrick had 'six chains of playn goulde of several facions' in his stock,[98] and the links of whatever shape – round, oval, rectangular or lozenge – were variously textured to enhance their effect. Flat overlapping links were called flagons; the name was also applied to overgrown tankards in the reign of James I.[99] Mary Gifford (†1542) is shown in her brass at Middle Claydon, Bucks. (MS III), with a chain of close-set rectangular links engraved like two rows of bricks. The open gold rings in the chain worn by Edward Lyttelton in a portrait of *c.* 1563 are tightly meshed together, and interspersed with two narrow plaques engraved with figures[100] (Plate 50).

Most chains were enamelled – either in black and white (Plate XII), or in bright colours often combined with white: purple, red, green and blue; and they could be further enriched with pearls and precious stones. The Duchess of Somerset had a sober 'chayne of fayer pearl furnished with pipes of gold inamyled with blacke', and Elizabeth I owned 'a small Chayne of golde ennameled grene contayninge a hundreth and one knobbs of golde sett with small sparkes of diamondes Rubies and Emerodes and CCiiij small pearles betwene them'.[101] Diamonds were also simulated by the gold being worked in points, and also by 'jet and mother of pearle diamond wise'.[102] Links

50 Edward Lyttelton wearing gold chains round his neck, clasped with panels representing soldiers. Portrait, *c.* 1563. Collection of Viscount Cobham, Hagley.

were made in varied forms: friar's knots,[103] roses 'enameled blacke',[104] daisies and little oranges,[105] fishes and snakes[106] (Plate XIII). More exotic designs owned by Queen Elizabeth I included blackamoors climbing a 'webbe chayne of gold made like a ladder' and another chain in which blackamoors climbed ragged staves. These ragged staves, the badge of the Earls of Leicester and Warwick, were used as spacers in a chain of 'pillars garnished with small pearles whereof five like lillies, five like Ha[w]thornes and five like dayses'.[107] The queen had chains composed of the knots of the Bourchier and Maltravers families combined with roses and other flowers;[108] these are comparable to another heraldic chain of Stafford knots and double crescents which has survived.[109] (Plate 33) A large jewelled chain owned by Anne of Denmark consisted of 'one hundreth pieces of openworke, whereof fiftie haue sondry Romane letters set with small table Diamonds, and fifty with ij of Pearles and one sparke of a Ruby'.[110]

Not all chains were made of gold. Besides the mother-of-pearl, crystal and coral stocked by John Mabbe,[111] there were amber with flies in the beads, lapis lazuli, opal, jasper and agate carved into both round beads and hour-glasses; while marble stones, lightly garnished with gold, formed part of a chain of Paris work.[112]

Pearls were part of Queen Elizabeth I's calculated and majestic presence, and all the great ladies of the court followed her example (Plate XIV). Earlier, the Duchess of Somerset could choose from: a rope of about a thousand small pearls, a double rope of pearl about one ell long, a double rope one-and-three-quarter yards in length, a great chaine of pearls with true-love knots and a chain of pearl and gold with friar's knots.[113] The coloured silk used for stringing the pearls contrasted with their sheen and ended with ribbons tied in decorative bows to fasten the pearls. Anne of Denmark added to the large collection owned by Queen Elizabeth and, besides ropes, owned more elaborate designs threaded into patterns like a trellis, and mixed with gold beads. The type was exemplified in her 'Chaine of gold & pearl conteining fifteene knobbes of gold, whereof eight set with threes of pearle, fower with threes of rubies; interlaced with six rowes of very small pearle, at everie end thereof one great round Pearle . . . being xiiij of such interlacings'.[114] The most magnificent chains combined diamonds and pearls, like the one given by James I to the Marchioness of Buckingham at New Year in 1622: 'a fayre cheyne of gold having sixty pieces with four diamonds in each piece and sixty great round pearls'.[115]

Pearls were not reserved exclusively for the court, and Fynes Moryson noted 'the better sort of women commonly wearing rich chaines of pearle' at the beginning of the seventeenth century.[116]

PENDANTS

One of the most commonly surviving Renaissance jewels, apart from rings, the pendant was worn in many ways: hanging from carcanets, chains and necklaces, and worn on the clothing. Some were worn singly, like the Duchess of Somerset's pendant of 'mother of pearl flourished with gold, like an S';[117] others were worn in pairs, like those given to Elizabeth I in 1599–1600 by Sir John Stanhope, fashioned 'like gates garnished with sparks of rubies and each with three small pearls pendant'.[118]

Some of Queen Anne of Denmark's best diamonds were made into pendants, and pear pearls from other jewels added to them as required.[119] Diamonds of different cuts and sizes were combined, as in a pendant 'garnished with Lozange, table and triangle small Diamonds having v triangle Diamonds pendant all in Collets'.[120] Multi-faceted stones were set clear, briolette-style: 'a pendant of one faire Diamond of divers cutts, set in gold without clawes without foyle, being in figure of eight sides; with a faire pendant of a Diamond of divers cuttes peare fashion, hanging by a small Loope of gold, without any other goldsmithes worke'.[121] The diamond bought of Stephen Le Gouch in 1612, 'cut with fancies on all sides and pierced at the top', would perhaps have been used in a pendant.[122]

Brightly coloured stones were contrasted with the diamond: 'a pendant of a small knotte, garnished with Diamondes, having fiue rocke Rubies pendant & one diamond without foil' or the 'pendant of a small blew Saphire full of cuttes in the forme of a Harte, with a stalke of gold through it, pendant with fower sparkes of Diamonds in Colletts'.[123]

Anne of Denmark had many pearl pendants – pear, ragged and round ones are specified[124] – and others with stones set simply or in a border of enamelled 'flowers and Frutage', or with an appropriate motto.[125] Figurative or symbolic subjects are rare; a jewelled slipper and a design with a crown and heart are exceptions.[126] Since most of the pendants ordered from George Heriot were in pairs, they would have been used as earrings (see pp. 120–1 above).

CROSSES

The cross was worn throughout the period and took many forms: Latin, Greek, Tau, St Andrews, Lorraine and Jerusalem crosses are all named, and they could be decorated with other Christian symbols and inscriptions. They were usually worn from a chain at the neck and, like that worn by Katherine of Aragon at Canterbury Cathedral in 1520, they were valuable.[127]

There was a diamond rose in the centre of a ruby St Andrew's cross belonging to Henry VIII in 1519.[128] The cross could be set within a larger jewel, as in the double cross crosslet of diamonds in a lozenge with filigree knotwork and three pendant pearls worn by the Princess Elizabeth in the portrait *c.* 1546–7 attributed to William Scrots.[129] Mary I wears a jewelled Tau cross on a necklace of pearls and sapphires in a portrait by Hans Eworth,[130] and the St Anthony's (or Tau) cross bequeathed by Thomasine Bussey in 1547 had St Anthony's bell hanging from it; it is perhaps related to the confraternity or order of St Anthony in Hainault.[131] The figure of the Virgin or a saint could be engraved on one face of the cross.[132] The Five Wounds were another common addition; they are depicted on the cross worn by Sir Brian Tuke in his portrait by Holbein (Plate 51) and on the back of a crucifix bequeathed by Sir Brian Stapilton in 1518.[133] Crucifixes are also seen in portraits, and both the first and second wife of St Thomas More wears one in the family group portrait.[134] A cross which had belonged to the saint was mentioned by Mary Basset in her will proved in 1572: 'a crosse of gold set of each corner with three pointed diamonds, and three pearls hanging at it, which was my grandfather More's'.[135]

Crosses are less often mentioned in the second half of the century, and five of those owned by Elizabeth I in 1587 had belonged to her father.[136] Another, given to her by Sir

51 Sir Brian Tuke with a gold cross showing Christ's wounded hands and feet and the Crown of Thorns in the centre. His coat is fastened by a gold button with knotwork ornament. Portrait by Hans Holbein, *c.* 1540. National Gallery of Art, Washington.

Christopher Hatton, had her own portrait on the back.[137] They were worn, not only at the neck, but also on the breast or over the heart and were more often richly jewelled, like the emerald ruby and pearl cross owned by John Mabbe.[138]

Three of the crosses owned by Anne of Denmark were 'of the old making' and 'of antient work'. They were set with diamonds, sometimes on both sides, and could be large, like the Lorraine cross she wears in a portrait by Marcus Gheeraerts.[139] Another was inscribed with the motto IN HOC SIGNO VINCES,[140] but the most important was one made from six great emeralds hung from a magnificent emerald collar.[141]

GARTER INSIGNIA

The precise form and weight of the collar for the Order of the Garter were laid down in 1522 when Henry VIII revised the statutes, and have remained unchanged to the present day. Twenty-six Tudor roses, within Garters separated by knots, represented the number of the knights established by Edward III, and from it hung an image in the round of the patron saint on horseback slaying the dragon.[142] The collar with the Great George would be worn on 'collar days' – that is, the principal court feasts of the year and at the Garter feast in April. Henry also introduced the Lesser George, worn on a ribbon or chain about the neck, for daily wear (Plate VIII).

According to the statutes, the collar could not be set with gems, although the Garter and both Greater and Lesser Georges could be and were so adorned. One of Henry VIII's Garters had 'gold letters, castles, and pomegrantes, ruby on the buckle, a turquoise on the pendant and a hanging pearl'.[143]

At his investiture each knight was given the insignia of the order in a series of ceremonies and, at his death, these had to be returned to the sovereign, although this was not always done by foreign princes who had received the order. Wills and inventories make it clear that many of the knights owned more than one set of the insignia, and these were often richly jewelled. Henry VIII had several Georges, one of the more elaborate being the 'George on horseback the foreparts of the George of dyamontes the mayle of his curates [i.e., cuirass] and rivetts of the same of silver demi-gilte with a swerde in his hande of gold, a lozenged diamond like a shield and a dragon of gold'. Another had the body of the dragon made from a baroque pearl.[144] The richly jewelled insignia presented to Philip II on his arrival in England, at his marriage with Mary I and subsequently, was meticulously documented in an inventory drawn up by the king when he returned it to his sister-in-law, Elizabeth I.[145] Among the items was another George, using a baroque pearl for the belly and haunches of the horse.

As one of the Five Orders of the Collar, with a very limited membership, it was highly prized. It was said of Thomas, Earl of Ormonde (1531–1614), that he wore both day and night the George given to him at his investiture in 1588.[146] Sir Thomas West's inventory of 1554 lists his insignia with weights and valuations, and in 1583 the Earl of Sussex bequeathed his collection of Garter insignia to the queen.[147] The Earl of Leicester had the rare distinction of belonging both to the French Order of St Michael and to the Garter who had a double-sided jewel with both insignia made for daily use. This he bequeathed to his brother: 'a George with the french Order and the Englyshe in one with a playne gold chaine at it, this token he muste keepe in remembraunce that his brother was of both the orders and not only soe but almoste the eldest of bothe the Orders in bothe the Realmes'.[148] He also bequeathed insignia to Sir Christopher Hatton and to his son-in-law, the Earl of Essex, in the well-founded expectation that they would soon be entitled to wear them.

Elizabeth I, like her father, owned several jewels of St George, hung from a variety of necklaces and collars and richly embellished with various gem-stones, such as a 'George on thone side a sparke of a diamond in his Targett and eight little Rubies about the same George And on the other side an Agatt with a face, and eight small diamondes about the face with a pearle pendaunt at it'.[149]

In the next reign the insignia became even more splendid. James I wore the Great George pendant to a collar of clusters of pearls and large square table-cut diamonds with enamelled S motifs in a portrait attributed to John de Critz.[150] Prince Henry also owned richly jewelled Georges, set with diamonds on both sides or with diamonds on the front and rubies behind;[151] the figure of St George himself might be worked in diamonds.[152]

A complete set of late-sixteenth-century Garter insignia has been preserved at Rosenborg Castle in Denmark. Presented to Christian IV (1577–1648), brother-in-law of James I, it is believed to have been the set given earlier to his father. The Lesser George is apparently the same as one shown in a portrait by Marcus Gheeraerts in 1614. The complete robes of the Order have also been preserved, although the cassock had been wrongly attributed in later catalogues.[153]

In the sixteenth century the use of the collar of Esses became restricted to heralds, certain other royal officials and members of the judiciary. Memory of its older significance as a token of personal allegiance lingered on for some time. In 1527 Sir Thomas More was painted by Holbein wearing a gold collar of Esses with the Tudor pendant of portcullis and double rose; and it is recorded that when he was being taken to the Tower of London, he refused to remove it (knowing that it would be confiscated on arrival) as this could be construed as an act of treason.[154] The only surviving Tudor gold livery collar, still worn by the Lord Mayor of London and bequeathed for this purpose by Sir John Alleyn, is of similar design.[155]

FLOWERS AND JEWELS

In 1548 flowers were defined as the 'hanging owche or flowers that women use to tye at the chayne or lace that they weare about their neckes'.[156] Sixty 'Flowers or ouches' were listed in Elizabeth I's 1587 inventory, but only one in 1606 for Anne of Denmark: 'a Jewell of gold being a flower with three stones, viz. one square table Ruby one square Emeralde and one Collet for a stone wanting'.[157] Flowers – or jewels, as they became known – were worn in various ways: hung from the collar or necklace, or fastened to the breast or sleeve; they were suspended by a ring or by small chains The chains could also be jewelled and often ended in a knob similarly adorned.

Some were designed to show off special stones of exceptional size, cut and colour, such as the Burgundian jewel called the Three Brothers (see above, pp. 65, 68), worn by Elizabeth I in the Ermine portrait at Hatfield.[158] The natural beauty of the stones was enhanced by the richly chased and enamelled mounts, the decoration of which also covered the back of the settings. Raised enamelling was also used. Anne of Denmark had a 'faire Jewell of gold enameled with many round small balles or peares of blewe & white having, one very faire square table Diamond, and five greate and faire pearles fixed'.[159] Most terminated in hanging pearls, round or pear-shaped, single, multiple or clustered like grapes, or with other gem-stones, like the 'Jewell of golde, garnished with two spynnelles and sparkes of dyamondes about yt, and 3 small pendantes like sparkes of diamonds' which Sir Edward Stafford gave to Elizabeth I in 1599.[160]

Gem-stones might be mounted between 'antiques': classical motifs, terms, putti, cornucopiae, nymphs and satyrs, columns and pediments, or framed within borders ornamented with shells, masks and bucrania.[161] John Mabbe had a representative collection of figurative jewels in his stock depicting the more popular subjects from mythology and Roman history. These included Phoebus and Daphne, Mars, Venus and Cupid, Neptune, Victory and Lucretia.[162] Leda and the Swan are modelled in relief in the pendant worn by 'Mary Boleyn' in a portrait (Plate 52). 'Orpheus sitting on a hill' was among jewels valued by William Herricke in 1596,[163] and the same subject is seen in a large pendant jewel worn on the left breast by Mrs Ralph Sheldon in her portrait.[164]

52 A lady, called Mary Boleyn, wearing an oval pendant with Leda and the Swan. Portrait, perhaps by William Scrots, *c.* 1540. Private collection.

Another musician, the Greek boy Arion, appeared on one of Elizabeth I's jewels riding on the dolphin which, charmed by his music, saved him from drowning.[165]

Personifications such as Fama Perennis, Charitas and Prudentia in Mabbe's stock[166] were comparable to jewels owned by the queen – a woman holding a diamond and ruby anchor, who is perhaps Hope, or the woman on a rainbow holding a pair of compasses and a garland with the inscription VIRGO.[167]

Other designs drew on the emblems created by the Humanists. A diamond and ruby 'juell of gold wherein is a dog leading a man over a bridge', given to Elizabeth I by Sir Christopher Hatton in 1577,[168] could derive from the device on the reverse of a medal of Michelangelo by Leone Leoni in 1561. There the dog leading a blind man is coupled with the words from Psalm 51: 'I shall teach transgressors the way to you, and to you sinners will return.'[169] Other gifts to the queen carried emblematic meanings: a diamond anchor, a lamp with a flaming heart, a rainbow with eleven pillars, a snake pierced by an arrow and a fly hovering over a candlestick.[170] According to Whitney, this last was a warning against the dangers of desire, as the fly risked being consumed by the flame to which it was drawn.[171] From Lady Cobham's carcanet in a portrait of 1567 hangs a diamond and ruby ship with a pear pearl; a ship, with or without crew or musicians aboard, was a symbol of happiness.[172] Ships continued to feature in early-seventeenth-century jewels, even though the figurative and the emblematic were no longer so fashionable. George Heriot supplied Anne of Denmark with 'a brilliant in form of a ship'; another was worn by Prince Henry (see p. 117 above).[173]

Other emblematic jewels paid homage to Elizabeth I's wisdom, learning and vigilance, and her military prowess by proxy was not neglected. A jewel of an armed man, 'the head and body of mother of pearl bordered with garnets and enamelled with thirteen true-love knots each knot with two sparkes of emeralds', another jewel of a ruby and diamond helmet,[174] and the crowned 'quiver of arrowes and artillery behinde it' with a pendant heart, all illustrate the latter theme.[175] A diamond warming-pan and an opal and diamond lamp[176] may be allusions to her care for the realm as her house.

Naturalistic motifs were used in jewels made for Henry VIII: a spinel pansy and a hand holding a rose-bud, for example.[177] Their continuing popularity is shown by the ones stocked by John Mabbe in 1576: 'a Bay Leaf havyng two Pescoddes with Pearles and a Jasent [Jacinth]', a 'Jewell like a Burrage Flower', and a 'Jewell with Cristall, havyng dyvers Flowers of Gold sett in the sayd Cristall'.[178] Insects and other creatures added a touch of realism to some of Elizabeth I's jewels of fruit and flowers: a mother-of-pearl and ruby snail in the midst of flowers,[179] an opal butterfly perched on two cherries or a ladybird, a snake and a lizard on a fern frond.[180] That this taste for natural motifs was widespread is seen in the bequest by Anne Brearton in 1588 of a 'leaf of gold enamelled green hanging from it a snail'.[181] Similar jewels were owned by Anne of Denmark: a 'Jewell beinge a vine Leafe of gold enameled greane, having three pendants of rocke Rubies in clawes without foils, and a frogge upon the Leafe garnished with Diamonds';[182] and others she ordered, such as a diamond rose costing £1,500 from Peter James, and diamond lilies, a gillyflower, butterfly and honeysuckle from George Heriot.[183]

Many of Queen Elizabeth's jewels used birds: a sapphire ostrich, the symbolic phoenix and pelican, a nightingale on a hill, and a ruby-breasted cock.[184] A homely pigeon, albeit set with diamonds, bequeathed by Anne Brearton to Lady Eleanor Percy,[185] contrasts with the more exotic birds like the parrot made for Queen Anne.[186]

The courtiers must have known that Queen Elizabeth liked animal jewels, since she was so often given them. Among them were: a white hare and a hind, both made from mother-of-pearl; an agate ram; a squirrel; a golden greyhound with a diamond collar; a white lion with a fly on his side; several jewels with a frog; a ruby tortoise; a knot of eleven emerald snakes; and a cat playing with mice.[187] Mythical creatures were also used: a Triton with a woman on his back and a mermaid admiring herself in a diamond glass.[188]

Henry VIII ordered cipher jewels with his initial and those of his wives, and they never went out of fashion; James I and his queen also wore them.[189] Mottoes and compliments too were inscribed on jewels – on the sail of a ship or the back of a hand holding a dice[190] – and some were so abstruse as only to be understood by donor and recipient, thus affirming the link between them.

Each jewel was created as a miniature work of art, with the back as carefully finished as the front. On the back of Elizabeth I's jewel of a man riding a whale was a woman shooting a hind, and two of her diamond jewels had a ruby at the back and an enamelled sun.[191] In Anne of Denmark's inventory there was 'A Jewell of gold the back side enameled blewe & white, having a greate & faire rock Ruby, a faire square table Diamond, and a faire peare pearle pendant'.[192]

TABLETS

In 1538 Anne Basset asked Viscountess Lisle for a tablet, an essential part of court dress, to wear at her girdle.[193] The tablet was a double-sided jewel designed to open to reveal its contents; in the second half of the century, it often contained a portrait miniature and could be hung at the throat or breast. It could be a simple geometric form – round, rectangular or lozenge-shaped – but some were made like hearts or even a steeple.[194] Like the flowers, tablets had pendant pearls or gems and enamelled finials added to them. The front and back covers were not always identical in design, and could be made of various materials, but gold – gem-set or worked with trellis patterns or historiated reliefs – was most common.[195]

Religious iconography was used, like the Trinity, the Crucifixion and the saints, but this was gradually replaced by classical imagery. Henry VIII had a 'plain tablet of gold antike work sett with ten emerades with little white children', presumably putti;[196] and from mid century such subjects predominate. Heroes and heroines of mythology and Roman history occur, like the virtuous Lucretia and the patriotic Mucius Scaevola, while busts of Mars and Hannibal signified military valour, as did Elizabeth I's 'Tablett of golde made lozengewise havinge therin a man on horsbacke with a targett in his hande and therin a lozenged diamonde'.[197] This was set with rubies and diamonds.

Heraldry, ciphers and mottoes gave an individual stamp to the tablets. Lady Stafford (*c.* 1548) at Blatherwyck, Northants. (MS I), displayed the arms of her husband, Sir Humphrey, *Gold a chevron Gules, a canton Ermine*, on a shield in the tablet shown on her brass. The Duchess of Somerset in 1586 owned 'a fayer square tablette of golde like an H, with fower diamondes, and a rocke rubie or ballast in the middeste, garnished with pearles, and a pearle pendant'[198] – perhaps a gift from Henry VIII to her husband, the brother of Jane Seymour. Tablets bearing the initials, mottoes and devices of Philip II and his father, the Emperor Charles V, in the collections of the Earl of Pembroke and Elizabeth I could have inspired the lines spoken by Count Ferneze of his late son, Camillo, in Jonson's play, *The Case Is Altered*:

> I cannot well remember his attire,
> But I have often heard his mother say
> He had about his necke a tablet,
> Given him by the Emperour Sigismund,
> His godfather, with this inscription,
> Under the figure of a silver globe:
> *In minimo mundus*.[199]

A profusion of mottoes, ciphers and emblems covers every surface of the heart-shaped Darnley jewel (Plate X). Figures representing Faith, Victory, Truth and Hope surround a crowned, winged heart set with a cabochon sapphire, framed in a white border with the Scots inscription QUHA HOPIS STIL CONSTANTLY WITH PATIENCE SAL OBTAIN VICTORIE IN YAIR PRETENCE. The inside has an anthology of emblems enamelled in *basse-taille*: a crowned salamander, the pelican in her piety, the phoenix in flames, united hearts pierced by arrows, *memento mori* symbols, Time, demon warriors (one grabbing a woman by the hair), with more inscriptions. The initials MSL stand for Matthew and Margaret Stewart Lennox, to whom the devices and heraldry refer. The tablet has been interpreted as a memorial to Matthew Lennox (†1571) commissioned by his wife, and the devices can be related to events in their life together, and to their hopes for their grandson, James VI of Scotland, the future James I of Great Britain.[200]

The next stage in the development of the tablet came with its use as a miniature case. Although portraits and pictures, including enamelled gold reliefs and cameos, had been enclosed in tablets or set in the covers from the 1530s,[201] it was not until the mid 1560s that they are shown being worn. A miniature of Catherine Grey, Countess of Hertford, has one, and the 1572 portrait of Lady Walsingham depicted her holding a round tablet with a miniature of a man in a gem-set border, with a hinged lid.[202]

The superb quality of some of the surviving miniature cases, three of them with miniatures by Nicholas Hilliard, is proof of their importance in Elizabethan and Jacobean jewellery. The cover of the pedimented jewel enclosing the Hilliard miniatures of Catherine Walsingham and her husband, Sir Thomas Gresley, is set with a sardonyx cameo of a Negress framed in a white band set with table-cut rubies and emeralds between flowers, flanked by cornucopiae holding black boys shooting arrows. The floral border on white is repeated on the back, framing a panel of symmetrical scrollwork. It is worn, suspended by three small gold chains, in a portrait of 1585, and may commemorate her marriage.[203]

The cameo on the cover of the jewel which Elizabeth I gave to Sir Francis Drake, another sardonyx with a black man and a white woman, is framed in a less sculptural but richly scrolled mount studded with table-cut rubies and diamonds and with pearls hanging from it like a cluster of grapes. The miniature of the queen is by Hilliard, and Sir Francis bears it in two portraits[204] (Plate IX). The equally celebrated Armada jewel also has the queen's portrait inside, and it is echoed on the cover by a medallic portrait, comparable to that used in the Phoenix jewel and in a medal of 1585, framed by an open border with table-cut rubies and diamonds. Inside, the lid is enamelled with a Tudor rose and with a Latin inscription by Walter Haddon, the queen's Master of Requests: NEI MIHI QUOD TANTO VIRTUS PERFUSA DECORE NON HABET ETERNOS INVIOLATA DIES (Alas, that so much virtue infused with beauty should not last forever inviolate). On the back, the Ark on a stormy sea symbolised the queen's care of her Church with the inscription SAEVAS TRANQUILLA PER UNDAS (Safely through the waves). This is also found on a mother-of-pearl plaque from another tablet.[205]

About 1600, openwork covers appear. A ruby and diamond star amidst knots and scrolls is an appropriate cover for a Hilliard miniature of the queen called Stella Britannis; the back has a magnificent dense composition of stylised foliage and a dolphin in champlevé and cloisonné enamels.[206] Another case, lacking the original miniature, has an openwork lid with the Heneage knot in rubies and the motto FAST THOUGH UNTIED, which is comparable to one in Anne of Denmark's inventory.[207] Not all of those listed were used for miniatures, as is shown by one made 'of gold like a pin-pillowe garnished with fifteen diamonds of divers forms and bignesse with four sparkes at the corners hanging at small chains of three knoppes'.[208] The inventory of the Earl of Northampton in 1614 included his 'Tablett of gold with a picture of my Lord of Essex',[209] and at this time the tablet and miniature case became almost synonymous. Anne of Denmark wore miniatures of her brother, Christian IV, and of her husband in jewelled cases hanging from a ribbon over the heart. She ordered cases from George Heriot, two with naturalistic designs of a bay leaf and a rose, and in 1610 he delivered a case set with diamonds on one side and the initials A and C.[210] This might be the red

53 Lady Ann Liviston, Lady-in-Waiting to Queen Anne of Denmark. Collection of the Earl of Seafield.

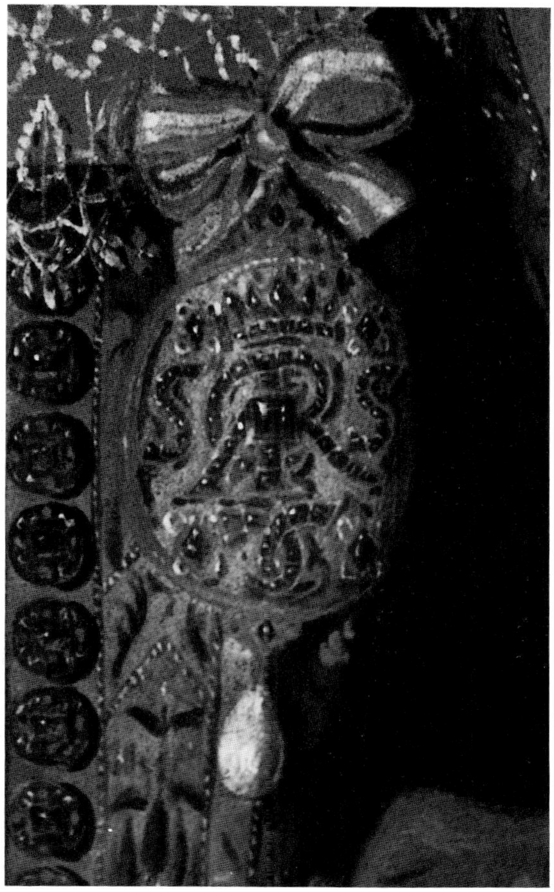

54 Detail of Plate 53, showing miniature pinned to bodice.

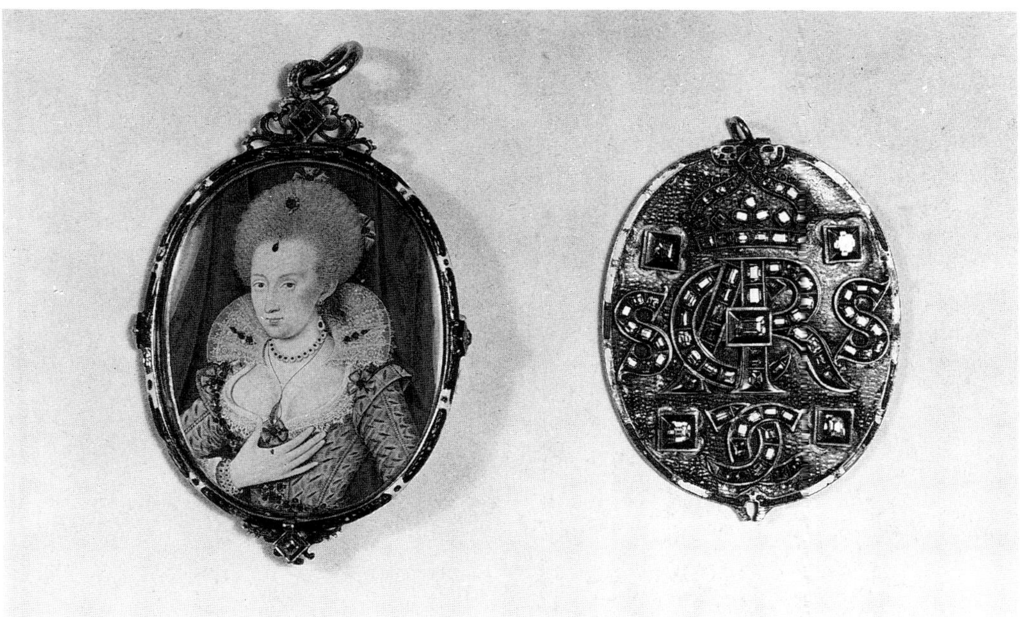

55 Miniature of Queen Anne of Denmark, the cover with her crowned cipher ARC, esses and two Cs on a red ground. *c.* 1610. Fitzwilliam Museum, Cambridge (formerly Earls of Eglinton).

enamelled miniature case with a crowned diamond cipher ARC, two Esses and a double C on the front and white on red ciphers on the back, worn by Anne Liviston, her Lady-in-Waiting, in a portrait done at the time of her marriage in 1612 (Plates 53 and 54); the case descended to the Earls of Eglinton and Winton, one of whom sold it in 1922[211] (Plate 55).

The remarkable locket which James I sent to the Emperor Rudolph II soon after his accession is set with a cameo of a Roman emperor, and is related to another in the Waddesdon Bequest chased with a finely enamelled radiating pattern, in the style of Corvinianus Saur, goldsmith to Christian IV.[212] There are other miniatures of James I in the original cases. A small example, of the school of Hilliard, is framed in a sunburst, with Queen Elizabeth's symbol of the Ark on waves inside the lid and the motto STET SALVA PER UNDAS (May it go safely through the waves); the outside of the oval case is enamelled in translucent red over a coffered ground.[213] The other, by Hilliard himself, is in the magnificent jewel given to Thomas Lyte in 1610 (Plate 56) and worn from a blue ribbon in his portrait. The openwork front has the royal cipher I R in diamonds amidst trails of plants with enamelled pea-pods, five diamonds in petal-shaped collets and a border of table-cut diamonds. The fine arabesques in red on white in the blackwork style of Guilhelmus de la Quellerie and Michel Le Blon show how closely the London jewellers followed developments abroad.[214]

Some of the tablets were designed like books, and these too could be used for miniatures.[215] There was Princess Mary's 'Boke of golde with the kinges face and hir graces mothers',[216] and the gold book, set with gems, holding miniatures of Sir William Cavendish and his wife, Bess of Hardwick. She treasured it all her life and bequeathed it to her daughter, Frances, in 1607.[217] Henry VIII and Elizabeth I both owned jewelled tablets for writing in, the later ones called books, and one of them had 'leaves of the ruines of Rome'.[218] Yet others were used by Henry VIII as pomanders.[219]

DEVOTIONAL BOOK JEWELS

Sometimes confused with the tablet, the girdle book formed a related but separate group. In 1580 John Lyly wrote of 'the Englysh Damoselles, who have theyr bookes tyed to theyr gyrdles, not fethers, who are as cunning in ye scriptures, as you [Italian women] are in *Ariosto* or *Petrarck*'.[220] These devotional books had enamelled gold covers, closed by twin clasps, with a ring on each cover to hang them by chains from the girdle, so as always to be at hand for prayer or meditation.[221] They can be seen in several brasses and portraits; exceptionally, in one of the latter, attributed to John Betts, the book is open.[222] Perhaps a Spanish fashion introduced by Katherine of Aragon, they were worn from the reign of Henry VIII onwards. In 1604 Peter Bales, Prince Henry's writing master, asked for payment for writing James I's 'Basilicon Doron for the Prince, in a small volume to be worn as a tablet book'.[223]

56 The Lyte jewel with miniature of James I by Nicholas Hilliard. Cover royal cipher set with rose- and table-cut diamonds amidst trails of plants and pods. Back: symmetrical ornament of broken scrollwork. 1610. British Museum.

Two of Holbein's designs for girdle books have arabesques with the initials T W, and T I W or W I T, perhaps for Thomas Wyatt and Jane Hawte, who were married in 1537, whose descendants own a book in a very similar style.[224] Another book in the British Library has covers with open-leaf tracery and black enamel ornament on the spine; it contains a portrait of Henry VIII and consists of the Penitential and other Psalms translated into English verse by John Croke.[225] Similarly sober is the book given by Elizabeth I to her cousin, Lord Hunsdon, containing the prayers said by Edward VI on his deathbed. The covers are enamelled with black arabesques with a white rosette in each corner, framing on the front a shell cameo head of a warrior and on the back a roundel of translucent red and green enamel.[226]

Two sets of covers for girdle books with Old Testament scenes are in the British Museum; the earlier pair, lacking the spine, depicts the Judgements of Solomon and Daniel with Latin inscriptions. The panel of the Judgement of Daniel is identical with that on a girdle book worn by Dame Philippa Speke in a portrait of 1592. Her husband, Sir George Speke, was descended from Sir Thomas Speke (1508–51), who was well-known at the court of Henry VIII, and the book was presumably an heirloom of the Speke family.[227] The other covers, which have the black enamelled spine, combine the Judgement of Solomon with the Brazen Serpent and have the texts in English, taken from the Bibles of 1539 and 1540. Stylistically, the book can be attributed to the London workshop of Hans of Antwerp *c.* 1540–5.[228] A book cover in the Pembroke inventory had David dancing before the Ark, set with sapphires, and other covers were similarly embellished, although not necessarily with historical scenes.[229]

BROOCHES

Brooches, fastened by a pin at the back, were made even more secure by ribbons. They were worn in the cap (see above, p. 114) or pinned on the bodice, usually at the neck, as on the brass to Dorothy, Lady Cobham (*c.* 1529), at Cobham, Kent.

Most of the numerous brooches in Henry VIII's inventory were jewelled, but others had various subjects: portraits and scenes, sometimes religious or classical in character.[230] There were some other scenes, notably the 'very faire brouche of golde wherein is made wrought and devised a tenys play and men playing at tenys with rackettes in their handes being set in the same brouche iij faire saphire and one lesse sapphire with also xxv small rubies'.[231] Since John Mabbe had over thirty brooches in his stock in 1576, it is surprising that only three are listed among Elizabeth I's jewels in 1587.[232] Other jewels took over their role in hat and dress ornament and they disappear from the inventories.

GIRDLES

Chains of gold links of different patterns were worn at the waist, often reaching to the hem of the skirt, and ending with a tablet, pomander or other pendant. Girdles were also designed to match the jewelled borders edging hood and neck – a style exemplified by Elizabeth I's 'shorte girdle with xiiij Rubies and xiii diamondes sett in golde like buttone and xxvij Scinques of pearle sett betwene them'.[233] Contrasting enamels also provided effective designs, as in the girdle of 'golde enameled blacke and white conteyninge cvi great links with clasp xi pillars and a knoppe likewise enameled' in the Pembroke inventory.[234]

The favourite knots – heraldic, decorative and friar's – enamelled, jewelled or pinned with pearls, are recurrent motifs for girdles, occasionally combined with other kinds of links, such as flowers or inscriptions. Mary I had a girdle composed of 'xv diamountes and xv Rubies set together by twoes between every two knottes the words of the Gartier enameled blacke and with iiij diamountes set by twoes and one table diamounte set above to bocle the girdle together';[235] and there was a 'waste girdle of golde with xv bowsers knottes and xvi roses and other flowers garn[ished] with small sparcks of Rubies' in Elizabeth I's inventory.[236] The latter type was the short girdle seen in portraits, fitting round the base of the bodice at the junction with the farthingale.

Corses of silk and velvet were studded with enamelled and jewelled buttons and knobs with clusters of small pearls in between them, and fitted with ornamental buckle and pendants. A belt fitting of the type worn by Baron Wentworth in a portrait of 1586 survives to illustrate the character of goldsmith's work of the period.[237] The dome-shaped head is enamelled with red flowers in a border of green leaves, and the openwork ends, ornamented with classical masks, have raised gold bars at the back, through which the end of the corse might pass.[238]

Anne of Denmark's girdles used ash- or carnation-coloured velvet, satin or black ribbon, and were sewn with jewelled links similar to those used in her collars and chains: blue snakes set with rubies, knots, crescents, inscriptions, and work in 'Spanish' style, 'open goldsmith's work', and cut-work enamelled red and jewelled, set over a mother-of-pearl base.[239] The trend was towards larger stones in simpler settings, and the belt worn by the Duchess of Lennox in a portrait by William Larkin *c.* 1625 has a double row of table-cut stones alternating with pearls in the plainest gold collets.[240]

BUTTONS

Buttons were one of the most common items of sixteenth-century jewellery, and some craftsmen specialised in their making (see above, pp. 87). Henry VIII owned many sets of jewelled buttons,[241] which were used not only to fasten the doublet but to ornament caps.[242] The importance of the button to the trade is illustrated by John Mabbe's stock

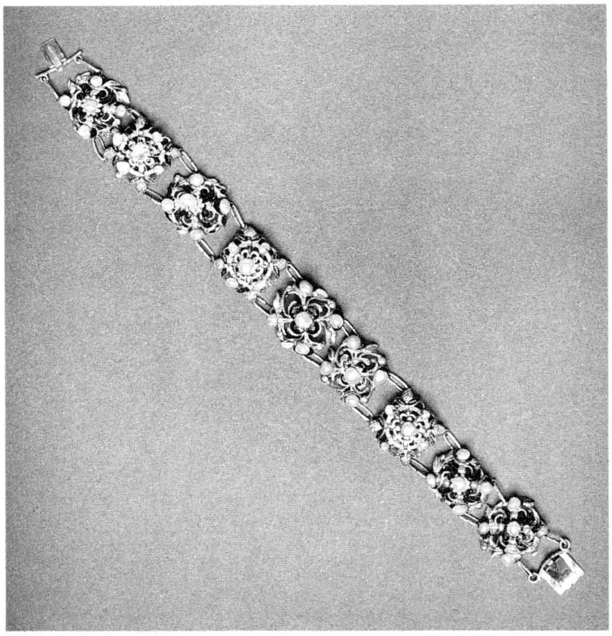

57 Cluster buttons in black and white enamelled gold, some with leaves and berries, now linked into a bracelet. One of a pair: *c.* 1600. Collection of Mr Alick Hay of Duns Castle.

of over two thousand for gowns and caps, and a further ninety-five for jerkins.[243] They were made in matching sets, and the same materials and techniques, including casting, were used as in the manufacture of other jewels. The most expensive were set wth gem-stones and pearls, but most were enamelled. Their small size did not inhibit the range of designs used: Catherine-wheels, roses, and red and white faces were all to be seen in Henry VIII's collection.[244] Two of the Earl of Sussex's cap bands were sewn with marigold buttons set with rubies: cabochon in one case and table-cut in the other,[245] while the Pembroke inventory includes buttons of white snails, pansies and blue snakes; others were 'fasshioned like the sonne' or enamelled with blue and white Cupid's bows.[246] Equally light-hearted were the green tortoises, lizards, peascods, roses and acorns belonging to Elizabeth I, who also owned buttons with ruby and pearl stars, heraldic ragged staves, true-loves, knots and double hearts.[247] In the seventeenth century, designs were simpler, following the fashionable trend, and consisted of large single stones, or clusters with pearls pinned to the centre of rosettes (Plate 57).

AGLETS

Slashes and seams were linked together by cords tied in bows ending in pairs of tags or aglets, made in sets of silver, silver-gilt and gold, and enamelled or set with pearls and gems. They were also worn in the hat.[248] Henry, Duke of Richmond's gold-embroidered crimson damask fur-lined gown was trimmed with 'seven grete buttons and foure paire agelettes',[249] and Viscountess Lisle owned 'xviij payer of Aglettes of golde upon ij payre of Sleves of clothe of gold'.[250] A 'cap of black velvet with white plume laced with aglets' was sent to Lady Jane Grey.[251] As no example of an aglet has been identified, our information about their design comes from portraits and inventories. Many of Queen Elizabeth I's aglets were white, enamelled with crosses[252] or contrasting with red, purple and blue, sometimes studded with garnets or rubies, while one had a spiral pattern 'enamelled and wreathed about with small and large pearls'.[253] Those in Queen Anne of Denmark's collection were larger, some shaped as square pyramids or elongated triangles [254] thickly set with table diamonds, rubies, opals and pearls. A carcanet and a pair of bracelets were broken up to make a splendid set of 'xxiiij long Aglettes of three sides, every Aglett having 27 Diamondes in the sides, and one in the top, conteining 672 diamondes', which were delivered to her in 1607.[255] The brilliant effect of such jewels was described by Spenser:

> All in a silken Camus lylly whight,
> Purfled vpon with many a folded plight,
> Which all aboue besprinckled was throughout
> With golden aygulets, that glistred bright,
> Like twinckling starres . . . [256]

BRACELETS AND ARMLETS

Although in 1551 Lady Tirrell declared that 'all the gentlewomen did wear bracelettes about their arms which they were not wont to do',[257] earlier examples are known. Henry VIII gave a pair to Anne Boleyn: 'I send you . . . my picture set in bracelets'.[258] Their role as tokens of love and remembrance was echoed by the couplet:

> Lady your hands are fallen into a snare;
> For Cupid's manacles these bracelets are[259]

which accompanied the gift of a pair to Elizabeth I at Hatfield in 1601.

Bracelets could take many forms: simple chains set with gem-stones, like Dame Maud Parr's 'braselet chayne facyon with a great jacent at it',[260] or ornamental links, like the Duchess of Somerset's 'payer of bracelets of golde wrought like scallop shelles with hollowe worke'.[261] In 1556 Queen Mary I was given a pair 'of stele set in gold enamuled blacke garnished eche with ix small Diamountes and iii grete'.[262] Henry VIII owned many bracelets of different designs,[263] as did Queen Elizabeth I, who continued to receive them at New Year. In 1587 the Earl of Leicester gave her 'one bracelet of golde contayning VI peeces, IV peeces like crosses, II peeces like half crosses, fully furnished with diamondes, rubyes, and perls of sundry bignesses, on thone side, with a rowe of perles and smale rubyes on eche side of the said bracelett, enamuled'.[264] Her collection ranged from very simple bracelets, such as the two pairs enamelled with the

Tudor colours (one pair of green and one of white), one with 'sundrie devises', and both 'made like hoopes', to more elaborate examples made with a wide range of motifs.[265] Links were made like knots, true-loves of pearls or diamonds, diamond and ruby fishes, or opal and ruby snakes.[266] Another pair were made of 'Jett like eyes havinge tenn pearles sett in twoes betwene them', a motif found in portraits.[267]

Another of her bracelets, 'made hoopwise called Persia worke', came from a South Indian workshop; it was given to the queen's cousin, Lord Hunsdon, and is preserved at Berkeley Castle.[268]

Initials and mottoes were also used. Henry VIII had a bracelet inscribed PLUS TOST MORIR QUE CHANGER MA PENSEE sent to Windsor Castle in 1535.[269] Another pair had 'letteres of .H. and .K. . . . thynner parte . . . made with Caracters of Astronomy', and another with the same initials and his motto DIEU ET MON DROIT.[270] Elizabeth I had several similar bracelets, including one spelling out the name of one of her suitors, FRANCOS DE VALOS (*sic*), and others with the mottoes CARUM QUOD RARUM or SINE FINE.'[271] The clasps of the gold chain bracelets worn by Lady Speke in her portrait of 1592 were enamelled with E R, for her mother, Elizabeth Rosewell.[272] A 1591 portrait of Dame Elizabeth Knightley shows her wearing a pair of bracelets composed of large gold letters over her lace cuffs (Plate 34).[273]

Anne of Denmark also had a number of inscribed bracelets; some had belonged to Elizabeth, including the pair with CARUM QUOD RARUM and others with the ciphers I R and A R.[274]. Interestingly, although she continued to buy jewelled bracelets from George Heriot, she was not painted wearing them, but only with rows of pearls with jewelled clasps,[275] and it is these that feature in the later orders. The changing fashion in bracelets can be clearly seen in the criticism of the once-fashionable 'flagon' bracelets – owned by the Duchess of Somerset, and the Earls of Shrewsbury and Pembroke, and stocked at his death by Nicholas Herrick[276] – made by John Marston's Donna Garbetza in his play, *Parasitaster or The Fawne*, in 1606:

> alas I was a simple country Ladie, wore gold buttons, trunck sleeves and flagon bracelets, in this state of innocency I was brought up to the Court.[277]

ACCESSORIES FOR DRESS, ETC.

SQUARE

Holbein painted Jane Seymour with her tight-fitting bodice bordered at the neck with a band of table-cut stones in quatrefoil collets alternating with pearl clusters.[278] A variation of this jewelled trimming is recorded in a royal inventory of 1541: 'one square of Goldesmythes werke conteignynge xxvij table Diamondes and xxvj Cluster of pearl's being vj in every Cluster'.[279] By 1587 they had gone out of fashion and none was listed in Elizabeth I's inventory.

BORDERS AND EDGES

These were jewelled bands with brightly enamelled gold pieces and clusters of pearls worn as garnishments at the neck and on the sleeves, and could be of Paris work and set with diamonds and other gems.[280] In 1576 John Mabbe had fourteen borders in his stock,[281] and among those belonging to Nicholas Herrick were nine of enamelled wirework, two 'graven borders enamelled' and one set with turquoises, opals, thirty-two pearls and seventy-nine small table-cut rubies.[282]

58 Gold spherical pomander case,
formerly enamelled and covered with pearls threaded on wire.
Found in the River Thames. British Museum.

POMANDERS

Mixtures of aromatic substances – cloves, cinnamon, musk, ambergris and civet – were rolled into balls and caged or netted in gold (Plate 58) or silver, enclosed in hollow enamelled gold tablets, pendants, bracelets, aglets, buttons, necklaces, chains and girdles, both to scent the foul air and to protect against infection.

In 1520 the Duke of Buckingham ordered 'a powmander of gold to be made with the kynge and quenes badgeys for a new yers gyfte for the quene and a chain of gold to hang the powmander at her gyrdyll'.[283] Worn in this way, they could be held in the hand to smell when desired. They were not only used at the court and in 1538 Mr Walden tried to buy one for the wife of the High Master of St Paul's School in London while he was visiting Cambrai in Flanders; he wrote that he could only find small tablets no bigger than a rial coin, 'of diver colours, most commonly, and openeth with a vice, that there be put within musce or sweet powders. Such may be had for 30*s*., with the fashion for which they ask a noble or a crown.'[284] In 1576 John Mabbe had more than 224 pomanders in his stock,[285] and they could take many shapes, ranging from a pear, sphere or book to a bird; some were of filigree of enamelled gold, and some set with precious stones.[286]

Pomander for bracelets, chains and girdles was caged in silver or gold filigree, frequently threaded with seed pearl, and laced with amber, coral, jet or gold beads and cameos.[287] The Earl of Leicester had two-and-a-half dozen buttons filled with pomander and set with diamond sparks on the top,[288] and Elizabeth I had a set of eighty-six 'in twoes' made like oranges with seed pearl.[289]

Anne of Denmark inherited Queen Elizabeth's collection of pomander jewellery and added to it, owning not merely the separate items but a complete parure of chain, sixty buttons and sixty-five aglets of Spanish work, all with white ambergris.[290]

WATCHES

Many watches had a bell to sound the hours, and so were called clocks after the French 'cloche' for a bell. Hung from the neck or waist by cords, leather or velvet ribbons, they were highly visible and prized, and the covers could be set with precious stones. The thick round pendant which Henry VIII has on his chest in portraits of 1537 and 1540 could be a watch, comparing as it does with continental examples;[291] while one worn by Lady Petre in a portrait of 1567 at Ingatestone, Essex, is a compact round box open to show the dial. (Plate 59).

Movements could be incorporated in tablets, flowers, and the clasp of an armlet.[292] In the second half of the century, hardstone cases with gold mounts were made, like Elizabeth I's watches 'of agatt made like an egg', of 'christall garnished with golde' and of 'Eliotropie'; others were encrusted with precious stones, wrought with daisies and pansies and enamelled, one of the latter with 'thistorye of time'.[293] A set of drawings made in 1575 depicts eight devices for the cover, sides and back of a watch case made for Mary, Queen of Scots, alluding to her fortitude in adversity; esoteric and complex, they can be compared with the imagery on the contemporary Lennox jewel.[294] The taste for hardstone cases was shared by Anne of Denmark, and these, with others set with diamonds, were purchased from George Heriot.[295] The few surviving watches of the Elizabethan and Jacobean period are not jewelled, however, but the cases were engraved with heraldry and religious and classical subjects, such as the heads of Roman emperors.[296]

MISCELLANEOUS

Whistles, used for summoning servants or hounds as well as at sea, were made with figurative designs such as sea-monsters or dragons, studded with gems and hung with pearls.[297] Equally useful were the tooth and ear picks, wrought as sickles or eagle's claws, three of which were fitted in a miniature wheel-lock pistol belonging to the

59 Lady Petre holding a girdle prayer book and wearing her watch on a ribbon at the neck. Portrait, 1567. Petre collection, Ingatestone.

60 The Pasfield jewel. Miniature wheel-lock pistol enamelled black, formerly set with three diamonds, containing tooth and ear picks and a tongue-scraper. *c.* 1600. Victoria and Albert Museum.

Pasfield family[298] (Plate 60). Dating from *c.* 1600, the blackwork case with scrollwork reserved in the enamelling was formerly set with three diamonds.

From the mid sixteenth century, rich dark sable or marten's furs were given heads and feet of goldsmith's work set with gems and carved crystal. They are seen in portraits hanging close to the body, and stroked like living pets.[299]

Fans also were highly valued, made from the feathers of exotic birds, with handles of rock crystal or agate encrusted with gold and gems.[300] In portraits they were a token of rank, comparable to the baton held by military commanders. More generally used were mirrors[301] and casting-bottles for perfumes, both of which were hung from the girdle and could be as richly adorned as the owner could afford.

RINGS

The medieval scalloped collet developed into a raised quatrefoil or multifoil bezel with the 'shields' at the sides chased and, from the 1540s enamelled, with the shoulders emphasised by volutes and strapwork in high relief. Around 1600, gem-set rings have simpler box bezels and less ornament at the sides; the shoulders diminish in importance and become one with the hoop.

DECORATIVE RINGS

On St George's Day, 1515, Henry VIII received the Venetian ambassador, who noted that his fingers were 'one mass of jewelled rings'.[302] When Henry died in 1547 he owned ninety-nine diamond rings.[303] In 1587, nearly a third of those owned by Elizabeth I were set with diamonds, including pointed, table-cut and triangle stones.[304] The preference for diamond rings was widespread and, according to Fynes Moryson, they were affected by the English 'to great excesse'.[305] Enamelled settings were usually black and white, red and green being rarely recorded.[306] Particularly fine stones were set *à jour*, like Elizabeth I's 'ringe of golde ennameled blacke with a pointed diamonde sett without foyle like fower clawes holding it'.[307] The ring delivered to Anne of Denmark in 1605, 'set all about with diamonds with one diamond in the topp cutt in the form of a rose',[308] seems to be an early example of the rose cut.

The largest stones were mounted as solitaires, and the smaller grouped in clusters like Elizabeth I's 'ring of golde with a mounte of dyamondes, containing a lozengie dyamonde in the toppe, with 3 dyamondes on eyther syde of the ring' or John Mabbe's 'very fayre Ryng with nynten fayre table Dyamondes'.[309] These might take more specific forms: a diamond rose, fleurs-de-lis, four half-circles, St Andrew's and Jerusalem crosses.[310] Queen Elizabeth's cipher E R, in table-cut diamonds, was set in the cover of the bezel of a locket ring opening to show an enamelled portrait of herself wearing a ruby brooch facing another lady with a diamond brooch. On the back of the bezel is the phoenix device of the Seymours and the queen.[311] Thomas Cromwell had commissioned a portrait ring in 1536: the figures of the king and queen in relief on one side and that of their daughter, Princess Elizabeth, on the back were framed in a scroll inscribed in Latin.[312]

Anne of Denmark had many diamond rings with the stones set in an emblematic heart, winged, burning, wounded, encircled by a snake signifying eternity or held by hands. Others were set in flowers (pansy, daisy) or in a leaf, a frog, a lizard or a pair of doves. Diamond ciphers of A and S (perhaps for Souveignez or remembrance) in rings reflected the larger cipher jewels she owned. George Heriot also made locket rings for her, one with a miniature of James I in it, and two others with scallop shell and frog bezels.[313]

When his inventory was compiled, Thomas Cromwell wore a cabochon ruby ring and four others set with table-cut stones in white enamelled settings, one 'wrought antique'.[314] Rings with rubies formed the second-largest group in Elizabeth's 1587 inventory, twenty-two in all, and nine of Mabbe's rings were so set, some in white, others 'of divers colours' or 'chased with frutages'.[315] Another ring had 'the sockett wherein the Rubie is set being facyoned like an Aulter'.[316] Large rubies and spinels could be claw-set without foiling; smaller stones could be set in clusters, lozenges and stars, alone or combined with emeralds, opals and diamonds.[317]

There were thirty-six emerald rings in Henry VIII's collection and ten in Elizabeth I's 1587 inventory, and although others are listed in various late Tudor or Jacobean inventories, only 'rocke' (cabochon) and square stones are ever specified. The colours of the settings are seldom mentioned, except for Thomas Cromwell's emerald ring enamelled white and Elizabeth I's in black, red and white.[318]

Since Henry VIII had only fourteen sapphire rings, Elizabeth I four and John Mabbe only stocked two, [319] this stone seems to have declined in prestige. The sapphire in a ring bequeathed by the Countess of Oxford in 1537 was faceted with 'divers squares', and two of Elizabeth I's rings had stones described as 'square' or 'cutt'.[320]

Thomas Cromwell wore a large turquoise ring in his portrait, which may be the one in his inventory 'like a heart'.[321] In 1587 Elizabeth I had nine turquoise rings, and those stocked by Mabbe in 1576 were enamelled black and white. Smaller stones, set in rows or clusters, could be owned by people of modest means like Thomas Patenson, one of the Yeomen of the Queen's Chamber.[322]

The range of gems used in rings was wide and included amethysts, chrysolites, topazes, garnets, jacinths, opals and aquamarines or pearls, set alone or in combinations, sometimes with the more precious diamonds, rubies and emeralds.

SIGNETS

Indispensable for business, signets were worn every day, and their designs were practical and simple, with broad convex hoops supporting round or oval bezels with a beaded or cable border framing the device. Armorial signets were engraved on the metal, or more rarely on crystal, foiled and painted to give the tinctures. Archbishop Cranmer and the Chancellor, Sir Nicholas Bacon, display them in their portraits;[323] and when the penniless young lawyer, Robert Boyle, created Earl of Cork in 1620, arrived in Dublin in 1588 to seek his fortune, his signet, of this crystal and gold armorial design, proclaimed his birth and intention to succeed.[324] Sir Thomas Gresham distributed five such signets to his friends, each enamelled behind the bezel with a green grasshopper, the Gresham crest[325] (Plate VI). Rarest of all were diamond signets, such as one with H and I for Henry VIII and Jane Seymour, or one with the arms of James I supplied by George Heriot and Nathaniel Gheraet in 1621, at a cost of £1400.[326]

Merchants used signets with their marks or personal devices, like the cock and star used by Humphrey Revell, a brewer; or else initials.[327] Signets with initials usually had the letters tied by an elegant knot, as is seen on that of Lord Darnley, which has the initials H and M on the front of the bezel and his crest at the back.[328] Crown servants also had signets, apparently for use in their office, like that of Richard Warde, Sub-Treasurer to Henry VIII, with the crowned initials H R.[329] Another group has Tudor roses on the bezel – but are otherwise different: one with saints on the shoulders, another with the names of the Three Kings of Cologne inscribed on the hoop.[330]

POSY RINGS

Posy rings were made of gold, silver and jet lined with silver, the outer face rounded, with moulded edges, and the inscription hidden inside the hoop. From mid century, Roman capitals replaced black letter and, although Latin continued in use, English became more usual. By 1596 it was possible for a collection of posies from over a hundred rings to be compiled.[331] Some had a strong religious character, such as Edward Coleman's I JOYE IN CHRIST AND I LYVE IN HOPE, while others, such as I LIKE MY CHOICE were obviously chosen as wedding rings.[332]

GIMMEL RINGS

Double hoop rings joined together at the base, with twin bezels, symbolic of the married state, were also inscribed. The ring allegedly used at Sir Thomas Gresham's marriage was of this design, and the inscription QUOD DEUS CONJUNXIT HOMO NON SEPARET (Matthew 19.6) affirmed the indissolubility of the union. Beneath the bezel are cavities enclosing an infant and a skeleton, emblems of the life cycle and the vanity of possessions (Plate VII).[333]

REMEMBRANCE

Rings were bequeathed as keepsakes, and if they were too large for the finger they were secured by a thread wound round the wrist, or else, it might be, hung around the neck. Gyles Blofeld of Mepershall, Bedfordshire, bequeathed a plain gold posy ring in 1591 to his sister-in-law, Ann Thomas, 'to be her own as a token of the true and faithfull love and great goodwill and kyndness which hathe byn betwixt her and her said sister and myselfe ever sythence our first acquaintance'.[334] Increasingly, rings were bequeathed in wills as mementoes of the testator, and the most common design in the sixteenth century was a gold ring with a white skull enamelled on the bezel; just such a 'Ringe of golde with a deathes hedde' was listed in Henry VIII's inventory.[335] The type is exemplified by a ring from the second half of the century, the inscription NOSSE TE. PSUM (*sic*) for 'Know thyself' around the skull and DYE TO LYVE on the edge.[336]

CRAMP RINGS

Rings blessed on Good Friday after the veneration of the Cross, at one of the major ceremonies of the Tudor court, were believed to have the power of curing cramp, epilepsy and palsy. The custom arose from an offering made by the English kings at this time to buy medicines for epileptics. By Henry VIII's reign this had developed into a ritual whereby gold and silver rings were handled by the king to bless them, so that they could effect a cure by the royal touch, which derived its merit from the coronation unction.[337] The practice survived the Reformation under Edward VI and Mary I, who blessed the rings with great devotion.[338] They feature in her inventory[339] and in 1554 she sent bunches of them to the Emperor Charles V, the Queen of France, the Queen of Hungary and the Duchess of Lorraine, by way of the Bishop of Arras. Acknowledging their safe arrival to Simon Renard, the Spanish ambassador in London, the bishop expressed the hope that the consignment would prove more efficacious than those blessed by some of the queen's predecessors.[340]

Whatever doubts might be expressed, there is evidence that such rings were eagerly sought after, and that those close to the throne, like Cardinal Wolsey, Bishop Fox and Thomas Cromwell, were continually asked for supplies.[341] Cramp rings of gold and silver are the most frequently mentioned item of jewellery in the *Lisle Letters*, although sometimes they were in short supply.[342] They were also regarded as efficacious in other circumstances; and Edward Fox, Bishop of Hereford, wrote to Viscountess Lisle in 1537 about cramp rings she had asked the London agent to obtain 'against the time that you should be brought abed'.[343]

5

The social context of Stuart and Commonwealth jewellery, 1625 – 1714

The reign of Charles I saw the full development of the style of jewellery in which gem-stones rather than wrought gold became the principal concern of the jeweller. The century also witnessed the predominance of French influence on design – either directly from Paris and the court at Versailles, or through the Huguenot goldsmiths who worked abroad after the Revocation of the Edict of Nantes of 1685.

ROYALTY

Charles I, who had pinned the Three Brothers to his hat as a boy, grew up accustomed to magnificent stones.[1] The fine art collection which he assembled is proof of the excellent taste which must also have extended to the jewellery he bought for himself, his wife and their children while his agents, Sackville Crowe and Philip Calandrini, tried to dispose of the remainder of the ancestral treasure on the Amsterdam market.[2] He began in 1625 with the purchase of a fine multi-faceted solitaire in a gold collet and other diamonds in rings and miniature cases.[3] Queen Henrietta Maria, who received splendid diamonds and pearls on her marriage, continued to add to her collection[4] (Plate 61), and was able to acquire the jewels which her mother, Queen Marie de' Medici, had to pawn.[5]

When money was needed for arms in 1642, and Parliament had issued an injunction against the disposal of the Crown Jewels (so strongly worded that no one would buy or lend on their security), the king sent personal jewels to the queen in Amsterdam for sale. She wrote to say how she regretted parting with his pearl buttons: 'You cannot imagine how handsome the buttons were, when they were removed out of the gold and strung into a chain, and many as large as my great chain. I assure you, that I gave them up with no small regret.'[6] She also pawned her own jewels for the king's use.[7] After the execution of Charles I in 1649, she wore few jewels with her widow's weeds and during

61 Queen Henrietta Maria wearing a pearl choker and chain, a large diamond set in a pendant and a lace collar pinned with bow-knot brooch. Portrait after Sir Anthony van Dyck. National Portrait Gallery.

the years of exile was obliged to sell them – with everything else of value – to buy food and fuel.[8] After the Restoration she was once again majestically jewelled: the inventory of her jewels when she died in 1669 listed bodkins, earrings, crosses, rosaries, rings, bracelets and sixteen watches. These she left to her son, Charles II, and her daughter and namesake, the Duchess of Orléans.[9]

In 1649 the House of Commons ordered that the regalia and personal ornaments of the late king and his queen 'be totally broken . . . and that they melt down the Gold and Silver of them: and to sell the jewels for the best Advantage of the Commonwealth'.[10] One of the first acts of Charles II was to appoint a committee to investigate this dispersal and to recover as much as possible.[11] Thus, in 1663, he paid £9,750 for diamonds and £1,200 for pearl pendants from the estate of his sister, the Princess of Orange.[12]

The model for the splendours of the Restoration court was France, where so many of the royalists had spent their time in exile. In 1661 the royal jewellers, Francis and John Simpson, were paid £4,840 for jewels which included presents to ambassadors and other servants of foreign princes.[13] The Lord Chamberlain's Office kept a record of all such gifts.[14] Among those rewarded for services was Jane Lane, who had helped Charles escape after the Battle of Worcester; she was given a pension, his picture and a gold watch.[15] Courtiers also received valuable presents: in 1664 the Count de Grammont was given a jewel worth £1,260 at his marriage,[16] while the previous year Pepys recorded how Lady Castlemaine 'had all the King's Christmas presents made him by the Peeres given to her . . . and that at the great ball she was much richer in Jewells than the Queen and Duchesse put both together'.[17]

Although part of Catherine of Braganza's dowry was paid in jewels, most were returned to Lisbon because of a dispute over their real value.[18] Queen Henrietta Maria gave her 'a complete headdress of diamonds and emeralds, with a watch dial to match, estimated to be worth 12.000*l.* sterling, of extraordinary beauty and incomparable workmanship'.[19] Valuable presents also came from the king: a jewel worth £2,800 bought from Isaac le Gouch, a yellow stone twice the size of the Sancy diamond, blue and white sapphires and a huge pearl.[20]

Lady Peterborough remarked on the quantities of jewels amassed by Anne Hyde, Duchess of York,[21] and when the Duke of York remarried he sent jewels valued at £20,000 to his bride, the Italian princess, Mary of Modena.[22] Her elegant style was portrayed by William Wissing: sets of shoulder brooches, a chain across the shoulders, pearls at her throat and ears, with a wide breast jewel of diamonds, acanthus leaves and a pearl pendant.[23] In exile after 1688 she kept up appearances, wearing a black velvet dress and 'a very fine diamond parure' at the wedding of the Duke of Burgundy on 7 December 1697.[24] James II must have succeeded in removing most of their personal jewels to France in 1689, for he still had sufficient to sell for the relief of needy Jacobites in 1698 after ten years of exile.[25] He then parted with pearls and diamonds, a pair of pendants, a bodkin, seven 'attaches', a pair of buttons, a girdle, a set of twelve loops,

62 Queen Mary II wearing pear pearl earrings, choker and diamonds set in a large brooch at the neckline, and clasps for her sleeves. Portrait after William Wissing. National Portrait Gallery.

buttons and a buckle, a pair of shoe buckles and the coulant of a cross. He still retained various items: two pairs of shirt buttons, seals, five gold watches, and his best Garter insignia.[26] These were inherited by his son, styled James III, the Old Pretender, along with what remained of Mary of Modena's jewellery.

Crowned in April 1689, William III and Mary II maintained a court described by a French visitor as only a pale reflection of that at Versailles.[27] The accounts of their jeweller, Richard Beauvoir, in 1694 do, however, suggest that this was a partisan view, since he was supplying brilliant and ruby earrings, sets of jewelled tags, buckles, loops and sleeve clasps, sixteen diamond stars, a diamond locket and a pearl necklace[28] (Plate 62). The huge sum of £12,000 was spent on an unpolished diamond to 'make a perfect hart for the head or breast. Her Majesty wil wear it Distint it having so great a light in it will play with the greater vigour.'[29]

After the death of Mary II in 1694 some of her jewels passed to her sister, the future Queen Anne, who on her accession pressed strongly for the return of others which William III had sent to Holland.[30] This may have been more from a sense of duty to the Crown rather than for her own pleasure, for unlike the other Stuarts she seems to have been indifferent to luxury.[31] According to the Duchess of Marlborough 'she was never expensive nor made any foolish buildings nor bought one jewel in the whole of her reign'.[32] As Mistress of the Robes the duchess was furious when the queen refused to wear any jewels to the thanksgiving service held at St Paul's for the victory at Oudenarde in 1708. The queen, whose husband was at the point of death, thought it inappropriate, while the duchess – who had spent hours laying the jewels out – thought she should have been ablaze with them.[33]

ARISTOCRACY

In 1625 Van Miereveld portrayed George Villiers, Duke of Buckingham, at the height of his career, resplendent, with pearls sewn all over his doublet, in rows round his waist, and hanging in long ropes below his collar.[34] Documents confirm that this dashing style was emulated by the nobility both before and after the Civil War and Commonwealth, although few wear jewels in their portraits. In her will of 1639 Frances, Duchess of Richmond and Lennox, bequeathed her jewels for the use of the men of her family: pearls for their clothes, gold and diamond chains for their hats, and to her nephew, the then duke, 'a Chaine of pearle which is 500 and odd to serve as a hatband, and his wife for a chaine when shee pleaseth'.[35] One of the most detailed documents for a private collection of jewels is the codicil of 1674 disposing of her jewellery made by Christian, Countess of Devonshire. In it she singled out eight of the parcels in her inventory – a 'great Diamond Chaine', two diamond lockets, 'one Rosse Jewell', two diamond bracelets and two groups of pendant pearls – as 'the Choysest of my Jewells' and designated them to be kept by her son and heir for 'the use of the Heire Male of the Earls of Devonshire'. Other of her jewels were bequeathed with notes of their sentimental value to her: a 'great Saphire Jewell' was given to her eldest son to 'weare it in memory of mee it beeinge bestowed on mee by my deare Mother' and therefore 'by mee most valued' and her wedding ring and the ring 'set with a Turkie Stone which I weare it beinge the Last gieft of my deare Lord and Husband'.[36] Such men bedecked themselves at court, and at the Queen's Birthday Ball in 1666 Lord Herbert estimated that there were 'a hundred vests that at the least cost a hundred pounds. Some were adorned with jewels above a thousand. The Lord Chamberlain's was one.'[37]

The unusually detailed will of Elizabeth, Countess of Devonshire, in 1642 reveals the splendour of the jewellery worn at the court of Charles I. Her two best pearl necklaces were left to her daughter, Eleanor, Countess of Sussex, and her daughter-in-law, Lady Wortley; a third rope was divided into three for her granddaughters. The

Countess of Sussex also received a large diamond pendant with a hanging pearl, and three out of five-dozen diamond and pearl buttons. Lady Wortley had received a miniature of Charles I in a diamond-studded case and a magnificent girdle of sixty-three diamond links. More diamonds were set in a cross, in chains, in chokers, and in the heraldic Cavendish snakes alternating with clusters of pearls and rubies in a necklace. She had another necklace set with rubies, and others were mixed with topazes in a 'Syphany' – perhaps a cipher – or with blue cornelian beads in a chain. Her husband, William, the second Earl of Devonshire, had been one of the first adventurers to Virginia, which may account for her girdle, threaded with barrel-shaped 'Virginia' stones. She had many sets of buttons, some with clusters of diamonds in black scrolled mounts, others of gold borage leaves, and many with rubies and pearls. Pearls were favoured for hair ornaments, and those in her three coronets were Persian, ragged (baroque) and pear-shaped, the last also being hung in the hair as an alternative to a diamond feather. Finally, each grandchild received a diamond ring inscribed with the posy 'Fear God', in the hope that 'God will blesse them all which shall followe the Councell conteined in that posey to feare and truly to serve God and value my love to them.'[38]

Some courtiers were even depicted wearing more splendid jewels than they owned in reality. Eleanor, Countess of Sussex, wrote of her portrait by Van Dyck in 1640 that it was 'no great mater for another age to thinke me richer than i was'.[39]

While it might be supposed that the aristocratic ladies with strong Puritan views might have adopted a simpler style of dress and refrained from wearing elaborate jewellery, this does not seem to have happened. In Scotland the second Marchioness of Hamilton, who rode at the head of her own troop of Covenanters, had a fine collection of jewels which she delighted to wear.[40] During the Civil War, social life was largely disrupted but, during the Commonwealth, life returned to more normal conditions. In 1653 Christian, Countess of Devonshire, wrote to her brother, Lord Bruce, that 'The garb in town is Ladies all in scarlet, shining and glittering as bright as "anty maske". You would wonder to see such stars in these our cloudy days.'[41] The Countess of Sussex, then remarried to the Earl of Warwick, and stepmother-in-law to Oliver Cromwell's daughter, was portrayed wearing all her jewels.[42] Good stones could be bought: those set in one of the Countess of Devonshire's best diamond lockets were acquired by her from William Gumbleton in 1655.[43]

At her death in 1674, the codicil listing the jewellery that Christian, Countess of Devonshire, had accumulated from the reign of Charles I onwards shows how many items could be owned by one person – and the care taken over their acquisition and disposal. Her daughter-in-law, the next countess, Elizabeth Cecil (1619–89), left most of her jewels to her daughter, Anne, Countess of Exeter (1649–1703), and these included sixteenth-century figurative pendants as well as the fashionable diamond tags, pearl necklaces and bracelets.[44]

Although Charles II's Portuguese queen was 'much concerned that the English ladies spend so much time in dressing themselves – she fears they bestow but little on God Almighty and in housewifery', it remained true that the 'most effectual method to pay court to the king, was to outshine the rest in brilliancy and grandeur'.[45] There was much rivalry between the court beauties, and at the wedding of the Duke of Monmouth, the Duchess of Cleveland tried to eclipse all others, especially Frances Stuart, by the magnificence of her jewels. At the Queen's Birthday Ball in 1666, Samuel Pepys recorded that 'It was indeed a glorious sight to see Mrs. Steward in black, and white lace – and her head and shoulders dressed with Dyamonds.'[46] Lord Herbert, who was also present, told his wife that he 'never saw greater bravery'.[47] In 1675 at a performance of *Calisto the Chaste Nymph*, a pastoral acted by the younger ladies at court, the diarist Evelyn noted that 'They were all covered with *Jewels*' and that his friend Mrs Blagg wore 'neere 20000 pounds worth of *Jewells*'.[48] Other opulent collections were owned by the Duchess of Albemarle (†1669) and the Countess of Lauderdale (†1671), both wives of leading statesmen. Instead of distributing the jewels – which may have been reset while the countess was living in Paris towards the end of her life – among their children as specified in her will, the Earl of Lauderdale seized them and gave them to his new wife. They are described in the documents of the subsequent litigation.[49]

Fashions changed more rapidly in France, and Baroness Aulnoy, who visited England in 1675, remarked on the antiquity of the jewels worn by a lady dressed as Diana whom she saw in a boating party on the Thames.[50] Even the less fashionable court at Vienna appears to have outshone that of London, for in 1685 Sir George Etherege concluded his description of the elaborate jewels worn by a lady at court:

> *The like in* England, *ne'r was seen,*
> *Since* Holbin Drew, Hal. *and his* Queen.[51]

By the turn of the century, however, the fashion-conscious court ladies had become the target of satirists who contrasted their extravagance with the sober habits of a former Golden Age, when wives were frugal and happy with no more than a ring, a pearl necklace and a locket. Mary Evelyn mocked the new fashion in a poem published in 1690 (see p. 217 below); but John Gay's description of a court beauty in her jewels is more dazzled and admiring:

> Her new-set Jewels round her Robe are plac'd,
> Some in a Brilliant Buckle bind her Waist;
> Some round her Neck a circling light display,
> Some in her Hair diffuse a trembling Ray;
> The Silver Knot o'erlooks the *Mechlen* lace,
> And adds becoming Beauties to her Face.[52]

One of the great court occasions of the year was the Queen's Birthday. After the celebrations of 1712 Lady Stafford wrote to her husband: ''twas allowed I had the most

Jewells of any body there, and the Queen told me I was very fine and my cloths was very handsome'; she claimed that 'My diamond necklace is now the finest as well as my earrings of any body's in town.'[53] She was the heiress of a rich ship-builder. Even her display was outshone by Sarah, Duchess of Marlborough, whose jewels, like the ducal palace at Blenheim, symbolised the success of her brilliant husband. In addition to the fine stones given to him by grateful heads of state, she was rich enough to acquire all the important pieces which came up for sale: the Duchess of Beaufort's pearl necklace, the Duchess of Shrewsbury's pear pearls, the pearls given to the Princess Royal by the City of London at her marriage in 1613 and Stuart family diamonds. It is clear from the number and variety of the diamond, ruby and sapphire parures in her inventory, from the weights and valuations of the most important stones (drawn in plan showing the facets), that this was the pre-eminent collection of the time. The Duke of Marlborough also cut a fine figure in public with his diamond buttons, loops and hatband, Garter insignia, huge rings and jewelled sword – the rewards of military victories and the highest political office[54] (Fig. 14).

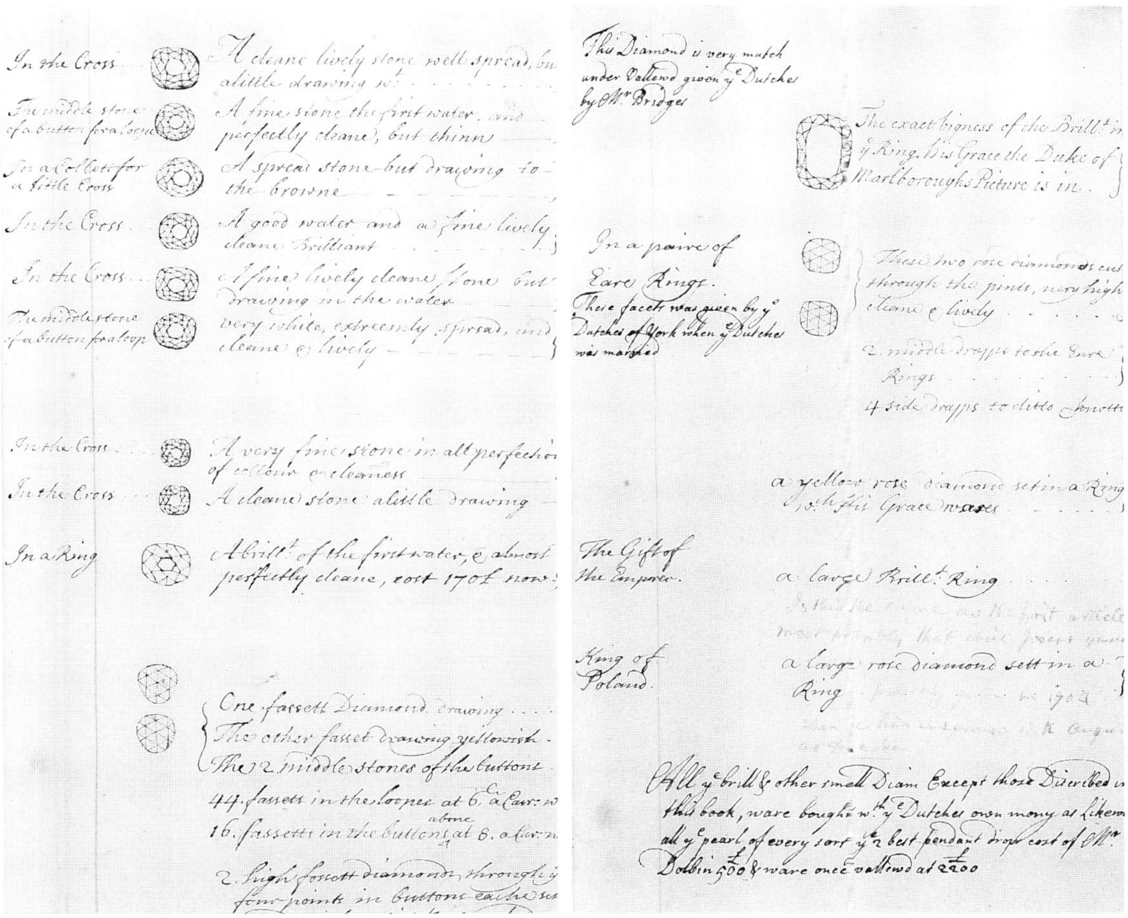
In the Cross — A cleane lively stone well spread, but a little drawing w:
The middle stone of a button for a loope — A fine stone the first water, and perfectly cleane, but thinn
In a Collett for a little Cross — A spread stone but drawing to the browne
In the Cross — A good water and a fine lively cleane Brilliant
In the Cross — A fine lively cleane stone but drawing in the water
The middle stone of a button for a loop — very white, extreemly spread, and cleane & lively
In the Cross — A very fine stone in all perfection of colour & cleaness
In the Cross — A cleane stone a little drawing
In a Ring — A Brill.t of the first water, & almost perfectly cleane, cost 170£ now
One fassett Diamond drawing
The other fasset drawing yellowish
The 2 middle stones of the buttons
44. fassets in the loopes at 6.£ a Carr:
16. fassetts in the buttons above at 8. a Carr:
2. high fossett diamonds, through the four points in buttons
This Diamond is very mutch under valewd given ye Dutches by Mr. Bridges
The exact bigness of the Brill.t in ye Ring his Grace the Duke of Marlboroughs Picture is in.
In a paire of Eare Rings. These facets was given by ye Dutches of York when ye Dutches was married
These two rose diamonds cut through the pints, very high cleane & lively
2. middle drapps to the Eare Rings
4 side drapps to ditto
a yellow rose diamond set in a Ring w.th his Grace wares
The Gift of the Emperor. — a large Brill.t Ring
King of Poland. — a large rose diamond sett in a Ring
All ye brill & other small Diam Except those Discribed in this book, ware bought w.th ye Dutches own mony as likewise all ye pearl of every sort ye 2 best pendant drops cost of Mr. Dolbin 500£ & ware once vallewd at 2200£

Fig. 14 Details from the Marlborough Inventory listing diamonds: 1716. British Library.

MERCHANTS AND GENTRY

In 1626 Dame Anna Cromwell, a provincial lady of standing, bequeathed her jewels: a gold bodkin, seed pearl carcanet, gold chain, sets of jewelled buttons, crystal, diamond and pearl bracelets, an agate cameo of Queen Elizabeth, and numerous rings, all decorative except for one *memento mori* and several jet hoops.[55] Sir Hugh Middleton, a former Lord Mayor of London who devised the New River Water supply, bequeathed several jewels in his will in 1631. To his wife he gave 'all the chaines, rings, jewells, pearles, bracelettes and gould buttons which shee hath in her custodie and useth to wear at festivals' and also the jewel presented to him by the Corporation of London and shown in his portrait. His friends had mourning rings each worth £10.[56] The letters of the Oxinden family in Kent also allude to the jewels used by a minor gentry family – notably Thomas, the man-about-town, with 'his silver hat-band, silver-hilted sword, his mother's diamond ring on his finger, Henry's [his father's] pearl in his ear'; by 1641, it was thought that 'in these dead times such toyes might be had at the easiest rates'.[57]

While little might distinguish the aristocratic Puritan ladies and gentlemen from others of their rank, those of the gentry and merchant classes adopted a simpler style, although adornment was not wholly eschewed.[58] General Harrison declared that 'gold and silver did not become saints' but he dressed very well indeed; and Colonel Hutchinson aspired to look 'pretty rich but grave', wearing sober-coloured suits embellished with buttons and points of gold and silver.[59] The fanatical extremists who wanted to abolish the wedding ring were motivated not so much by a dislike of personal adornment as by a hatred of all religious ritual shared with the Roman Catholic Church; their campaign did not, however, meet with wide support.[60] After the Restoration, the Puritan tradition of plain dressing was maintained by the Quakers, who could be recognised by their grey homespun cloth and lack of ornaments. Although the daughters of Margaret Fox, step-daughter of George Fox, the founder of the sect, wore brighter clothing than was general, trimmed with ribbons, they used no jewellery apart from watches and a pocket looking-glass.[61]

The jewels of the richest City wives compared with those of the court ladies. When Mary, wife of the then Lord Mayor and royal goldsmith, Sir Robert Vyner, sat next to Charles II at her husband's banquet in Guildhall in 1674, she was 'all over scarlet and ermine, and half over diamonds'.[62] She was the heiress to a great fortune, but even the wives of senior officials like Samuel Pepys owned collections of jewels. After thirteen years of marriage Mrs Pepys had a three-row pearl necklace, two good rings set with a diamond and a turquoise, and perhaps a gold or silver watch. She could have acquired more if her husband had allowed her to receive all the presents offered to her by friends and by those looking for his help.[63]

Sir Miles Stapleton in 1707 bequeathed to his wife all her jewels: 'one diamond locket set with eight and forty diamonds for which he paid £100, and one diamond ring with a necklace of pearls and a gold watch'.[64] One of the characters in Aphra Behn's play, *The Rover; or, the Banish'd Cavalier*, in 1677 had the following jewels: a gold watch, a bunch of diamond rings, an armorial signet, a miniature of his mother and a bracelet given to him by his sister.[65] It was easy for those who wished to make a fine show on a special occasion to borrow. The custom is referred to in a letter from John Lawrence in London to Owen Wynn on 2 November 1639 concerning jewellery that had been altered: 'I conceive they weare hired out, to be worne (as is usuall in this cittie) and soe the stones might well be lost.'[66]

THE ROLE OF JEWELS IN DIPLOMACY AND SOCIAL LIFE

The custom of presenting foreign envoys and their staff with valuable presents continued throughout the century, which had become formalised according to the standing of the state they represented and their position within the embassy. Before Vincenzo Gussoni returned to Venice in 1629 the king gave him the ordinary present of a silver-gilt chain for the secretary Agustini. The day before I left he sent me a ring as a token of his appreciation for my services in concluding the peace . . The Queen gave my nephew Vincenzo a small diamond as a memento.'[67] When the painter and diplomat, Peter Paul Rubens, was knighted in 1630 Charles I also gave him the diamond ring from his finger, with other gifts.[68] Occasionally these were not ready, as happened with the Duke of Vendôme, 'whose gift through some defect in liberality was not ready in time before he left, and so they had to send it after him. It was a diamond worth 6000 ducats.'[69]

The Commonwealth government continued the tradition,[70] and their envoys abroad were likewise honoured. The journal of the embassy to Sweden in 1653–4, written by Bulstrode Whitelocke, describes in detail the presents received: a diamond-set gold and enamel miniature case with the portrait of Queen Christina was given to him, and gold chains with medals, varying from five to two links and in value from four hundred to a hundred ducats, were given to his sons and the members of his staff. Some of the latter felt that they had not received good enough presents and Whitelocke had to restrain them from returning them.[71] He also gave a gold medal 'very like him' to the Spanish envoy;[72] and, following the abdication of the queen at the end of his embassy, received another miniature from her successor before leaving the capital.[73] A double gold chain with a portrait medal hung with pearls was also sent by the queen to Cromwell.[74]

After the Restoration these customs continued, and gifts were supplied by the court jewellers, Isaac le Gouch, Christopher Rosse, Sir Francis Child and Sir Stephen Evance.[75] Such presents were rarely refused, and in 1679 Henry Savile wrote to Sir Leoline Jenkins to explain that

As for yr refusing the jewell, I thinke that is without other president then that of my Lord Holles who, leaving this place before our first warr with Holland, and not beeing able to gett this King on our side (who was soe soon after against us), said hee would not doe his own businesse if hee could not doe his master's, and soe would not accept a rich diamond that was offer'd him.[76]

Savile was well aware of the subtleties of diplomacy, for having been singled out by Louis XIV for a private conversation in 1672, he speculated on how the king would demonstrate this particular favour 'by his jewels'.[77]

Often such gifts were sold, like the miniature of Louis XIV framed in diamonds which Henry Cope bought from the Earl of Oxford in 1680 for £750.[78] The full value was not always realised; when Lady Bolingbroke had to sell a diamond ring given to her husband by Louis XIV, valued at £5,000, she could only get £2,000 for it in 1714–15.[79] Others treasured them and they were handed down as heirlooms. The Earl of Cork gave his son, Richard, the gold chain and medal

which His Majesty of Denmark with his gracious letters sent unto me as a royal demonstration of his princely acceptance of my endeavours for preserving and supplying his great ship and men by that extraordinary tempest were put in at Youghal, with express charges to my son never to part with it, but as I had given it to him he was to leave it to his heir, to be for ever continued to the house of the Earls of Cork, which house's unspotted honour and integrity, I desire the Almighty for ever to uphold it with his Grace.[80]

Similar chains which the Elector of Brandenburg and the King of Denmark gave to Elias Ashmole are kept in the Ashmolean Museum, Oxford. Acknowledging the gift to Count Greiffenfeld, he said that after his death they would be deposited in a 'publique Musaeum', so that 'Posterity may take notice of his Bounty to an English Gentleman.'[81]

Similar gifts were also made to reward subjects for their services or notable exploits. A miniature of Oliver Cromwell set in diamonds by George Alkington was given to Admiral Blake,[82] and one of Charles II, also set in diamonds, to Sir Richard Fanshawe. Sir Richard prized it greatly, for – unusually – it depicted the king as a child and, while in Spain as ambassador, he wore it on a 'rich curious wrought gold chain made in the Indies'.[83] Gold medals and chains were also given as rewards for military and naval exploits, and are recorded in the Jewel House Warrant Books.[84]

THE OFFICE OF MASTER OF CEREMONIES

From 1605 the English court had a Master of the Ceremonies whose duty it was to receive and entertain all foreign visitors, especially ambassadors; the first was Sir Lewis Lewkenor – 'a gentleman well languaged, of good education and discretion'.[85] He was succeeded in 1619 by Sir John Finett, whose record of his duties was published in 1656.[86] Sir Balthasar Gerbier, the next Master, who took over in 1641, was suspended from office and not reappointed. At the Restoration, Sir Charles Cottrell (1615–87) was granted the office and relinquished it in favour of his son, Sir Charles Lodowick Cottrell, who had been his assistant for many years. In 1714 he in turn was succeeded by his son, Sir Clement Cottrell, later Cottrell-Dormer (†1758), who kept notes of his duties, and recorded all presents given and received.[87] He was succeeded by Sir Charles Cottrell-Dormer (†1779) and Sir Clement Cottrell-Dormer (†1808).

The chain and jewel of office which Charles II gave Sir Charles Cottrell on the eve of the coronation in 1660 are shown in his portrait.[88] As the jewel bears the Biblical motto of James I, BEATI PACIFICI, the design was probably established when Lewkenor was appointed in 1605. The warrant for the badge given to Charles Cottrell in 1686 ordered the Master of the Jewel House to 'provide and deliver . . . A chaine and Medall of gold of the same fashion as that which his father wears as Master of the Ceremonies the same not to exceed tenn Ounces'.[89] Similar warrants were issued for new badges in 1714, 1727, 1758 and 1779; the first two dates suggest that new badges were issued at each coronation or succession.[90] The assistant Master had a 'gold chain and Medall of the same value and Fashion as was provided for the Master of the Ceremonys', according to the warrant for John Inglis in 1711.[91] A design by Marcus Gunter dated 1725 (Fig.15) illustrates the two sides of the medal. On the obverse is a hand amidst clouds, holding an olive branch, and the motto BEATI PACIFICI; and on the reverse a gauntleted hand issuing from thunderclouds, with the motto DIEU ET MON DROIT, framed in a laurel wreath surmounted by the royal crown.[92]

Fig. 15 Design by Marcus Gunter for the badge of Master of the Ceremonies: 1725
Röhsska Konstlöjdmuseet, Goteborg.

The Restoration badge, with the crown and border set with diamonds, is still in the possession of the Cottrell-Dormer family.

VALENTINES

It was customary on St Valentine's eve for men and women to assemble in equal numbers to draw lots to pair themselves, whereupon each man gave his lady a present. Worn over the heart for several days, most Valentines were modest, like the 'golden flower for a Valentine' noted in 1637 or the enamelled gold Valentine among the Eglinton jewels in 1652.[93] Samuel Pepys (who agreed to be his wife's Valentine every year) gave her a ring worth four or five pounds in 1665.[94] In 1668 the Duke of York drew the beautiful Frances Stuart, whom he was hoping to make his mistress, and gave her a jewel worth £800.[95] According to Lady Wentworth, Charles II abolished the custom because of such extravagances.[96]

BRIBES

During the reign of Charles I, the Dutch Admiral Van Tromp promised Sir John Pennington, a British vice-admiral, a very rich diamond on condition that he did not 'interfere with his plans'.[97] Samuel Pepys, too, recorded gifts from those seeking his help in advancing their career in the Navy. In 1665: 'This night I did present my wife with the Dyamond ring a while since given me by Mr . . . Dicke Vine's brother, for helping him to be a purser – valued at about 10*l*.'[98]

MARRIAGE CASKETS

Jewels were presented to ladies prior to their marriage. In 1713 the Duke and Duchess of Somerset called on Lady Frances Thynne shortly before her marriage to their son –

> each of them with a chagreen box in their hand, which they presented to Miss Thynne, who having previous instructions from her mother not to open them in their presence, she forebore doing but I have heard her say she was never so impatient for anything in her life as for their going away that she might see what they contained. One of them was a pair of diamond earrings from the Duke, the other a diamond necklace from the Duchess.[99]

PRECIOUS STONES AND METALS

In 1630 Sir Thomas Roe, acting in partnership, sold Queen Henrietta Maria two briolettes for £3500. Obliged to wait until 1635 for the first payment of £1500, he calculated that, even after the deduction of that sum, with interest charges the queen still owed £3761.[100] The risks in diamond trading were not merely financial but physical too, for many a ship's officer bringing stones to London from the coast was robbed by highwaymen. There was no organised system for imports, and it was from a chance purchase of bags of diamonds from a sailor who happened to pass his shop as he stood outside that William Ward, ancestor of the Earls of Dudley, began his career, ending as a rich banker (see below, p. 170). They were brought in by irregular shipments,[101] by foreign merchants like Melchior Rodriques,[102] and by the officials of the East India Company, who invested their money in stones. Apart from such officials, Englishmen only rarely travelled to the East, but those who did, like Lord Denbigh, could return from a visit to the Great Moghul 'full of jewels'.[103] When Nathaniel Harley was in Aleppo as a merchant he could send back animals and birds, pistachio nuts, and a packet of precious stones worth £3,000.[104] Another occasional source was plunder. In 1685, according to Pepys, eight bags of diamonds and rubies were captured from a Dutch vice-admiral and brought to London for sale.[105]

The decision by the East India Company in 1664 to permit outsiders to trade in precious stones, albeit subject to their regulations, ended their own monopoly.[106] The change of policy coincided with the settlement in London of Portuguese-Jewish merchants, who brought their financial and gemmological skills to the business, which for the first time was organised on a professional basis. Their synagogue in Bevis Marks made a great impression on visitors and in 1662 Joseph Greenhalgh noted: 'about or above one hundred right Jews . . . they were all gentlemen (merchants) . . . most of them were rich in apparel, divers with jewels glittering (for they are the richest jewellers of any)'.[107] They exported silver, coloured stones, amber and coral to India and imported uncut diamonds; these were then forwarded to Amsterdam for cutting and polishing. A proportion came back to London, where they were sold to jewellers and their craftsmen. As a result of their expertise, London became the centre of the international trade, and in 1695 the merchants could declare in a petition to the East India Company that the diamond business 'formerly driven by way of Italy or Portugal is become almost a sole English trade'.[108]

The rapid expansion of the diamond market was to some extent due to the grandiose court life which enshrined the baroque monarchy. Demand for diamonds, so eminently suited to displaying wealth, always increased at the time of royal weddings and coronations. A stable political situation was essential for business, as the Parisian jeweller, Philip Masson, explained to Sir Richard Hoare: 'in order to sell diamonds people must be at their ease, money must circulate and there must be as t'were, a superfluity'.[109] Some disasters could present opportunities, and in 1669 Robert de Berquen was hoping to buy good-quality diamonds from people obliged to raise money on account of the Great Fire of London three years before.[110]

Although Amsterdam was the main centre for cutting and polishing diamonds, there were competent lapidaries in London too, and in 1710 Joseph Cope faceted the 410 carat diamond named in 1717 after Thomas Pitt, Governor of Fort St George in India, and which is now in the Louvre. Since this diamond was so much bigger than any other previously sold, it was difficult to determine its value. The cleavage material was soon disposed of but it was not until 1717 that the cushion-shaped brilliant itself was sold to the Duke of Orléans, Regent of France, who never paid in full.[111] The stone, which was the size of an egg, aroused great interest; crystal models were sold, and Lady Wentworth declared that the City of London ought to buy it for the queen's crown.[112]

Brilliant-cut diamonds are recorded from the reign of Charles II, when Christian, Countess of Devonshire, bequeathed a ring with a 'Diamond Cutt eight square'.[113] In 1680 a London jeweller had '22 faucet diamonds sett in silver' in his stock.[114] By this date, when faceting was so much more evolved, silver settings were preferred to gold, which cast yellow reflections over the white brilliance of the diamond. While many were still foiled to disguise flaws and for additional brilliance, the finer stone would be 'sett transparent'.[115]

The variety of stones in the Cheapside Hoard – Colombian emeralds, topazes and Amazon stones from Brazil, chrysoberyls, spinels and iolites from Ceylon, Indian rubies and diamonds, lapis lazuli from Afghanistan, turquoises from Persia, peridots from St John's Island in the Red Sea, amethysts, garnets and opals from Bohemia and Hungary – is proof of the importance of the London market in the time of Charles I. While some of the stones were simply polished *en cabochon*, others were table, trap, rose and star cut.[116] Clear and well-coloured rubies and large sapphires were more expensive than diamonds. Emeralds were not so rare and, like rubies and sapphires, were often set with diamonds, as the contrast enhanced their colour. Coral from Leghorn was handled by the London diamond merchants, who sold large quantities to India for the local and Tibetan markets, although much was used here as well. Amber, sold by an itinerant Armenian in Burnaby's play, *The Ladies' Visiting Day*, was equally in demand for necklaces and bracelets.[117]

The increased supply created a demand for information about relative values, and Rice Vaughan, a lawyer, published tables setting out the prices of pearls, rough and polished diamonds and gold and silver, according to weight. Yellow diamonds, often listed in inventories, were reckoned at one-third of the value of good white stones.[118] Two important studies on gem-stones and their properties were published by British authors: Thomas Nicols in 1652 and Robert Boyle, one of the founders of the Royal Society, in 1672 (see Bibliography).

IMITATIONS

In 1635 Sir Nicholas Crisp obtained a patent from Charles I 'for the sole making and vending of Beads and Beangles'.[119] During this reign imports of imitation stones reached such proportions that in March 1636 the government resolved by Order of the King in Council to prohibit counterfeit jewels, pearls, chains, pendants and false stones upon consideration of the great quantities of money exported to buy them. The order also provided that

> no person, or persons, of what estate, degree or qualitie soever do presume to wear, or use upon their persons or apparell, or to buy, sell, exchange or utter any counterfeit Jewels, Pearls, pendants, Chaines, or false stones whatsoever . . . Upon paine as well of forfeiture and losse of the same, as also of incurring His Majesties high displeasure.[120]

False pearls were imported from France,[121] and an excellent turquoise paste from Venice,[122] where in 1645 John Evelyn saw examples of the pastes made to 'emulate the best diamonds, Rubies etc.'[123]

From the Commonwealth onwards, there was a proliferation of what Samuel Butler called those 'paltry counterfeit French stones' and 'false St Martin's beads',[124] for, despite the efforts of the City authorities, the production of counterfeit plate and jewellery within the Liberty of St Martin le Grand continued. Glass coloured to imitate precious and semi-precious stones was sold by the pound.[125] Thomas Nicols described how imitation pearls were made in 1652:

> There are factitious jewels made of double glasse which being set in gold, jewellers cannot discern from *Pearl*, except they take them out. Some will adulterate them with the powder of the shell of the *Margarite*; and others with chalk covered over with leaves of silver, and then anointed with the white of an egg. Some adulterate them with the powder of *Margarites*, mixt with the white of an egge, and dried, and then polished, but these will easily be discovered from the true by the weight and colour.[126]

The English edition of François Haudicquer de Blancourt's book on artificial gems and pearls, published in 1699, claimed that his formulae were superior to all others.

Almost every dealer stocked imitations. The volume of imports from Venice,[127] Holland and Germany[128] was considerable. In 1654 Francis Cole owned six gold rings with counterfeit stones,[129] and there were three pairs of false pendants, a pair of false stone bracelets, three pairs of false stone buckles and pieces of amethyst and opal paste in the stock of John Keech in 1680.[130] Lancelot Baker had twelve pairs of false earrings set in gold and silver valued at £3 in 1701.[131]

In 1677 trinkets of this kind were given to Indian tribal chiefs in Virginia; Lord Arlington ordered 'a necklace and a pair of braceletts for the Queen of Pamunkey of false stones' and 'four small crowns or coronets of thinne silver plate gilt and adorned with false stones of various colours with this inscription "A Carolo secundo Magnae Britanniae Reg."'[132]

Although some, like Sir Feeble Fainwou'd in Aphra Behn's play, *The Chance; or, An Alderman's Bargain* (1687), could tell his future bride, on giving her a box of jewels, to remove

> this St. *Martin's* Trumpery, these Play-house Glass Baubles, this Necklace, and these Pendants, and all this false Ware; ods bobs, I'll have no Counterfeit Geer about thee, not I. See – these are right as the Blushes on thy Cheeks, and these as true as my heart.[133]

Others of good birth had no such concern. There was a 'false gioell with eight stones' owned by Lady Wrottesley in 1692,[134] and even the Duchess of Marlborough had several. Not all of the rubies in her diamond and ruby parure were genuine; pendants of green and blue glass hung from her girandole earrings instead of emeralds and sapphires, while some of her pearls were French imitations mixed with diamonds.[135]

Speculation on whether jewels were genuine or not was always a subject for gossip. The 'Journal of a Rich Maiden Lady of good fortune' published in *The Spectator* noted: 'Found Mrs. *Spitely* at home. Conversation: Mrs. *Brilliant's* Necklace – false Stones'.[136] Widespread as the custom was, no one wanted it to be thought that her jewels were not genuine and worth a fortune, as Lady Lovetoy declared in *The Ladies' Visiting Day*: 'I shou'd be as much asham'd to have anything about that *I* cou'd not say was right *French*, right *Mechlin* or right *Indian* as *I* shou'd to wear false Diamonds, or false Teeth.'[137]

HARDSTONES AND ROCK CRYSTAL

Hardstones, besides being worked in relief and intaglio to set in rings, were also made into beads for bracelets and necklaces. They appealed, not only for their aesthetic qualities, but also on account of their amuletic properties (see below, pp. 195–6). Robert Boyle wore

> a Ring a small Sardonix that was once a great Princes, wherein there are three Portions one within another, the uppermost, Black, the middlemost of a kind of Chesnut colour, the other of a Blew; almost like a Turquois, each of which proportions is exactly of a fine Oval figure, and each of the two uttermost is throughout of a very uniform Breadth as well as colour.[138]

– a combination of phenomena which obviously delighted and intrigued him. Moss agates, with inclusions forming trees, landscapes and even human profiles, were also sought after and set to advantage in bracelet clasps and rings.[139]

On account of its hardness and transparency, rock crystal was faceted and set in

63 The Avon Gorge and Bristol Hotwells, where 'Bristow' crystals were mined. Drawing, English School, *c.* 1750.

memorial jewellery and miniature cases to protect the contents. The London jewellers, like John Austen in 1670 and Hector Moore in 1696, had a few crystal lockets and pendants in stock.[140] It could be obtained from Cornwall and from near to the hot well at the foot of St Vincent's rock outside Bristol[141] (Plate 63). According to Celia Fiennes, these 'Bristow diamonds' were

> very bright and sparkling in their native rudeness and have a great lustre and are pointed and like diamond cutting – a piece from the rock appeared to me as a cluster of diamonds polished and irregularly cut. Some of these are hard and will endure the cutting and polishing by art so they make rings and earrings of them.[142]

PEARLS

Henry Hawkins, the author of *Partheneia Sacra* (1633) explained why pearls were so highly valued:

> If you would epitomize an ample estate, & put the same into a little *Compendium* with *Bias* to carrie your wealth about you, sel what you have, and put it into a *Pearl*. If you have anie suit in Court, it wil purchase greater friends, and procure you better preferments, then the best deserts . . . It . . . wil make you more place in a throng of people, of meer respect, then a rufling Whifler shal do with torch in hand.[143]

Each pearl was a jewel in itself, requiring no setting. They blended well with the skin, and so looked best when worn in the ears or in bracelets and necklaces. Pear pearls were favoured for the ears, and the roundest, whitest pearls were carefully graduated for threading as necklaces. During the Commonwealth, pearls were in short supply. In 1659 William Dolben sent from London to Lady Grace Wynne a necklace for which John Lawrence demanded £52 10*s* and would not take a penny less for 'Pearle is now extraordinary deare and very scarce to come by . . . Lawrence hath but one rope more and that he prices at £150.'[144] Cosimo III, Grand Duke of Tuscany, observed during his visit to England in 1669 that of all jewels English women preferred pearls, 'which they wear in necklaces of very great price'.[145] The purchase of a pearl necklace was an important event, and Samuel Pepys describes the time he spent comparing prices and quality, and notes that his wife, too, was 'mighty busy' doing the same, until their choice was made: a necklace which family tradition believes to have survived On 17 December 1666 he noted with pride that she had gone to the theatre, 'having her necklace of pearl on'.[146]

Inventories, like that of John Keech's stock in 1680, differentiated between ragged, oriental and Scotch pearls.[147] Pearls were also found in Irish rivers, and in 1634 the Earl of Cork gave his daughter-in-law, Lady Dungarvan, a necklace of twenty-five large and one-hundred-and-fifteen smaller pearls, all from the Brandon river – with one very large round pearl fished just before her marriage.[148] Oriental pearls from the Persian Gulf were supplemented by others from South America, but there does not seem to have been any demand for the West Indian black pearls, as it was the whiteness which was esteemed above all. The very small seed pearl was also used and cost about 10*s* an ounce according to size and quality.[149]

JEWELLERS AND MERCHANTS

Relatively little attention has been paid to the history of the Goldsmiths' Company at this period for either plate or jewellery, owing in part to the fact that no records of the makers' marks survive until 1697. It is certain, however, that the specialisation already noted in the later Middle Ages and the Renaissance continued and grew. In 1671 Leonard Collard, a London goldsmith and jeweller, died owing money to his 'Ringmaker' (£1) and 'Ingraver' (£5 3*s* 4*d*).[150] The dependence on specialist craftsmen for the supply of jewellery is demonstrated by the fact that only a very few of the London inventories make mention of the tools of the trade. Apart from scales, such as the '3 pairs of Scales and 1 pile of weights' owned by Henry Weare in 1669,[151] only two seem to have been equipped to make items of jewellery; in 1709 Michael Wilson had mainly engraving tools.[152]

The kind of documentation available changes during this period. After the reign of Charles I, the civic authorities no longer kept detailed records of resident aliens, despite the large influx of Huguenot refugees after the Revocation of the Edict of Nantes, which reached a peak in the 1680s.[153] From 1662 the Court of Orphans kept detailed inventories of the parents' goods, including their stock-in-trade and tools, and these provide a very complete picture of the jewellery trade in London in the last part of the period.[154] The stray references in the State Papers Domestic to the purchase of jewels by the king can also be supplemented by the Jewel House Warrant Books for the suppliers of regalia, order insignia and diplomatic presents.[155]

James Heriot, who had worked for Charles I before his accession, continued to supply him with jewels, and Jan van Lore provided rings and other jewellery for Henrietta Maria to give away when she left France in 1625.[156] William Ward, Christopher Favell, William Rogers and John Acton supplied diplomatic and other jewels to the Caroline court.[157] Although the names of many of the London jewellers and makers of rings were recorded in a petition of 1628, little is known about them.[158]

The 1635 Return of Aliens in London included thirty-one jewellers, mainly of Dutch or French extraction, but there were also Walloons, Germans and one Pole.[159] As in the late sixteenth century, many had been resident for long periods; some worked for English masters, and not all – like the Frenchman who mounted some seals for Dorothy Osborne – satisfied their clients.[160] Quite apart from the French origin of the queen, the growing prestige of the French court would have ensured the influence of French jewellers, and the names of those patronised by Charles I and his queen are known, among them François Dujardin, Jean Vaulier, the Muscardets, and Jacques

Duart, appointed the king's jeweller in 1636.[161] The London Port Books show that large quantities of jewels, pearls and precious stones, beads and buttons were being brought into the country for the trade.[162] Travellers also took advantage of being in Paris to purchase jewels at first hand.[163]

During the Commonwealth, state patronage continued, albeit on a diminished scale, and portrait jewels of the Protector were commissioned from George Alkington and Thomas Simon.[164] Medals were also presented to General Fairfax and the Earl of Leven, made by Francis Allan,[165] while foreign merchants like Antony Poretch or John Almann supplied jewels.[166]

William Gumbleton, who had petitioned Parliament for permission to do business in 1650, established an aristocratic clientèle – the Earl of Rutland and Christian, Countess of Devonshire, among them.[167] At the Restoration he worked for the court, enamelling some of the regalia and lending stones to be set in them for the coronation, selling the king a ruby and diamond heart ring for £2,220 in 1661 and more jewels for the queen in 1662.[168] He also supplied the Duke of Monmouth's Garter insignia, and jewels for diplomatic presents.[169] His success was resented by Francis and John Simpson, who claimed that Gumbleton, a former Oxford ribbon-seller, had incited the royalist army to mutiny and was undeserving of royal patronage whereas they had always supported the king, and had had property worth £20,000 plundered and sequestrated.[170]

The Restoration saw the rapid rise of the banking system in London, and several of the major suppliers of jewellery to the court were primarily bankers and not working goldsmiths. One of the most successful was Sir Robert Vyner (1631–88), who supplied the major items – crown, sceptre and orb – for the coronation, and the new Garter insignia for the king. His wife, Mary, with whom he was painted, together with their children, by J. M. Wright in the garden of his country house, Swakeleys, in Middlesex, was a great heiress; after a visit to Vyner, Pepys wrote that 'now he lives no man in England in greater plenty, and commands both King and Council with his Creditt he gives them'.[171] This led to Vyner's eventual ruin when the government stopped payment of the loans made to them in 1672. Another casualty was Edward Backwell, who was obliged to raise money by a sale held on 18 January 1673 'at Widow Kemp's Coffee House, Exchange Alley at 2 in the afternoon in small lots numbers from 1–100 for which he will take in payment any bonds bills and notes with interest due upon the same'.[172]

Charles II also patronised foreign artists and craftsmen. Abraham Walkhert, who had served him in exile, petitioned for the office of jeweller in 1660, and Jasper Duart asked for the place formerly held by his brother, Jacques.[173] Isaac le Gouch (1628–85), great-nephew of Stephen who had been jeweller to the first Duke of Buckingham, was appointed to succeed the Simpson brothers. He had come to England in 1655, supplied jewels worth over £9000 for Catherine of Braganza, and in 1667 was given the right to make the medals and other jewels for diplomatic gifts. Delays in payment caused him financial difficulties and once he refused to deliver a diamond miniature case, to be given to Admiral van Tromp, until paid in cash.[174] The most celebrated of the foreign jewellers was Sir John Chardin (1643–1713), who settled here in 1681, having travelled widely in the Orient, and was given an appointment to Charles II.[175]

James II's principal jeweller was Christopher Rosse, who valued Prince Rupert's jewels which were sold by lottery in 1683.[176] Richard Beauvoir, of the Silver Ball in Pall Mall, supplied Mary II.[177] The ledgers of the great banker, Sir Francis Child, record items supplied to William III, his queen, and his sister-in-law, the Princess Anne.[178] The princess bought a diamond ring costing £170 to give to the Duchess of Marlborough.[179]

The same jewellers were patronised by the aristocracy. Gumbleton, who supplied jewels to Christian, Countess of Devonshire, from 1655, and the Earl of Rutland in 1658,[180] also sold a 'fasset diamond ring' (£625), a great table ruby (£250), and a pair of diamond ear-rings, each with only one great diamond (£1120), to the Countess of Lauderdale shortly before she left to live in Paris.[181] According to the Count de Grammont: 'with regard to more solid presents, such as earrings, diamonds, brilliants, and bright guineas, all this was to be met with of the best sort in London, and the ladies were as well pleased with them as if they had been brought from abroad'.[182] The range available in the jewellers' shops in London is seen in the Orphans' inventories, ranging from diamond and gem-set jewels to pastes and less expensive stones and beads.[183] Like the king, the great ladies patronised not one but several jewellers: Christian, Countess of Devonshire, bought gem-stones and pearls not only from Gumbleton but also from five others,[184] while the Countess of Lauderdale dealt with five.[185] That the London jewellers dominated the trade cannot be doubted and references to provincial men, like the Oxford jeweller from whom the Countess of Lauderdale had purchased a ring, are rare. Two Bury St Edmunds inventories, for a Mr Tylor in 1664 and Isaac Hurst in 1710, list only coral and pearl necklaces, gold rings and buttons.[186]

MOTIFS

The Cheapside Hoard offers a conspectus of the motifs used in English jewellery in the first half of the seventeenth century. Except for the engraved gems, clasical themes are absent, apart from an enamelled socket in the shape of a caduceus.[187] Another socket, like a tulip, belongs to the large group of floral and foliate designs enamelled on the backs of brooches and pendants (albeit in the stylised pea-pod form) or wrought into chains of star-like flowers, roses and daisies, interspersed with green leaves.[188] Equally naturalistic are the bunches of grapes carved from amethysts and emeralds[189] (Plate 64). A bodkin with a diamond and ruby head like a shepherd's crook strikes a pastoral note, and there is a lively little salamander or lizard.[190]

64 Bunches of grapes carved from emeralds and amethysts. *c.* 1640. Museum of London, from the Cheapside Hoard.

Knots appear in some of the chains, and in a ruby and diamond bow for the breast.[191] These breast knots are perhaps one of the most characteristic jewels of the period and, towards the end of the century, were hung with pendant drops.[192] Knots were also used as links between the top cluster and triple drops of girandole earrings; the Duchess of Marlborough owned several pairs of this design.[193]

The clusters worn by ladies in the portraits by Van Dyck and Lely are exemplified in the Cheapside Hoard by a rosette of six foiled rose-cut amethysts and seven diamonds.[194] In the ledgers of Sir Francis Child, they are called roses, and smaller versions were set in rings.[195] Other brooches and pendants used geometric designs – ovals, squares and circles – and large lozenge-shaped jewels were worn at the neck of the dress by Lady Arundell and her sister-in-law, the Hon. Henry Arundell's wife, in portraits by J. M. Wright dating from the 1660s.[196]

The moonstone cameo of a cherub in the Cheapside Hoard[197] introduces a motif interpreted on a grander scale in gold and precious stones. Small diamond-breasted cherubs in sets clasp the sleeves and bodices in portraits of both Queen Henrietta Maria and the Countess of Cleveland.[198] Larger versions were worn at the neckline. An elaborate brooch with a cherub, the head crowned by a large gem and a pear pearl pendant, was worn by Mary Villiers, Duchess of Richmond;[199] another, with a slightly different design, was pinned to the edges of the lace collar in the portrait of Mrs Richard Lucy at Charlecote (Plate 65).

65 Mrs Richard Lucy with her lace collar pinned with a cherub brooch over a ribbon bow-knot. Portrait, *c.* 1630. Charlecote, National Trust.

The hardstone hearts in the hoard have their counterparts in the inventories, like that of 1632 for Lady Anne Hamilton, which mentions 'a red blood stone set in gold, in the form of a heart'.[200] The Burghley Schedule of 1690 has three heart jewels: one with two diamonds set in black enamel, a heart-shaped garnet in white enamel, and another made of a ruby with a coronet over it.[201] In 1695 Lady Mary Kemys bequeathed two such jewels: 'a little heart with a pearle in it' and another 'with a blew turkey stone'.[202]

More elaborate was the jewel in the Child ledgers, 'containing 9 Faucet Diamonds or thereabouts the middle stone Heart Fashion'.[203] A silver heart-shaped locket with a Cupid with his quiver embossed on the cover and the inscription NOE HEART MORE TRUE THEN MINE TO YOU is in the Victoria and Albert Museum[204] (Plate 66). Massinger's *The Roman Actor* alludes to the power of Cupid's weapons:

And from thy never emptied quiver take
A golden arrow to transfix her heart
And force her love like me.[205]

A wounded heart, transfixed by two arrows, with an anchor below, flanked by tulips, formerly in the Hay collection of Duns Castle, Berwickshire, illustrates this type (Plate XVI). It is inscribed on the back, round the heart, THO I BE CROST MY HOPE IS SURE THO I BE HURT A CROWNE I BEARE.[206]

66 Silver heart locket embossed with Cupid taking aim with his bow and inscribed NOE HEART MORE TRUE THEN MINE TO YOU. Maker's mark: RA. Victoria and Albert Museum.

In a long poem, *The Lover's Watch*, translated by Mrs Aphra Behn from Baltazar de Bonnecorse's French original in 1686, the watch is minutely described: the dial with a Cupid, arrow in hand; the case made heart-shaped and adorned with amorous symbols and sets of initials for the lovers and their extreme, reciprocal, constant and secret love; the joined hands on the clasps standing for inviolable faith.[207] A list of lovers' tokens, to relieve the distress of separation, appeared in *The Spectator* in 1711.[208]

Apart from sealstones, classical themes remain rare in jewellery design at the end of the period. However, tableaux of the Rape of Europa and of Diana and Actaeon, mounted in slides of *c.* 1700, provide exceptions to the rule.[209]

Apart from their use in sentimental and mourning jewels, ciphers were also used on seals and – engraved, enamelled or gem-set – on snuff boxes, watch cases and miniature cases; they could also be worked into links for chains. Their increasing importance is attested by their inclusion in pattern books.[210]

Pattern books and sheets of engraved designs were being published in increasing numbers during this period, although few copies survive as most were worn out by use or discarded when new fashions came in. Several were by French artists: Balthasar Moncornet, Giles Legaré and Daniel Mignot gave patterns for pendants, sprays, breast knots, chains or necklaces and rings. German designs were also represented: Friedrich Jacob Morison and J. B. Herbst, whose book, published in 1710, gave variants on the favourite classical motifs of acanthus and scrollwork.[211] Acanthus also played an important role in the breast jewels of Marcus Gunter (†1733), the Leicester-born goldsmith who made his living designing jewels on the continent from the 1680s, as well as in London. His figurative bodkins are topped with busts of blackamoors exotically turbanned and habited with jewels.[212] (Fig. 16).

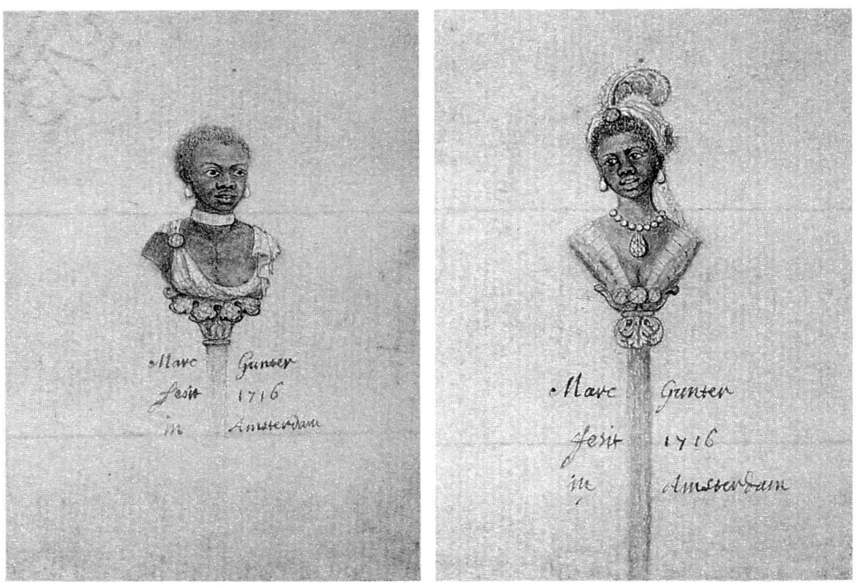

Fig. 16 Designs by Marcus Gunter for bodkins with blackmoors' heads: Amsterdam, 1716. Röhsska Konstlöjdmuseet, Goteborg.

TECHNIQUES

The change of style from wrought gold jewels and chains to designs in which the gemstones played the major role was accompanied by new techniques for their setting. Whereas previously stones were almost always set in colletts, the new claw setting allowed for a greater freedom in design. Closely packed together in clusters or lines, the stones, afire with reflected light, themselves formed the patterns, seemingly without support. As the role of metal was reduced, so too was that of enamel, which was increasingly relegated to the back of settings. Steele, in an article in *The Tatler*, discussed in 1710 the way to show off diamonds:

When artists would expose their diamonds to an advantage, they usually set them to show in little cases of black velvet. By this means the jewels appear in their true and genuine lustre, while there is no colour that can infect their brightness, or give a false cast to the water.[213]

In accordance with this principle, diamonds and crystals were often set in silver soldered to the gold of the main jewel, in the same way as platinum is now used, and in another article the list of 'Lady Farthingale's' stolen goods included: 'a crochet of 122 diamonds, set strong and deep in silver, with a rump jewel after the same fashion'.[214] From the mid seventeenth century, the edges of both gold and silver setting were often engrailed – a custom which lasted into the early eighteenth century.

Gold and silver-gilt filigree of an Eastern inspiration was introduced from Holland for certain types of jewellery: buttons, mirrors, watch cases and miniature cases.[215] This was easily damaged in use and few pieces have survived; the vases, scent-bottle cases, candlesticks and baskets wrought in feathery scrolls, birds, tulips and daisies in the Marquess of Exeter's collection are rare examples of the technique.[216] The cover for the watch in Aphra Behn's translation, *The Lover's Watch*, is described as 'like those delicate ones of Filligrin Work which do not hinder the Sight from taking a View of all within'.[217]

A new technique of painting in enamels was developed by the Toutin family at Blois, and introduced from France into England by Jean Petit and Jacques Bordier during the reign of Charles I. Using a wide range of vitrifiable colours on a white or tinted ground, the depiction of botanical ornament, still-life subjects, narrative scenes or portraits, unrestrained by the confines of the older cloisons, could be used to decorate the backs of jewels, and for snuff boxes, miniature cases and watch cases.[218]

ENGRAVED GEMS

Mirtilla, in Massinger's play, *The Guardian* (1655), admired the art of the cutter who engraved the Rape of Proserpine 'to the life' on a small cameo offered as a token for a lover to wear in his hat.[219] Not all engraved gems in the seventeenth-century shops were new; those in the Cheapside Hoard comprised Roman, Byzantine, medieval, Renaissance and later hardstones and pastes, some in enamelled gold settings.[220] A receipt for 'one picture of a Cleopatria sett in Gold, one red stone sett round with sixteene Diamonds with a large pearle hanging to it' in 1677 shows how valued such stones were.[221] Typical of the stock of the London jewellers after the Restoration was that of John Keech in 1680, many of the stones being set in rings, though not all were engraved:

73 Cornelian rings valued at 2*s*. 6*d*. a peece . . . One hundred & fifty Cornelian stones . . . one Sardones sett in gold with a pearle 001:15:0 [i.e., £1 15*s*] . . . 6 Cornelian head rings . . . 18 seal rings a greate onix engraven . . . one Cornelian head att 2*s*. 6*d*. a peece . . . 4 Cornelian sealess sett in gold enamelled . . . one onix engraven 000:05:0 . . . 3 large Cornelian stones engraven 000:12:6 a Jacinth engraven with a head 000:15:0 . . . 7 agatt heads in releife 000:07:0.[222]

The small number of stones described as cameos is paralleled in the Cheapside Hoard, where there are two rings (an onyx St George and an opal frog). Two of the signets in the hoard had Roman nicolo intaglios – a hippocamp, and a trussed chicken, fish and knife. Several of the loose post-classical ringstones were engraved with the imperial eagle or the heads of the Roman emperors Hadrian and Titus.[223] Lady Anne Hamilton's signet 'with a great bloodstaine with a face sunk into it' may have had just such an imperial portrait.[224] The heads of illustrious Englishmen – Shakespeare, Milton, Newton, and Archbishop Sancroft and the other bishops imprisoned by James II in 1688 for refusing to have the Declaration of Indulgence read – could all be had by their admirers for sealing letters.[225]

Some royal signets were made from gem-stones: Charles I commissioned a diamond with the arms and cipher of his queen, Henrietta Maria, in 1628. This gem disappeared after the Civil War; it was seen in Persia by J. B. Tavernier, bought by a Dutchman and passed to the French royal collection. It was sold again after 1789, and in 1887 it was presented to Queen Victoria for her Golden Jubilee by the antiquary C. D. Fortnum. Ten years later he was able to present her with another historic royal signet, a sapphire with the arms of Mary II in its original setting, with red roses on the shoulders [226] (Plate 67).

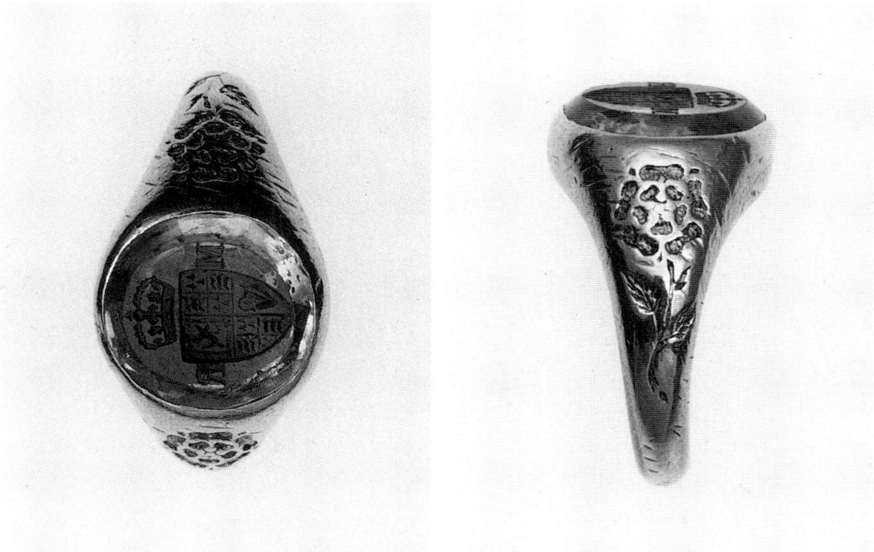

67 Gold signet set with a sapphire engraved with the Royal Arms of England beneath a crown and between the initials MR; shoulders with Tudor rose sprig. The signet of Queen Mary II. *c*. 1690. Collection of H.M. Queen Elizabeth II.

Jeremiah Marlow of Lombard Street advertised in 1677: 'You may have coats of arms, cyphers and other devices curiously engraved on any sort of stone.'[227] Such specialists were increasingly supplying the English market, despite the prestige of Italy. Sir Ralph Verney wrote home from Florence in 1651 that 'one Col. Atkins in Florence, at Mr. Amies the English House, hathe more varietyes of stones with seales than all Italy besides'.[228] There had been a decline in the art of gem-engraving in England after the death of Queen Elizabeth in 1603, especially in portraiture, but it was revived in the reign of Charles I. In 1625 the French medallist, Nicholas Briot (1579–1646), came to London and in 1633 was appointed chief engraver to the Mint. While no gems can be attributed to him, his influence was transmitted through his pupils. Thomas Rawlins (1620–70) and Thomas Simon (1618–65), who were both distinguished medallists and gem-cutters.[229] They began working under Charles I but joined opposite camps in the Civil War. Rawlins went to Oxford with the king in 1642 and, on the death of Briot, was appointed royal medallist and engraver. His cameo portraits of the king are closely related to those on his medals. Two ringstones were engraved in the years immediately before the execution of the king in 1649, both based on the portraits by Van Dyck. One is now reset in the Devonshire parure, but the other is still in the original enamelled gold ring.[230] A larger portrait, using the *cameo relievo* technique favoured in the sixteenth century, now in the Hermitage, is associated with the posthumous medals and badges designed by Rawlins after 1649. Charles I is shown in profile, wearing cuirass and cloak, a laurel wreath round his head, and with an expression of suffering.[231] A cornelian cameo of this type is in the collection of the Duke of St Albans, and is said to have belonged to Bishop Juxon[232] (Plate XVII).

Rawlins had a difficult time during the Commonwealth, but was reinstated as Chief Engraver to the Mint after the Restoration. He was, perhaps, responsible for two cameo portraits of Charles II which have the same aloof, impersonal character as his medals. In 1653 the poet Richard Flecknoe described Rawlins as a sculptor who worked in gold and precious stones, and another contemporary, John Evelyn, said that he was 'very good in cameos and intaglios'.[233]

Thomas Simon was also a gem-engraver of outstanding talent.[234] His hardstone portraits of Oliver Cromwell were based on models made by his brother, Abraham, but he was also influenced by the miniatures of Samuel Cooper. In order to emphasise Cromwell's military authority, he first portrayed him in armour after the Dunbar Victory medal of 1650, and a series of cameos with idealised features has been tentatively attributed to him.[235] In a large onyx cameo in the Cromwell Museum at Huntingdon, the Protector is shown, not as a Roman emperor, but in contemporary dress, armour, sword and cloak, as in the Inauguration medal of 1654. The gold mount is inscribed on the back OLIVER CROMWELL ANG : SCO : FRAN : ET HIB : PRO : AN : DOM : 1657 with the crowned arms of the Commonwealth. It has an open border of oval collets with engrailed edges set with table-cut pastes (Plate 68). In John Michael

68 Pendant set with onxy cameo portrait of Oliver Cromwell, the frame set with table-cut pastes. Back: inscribed OLIVER CROMWELL ANG : SCO : FRAN : ET HIB : PRO : AN : DOM : 1657 around crowned coat-of-arms of the Commonwealth. Cromwell Museum, Huntingdon.

Wright's 1658 portrait, Mrs Claypole, Cromwell's daughter, holds a gold chain with a jewelled pendant set with a cameo of her father, his wreathed head in profile to the left[236] (Plates 69 and 70). Simon engraved other portraits of Cromwell for rings, mainly small intaglios, and also portraits of other political and literary figures of the time, including the printer John Lillburne, John Milton, a close friend called Gifford (possibly George Gifford the engraver) and even Archbishop Laud. Although deprived of his office as Chief Engraver at the Restoration, he remained at the Mint, and two sapphire seals (for Charles II and Lord Clarendon) and the cornelian head of a god have been attributed to him.[237]

The Antwerp artist Jan Roettiers, whose father had helped Charles II during his exile, was invited to England in 1661, and although he was a less imaginative artist, he made a lasting impression on English medallic art until the end of the century. A sapphire seal with busts of Mars and Venus, and another with a portrait of the king derived from one of his medals, are both attributed to Roettiers.[238] Other gem-engravers known to have been working in London as independent craftsmen were the Englishman, Henry Harris,[239] and Christian Reisen (1637–97), who came from Trondheim and, after two years in Aberdeen, moved to the south in 1666.[240]

69 Mrs Claypole, daughter of Oliver Cromwell. Portrait by J. M. Wright, 1658. National Portrait Gallery.

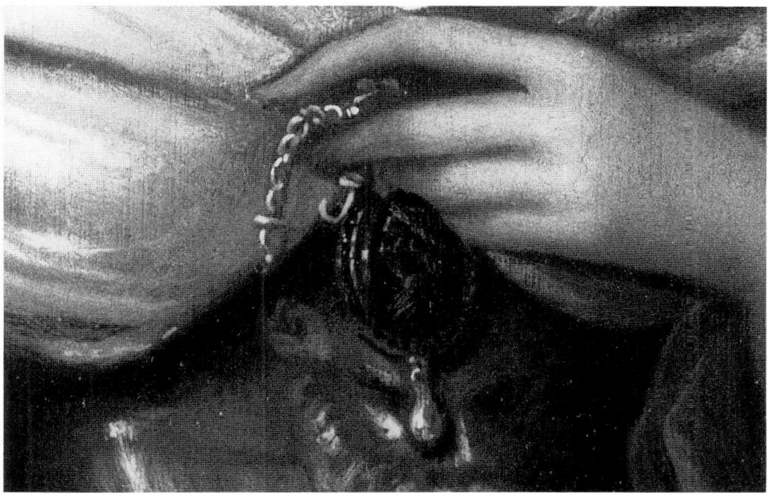

70 Detail of 69, showing cameo head of Oliver Cromwell set in pendant.

In the second half of the seventeenth century there were changes in the way intaglios were used. Increasingly they were set in wrought gold or silver mounts, enamelled and enriched with gem-stones, which served as handles during use, and hung with the watch by suspension loops. The 'seal of Caesar's head in olive sett in gold enamelled with green transparent' in the 1690 Burghley Schedule was of this kind.[241] Another 'cornelian seal set, ye bottom of a Crown with a lion att the top in gold' in the Marlborough inventory may have been of the same type.[242] Flat seals could be engraved on both sides, and triangular stone or metal seals were engraved with shield, crest and cipher on the different faces – a type perhaps alluded to in the description of 'A prettie seale containing three one within another, of gold' in the Eglinton inventory of 1652.[243] There were sculptural mounts, too. One with the agate handle carved as a blackamoor, recorded in 1691, is comparable with a surviving example from the Fountaine collection.[244]

Not all intaglios were used as seals. Dorothy Osborne wrote to Sir William Temple that the 'fair Sacharissa' (Dorothy, Countess of Sunderland) wore chains with as many as twenty engraved gems strung on a ribbon, 'like the nuts boys play withal . . . the oddest and oldest are the most prized'.[245] Lady Jeane Wemyss wore a bloodstone intaglio mounted in gold hanging from a small gold chain, but it is not clear whether she wore it round her neck, at her wrist or at the waist.[246] There is a locket set with bloodstone cameos of Christ and the Virgin at the front and back in the Cheapside Hoard. A watch case (now in the British Museum), given by James II to his daughter, Catherine, Countess of Anglesey, later Duchess of Buckingham, is set with the wreathed cameo head of a Roman emperor in the centre[247] (Plate 71).

71 Watch case set with cornelian centred on the cameo head of a Roman emperor. Given by James II to his daughter, the Countess of Anglesey. British Museum.

INSIGNIA OF THE ORDERS

In England the Order of the Garter retained its pre-eminence, and the insignia made for the king and for foreign princes were magnificently jewelled. The knights also continued the custom of having duplicate insignia made for themselves. The high standard of craftsmanship is exemplified by the complete set – Garter, Collar (often referred to in the contemporary inventories as a collar of Esses) and Great and Lesser Georges – made in 1629, the year before he died, for William Compton, created Earl of Northampton. Now in the British Museum, it is the earliest complete set of the insignia in Britain. The Garter has the buckle plate and buckle enamelled with pea-pod ornament and is set with diamonds – rose-cut in petal-shaped collets, and table-cut in square collets. The two Georges are both jewelled; the Great George, in the sixteenth-century style, is richly studded with diamonds of various cuts, including two large clusters on the horse trappings. The Collar follows the usual pattern and style of workmanship, plain gold and enamel, but has only twenty-five roses.[248]

During the Civil War and its aftermath, the richly jewelled duplicate insignia had sometimes to be sacrificed. Lord Ormonde, for example, sold a diamond George, his last remaining jewel, to finance the journey of the Duke of York from France to meet his elder brother in Cologne.[249]

There were two changes in the insignia in this period. Charles I introduced the breast decoration, the Star with the shield of St George encircled by a Garter, to be worn on the mantle and also on the cloak or coat.[250] From 1682 the Lesser George, 'for the more Conveniency of Riding or Action' according to Ashmole, was worn on a blue ribbon over the left shoulder and under the right arm.[251] In this, the example of the French Order of the Holy Ghost may be discerned. An earlier example of the Lesser George worn with the ribbon as a sash is, however, seen on a miniature of Prince Henry by Isaac Oliver in the collection of H.M. The Queen.[252]

The history of the insignia used by Charles I is confused for, although Charles II tried to reassemble his father's collection after its dispersal, James II seems to have removed whatever had been recovered when he went into exile. He is said to have used Charles I's George at an investiture shortly after his exile in 1689.[253] Ashmole published an engraving of Garter insignia by Hollar which included a locket said to be the Lesser George of Charles I. It contained a miniature of Queen Henrietta Maria; the Garter was set with table-cut diamonds and the back enamelled with flowers[254] (Plate 72).

Immediately on landing at Dover on 15 May 1660, Charles II held a Chapter of the Order of the Garter at Canterbury, where he invested General Monk, later Duke of Albemarle, and Admiral Edward Montagu, later Earl of Sandwich, who had done the most to bring about his restoration.[255] Pepys was impressed by the 'rare George all of diamonds' which the Earl of Sandwich always wore.[256]

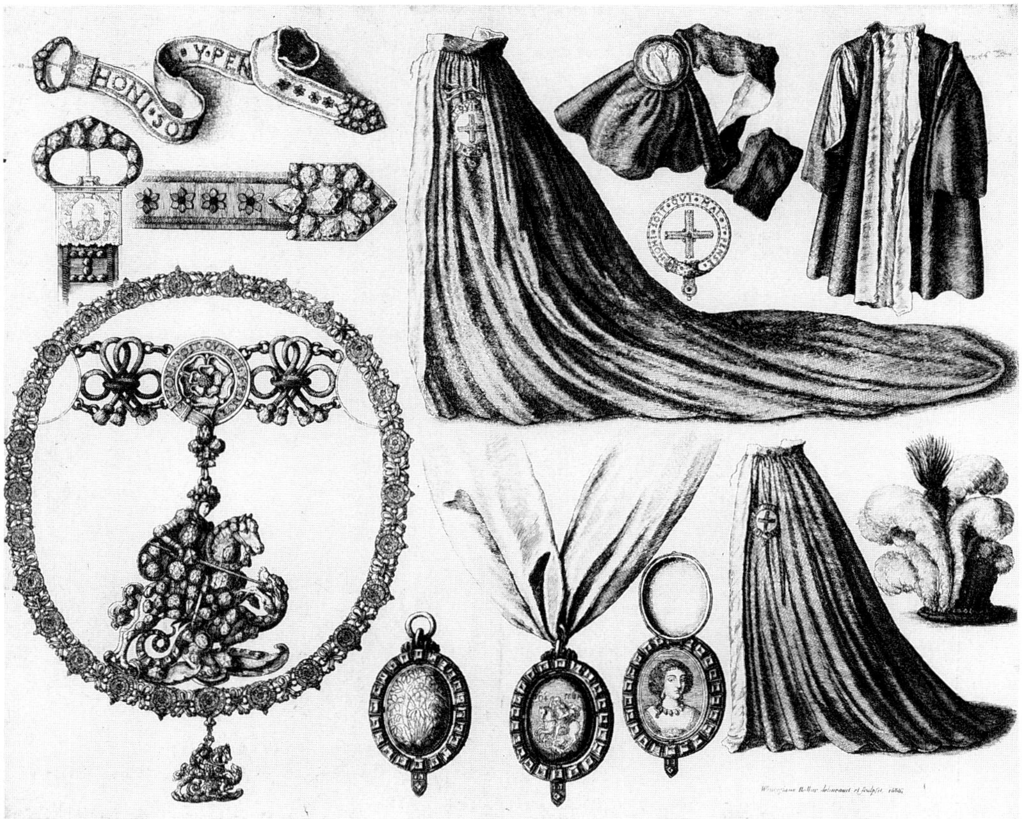

72 Garter insignia of King Charles I. Engraving by Wenceslas Hollar. 1666. British Museum.

The 1662 inventory of the king's insignia, drawn up by Lord Mansfield, the Keeper, shows the importance Charles II attached to his most venerable chivalric Order. Four Lesser Georges were set with cameos framed in diamonds, and there were others enamelled, one on both sides – described as 'very rare'. A Garter was set with eighteen large and two-hundred-and-twenty-two small diamonds; and his Great George was also set with diamonds.[257] A portrait of the king at Gray's Inn, London, shows him wearing a magnificent collar, perhaps that of 'massy gold' in the inventory, with a George enclosed in a diamond lozenge with a pear pearl drop (Plate 73). Likewise worthy of a king was the George which Queen Anne gave to the Duke of Marlborough, the front studded all over with diamonds and the whole hanging from a fleur-de-lis set with diamonds. George IV presented it to the Duke of Wellington and it remained at Apsley House until it was stolen in 1965.[258]

The Lesser George was one of the distinctive products of English glyptics from the late sixteenth century, and the special quality of these cameos was well described by Elias Ashmole:

exquisitely cut in Onix's and also in agats and therin such happy choice of the Stones that by joining thereto the Workmans skill in designing and laying out the Figures to express the History the natural tinctures of the Stones have fitted them with Colours for Flesh, Hair, and everything else even to admiration.[259]

Many of these miniature works of art have, fortunately, survived to show the quality of seventeenth-century English work in hardstones. There is a large group at Windsor, others in the British Museum, the Hermitage in St Petersburg, the Cabinet des Médailles in Paris and in private collections. Not only did the choice of stone vary – onyx, sardonyx, lapis lazuli and heliotrope are found – but there were also striking variations in the details of the composition. The saint may be bearded or clean-shaven; he may move to either right or left; the sword may be brandished at various angles; and the dragon be placed either under the horse's belly or at one side. The shield may bear a variety of crosses, not just the plain cross normally associated with the saint in English art, and the helmet may or may not be plumed. In the larger examples, and where the stone lent itself to the purpose, the edge could be carved with the Garter and its

73 King Charles II wearing Garter collar and George. Portrait detail, Gray's Inn.

74 Onyx cameo Lesser George framed in buckled Garter with motto.
Back: enamelled relief of St George amidst flowers.
Collection of H.M. Queen Elizabeth II.

motto.[260] More usually, the stone was set in an enamelled gold Garter or a border of precious stones. A fine example of a Lesser George framed by large red stones, perhaps garnets, hanging from a broad blue ribbon round the neck, is to be seen in a Van Dyck portrait of Philip Herbert, Earl of Montgomery and Lord Chamberlain to Charles I[261]. The treatment of the back also varied; some had the George repeated in silver-gilt reliefs, enamelled with flowers.[262] An example associated with Charles II at Windsor is framed in an enamel border with the George repeated on the back in relief amidst a beautiful bouquet of flowers[263] (Plate 74). Another has a silver-gilt portrait of Charles I on the back,[264] while Charles II had one 'with an Oneix on the one side and an Aggot on the other sett on both sides with Dyamonds fifty two in all'.[265] The subject of the cameo at the back is not stated but it could be another figure of the saint, as on a Lesser George owned by the Duke of Buccleuch[266] (Plate XIX), or an allegorical scene like those on two in the Hermitage. One of these represents the Victory of Christianity, personified by the princess rescued by St George, and the other has Diana escorted by a flying putto with a scroll below reading VIS CEDIT AMORI[267]. A third cameo in this allegorical group alludes to the Revolution of 1688 when William III established himself on the throne of his father-in-law, James II.[268] In the George on the other side the saint wears the Garter on his leg, a rare detail. The use of cameos for the Lesser George continued into the reign of Queen Anne, and John Evelyn described that worn by the Duke of Marlborough in 1705 as having 'a most rich George in Sardonix set with Diamond of an inestimable value' (Fig. 17).[269]

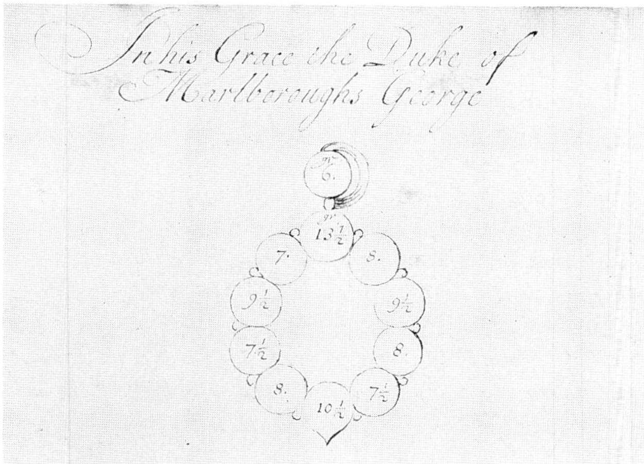

Fig. 17 Diamond frame to the Duke of Marlborough's George: 1716. British Library.

The hiatus of the Commonwealth meant that many sets of insignia needed to be replaced at the Restoration. Apart from the jewellers who supplied the Lord Chamberlain's officials at the Jewel House with the insignia needed for investitures, other jewellers had Georges in their stock, as did John Keech and Richard Beauvoir.[270] In 1663 William Gumbleton was paid £500 for a diamond George and Garter to be given to the Duke of Monmouth[271] – perhaps the same jewel that, according to Evelyn, betrayed Monmouth's identity in Dorset after his defeat at Sedgemoor: 'his beard being grown so long, and so grey as hardly to be known, had not his George discovered him, which was found in his Pocket'. This George, according to family tradition, is the one still in the ownership of his descendant, the Duke of Buccleuch and Queensberry[272] (Plate XX).

In 1687 James II established the Order of the Thistle, under the patronage of St Andrew, as the equal of the Order of the Garter in Scotland. The twelve knights had a collar of thistles and rue, with a pendant of the patron saint enamelled, within a frame inscribed with the Scottish royal motto, NEMO ME IMPUNE LACESSIT. It ceased to be given under William III, but was revived in 1703 by Queen Anne.[273] Although some sixteenth-century depictions of the Scottish royal arms have a collar resembling that of the later Order about the shield, there does not seem to be any firm evidence for its being generally worn, or that any statutes for an Order existed.

Although Knights of the Bath had been created with the full late-medieval ceremonial by the English kings since 1399 at coronations and a few other occasions, it was not until 1603 that they were given a jewel to wear to denote this. The design commemorated the union of the two kingdoms by James I. It was worn round the neck suspended from a red ribbon, like the Lesser George. In 1626, when Charles I made his first creation of Knights of the Bath, the Earl Marshal ordered that they, and the survivors of the Jacobean creations, were 'continually to wear the ensign of that Order about their necks as a mark of honour'.[274] The last creation was at the coronation of Charles II; the custom lapsed until the creation of a new Order in the next century. A very few examples of the seventeenth-century insignia have survived, and it was shown in portraits; a few engravings depict some variants from the normal pattern.[275]

POLITICAL JEWELLERY

THE MONARCHY

Writing to Henry Oxinden in 1635, Sir Thomas Peyton made the comparison between 'the Diamond', which 'showes best when 'tis sett in gold', and a comely face, that 'looks sweeter when it stands by the king's picture, by whose secrett power the estimation is advanc't'.[276] Within a few years, the wearing of a royal portrait was not so much a sign of royal favour as of support for the king's cause. In 1642, on her return from Holland, Queen Henrietta Maria distributed inexpensive rings, lockets and slides with the royal cipher and portrait to those supporters who lent money, promising an honour or repayment once the monarchy was again firmly established.[277] One such ring, the bezel set with a miniature of the king and the shoulders with rose-cut diamonds and paste, was passed down, in its original presentation box, in the Gresley family of Drakelow in Derbyshire.[278] Others might wear the silver medallic portraits of the king and queen in a laurel frame made by Thomas Rawlins, hanging from a blue ribbon.[279] For the royalists, the execution of Charles I was a crime, and they never ceased to mourn him. Commemorative jewels of the royal martyr, with his portrait, cipher, palm branches, symbols of mortality and appropriate mottoes, appeared soon after his death and were also worn as badges of loyalty to his children.

Rings were particularly favoured for this purpose. The earliest bear the date 1648 (the year of his execution according to the Old Style calendar, which began the year on 25 March) and the cipher CR with a skull and cross-bones[280]. Many included miniatures, either painted or enamelled, set in oval or heart-shaped bezels under glass or, exceptionally, a flat picture diamond.[281] The more elaborate rings had this crowned and framed with rose-cut diamonds, the shoulders either chased or similarly set, while the hoop might be enamelled with a laurel wreath or motto. Among the latter we find: GLORIA VANITAS. EMIGRAVIT GLORIA ANGL[IAE] IA: THE 30, 1648; SIC TRANSIT GLORIA MUNDI; QUIS TEMPERAT A LACHRIMIS JA 30 1648; and PREPARED BEE TO FOLLOW ME.[282] The miniatures were usually copies of a melancholy version of a Van Dyck portrait on a celestial blue ground, and the back of the bezel was enamelled with the royal cipher and 1648. More cautious royalists concealed their miniatures in rings with locket bezels, the hinged lid set with a diamond or a non-political motif, such as a flower or the Four Cardinal Virtues, in enamel.[283] A more elaborate ring has a swivel bezel, set with a cornelian intaglio of the king on one side, and the back engraved with a sun in splendour on a pedestal, surmounted by a royal crown between two cherub's heads. The arcaded sides are filled with black enamel and the hoop, composed of six oval enamelled loops, has rose-cut diamonds between them.[284]

Immediately after the execution, those able to approach the corpse and scaffold dipped their handkerchiefs in the blood, and the block was cut up into splinters to make more relics – a scene included in a painting of the execution attributed to the Flemish painter Weesop.[285] Relics of hair and sand were also cherished, and in 1685 John Evelyn recorded hearing the Bishop of Bath and Wells telling Charles II 'of the sanatory effect of *K. Charles* his Majesties fathers blood, in healing one that was blind'.[286] Pendant reliquaries might be designed as books,[287] but more frequently hearts, like the red enamelled heart-shaped reliquary worn by Henrietta Maria's page, Ralph Creke.[288] Many were of plain silver, pierced with arrows, engraved with weeping eyes and royal or celestial crowns, and inscribed.[289] One has three mottoes: BE PREPARED TO FOLLOW ME on the front, LIVE AND DY IN LOYALTY on the back and I MOURN FOR MONARCHIE within.[290] More elaborate versions were made with gold foliage and set with rubies and diamonds.[291] The most important surviving example is a large gold and pearl heart-shaped locket enclosing a miniature with the skull and cross-bones below and a royal crown above, on hair and a piece of blood-stained linen. It hangs by three chains from a loop and is in the National Museum of Scotland. The style of the frame is old-fashioned for a mid-seventeenth-century jewel, and the threaded pearls laced round the circumference resemble those on the Penicuik jewel associated with Mary, Queen of Scots[292].

After the Restoration the date of the execution was observed as a day of national mourning; a special service was added to the 1662 Book of Common Prayer, and commemorative jewels continued to be worn. Multiple relics might be set in clusters under faceted crystal covers.[293] Miniatures framed in acanthus scrolls studded with rose diamonds are quite likely to have been worn by the Jacobites at the time of the accession crisis in 1714.[294]

As a boy, Charles II had been portrayed with his parents in a ring, and also with his father in slides and pendants worn by supporters[295] (Plate 75). His escape from capture after the Battle of Worcester by hiding in an oak tree at Boscobel House provided another theme for royalist jewellery and medals. The idea of creating a new decoration to reward the services of loyalists during the Civil War and Commonwealth was taken so far that the medal was designed and a list drawn up of the proposed members. It was not, however, proceeded with; 'it was thought proper to lay it aside, lest it might create heats and animosities, and open those wounds afresh, which at that time were thought prudent should be healed'.[296] This did not inhibit private commissions. A heart-shaped silver locket set with diamonds with a miniature of the oak tree on ivory and on the back the cipher and date C R 6 SEPT. 1650 belonged to the wife of Sir William Murray of Stanhope, a devoted supporter of Charles I.[297] A gold locket has the whole

75 Enamelled gold loyalist slide with double portrait of Charles I and Charles II. Back with botanical enamel. *c.* 1650. Victoria and Albert Museum.

scene on the back: Charles II and Major William Carlos hiding in the oak, while the Parliamentary soldiers ride under it. The front has the Carlos arms, and inside a long inscription tells the story and alludes to the public festivities after the Restoration, on the anniversary.

Renowned Carlos! Thow hast won the day
(Loyalty Lost) by helping Charles away,
From Kings-Blood-Thirsty-Rebels in a Night,
made black with Rage, of theives, & Hells dispight
Live! King-Loved Sowle thy fame by Euer Spoke
By all whilst England Beares a Royalle Oake.[298]

Rings, slides, medals and lockets with portraits and ciphers of Charles II were widely used during his reign, and mourning rings commemorated his death on 6 February 1685.[299] Another group of memorial jewels has the crowned ciphers of Charles and Catherine of Braganza and their hair; the queen may have had them made for those in her court after the king's death.[300]

The general air of foreboding which greeted the accession of James II was not shared by one loyal supporter, who had the following verses written on paper and set under the heart-shaped bezel of a mourning ring:

On the death of K. Charles the II
A greater Prince the Throne did never grace
Nor to a better left his Place:
Charles is reviv'd while Royal James does reign;
And all our loss well paid in such a gain.
Died Feb. 6 1684.[301]

Few would have shared these views at the time, and James's short, troubled reign produced few jewels to commemorate it. One given to his staunchest supporter, John Graham, whom he created Viscount Dundee in 1688, took the form of a ring. The locket bezel contains hair under a coronet with the initials VD, and on the hoop GREAT DUNDEE FOR GOD AND ME J. REX.[302]

Of the numerous portrait rings, slides and pendants commemorating William III and Mary II,[303] the most important are an enamelled miniature of the king and a locket with a relic. The former depicts William III in wig and armour, framed in black and white enamelled acanthus scrolls, set with rose-cut diamonds in collets with serrated edges, the whole surmounted by a royal crown.[304] The other, owned by the Walsingham family, was a locket 'in wch was enclosed a piece of King William's coat, wch was extracted out of a wound given by a comon bullet at ye battle of ye Boyne, wch Lord Coningsby got, &c., he being by his side at ye time'.[305]

Mourning jewellery was produced in large quantities on the death of Mary II, and when William III died some of the pieces were strongly political in tone. A memorial locket containing his hair surmounted by the royal cipher under a red canopy includes figures of Britannia and an angel, who points upwards to a celestial crown, exchanged for that of England which rests on a cushion, and has the inscription OB MAR 1702.[306] A long adulatory inscription adorned a slide: 'On ye death of K. WILLIAM III. Mourn Justice Liberty Religion Peace Lament your Royal Patron's sad Decease. Your brave Protector Peace, is now no more, whose greatness was all good, & kind his pow'r: Whilst widow'd Europe fills the Air with Cries Defenceless nations weep his obsequies. Ob. Mar . . .'[307]

PARLIAMENTARIAN AND OTHER

Jewels were presented by Parliament to Sir Thomas Fairfax and the Earl of Leven in acknowledgement of their outstanding military service during the Civil War; a deputation of Members of Parliament gave his jewel to Sir Thomas at Ottery St Mary in November 1645. Worn from a blue ribbon around his neck, it was made by Francis Allen at a cost of £800. It could have been designed for use as a watch case, having two convex covers, framed with diamonds, and enamelled inside and out. One scene showed Sir Thomas in armour on his chestnut mare before the Battle of Naseby, inscribed SIC RADIANT FIDELES and signed P B; the battle was shown on the back with the inscription NON NOBIS, and the House of Commons in session was also depicted.[308]

The Earl of Leven's jewel, also made by Allen, was presented to him in February 1646 before the departure of his army; it was similar to that given to Fairfax. It was

> made in the fashion of a Mary-gold conteyning one rose diamond one table diamond both very faire ones twelve lesser table diamonds and eight more of a lesser sort and thirty small diamonds and one pendant. On the backside of the jewel is drawn the general on horseback and the Army upon their marche with this inscription Donum Domus Co. Parl. Angliae An. Dom. 1646. On the other side of the cover is an emblem of the present union of the kingdoms of England and Scotland and within the jewel is represented the House of Commons sitting in Council.[309]

During the Commonwealth, jewels with the portrait of Oliver Cromwell were given: cameos, and miniatures by Samuel Cooper; after his death his relics were accorded, by a few Puritans, the kind of veneration the royalists had given to mementoes of Charles I. Cromwell's hair was worn in sleeve buttons.[310]

In 1688 seven bishops, including Archbishop Sancroft, refused to have James II's Declaration of Indulgence read. Sent to the Tower, they were acquitted at their trial amid popular rejoicing. Their portraits were widely disseminated in prints, and one supporter commissioned a cornelian intaglio of all their heads, the archbishop's in the middle.[311] In the following reign, the protest of John Lake, Bishop of Chichester, and Thomas White, Bishop of Peterborough, the two Non-juring bishops, was supported by a person who wore coloured engravings of their portraits under glass set in a pair of slides.[312]

DEVOTIONAL JEWELLERY

While the Protestant majority had very little devotional jewellery, the Catholics continued to wear it. Queen Henrietta Maria hung an Agnus Dei on a gold chain,[313] and Cardinal Francesco Barberini sent religious jewels to her from Rome: jewelled reliquaries, rosaries of agate and buffalo horn beads carved like cameos, and a diamond cross worked with the Barberini bees.[314] There are various sizes of cross shown in her portraits, and some of her largest stones were set in the cross that can be seen in the portrait painted by Van Dyck as a pattern for Bernini to use in making a bust. It is an unusual design, perhaps the headless cross mentioned in some of the royal inventories; it had three long stones in the arms and upright with a lozenge-shaped setting above the crossing, two round pearls under the arms, and a pear pearl at the foot.[315]

Anne Dacre, Countess of Arundel, was a devout Catholic and her biographer recorded how

> Upon great feasts and the principal holy dayes in honour of the solemnity she used to wear about her neck either a cross of gold in which a particle of the Holy Cross was inserted, or an Agatt in which a picture of the Blessed Virgin's Assumption was engraven, or else a plain pair of beads sent to her by Father Claudius Aquaviva, General of the Society of Jesus, the which she much esteemed kept and used until her death and then left as a legacy to a great lady and a special friend of hers.[316]

She also showed her piety in leaving to some special friends

> Crosses of gold enamell'd with azure, on the one side of which was the Holy Name of *Jesus* in the midst, and on the other, the name of his Blessed mother *Maria*, and in the corners thereof these words, *Miseremini mei An. Ar.* on the one part: and *Parce mihi Domine* on the other: . . . Ande she procured that every one of these Crosses should be made graines of S. *Ignatius* and the other four Saints canonized with him; to the end that those her friends by doing such pious works as are appointed unto the enjoyers of those graines, might gain Indulgences both for her soul and themselves.[317]

76 Susan, Lady Bathurst, with pearl earrings similar to those in Plate 82 and an anchor cross like that in Plate XX hanging from her necklace. There is a miniature inside the lid of her watch case, and rings are pinned to the bow-knots on her dress and collar. Portrait, *c.* 1630. Collection of Lord Bathurst, Cirencester Park.

Other recusant families possessed such jewels,[318] but prudence meant that few were recorded, although in 1713 Mary Weld left a gold cross to her sister[319] – a bequest which, like the alleged gift of a gold cross by Charles II to Lady Lilias Murray, would not of itself be incriminating.[320] It is interesting to note that some of the items in the Cheapside Hoard had an uncompromisingly Catholic character. The most important piece of this kind is an enamelled gold locket ornamented with the Instruments of the Passion and set with bloodstone cameos of Christ and the Virgin. Three others, all cruciform, were enamelled with leaves and flowers. Another three crosses in the hoard were enamelled in this way on the back, and their fronts were set with various coloured stones: rose-cut amethysts, water sapphires, pink spinels with table-cut diamonds, and cabochon emerald borders.[321] They are similar to a cross owned in 1651 by Anne Lewis, and described as 'one Jewell in forme of a Crosse with five greene stones'.[322] An anchor-shaped cross signified hope:

> the anchor doth declare
> That Hope which keeps us from Despairing quite.[323]

Such a cross, hung on a necklace by Susan, Lady Bathurst (Plate 76), compares with a surviving example which has a heart on the upright (Plate XVIII).

Jewelled crosses feature prominently in both shop and personal inventories of the second half of the century. Shop inventories are exemplified by those for John Austen in 1670 and Gabriel Cox a decade later,[324] personal ones by those of the Countess of Lauderdale in 1671 and the Countess of Devonshire in 1689.[325] One of the four crosses bequeathed by the latter to the Countess of Exeter represented the four elements: an emerald (earth), a long ruby (fire), a sapphire (water) and a diamond (air).[326] In 1705 the future Duchess of Montagu had two diamond crosses (with other jewels) reset, one with rose-cut and the other with brilliant-cut stones.[327] Both hung from coulants, jewelled runners through which a ribbon could be passed, which had originated in France where they were first mentioned in 1688.[328] The coulant and cross could also be attached to a pearl-or gem-set necklace, like one in Michael Wilson's stock in 1709: 'a string of diamonds, runner and cross'.[329] Worn high on the neck, their effect was mentioned by Pope – 'on her white breast a sparkling cross she wore'[330] – and the Duchess of Marlborough had some of her best diamonds, recorded in drawings, set in crosses and coulants. The most magnificent of all was set 'with five large diamonds one very large for the middle collet and 1 large to buckle it behind with two little ones in all nine'.[331] This category of early-eighteenth-century aristocratic jewellery is illustrated by a drawing of a ruby and diamond cross belonging to the Duchess of Montagu *c.* 1710 (Fig. 18). The emphasis is on large stones, the warm glow of rubies being enhanced by the glitter of rose-cut diamonds radiating from the centre and in trefoils at the end of each arm.[332]

Religious belief was also expressed by two types of ring. Silver decade rings, the bezel

Fig. 18 The Duchess of Montagu's ruby and diamond cross *c.* 1710. British Library.

inscribed IHS with a cross and three nails, and ten bosses, for the Aves, on the hoop, are associated with recusant families in the Liverpool area. Unlike rosaries, they were tolerated by the authorities.[333] Posies on wedding rings, like that of 1660 with JOYNED IN ONE BY CHRIST ALONE, could affirm the Christian ideal of marriage.[334]

MAGICAL JEWELLERY

Sidrophel, the astrologer in Samuel Butler's poem *Hudibras*, made his living by selling amulets and charms:

> Engrav'd in *Planetary hours*,
> That over *Mortals* had strange powers
> To make 'em thrive in *Law*, or *Trade*;
> And stab, or poyson, to evade;
> In *Wit*, or *Wisdom* to improve,
> And be victorious in *Love*.[335]

Queen Henrietta Maria was much attached to a heart which her mother, Marie de' Medici, had sent her when she was expecting a child in 1630; in her letter of thanks she wrote: 'I always wear it on my neck as I fancy it brings me such good fortune that I am always afraid without it.'[336] The Duke of Monmouth was also very superstitious. According to Archbishop Tenison, he carried a charm under the stone in his ring, bought from a German mountebank, in the belief that it would protect him from danger and defeat in battle.[337]

Talismanic powers were still attributed to precious and semi-precious stones; according to Thomas Nicols they had the power to

> make men rich and eloquent, to preserve men from thunder and lightning, from plagues and diseases, to move dreams, to procure sleep, to foretell things to come, to make men wise, to strengthen memory, to procure honours, to hinder fascinations and witchcrafts, to hinder slothfulnesse, to put courage into men, to keep men chaste, to increase friendship, to hinder difference and dissension, to make men invisible . . .[338]

But such properties were increasingly questioned. Nevertheless, Nicols ends his survey of each stone with an uncritical summary of their magical properties, quoting from Pliny and such later writers as Albertus Magnus, Anselm, Boethius, de Boot and Andreas Baccius. Twenty years later Robert Boyle, one of the founders of the Royal Society, while admitting that he 'never saw any great feats perform'd by those hard and costly Stones, (as *Diamonds, Rubies, Sapphires*) that were wont to be worn in rings', did not entirely reject the possibility of their having some medicinal value, and referred to the alleged cure of a scholarly friend's severe nose-bleed by a bloodstone the size of a pigeon's egg which had been hung round his neck by an old woman.[339]

This supposed property of the bloodstone in stemming bleeding was the cause of its popularity in seventeenth-century jewellery. Lady Elcho's will in 1649 referred to 'the bloudstone braislett with Dr. Arnot's stone that is for women in travail',[340] and she also bequeathed a toadstone ring. According to Nicols, the toadstone 'was good against poison if it be worn so as it may touch the skin'.[341] In 1680 John Keech had several toadstones in stock, some loose and some set in gold or silver rings, one in a silver seal, and three of large size mounted in loops.[342] Elk horn, imported from the Baltic, was worn in bracelets, set in gold and mixed with pearls, as a 'sovereign remedy for the falling sickness'.[343]

MEMENTO MORI, MEMORIAL AND SENTIMENTAL JEWELLERY

Several strands of thought – both pagan and Christian – can be discerned in the *memento mori*, memorial and sentimental jewellery of the seventeenth century: the belief in the need to prepare for a good death, the memory of deceased relatives and friends, and the expression of love and devotion all appear. The Anglican clergy were much concerned with preparing their congregations for death. Jeremy Taylor (1613–67), Bishop of Down and Connor, won a large following for his treatise *Thoughts on Holy Dying* (1651), which taught that it was 'a great art to die well and to be learnt by men in health'.[344] It was in this spirit that his friend, the diarist John Evelyn (1620–1706), was depicted in a portrait by Robert Walker of 1648 holding a skull and a copy of Seneca's *De Brevitate Vitae*, recommending the proper employment of time during life's brief span.[345]

The Puritan Countess of Warwick, Mary Rich, overcame her natural horror of death by thinking of it as the harbour in which she would find rest from the troubles of this world and release from the burden of sin. She confided her thoughts in her diary of 1671:

> In the morning as soon as up, I had whilst my Lord slept, very large meditations of death . . . I found the thought of my lying in my cold bed and of the worms feeding upon me and of my

turning to dust to be a little frightful and amazing to me, but it pleased God to let me all of sudden find an extraordinary and reviving joy to think that . . . my body should be raised and made a glorious one.[346]

This Christian view of life as a preparation for holy death is mirrored in jewels, particularly rings, watches, pendants and slides ornamented with skulls, cross-bones, skeletons (or 'death at length') and hour-glasses – reminders of the hour of death. There is an allusion to them in Fletcher's play, *The Chances*, where one of the characters says:

> And keep it, as they keep deaths Heads in rings,
> To cry *Memento* to me . . .[347]

It has been suggested that the custom fell into disuse during the Commonwealth, but *memento mori* rings are mentioned in the wills of that period.[348] Jasper Despotin of Bury left ten rings with death's heads to friends in 1648, and in 1656 Jane Dixon bequeathed such rings 'to wear in remembrance of my love', and others were given by Dorothy Coleman in 1659.[349]

The skull might be engraved on either the front or the back of the bezel or carved in relief or intaglio on a ringstone – as in the amethyst among the Binyon jewels or Frances Dobson's 'ring with the agott stone cut like a death's head'.[350] Others were enamelled white *en ronde bosse* with jewelled eye-sockets; just such a ring with 'a gold death's head with diamonds' was in the stock of Michael Wilson in 1709.[351] The message of the symbol could be reinforced by inscriptions such as HODIE MIHI CRAS TIBI or MEMORARE NOVISSIMA.[352] Such images could intimidate. When Colin, third Earl of Balcarres (1652–1721), forgot the ring for his mariage to Lady Mauritia de Nassau, he borrowed one from a friend, and when the bride saw the skull and cross-bones she fainted, perhaps fearing her death in childbed, which took place a year later.[353]

From the mid century, memorial rings were often given a more personal touch by adding names, ciphers and dates or by enclosing hair within them. When Anne Maria Verney died aged four, her father Ralph promised his brother Henry that 'You shall herewithal receive a ringe filled with my deare gerle's hair; shee was fond of you . . . therefore I now send this to keepe for her sake.'[354] Sometimes the hair was enclosed in the hollowed hoop of the ring, as in one enamelled with two coats-of-arms and a skull and cross-bones, inscribed SAMUELL NICHOLETS OBIJT 17 JULY 1661 CHRIST IS MY PORTION.[355] This design was still in fashion fifty years later, when it was used for another ring commemorating M. Frend.[356] Hair could also be put in an oval, round or octagonal bezel over corded silk, with the cipher of the deceased worked in gold wire covered by a slab of rock crystal with faceted edges.[357] There were many variations in design. Rear-Admiral Sir John Chicheley ordered in his will: 'I desire you will give to Lord George a Mourning Ring according to the new fashion with my haire and Cypher and two small Diamonds on each side somewhat better than ordinary', which shows the prevalent fashion *c.* 1691 when he died.[358] Coffin-shaped bezels, sometimes with white skeletons under the glass or crystal, and the name of the deceased inside the hoop, are found about the end of the century.[359]

The Burghley Schedule of 1690 lists several *memento mori* jewels of the older type: an hour-glass, skulls like the 'death's head enamelled in white hung in gold' and the 'square locket set round with diamonds with a death's head in it made of opal'.[360] Other variations on the theme include a skull-shaped gold locket enclosing a skeleton and hour-glass, or the coffin pendant with a death's head within and the cipher P B, and on the outside P.B. OBIT YE 17 MAR: 1703 AGED 54 YEARS.[361] In similar mood is the skull-shaped pomander inscribed MAN PROPOSES BUT GOD DISPOSES, with the date 1679.[362]

From the reign of Charles II, slides were the most usual form of memorial jewellery after rings. Oval or heart-shaped, mounted in gold and framed in pearls, rose-cut diamonds, coloured stones or paste, they had twin loops at the back through which a ribbon could be threaded, for wear at the neck or wrist. Ciphers and other symbols were worked in gold thread and enamel and laid over a ground of hair or corded silk, often red, and covered with thick tablets of faceted crystal. The back could be engraved or enamelled with ciphers, dates and floral or acanthus patterns. Again, designs were open to individual interpretation: one enclosed an enamel coffin and skeleton with I REST beneath a cartouche with the initials M T held by two angels.[363] Another shows the skeleton emerging from a tomb with angels at each side trumpeting the good news of the Resurrection, the text COME YE BLESSED and the cipher M K for Margaret Keith, wife of George Graeme of Inchbraikie in Scotland.[364] An engaging version shows a small boy reading the Bible at a table, candle and skull beside him, the cipher F H and, below, the injunction LEARN TO DIE[365] – an image from Wither's *Emblemes* (Plates 77 and 78):

> When, on this Child-like figure, thou shalt looke,
> Which, with his Light, his Houre-glasse, and his Booke,
> Sits, in a watching-posture, formed here,
> And, when thou hast perus'd that Motto, there,
> On which he layes his hand; thy selfe apply
> To what it counselleth: and, learne to die,
> While that Light burnes, and that short houre doth last . . .[366]

Slides might be mounted together in necklaces. There is one of thirty-one memorial slides, each with a gold monogram over the hair and ciphers on the back; another has blue foil insets painted in white with skulls, crossbones, angels bearing crosses, a skeleton in the tomb with I REST, and winged and crowned skulls with GLORIA and VANITAS[367]. The collection of Mrs Phillips was made up into a necklace in this way[368] (Plate XXI). The Duchess of Marlborough had a luxurious version, with sixteen collets, each with hair under the crystal and sixty brilliants set in the spacers between them.[369]

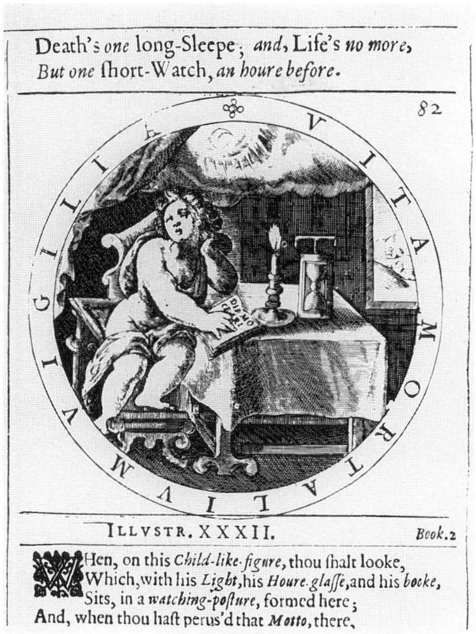

Death's *one* long-Sleepe; *and*, Life's *no more*,
But one ſhort-Watch, *an houre before.*

82

VIGILIA VITA MORTALIVM

ILLVSTR. XXXII. Book.2

WHen, on this *Child-like-figure*, thou ſhalt looke,
Which, with his *Light*, his *Houre-glaſſe*, and his *booke*,
Sits, in a *watching-poſture*, formed here;
And, when thou haſt perus'd that *Motto*, there,

77 A page from George Wither's *Emblemes* (1635) illustrating the brevity of life. Private collection.

78 Memorial pendant derived from the emblem in Plate 77, with the infant seated at a table with skull, hour-glass, candle and book, with the inscription LEARN TO DIE and gold wire cipher FH. E. Donohoe, London.

Not all such slides commemorated the dead. Among those described as being stolen from 'Lady Farthingale' in 1710 were 'lockets with the hair of dead and living lovers'.[370] Earlier, Dorothy Osborne had told Sir William Temple what it meant to her to possess a lock of his hair: 'I am combing and curling and kissing this lock all day and dreaming on't all night.'[371] In 1672 Thomas Isham described how he had bought from a French jeweller, Ricarfeild, 'a ring with a cavity in which a lock of hair of a lover might be placed to keep him in remembrance'.[372] According to Grammont, the Restoration beauty Lady Shrewsbury gave bracelets of her hair to three or four gentlemen,[373] and a bracelet of hair and balls of pomander with seed pearl, inscribed JOHN SYMES WAS BORNE AUG 26, 67, OB 7 OF JULY 1687 BURIED 11 OF JULY on the gold clasp, is in the Museum of London. In her will of 1686 Sarah, Duchess of Somerset, bequeathed to the eldest daughter of her niece, Lady Delamer, 'one hair broad bracelet for the arm curiously wrought in flowers with hair of several colours'.[374]

Such slides could have ciphers or amorous symbols under the crystal, such as a pair of putti shooting arrows at a target with the motto AU PLUS ADROIT,[375] a ship with the message I WILL FOLLOW YOU EVERYWHERE, turtle doves billing, and a flaming heart.[376] The hair could itself be arranged decoratively, as in the gold locket advertised in the *London Gazette* for 1702 as being 'striped with dark brown and fair hair wrought like a camlet, over the hair a cypher of four letters R A M L under a cut crystal and set round with rose diamonds'.[377] After discussing various remedies to alleviate the pains of separation, a writer in *The Spectator* in 1711 declared that, having tried many, he never had 'so much benefit from any as from a Ring in which my Mistress's Hair is platted together very artificially in a kind of True-Lover's knott'.[378] The Duchess of

Marlborough (who wore bracelets with 'hair lockets' and a ring with her mother's hair) instructed her jeweller to make a ring with love symbols:

> You must set the ring with this ruby heart and a crystal heart of the same size with this hair put loose into it without being wove. The hoop must be light blue enamel with the following motto round it in good letters, the two hearts must be crowned with these other diamonds.[379]

After Lord Petre had forcibly taken a lock of Miss Arabella Fermor's hair, Alexander Pope described in his poem, *The Rape of the Lock*, how it would be set in a ring:

> And shall this Prize, th' inestimable Prize,
> Expos'd thro' Crystal to the gazing Eyes,
> And heighten'd by the Diamond's circling Rays,
> On that Rapacious Hand for ever blaze?[380]

DRESS AND JEWELLERY

Portraits are more widely available for evidence as to how people dressed and wore their jewels; they document the changing fashions, not only of the court, but also of the country gentry, rich merchants, and their wives. Diarists like Samuel Pepys also provide well-dated information about new fashions.

The fashions of the Caroline court, as they appear in the paintings of Van Dyck, were elegant and picturesque, following the example set by the king and his queen.[381] In 1640 Wenceslas Hollar, the Bohemian artist introduced to England by the connoisseur Earl of Arundel, published the first, and one of the finest, costume books devoted to this country. It illustrated the 'Severall Habits of Englishwomen from the Nobilitie to the countrywomen' – a restriction also followed by some of the continental costume books.[382]

For the ladies, the high waistline was emphasised by a girdle, the ample skirts of the gown falling in graceful folds, with the back prolonged, for court dress, to make a short train. Pearls were worn in the ears, about the neck, and in long ropes looped about the shoulders and caught in the centre of the low neckline of the bodice under a jewel pendant from a bow-knot. The sides of the bodice could be closed with more strands of pearls or, like the sleeve seams, clasped by small brooches, which could be used also to fasten the falling lace collars (Plate 79).

During the Commonwealth, dress was more restrained; the expensive materials of the preceding period and the low necklines were particularly abhorrent to the Puritans. After the Restoration this changed rapidly and the court followed the French styles (Plate 79). When Catherine of Braganza arrived in England, her dress, and that of her ladies-in-waiting, gave rise to much comment, as the Portuguese court dress followed a long-outmoded style with farthingales and black fabrics.[383] The appearance of Charles II's court was immortalised in the paintings of Sir Peter Lely, especially his series of the

79 Lady Hewett wearing pearls in her hair, ears and neck, her dress clasped with diamond and pearl brooches, and a diamond pendant at centre of the neckline. Portrait detail, *c.* 1640. Shrublands collection.

beauties at Hampton Court Palace.[384] Jewellery became more elaborate again, and even buckles for stays could be set with diamonds.[385] At the end of this period the extravagant fashions of the court and the *nouveaux riches* became the target of satirists like Mary Evelyn, whose *Mundus Mulieribus* appeared in 1690, and the essayists in *The Spectator* and *The Tatler*.

Just as ladies' dress assumed a more familiar appearance, so, too, did that of the men. Van Dyck's portraits show them wearing fine linen shirts with lace collars, a short closely-fitting coat with lace cuffs on the tight sleeves, knee breeches, stockings, and shoes with rosettes to hide the laces. The shirt could be fastened with a large diamond set in a button,[386] and other buttons were used for the coat. High-crowned hats were worn out of doors, with a band which could be of gold or silver and set with precious stones, while the cloak would be embroidered in silver thread with the Garter star.

80 Detail from portrait of Admiral Sir Jeremiah Smith († 1675) with sleeve buttons fastening his cuff. Portrait by Sir Peter Lely. National Maritime Museum.

At the Restoration, after a period of relative austerity, richer fabrics returned and also new styles. The combination of a long coat, worn over a shorter tightly-fitting vest, the shirt with lace cravat, knee breeches and shoes fastened with buckles, set the pattern for the future.[387] The king led the way in matters of fashion, and introduced new styles.[388] At the English court, as in France, much jewellery was worn, such as diamond buttons and buckles; gold-headed canes might be carried, and the snuff box and small-sword became essential accessories. An innovation was the linked sleeve button, often set with stones, the ancestor of the modern cuff-links[389] (Plate 80). The wearing of chains, except when required by insignia like that worn by the Master of the Ceremonies, was not revived and the insignia of the Garter and Thistle worn like a sash under the coat, the breast of which would be embroidered with the star.

6

The categories of Stuart and Commonwealth jewellery 1625 – 1714

JEWELLERY FOR THE HEAD

CROWNS AND CORONETS

After the execution of Charles I in 1649 Parliament ordered that the regalia should be broken up; when the Restoration of Charles II took place, one of the first duties of the Master of the Jewel House was to have new regalia made.[1] This was duly done, and although the designs were not always identical with those of the old items which had been destroyed, the ancient names, like St Edward's Crown, were kept.[2] Neither then, nor for most of the next century, were the diamonds which blazed in the crowns, etc., at coronations permanent; many were hired for the day.[3]

Except at coronations and formal court ceremonies, like the Proceeding to Parliament at the beginning of a new session, coronets had ceased to be worn by the nobility. The baron's coronet was created for the coronation of Charles II, and successive Earls Marshal or their deputies issued orders prior to coronations that the circlet of the coronet must not be jewelled, but only chased as jewelled.[4] Portrait painters and herald painters, however, frequently ignored these orders and depicted the coronets as if they were set with pearls, rubies and sapphires or emeralds.

JEWELS FOR THE HAIR

In contrast to the tall padded coiffures of the Jacobean period, during the reigns of Charles I and his son, Charles II, the hair was worn flat, drawn up into a chignon at the back with ringlets framing the face. In 1636 Alice, Countess of Derby, left each of her granddaughters a string of pearls to wind round the chignon or entwine in their hair,[5] perhaps with pear pearl or drop-shaped gems attached. There were three bodkins in the Cheapside Hoard: one of them, set with a golden table-cut topaz bordered with tiny rose-cut diamonds, could be the counterpart of the topaz bodkin in the will of Lady Jeane Wemyss in 1655.[6] The other two are made like shepherd's crooks, one with the head set with diamonds and rubies, the other with turquoises.[7] One of the four jewelled

81 Young woman with an insect bodkin in her hair, similar to that in Plate XXII. Portrait detail, Flemish school, 1650–60. Collection of Lord Talbot de Malahide.

insects in the Burghley Schedule 1690 survives (Plate XXII), and although there is no bodkin, it was most likely to have been worn in the hair[8] (Plate 81). It is set with rose-cut diamonds, cabochon rubies, cat's-eyes and opals in the same style as the Cheapside gems, and is enamelled blue and green.[9] Rich ladies, like the Duchess of Marlborough, wore their largest diamonds in bodkins for the hair,[10] and in a jewel casket described in 1690 were to be found

> A Saphire Bodkin for the Hair
> Or sparkling Facet Diamond there.[11]

By this time the hair was again being worn piled high, padded out with tours, and the effect of the jewels in the hair was thus described: 'Diamonds or other precious Stones heading the *Pins* which they stick in the *Tour*, and Hair, like stars'.[12] The feathers and sprigs, which had gone out of fashion in the 1630s, reappeared. Lady Wrottesley wore a sprig of eleven diamonds, six large and five small,[13] and the Duchess of Marlborough had one with six briolettes.[14] The sprigs, aigrettes and girandoles of Marcus Gunter must have been designed for such clients; his drawings show leafy branches, studded with rose-cut stones, apparently drooping under the weight of hanging pearls and briolettes[15] (Fig. 19).

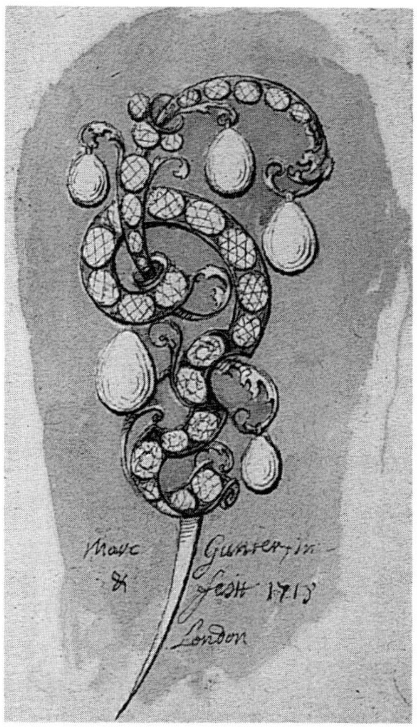

Fig. 19 Design by Marcus Gunter for an aigrette: London 1718.
Röhsska Konstlöjdmuseet, Goteborg.

Celia Fiennes noticed the diamond bows which the Countess of Pembroke had in her hair at the coronation of Queen Anne, adding that the tresses of the other peeresses were 'full of diamonds'.[16] The funeral effigy of Frances Stuart, Duchess of Richmond, is dressed in the robes she had on at this coronation and the jewellery she wore fits this description. She has the formal 'Fontange' hair-style with a 'Top-Knot' or Tour on the forehead. Her coronet is tilted over the chignon at the back of the head, the side tresses are entwined with pearls, and a great aigrette over the brow is crowned by a jewelled bodkin. The funerary jewels are set with faceted crystals, but the rose-cut diamonds of the originals would have made a fine show, diffusing what John Gay in *Araminta* described as a 'trembling ray' over the duchess's fine features.[17]

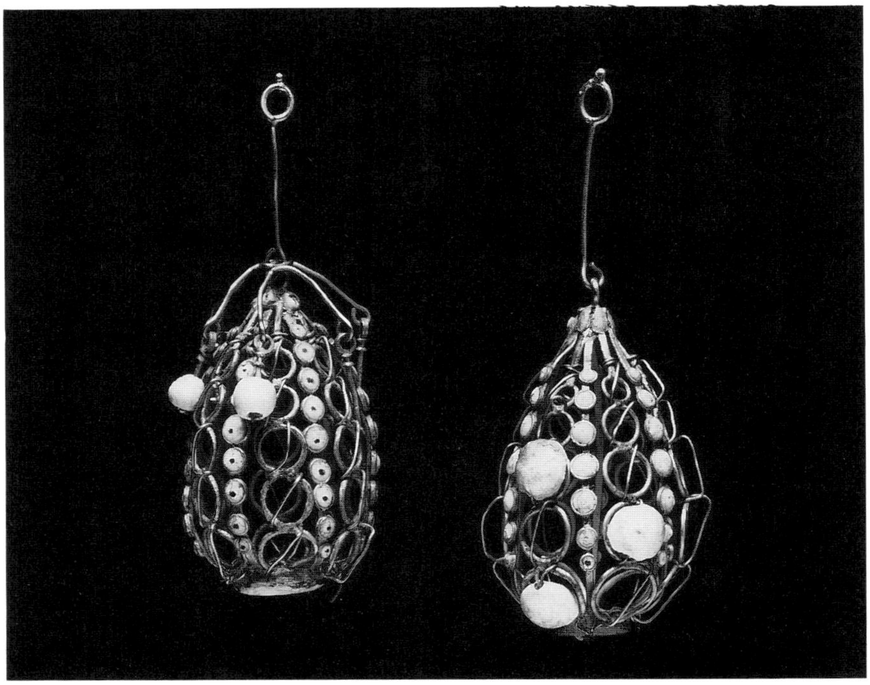

82 Pair of pendants formerly threaded with pearls similar to the earrings worn by Lady Bathurst in the portrait at Plate 76. British Museum, from the Cheapside Hoard.

EARRINGS AND PENDANTS

Pearls, which enjoyed a prestige eclipsing all other gems, were worn singly and in pairs or clusters of two or three hanging from gold hooks, jewelled studs or wrought mounts, in the ears. Since it was rare to match the largest pearls, one alone might be used, like that worn by Charles I to his execution. His pear pearl, which has been preserved at Welbeck Abbey, is mounted in a diamond-set imperial crown.[18] Another instance of this motif occurs in the inventory of a Mrs Brett *c.* 1670, though in her case the crowns were enamelled, not jewelled.[19] Although numerous pairs of diamond and coloured stone pendants are listed in pre-Restoration inventories, designs are not specified – with rare exceptions like the 'pair of litill bell pendants for the eare set with lytill dyamondes' owned by Lady Binning in 1635.[20] Pear-shaped drops of pearls threaded on gold wires found in the Cheapside Hoard (Plate 82) compare with those worn by Lady Bathurst in her portrait *c.* 1630 (Plate 76).

In the reigns of Charles II and his successors, earrings, like pearl necklaces, were essential to fashionable dressing and were often given as wedding presents, like the 'pair of diamond pendants' given to his wife by the Earl of Devonshire in 1688.[21] Sir Charles Sedley, in his poem, 'The Happy Pair', describes how they caught the eye:

> Her Face he praises, but he courts her Ears,
> Catching the glitt'ring Pendants that she wears.[22]

The schedule of her jewels annexed to the will of Christian, Countess of Devonshire, lists many important pendants of pearls, diamonds and emeralds, and 'a little pendant like a chayne for the eares Containeinge Nine diamonds two little Fosett Diamonds and at the end five pendant rubies and two table rubies', and amply demonstrates how important earrings had become.[23] A rosette design is described in the inventory of Anne, Countess of Lauderdale: 'a pair of great diamond earrings or buckles each of them containing a great diamond in the middle and eight lesser ones about it'.[24] A pair of top and drop earrings set with crystals, the backs enamelled with botanical motifs, is worn by the funeral effigy of the Duchess of Richmond[25] (Plate 83).

At the end of this period, the collection of the Duchess of Marlborough included several pairs of earrings, notably a superb pair with 'Two very Large Pendant Pearls that

83 Funeral effigy of the Duchess of Richmond and Lennox in the jewellery and robes she wore at the coronation of Queen Anne. 1702. Westminster Abbey.

cost £500 but were valued at more than double the price set in earrings with two brilliant diamonds'.[26] Among the others were girandoles with large rose diamond tops and three brilliant drops bequeathed to her grandson, John Spencer.[27] Another pair of this pattern, all set with rose-cut diamonds, with ribbon bow-knots linking the tops and drops, had been given to her at the time of her marriage in 1678 by the Duchess of York.[28] Others had coloured drops hanging from diamond tops and bow-knots, rubies, imitation emeralds and sapphires.[29] Marcus Gunter gave this style a classical character by introducing acanthus leaves, mounted with coloured stones or rose-cut diamonds and hung with pearls, into the designs for his clients[30] (Fig. 20).

Fig. 20 Design by Marcus Gunter for girandole earrings: Siena, 1703.
Röhsska Konstlöjdmuseet, Goteborg.

NECKLACES AND JEWELLED CHAINS

Throughout the period, pearls were the most popular kind of necklace, although not all were so large as the 'collar of pearls, each as big as the top of one's finger', worn, to the admiration of the great crowd which stared at them, by the Lord Mayor's wife in 1679.[31] They could be threaded into short chokers, multiple-rowed necklaces or chains several feet long, and if the pearls were oriental, round and white, they enjoyed the greatest prestige. They could also be set in goldsmith's work, like the chain with a pearl in each link of green leaves from the Cheapside Hoard,[32] or the 'chaine of small pearl with bars of gold enamelled black' bequeathed by Alice, Countess of Derby, in 1636,[33] and the 'necklace of pearls and amythyst set in gold' bequeathed by Ann

Wharton, wife of William Carr, who died in 1689.[34] Although a three-row necklace with four hundred pearls, owned by the Duchess of Marlborough, was fastened by a diamond hook,[35] ribbon ties were still in general use.

Elizabeth, Countess of Devonshire, bequeathed in 1642 a 'Chaine of Dyamonds conteininge fortie peeces everie other peece thereof having five Dyamonds a peece and the other peeces having but one diamond a peece'.[36] In the next generation Countess Christian owned a similar diamond chain, with eighteen large table-cut stones alternating with seventy rose-cut stones set in clusters.[37] Small table-cut diamonds are set in daisies with white petals in some of the chains from the Cheapside Hoard and could alternate with open oval links or turquoise spacers.[38]

As the supply of diamonds increased, and faceting and polishing improved, the wealthiest ladies wore them in rivières which encircled the throat with rays of light. The diamond necklace copied for the effigy of the Duchess of Richmond, based on the one

84 Silver and crystal parure of the Duchess of Richmond and Lennox. 1702. Westminster Abbey.

worn at the coronation of Queen Anne, is an example of this style, with rose-cut crystals set in silver collets, the backs enamelled with sprigs[39] (Plate 84). Others, like that of the Duchess of Marlborough, were set with brilliant-cut stones.[40] In Marcus Gunter's early-eighteenth-century design smaller rose-cut diamonds in groups of three alternate with pearls (Fig. 21).

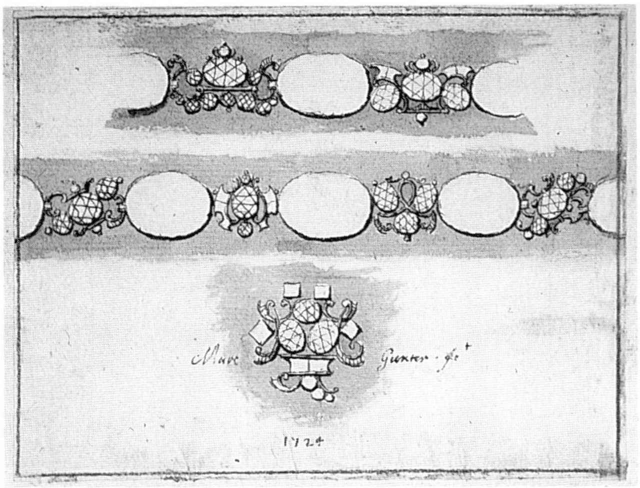

Fig. 21 Design by Marcus Gunter for a necklace: 1724.
Röhsska Konstlöjdmuseet, Goteborg.

The number of chains in the Cheapside Hoard, with many different designs of flowers, leaves, bow-knots and entrelacs, set with fancy-cut amethysts, turquoises, garnets and cabochon or trap-cut emeralds, demonstrates their importance in the first half of the seventeenth century.[41] In 1642 Elizabeth, Countess of Devonshire, bequeathed a chain of pearl and ruby clusters, linked by diamond-headed snakes taken from the Cavendish family crest.[42] Three decades later, in 1670, the Countess of Lauderdale had a 'chain of Emerods and Diamonds to hang upon the breast containing sixteen little roses and a big rose at the end',[43] but not all chains used the more precious stones. In the 1675 Devonshire schedule there was a garnet and gold bead chain, and even the Duchess of Marlborough owned one with imitation rubies.[44]

In 1637 a London jeweller, Ezekiel Major, had 'amber beades' among the 'chaines and Cornelian beades' in his stock,[45] and in the Restoration period these were so popular that Sedley could accuse the husband in his poem, 'The Happy Pair', of marrying his wife for her 'Jewels, and her Amber-Chains'.[46] Although the jewellers' inventories show that they stocked quantities of amber, coral, and other hardstone beads, particularly cornelian, there is no description of the appearance of the necklaces and chains into which they were threaded.[47] A rare survival in the Cheapside Hoard of a chain of lapis lazuli beads in oval links, alternating with white daisies, alone gives a clue to this.[48]

BREAST JEWELS

The most important pieces of seventeenth-century jewellery adorned the breast, either joining the edges of the falling collar together or in the centre of the neckline of the bodice. In the latter position, the rope of pearls could be looped under it and the jewel pinned through a ribbon bow-knot.

Large stones were framed like pictures in bold gold cartouches: square, octagonal or lozenge-shaped, embellished with round and pear pearls. Figurative designs are rare, except for the gold cherubs, their breasts set with a large gem and a pearl pendant, seen in several portraits, like that of Mrs Richard Lucy, at Charlecote Park. Smaller stones would be composed in clusters, like Lady Binning's 'ane starre having in it seven dyamondes' in 1635,[49] the Earl of Roxburgh's 'round jewel for the breast with thirty nine diamonds' in 1644,[50] or the Countess of Warwick's 'greate round jewell of gold set round with Rowes of diamond & one great diamond in the middle'.[51] A remarkable diamond jewel, the round pendant hanging from a ribbon bow-knot, with botanical enamelling at the back, sold from the Hay of Duns Castle collection in 1971, was described in the inventory of William Hay, 6 January 1725: 'A large breast jewell sett with diamonds cutt after the old Fashion compleat so that none of the diamonds are lost'[52] (Plate 85). Coloured stones were also used; in 1636 Robert Rogers owned 'a greene stone called an Emerald set in Gold of an Ovall fashion and encompassed with small Rubies' valued at £5,[53] and they could be combined with diamonds, as in the Earl of Eglinton's 'great jewell set with diamonds, rubies and pearles'.[54]

85 Diamond breast jewel with round pendant hanging from bow-knot; the stones are table-cut. Back: botanical enamelling. Christie's (formerly Hay of Duns Castle), now private collection.

After the Restoration, breast jewels were larger, and could be divided into sections, like William Boteler's 'i brest diamond Jewell in 3 part cont[aining] 53 Stones', valued at £32 in 1680.[55] Jewels were reset to make these fashionable items. Elizabeth, wife of the fourth Earl of Devonshire, had the large diamond given to her in a ring at her marriage reset with many others, including seven diamond drops bought from William Gumbleton, in one great cluster.[56] So, too, did Lady Yester when in 1694 she had two crosses, earrings, a locket and one of her husband's old jewels broken up to obtain fifty-seven diamonds for a new breast jewel commissioned from Mr Main.[57] Pendant gems often formed an important part of the design, like William Waller's 'brest Jewell with four Emerald Drops sett in gold' in 1696 or the pear pearls also mounted in a gold pendant from Alice Thornton's green jewel in 1705.[58]

Another popular design was a ribbon-like bow-knot; one set with table-cut diamonds was in the Cheapside Hoard[59] and, from the mid century, references to them become more common. The Countess of Warwick had a 'faire knott of gold enamelled with tulips set with diamonds', and Thomas Knevet bequeathed a diamond bow-knot in 1658.[60] In 1670 John Austen had two in his stock, one set with chrysolites, the other with diamonds.[61] The Countess of Lauderdale not only had the customary bow-knots – one set with 'twelve rubies and several small rubies' – but also croches or croshettes, breast jewels with a hook at the back, set with various combinations of precious and semi-precious stones.[62] They remained in fashion, and Lady Pawlet went to a wedding in 1712 'in all her finery of true lovers knots of diamonds set in as much silver as would make a pair of candle-sticks'.[63]

Other breast jewels were designed as roses. One with a topaz in the centre of the diamonds belonged to Christian, Countess of Devonshire,[64] and others, set with diamonds, were owned by the Countess of Lauderdale and Margaret Scott of Rossie, the latter a 'small jewel for the breast set like a large rose'.[65]

A portrait by Robert Lovejoy of Mary, wife of the seventh Duke of Norfolk, now at Kedleston, shows her wearing a breast jewel in the form of a Brandenburg, a wide bar derived from the frogging on Prussian uniforms, and introduced as a jewel design in France from the late 1670s. Another forms part of the jewellery on the effigy of the Duchess of Richmond.[66] Both have similar designs: acanthus with the leaves spread out and studded with large and small stones. It was a common element in the designs by Marcus Gunter, and his Brandenburgs were also designed in graduated sizes in sets of three or more (Fig. 22), as worn by Queen Mary II in her funeral effigy in Westminster Abbey (Plate 86). The acanthus was set with small table- or rose-cut stones, with a larger white or coloured stone as the centrepiece.

Another of his designs, dated London 1689 (Fig. 23), was made to fill more of the triangular space between the neckline and waist. This stomacher has luxuriant acanthus with pendant briolettes from the branches laden with rose-cut gems.[67]

Fig. 22 Design by Marcus Gunter for a Brandenburg: 1695.
Röhsska Konstlöjdmuseet, Goteborg.

Fig. 23 Design by Marcus Gunter for a stomacher: London, 1689.
Röhsska Konstlöjdmuseet, Goteborg.

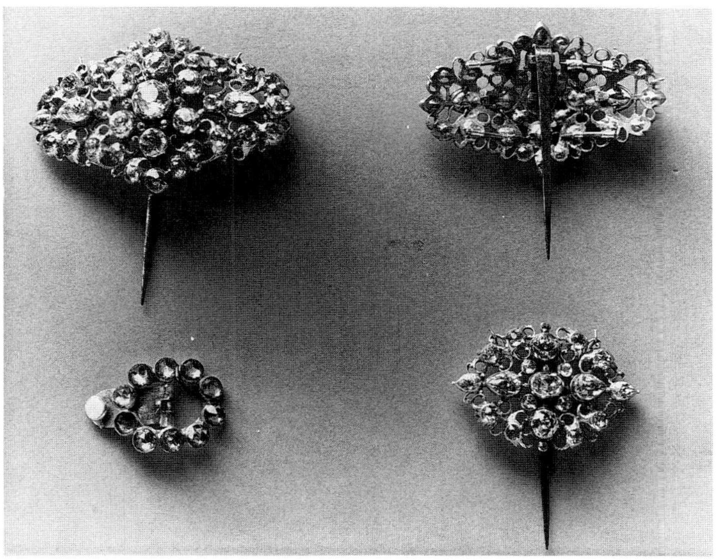

86 Breast jewels and buckle set with rose-cut crystals from the funeral effigy of Queen Mary II. *c.* 1700. Westminster Abbey.

Even more ambitious designs from the early eighteenth century, from Leghorn, Rome and Florence, were wide enough to cover the entire front of the bodice and, sewn over the coloured silks, these stomachers made a great show at the coronation of Queen Anne in 1702.[68]

MINIATURE CASES

Henry Oxinden wrote in 1641 to Elizabeth Dallison: 'I desire that I might have your picture by mee, that I might take pleasure in beholding it.'[69] Like the royal miniatures, those of family, friends and lovers were cased as handsomely as the owner could afford. Alice, Countess of Derby, wore the picture of her late husband, Ferdinando, in a case with the front thickly set with diamonds and his cipher F D on the back.[70] While the role of enamel declined in other jewels, it assumed a greater importance for both miniature and watch cases, and surviving examples show the excellent standard of the craft in England.

Although the front of the Grenville jewel *c.* 1635, called after the miniature of the royalist hero Sir Bevil Grenville (1596–1643), is embellished with a large sapphire, opals, table-cut rubies and diamonds, they do not dominate the composition, but blend with the brilliant colours of the bouquet of flowers – roses, daisies, etc. – on a black ground[71] (Plate 87). Similarly accomplished decoration, with the flowers standing out against the burnished gold ground of another miniature case of the same date, illustrates the high standard of enamelling attained during the reign of Charles I.[72] Unfortunately, nothing is known about the design of the black cases for the miniatures of her husband and son listed in the schedule of Christian, Countess of Devonshire's will.[73]

Charles I's patronage of the French enamel painters (see above, p. 177) meant that miniature portraits could now be executed in enamel. Such pictures could be worn framed under a crystal, without a cover of the sort that was needed to protect a painting in watercolours from fading. The back and sides of the case would be enamelled with sprigs and other motifs.

The care taken over the setting of miniatures is illustrated by the letters of John Hervey, first Earl of Bristol, to his father. Having decided on a miniature of his late wife for a memorial, he consulted his father:

> Sir, having made Cross the limner take a copy in miniature from the picture Brook drew at Bury for my dear wife, and being very desirous to have something engraved on the backside of it which might be some epitomy of her beautifull soul, I have sent you this inclosed (being well acquainted with your happy genius to poetry) not for an approbation but for your correction . . . The size of the paper being that of the picture will confine you to a dozen lines to represent infinite vertues in.

87 The Grenville locket, containing a miniature of Sir Bevil Grenville (1596–1643), the front with botanical enamelling on black ground and set with a large sapphire, opals, table-cut rubies and diamonds. Hanging pearl. Back: lozenges, octofoils and drop motifs on a ground of arabesques, framed in scrolled border. 1635. British Museum.

He recurred to the subject in another letter, this time requesting advice about the text for the back, desiring that

some fuller memorandum might be made of all those various graces God and nature had adornd her with, to remain in our family as an incentive for future daughters of it to emulate in ye imitation of. Something of that sort I must beg your assistance in. They are both for my private wearing.

His proposed text was given in a postscript:

Domina Isabella Hervey. O decus! O dolor! Una tecum tota domûs nostrae gloria occidit. Multae faeminae egerunt probe, tu vero omnes superâsti, dilecta Deo, chara mortalibus. Ob. 7 March, 1692.

Six years later he remarried and, on being sent a miniature by his wife, wrote: 'I put it on my arm ye moment I beheld it, & there have kissd it ore & ore till I have almost spoild ye crystall.'[74]

An enamelled miniature of a man in armour *c.* 1690, with a crowned, interlaced cipher at the back with two loops for a ribbon to pass through, is in the Devonshire collection and would have been worn on the wrist.[75] According to the Duchess of Marlborough this was a Dutch fashion; she wrote from Holland that 'It is the fashion in these countries to wear bracelets of dyamonds and pictures about their rists, buckled on in a manner that they cannot come off without undoing.'[76] It was a custom she herself adopted, wearing the duke's picture set in the clasp of a pearl bracelet.[77] She also had other jewels set with miniatures: a ring with the miniature covered by a thin diamond, a gift from the Duke of Bridgwater,[78] and another in a buckle framed by diamonds with a pearl pendant. The miniatures of her daughters were set in this manner; that of her friend Madame d'Escalache was enclosed in a locket.[79]

BUTTONS AND OTHER FASTENINGS

Although some of the ways in which buttons had been used to adorn dress fell out of favour, they continued to be worn by both men and women. They were no longer sewn to hats as in the early seventeenth century, but changes in male dress, especially the introduction of the vest, actually increased the number required, and the turned-back cuffs of the coat were often fastened with one or more buttons. They could be made of base and precious metals, in filigree and enamel work, and were often set with pearls and gem-stones; they could even be made of glass from Nottingham, which was said in 1697 to be 'very strong and will not break'.[80]

Although the designs are not always specified, wills and inventories give a view of the types of button used, and sometimes their function and value. For festive occasions at court, the diamond-set buttons could be costly, as well as shedding a brilliance on the scene. In 1642 Elizabeth, Countess of Devonshire, could bequeath 'five dozen . . . pearle buttons haveng a sparke of a Diamond upon each of them . . . seaventeene gold buttons sett with sixe Diamonds a peece . . . my great buttons sett with seven Dyamonds a peece . . . my Burrage [borage flower]) Buttons . . . two and Twentie gold buttons set with one Rubie upon each of them'.[81] At the end of the period the collection of the Duchess of Marlborough shows that buttons were often associated with loops: '12 Buttons of the same sort [set round with brilliants] for the Bodyes value 335*l.* /& 13 Loopes that goes with them val 135*l.*'.[82] Three different (but unspecified) 'fashions' for the buttons were distinguished in the inventory made around 1715–18. One set, described as 'smaller', comprised '4 Buttons with 9 diamonds in Each val 50[*l.*]'. 4 loopes with 10. diamonds in Each loop val. 25[*l*]'.[83] The preceding entry, presumably of a middling size, had '2. Buttons with 7 diamonds about each of them about the bigness of the middle stone val. 130*li.* 2. loopes with 13. diamonds in each, & one larg diamond at the bottom of each loope val. 210[*l.*]'.[84]

In Mary Evelyn's poem the heroine had

. . . Diamond Buckles too,
For Garters, and as Rich for Shoo . . .
A *Manteau* Girdle, Ruby Buckle . . .
Besides these Jewels you must get
Cuff Buckles, and a handsom Set
Of Tags for Palatine, a curious Hasp
The manteau 'bout her Neck to clasp.[85]

Such jewels existed not just in the satirist's imagination but in reality in the Duchess of Marlborough's collection:

A Large Buckle for a Girdle of fossets . . . Four diamond Buckles & loopes to put upon the Net [*sic*] of a Manteau. Six diamond buckles and loops for a Manteau sleeves. There is in the loops for the sleeves 124 diamonds some brilliants and some fossets.[86]

Tags, some set with diamonds, were included in the 1670 Lauderdale inventory,[87] and in 1718 the Duchess of Marlborough owned 'Eight little square buckles for a wastecoat, fosse [i.e., fosset] and ten tags'.[88]

In 1639 Margaret Verney bequeathed her diamond clasps to Ralph Verney's wife,[89] and in Restoration documents the term was usually used for a cloak fastening. In 1680 John Keech had in his stock 'a Mantua Claspe with false stones',[90] and in 1683 Frances Dobson bequeathed 'my mantle with the silver clasps'.[91] Some consisted of several parts, like the 'Mantua Clasp in 3 pieces sett with rose Diamonds' in the Orphans records,[92] and perhaps inspired Mary Evelyn's description.

BRACELETS

Bracelets, singly or in pairs, were worn by both men and women. Most were strings of hardstone, coral or amber beads and pearls, but others were of wrought gold, like the chain of 'prettie bose gold work' in the 1652 Eglinton inventory.[93] These could also be jewelled, like Lady Binning's pair of 'carved gold brasselets vii rubies in everie of them',[94] or the Eglinton bracelet of '7 table diamonds and on of litle value 52 litle table diamonds set in fours'.[95] Pearls, so often worn as bracelets in portraits, occur in a list of jewels belonging to Lady Jeane Wemyss, one with a matching belt, another mixed with banded agate beads, and a third 'of goldsmith's work with emerauds'.[96] Four small lengths of jewelled chain in the Cheapside Hoard, set with faceted crystals, amethysts, emeralds and diamonds, and diamonds with turquoises, may have been intended as bracelets.[97] The royalist exile, Ned Blunt, in Aphra Behn's play, *The Rover or The Banished Cavalier*, wore 'a Bracelet of bow'd gold' which his sister had 'ty'd about his Arm at parting'.[98] Ribbon ties remained the usual fastening; there is an exceptional 'double bracelet with a "look" of gold enambled' in the Eglinton inventory.[99]

Bracelets also served as lovers' tokens; Rinaldo in Aphra Behn's novel, *The Lucky*

Mistake, renewed his vows by tying a diamond bracelet around the arm of Atlante in return for one of hair.[100] In the schedule of jewels belonging to Christian, Countess of Devonshire, there are two diamond bracelets, one set with forty-seven and the other with forty-nine 'fosset diamonds', while another was described as a 'Turkie bracelett in eight peacs sett with a Turkeisy & Sixeteen Table diamonds'.[101] An unusual pattern was described in the Countess of Lauderdale's list as a

> great locquet of diamonds a bodkin of a great saphier and small Diamonds a bodkin a great Rubie and small Diamonds A bodkin of a great Diamond and eight Diamonds of a smaller syse A bodkin of a great Turkess and small Diamonds of a smaller syse A bodkin of a great Turkess and small Diamonds A bodkin of a great Emathist and small Diamonds. All these seven sewen upon a black ribbon in fashion of a bracelett.[102]

88 Lady Mary Montgomerie wearing a slide on her wrist, mounted on a dark band. Portrait, 1672. Private collection.

A similar type is recorded in the Tweeddale papers: '9 turquoises set in silver enamelled for a bracelet with diamonds sewed to a black taffetas eight cinques and two long single diamonds for the ends of the bracelet which 9 turquoises with ye 8 cinques and two long diamonds make up the bracelet'.[103]

Three bracelets in the Lauderdale collection used rosettes: a 'Diamond bracelett sett upon jeatt containing nineteen roses', another with 'fifteen little roses of diamonds each rose having a pretty big diamond in the middle' and one 'of great Rubies and different great and small Diamonds containing fourteen roses'. Others had diamonds set in cinques or fives, combined with turquoises; one had 'great Turkeses' and the gold settings enamelled. In some the enamel was an important element in the design, like the 'Bracelett with fourteen stones of severall colours enamelled in gold' or the 'Diamond bracelet enamelled in gold in fasion of crosses and containing ten crosses and eleven little sparks of diamonds'.[104] The cross motif also appeared in a bracelet in the Marlborough collection.[105]

The best bracelets in the Duchess of Marlborough's collection were made of pearls, one having a clasp with the duke's miniature. Less expensively, such miniatures could be set in slides, through which the ribbon of a bracelet could be passed, a fashion depicted in a portrait of Lady Mary Montgomerie dated 1672 (Plate 88). There, a jewelled slide is shown on a wide band of silk or velvet which she holds in her hand.

According to their inventories, London jewellers sold bracelets of white and gold amber, coral and hardstones. The latter could be chosen from black and moss agates, 'blew-stones' and bloodstones, and might be mounted in 'gold wyer work' or filigree.[106] Lady Tweeddale recorded that Queen Catherine wore cornelian bracelets: 'I am glad Lady Yester is pleased with hir bracelet . . . such a on as ye Queen weares cornelliens being att this time much in fashion'.[107] Margaret, Countess of Wemyss, owned in 1683 a splendid 'breslit of cornelians, persed, and dymunts on the cornelians, and a jerb [?garb or sheaf] of many dymunts betwix'.[108]

LOCKETS

In 1656 Lord Digby and his wife owned a 'Jewell of gold called at [*sic*] locket' and two other lockets 'set with diamondes', the second with twenty-five stones;[109] these jewels, successors to the earlier tablets, were named after the tiny latch which secured their hinged covers. They became very fashionable, and in 1668 a family friend, Mr Hewer, wanted to give one worth £40 to Pepys's wife.[110] This was made of diamonds, but others were set with rubies or with diamonds framing a large sapphire or emerald, or combined with pearls. In 1671 Francis Manby, a London Merchant Taylor, owned a 'Lockett sett with three bigg Foset Diamonds & 20 small Diamonds with 59 Pearls' valued at £50.[111] The less valuable but colourful semi-precious stones were widely used; the cheaper ones were set in silver or silver-gilt. The locket was decorative but it could also be functional: in 1683 Frances Dobson distinguished between lockets for the hair of her friends and one with a miniature of Charles II set inside it.[112]

Lockets could be worn at the wrist (see above, p. 216). In 1662 Speaker Lenthall bequeathed to his daughter-in-law, Lady Stonehouse, 'that jewelle which my wife wore at her arm I mean the locket'.[113] Henrietta, Duchess of Orléans, gave the daughter of Sir Thomas Bond, Comptroller of the Household to Queen Henrietta Maria, a bracelet with several lockets, one with her own portrait enamelled and 'sette with fourteen bigge dyamondes' and another with her pet dog, Mimi, also 'sett round with twenty little dyamondes'.[114]

Lockets were also hung from necklaces, like the 'one Lockett or Jewell Consisting of three drops Conteineing therein thirty eight Diamonds greate and small, one necklace of pearl Conteineing one hundred & Fifteene pearles one Lockett or Jewell fastened to the end of the said necklace conteineing twenty nine Diamonds' valued at £170 1*s*, owned in 1672 by Thomas Veale of Middlesex.[115] An emerald locket and necklace, and a locket set with sapphires, emeralds and rubies hanging from an oriental pearl necklace, were given by the eccentric Mr Would-be King in Aphra Behn's novel *At the Court of the King of Bantam*, published in 1684.[116] They could also be worn with the watch.

RINGS

Rings are perhaps the most common surviving item of seventeenth-century jewellery and their popularity is witnessed by their being frequently bequeathed as mementoes, and the way in which some were handed down in families from one generation to another. Thomas Gore of Alderton, Wiltshire, for example, after giving a diamond ring to his wife left the remainder to his son, singling out for special mention his grandmother's wedding ring which had an unusual posy: GOD HAS BROUGHT TO PASS THAT WHICH UNLIKELY WAS.[117] About the same time, in 1683, Robert Price, a haberdasher, divided his collection of rings between his sisters, nieces and friends, while his cousin and executor was to have the best diamond ring.[118]

Like other jewels, the design of rings was simplified in the seventeenth century. Relief decoration on the shoulders almost disappeared, the hoop merely broadening out at the junction with the bezel, and ornament (if any) was either engraved foliage or small gems in raised collets. The entire hoop and the sides and back of the bezel could be enamelled in black, blue or white opaque colours with spots of translucent red enamel over them. The enamel was often kept for the back, and sometimes as a filling for the arcades on the sides of the bezel. Stones could be given extra security by small claws at the corners, called 'greiphins feitt' in the list of Lady Binning's jewels.[119]

The rings in the Cheapside Hoard illustrate these styles. Clusters predominate:

rosettes of small cabochon emeralds or garnets grouped round a large central stone glow with colour against the opaque white enamel. Smaller stones could be set side by side across a bezel only slightly wider than the hoop, a style still used. The largest stones – cat's-eyes, a table-cut diamond, fancy-cut sapphire and garnet – were set in substantial 'pie-dish' bezels. There are no examples of heart rings in the hoard, but two occur in the 1652 Eglinton inventory: 'A diamond ring, set in the forme of a hart, enambled green' and another 'set in the forme of a crowned hart with 4 diamond'.[120]

A number of rings could be worn at the same time and when the newly married Mrs Wood visited Pepys, he was impressed by her appearance: 'mighty rich in rings and fine clothes, like a lady'.[121] The sparkling brilliant cut, available from the mid 1670s, made the diamond more attractive than ever before, effectively emphasising the gestures of the hand. Knotting was recommended as a means of showing off the diamond ring embellishing a white hand, and John Gay observed that 'a pinch of snuff judiciously taken will display the glittering ornament of her little finger'.[122]

Large stones, like the Countess of Lauderdale's ruby or her rose-cut diamond, were either set as solitaires or enhanced by a border of smaller diamonds in oblong or oval bezels.[123] Clusters or roses predominate, but several inventories have a design for seven stones, the largest in the centre, flanked by three smaller stones at either side.[124] Eight small rose-cut stones are set in a fleur-de-lis ring in the Hay of Duns Castle collection. Unusually a turquoise and diamond ring in the Burghley Schedule was 'sett in fashion of a cross'.[125] Exceptionally, some rings had gem-studded hoops; the ruby coronation ring of Mary of Modena took this form,[126] as did a brilliant diamond ring supplied to Lord Bolingbroke in 1714.[127]

Signet rings, the plain hoops expanding to the flat bezel, sometimes with an inset hardstone, continued to be engraved with heraldic and emblematic devices and initials.[128] The outstanding signet of the time was made for Charles II in the auricular style of Paul Van Vianen, the bezel engraved with the royal arms, his cipher in a cartouche inscribed round the sides with the motto DIEU ET MON DROIT, and the lion and unicorn supporters worked in relief on the shoulders.[129] The signet, however, declined with the growing use of fob seals, often worn with the watch, though in the inventories of London jewellers it is not always easy to distinguish these from the small desk seals which were also being made.

A special category of enamelled gold rings was described by Elias Ashmole as

> cast into the figure of Garters the ground on the outside enamelled with a deep blue through which the golden letters of the motto appearing set them off with an admirable beauty. And it seems such Garter rings have been of ancient use since the Preface to the Black Book of the Order taking notice of the wearing of the Garter on the left leg and shoulder adds also the Thumb: by which we suppose is meant Gold rings made into the fashion of Garters and bestowed by some new installed knights upon their Relations and friends to wear in memorial of so great an honour conferred upon them.[130]

No surviving statute of the Order of the Garter makes any reference to the wearing of the Order's insignia in this fashion by the knights, let alone to their giving it to relations and friends. A solitary example seems to be a mourning ring left in 1626 by Lancelot Andrewes, the Prelate of the Order, and now kept in the treasury of his cathedral at Winchester. The bezel is formed by the buckle of the Garter and is set with a diamond.[131]

Not only gem-set rings were used as love tokens. A heart flanked by the couple's initials appeared on the outside of an enamelled hoop ring, with the arms of Wilmer, Chibnall, Haselwood and Andrews on the inside, made to commemorate the marriage of Sir Anthony Haselwood and Elizabeth Wilmer before 1631.[132] The heart was a favourite symbol. In 1680 John Keech had in his stock 'one heart ring with a turquoise stone' and another with the popular *fede* motif: 'one turkey ring cut hand in hand'.[133] The motif also appears amidst flowers and accompanied by appropriate posies like LET VERTU BE THY GUIDE.[134] A wedding ring with a pair of white hands clasping a crowned diamond heart is inscribed DUDLEY AND KATHERINE UNITED 26 MARCH 1706.[135]

Not all posy rings were enamelled; the outside could be decorated in various ways with engraving or chasing, and many were obviously used as wedding rings. John Keech had forty-six in his stock in 1680, and these would be engraved with the purchaser's chosen posy.[136] Care was taken over the choice of such mottoes and in 1660, while their lamb was stewing, the Pepys family passed the time composing a suitable posy for the wedding ring of Roger Pepys.[137] A collection of posies published in 1658, *The Mysteries of Love and Eloquence or the Art of Wooing and Complimenting*, included individualised examples with different Christian names.[138] With their carefully chosen posies and associations, such rings were treasured, and on the husband's death, the widow might add *memento mori* emblems to the outside of the hoop, converting it into a mourning ring.[139]

An unusual design which appeared in Restoration England was a chain ring. On his return in 1660 Charles II gave the captain of the ship that brought him to Dover a ring made of minute gold chains, which became a family heirloom.[140] It was with such a ring, the gold chains studded with table-cut rubies, that the future James II married Mary of Modena at Dover in November 1673,[141] and the 'chained ring with 7/8 turkases in it' mentioned in the inventory of Margaret Scott of Rossie was probably of the same style, like a miniature bracelet.[142]

Some broad hoop rings were enamelled with figurative subjects on a white ground. One depicts Biblical scenes, another an arcaded market with traders. The latter is inscribed RL TO T AND T TO K:L.[143]

The black cords attached to rings, which appear in Jacobean portraits, were still worn (see Plate XII), and the custom was explained by Lady Brilliana Harley in a letter to her son, Ned, in 1638: 'Sence you keep the britell ringe tell it brake, I have sent you on of more dureing substance and that you may know I have worne it I have left the ribon upon it which did help to make it fite for my finger.'[144] Rings might also be attached to bracelets, and Anne Hill of St Brides in 1626 bequeathed 'two paire of best braceletts and the two ringes tyed thereunto',[145] and in 1662 Speaker Lenthall enjoined in his will 'that my son will weare his mother's wedding ring about his arme in remembrance of me'.[146]

WATCHES

Although watches were unreliable time-keepers for the first three-quarters of the seventeenth century, this did not deter people from owning them. Cases varied from the severely simple to the magnificent.

An example of the simple 'Puritan' style, usually oval or egg-shaped, is a watch with a movement by John Midnall, now in the British Museum, attached to a short fob chain with a medallion engraved with the crest and cipher of Oliver Cromwell.[147] No doubt the many gold and silver watches listed in the inventories of London jewellers were of this simple type.

For the production of more ambitious and decorative watches, the goldsmiths and enamellers collaborated. Cases were designed in a variety of naturalistic shapes – pumpkins, cockle-shells, sea-urchins or a Tudor rose – and such Form watches, whose cases disguise their purpose, have English movements.[148] Some had a striking mechanism and were supplied with pierced openwork backs or sides, which could be engraved with flowers – lilies, daffodils and roses – either in all-over patterns or radiating from a central motif – a style illustrated by the silver case of a striking clock made for Charles I by Edward East.[149] A circular case, also with a movement by East, is enamelled in the Toutin technique with small flowers in relief on a pale blue ground on the outside, and with a landscape, buildings and figures in black on a blue ground inside.[150] A watch by Samuel Betts has the case enamelled on the outside with translucent green, a central white daisy and a border of white flowers tinged with pink; inside, there are pastoral scenes on the covers, and the dial is also enamelled with translucent green, with a sunflower in the middle and a border of flowers.[151] Some of David Bouguet's watches have floral ornaments engraved on their dials but, fine as they are, they cannot compare with the rich effect of polychrome enamel.[152] The superb flowers on the dial of a watch by Henry Jones, said to have been given by Charles I to his servant, John Ashburnham, is certainly worthy of the king's fine taste.[153]

One of the two watches in the Cheapside Hoard was set in an hexagonal block of emerald, the dial also being enamelled green.[154] Two watches in the Countess of Lauderdale's collection in 1670 were jewelled: one an 'enamelled gold watch sett with diamonds', the other an 'enamelled gold watch sett with Diamonds and Turkeases one of the keys is plain and the other enamelled with one Turkess'. Both had chains *en suite* and were valued at £100 and £60.[155] They compare with the 'Watch case, Chaine and hooke contayneing . . . one hundred ninety seaven Diamond' bequeathed by Lady Katherine O'Brien to her granddaughter, Katherine Hyde, in 1705.[156]

With the introduction of the balance spring after 1675, watches became more reliable as time-keepers but, paradoxically, their cases became less decorative. They were larger, to accommodate the more powerful spring, and were fitted with minute hands. Some were inlaid with coral or polished hardstone plaques, the bright colour contrasting with the gold mounts.[157] An innovation was the adoption of tortoise-shell for the outer, or pair, cases usually inlaid with silver or more rarely gold, with patterns of birds and flowers, ciphers and coats-of-arms upheld by putti. Such protective cases were found as early as 1658, when John Knight owned a 'Gould inamelled watch with a Silver outcase & Silver Chaine';[158] Philp Trahearne's stock in 1679 included a 'Silver watch with A Studded Case'.[159] A great many watches were stocked and sold by the London jewellers, and Misson gave the widespread use of watches as a reason for the small number of public clocks in London.[160]

ACCESSORIES

Other trinkets besides watches were worn hanging from chains or ribbons. The wife and daughters of a prosperous merchant, Sir Frugal, in Massinger's play, *The City Madam*, first appear on the stage 'in several postures, with looking glasses at their girdles'.[161] The handles may have been like those, described as fan-holders, in the Cheapside Hoard: enamelled and gem-studded, perhaps shaped like a flower on a stem or a caduceus, with a suspension ring at the base.[162]

Pomanders continued to be used, and might be combined with gold and pearls into bracelets[163] or placed in a container. These were pear- or flask-shaped, made of engraved or enamelled gold and silver, or inlaid with hardstone plaques, like the sole example in the Cheapside Hoard.[164] They hung from the girdle, like

> . . . the Bob of Gold
> Which a *Pomander* Ball does hold,
> This to her side she does attach
> With Gold *Crochet*, or *French Pennache*

in Mary Evelyn's poem.[165]

The kinds of items that might be hung with the watch were enumerated in the 'advertisement' inserted in *The Tatler* of the jewels stolen in 1710 from the fictitious Lady Farthingale:

> a large new gold repeating watch, made by a Frenchman; a gold chain, and all the proper appurtenances hung upon steel swivels, to wit, lockets with the hair of dead and living lovers, seals with arms, emblems and devices cut in cornelian, agate, and onyx, with Cupids, hearts,

darts, altars, flames, rocks, pick-axes, roses, thorns, and sunflowers; as also variety of ingenious French mottoes; together with gold etuis for quills, scissors, needles, thimbles, and a sponge dipped in Hungary water.[166]

For greater convenience in carrying these items, the chatelaine was devised. The top was a deep hook of flat metal to go over the waist band, broadening out to accommodate a number of hinged pendants with spring swivel catches for the watch, etc. The face of the hook was embellished with a plate of gold or silver, with relief ornament. Less frequently, the whole was made of gold or silver. An early example with chains and swivels has a watch by Thuilet, the outer cover of which is engraved with the arms of Queen Anne *c.* 1705. The gold pendants, hook plate, key and watch case are inlaid with mother-of-pearl and set with garnets in a chased border enamelled black with touches of red.[167]

SNUFF BOXES, ETC.

The practice of inhaling powdered tobacco, or snuff, arose in the later seventeenth century, and by 1680 jewellers could be found stocking a 'gold snuffbox'.[168] The 'Gold Snuff Box that has in it Two pictures of her Father [the Duke of Marlborough] when he was an youth' which was bequeathed to her daughter, Mary, Duchess of Montagu, by Sarah, Duchess of Marlborough, in 1744 was probably a late-seventeenth-century box.[169]

Perhaps the oldest and finest example of a snuff box with an English association is a jewelled box made for Mary II by the Dutch goldsmith, Adam Loofs. It is an oval box with her monogram reserved in red enamel on the lid, the crown and border set with diamonds; on the sides, a trail of Tudor roses and foliage is also enamelled, while the base is engraved with an oval rosette and border.[170] There is a fitted mirror inside and it may have been used for comfits.

SMALL-SWORDS

Samuel Pepys provides a date for the new style of sword when he records on 3 February 1661 that 'This day I first began to go forth in my coate and sworde as the manner now among gentlemen is.'[171] The small-sword became an indispensable part of a gentleman's dress, particularly at court, and the hilts were often made of gold or silver and decorated with floral motifs and, between 1680 and 1700, with Biblical and military figures and other small scenes.[172]

7

The social context of early Georgian jewellery 1714–89

This was the golden age of the decorative arts in Britain and jewellery attained a high level of craftsmanship and design, for although Paris still retained its supremacy, Huguenot immigrants had brought French standards of excellence to the London trade. Improved faceting and foiling revealed the beauty of white and coloured stones, which looked their best by candlelight. Designs and the style of mounts reflect the succession of styles in painting and architecture: late baroque, followed by rococo *c.* 1740 and, from the 1770s, neo-classicism.

ROYALTY

George I, who had divorced his wife, Sophia Dorothea of Zell, gave some of Queen Anne's jewellery to his German favourites, though his daughter-in-law, Princess Caroline, received her share.[1] As consort to George II she was ablaze with jewels at the coronation:

> The dress of the Queen was as fine as the accumulated riches of the city and suburbs could make it, for besides her own jewels which were of great number and very valuable she had on her head and shoulders all the pearls she could borrow of the ladies of quality at one end of the town – and on her petticoat all the diamonds she could hire of the Jews and jewellers at the other.[2]

At the wedding of her daughter, the Princess Royal, to the Prince of Orange in 1733 her head was 'loaded with pearls and diamonds'.[3] The bride was dressed in white damask, with

> The finest embroidery of rich embossed gold and festoons of flowers intermixed in their natural colours. On one side of her head she had a great green diamond of a vast size, the shape of a pear, and two pearls prodigiously large that were fastened to wires and hung loose upon her hair: on the other side small diamonds prettily disposed; her earrings, necklace and bars to her stays all extravagantly fine, presents of the Prince of Orange to her.[4]

The green diamond was sometimes hung as the pendant to a necklace of twenty-two large rose diamonds which she had at this time.

When Queen Caroline died in 1737, the Dowager Duchess of Marlborough wrote that 'she gave no legacy to anyone but left it all to his Majesty – her jewels are worth a very great sum'.[5] On ceremonial occasions the king's Garter star and George and his coat and hat buttons 'with prodigious fine diamonds' shone forth with great splendour, and the Lesser George is clearly displayed in his portrait by Pyne in 1759.[6] He did not give much away: in his younger days he was known to bring out of his pocket a 'handful of maimed topazes and amethysts and give them to be raffled for the Maids of Honour',[7] and he was notoriously mean to his favourite, the Countess of Albemarle.[8] The only jewel with which he rewarded the statesman, Sir Robert Walpole, was 'a large diamond cracked right through'.[9]

At the time of the Jacobite rising of 1745 he sent to Hanover for safekeeping some valuable jewels, which he later bequeathed to his grandson and successor George III;[10] all those which had been left in England went to his son, William, Duke of Cumberland (1721–65). On his accession in 1760 George III brought the jewels back from Hanover, and acquired the Duke of Cumberland's share for £54,900 – which the duke later complained was a bargain.[11]

Princess Augusta, the wife of Frederick, Prince of Wales, was a client of Peter Dutens and of Isaac Lacam, and also borrowed jewels to ensure that she stood out at masquerades and other social events.[12] When her collection was dispersed by Christie's on 1–3 February 1773, her son, George III, bought a pair of diamond and emerald earrings and other gem-stones for his wife, Queen Charlotte.[13]

Queen Charlotte was the first queen since the early seventeenth century to possess jewels rivalling those of Continental royalty, having at her disposal the reunited collection of hereditary pieces. Among her jewels were: a necklace of twenty-six large brilliants, a big cross, a pair of three-drop brilliant earrings, two large single drops, two brilliant rosettes (one with a drop in the centre), two brilliant sleeve knots, a large diamond bouquet, a small crown with pendaloque diamonds hanging from four gold rods, and three pearl and brilliant bow-knots. John Duval restrung the pearl necklace, which is believed to have descended from Mary, Queen of Scots, through George I's mother, the Electress Sophia, and added a drop which Queen Charlotte had brought from Germany with her pear pearl earrings framed in diamond chains. Her stomacher was the 'finest piece of magnificence and workmanship' ever seen, 'the fond is a network as fine as cat gut of small diamonds and the rest is a large pattern of natural flowers composed of very large diamonds'.[14] A Quaker lady who watched the queen on a state visit to the City shortly after her marriage was equally impressed by this piece: 'the lustre was inconceivable . . . which was represented by the vast profusion of diamonds placed on it by the magnificence of so great a king'.[15] They were considered as Crown property, for the queen's use during her lifetime, and were separate from the personal jewels which the king gave to her on birthdays and to commemorate the birth of their sixteen children and his recovery from illness.[16]

An important source for the royal collection was India; gifts were made both by the Indian Princes and by the wealthy English who had made their fortunes there. In 1765 the Mughal Emperor Shah Alam sent a collection of precious objects to George III, and the queen received a share of the diamonds and pearls;[17] the Nawab of Arcot sent seven superb brilliants,[18] and others were given by a Mr Errington.[19] A carved emerald grape presented by Mrs Warren Hastings was hung on the queen's diamond and emerald necklace.[20] By 1769 Lady Mary Coke was able to observe that

> The Queen's diamonds seem to have surprised everybody: many of them we have all seen but she had so many additional ones and of such extraordinary size that the Princess Amelia said (in which the ladies agreed) that the description sounded like a fairy tale . . . she had another of surprising magnitude which was placed in the middle of a nosegay of jewels.[21]

Her dazzling appearance was caricatured in an anonymous print of 1786 entitled 'The Queen of Hearts bedecked with diamonds': she is covered with jewels and beside her is a crowned heart and a bulse of diamonds.[22] The effect was so astonishing that some people doubted whether the stones were genuine. Lady Holderness, wife of the Governor to the Prince of Wales, told Lady Mary Coke that she overheard two gentlemen who 'agreed when they considered the quality and fitness of the Queen's jewels that they must be false, for said one of them, were they real diamonds I don't think the whole kingdom would be able to purchase them'.[23]

Queen Charlotte kept her jewels in a special cabinet made by William Vile in her bedroom at Buckingham House, and her collection of twenty-five watches hung in a glass case beside the bed.[24] The collection was world-famous, and among the foreign visitors who asked if they might see it were an Austrian archduke and archduchess and the Prince and Princess Albani from Rome.[25] The most important pieces were deposited at the Bank of England each year after the last Birthday Drawing-Room, while the court was at Windsor and Kew from July to January.[26]

This might have been a relief to the queen, who complained of their excessive weight,[27] and even admitted to Miss Burney that they were a worry:

> it is the pleasure of a week, a fortnight at the most to return no more. I thought at first I should always choose to wear them but with the fatigue and trouble of putting them on and the care they required and the fear of loosing them, believe me Ma'am in a fortnight's time I longed for my earlier dress.[28]

She left her personal collection to her four youngest surviving daughters, who sold some pieces, including the Nawab of Arcot's diamonds, to the firm of Rundell, Bridge and Rundell. The remainder was auctioned by Christie's on 7 May 1819.

George III preferred a quiet family life at Windsor or Kew, for which he created the Windsor uniform which he wore with a Garter and breast star,[29] but on festive occasions he could cut a fine figure. *The Lady's Magazine* described his appearance at his birthday court in 1779, wearing

> an elegant set of mother of pearl buttons, set round with small brilliant diamonds . . . a garter, the george, and a star . . . His shoe and knee buckles were diamonds . . . a sword elegantly

ornamented with jewels: likewise a brilliant diamond ring: but what rendered it truly estimable was the amiable miniature of her Majesty with which it was embellished.[30]

The magnificent Great Georges in the royal collection which belonged to George III, with rider, horse and dragon modelled in the round and entirely paved with diamonds, exemplify the high standard of stone cutting and setting attained in his reign (frontispiece).[31] The Prince of Wales, who became a great collector of art, was the one member of the family who developed a passion for jewels, and the archives at Windsor which document his purchases for himself, his brothers and sisters, and for Mrs Fitzherbert (whom he had secretly married in 1785), provide a guide to the most elegant taste of the time.

ARISTOCRACY

Like retainers, carriages and fine houses in broad parklands, jewels formed part of the outward display of the British nobility, representing a substantial investment and for the wearers a great responsibility. When the newly married Lady Louisa Connolly inadvertently left her jewels behind at Dublin in 1759, she dreaded having to face her mother-in-law without them, and told her sister that 'the uncertainty of what has become of them has made my blood circulate so well that I shall never forget it, the longest day I live'.[32] Family pride was at stake: when Sophia, the young wife of the elderly Earl Granville, complained that her head ached with the weight of her diamonds, her mother, the Countess of Pomfret, explained that 'Her husband is not pleased unless she be magnificent – he would have her covered with jewels.'[33] It was customary for the family jewels to be reset when the heir married and the splendid jewel casket ordered from Peter Dutens by Richard Lumley, fourth Earl of Scarbrough, for his wife, Barbara Savile, when they married in 1753 comprised:

	£	*s*	*d*
A necklace of brilliants which cost	346	5	0
A nesclavage girdle with tossells [*sic*], knot and ends	265	7	6
The horn of plenty which hangs to the necklace	167	7	6
As the esclavage was made too short an addition had to be made which cost	37	7	0
The cross	187	7	6
A fine aigrette representing an eagle	96	0	0
One aigrette of different flowers tied with a knot	136	0	0
An aigrette pompon	98	0	0
Four circles of brilliants for the hair	41	0	0
A girdle buckle	108	0	0
A pair of 3 drop earrings in which my lady employed her two large drops and in which she furnished 6 side drops	130	0	0
Total price of the earrings in addition to stones supplied	325	15	0
A sett of five fine starrs	330	15	0
A brilliant hoop ring and a gold one	14	0	0
TOTAL	2024	4	6
[Should be	2283	4	6]

[*continued from previous page*]

A small ring with flowers tyed with a knot of brilliants		5	5	0
His Lordship's seal		13	17	0
For some brilliants for form several ornaments, watch and chain, etc.		74	5	0
	TOTAL	2117	11	6

34

Jewellers proudly showed off commissions of this grand nature to clients such as the Countess of Hertford, who wrote to her friend the Countess of Pomfret in 1741:

I have been at this moment agreeably interrupted by a jeweller who said he was carrying home some jewels for a wedding which he wished to let me see. He shewed me the very finest pearl necklace I ever beheld with three dropt earrings belonging to it and a pair of most magnificent brilliant earrings with single drops I think finer than those of the Princess of Hesse. He told me he had a solitaire at home for the same lady which surpassed what he then showed me: besides a watch set with diamonds to the value of £1600.[35]

The greatest quantity of jewels were paraded at the Drawing-Rooms held in honour of the birthdays of the king and queen. Members of the royal family commented on them as they moved among the courtiers. In 1729, for example, at her Birthday Drawing-Room, Queen Caroline admired Mrs Delany's jewels and, when told that they had been borrowed from Lady Sunderland, laughed and said she had assumed they were a present from Lord Selkirk, a rich bachelor admirer.[36]

Receptions at private houses also provided occasions for the display of jewels. Lady Betty Germain was a celebrated hostess who, according to Mrs Delany, owned as many jewels as would deck out a Sultana of the Indies; at one of her parties in 1752 'great numbers came to show themselves . . . Lady Coventry, Lady Catherine Petersham and Mrs Watson, were allowed the finest: their clothes all had silver ground and coloured flowers with silver mixed and a great quantity of jewels in their hair.'[37] There were also rich displays at the ridottos, balls, masquerades and gala fetes held in the rotunda at Ranelagh. Nor were these confined to London; they happened in the provinces, too. At Chester in 1773, Lady Watkin Williams Wynn, whose husband was mayor, struck one observer as

very brilliant. She looked very handsome and the picture of good nature and happiness. Her gown was something of gold but I don't know what. A finer necklace than Lady Grosvenor's, earrings, watch and chain all Diamond a stomacher with four Bows all Diamonds so that she was quite dazzling. Her bracelets were pearls and she had a row with a large drop falling below her necklace which was the princess Dowager's and cost five hundred guineas. She was valued at £20,000 exclusive of her inestimable self.[38]

In 1781 Mrs Lybbe Powys wrote that at Yarmouth, 'In the evening our very large party met at the ball, a very numerous assembly and numbers of the ladies were profuse in jewellery – particularly the Ladies Buckingham and Astley.'[39] It was the same in

Ireland. Caroline Dawson wrote from Dublin in 1778 to Lady Louisa Stuart that 'everything seems to go on in great state here. The Duchess of Leinster appears in sack and hoop and diamonds in an afternoon, French horns playing at every meal, and such quantities of jewellery that one would imagine oneself in a palace.'[40]

Foreigners were impressed by English magnificence. After dining in Germany with one of the Electors at Bonn, the Duchess of Northumberland wrote that 'the ladies did me the honour to admire my diamonds so much I really thought they would have pull'd me to pieces. The ladies of this court have few of them any jewels.'[41] At a celebration held after the king's recovery from illness in 1789, the splendour was quite overwhelming, and Lady Louisa Stuart declared: 'I do not think any country could show a more magnificent spectacle.'[42] Curiously, this splendour was seldom reflected in the portraits, which favoured either the Van Dyck or a less formal style of dress for both ladies and gentlemen.

NABOBS

A new element in English eighteenth-century society was the nabob. They were characterised by the playwright, Samuel Foote, in 1773 as 'these new gentlemen, who from the caprice of fortune, and a strange chain of events, have acquired immoderate wealth, and rose to uncontroled power abroad, find it difficult to descend from their dignity, and admit of any equal at home'.[43] Lord Macaulay drew attention to the fact that they were often of neither 'ancient nor opulent families', a fact which doubtless contributed to their unpopularity.[44] They transferred their wealth from the East in the form of gem-stones, following a long tradition; in Oliver Goldsmith's *She Stoops to Conquer*, Miss Neville's fortune from her uncle, 'the India Director', consists chiefly of jewels.[45]

The most successful of all the nabobs was Robert Clive (1725–75), created Baron Clive of Plassey, who lived as splendidly as any of the old nobility. According to Horace Walpole, he had remitted home 'all the Mogul's pearls and rubies', some being sold in bulses to Yehiel Prager and Peter Duval.[46] Others were made up into jewels for his wife and himself, his diamond badge of the Order of the Bath being particularly splendid.[47]

Although all nabobs' wives wore 'more pearls and diamonds than would fill a peck measure', according to Mrs Delany,[48] they were eclipsed by Mrs Warren Hastings. Even her black satin riding-dress was jewelled:

> the jacket and bottom of her petticoat were edged with pearls and the buttons of her sleeves were diamonds. On her left shoulder was a valuable diamond star and two large diamonds marked the length of her waist. Her underjacket or waistcoat was of white satin ornamented with buttons of good size. Her hat was black edged with large pearls, the button and loop were of diamonds and could not be worth less than £4–5000. Pendant to a black feather which nodded over her left eye was a large drop diamond and in front of the hat was another of large size.[49]

GENTRY AND MERCHANTS

All who could afford to do so imitated the nobility. Samuel Richardson in *Clarissa Harlowe* (1747–8) expressed the generally accepted view that the jewels of a man or woman should be 'the newest, richest we could procure answerable to our fortune'.[50] Those without ample means aspired to be thought rich, as when the wife of Goldsmith's *Vicar of Wakefield* asked the painter of her portrait 'not to be too frugal of his diamonds in her stomacher and hair'.[51] According to Casanova, the jewels of the actress, Kitty Fisher, were the envy of London,[52] and Mrs Abington wore her own splendid jewels on stage when playing the part of a lady of fashion.[53]

Girls wore jewels long before they married. Sir Thomas Grandison, in Richardson's novel *Sir Charles Grandison* (1753–4), tells his daughter, Caroline, 'to stick some of your mother's jewels in your hair and bosom to draw the eyes of followers' when he takes her to London in search of a husband.[54] Similarly, the heroine of 'The History of an Heiress', published in *the Lady's Magazine* in 1773, goes to a ball 'covering my head, neck, ears and stomacher with diamonds so I glittered like a star of the first magnitude'.[55]

The gifts made by a gentleman like Edward Weld to his bride in 1740 followed the pattern set by the aristocracy: diamond keeper and wedding ring, earrings, watch and chain, and the family diamond necklace – reset, 'to make it more useful and genteel'.[56] Exceptions were so rare that when Mr Blount of Mapledurham married in 1731, he made a point of recording for posterity his gratitude to his wife for being 'so provident as not to accept diamond earrings' at a time when he was short of money.[57] The will of Philip Stapleton in 1782 lists the typical jewels of a middling landed gentry family:

> One breastbuckle, with Bristow stones set in silver, and two mourning rings . . . my pinchbeck watch, silver-hilted sword, and King William's picture . . . two pair of sleeve buttons set in gold, one gold ring with a pebble set in gold . . . one gold ring with two diamonds set in it.[58]

Unmarried women of similar status could expect to own jewels like those bequeathed to her friends by Clarissa Harlowe in the novel: a watch and equipage, lockets with miniatures, several diamond rings, and her mother's parure of diamond necklace, solitaire and buckles.[59] The jewels of a gentlewoman of more limited means were listed in the will of Abigail Gregory in 1739: gold watch, amethyst earrings, lockets with miniatures, rings and buttons with her mother's hair, diamond and turquoise rings and a seal engraved with the head of Socrates.[60] The only jewels which Elizabeth Hurst, a Dissenting spinster of Bedford, owned were rings, and she left money for her relations to buy gold rings to wear in her memory.[61] It was this mourning and sentimental jewellery that was most widely diffused through all classes of society.

I Crown of Princess Blanche: gold set with sapphires, rubies, diamonds and pearls in twelve lilies rising from the circlet of traceried medallions: 1370–80. Bayerische Verwaltung der Staatlichen Schlössen Garten und Seen Munich.

II Crown of Margaret of York: silver-gilt, enamel, pearls, diamonds, sapphires and rubies: 1461, restored 1865. Cathedral Treasury, Aachen.

III Gold jewel consisting of two ring brooches each set with four blue pastes joined by twin links similarly set, gripped by dragons and centred on a cabochon sapphire. 13th century. Sotheby's.

IV Silver-gilt ring brooch with granulation, formerly set with eight gems: fourteenth century, from Blackthorn, near Bicester. Finder: Len Rees.

V Annunciation jewel formed as a Lombardic letter M: silver-gilt, rubies, emeralds, pearls and a diamond: late fourteenth century. The Warden and Fellows, New College, Oxford.

VI Gold signet set with crystal engraved with the arms of Robert Taylor over foil.
Back: the grasshopper device of Sir Thomas Gresham: 1575. Private collection.

VII Two views of the marriage ring of Sir Thomas Gresham,
showing it closed and open. 1544.

VIII Enamelled gold Lesser George with twenty-four hog back diamonds
set in the armour and horse trappings, enclosed in deep blue enamel.
Garter inscribed with motto. 16th century. Christie's.

IX The Drake jewel, set with a sardonyx cameo of a blackamoor and a white woman, the enamelled frame set with table-cut rubies and diamonds. Inside: miniature of Queen Elizabeth I by Nicholas Hilliard, 1575, with phoenix emblem on the inside of the lid. Collection of Sir George Meyrick, Bt.

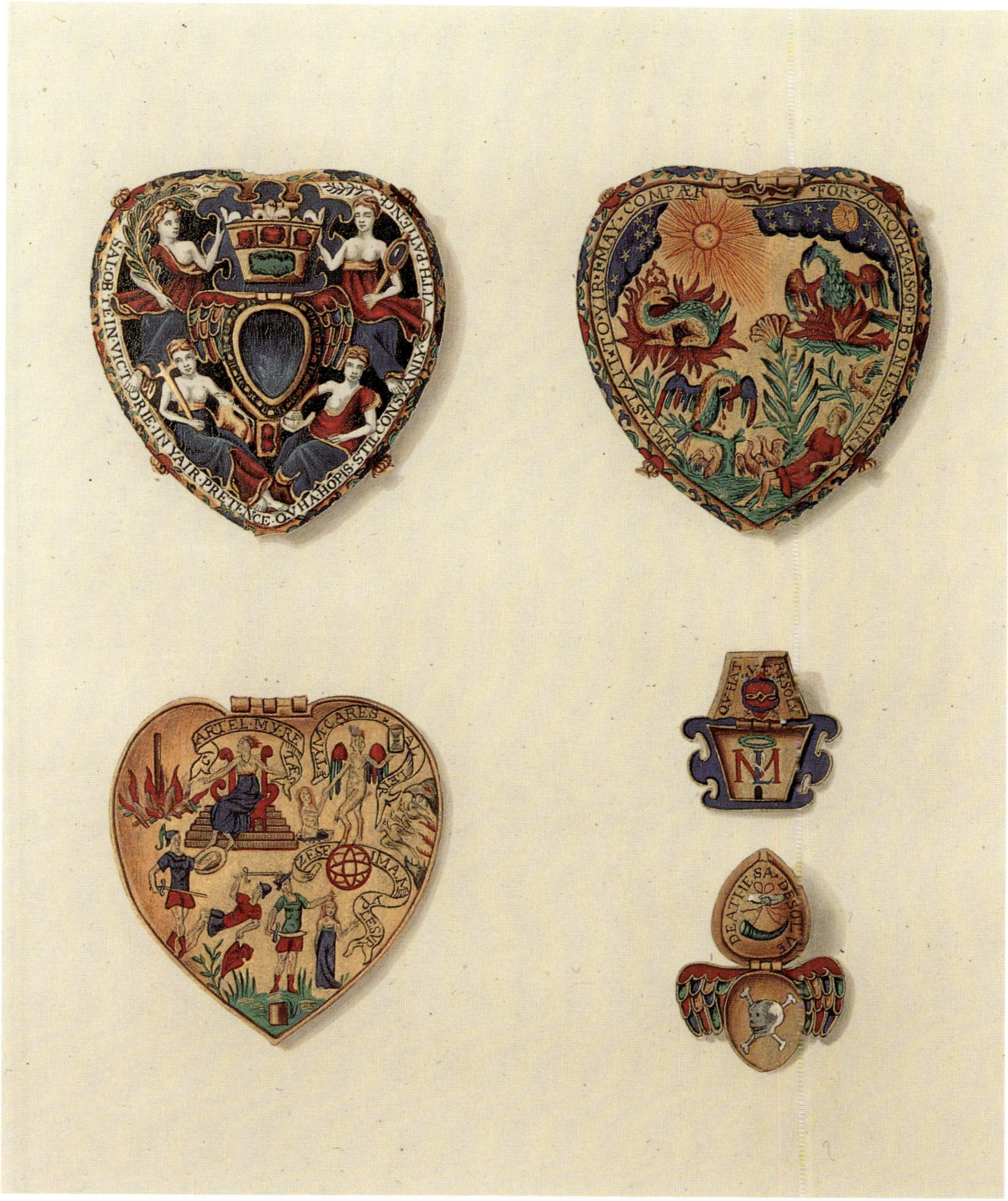

x The Darnley jewel, heart-shaped, the front set with a sapphire in a winged and crowned heart flanked by Faith, Hope, Victory and Truth within a border, with inscription contained on the back, framing other emblems including a salamander and a phoenix. *c.* 1571–8. Collection of H.M. Queen Elizabeth II.

XI Lady Lovelace wearing a monogram jewel in her hair, a locket set with a cameo, chains of pearls and pomander, a jewelled pendant at her neck and a cruciform diamond brooch fastening her collar. Portrait by John de Critz, *c.* 1615. Sotheby's.

XII A lady wearing a chain of enamelled flowers and diamond links, with a ring attached to a black cord on her wrist. Portrait, English School, *c.* 1610 Christie's.

XIII Chain of snakes and ruby esses, said to have been a gift from Mary, Queen of Scots, to Mary Seton. The back showing enamels: *c.* 1580. Collection of Mr Alick Hay of Duns Castle.

XIV Elizabeth Vernon, Countess of Southampton, with her jewels laid out beside her. Portrait, *c.* 1600. Collection of the Duke of Buccleuch and Queensberry, K.T.

XV Portrait of a lady of the Howard family arrayed like a nun at her profession wearing devotional jewellery with court dress. *c.* 1610. Private collection.

XVI Enamelled gold crowned wounded heart brooch, with a cross at the top and an anchor below between yellow tulips. Back: inscribed with the letter M behind the crown, and round the heart: THO I BE CROST MY HOPE IS SURE THO I BE HURT A CROWNE I BEARE – alluding to the symbols on the front. Collection of Mr Richard Falkiner (formerly Hay of Duns Castle).

XVII Cornelian cameo of Charles I set in an enamelled ring. Collection of the Duke of St Albans.

XVIII Enamelled gold anchor-shaped cross set with table-cut diamonds in box collets and petal-shaped drops. Back: showing red heart enamelled on upright and pea-pod enamel on drops. A similar cross is worn by Lady Bathurst in Plate 76. Private collection.

XIX Lesser George set with an onyx cameo in frame of rose-cut diamonds. Back: cornelian cameo St George in buckled Garter with motto: *c.* 1660. Collection of the Duke of Buccleuch and Queensberry, K.T.

XX Enamelled gold George set with rose-cut diamonds: *c.* 1660. Collection of the Duke of Buccleuch and Queensberry, K.T.

XXI Slides from a necklace with a miniature of Mary II as a pendant. Back: showing acanthus-style enamels. Mrs Phillips collection, Christie's.

XXII Gold dragonfly set with rubies, opals, cat's-eyes and diamonds, as worn by the young woman in Plate 81. Back: blue and green enamels. Burghley House, courtesy Lady Victoria Leatham.

XXIII Pendant composed of miniatures of Charles I and Queen Henrietta Maria, painted in profile on lapis lazuli framed in diamonds and hanging from a knot similarly set. Setting 18th century, miniatures earlier. Christie's.

XXIV Locket with a miniature of George II with diamond and ruby frame surmounted by a crown; hanging pearl below. Back: showing hair, gold wire royal cipher within star and buckled Garter with motto. David Lavender, London.

XXV Suite of Scots pebble necklace, earrings and buckle: by David Deuchar of Edinburgh. National Museum of Scotland.

XXVI A young girl wearing a jewelled cross on a ribbon at her neck.
Bardwell. Christie's.

XXVII Silver cross with lilies between the arms, set with rose-cut diamonds. Collection of Mr Alick Hay of Duns Castle.

XXVIII Shuttle-shaped locket with seed pearl bouquet inscribed AMITIE : *c.* 1770. Glasgow Museum and Art Gallery.

XXIX Diamond and sapphire brooch pendant with briolette drops. A gift from Warren Hastings to Mrs David Anderson of St Germans: *c.* 1780. S. J. Phillips.

XXX Designs for jewels for the hair by Christian Taute. Victoria and Albert Museum.

XXXI Design by Christian Taute for brooch with bouquet in vase and top and drop ruby earrings. Victoria and Albert Museum.

XXXII Designs for flower jewels by Christian Taute. Victoria and Albert Museum.

XXXIII A viscountess wearing diamond pins in her hair, diamond and pearl earrings, a pearl choker, diamond and lace sleeve clasps and a large V-shaped stomacher. Portrait by Carl Marcus Tuscher, *c.* 1741. P. and D. Colnaghi.

XXXIV Pair of bracelet clasps of enamelled gold, after the figures of Faith and Hope by Sir Joshua Reynolds for the stained-glass windows in the chapel of New College, Oxford: *c.* 1775. Victoria and Albert Museum.

XXXV Pair of diamond bracelets, the centrepieces with a rose-cut diamond royal cipher and a maritime trophy of anchor, trumpet, flag and cannon on blue enamel, given by George III to Countess Howe: 1794.
Collection of Lady Mary-Gaye Bonas.

XXXVI Back of watch case enamelled by G. M. Moser with portraits of George, Prince of Wales, and Frederick, Duke of York, in Van Dyck costume standing beside a pedestal with a relief of Britannia and vase of flowers. Movement by Augustin Henckel of Vienna; case signed GMMF [ecit]: *c.* 1766. Trustees of the Grimsthorpe and Drummond Castle Estates.

XXXVII Chatelaine with watch case enamelled in neo-classical style by William Craft with a sacrifice, profiles of Medusa and Hercules, a swan and portraits of George III and Queen Charlotte: 1777. British Museum.

XXXVIII The Marchioness of Londonderry dressed for the coronation of William IV in 1830. Portrait by F. Dubois Drahonnet. Collection of the Marquess of Londonderry.

XXXIX Enamelled and jewelled cross given by the Prince Regent to the Marchioness of Londonderry in 1819. Back: showing Gothic tracery. Made by Rundell, Bridge and Rundell. Collection of the Marquess of Londonderry.

XL Hoop ring with a cameo portrait of George IV, the hoop inscribed VIVE LE ROI in Garter blue. Trustees of the Chatsworth Settlement.

XLI Coronation suite of necklace with emblems of England, Scotland and Ireland and Garter collar knots, and matching brooch and earrings of orb and cross. Made by Rundell, Bridge and Rundell, 1821. Trustees of the Grimsthorpe and Drummond Castle Estates.

XLII Pearl, diamond and enamel locket with Nelson's ship, the *Victory*, surmounted by his cipher HN between laurel branches. Charlecote, National Trust.

XLIII Memorial jewel for Princess Charlotte, showing her miniature on the front and hair in urn below: 1817. Victoria and Albert Museum.

XLIV The Marchioness of Sligo in Mary Stuart costume.
Portrait by Sir William Beechey. Sotheby's.

XLV Pink topaz parure made for Laura, wife of Sir Robert Mowbray of Cockairny House, Fife: 1804. Private collection.

XLVI Pink topaz necklace given by George III to Frances Honeywood, lady-in-waiting to Princess Charlotte: *c.* 1800. Harvey and Gore.

XLVII Emerald and diamond cross: 1819. Cluster necklace: 1830.
Sotheby's (formerly Viscount Windsor).

XLVIII Necklace of pansies alternating with pearl and coloured stone links set with amethysts, topazes, emeralds, sapphires and diamonds: *c.* 1800. Said to have been worn by Emma, Lady Hamilton; sold to the Countess of Aldborough, who gave it to Harriet, Lady Campbell of Barcaldine, who bequeathed it to Miss Erica Rose Campbell of Barcaldine. Christie's.

XLIX Diamond and blue enamel suite of engine-turned locket bearing the cipher of Alexander I with matching earrings. Back inscribed: THIS LOCKET AND A PAIR OF EARRINGS WERE MADE FROM A BOX PRESENTED BY THE EMPEROR ALEXANDER OF RUSSIA IN 1812 TO RR. ADMIRAL THOMAS BYAM MARTIN FOR THE DEFENCE OF RIGA AND OTHER SERVICES IN THE BALTIC. S. J. Phillips.

L Diamond butterfly brooch. Collection of the Duke of St Albans.

LI Gold filigree lyre pendant entwined with vine leaves, the stones spelling out the message REGARD. *c.* 1800. Collection of Mr Richard Digby.

LII Diamond flower brooch tied with bowknot. Bought in 1799 from Jefferys, Jones and Gilbert of Cockspur Street, by the seventh Earl of Elgin for his bride, the heiress Mary Nisbet, it has been listed in all subsequent inventories of Elgin jewellery. Private collection.

SOCIAL AND ECONOMIC USE OF JEWELLERY

Jewels were given as bribes by those wanting advancement at the court of George I. It was rumoured that a Mr Chetwynd obtained a position at the Board of Trade in return for a fine pair of earrings he had given to one of the king's favourites, Madame Kielmansegge.[62] In the next reign Lady Sundon, Mistress of the Robes, used her influence on behalf of the Earl of Pomfret, who became Master of the Horse. Her reward, diamond earrings worth £1,400, was noticed by the Duchess of Marlborough, who commented to Lady Mary Wortley Montagu: 'How can that woman have the impudence to go about in that bribe', to which the neat riposte was 'Madam, how can people know where wine is to be sold, unless there is a sign hung out?'[63]

Portraits of the king and queen, distinguished soldiers, statesmen and poets might be worn in rings and lockets (Plate XXIV). Medals were struck to celebrate the recovery of George III in 1789 and were worn round the neck at the thanksgiving celebrations; enamelled in red, white and blue, they cost five guineas apiece.[64] Tassie had some in his 1791 catalogue, either with Britannia holding a medallion with the king's head and accompanied by Aesculapius, or with a symbolic design using the zodiac to indicate the month (March) of the king's recovery.[65] Later in 1789, the Spanish embassador invited the queen to a celebration at Ranelagh on 9 June, when

> there was a new invention of a lottery, a ticket being given to every lady as she came in: then when you pleased you went to draw a number and took your prize which was generally a purse, a little smelling bottle etc. A Miss Sturt won the lot 205 – a fine watch set with diamonds – and a few other people handsome trinkets. Some say the Queen won the King of Spain's picture adorned with jewels.[66]

DIAMONDS AND COLOURED STONES

As a result of the discovery of diamonds in 1725 at Minas Geraes, Brazil rather than India became the main source of supply, and stones were more plentiful. London was the centre of the trade, as the statute abolishing customs duties on diamonds and other precious stones acknowledged: 'this kingdom is now become the great mart for diamonds and other precious stones from whence most countries are supplied'.[67] This was due in part to the stable political and economic circumstances of Britain, and to the increasing importance of the country as a maritime power with a large merchant fleet. The home market was good and was encouraged by events at court: coronations, royal marriages, the return of the king from Hanover or recuperation from illness – all could raise demand, and prices.

Before the trade was properly organised, it could be difficult to dispose of diamonds independently, as is witnessed by the predicament of Lady Mary Wortley Montagu in 1722. She wrote to her sister, Lady Mar, who was in Paris at the time of Louis XV's coronation: 'I beg you would let me hear soon from you, and particularly if the approaching Coronation raises the price of Diamonds. I have some to sell and cannot dispose of 'em here.' The reply was discouraging: 'This is the worst time to think of selling anything here. Money is so scarce that I question whether anybody could be found to buy such a diamond as you speak of. Everything is very dear, which makes people retrench their expence to what is absolutely necessary, and jewells you know cannot be comprehended under that head'; and Lady Mary was still trying to dispose of them two years later, writing that 'till a fit Occasion [arises] of disposing of some superfluous Diamonds I shall remain in this sinfull Sea cole Town'.[68]

By the end of the century the price of diamonds had been fixed at a high rate by the efforts of the

> East India Company, the Portuguese and their retailers who in that quality have done the business of their employers and by exaggerated praises of the diamond above any fine stones have raised it to an unconscionable price even beyond what it cost 100 years ago at the time of Tavernier.[69]

The three most important firms were Gompertz, Prager and Norden. In order to end the confusion about the value of stones, cut and polished, Desaguliers in 1734, and Jeffries in 1751, published tables from which the price of diamonds could be calculated. Jeffries's system was based on the assumption that a diamond increases in value in proportion to its weight in a direct ratio to the square of its weight. Thus, if a one carat stone was valued at £8, a stone of two carats would be worth 2 x 2 x 8 = £32; and he continued on this basis to calculate the value of stones weighing up to 100 carats. One-third of the value was deducted from ill-coloured or flawed stones.[70]

Although Amsterdam continued to be the great centre for cutting and polishing diamonds, there were craftsmen in London, one of whom, Joseph Cope, had cut the celebrated Pitt diamond. The British ambassador to Portugal declared in 1732 that the best diamond-cutters were in London.[71] Some were probably of Dutch origin, some were English and others Jews, including Levy Norden who, in 1764, described himself as an 'opulent and very considerable jeweller in London having diamond mills in Wheeler Street, Whitechapel'.[72] Apart from preparing new stones from the rough, they were kept busy recutting rose diamonds into brilliants, an operation deplored by Jeffries because it lessened the weight.[73] Fashion was all in favour of the transformation, and Goldsmith derided rose- and table-cut stones as 'things which would make you look like the court of King Solomon at a puppet show'.[74] A sale in 1778 of the 'Stock in Trade of a Goldsmith, Toyman and Jeweller', including a 'Pair of brilliant diamond frames for single drop earrings and a pair of ditto for drops containing 160 English cut brilliants', points to the success of the London craftsmen.[75]

Whether on its own, set in rows or clusters, in rings, pins, necklaces or earrings, the diamond was the status symbol *par excellence*. André Rouquet observed the preference for the diamond in England: 'the use of diamonds is more received in England than that of other jewels: they are richer, less variegated and less liable to imitation'.[76] Because of this preference, English jewellers 'would not have often an opportunity of displaying their abilities on pieces of any great consequence especially in colours if they were to work only for their own country'.[77]

Notwithstanding Rouquet's opinion, jewels set with emeralds, rubies, amethysts, cornelians, opals and topazes are recorded regularly in accounts and inventories. Of the less expensive semi-precious stones, almandine garnets were most in demand. This was due to the skilful foiling, which transformed the colour of the stone into a most attractive velvety crimson. Thinly cut into variegated shapes, the garnets were set over the rose-red foil in silver-gilt mounts for earrings, necklaces and bracelets.[78] Garnets could be worn with mourning; the Marchioness of Rockingham asked her husband to buy her a pair of round garnet earrings from Russell's in London, like those of the Duchess of Grafton, at a cost of two-and-a-half guineas, as 'they will really be of great service to me not having any to wear in this deep mourning'.[79]

From the 1740s garnets were combined with mocha stones – a variant of chalcedony with inclusions resembling trees – into necklaces, earrings, buttons, watch cases and rings.[80] Mochas of the best quality, such as a moss agate with markings resembling a landscape, once owned by the artist Gainsborough,[81] were set in bracelet clasps, crosses and brooches framed in precious stones. A particularly splendid pair of bracelets, sold in 1772, combined mocha stones with 'diamonds rubies and emeralds strung with 900 pearls', the property of a 'noble lady'.[82] The importance of such stones was recognised by Louis Dutens (1730–1810), who in 1776 published *Des pierres précieuses*, a guide to both precious and semi-precious stones which supplemented Jeffries's book, which had dealt with diamonds and pearls only.

PEBBLE STONES AND BRISTOWS

When Mrs Delany visited the famous lapidary Faulkner in 1740, she was impressed by the 'abundance of fine things and the manner of cutting and polishing pebbles'.[83] These stones, crystals and agates, were popular, and in 1750 Lady Jane Coke said of a 'pair of Scots pebble earrings and cross' which she had bought for her friend, Miss Cotton, that they were 'extremely the fashion and very pretty'[84] (Plate XXV). The Dowager Marchioness of Tweeddale wore her pebble beads simply strung into a necklace, but she also had them set with diamonds in earrings listed in an inventory of 1789.[85]

Bristows still came from Bristol, and *The Lady's Magazine* described St Vincent's rock as being 'stocked with a kind of precious stones which would be more valuable if they were scarce. In transparency they vie with those of the Indies and are inferior to them in no respect but hardness.'[86] They were set in girdle and shoe buckles,[87] in aigrettes and necklaces[88] and in buttons.[89]

PASTE

All the best jewellers sold paste. George Wickes's trade card in 1759 advertised 'False Stonework in Aigrettes, Earrings, Buckles etc', and the ledgers record many sales of 'French drops' and 'paste tops'.[90] Available in white, pink, red, yellow, green and purple, as well as imitating garnets, opals and golden-flecked aventurine, paste was set in the most up-to-date, elegant styles. Mrs Hardcastle observed in *She Stoops to Conquer* that 'half the ladies of our acquaintance, My lady Kill Daylight and Mrs Crump and the rest of them carry their jewels to town and bring nothing but paste and marquisites back.'[91] It appealed to those of modest means, like Mrs Delany, and also to the rich, like Lord Egremont and Lady Burlington, for not the least of its attractions was that it could be worn without having to worry about thieves.

The quality was so good that Horace Walpole wondered why the stained glass used for windows was so bad in comparison, for 'every necklace-shop sells rubies and emeralds which jewellers must take out of the setting to be sure they are not true and what are these counterfeits but coloured glass?'[92] The best paste was imported from France for, as the writer of the introduction to the translation of Fontanieu's book in 1787 admitted, while in England 'the art of making glass is arrived at the highest perfection, the manner of colouring it is not so generally understood'.[93] French paste was usually set in silver, and its quality was such that many were deceived by it. Dr Schomberg was given a ring set with a deep-blue stone, inscribed POUR L'AMITIE in brilliants, by the Duchess of Kingston, and wore it everywhere, extolling her generosity, until one of the brilliants fell out. The jeweller to whom he took it for repair told him the stone was a composition, imported from Paris, and worth no more than thirty-six shillings.[94] The subject had long been a topic for gossip.

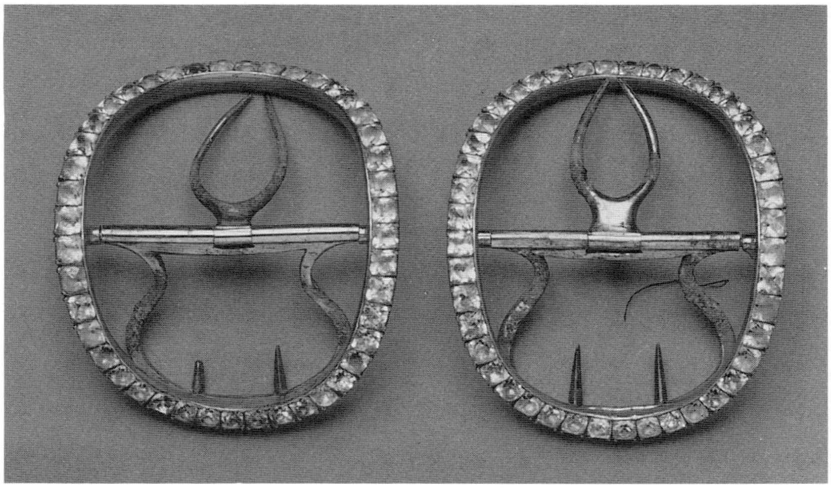

89 Pair of shoe buckles set with white paste. Collection of Mr Alick Hay of Duns Castle.

90 Coq-de-perle earrings. Detail of the portrait of Mrs Marton by George Romney. Southampton Art Gallery.

The best and most characteristically English product was white paste, brilliant-cut and set in simple, well-proportioned and substantial mounts, for buttons and for shoe, stock and knee buckles [95] (Plate 89).

COQ-DE-PERLE

According to Pouget's *Traité des pierres précieuses* (1762), coq-de-perle was the shell of a snail found only in the East Indies. Only one *coque* could be obtained from each snail and, being thin, it had to be filled to give it body. In spite of this disadvantage, coq-de-perle was much prized for its beautiful mother-of-pearl iridescence (Plate 90).

DOUBLETS

A well-established method of economising in the use of precious stones was to make doublets: a thin layer of the genuine stone cemented to a glass or crystal back. George Wickes supplied doublets as drops to earrings, set in stay hooks, buttons and rings, and sometimes combining the doublet with genuine stones, as in the brilliant solitaire with a red doublet in the middle stone and drop.[96] An 'emerald doublet set round with brilliants' was sold at Christie's in 1772.[97]

MARCASITE (IRON PYRITES)

A crystalline form of iron pyrites was called maracasite and had been used in ornaments since the sixteenth century. Rose-cut and polished, it shimmered by candlelight so attractively that it was worn by the rich for its decorative quality, and by those who could not afford diamonds. It was mounted in silver buckles, brooches, top and drop earrings, necklaces, chatelaines and rings, in openwork floral designs or in clusters.[98] As a substitute for diamonds it framed jet, mother-of-pearl and coq de perle,[99] enamels and glass,[100] and might be worked into floral sprigs and ciphers over domed cabochon gem-stones or coloured grounds.[101]

WEDGWOOD

Josiah Wedgwood (1730–95) was confident of the potential of his products for jewellery as well as for table-wares and architecture. In 1773 he predicted that if Wedgwood buttons sold well, this would be 'a fine leader to the wearing of cameos'.[102] With this in view, he persevered until the formula for Jasperware was perfected, and wrote in 1777 to his partner, Thomas Bentley: 'I shall not sit down content with bracelet and ring cameos till I can make most of them with color'd grounds, polished and without staining and if I succeed, that branch alone, I am fully persuaded, would be a capital business.'[103]

The fruits of his success were cameos with pure white figures standing out in relief on tinted grounds, both matt and glossy. They were produced in various sizes, not only for rings and bracelet centrepieces, but also for neck pins, brooches, lockets, watch cases, shoe and belt buckles, and large drops for the ears (Plate 91). Sets were linked together for chatelaines, bracelets and necklaces; and the colours – green, lilac, black, grey, yellow, brown, dark blue and light blue – combined well with gold, silver and cut-steel mounts.[104] Unusually, pearls embellished the suite composed of necklace, bracelet, earrings, brooches and waist buckle, worn by the wife of John Flaxman, the sculptor, who designed many of the cameos for Wedgwood.[105]

Most designs reflected fashionable neo-classical taste. The comprehensive sale catalogue of 1781 lists portraits of divinities, portraits of ancient and modern illustrious men and women, and versions of classical sculpture and of wall paintings from Herculaneum.[106] Twin themes, such as Night and Day or Victory and a Conquering Hero, were produced in pairs for earrings, bracelets and waist buckles. Others allude to particular professions: cameos of the Roman patriot Mettus Curtius, of Aesculapius the God of Healing, and of priests sacrificing, were intended to appeal respectively to the wives of soldiers, doctors and clergymen.[107]

Like Matthew Boulton, Wedgwood liked to anticipate fashion and much regretted that he had not foreseen the huge popularity of Admiral Viscount Keppel (1725–86),

91 Two pairs of lilac-dip Wedgwood earrings with classical figures. Castle Museum, Nottingham.

who was tried for neglecting his duty in 1779. So many admirers demonstrated their support by parading the admiral's portrait in rings and bracelets that Wedgwood admitted that 'if we had our wits about us as we ought to have done two or three months since we might have sold £1000 worth of the gentleman's head in various ways'.[108] He learnt his lesson, and when it came to promoting a cause dear to his own heart – the abolition of slavery – he commissioned a relief of a slave from William Hackwood in 1787. The kneeling slave, bound in chains, inscribed AM I NOT A MAN AND A BROTHER?, was reproduced in thousands for men's seals, rings, shirt pins and coat buttons, as well as for women's ornaments, including hairpins, as the campaign gathered momentum.[109]

Appealing to those who found classical and political themes too severe were bouquets of flowers and scenes from contemporary literature. These include Goethe's

Charlotte mourning Werther, and two designs by Lady Templeton: the Bourbonnais shepherd, and Maria, from Sterne's *Sentimental Journey*.[110] A medallion of Maria, seated forlorn under a weeping willow with her faithful dog, Silvio, beside her, is set in the belt clasp worn by the Duchess of Orléans in her portrait by Mme Vigée le Brun,[111] formerly in the collection of the Comte de Paris.

ENAMELS AND OTHER CERAMICS

In the mid eighteenth century, an enamel manufactory was set up at Battersea and started making fine painted enamels, snuff boxes and the like. The floral designs derived from the types found on Chelsea porcelain, and copperplate transfer prints were used for figurative subjects.

White carnival masks, the eyes set with brilliants and the mouths painted red, are attributed to the Chelsea porcelain factory *c.* 1752–3.[112] They were either set in brooches or mounted in pendants and, when used in pairs, could be inscribed UNIS PAR AMITIE.[113]

Enamels were also a speciality of Bilston and Wednesbury in south Staffordshire. Bright turquoise, green, rose-pink, and royal blue portraits, pastoral scenes or flowers were painted on opaque white or coloured grounds.[114] They were set in cut-steel, pinchbeck and gilt-metal brooches, pendants, watch cases, chatelaines (Plate 92), etuis and plaques for threading onto ribbons for necklaces and bracelets.[115]

PINCHBECK

An alloy of 90% copper and 10% zinc was invented by Christopher Pinchbeck (†1732), using purified rose copper and pure zinc from China. This could be made into articles like watch cases or cast in clear-cut relief, and by processing after making the object, a reddish-gold hue resembling that of 18 carat gold was obtained. It did not tarnish or wear like ordinary alloy or plated base metal, and so appealed to many who could not afford real gold for their ornaments. Edward Pinchbeck, the son, claimed not to 'dispose of one grain of his curious metal which so nearly resembles gold in colour, smell and ductility to any jeweller whatsoever'. Its success inspired many imitations, including similor, which was made in France.[116]

CUT STEEL

In 1728 Monsieur de Muralt criticised the quality of British cut steel, which he considered neither well-made nor well-finished, although he did concede that the case hardening was excellent.[117] Nonetheless, it went from strength to strength, and developed into a national speciality. Sophie von La Roche, who was in London in 1766, visited Charles Towneley's celebrated collection of antiquities, and then

92 Gilt metal chatelaine with étui and two egg-shaped cases enamelled with birds and landscapes. Made in Staffordshire or Birmingham, 1750–60. Bantock House Museum, Wolverhampton.

arrived at Mr. Gray's to inspect the steel work of the Moderns, and admire a thousand delicate ornaments and instruments made from this metal. For whatever the most skilled gold craftsmen or diamond polishers can show, may be found in steel here artistically wrought, and most tempting, so tasteful is the moulding of every separate piece, to which the pleasant, I might almost say modest, tone of the steel contributed largely.[118]

From Rome, Charlotte, Duchess of Albany, ordered English cut-steel chains for herself and her friend, the Princess of Santa Croce,[119] and in Florence Horace Mann delivered cut-steel buckles sent by Horace Walpole from Woodstock to the Prince de Craon.[120] John Worralow of Wolverhampton, who received the royal appointment in 1782, also exported to the courts of France, Spain and Russia. Stamped with the letter W in minute script, his products were copied by French makers.[121] From 1780 a Mr Sykes from Yorkshire dealt in cut steel from a shop in the Palais Royal in Paris, and there was a 'fureur d'acier' after the commercial treaty of 1786 permitted unrestricted imports from Britain.[122]

Over twenty persons were employed by Queen Charlotte's worker in polished steel at Woodstock in 1771, and the industry, which had been there since the seventeenth century, flourished.[123] Besides everyday items – watch chains, buckles and necklaces – Mrs Lybbe Powys, who was there in 1775, noticed sword-hilts and stars. She commented: 'they are beautiful – the latter [stars] are not dear about 20 guineas each'.[124] According to Sylas Neville in 1781, Woodstock work was 'more highly polished and better studded than that of Birmingham. They polish all by hand. Their studs and screws and everything they make can be taken to pieces and cleaned whereas the Birmingham studs are rivetted.'[125]

There was also a long tradition for making cut steel in Birmingham, with several firms competing for business, notably John Taylor. The most successful, however, was Matthew Boulton at Soho, who produced efficiently a wide range of personal ornaments and marketed them without an intermediary. A foreign visitor to his factory in 1775 described the scene:

seven hundred persons daily engage in making buttons, watch chains, steel buckles, sword hilts . . . all manner of silver work, watches, every imaginable kind of ornament in silver and in pinchbeck and other compositions . . . each workman has only a limited range so that he does not need constantly to change his position and tools and by this means an incredible amount of time is saved.[126]

Buttons, uniform in size and design, were the sheet anchor of Boulton's business, with buckles and chains next in importance. His first goal was cheapness, to which he attributed his successful export figures, and he was also determined to maintain quality and keep abreast of changing styles. He collected ideas from sources as diverse as La Fontaine's book on buckles and the plates in D'Hancarville's *Antiquités Etrusques, Grecques et Romaines* (1766). In 1775 he asked James Watt to call on James Tassie to 'see if he has any pretty things that would do for watch chains'. Other motifs in his pattern book of 1470 designs derived from Egyptian art. As he always had some novelty to offer, Boulton approached the nobility, sending samples to the Duke of Marlborough, Lord Charles Spencer and the influential blue-stocking, Mrs Montagu. He despatched steel buckles to Lady Hamilton at Naples, to set a fashion which might be taken up by the ladies at the Bourbon court. It was his salesmanship that prompted Lady Claremont to persuade her husband to wear a set of Boulton's buttons to Her Majesty's Birthday in 1771, and Boulton wrote to his wife that he expected to sell a large quantity as a result of this. As early as 1767 Queen Charlotte had accepted a watch chain from him. Mrs Siddons was a customer and Lady Shelburne, who visited the factory, was amazed at how cheap everything was.[127]

Beads and round studs of faceted steel, cut flat, concave or convex, and burnished, were strung into chains and hat loops, or packed closely into brooches and buttons. The smaller the studs and the greater the number of facets, the more points of light would be reflected, and the more effective the ornament. Necklaces were composed of rosettes, linked together with long pendant fringes, with matching pendants for the ears. The polished black lustre combined well with other materials such as coral, crystal or cornelian beads in chains, or with Bilston enamels or Wedgwood jasper cameos and beads in chatelaines, buttons, brooches and waist buckles[128] (Plate 93). The matt surface of the jasperware toned admirably with the brilliance of the polished steel.

93 Cut steel buckle with Wedgwood plaque of Minerva beside an olive tree. *c.* 1770. Castle Museum, Nottingham.

The withdrawal of Matthew Boulton from the 'toy' business in 1780 left the field clear for his many competitors in Wolverhampton and Birmingham, who were responsible for the large output in the last two decades of the eighteenth century and the early part of the next. Lady Lonsdale, who was in Birmingham in 1806, was impressed by the quality of the cut steel on sale; and these makers, like Boulton, kept abreast of fashion and were particularly successful with neo-classical designs.[129]

For the head, they made bandeaux with studs arranged in Greek key fret pattern, or composed of rows of steel, Wedgwood or glass beads; tiaras with rosettes enclosed in laurel wreaths; and open circles linked by swags with pendant enrichments hanging from the more elaborate designs. Similar patterns were adopted for tortoise-shell combs, while those of smaller size were topped with arrows, palmettes, wheat ears, layered flowers, butterflies and moths. Rosettes and star motifs were linked together into short necklaces or draped into long festoons with pendant fringes or crosses attached. Diamond-cut steel studs were also combined with fashionable blue enamel into necklaces. Such designs might be repeated in matching ornaments, such as the 'elegant necklace, bracelets and ear drops formed of imitative garnets and cut steel beads', or demi-parures with sets of a necklace and either bracelets or earrings. Earrings of the pendant or drop type might be combined with gold, and gold clasps and inlay contrasted with steel in bracelets. Flexible chains of interlocked circles, rectangular patterned plaques or rows of rosettes with the largest in the centre for the clasp were worn round the wrists.

By the second quarter of the nineteenth century these items were no longer fashionable, except for watch chains – worked in meshes as well as composed of beads – buttons, sword knots and purses.

LONDON JEWELLERS

In the opinion of the Swiss enameller, André Rouquet, who had spent some years in London, the 'English jewellers are very expert in their profession' and he thought that their best commissions came from abroad.[130] Mrs Poyntz, whose will is dated 1771, was proud of 'the equipage set with diamonds left me by my sister-in-law the Right Hon. Lady Mohun . . . three score years ago the equipage was sent abroad to shew the French how well diamonds could be set in England. I would by no means have it unset'.[131] Much of the trade was in the hands of specialists, who supplied the retailers. There were necklace makers: James Howard, at the Hand and Beads on London Bridge *c.* 1735–60,[132] and Mary Phillips of 20 Green Street, Leicester Fields.[133] John Raynes, at the Sign of Pallas in Foster Lane *c.* 1743, dealt in 'gold chains, buttons, earrings and all sorts of gold, silver and jewelling work'.[134] Light-hearted compositions of seed pearl, or 'pearl fancies', could be bought from James Hill at the Arms of France *c.* 1787.[135] Some craftsmen specialised in mourning rings: Thomas Wallis of 54 Red

Lion Street, Clerkenwell;[136] George Heming at the Hand and Hammer opposite the Black Bear in Piccadilly; and John Alderhead of the Ring and Pearl in Bishopsgate Street.[137] Mottoes were engraved by Sutherlands of Orange Street, Leicester Square; and J. Walker of 16 Rolls Buildings, Fetter Lane, specialised in hair work.[138]

Some of the grander jewellers can be identified by the stock-in-trade advertised on their trade cards, such as William Park Fisher of Covent Garden, or Robert Parr of the Diamond Cross, Salisbury Court, Fleet Street.[139] Rococo jewellery is displayed on the trade card of Samuel Taylor of Lad Lane, Wood Street, *c.* 1744–57: rose diamond earrings, necklaces, brooches, aigrettes with pear pearls, miniatures in jewelled frames, seals, rings with heart-shaped and fleur-de-lis bezels, and keepers to protect them.[140] Among the subscribers to David Jeffries's *Treatise on Diamonds and Pearls* (1751) were several jewellers: Stafford Briscoe, Thomas and Nicholas Crisp, Thomas Leach, Thomas Postell and Henry Stacey, all of whom are likely to have been dealing in precious stones.

One of the most talked-about jewellers was James Cox, who was in business from 1749 at the Golden Urn, Racquet Court, Fleet Street. He had a great reputation as an innovator and was famous for his jewelled automata, some of which were sold by lottery in 1773.[141] His jewellery attracted the attention of the Princess of Orange,[142] and other clients included Sir John Delaval[143] and Viscount Galway, who was impressed by his honesty.[144] Sylas Neville, who had met him in 1767, commented that 'he is an extraordinary person who has acquired his great knowledge of precious stones by force of unnatural genius – he cannot keep his own accounts'.[145] This may have been his undoing, for he was declared bankrupt in 1778. Three sales of his stock were held by Christie's: 1–2 July 1772, 16–17 December 1779 after his bankruptcy, and finally on 16 February 1792 after his death.

Like Cox, Christopher Pinchbeck (1670–1732) was more successful as a craftsman than as a man of business. He dealt from a trinket shop in Fleet Street where he sold the great range of items made from the alloy he had invented, and to which he gave his name, as well as repairing watches and clocks, supervising a pastry-cook's shop, and exhibiting at fairs. His stock-in-trade, library, furnishings, paintings and working tools with all the contents of his home and shop are recorded. His two sons quarrelled after his death but one of them, Christopher, settled down to a prosperous career as a jeweller in a shop in Cockspur Street opposite the Haymarket.[146] His clients included Lady Monson and the dandy, Benjamin Mildmay, Earl Fitzwalter.[147] His stock-in-trade, with paintings, miniatures, drawings, prints and library, were sold by Christie's in 1784 and 1788.[148] Christie's sold the stock of other jewellers: that of George Robertson of Frith Street, Soho, in December 1777 and on 3 May 1778, and that of James Bellis of Pall Mall on 13 May 1780 and 12 June 1782.

These catalogues provide a guide to what was on sale at a particular time; the ledgers of a firm, like that of George Wickes from 1731, are even more useful. Series of invoices, like those of Gavin Shiells for Thomas Fisher and his family for 1751–61, also give an idea of what was being purchased at that time.[149] Misunderstandings about price could arise. In 1776 the antiquary and Norfolk landowner, Sir Martin Folkes, believed that he had been quoted £400 for a pair of diamond earrings, while the jewellers, Jeffreys and Jones of Cockspur Street, politely stood their ground and insisted that the price of £420 only gave them a profit of 10%.[150] Their shop was visited by Sophie von La Roche in 1786 and she noted that 'the shelves and the window and the tables contained a number of indefinable but delicately wrought trifles, for instance rings, needles, watches and bracelets showing an inventiveness and craftsmanship almost past imagination'.[151]

Nathaniel Jeffreys of Piccadilly was involved in the Diamond Necklace Affair in 1785 when M. de la Motte came to London to sell the stones from the famous jewel which had been offered to Queen Marie-Antoinette, and which she had refused. Jeffreys was surprised at the low price asked for such good stones, and also the willingness of de la Motte to take payment in goods; diamond medallions, rings, earrings, a necklace, pearl bow, diamond aigrette, brilliant star, and bracelets of steel and gold.[152] Some of the diamonds were sold in 1790 to the Duke of Dorset and were remodelled by Lady Sackville, the wife of one of his descendants, early in this century. Others stones were bought, also by exchange, by the firm of Robert and William Gray of New Bond Street. These were made up into a rivière for the Marchioness of Stafford.[153] The Prince of Wales patronised Rundell, Bridge and Rundell, but also acquired jewels from others: Thomas Gray,[154] James Shrapnell,[155] Stephen Rice[156] and F. Satchell.[157]

Payments to British jewellers are recorded in the papers of the fourth Duke of Bedford: Richard Arundell, who was paid £800 for two pearl drops in 1737, and John Eyemaker, who received £520 6*s* for diamond earrings, a pair of bow-knots and a girdle in 1737. Garnets for Lady Caroline Russell were acquired from Francis Sutherland in 1756, and in 1761 Andrew Hunter wrote to the agent soliciting business in connexion with the marriage of George III:

> Pray excuse this trouble, you have been so kind to recommend me to the Duke for which I am under great obligations to you. Lady Caroline is to be one of the bridesmaids and will want several things in my way. I have among other things a diamond nosegay of £1000 by me – your recommending of me by a line to his Grace would perhaps do me much service. I have lately met with some things that have not gone quite to my mind having been supplanted by foreigners. I therefore beg your interest for me at Bedford House.[158]

THE HUGUENOTS

The Huguenots had emigrated from France after the Revocation of the Edict of Nantes in such numbers that they dominated the London goldsmiths' and jewellery trade. In 1706, the Dowager Duchess of Orléans observed that it was no longer necessary to go to Paris for fine jewellery.[159] The Huguenots had been trained in a harder school than their English contemporaries who, in the opinion of Monsieur de Muralt, who had visited London in 1728, were not encouraged to excel by their patrons:

> La plupart ne jugent d'un ouvrage que par le prix qu' on y met – vous croiez bien que l'ouvrier n'ayant pas de peine à les contenter et pouvant s'enricher à son aise se souciera peu de s'appliquer à son metier et n'y excellera pas.[160]

Augusta, Princess of Wales, patronised Isaac Lacam, as did Lady Monson and the second Marquess of Rockingham.[161] The trade card of Paul Daniel Chenevix of A L'Enseigne de la Porte D'Or in Suffolk Street was written in French, and his clients included Lord Fitzwalter and the handsome and grand 'Dame Palladio', Lady Burlington.[162] His widow Elizabeth, daughter of the fashionable toyman, William Beard, married Peter Russell, who took over the business when she died in 1755.[163] Their impressive shop front was depicted in a satirical print published in the *General Advertiser* for 18 January 1751,[164] and their clients included the Duchess of Leinster, the Marquess of Rockingham and Lady Jane Coke, who considered Russell's setting superior to all others.[165]

From 1726 to 1765 Peter Dutens and his wife, Elizabeth, at the Golden Cup in Chandos Street, dealt with an equally elegant clientèle, and it was from them that Barbara Savile ordered her casket of jewels on her marriage to the Earl of Scarborough in 1753.[166] The impressive scale of their business can be judged from a bill for diamond jewellery sold to Richard Tournour, the future Earl Winterton, comprising a necklace (£556), esclavage with knot (£251), cross (£227), aigrette (£240), earrings (£650), and buckle (£97).[167] In 1756 Lady Burlington bought amethyst and brilliant jewels from them, and a ruby and brilliant heart ring.[168] They had an extremely high reputation, and the richness and variety of their workmanship exercised a powerful attraction; the Countess of Kildare exclaimed ruefully in a letter to her husband, 'such contrivances have they now got to pick one's pocket, and you know your poor Emily cannot resist temptation'.[169] Two other members of the Dutens family were connected with the trade: James, who supplied Lady Monson in 1764,[170] and the gemmologist and antiquary Louis, whose book, *Des pierres précieuses et des pierres fines avec les moyens de les connoîtres et de les évaluer*, was published in 1776. Four Huguenot jewellers were patronised by the Marchioness Grey: Philip Hardel, Stephen Artaud, Peter Castelfranc (who also supplied Sir Martin Folkes and the Princess of Wales) and Thomas Harrache.[171] On Harrache's retirement from the Golden Ball and Pearl in Pall Mall, his stock and household effects were sold by Christie's on 13 and 14 March 1778, 19 June 1778 and 3 May 1780. A similar dispersal was made of Mr Courte's stock from his shop in Northumberland Street on 8 July 1774.

Other Huguenot jewellers are known from their trade cards or accounts surviving in family archives. One of them, Elizabeth Godfrey of Haymarket, is described on her trade card as silversmith and jeweller to the Duke of Cumberland.[172] Peter Romilly supplied the third Earl of Egremont between 1763 and 1776, and Lady Watkin Williams Wynn in 1774.[173] John Duval remodelled some of the jewels brought back from Hanover by George III in 1761 for Queen Charlotte and supplied the Prince of Wales two decades later.[174] He also made valuations of the jewels of Lady Sarah Featherstonehaugh of Uppark in 1781 and 1789.[175]

Not all the foreign jewellers in London were French in origin. The Swede Peter Wirgman II traded in Denmark Street and in 1778 in St James's Street – where Dr Johnson bought a pair of shoe buckles from him.[176] Two members of the Dinglinger family from Saxony were active in London: Sebastian Henry Dinglinger published *A New Book of Designs for Jewellers Work* in 1751, and the trade card of Sigismund Godhelp Dinglinger, a jeweller of the Diamond Cross, St Martin's le Grand, is known.[177]

PROVINCIAL JEWELLERS

Jewellers were established in Bath and the other fashionable watering places – Tunbridge Wells, Buxton, Scarborough, Matlock, Bognor and Harrogate – to supply the needs of visitors during their seasons. County towns also had their own jewellers, who could deal in other wares as well. Nathaniel Rose, formerly of Foster Lane, London, was sheriff of Norwich in 1737, and sold china, glass, tea, coffee, chocolate and snuff besides jewellery and watches, all luxury items.[178] In Glasgow James MacEwan's trade card shows that he could supply canteens of flatware, musical instruments and scores, as well as rings, buckles, seals, watches and earrings.[179] Manufacturing jewellers were beginning to concentrate in Birmingham. In 1767 there were twenty-five jewellers who 'held the first rank among mechanics for the elegance of their Work: they are the makers of Necklaces, Ear Rings, Rings, Buckles, Sleeve Buttons and Studs, Seals &c'; and on his trade card John Smith claimed to make 'all sorts of Jewells, stone buckles buttons rings and seals as neat and cheaper than in London'.[180]

Jewels could also be disposed of by lottery,and there is an advertisement for one such in the *Derby Mercury* for 15 May 1735. Tickets cost 5*s*, and if all the 1440 were sold the organisers would have covered the advertised value of the prizes. The latter included:

> 1 Large Brilliant Diamond Buckle, 16 0 0 – 1 Gold Chas'd Watch, 18 0 0 – 1 Single Brilliant Diamond Ring, 16 0 0 – 1 Pair large Night Earings, 14 0 0 – 1 Pair of smaller Ditto, 10 0 0 – 1 Large Ring with five Brilliants, 9 0 0 – 1 Ditto smaller, 8 0 0 – 1 Solitaire with five Brilliants and five Garnets, 7 0 0 – 1 Ring with five Brilliants, 6 0 0 – 1 Hoop ring set round with Brilliants and Rubies 5 10 0 ... 1 Pair of Rose Diamond Night Earings 3 10 0 – 1 Saphire Ring with six Rose Diamonds 3 10 0...

and other lots of rings, not separately described.

EXPORTS

English jewellery was being exported on an increasing scale of business in the eighteenth century, partly for sale to foreign jewellers and partly for barter. Joseph Greenshill of the Strand, a working jeweller, goldsmith and cutler, advertised a large stock for export as well as for wholesale and retail trade.[181] The trade card of Wetherall and Janaway, goldsmiths and jewellers of Cheapside who had the appointment to the Princesses Mary, Sophia and Amelia, also offered to 'Merchants and Captains . . . a curious assortment of Goods of foreign trade of our own manufacture'.[182]

Thomas Harper of Bristol emigrated to Charlestown, South Carolina and announced in the *South Carolina Gazette* for 14 January 1774 that he had opened a shop in Broad Street and had imported 'a neat assortment of jewellery'; on his return to England *c.* 1784 he specialised in Masonic jewels.[183] James Henry Cox, son of the jeweller James Cox, was established as a private merchant for the Chinese market by 1783 when he dealt 'largely in all sorts of clockwork and jewellery and is the consignee of most of these articles brought to Canton'.[184] Others were concerned with the Russian trade: Thomas Meux sending clocks and watches, among them a watch with 'the outward contour adorned with the Czar's picture enriched with diamonds the work new and if possible very like him'.[185] Thomas Copestake, a jeweller, lapidary and engraver, who employed over one hundred workers at Uttoxeter also exported much of his production to Russia.[186]

While she was in Venice, Mrs Piozzi met a lady who told her: 'You do very right to look at our churches as you have none in England I know, but then you have so many other fine things – such charming steel buttons for example.'[187] The trade card for the Birmingham firm of R. Moor, one of the many button manufacturers to be found there, specifies that they made them for 'Wholesale and for Export'.[188]

PURCHASES ABROAD

Despite the improved reputation of the English jewellers, purchases continued to be made abroad, especially in Paris. It was there in 1769 that the rich Welsh landowner, Sir Watkin Williams Wynn, a great collector and patron of Robert Adam, bought a watch in a diamond-studded case for £404 10*s* and a pair of lady's shoe buckles for £168.[189] It was in Paris in 1749 that Lord Hervey bought a new pair of diamond shoe buckles to wear at Madame de Boufflers's ball.[190] The services of friends visiting Paris were also employed. David Garrick asked the famous fencing-master Angelo, who was travelling through Paris on his way to Turin, to deliver designs for a George, hat button and loop to the jeweller Weillard, and to collect them on his return journey to London.[191]

Elsewhere, little of high quality was to be found, and travellers sometimes found it difficult to buy presents. In 1763 all Lady Holland could find in Spa were three Geneva stone necklaces; in Italy she complained that 'nothing is to be got a comfortable way' and sent only a pair of gold scissors, fan mounts and a cameo ring.[192]

REMODELLING AND TECHNIQUES

The new, lighter designs called for changes in the way in which stones were set; collets became more delicate and were barely visible, so that the stones apparently formed an unbroken mosaic of light and colour. Fine stones were set transparent, especially in earrings.[193] The general use of silver for setting diamonds meant that tarnishing of the back of the mounts was a problem, and to avoid soiling skin and fine fabrics, brushes and powder for cleaning them were also bought. In 1767 Sylas Neville noted an innovation by James Cox, who 'called after dinner to show the costly neck or breast ornament made of diamonds for the intended Princess of Orange . . . the back of the setting is lined with gold, a new improvement to prevent cleaning or brushing'.[194] The beauty of stones set in closed collets could be enhanced by foiling, which transformed dullish stones into richer, more brilliant tints, and excellent results were obtained with garnet jewellery by these means.

The skills of the goldsmith were exercised in making gold boxes, watch cases, chatelaines and etuis. Craftsmen like George Michael Moser (1707–83) and James Morisset (active from 1764) (Plate 94) worked in gold; from the 1770s gold alloys were combined for pictorial effect and both chasing and enamelling reached a high point. The English gained a reputation for the smoothness and translucency of their dark, midnight-blue enamel fired on engine-turned grounds. This was a trade secret which the Spanish goldsmith and jeweller, Antonio Martinez (founder of the royal factory for silversmiths in Madrid), who was in London in 1775–6, succeeded in obtaining by bribing the servant of the expert enameller, Jusen. On the same visit he also learnt how to matt finish and inlay gold for ceremonial sword-hilts, and to make convex crystal covers for miniatures.[195]

Engine-turned, or guilloché, grounds overlaid with translucent enamel were used not only for watch cases but for other jewels as well. In 1786, for instance, the Prince of Wales bought 'a pair of engine-turned clasps to a pair of bracelets'.[196] From the 1780s, tiny gold beads and bright-cut ornament appeared on the rims of lockets and ring bezels, balancing the severity of the geometrical shapes.

The trend towards lighter designs and the improvements in techniques combined to ensure that jewels could never remain fashionable for long and remodelling was a continuous process. Emily, later first Duchess of Leinster, wrote to her husband in 1747: 'my chain I am altering into a very pretty thing like a peacock's feather; this you gave me leave to alter when I pleased'; and next day: 'You know, my dear Lord Kildare you did once consent to altering my buckle. Now I wish it more than ever because hardly

94 Enamelled plaque inscribed 'Aesculapius Conducts Hygeia and Telesphorus to Neptune, Margate 1772'. Telesphorus was a child god associated with Aesculapius. Maker's mark of James Morisset on the loop. Royal Museum and Art Gallery, Canterbury.

anybody now wears a buckle at all and this same buckle will set into another thing just like my coulant: which being then alike are to be set so as to be worn in bracelets, in earrings, in my head, or in short anyway.'[197] Few ladies could resist the desire to keep up with the latest fashion, and the resetting of jewels was the subject of discussion among family and friends. Writing in 1759, Lady Sarah Lennox, sister of Emily, Duchess of Leinster, reported: 'Talking of diamonds, I am advised by my sister, my brother and the Duchess to new set my poor humble diamonds. The cross and feather will Mr. Dutan says make me a pair of clump earrings: for I would have them so, for I am tired of the round ones and a pair of peepers.'[198] The transfer of family jewels to a daughter or daughter-in-law almost always led to remodelling, as Lady Louisa Connolly observed after the marriage of William, second Duke of Leinster, in 1776: 'the little Duchess's diamonds are all going to be metamorphosed. I am sorry to part with the fine knot I have admired all these years.'[199] Mrs Delany commented of the rich Lady Temple that she was 'dressed in all her diamonds which she had new set and are prodigious fine'.[200]

DESIGNS AND MOTIFS

There were two major changes in eighteenth-century taste which affected all the arts: the transition from baroque to the lighter rococo style, with its emphasis on asymmetry and delicate floral and scroll-work, and the introduction of the severer neo-classical style associated with the Adam brothers and 'Athenian' Stuart. In jewellery the changes can be followed in a series of designs and published pattern books. The transition from the more massive baroque style is found in Marcus Gunter's designs *c.* 1718–38 for asymmetrical brooches and aigrettes, composed of tall stalks and flat ribbon-like plants with jagged edges instead of acanthus foliage.[201] The high rococo style is illustrated in a series of pattern books – Thomas Flach's *A Book of Jeweller's Work* (1736) (Fig. 24), William de la Cour's *Eighth Book of Ornaments* (1747) – which culminated in S. H. Dinglinger's book of 1751 (see above, p. 248) and *A Book of Ornaments Useful for Jewellers Drawn and Invented by Christian Taute* (1750) (Fig. 25).

Other designs, like those of Peter Glazier for chatelaines and bracelet clasps, are also known.[202] The flowers are recognisable: trumpet-shaped tulips, star-shaped jasmine and open sunflowers, entwined with the flexible ribbon-work, tumbling out of cornucopiae, making the jewels into bouquets or garlands. This style remained popular after the earliest neo-classical designs had appeared; T. D. Saint's *New Book of Designs for Jeweller's Work* (*c.* 1770) contained twenty-three plates of bouquets of all shapes and sizes for the hair, ears, neck, wrists and dress. The character Miss Sterling in the play *The Clandestine Marriage* (1766) enthused about her flower jewels: 'I have a bouquet to come home tomorrow, made up of diamonds and rubies, and emeralds, and topazes, and amethysts: jewels of all colours, green, red, blue, yellow, intermix'd: the prettiest thing you ever saw in your life.'[203] They were a speciality of James Cox, who exhibited them and, in 1774, sold them by lottery. In a catalogue, he emphasised that his flowers were 'copied from nature in all its infinite variety of tints and forms with different coloured gems – all in motion being fixed to springs of tempered gold which gives them vibration as if they were blown by the wind – innumerable flies and insects all of jewellers work hover upon and amongst the flowers', and the stones for these were 'cut and proportioned to every shade of the insects as they are to every flower'.[204]

Neo-classical design had been introduced in architecture and interior decoration by Robert Adam in the 1760s, and after 1770 it became the rule, with symmetry and classical proportions replacing the asymmetry of the rococo. The geometric outlines of lozenges, octagons, ovals and circles were adopted for rings, lockets and clasps, and classical imagery – Muses, divinities (Plate 94) and heroes – was introduced again into the repertory of designs, along with the Greek key fret pattern. The severity of the style was softened by the continuing use of flowers and foliage, with festoons of husks and the classical repertory of anthemion and palmette ornament.

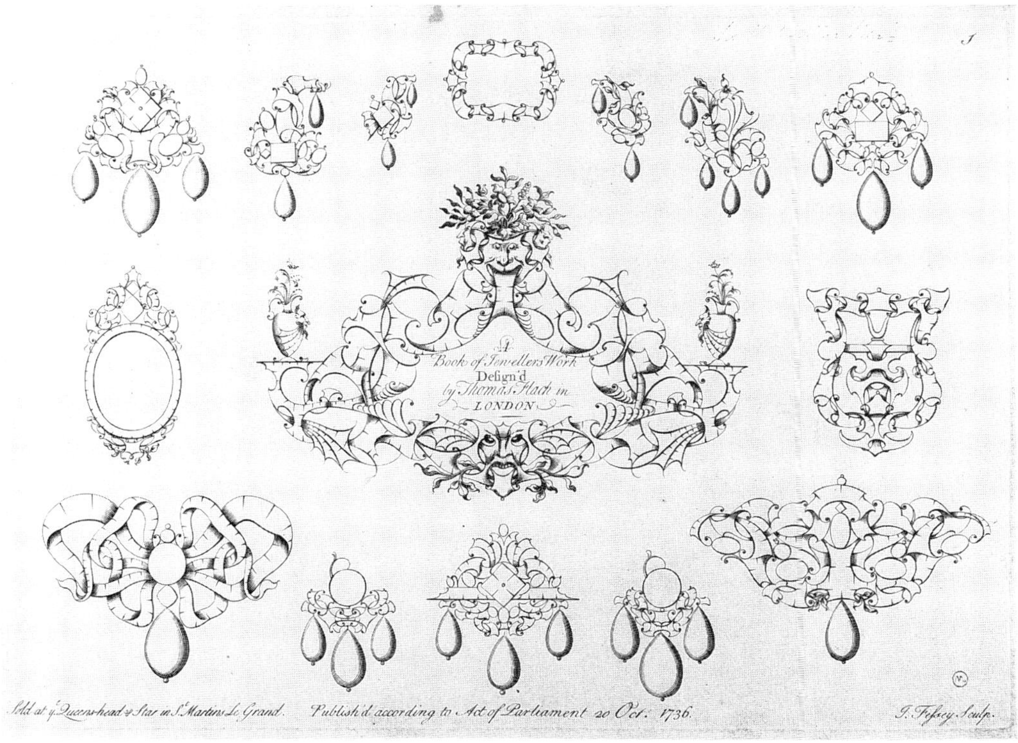

Fig. 24 Title-page of *A Book of Jeweller's Work* by Thomas Flach (1736).

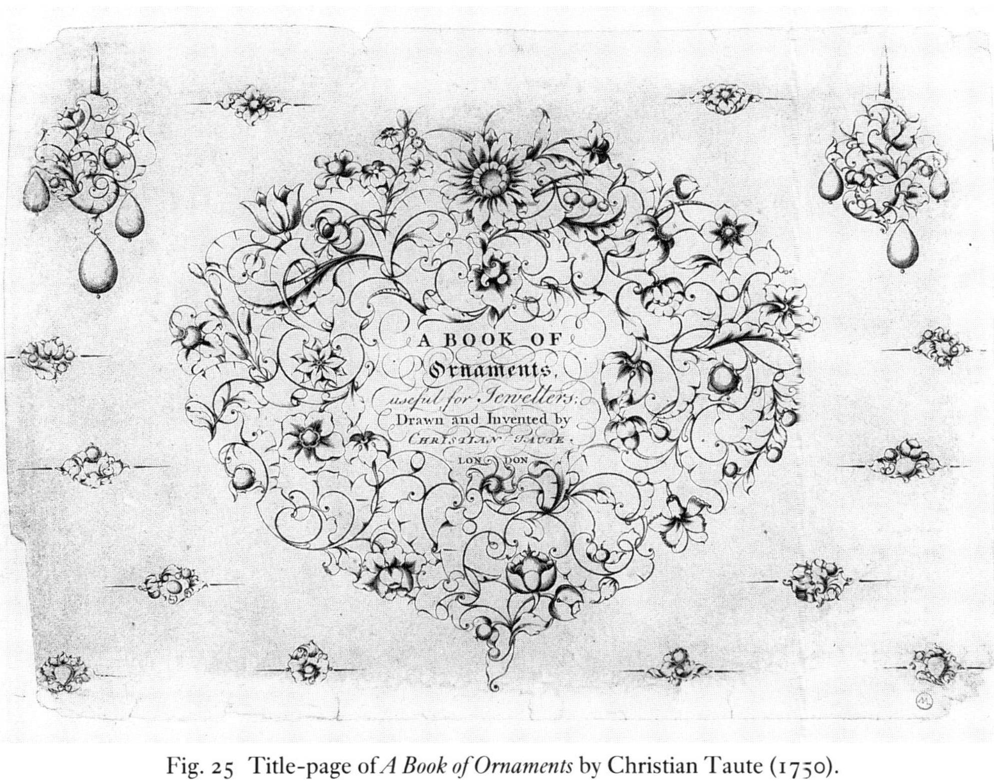

Fig. 25 Title-page of *A Book of Ornaments* by Christian Taute (1750).

The eighteenth century witnessed an increased use of ciphers, both for seals, and – worked in gold, marcasite or gem-stones – to embellish lockets, clasps and rings. Several collections of ciphers were published: by Benjamin Rhodes in 1723, Bowles and Carver *c.* 1770 (Fig. 26) and Garnet Terry, an undated collection.[205]

Fig. 26 Designs for ciphers by Bowles and Carver.

Rhodes, who had been active in the reign of William III, is best known for his engraving on plate executed for Sir Richard Hoare. Terry, described as an engraver and jeweller on a billhead of 1780, engraved several bookplates *c.* 1760–80.[206]

ENGRAVED GEMS

Glyptics reached a high standard as English collectors encouraged the work of engravers at home by buying modern as well as ancient gems. Several of the craftsmen combined engraving seals with other types of work, bookplates and the like, and the number of craftsmen practising in London in 1784 is known from the trade directory for that year. Of the seventeen names, eleven are simply described as 'Seal Engraver' and five as 'Jeweller & Seal Engraver' or 'Maker'; and at least one, Edward Parker, had two shops in the West End.[207]

The engravers could thus serve their public directly, as well as by working for other jewellers. Robert Wray (1715–79) is one of the first to emerge with an identifiable group of works, recorded by impressions made in his account book, and with a known clientèle. The latter included the Dukes of Marlborough and Kingston, Charlotte, Duchess of Somerset, and Lord Ilchester.[208]

In the mid century, Rouquet was impressed by the number of talented English engravers, although he doubted if modern works could ever equal those of antiquity.[209] Foreign engravers also made careers here: the Norwegian Christian Reisen (1685–1725) taught Claus Smart (†1739) and Christopher Seaton (†1768); and the Huguenot modeller and engraver, Matthew Gosset (1683–1740), had taught Robert Wray. The German engraver Lorenz Natter (1705–63) was in England between the 1740s and 1760 cataloguing collections and engraving gem portraits of eminent men and women, including that of Frederick, Prince of Wales.[210] In the second half of the century a large group of talented indigenous engravers appeared: John Kirk (1724–76), Richard Yeo (1720–79), Richard Dean, R.A. in 1777–8, William Barnet, R.A. in 1786, Thomas Pownall, R.A. in 1778, William Pownall, R.A. in 1782, William Harris, R.A. in 1788, Edward Burch senior (1730–1814) and his son, Edward, R.A. in 1787, Nathaniel Marchant (1739–1816) and the brothers William Brown (1748–1825) and Charles Brown (1749–95). Public exhibitions and the encouragement of the Royal Academy and the Royal Society of Arts, as well as private patronage, contributed to this remarkable flowering of native talent in glyptic art.

As all business documents and private letters were sealed with wax, there was a steady demand for small, modest seal-stones. What interested clients was iconography rather than a standard of artistry comparable to that of the ancients. Some seals were purely armorial; a three-sided stone with the arms, crest and cipher each occupying one of the faces was a popular type. Other favourite devices were the heads and busts of classical writers, of heroes and heroines, and of English poets. Robert Wray's account book is a guide to taste in the years 1738–43. He cut 'fancy subjects in the antique manner' – that is, the classical divinities and personifications such as Diana, Mercury, Minerva and Fame; portraits of illustrious men of antiquity: Alexander, Mark Antony, Socrates and Virgil; and, for the moderns, Queen Elizabeth, Cromwell, Newton and the literary trio, Shakespeare, Milton and Pope.[211] Gems also expressed political opinions. Sylas Neville, who was a republican, ordered devices which demonstrated his point of view. On 21 October 1768 he called at Mr Bellis's 'for a seal he has engraved for me by Pownal, which I intend to use when I write etc. in my real character The device is an exact representation of the Pileus on the medals of M. Brutus, above it a star and this motto, CAUSA ARDENS. On the white side of a red and white cornelian, O eternal Father of Life & Liberty'.[212] Conservative upholders of the established order used seals with intaglio portraits of Julius Caesar or of the Hanoverian monarchs. The Prince of Wales, who had many friends in the Whig party, ordered from Benjamin Laver of Bruton Street in April 1785 'a curious matchless ring of sardonyx elegantly engraved in the natural colours with the striking likeness of the bust of the Rt. Hon. Charles James Fox neatly mounted in gold and set round with brilliants of the first water'.[213]

From the late 1770s, as neo-classical influences grew stronger, more accurate depictions of classical subjects were commissioned. Thus, the Countess of Pembroke ordered from Nathaniel Marchant, who was then in Rome, a ringstone engraved with a figure of a Bacchante from the Villa Borghese.[214] Because of their small size, engraved gems were best displayed in rings. Around 1720 the second Duke of Devonshire mounted several intaglio portraits of Roman empresses in impressive ring settings, with his cipher and coronet on the back of the bezel.[215] Most such collection mounts were simple in design and not intended for wear. More luxurious rings, like the 'onyx cameo ring of a blackamoor's head with diamond collar set round with twenty six brilliants' or the 'garnet engraved with Jupiter and Leda also set with brilliants in a ring' combined sparkle with hardstone engraving for wear and display.[216] From the 1770s plain gold channelled rims or Roman ring settings were offered for sale, and the Hon. John Smith, M.P. for Pontefract (1748–1811), wears such a ring in his portrait, done at Rome in 1773 by Pompeo Batoni.[217] These rings were the badge of the 'man of taste', and the Prince of Wales, that pre-eminent arbiter of fashion, had a pair of portraits of the late and present Kings of Prussia mounted in a 'very large Roman setting swivel ring'.[218]

The setting of cameos and intaglios in necklaces and bracelets seems to have been a fashion imported from Italy: in a letter from Brighton in 1779 the Countess of Pembroke described the Lucan family, just back from Rome: 'they have bought [*sic*] over long necklaces of them [cameos] for all their family and some very pretty ones. I should like very well to have two pretty cameos not bigger than this [large circle in MS.] for lockets, bracelets etc. I don't desire this if it costs much money.'[219] In fact they were not likely to be cheap, as a letter from Dr Moore, tutor to the young Duke of Hamilton on the Grand Tour, pointed out when writing to his pupil's mother from Florence: 'It was with infinite difficulty I got him turned away from giving £250 for a little cameo of Caligula. The thing was fine to be sure but I'm sure £250 are finer . . . He gave up also after much persuasion a necklace of antiques which he intended as a present for your Grace.'[220] Attractive cameos were rare, as Lady Holland informed the Duchess of Leinster in 1767: 'Your cameo is antique undoubtedly: to be sure some modern ones are prettier to look at, but in general one finds few pretty cameos.'[221] Matching pairs, of hardstone or shell, were mounted in jewelled bracelet clasps. They might be portraits of kings and queens, such as Henri IV and Maria de' Medici,[222] or a depiction of the

Rape of Europa with a Triton and Cupid in an extraordinary fine agate of many colours and Galatea upon a dolphin with two Tritons curiously variegated. These two cameos are of uncommon largeness and of most exquisite skill neatly mounted in gold and extremely proper for bracelets.'[223]

Shell, which was far easier to carve, was used for buttons, such as those bought by the Prince of Wales from Thomas Gray: 'a set of Sicilian shells mounted in gold containing thirty buttons'.[224]

In the foreword to the 1791 Tassie catalogue, Raspe drew the parallel between classical and contemporary custom; in both ages, 'the poorer and lower sort of people would imitate the great and rich and figure away [i.e., cut a dash] by external form and show of things or fashions which surpassed their faculties'.[225] To meet this demand Tassie had first issued a catalogue in 1775 of cheap glass reproductions of famous engraved gems for mounting as rings, seals, necklaces, lockets or bracelets. The connoisseurship of engraved gems was also aided at this time by the production of collections of plaster casts of examples from the major collections, which could be bought in sets and mounted in trays or false books, with a note of the subject, engraver and collection.

INSIGNIA

All the talents of enamellers, gold-chasers, gem-engravers and stone-setters were enlisted for the creation of the insignia of the Orders of Knighthood. The Garter retained its pride of place except in Scotland, where the Thistle was the premier Order, and both were joined after 1725 by the newly revived Order of the Bath. The latter was then regarded as a stepping-stone to the higher Order, and it was the custom, as in the Russian Imperial system, to surrender it on receiving the blue ribbon. Finally, in 1783, the Most Illustrious Order of St Patrick was created as the premier Order for Ireland.

There were no changes in the Garter insignia, apart from those of style and taste. The earlier insignia continued the late-seventeenth-century style,[226] but the ribbon-work frame for a Lesser George designed by Thomas Flach in 1736 (Fig. 27) introduces a rococo element which was repeated in the designs by Taute.[227]

Brilliants replaced rose-cut diamonds,[228] and engravers of the calibre of Charles Brown made cameos in opaque and transparent stones for the Lesser George; one was cut from an almandine garnet and sold to the Empress Catherine II,[229] others were stocked by dealers.[230] Moser made a setting for a Lesser George, which was reset in 1807 with a 'very fine sardonyx George in cameo with diamond cut Garter and diamond motto fine chased gold George at the back by Moser'.[231]

The most obvious outward sign of membership of the Order in daily life was the breast decoration or star worn on the coat. Originally worked in silver thread and then

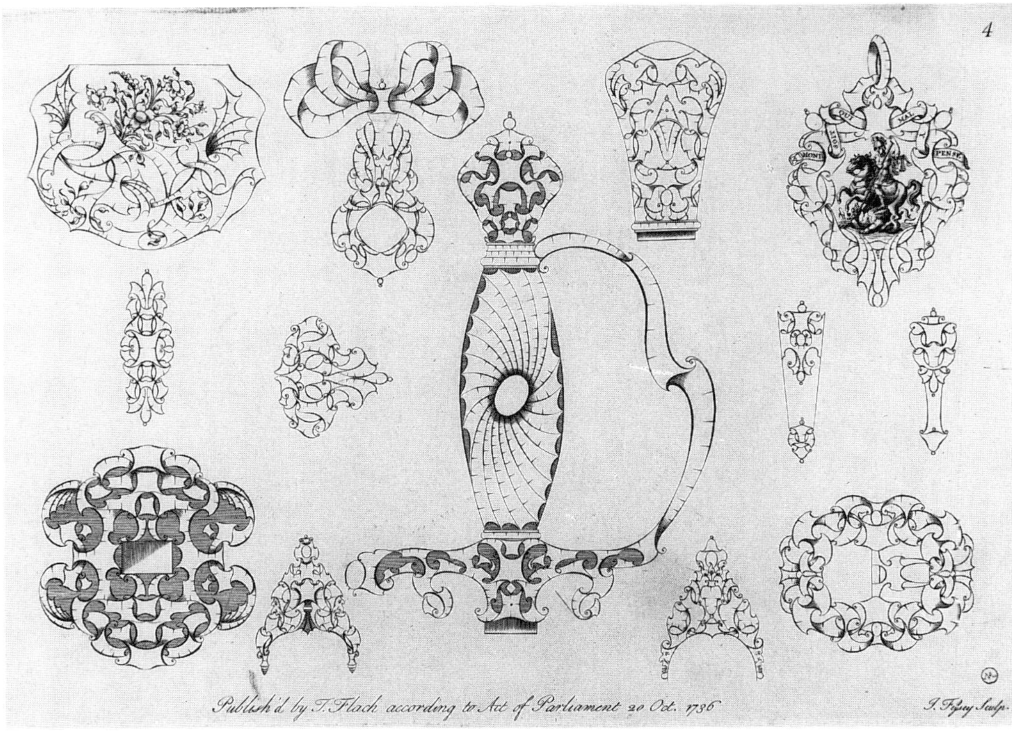

Fig. 27 Designs by Thomas Flach, including a rococo frame for a Lesser George, snuff box, cane handle, pendant, seal mounts, buckle, sword hilt and guard.

fashioned in silver, the star became more luxurious. In 1786 Thomas Gray supplied the Prince of Wales with a 'diamond badge of the Order of the Garter' which was twice remodelled, the last time at a cost of £498 6*s* for 'Remaking the diamond star with ruby cross gold back and furnishing 38¾ carats of brilliants 175 roses, 17 rubies'.[232]

As first conceived, the Order of the Bath was similar to the Garter in having only one class of members under the Sovereign and Grand Master; in 1725 the future Duke of Cumberland held this office. The first installation in Henry VII's chapel at Westminster Abbey was a splendid occasion, commemorated in a fine volume of engravings by Pine which was published in 1730.[233] The device was modelled on that used in the seventeenth century for the Knights of the Bath, and the colour of the ribbon established in Charles I's reign was maintained. To this was added a gold collar, a star or breast decoration, and insignia for the officials of the Order. There is a design by Marcus Gunter for the badge (Fig. 28), and a jewelled version has been acquired by the British Museum.[234]

The sumptuous appearance of the knights at George III's wedding was commented on by Mrs Lybbe Powys,[235] and whatever feelings of disappointment may have been felt at first by recipients who had aspired to the blue ribbon of the Garter, some of the knights, like Lord Clive, spent immense sums on their insignia.[236]

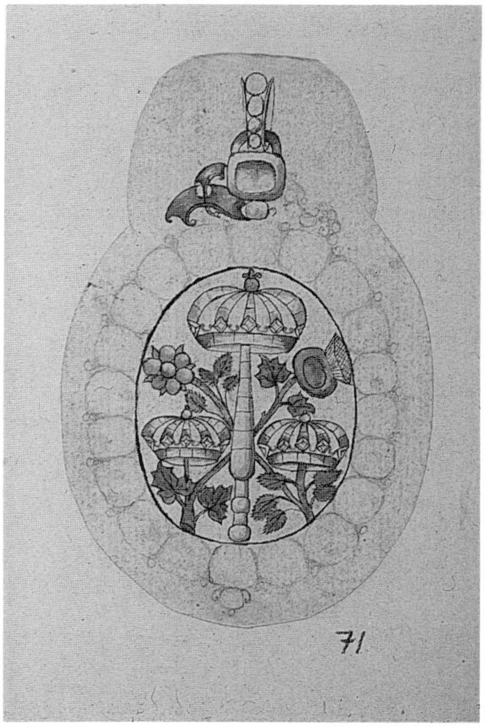

Fig. 28 Design by Marcus Gunter for badge of the 'Order of the Bath. Röhsska Konstlöjdmuseet, Goteborg.

95 Pendant enamelled with Masonic emblems. Collection of Mr Alick Hay of Duns Castle.

Freemasonry thrived in eighteenth-century England; the number of lodges multiplied and attracted membership from the aristocracy and professions. At a meeting of the Grand Lodge on 24 June 1727 it was resolved that 'in all private lodges quarterly communications and general meetings the master and wardens do wear the jewels of Masonry hanging to a white ribbon'[237] (Plate 95). Some of these jewels were designed by well-known artists. William Hogarth was reputed to have designed the Steward's jewel of 1735,[238] and the characteristically classical badges worn by officials at his lodge of the Nine Muses are attributed to G. B. Cipriani.[239] Quality varied from the Order of Masonry elegantly set with brilliant diamonds' sold with his blue silk apron by Earl Ferrers in 1788[240] to the more modest items depicted on the trade card of F. Fisher *c.* 1800.[241]

The eighteenth century was also the age when clubs and societies flourished, and some of these, like the Anti-Gallican Society founded in 1745 'to oppose the insidious arts of the French nation', had insignia to be worn at meetings by officials. The badge for the Anti-Gallican Society had a complicated design, repeated on the back, of a plaque enamelled with the assumed arms of the Society: St George mounted and spearing the flag of France, supported by a lion and a double-headed eagle, with a trophy of flags and cannon with a mask, framed in flowers and set with rock crystal, crowned by a naval crown with pennants, and a pendant of Britannia painted on glass, and the motto FOR OUR COUNTRY.[242] The Whig Club, founded in 1784, used an oval badge with a gold key on a blue enamel ground. Known only from a rare survival in the Museum of London, it represents what must have been a numerous class of political jewels.

RELIGIOUS JEWELLERY

The diamond cross hanging from the necklace of the great heiress, Miss Edwards, in her portrait by William Hogarth in 1742 was both a symbol of faith and a fashionable jewel.[243] The cross might be worn either high or low on the neck, as Lady Jane Coke explained in 1752: 'You can't make a mistake in putting a ribbon to it, and as to length, you may either wear the cross upon your neck or the bottom of it touch the top of your stays'[244] (Plate XXVI). The cross was attached to its necklace of pearls, precious stones or a ribbon by a runner or coulant. These might take the form of a cluster, a bow-knot, or even a coronet[245] (Plate 96). Displayed so prominently, the cross looked best when set with fine-quality rose- or brilliant-cut diamonds, like the one given to Queen Charlotte on her arrival in England,[246] or with rich coloured stones such as rubies framed with brilliants.[247] Cheaper versions could use semi-precious stones: amethysts

96 Silver cross set with rose-cut diamonds surmounted by a coulant shaped as a coronet over a bow knot. Private collection.

and garnets,[248] crystal,[249] and paste, both white and coloured.[250]

Designs for crosses set with rose-cut stones, in collets with saw-toothed edges and framed in acanthus leaves, were published in 1762; one design with fleurs-de-lis in the angles of the arms, copied the crosses for the French Orders, but strengthened the design[251] (Plate XXVII). The mid-century designs by Dinglinger and Taute have asymmetric floral decoration, the flowerheads set with pearls and precious stones, trailed along the arms and ending with trefoils. Women of taste collaborated on designs with their jewellers, and Horace Walpole complimented Lady Carteret at a Ranelagh ball by telling her: 'how charming your cross is – I'm sure the design was your own.'[252]

Religious iconography was rarely used for personal ornaments, but there were exceptions. A gold watch by Palue was enclosed in a case enamelled with scenes from the life of Christ after the paintings of Veronese,[253] and another was chased and embossed with the Presentation in the Temple after a design by Augustin Heckel in 1786–7.[254]

JEWELS OF LOVE, FRIENDSHIP AND MOURNING

Rigid observance of mourning affected both clothing and jewellery and was followed by the court and by society at large, with a distinction between full and half mourning. The types of fabric as well as the colours permitted were all regulated by the court and the only jewels permitted were black or jet beads, enamelled gold and marcasites, occasionally with garnets. Even buttons were affected, and in 1784 Mrs Papendiek, dresser to Queen Charlotte, recorded that a 'Mr. Clay introduced a button to London which he had for some time been perfecting. It was for gentleman's mourning attire and improving by wear was in use for many years.'[255]

The mourning regulations affected the regular court functions, and newly-married brides, like Mrs Damer in 1767, might be disappointed because they could not show off their new jewels.[256] Writing from Ireland just after the death of George II, Lady Caroline Fox told the Countess of Kildare that 'The mourning here is vastly strict, one must not even wear a bouquet or a garnet.'[257] The effect on business could be serious, and when news came of the death of the Duke of Cumberland in 1765 Matthew Boulton wrote that 'I am fearful this will be detrimental to our plating button trade as we begin already to want some orders for this article.'[258] His apprehension was well-founded, for polished buttons were contrary to the regulations for mourning attire.

Long periods of mourning were also observed in private families for husbands and parents. On 24 March 1724, alluding to the death of their father the previous December, Mrs Delany advised her sister in the country that she might 'wear black silk gloves, you might have worn black necklaces and earrings this last two months';[259] the length of time for full and half mourning was not so prolonged as at court.

Memorial jewellery to honour the dead is one of the largest categories of eighteenth-century jewellery to survive, and illustrates the sequence of styles from baroque through rococo to neo-classical. Rings outnumber the other types; they were worn by both sexes and were given by all who could afford them. A few retained the traditional *memento mori* symbols, but new motifs were introduced and the name of the deceased given more prominence. The grandest ring was a memorial to the pathetically short life of Edward Harley, the infant son of the Earl of Oxford. The octagonal bezel is set with an emerald with flaming lamps at the four angles, two panels at the sides enclosing hair, and on the back an enamelled shield with the arms of Harley quartering de Vere, Bampton and Cavendish, with the motto FIDE ET VIRTUTE. The inside of the white enamelled hoop had the inscription, UNE VIE SI COURTE UNE SI GRANDE AFFLICTION, and on the outside: EDWARD HARLEY NAT 18 OCT 1725 OB 22 OCT 1725.[260]

White enamel signified that the deceased was unmarried; black was used for married persons. The inscriptions could be in Latin, English or French. In the rococo period the design became standardised, with a small bezel having a reeded back and set with a gem-stone or crystal, the hoop broken up into scrolls inscribed with the name, age and date of death. The shoulders might be set with gems and hair enclosed in the bezel. Typical of the more expensive types were those directed to be given in her memory by Richardson's heroine, Clarissa Harlowe, 'with the cipher CL.H with my hair in crystal and round the inside of each, the day, month and year of my death, each ring with the brilliants to cost 20 guineas'.[261] Large numbers of rings might be given away. On the death of Robert Walpole, Earl of Orford, in 1745, George Wickes supplied seventy-two 'mourning rings' at £1 apiece.[262]

Around 1770 the bezel became larger, a pointed or rounded oval or an octagon, being filled with hair, plaited, set in a curl, knot or sheaf, and overlaid by a cipher in gold wire, seed pearl or diamonds. Neo-classical motifs were introduced; the Roman funerary urn appeared as an onyx cameo, enamelled white on a deep-blue ground with rose diamond handles and festoons, or worked in hair. The urn on its plinth could be crowned by a canopy painted *en grisaille* and mourned over by a genius or an allegorical figure of a woman in classical robes. The pathos was emphasised by inscriptions: SACRED TO FRIENDSHIP or NOT LOST BUT GONE BEFORE with an angel bearing a scroll inscribed TO BLISS.[263] The name of the deceased and the date of death were now inscribed on the back of the bezel. Other symbols used include obelisks, dogs, broken columns and the weeping willow. The willow had, from its appearance, a long association with mourning, and a poem by Robert Herrick celebrated its role for garlands to mourn lost loves:

> When once the lover's rose is dead
> Or laid aside forlorn
> The willow garlands 'bout the head
> Bedewed with tears are worn.[264]

Such 'crants', adorned with paper rosettes, were carried at the funerals of virgins and hung in the parish church in some parts of the country.[265]

Not only rings but lockets and brooches were worn in memory of the dead. One of the most pathetic is a brooch dated 1786 depicting the coffins of two children with the mourning parents.[266] Another, commemorating REBECCA DOBSON OBT 1787 AET 26, encloses a miniature of two allegorical mourners worked in hair, small pearls and gold.[267] Lockets were also popular, and an example in the form of a heart in rock crystal surmounted by a ruby and diamond heart, framed in black ribbon, is inscribed ELIZ EYTON OB FEB 1754 AET 81.[268] Many of the standard motifs could be bought ready-made, wanting only the cipher and inscription, but others were designed by relatives. When her brother Charles died at sea in 1788, Lady Louisa Cathcart wrote that 'Families have certainly a right to indulge themselves in any mournful fancy upon such an occasion', and she designed

a large lockit, with a little black ribbon bow, to be worn *always* with Hair which I have got enough of for four, and a little inscription in black & white enamel round the name on the back, and if you think of something short, pretty and applicable besides, we might have them all the same to wear always – I think it would be comforting.[269]

Another hair locket made for a widow has a miniature of a lady in contemporary dress mourning at a tomb inscribed MAY SAINTS EMBRACE THEE WITH A LOVE LIKE

97 Memorial locket depicting a widow and a dog, mourning by a tomb inscribed MAY SAINTS EMBRACE THEE WITH A LOVE LIKE MINE. Victoria and Albert Museum.

MINE, derived from an etching by John Raphael Smith in 1783 illustrating Charlotte grieving for Werther in Goethe's novel[270] (Plate 97). There is a memorial bracelet with pointed oval centrepiece,with frame inscribed CHARLES PETLEY RAYLEY OB 5 DEC 1785 and FORGIVE THE WISH THAT WOULD HAVE KEPT THEE HERE surrounding a lady in classical drapery grieving over an urn on a plinth inscribed CPR amidst weeping willows (Plate 98).

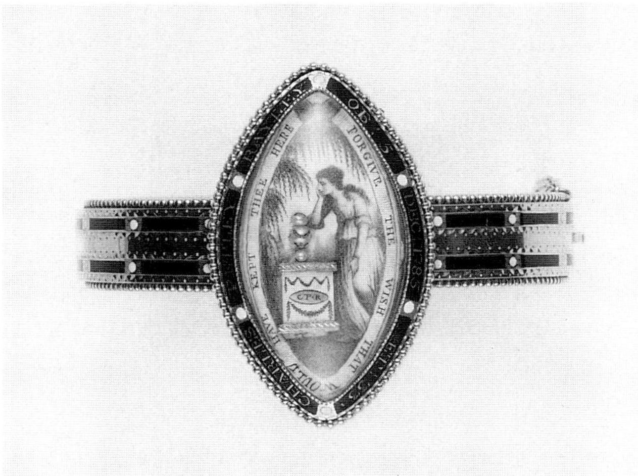

98 Memorial bracelet with centrepiece inscribed CHARLES PETLEY RAYLEY OB 5 DEC 1785 and FORGIVE THE WISH THAT WOULD HAVE KEPT THEE HERE. Christie's.

Not all hair jewels commemorated the dead. Richardson's Clarissa Harlowe described the 'four charming ringlets one of which the Colonel took for his locket which he says he will cause to be made and wear next his heart in memory of his beloved cousin'.[271] William Hickey was devoted to Tom Forest and, knowing their attachment, Miss Celia Forest gave him 'a lock of his hair observing it would be a melancholy memento of my deceased friend and companion. I immediately had the hair set in a pair of sleeve buttons with his cipher and have worn them from that time to the present day.'[272]

Jewels, with or without hair inside, exchanged by friends and lovers have a symbolism of their own. Many rococo heart-shaped crystal lockets were tokens of friendship. One is inscribed: PRUDENCE FIXES ME OCTR 15TH HAVE MY FRIENDSHIP FOR EVER AUG 16 1746[273] (Plate 99). In 1716 Countess Cowper sent Viscountess Sundon 'the heart I promised and am glad you should wear it to put you in mind that I have another heart most faithfully at your service'.[274] Heart lockets worn at the throat could also be made of amber, pebble stone and turquoise, or wrought in gold and enamelled with flowers and turtle-doves, set round with garnets and other stones. Hearts, single or twinned, surmounted by a crown or lover's knot, enamelled and set with rubies and brilliants,

99 Heart-shaped crystal locket mounted in enamelled gold set with emerald flanked by pairs of garnets, with white frame inscribed PRUDENCE FIXES ME OCTR 15 and on the back HAVE MY FRIENDSHIP FOR EVER AUG 16 1746. Victoria and Albert Museum.

were a favourite symbol on rings. The hoops might be inscribed with amorous mottoes in French: NOS DEUX COEURS SONT UNIS; VOTRE AMITIE FAIT MA FELICITE; and the simple GAGE D'AMOUR. They reached the height of fashion in 1755 when the future Earl Spencer gave Georgiana Poyntz a double-heart ruby and diamond ring and a billing turtle dove brooch for her riding habit on their engagement. The mottoes, MON COUER EST TOUT A TOI GARDES LE BIEN, and IMITONS LES EN AMITIE allude to the symbols of heart and turtle doves.[275]

The success of Rousseau's *La nouvelle Héloise*, published in 1761, made sentimental jewellery even more fashionable. Devotees of this novel extolling the virtues of the simple life and true love paraded their enamelled crystal lockets of hair and the miniature of loved ones as proudly as they wore parures of rubies and diamonds. Mrs Delany expressed the feelings which such jewels represented in her lines:

All things but friendship such as yours
Inconstant pass away
This lock the emblem of your love
Like that will ne'er decay.[276]

Hair was also made into bracelets. When Lord Bristol died in 1751 aged 86, he asked to be buried with the letters of his first wife by his left cheek, the turquoise ring she gave him on his finger, and on his wrist the bracelet of her hair which he 'ever wore'.[277] Catherine, first wife of Sir William Hamilton, the British Minister at Naples, wore a bracelet clasp with a lock of his hair from the time of their marriage in 1758 until her death in 1782.[278] Very grand versions of such clasps were given to Queen Charlotte by George III for her pearl bracelets. One had his miniature, the other his hair and cipher, and both were set round with brilliants.[279]

Not only the hair of friends, family and lovers was so cherished. At the time of Admiral Keppel's trial for neglect of duty in 1779, 'all the fine ladies', such as Lady Betty Compton and the Duchess of Rutland, wore his hair in lockets as badges of their support.[280] Gifts of hair from royalty were treasured. In 1772 Lady Mary Coke became friendly with the Empress Maria Theresa and was very disappointed when the promised gift of a bracelet clasp with the Imperial cipher 'set round with diamonds close and another border of diamonds round that' did not contain hair: 'I had some reason to flatter myself that I should have had that favour which would have been more to me than all the diamonds in the world.'[281] Mrs Delany was overjoyed when Queen Charlotte showed her affection with the gift of 'a lock of her beautiful hair, so precious a gift is indeed inestimable', and it was set in a pearl locket with the queen's crowned cipher.[282] The queen also gave away rings with the hair of her two eldest sons, woven emblematically – that of the Prince of Wales into an ostrich plume, and that of the Bishop of Osnaburgh into a mitre.[283] Already, at the age of seventeen, the Prince of Wales was asking women he admired for their hair and offering his own, enshrined in jewels inscribed with his name, his birthday and sentimental mottoes: GRAVE A JAMAIS DANS MON COEUR; TOUJOURS AIMEE; and TOUT CE QUI M'EST CHERE AU MONDE.[284] The fine pearl locket 'with gold enamelled plate, hair curl on diamond ornament' which he bought from James Shrapnell in 1783 could have borne a similar declaration.[285] Such lockets and brooches were advertised by the York firm of Etherington on their trade card in 1786: 'Devices in diamonds, pearls, hair etc. executed in the most pleasing taste'. They were shuttle-shaped, rimmed with pearls and had a central plaque inscribed AMITIE or SOUVENIR over the curl of hair[286] (Plate XXVIII). To a large extent these inscriptions replaced the hearts, turtle-doves, quivers, Cupids and other amorous symbols of the rococo period.

JACOBITE JEWELLERY

The Stuart cause was rekindled by the romantic adventure of the Young Pretender, Prince Charles Edward (1720–89), who landed in Scotland in 1745 without money or arms, and went on to capture Scotland and lead an army to within reach of London. His defeat at Culloden, followed by hair's-breadth escapes from his pursuers, and the inspiring devotion of his friends, made a strong appeal to the imagination. Until his death, his supporters continued to dream of his return, drank toasts to the King over the Water, and wore his or his Stuart ancestors' portrait on snuff boxes, in rings, in lockets and bracelets (Plate XXIII); and such jewels, if gifts from him, were treasured as sacred relics.

Rings were the commonest Jacobite badges. In 1762 James Boswell met Alexander Macdonald from Skye, who was

> warmly attached to the family of Stuart: and he said the Scotch Jacobites had great hopes of a restoration in which they were confirmed by a dream which he had. He repeated it to me with the greatest enthusiasm. It was very entertaining to see the superstitious warmth of the old Highland seer mixed with the spirited liveliness of a neat, clever young fellow. He had a picture of Mary Queen of Scots in a ring which he wore with much affection.[287]

Intaglio portraits of her grandson, Charles I, for setting in rings were a speciality of the engraver Christian Reisen (1685–1725).[288] Miniatures might be concealed in rings with locket bezels beneath a bust of George II, or covered by the broad hinged gold keeper.[289] Some portraits were worked in hair. Frances, Lady Shelley, daughter of Thomas Winckley of Brockholes in Lancashire, remembered her childhood in a High Tory home:

> We were all strong Jacobites – in our old house the Pretender had slept the night before the Battle of Preston and I still possess the bracelet given by him to my ancestor with a portrait of King Charles made of his own hair cut off on the scaffold and dipped in his blood. I recall the pride with which I wore this bracelet on state occasions.[290]

After James II died in 1701, Jacobites celebrated White Rose Day on the birthday of James III (1688–1765) by wearing white ribbons and white rose cockades. The latter symbol appears in jewellery, as in the four multi-petalled white roses on the hoop of a ring with an inscription calling the Pretender to return to his kingdom: QUAERIT PATRIA CAESAR— – the fatherland desires the king – in the collection of the Duke of Buccleuch and Queensberry.[291] It is associated with other Jacobite emblems in the ring given by Prince Charles Edward to Sir Hugh Cholmondley of Cheshire in 1745.[292] The bezel is set with a moss agate depicting a thistle, framed in brilliants, the back enamelled with the star of the Order of the Thistle and inscribed CAESAR CAESARIS. On one shoulder the white rose stands out in relief and on the other a closed crown; there is a trophy of arms in relief round the hoop.[293] Another moss agate, representing three crowns set in a ring inscribed JAMES III, brought about the conversion of a suspicious goldsmith who, having failed to prove that the crowns were not natural, declared, 'I was before a Whig but from this moment I am a Jacobite.'[294]

John Drummond, fifth Duke of Perth (1679–1757), fastened the fur cloak he wore over his armour with a brooch set with a cameo portrait of James III, and another such, carved in shell and crowned, is in the Drumlanrig Castle collection.[295] Two intaglio portraits of James III engraved by Carlo Costanzi – a garnet in a ring, with cipher and hair, and an emerald – were sent to Prince Charles Edward in 1750 by James Edgar, the devoted secretary of the Old Pretender in Rome.[296] James III's miniature was similarly set in rings or pendants, framed in acanthus, crowned and jewelled.[297] Gold filigree ciphers JR, set under crystal with hair, and stamped gold heads in medallions were widely distributed, one being inscribed JAMES III (OF ENGLAND) VIII (OF SCOTLAND) GOD SAVE YE KING 1710.[298]

From mid century, the portrait of Prince Charles Edward dominated Jacobite iconography. A report of 28 August 1750 from a government agent in Paris sent the following information:

> An Order is given by the Pretender's People here to an able Artist, who makes engraved Seals of compositions in Imitation of all Sorts of fine Stones, to get ready in a weeks times fifteen hundred Seals, with the Pretender's Eldest Son's Busto upon them, at the rate of 20 sols a Piece, and accordingly he has undertaken to get them ready by that time.[299]

The artist was later identified as 'le Sieur Malapert', and an escaped Jacobite, Tate, as the one 'who got the engraving made on metal from which the artist takes the Impression on his Composition'.[300] The latter was further described in a list of Jacobites abroad as 'Adam Tate – of Edinburgh, Master Goldsmith', then aged about 33.[301] A quantity of these intaglios, and small silver-gilt heads inscribed LOOK LOVE AND FOLLOW, were brought to London by an Irish priest appointed as chaplain to the Sardinian Minister.[302] A similar medallion, without the motto, is set under crystal in a ring formerly in the Seton family collection. The four scrolls of the hoop are inscribed C.P.R. DUM SPIRAT SPERO (Charles Prince Regent. While he breathes I hope) and there is a white rose and thistle on the shoulders.[303] Another such medallion in a ring is in the Museum of Fort William; it bears the same inscription and the date 1745.[304] A ring with a shell cameo and the inscription CR III 1766, asserting his claim to the throne, is at Chiddingstone Castle.[305] Even after his death in 1789 the demand for Jacobite jewels continued, and Tassie's 1791 catalogue listed a number for seals and rings, including one in Highland dress and the motto SUUM CUIQUE.[306]

A miniature of the prince as a boy wearing the Garter ribbon, after a portrait by J. F. Liotard, is set in a ring with the Garter enamelled on the back of the bezel,[307] and another, much smaller, is hidden in the shoulder of a ring he gave to John Farquharson of Allarque, with a foiled crystal bezel.[308] More important is the ring set with a turquoise cameo of a crown and other emblems of royalty and inscribed around the sides and on the back: BY EVERY CLAIM TIS YOURS and US DD AD NUPTIAS 1772, alluding to the marriage with Princess Louisa of Stolberg, in the Buccleuch and Queensberry collection.[309] The same collection has another ring with a turquoise crown cameo, a tiny pink heart at the base of the hoop and thistles on the shoulders, with initials and THOU SHALT TO FORTUNE VIRTUE RECONCILE BOTH DUE TO HIM. Both rings have been attributed to an Edinburgh goldsmith.[310] Small miniatures might be worn as scarf or neck pins,[311] and larger ones, like that enamelled by C. F. Zincke, could be set in a diamond frame with a bow-knot and hung from a ruby and diamond necklace.[312] Another was attached to a chain of white roses.[313] In another the prince is in Highland dress and wears a white rose, and the frame combines roses and thistles.[314]

The most famous of the jewels set with the prince's hair is the ring which he gave to Flora Macdonald, who had helped him in his flight when there was a price of £30,000 on his head. It is set under crystal with the white rose on the shoulder, a lyre on the back of the bezel, and LOVE AND HONOUR inscribed on the hoop.[315] An admirer of her devotion and courage had a locket made with both her hair and that of the prince.[316] A hair ring given to Alexander Stuart of Inverhayle by the Prince is set in a neo-classical ring with a pointed oval bezel and the cipher CR in seed pearls.[317]

The inscriptions AWA, WHIGS AWA; DO COME; THE ROSE THAT'S LIKE THE SNAW; and PRO REGE ET PATRIA on Jacobite rings echo the toasts drunk by members of clubs, like the Cycle of the White Rose in Cheshire and Denbighshire.[318] The Lady Patronesses of the club wore badges of an enamelled white rose framed in blue, inscribed CYCLE within a coiled serpent on white with their name and date of election on an outer band of blue, as for LADY WILLIAMS WYNN PATRONESS ELECTED 1780, and on the back the foundation date, INSTITUTED JUNE YE 10TH 1710, also on a blue ground.[319] The buttons worn by the members bore an oak wreath.[320]

The executions which followed the failure of the '45 were commemorated in jewels. The four peers – Lovat, Balmerino, Derwentwater and Kilmarnock – beheaded on Tower Hill in 1747, and the seventeen officers executed at Kennington Common, were commemorated by initials and dates on a ring with the headsman's axe, rose and thistle, and the initials and dates of the seventeen officers ingeniously arranged round the twin hoop.[321] Lord Lovat was also commemorated separately with a hair ring, the scrolled hoop inscribed on the outside with his name, date of execution and age, and on the inside with DULCE ET DECORUM EST PRO PATRIA MORI.[322] Robert Lyon, chaplain of Lord Ogilvy's regiment, was also commemorated on a ring with his name, date of execution and age on the outside, and within, PRO REGE & PATRIA TRUCIDATO.[323] Such rings vividly evoke the courage of the men of whom Robert Burns said that they 'shook hands with ruin for what they esteemed the cause of their king and country'.[324]

MINIATURES AND SILHOUETTES

Miniatures, enamelled or painted on vellum or ivory, were set in rings and bracelets surrounded by brilliants,[325] in lockets worn at the neck, as in a portrait by Gainsborough of Queen Charlotte, or hanging below the waist, as in another portrait by Wright of a lady in Van Dyck dress[326] (Plate 100); and on the watch chain.[327] Mrs Warren Hastings told Sophie von La Roche in 1786 that she proposed 'to set a new fashion of wearing men's portraits in the buckle of one's belt'.[328]

There are many references to miniatures being given as tokens of love between husbands and wives, and parents and children, in eighteenth-century literature. Samuel Richardson's heroine, Clarissa Harlowe, decided to leave in her will a miniature painted by an Italian 'to bestow upon the man whom I would one day be most

100 Susannah Hope wearing Van Dyck dress, a miniature at her waist.
Portrait by Joseph Wright of Derby. Sotheby's.

inclined to favour'.[329] In real life, the poet Richard Hayley wrote his first verses to the Miss Read who painted his miniature in Van Dyck costume for his mother's bracelet.[330] Tysoe Paul Hancock left the miniature of his wife by Smart, now at Jane Austen's old home in Chawton, to his daughter, Betsy, hoping that she would 'never part with it as I intend it to remind her of her mother's virtues as well as her person'.[331] Friends liked to wear each other's miniatures. The Prince of Wales showed his devotion to Georgiana, Duchess of Devonshire, by purchasing her miniature in 1788.[332] Political allegiance could also be displayed by wearing a miniature, like that of John Wilkes in a ring with the hoop inscribed FRIENDSHIP WITHOUT INTEREST.[333] The lace jabot could be fastened with an oval miniature depicting Venus reclining on her shell, dove on wrist, and framed in gem-stones.[334]

The quality of the settings – chased or plain gold set with diamonds, pearls or coloured stones – reflected their importance.[335] Lady Yorke proved her attachment to her husband by attending the Queen's Birthday Drawing-Room with her diamond earrings and a diamond-set miniature of her husband which had been painted at The Hague hung from her breast knot.[336] Settings could include the coroneted cipher, such as Lady Isabella Monck's 'Pearl bracelet with my father's picture in enamel done by Zincke set in gold with the cipher and coronet'.[337]

From the 1770s silhouettes were a fashionable alternative to the portrait miniature and, being cheaper, became very popular. Many were made by family or friends, but others were cut by professionals. John Miers (1758–1821) of the Strand excelled at this branch of portraiture, and had many clients, including the fourth Duke of Atholl.[338] These stark black images stood out against ivory behind crystal or glass covers, set in round or oval frames with bright-cut gold borders which might be embellished with pearls or little gems; and, like miniatures, they might have a lock of hair at the back of the frame with a cipher. They, too, were worn in rings, lockets, scarf pins and as bracelet clasps or on black ribbon bands.[339]

MAGICAL JEWELS

The introduction to the 1750 edition of Leonardus's *Mirror of Stones* (originally written in the sixteenth century) admitted that the book's ideas had been abandoned:

> the Author, falling in with the Maxims of the Age wherein he lived, has assigned such Virtues to particular Stones as will not be allowed by the Moderns; as that such or such a Stone shall give the Possessor of it Victory over his Enemies, make him successful in Love, in Litigations at Law, and other Undertakings, with other Fancies of the same Kind which have long since been exploded.[340]

Nevertheless, George Wickes set a toadstone in a ring for Arthur Onslow, Speaker of the House of Commons, in 1740, and Lord Baltimore wore a bloodstone necklace as a 'specific against violent bleeding'.[341]

DRESS

Distinctions were made between the dress worn at court and the simpler styles adopted by merchants and country gentry; and between the less formal, morning 'undress' and the formal clothes worn in the afternoon and evening.

The court dress could use embroidered silk shot with gold and silver thread, the skirts over wide panniers and the bodices laced with straps fastened with gem-studded buckles and partly covered by jewelled stomachers, and perhaps also pinned with brooches and loops; all was designed for the maximum effect by candlelight. Other jewels in the hair, at the ears and neck, on wrists and fingers, completed the ensemble. At the wedding of the Prince of Wales in 1736 the ladies were a magnificent sight:

> Some had diamonds set on ribbands on their heads . . . exceeding brilliant likewise in jewels, some had them in their necklaces and earrings, others with diamond solitaires to pearl necklaces of three or four rows; some had necklaces of diamonds and pearls intermixed, but made up very broad: several had their gown sleeves buttoned with diamonds, others had diamond sprigs in their hair. The ladies' shoes were exceeding rich, being either pink, white or green silk with gold or silver lace and braid all over with low heels and low hind quarters and low flaps and large diamond shoe buckles.[342]

Jewels were much in evidence at masquerades. At one held in 1770 by Mrs Cornelys at Carlisle House, Soho Square, Lord Galway's daughter, Miss Monckton, 'appeared in the character of an Indian Sultana, in a robe of cloth of gold and a rich veil. The seams of her habit were embroidered in precious stones, and she had a magnificent cluster of diamonds on her head'; the jewels were valued at £30,000.[343] From the 1730s Van Dyck costume was favoured for both masquerades and portraits, and seventeenth-century styles of jewellery were adopted for them[344]. Clarissa Harlowe appeared in her morning gown with no jewels but a pair of diamond snaps in her ears and neat buckles on her shoes,[345] but most women would have worn their watch and chatelaine with other accessories.

From 1770, dress became simpler (Plate 101), and the change coincided with the fashion for sentimental jewels in the severe neo-classical style. Lockets with hair and miniatures worn at the neck or in bracelets attracted attention because of their size. Belt clasps with hardstone cameos, or more usually glass or ceramic copies framed in cut steel, emphasised small waists.

The social season was in the winter and spring, and only then were rich ornaments worn. In 1761 Lady Grey wrote to her friend, Catherine Talbot, that 'Pomps and shows and finery belong to winter but not to summer or the country.'[346] This attitude explains the rare occurrence of jewellery in late-eighteenth-century portraits, which were often set out of doors or in less formal attire.

The gentlemen at court were seldom outshone by the ladies: the jewelled insignia of Orders, diamond buckles for shoes and breeches, diamond buttons and hat ornaments,

101 The Countess of Hopetoun. Portrait by David Allan, *c.* 1780. Private collection.

and sword-hilts of gold or silver sometimes set with precious stones, made a brave display. Even in less formal attire, the gold buttons of the coat, the star of an Order, watches and snuff boxes, buckles for shoes and breeches, seals, rings and hat loops, combined with fine, well-cut fabrics to set the gentleman apart.

8
The categories of early Georgian jewellery 1714 – 89

PARURES

On formal occasions parures – that is, jewels of uniform design set with pearls or gems: diamonds, sapphires, rubies, emeralds, topazes, each piece of the same colour as the rest – complemented the dress with greater elegance than a miscellany of magnificent but disparate ornaments. A full parure was extensive and expensive; one supplied to Sir Watkin Williams Wynn by Michael Shuckmell in 1769 comprised: sultana and sprig for the hair, earrings, necklace, five diamond bows, six buttons, chain and bracelet. This was set with diamonds and cost £5294 15*s*.[1] Others were less expensively mounted, with paste, coq de perle and semi-precious stones, like the garnet parure sold at Christie's in 1769. This comprised 'a pair of top and drop earrings, egret, knot, six stay buttons, two sleeve knots, buttons, and three hair pins'.[2]

JEWELS FOR THE HEAD

Eighteenth-century finery culminated in the show of aigrettes and pins worn in the hair or hat. Nature provided many of the motifs. Marcus Gunter's designs of 1724 (Fig. 29) introduce flowers in vases asymmetrically arranged, with tall leafy stems studded with gems and weighed down with pendeloques which shook with every movement.[3]

Fig. 29 Design by Marcus Gunter for aigrettes: 1724
Röhsska Konstlöjdmuseet, Goteborg

Whereas the sprigs that ladies wore to the wedding of the Prince of Wales in 1736 were set with white diamonds,[4] others were made with flowers and leaves of enamels and coloured stones[5] (Plate XXX); insects and birds added a further touch of realism. Sometimes birds carried flowers or jewels; Lady Jane Coke admired the diamond bird with outstretched wings holding a diamond drop in its beak perched in the hair of Mrs Watson, wife of the future Marquess of Rockingham, at Lady Betty Germain's in 1752.[6] An eagle is listed among the Scarbrough jewels in 1753.[7] Insects included brilliant gnats, and butterflies of white and coloured diamonds; and these, like the birds and flowers, were also made in paste and garnets. Diamond sheaves and ears of wheat, symbolic of plenty, were worn in the hair from the 1770s.[8]

In 1776 Lady Sarah Lennox described a new French fashion for the hair, which

> must be powdered, curled in very small curls, & altogether be in the style of L[ad]y Tavistock's, *neat*, but it must be high before & give your head the look of a sugar loaf a little. The roots of the hair must be drawn up straight & not fruzed at all for half an inch above the root; you must wear no cap, and only *little little* flowers dab'd in on the left side; the only feather permited is a black or white sultane perched up on the left side, & your diamond feather against it.[9]

Various feathers are mentioned in records: Lady Grey bought one from Philip Hardel in 1761 for £105,[10] and in 1769 Lady Isabella Monck ordered from Mr Champion 'a brilliant plume of feathers for the head consisting of 247 diamonds weight 12 carats 2 grs.' The stones cost £150 7*s* 6*d* and the setting £14 15*s* 9*d*.[11] Not only diamonds were admired. In 1774 the *Lady's Magazine* reported: 'Lady A—C— was dressed at Ranelagh, the last full night, with nothing on her head but a row of pearls in a chain, across her hair, and a beautiful pearl feather on the left side.'[12]

Jewelled pins could be scattered over the hair or used to attach the cap to the head. Mrs Greville's news from Paris was passed on by Lady Caroline Fox to her sister in 1758:

> Nobody can be dressed without diamond pins which one must have to the value of a guinea up to £20. The principal pin must be put in the poke of the cap and the ribbon round pinn'd on with them for those that wear caps, and those that don't stick them in the curls and pom-poms – in short nothing but diamond pins must appear in the head d'une femme accommode selon le bon ton.[13]

According to Lady Louisa Cathcart in 1776, it was important to place the pins to one side of the cap only – such were her instructions to Louisa Stormont.[14] The fashion lent itself to satire. When the rich and vulgar Miss Alscrip, her maid holding a box of diamond pins beside her, has her hair dressed by her valet-de-chambre, Chignon, in Sir John Burgoyne's play *The Heiress* (1786), all three discuss, as a matter of vast importance, how best to place the pins on the coiffure.[15]

Like Miss Alscrip, every woman of fashion possessed a collection of pins, which varied in design. A few were figurative, such as the 'gold enamelled pin for the hair in

102 Margaret, Duchess of Douglas, with cluster pin in her hair, top and drop earrings, and a double row of pearls at the neck. Portrait, 1760. Collection of Mrs A. V. C. Douglas of Mains.

the form of a hand embellished with diamonds holding a pearl drop circled with diamonds' auctioned in 1772,[16] or the 'large pin with trophies of war' sold in 1787.[17] Among the Scarbrough jewels bought in 1753 were 'four brilliant circles for the hair',[18] but most were set with a large solitaire or else a cluster of stones. Lady Isabella Monck, for instance, owned 'a brilliant diamond pin for the poke of the cap containing one middling sized diamond in the middle with eight small diamonds around it';[19] another, all diamonds, is worn by Margaret, Duchess of Douglas, in her portrait *c.* 1760 (Plate 102); and a similar pin with diamonds round a ruby was listed in the 1789 inventory of Frances, Dowager Duchess of Tweeddale.[20] Six- and eight-petalled jessamine flowers and pointed stars were attractive variants of the cluster; sprinkled on high, powdered headdresses they sparkled like a galaxy.[21] Some women such as Lady Guidon went to extremes: 'her headdress is high but is built up like a rock with diamonds, and indeed she is so much cover'd with jewels that they compare her to a lark wrapped in crumbs'.[22] Pins kept panaches of feathers and other ornaments in place; at a Devonshire House gala in 1782, 'the headdress chiefly consisted of artificial flowers and braided wheat ears fastened on with brilliant and pearl pins'.[23]

In 1757 the Countess of Kildare reported that 'Nothing is so very fashionable as a diamond ribbon which is worn on a black cap – the prettiest thing in the world.'[24] These jewelled trimmings continued in fashion. Lady Sarah Lennox described Lady Waldegrave in 1759:

> She had a great cold, but looked very handsome with a large blonde cap with wings poky up [and] a bead necklace . . . My sister said that she would be much obliged to her if she would let her see her diamond row to sew yours on by it. She did so. It was upon a pearl cap, but she has two rows of it, each a great deal broader than yours, and they don't look the least clumsy, but vastly showy and handsome. When I told her how yours was, she advised me to write to you to tell you it would be much better to pull t'other half of the feather to pieces, as the fashion is, only to wear peepers over the poke. I must tell you also of another fashion, which I like better than any, which is to have a great number of single diamonds about the size of your row put at the edges of a ribbon: – which ribbon is puffed round the cap . . .[25]

Other jewels, besides pins, fixing ribbons and feathers, were worn in the hat: buckles fastened velvet bands in the front, and buttons and loops caught up brims at the sides.

Although the coronet had ceased to be worn, except for coronations and the proceeding to Parliament, more substantial tiaras were introduced in the course of the eighteenth century. One of the earliest examples is seen in Joseph Highmore's portrait of Queen Caroline in the collection of H.M. The Queen. A broad gold band rising to a peak at the front has the upper edge trimmed with pearls and large rubies or garnets set at intervals on the band and with diamond pendants from the crest of the peak.[26] A similar tiara, with a double edge of stones, was worn by Sarah Siddons in her portrait by Reynolds as the Tragic Muse.[27]

EARRINGS

When his daughters left school in 1723 and required new outfits, Nicholas Blundell bought them earrings because, notwithstanding the ordeal of piercing which had to be endured, earrings were essential to the appearance of the well-dressed woman.[28] Whether dressed high or low, the hair was drawn back from the face leaving the ears showing, and as coiffures towered ever higher from the late 1760s, so pendants increased in length.

Still favoured for formal wear was the seventeenth-century girandole with three drops from a bow (Plate 103), but now softened with flowers and leaves. Three drawings have survived from the four submitted by the London jeweller, the Quaker

Thomas How, to his Yorkshire client, George Allan, in 1774 (Fig. 30). The fourth was returned for the design to be made but the others, all variants of the girandole type, have cornucopiae, sprays of flowers and ribbons entwined with flowers linking the top cluster – 'all according to the present taste', at prices from £40 to £50 according to the number of stones required.

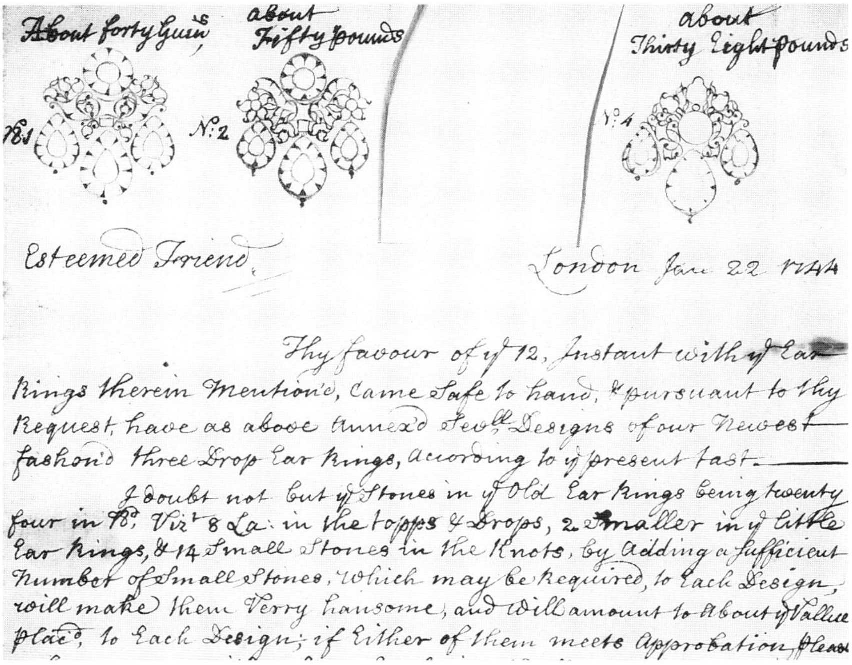

Fig. 30. Designs for girandole earrings sent by Thomas How to George Allan: 1774. Havelock-Allan Papers, North Riding Record Office.

Most of the stones had been broken out of an old-fashioned Allan jewel.[29] Similarly, the girandoles made for the Countess of Scarbrough in 1753 were set with some of her own stones; as Peter Dutens's invoice specified, a 'Pair of three drop earrings in which my Lady employed her two large drops and in which she furnished six side drops £130'.[30]

Single drops hanging from collet, lozenge or cluster tops were also fashionable (Plate XXXI). Sir Watkin Williams Wynn's 1769 inventory listed 'a pair of single drop earrings containing two spread brilliants (for tops) a pair of spread drops valued at £730 14*s*',[31] and in Lady Betty Germain's sale the following year were earrings with large single drops hung from cluster tops set with large stones.[32] They might be linked by knots[33] (Plate 104) or other motifs like fleurs-de-lis, as in a design by Jean Guien.[34] In 1736 George Wickes sold three pairs, to the Bishop of Norwich, and Miss Dodd and Miss Hippie.[35] From 1787 to 1789 the Prince of Wales bought earrings designed around sentimental motifs: heart, butterfly and pansy.[36]

103 Mrs Andrew Lindington wearing a jewel in her cap and girandole earrings. Portrait by Joseph Wright of Derby, 1760. Philadelphia Museum of Art.

Diamonds were the most esteemed stones, and both rose and brilliant cuts were combined in the same ornaments. Not only white but coloured diamonds were available. Two were bequeathed by Mrs Poyntz in 1771: 'my yellow diamond ring set with sapphires' and 'my ruby and blue diamond ring'.[37] Mrs Delany described a gift from the diplomat, Sir Robert Sutton, to his wife in 1724: 'The tops of the earrings are middling brilliants the drops are pink colour diamonds of prodigious size'.[38] With

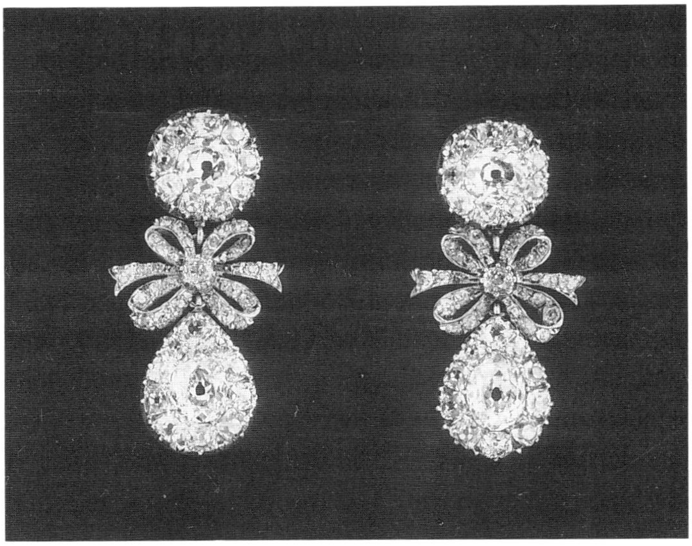

104 Diamond pendant earrings, with bow-knot linking top cluster and drop, similar to those worn by the Duchess of Douglas in Plate 102. S. J. Phillips.

skilful foiling and setting, the two drops might seem cut from the same unclouded stone of the purest water. The very best quality stones could be open-set, with the light entering from both front and back. Miss Sterling in *The Clandestine Marriage* (1766) was proud of her earrings 'set transparent',[39] and in 1769 Stephen Artaud supplied Lady Grey with a pair of 'single drop earrings containing 158 brilliants set transparent'.[40] The brilliance of the long pendant drops was enhanced by framing them in swinging diamond chains.

The tint of coloured stones could be intensified in such designs by setting them in borders of small diamonds. In 1747 Mrs Delany was pleased with her 'pretty birthday present – a pair of three drop amethyst earrings set round with diamonds'.[41] Among other examples are chrysoprases with diamonds or brilliants with ruby circles.[42] The effect was imitated with cheaper stones like the 'pair of three drop jacinth earrings clustered with Saxon topaz and mounted in gold' in the Wynn collection.[43]

All the fashionable styles were made with pearls. There was a 'pair of night earrings with pearl drops set with diamonds' in the sale of the jewels of the Dowager Princess of Wales in 1773,[44] and in 1769 Lady Isabella Monck had ordered rose diamond tops hung with Irish pearls.[45] Seed pearls were strung into knots linking the tops with pendants[46] or set in clusters (Plate 105), such as those bought by Lady Caroline Fox, who 'went to Chevenix about pearl earrings – there are none but seed pearl ones round with a little larger in the middle the price about 2 gns'.[47] Coq-de-perle was even cheaper: a pair sold by Thomas Fisher to Gavin Shiells in 1761 was invoiced at £1 7*s*.[48] Mounted in marcasite or combined with garnets, coq-de-perle could be set in disks or 'clumps' to cover the lobe of the ear as well as hung in pendants.

105 Pearl cluster earrings. Detail from the portrait of Lady Willoughby de Broke by J. Zoffany. Christie's.

Moss agate, crystal and Scotch pebbles were also fashionable. On 26 February 1756 Lady Jane Coke 'ventured to buy Miss Cotton a pair of Scots pebble earrings and cross with another pair of drops for her diamond cross [*sic*]. I met with them very cheap for the whole purchase is but 2 guineas and a half. They are extremely in fashion and in my opinion very pretty.'[49]

There were quantities of inexpensive earrings made of beads, mock garnet and paste, both French and English, in the stock of James Bellis, which was sold in 1782, and that of Christopher Pinchbeck, which was sold in 1784.[50] Several eighteenth-century

106 Martha Ray wearing dark green earrings. Detail of the portrait by Allan Ramsay. Collection of the Earl of Sandwich.

portraits illustrate a simple design consisting of two pieces of paste, one larger than the other, and a white trefoil between them. Martha Ray, mistress of the Earl of Sandwich, was painted by Allan Ramsay wearing dark-green earrings of this design[51] (Plate 106).

Some earrings, like those which Miss Sterling showed off in Colman and Garrick's play, could be taken apart: 'the tops, you see, will take off to wear in the morning, or in an undress'.[52] Others were specifically designed for day wear, such as the 'undress earrings containing two round brilliants' valued at £102 12*s* 11*d* in the Wynn inventory.[53] More luxurious were the 'pair of brilliant diamond negligee earrings with middle sized brilliants six small stones set round with twelve rows of small diamonds round each' sold in 1774 by Commodore Forrest of the East India Company.[54] The Dowager Princess of Wales had a pair of 'large jacinth undress tops of earrings set round with brilliants' in the sale of her jewellery.[55]

NECKLACES

According to the *Weekly Journal* of 1 May 1736, the necklaces of the ladies invited to the reception held at Windsor after the wedding of the Prince of Wales were particularly splendid: 'pearl necklaces of three or four rows . . . some had necklaces of diamonds and pearls intermixed, but made up very broad'.[56]

The length, size, number and quality of pearls strung into necklaces worn high on the throat varied considerably. On her wedding day in 1772 Mrs Nollekens, wife of the sculptor, wore 'a triple row of pearls tied behind with a narrow white satin ribbon'.[57] The Dowager Princess of Wales owned a single row of thirty-three pearls with a large drop in front, a triple row, one of twelve rows, and also a coq-de-perle necklace with matching clump earrings.[58] Other cheap necklaces could be made from Scots pearls[59] and seed pearls, either twisted into strands or made up into roses.[60] Pearls were also threaded into decorative necklaces with jet,[61] garnets,[62] coloured paste[63] and doublets.[64] One such necklace, centred on a large bow-knot with a drop, is worn by Lucy Ebberton in her portrait by George Knapton.[65] Knotted in chains, worn like a baldric across the shoulder, pearls were an essential part of the Van Dyck costume often adopted for portraits and at masquerades.[66] In 1773 *The Lady's Magazine* mentioned that, with full dress, pearls were worn in a bow at the centre of a narrow collar.[67]

Every woman of means aspired to the ownership of a rose– or brilliant-cut diamond necklace, perhaps with coloured stones set into clusters, or links of openwork floral and foliage motifs intertwined with ribbons and bows, sometimes set off by mounting on black velvet or coloured ribbon[68] (Fig. 31).

Fig. 31 Designs by Christian Taute for necklace, floral crosses, pendants and earrings: 1750. Victoria and Albert Museum

While smaller stones could be used in these ways, the more important gems were shown to advantage in clusters or plain collets strung into graduated rows or rivières, with the centre emphasised in some way. There was a bow-knot in the centre of a necklace of ten brilliant roses belonging to Lady Isabella Monck.[69] Others placed a large and choice gem there, as with Mrs Spencer's necklace centred on a stone set at the edge with small brilliants estimated at £1,000,[70] or Lady Watkin Williams Wynn's string of seventy brilliants with a magnificent 'oval spread' brilliant.[71] A slide with a cross or drop might hang from the front, like the 'brilliant diamond necklace consisting of seven pieces and a drop' owned by Elizabeth Wegg in 1777.[72] Sometimes this drop or pendant was linked to the band encircling the neck by a second band, called an esclavage, which hung down on the bosom. When Miss Sterling showed her jewels to her sister, Fanny, in *The Clandestine Marriage*, she pointed this out asking: 'How d'ye like the style of this esclavage?'[73]

A simpler style is represented by the 'brilliant necklace set with 55 round brilliants and two rows of ruby collets' made for Lord Egremont by Peter Romilly in 1776.[74] The trend is confirmed by a letter written in the same year about the resetting of the family jewels by the newly married Duchess of Leinster: 'in short a very very fine pair of earrings and necklace is the thing and the latter is a single row of diamonds'.[75] In 1787, the Prince of Wales bought a 'single row'd brilliant necklace' for £925 6*s* 6*d* from Thomas Gray.[76]

Many cheaper materials were available: coral,[77] turquoise,[78] topaz,[79] genuine and mock garnets,[80] Scotch pebble,[81] jargoons,[82] white, coloured and opaline paste,[83] enamelled, gilt, wax and barley-husk beads.[84] Stringing them into necklaces was an amusement for those clever with their hands like Nicholas Blundell who, in 1718, noted in his diary that he had spent several hours one day doing this for his wife and daughters.[85]

Some necklaces were fastened, not by tied ribbons, but by clasps, and a page of such clasp designs *c.* 1736 has survived. One was enamelled with a bust of George II, two with busts of the Prince and Princess of Wales, another commemorated the Act of Union with the crowned rose and thistle, another had the White Horse of Hanover, and three alluded to marriage with crowned turtle-doves, a crowned winged heart and a heart transfixed by arrows[86] (Fig. 32).

Some verses published in 1736 make a fitting conclusion to this subject:

To BELINDA: *The* Neck-lace

Thou pretty toy, emblem of joy!
  Which now provok'st my muse to sing;
The virgin's pride, joy of the bride;
  Thou sweet delightful thing!

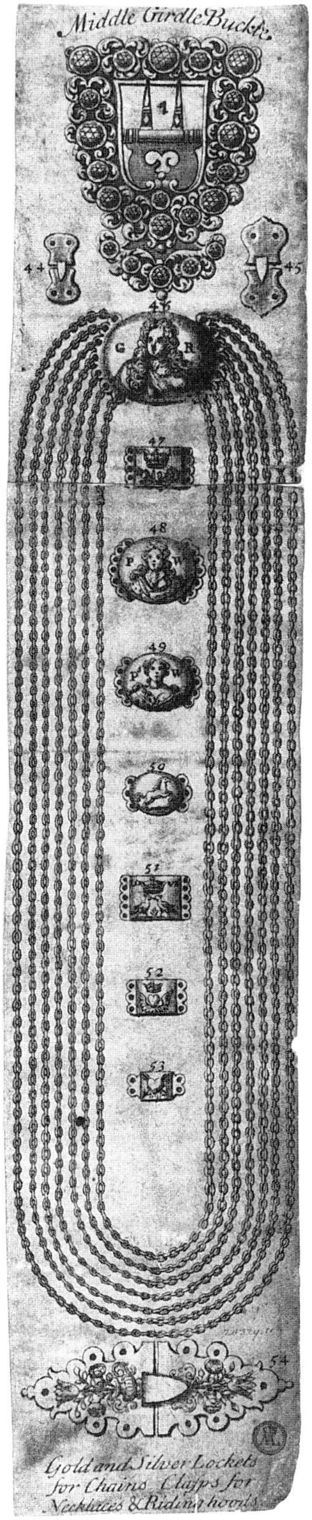

Fig. 32. Designs for clasps and buckle: *c.* 1736.
Victoria and Albert Museum

Sometimes thou'rt set with pearl and jet,
True sable, and the argent hue;
Sometimes thou'rt dy'd with ermin'd pride,
As often clad in azure blue.

Sometimes in green, thou'rt gaily seen;
As rival to the youthful spring;
As often drest in crimson vest;
And *Flora's* sweets to mem'ry bring.

The topaz rare, and diamond fair
In thee, their brilliant form express,
But those are found, where wealth abound,
And great or royal blood confess.

But azure bright, or lovely white;
Thou'rt still a favourite of the fair:
At balls display'd, on wife or maid;
Thou giv'st to charms a beauteous air! . . . [87]

LOCKETS

In her will of 1771 Mrs Poyntz left Grace Langdale 'a gold watch with a locket of my hair'.[88] Other lockets, containing miniatures as well as hair,[89] hung from the neck,[90] from the chatelaine beside the watch[91] and were mounted as clasps for centrepieces of bracelets.[92] The cases might be enamelled in one colour or with flowers,[93] or embellished with pearls,[94] brilliants,[95] garnets or amethysts,[96] coral and crystal.[97] Oval, round or heart-shaped, they could also be ornamented with ciphers,[98] or devices worked in seed pearl,[99] or inscribed with mottoes.[100]

SOLITAIRES

Although sometimes used as pins for fastening clothing,[101] solitaires were more frequently associated with neck jewellery; 'diamond solitaires attached to pearl necklaces' were seen at the wedding of the Prince of Wales in 1736.[102] Some were set with brilliant- and rose-cut diamonds[103] intermixed with topazes,[104] emeralds[105] or rubies.[106] The less expensive versions were made of garnet or stone[107] and doublets.[108] Drops formed part of some designs[109] and in 1740 George Wickes made a rose bow-knot solitaire for Mr James Theobald.[110]

PENDANTS

Pendants were drop-shaped (Plate XXIX) or designed as crosses, hearts, lockets, miniatures, tassels[111] and cornucopiae. Some could indicate personal loyalties, like the anchor and cable inscribed KEPPEL and L'ESPERANCE on a dark-blue ground, made at the time of the trial for treason in 1779 of Admiral Keppel (1725–86) and kept at Welbeck Abbey.[112]

107 Diamond bow-knot stomacher. *c.* 1750. Private collection.

STOMACHERS, BREAST AND SLEEVE KNOTS

In full dress, the section of the bodice between the neck and waist, the stomacher, was enriched with jewels which were given the same name. They derived from the graduated clasps worn earlier, and designs were conservative. Marcus Gunter's large V-shaped compositions of acanthus framing drops and rose-cut stones at the turn of the century[113] are similar to that worn *c.* 1740 by a viscountess in a portrait by C. M. Tuscher (Plate XXXIII). Thomas Flach's stomachers (1736) are elaborate versions of the bow-knot, and were later adapted to the rococo taste by Christian Taute (1750), who entwined flowers and foliage among the ribbons, which were sometimes tied double. Further refinements came with the addition of tassels, and the bow sometimes took the form of a lover's knot or the more complex Gordian knot.[114]

Single large bow-knots to be worn at the breast (Plate 107) occur in the accounts of George Wickes and in private inventories.[115] In 1778 Queen Charlotte was 'very finely adorned with jewels of emeralds and diamonds, particularly a vast knot which almost covered the stomacher'[116] – perhaps that sold after her death in 1819 and described as 'a magnificent brilliant and emerald bow, the brilliants large and of the purest water, the emeralds singularly clear'.[117] One of her wedding gifts had been a diamond stomacher arranged in a pattern of natural flowers composed of very large diamonds on a ground of small diamonds.[118]

Besides this large bow-knot, Queen Charlotte possessed sets of three or more, graduated in size, which made the front of her bodice appear to be entirely laced in diamonds, pearls or coloured stones. There is a set of five such bows in the Wynn inventory of 1769; valued at £2743, they are the most expensive item in the diamond parure.[119] A less expensive set, also of five, was made by James Cox for Sir John Delaval in 1772,[120] and another, of rubies and diamonds, was made by Peter Romilly for Lord Egremont in 1773.[121] The effect on rich fabrics when all were worn at once was impressive, and in 1777 Mrs Lybbe Powys described the dazzling appearance of the beautiful Miss Hodges when dressed for amateur theatricals in 'a pink satin suit of clothes elegantly trimmed with gauze and flowers, all Lady Villiers' diamonds valued at £12,000 four large bows making a complete stomacher and two of the same as sleeve knots'.[122]

Sleeve knots were usually made *en suite*. An exceptionally important piece was sold in 1774 by Commodore Forrest of the East India Company: a 'Brilliant diamond sleeve knot, large brilliant in the middle set round with 12 small brilliants with four rows of brilliants, six rows in each bow with four middle-sized brilliants in each bow having 49 brilliants except one with 26 brilliants at the end of the bow'.[123]

BUCKLES

The large and small buckles which were an essential part of dress for both men and women were sometimes made of gold or silver inlaid or enamelled and set with diamonds and coloured stones,[124] but they were usually made of cheaper materials: bronze, pinchbeck or Sheffield plate, and set with garnets, jet, topazes, pebble stones, Bristows, imitation pearls and white or coloured paste.[125] In 1742 Horace Walpole sent cut-steel shoe buckles as a present to the Prince de Craon at Florence,[126] and these, faceted and polished like diamonds, were fashionable throughout the century.[127] Round, oval, square, oblong and navette shapes were ornamented with interlaced ribbons, lover's knots, rosettes, openwork and chain patterns, stars and hearts.

Buckles fastened women's gowns, girdles,[128] glove strings,[129] hat bands and shoes. Girdle buckles were given as wedding presents, and in the comedy, *Money the Mistress*, the buckle given to the heroine, Mariana, is described by her father as 'the emblem of matrimony to twitch you together'.[130] In 1734 Lady Isabella Monck, daughter of the Duke of Portland, inherited £120 from his steward, which she spent on a girdle buckle set with thirty diamonds.[131] Small buckles of pearl or diamonds, or substitutes, in sets fastened stays and bodices.[132]

Clarissa Harlowe, Richardson's heroine in the novel, was wearing a pair of neat buckles in her shoes when Robert Lovelace first noticed her,[133] and shoes ornamented with 'silver spangles and square Bristol buckles' imparted the final touch of smartness to Mrs Nollekens's bridal attire in 1774.[134] In the 1770s ceramics were introduced:

wedgwood cameos and Liverpool pearl ware painted with blue and white or coloured flowers.[135]

Shirt buckles for men, worn to the side or else at the back of the neck, might be very expensively set with diamonds[136] or, more modestly, with garnets – sometimes heart-shaped or outlined with gold beads.[137] They were small, as were the buckles which fastened the breeches just below the knee, and the latter were made *en suite* with the shoe buckles, with fitted boxes to keep them together.[138] Sparkle was the chief concern, as Monsieur la Mode declared in *Roderick Random* in 1773:

> His buckles like diamonds must glitter and shine,
> Should they cost £50 they would not be too fine.[139]

Sir Walter Blount in 1771 proudly showed Mrs Lybbe Powys the pair of diamond shoe buckles which his rich cousin, the Duchess of Norfolk, had given him for his wedding present.[140] Bright and inexpensive substitutes were provided by paste, Bristows and faceted steel, and were popular with all.[141] From the reign of George II, buckles increased in size, so much so that in 1777 Sheridan's Lord Foppington in *A Trip to Scarborough* could declare that 'At first the buckle was used to keep the shoe on, now the shoe is of no earthly use except to keep the buckle.'[142] This was the year when the massive Artois buckles, named after Louis XVI's brother, were introduced; they remained in fashion until 31 May 1788, when the *London Evening Post* announced that 'The massy Artois buckle seems to be giving place to the shoe tie which whatever may be the fashion is surely lighter and more elegant at least for morning undress.'[143]

ROSES

Stays were fastened with roses – that is, pins set with gems in the petals of flower-like clusters – as well as by buckles. There were 'six roses all brilliants' on the bodice of Miss Poyntz's wedding dress, described and illustrated by Mrs Delany in 1756[144] (Fig. 33).

Fig. 33 Mrs Spencer's rose, drawn by Mrs Delany: 1756.
From Mrs Delany's *Autobiography* (1861).

A smaller set of 'three roses for the stays containing 56 rose diamonds' was listed in the 1759 inventory of Lady Isabella Monck,[145] and roses, set with brilliants, were among the jewels ordered from Philip Hardel by Lady Grey in 1762.[146]

BRACELETS

Lady Sarah Bunbury declared in 1762: 'My hoggy paws are pretty – very much improved by the pearl bracelets.'[147] Strung into as many as twenty-four rows, pearls were occasionally mixed with coloured stones such as rubies, or with diamonds.[148] On their own, diamonds were linked into strands, like the 'pair of brilliant bracelets set with 16 large diamonds and 16 small to fill up the intervals'.[149] They were also combined with amethysts, rubies and emeralds.[150] Cheap alternatives to precious stones were also used: garnets, 'elk's claws', mocoa stones and oval medallions of Bilston enamel.[151] The Prince of Wales bought a pair of enamelled gold pansy or 'Pensez-à-moi' bracelets in 1788, and his other purchases illustrate a wide range of materials: seed pearl and gold, gold and steel, diamonds and coloured stones, and cornelians.[152]

The chief decorative feature or centrepiece of the bracelet was the clasp, which was most often set with a miniature, framed in a gold rim studded with pearls, diamonds or garnets. So when Miss Sterling in *The Clandestine Marriage* (1766) showed her jewels to her sister, she asked: 'What d'ye think of these bracelets? I shall have a miniature of my father set round with diamonds to one and Sir John's to the other.'[153] Instead of another miniature, the pair might have a decorative cipher or motto, executed in pearls or rose diamonds on an enamelled ground, or else in marcasite on blue or red glass.[154]

Dr Johnson challenged the practice of carrying portraits of loved ones in this way in an essay published in 1759. He argued that, since 'the joy of life is variety', a wife might eventually tire of her husband's picture permanently on view on her wrist; he suggested that clasps might indicate other interests besides family affection. Thus, an authoress might have a picture of the Muses in a laurel grove, a housewife one of Penelope and her web, a gambler one of Fortune and her wheel, and, for a lady who wanted a permanent

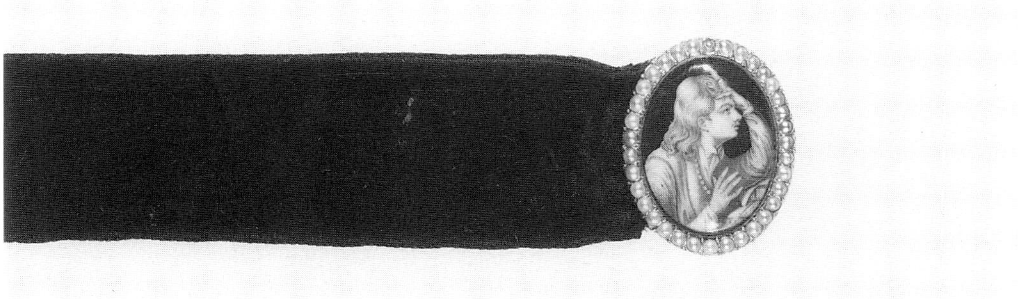

108 Peter Abelard bracelet clasp. Private collection.

109 The widowed Princess of Wales and her children. Portrait by George Knapton, 1751. Collection of H.M. Queen Elizabeth II.

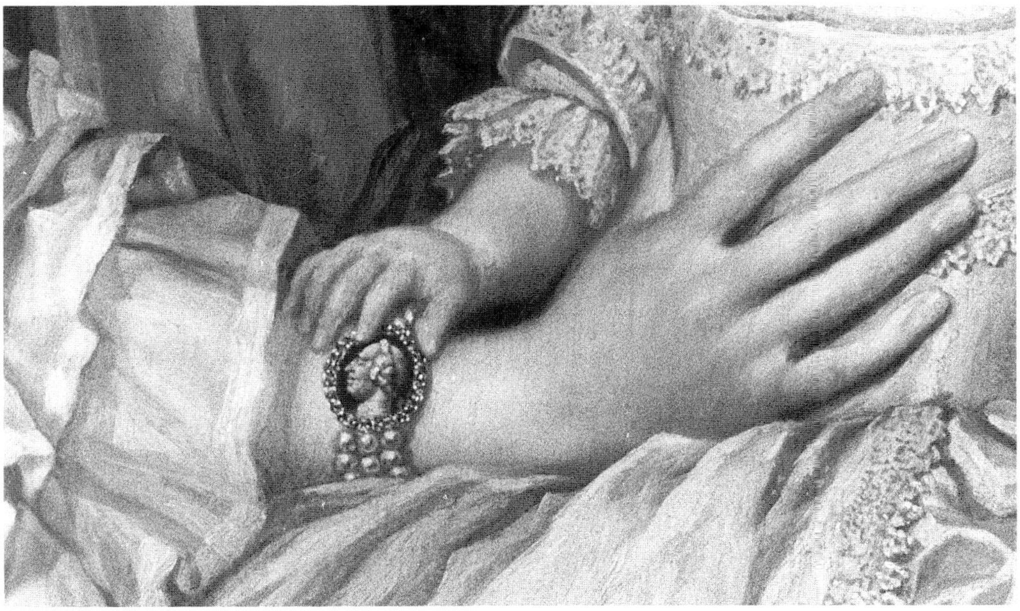

110 Detail of Plate 109, showing the cameo portrait of Frederick, Prince of Wales, in bracelet clasp.

source of pleasure, there might be a small convex mirror in which she could see herself whenever she raised her hand.[155] Enamelled clasps of this kind were exhibited by Augustin Toussaint at the Royal Academy between 1775 and 1778.[156] Copies were made, *en grisaille* on a warm blue ground, of the figures of Faith and Charity designed by Sir Joshua Reynolds for New College, Oxford, framed in wreaths of leaves wrought in two colours of gold[157] (Plate XXXIV). Others depicted illustrious ladies, carnival masks, and the romance of Eloise and Abelard[158] (Plate 108).

Cameos were also used for clasps, like the 'pair of historical cameos set in gold' or the 'lion and a lioness, curious stones',[159] and the heads of illustrious men and women past and present. The bracelet of the widowed Augusta, Princess of Wales, depicted in a family group by George Knapton in 1751, is clasped with the cameo portrait of her late husband, Frederick, Prince of Wales[160] (Plates 109 and 110). While hardstone cameos were costly, cheaper reproductions could be bought from James Tassie in Leicester Square, selected from more than 15,000 examples in his catalogue, priced from 10*s* 6*d* to 42*s*.[161] Plain clasps might be engraved, engine-turned and enamelled,[162] or set with gem-stones and pearls. The weeping willow, symbol of mourning, was used for clasps as well as rings, and the branches could be worked in hair.[163] Bands of braided hair or of velvet, fastened by clasps and buckles, were also worn as an alternative to rows of pearls or gem-stones, though pearls could be strung on the edges of the ribbon.[164] In 1776, forerunners of the wrist watch were sold: 'A pair of very singular bracelets with small watches'.[165]

BUTTONS

Ornamental jewelled buttons, designed as clusters, stars, flowers and leafy scrolls, might be included in a parure. The set in the Wynn collection, made by Peter Romilly, employed 182 brilliants and 81 emeralds.[166] Buttons could be sewn on gloves or stomachers,[167] and on sleeves. Brilliant- and rose-cut diamonds were used, sometimes mixed with topazes,[168] sapphires and emeralds, or clustered with rubies.[169] Crystal and paste substitutes were also used.

For the most part, ladies only wore buttons for practical purposes with riding-habits, but they were of greater importance in men's clothes.[170] Sleeve buttons fastened the shirt at the wrist; a coat would have large buttons on the front and smaller ones on pocket flaps, cuffs and back pleats; they appeared on the waistcoat and as an alternative to buckles below the knee for the breeches.[171] The buttons were not only practical but also emphasised the cut of the coat.

Visiting Birmingham in 1758, the poet John Hone was astonished at the number of button-makers established there; twelve years later there were eighty-three, each with his own speciality: gilt, plated, silvered, lacquered, pinchbeck, platina, inlaid glass, ivory, pearl, horn, Bath metal and brass.[172] John Taylor (1711–75) was the most successful, closely followed by Matthew Boulton, who specialised in cut steel (see pp. 242–3 above).

Men liked the bright, light-reflecting stones as much as women did. The sparkling India stones (piedro d'India), which Admiral Boscawen took as a prize in 1747 and sent home to his wife, were such a success mounted in buttons that she presented some to the Princess of Wales for the future George III to wear.[173] The young prince was fascinated by buttons and learnt to make them 'of a German in Long Acre' and he is reported as having said to a Mr Clay: 'send me several sets of buttons . . . I am called George the button maker I must give a lift to our trade.'[174]

Since buttons were bound to catch the eye, the chased, pierced or engraved devices on them often signified party allegiance or reflected the cultural and sporting interests of the wearer. The sporting button originated in England. A contemporary description of a sporting squire, 'whose ideas are wholly bent on guns, dogs, horses, game', notes not only that he adorned his house with 'stags' heads instead of busts' but that 'even the butons of his cloaths are impressed with figures of dogs, foxes, stags and horses'.[175] It was for such enthusiasts that enamel transfer-printed buttons were made with reddish-brown racing, hunting and stable scenes based on the works of Sartorius and Seymour.[176]

The subjects of the enamelled buttons in sales of stock are seldom specified; one exception is the 'Pair of gold buttons finely enamelled with Cupids' sold in 1778.[177] Mrs Siddons is said to have owned a set of buttons depicting sailors with young girls.[178] The range of materials used for buttons in the London trade was wide: gold filigree,[179] cornelian, cat's-eye, pebble, both brown and white crystal, 'elk's claw' and mother-of-pearl, a Birmingham speciality worn by George III.[180]

As the fabric of men's clothes became plainer after 1770, buttons increased in size, and in 1777 Mrs Lybbe Powys remarked on Lord Villiers's 'different and still finer dress, buckles and buttons quite in ton' – that is, excessively large.[181] A guide to fashionable designs in 1786–8 is provided by the purchases of the Prince of Wales, which included three sets of buttons in steel, a set of Wedgwood cameo buttons, a set of 'Sicilian shells mounted in gold' and a set of 'Button cameos'. Fifty-two buttons with his crest and the cipher PW proclaimed his identity,[182] and among his other purchases were decorative buttons made of sandalwood and buttons of white paste, some framed in amethyst, others bordered in blue-enamel.[183] He also bought large sets 'engraved with different devices in the best manner',[184] twenty silver buttons 'engraved with fancies'[185] and a set with views of Paris.[186]

PINS FOR SHIRT AND CRAVAT

Glittering pins fastened the ruffled white linen shirt-front or the pleated neckband of the man of fashion. Lord Lincoln's birthday present from his uncle, the Duke of

Newcastle, was a pin valued at 1100 guineas,[187] and Lady Pomfret bribed the young man's valet with a pin 'such as a gentleman might wear'[188] when she was scheming for a match between Lord Lincoln and her daughter.

Pins could be set with clusters of topazes, paste or marcasite, and antique heads.[189] The fichu trimming the neckline of a gown was also fastened with pins, either of plain gold or enamelled blue or set with brilliants in star patterns or festoons.[190]

Studs, sold individually or in pairs, were wrought in silver and set with crystals.[191] In 1788 the Prince of Wales had his ostrich feather badge reproduced in gold on a set of studs.[192]

RINGS

Decorative gem-set rings designed to display large stones on their own, and smaller stones in groups, were the most numerous category of eighteenth-century rings. A few brilliant- or rose-cut diamonds, white, foiled or coloured, were mounted as solitaires, but most were set with smaller stones, like the cluster with 'one large Brilliant and 24 small ones' bought by Lady Grey from Philip Hardel in 1762.[193] Small brilliants framing a larger stone in a contrasting colour made attractive combinations, and a wide choice was available for the centrepiece: rubies, emeralds, sapphires, amethysts, garnets, turquoises, amber, opals, topazes, mocoa and cat's-eyes. Lady Worsley had an amethyst set in a brilliant circle, and in 1770 a beautiful opal valued at £157 10*s* was 'set round with very fine brilliants in the antique manner for a ring' by George Robertson for Sir Watkin Williams Wynn.[194]

Some rings were made with multiple clusters. In 1762 Lady Grey bought a double cluster ring from Peter Romilly,[195] and the Wynn inventory has a triple cluster ring, also of brilliants and rubies, valued at £25.[196]

A variant of the cluster was the star motif, and rings 'star fashion' were bought from George Wickes in 1737 and 1740, set with rubies or sapphires and brilliants. Star cluster rings were listed in a sale in 1776,[197] and in 1788 the Prince of Wales bought a 'blue star ring' from Thomas Gray.[198]

In the rococo period, from about 1740, the shoulders of rings were emphasised in a way quite foreign to seventeenth-century ring design. Sometimes set with small stones, the juncture of hoop and bezel was forked, with a flower or leaf in the space between. In rare cases the whole hoop might be set with stones.[199] After 1770 rings became larger, with octagonal, pointed oval or lozenge bezels, ornamented with clusters, sometimes in enamelled borders,[200] or with brilliant ciphers on a red or blue ground.[201]

Notwithstanding their small size, rings were decorated with figurative subjects and symbols. There were single or double hearts, set with precious or semi-precious stones, enamelled,[202] tied with a lover's knot or crowned.[203] On a ring from the Spencer collection with clock-dial bezel there is a red heart instead of the figure XII; the hoop is

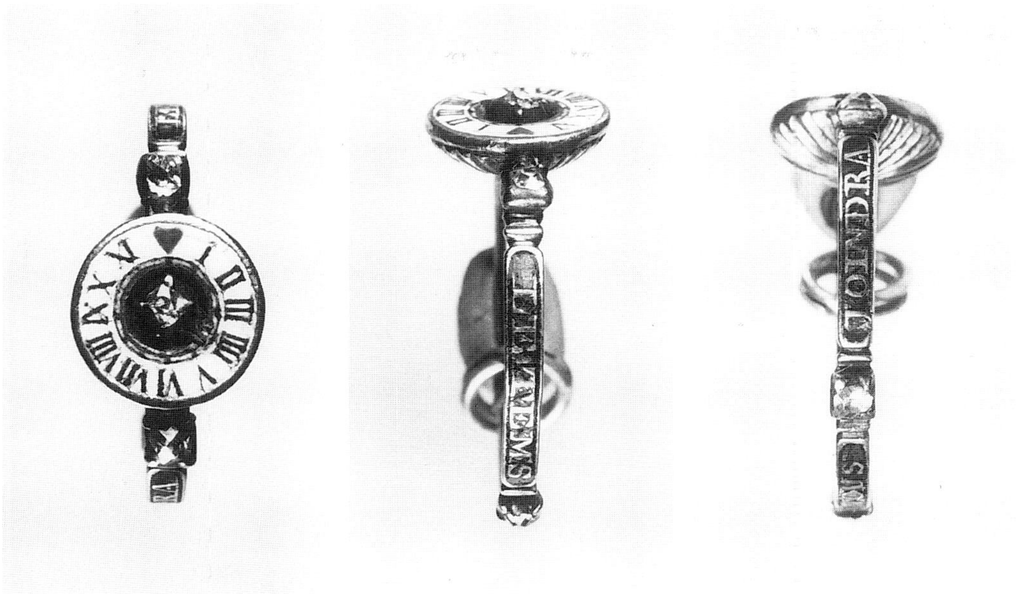

111 Gold ring with clock dial bezel, enamelled with a heart for twelve o'clock, the hoop inscribed LE TEMPS NOUS JOINDRA. S. J. Phillips (formerly Earl Spencer).

inscribed LE TEMPS NOUS JOINDRA (Plate 111). Sprays of flowers set in a basket or vase, flowerpot rings, were sold by George Wickes in 1736 and by Harrache in 1778: 'a fancy flower basket ring with diamonds, rubies and sapphires'[204] (Plate XXXII). Harrache also stocked rings with a squirrel or a bird, and these too were set with diamonds and coloured stones.[205] Lady Mary Wortley Montagu bequeathed a butterfly ring to Sir Joshua Reynolds, the wings studded with diamonds and fancy-cut rubies, the body with emeralds, the hoop engraved and chased with poppy leaves, buds and flowers, the petals set with amethysts, quartz, topaz and a single diamond. The inside of the hoop was engraved MARY WORTLEY MONTAGU TO JOSHUA REYNOLDS SIC TRANSIT GLORIA MUNDI 1762.[206]

Inscriptions, within and without the hoop, were a feature of commemorative and mourning rings, and also of the gold-band posy rings used at weddings. They might be protected by gem-set hoop or keeper rings set with brilliants, roses, coloured stones or pearls.[207] Some hoop rings were designed as chains,[208] while others were double or, like 'a three row'd diamond hoop ring' bought by the Prince of Wales in 1786, triple.[209]

The Prince of Wales liked to give rings with symbols and hieroglyphs which expressed his amorous inclinations – among them a pansy or *Pensez à moi* in diamonds on blue enamel,[210] an octagonal ring with the letter M (for *aimé*) in diamonds, another octagon with M MOI (*Aimes moi*) in pearls, and a Roman ring setting with J'M (*J'aime*) in diamonds.[211] To wish his friends good luck the prince gave them talismanic or zodiacal rings with the signs of the zodiac engraved in cornelian and the hoop and bezel set with diamonds.[212]

Mourning rings and those set with miniatures have been considered above (pp. 262 and 271). Signets were out of fashion for most of the eighteenth century, owing to the custom of wearing seals hanging from the watch-fob chain, or attached to the chatelaine.

ACCESSORIES

WATCHES

Watches, chatelaines, etuis, snuff boxes and small-sword hilts made of gold, silver, Sheffield plate and gilt metal illustrate the techniques of the eighteenth-century goldsmith (chasing, engraving and enamelling) as well as the changing fashions in style and iconography.

Travelling in Italy, the fourth Earl of Carlisle and Lady Mary Wortley Montagu both found that no present from England was so welcome as a watch,[213] and at home a gold watch was a sign of status. Edward Weld gave his wife, Mary Theresa, a chased gold watch on a gold chain valued at £25 at their wedding.[214] In 1759 the Countess of Kildare was amused by Moll Bath, a countrywoman, dressed for the races 'as fine as any lady with her cardinal and her silks and flounces and gold watch by her side'.[215]

Thus displayed, the decorative character of the watch and its pair case was of the greatest importance. Hardstone plaques, particularly bloodstone or moss agate, were mounted *à cage* in luxuriant gold scroll-work[216] (Plate 112), or the metal was embossed with figurative scenes, enclosed in asymmetrical cartouches of scrolls, flowers, shells and leaves, some parts left matt and others burnished. André Rouquet, however, wrote that

> the number of skilful chasers is not considerable in England. This conclusion is justified by experience: for I know but of one artist in this branch, whose abilities really deserve the approbation of the curious, and the approbation of his profession; this is Mr. Mosar who has been in possession of both for these many years.[217]

The technique of George Michael Moser (1706–83) is illustrated by watch cases embossed with classical scenes – Vertumnus and Pomona or Hymen crowning a bride – enclosed in cartouches rather more symmetrical than those of his contemporaries.[218] Working in the same manner were John Gastrell (†1772), with a case depicting Perseus and Andromeda, and Henry Manly (*fl.* 1735–70), one of whose cases has the Judgement of Hercules after a painting by Paolo de Matteis.[219] Another version of the subject, by an unknown chaser, still has its bill describing the subject: 'The story of the judgement of Hercules viz. Hercules is represented as determining between Virtue and Pleasure and gives the preference to Virtue.'[220] To Augustin Henckel (1690–1770) are attributed a watch case embossed with a scene from the Commedia dell'Arte, and the

112 Chatelaine by John Pyke with watch and key, set with panels of moss agate in rococo gold scrollwork highlighted with diamonds. Barclays Bank.

design for another watch case set with a plaque of Venus teasing Cupid, framed in asymmetrical rococo scroll-work with putti.[221]

Lord Egremont bought a 'gold carved watch' of this style in 1762,[222] but by the end of the decade taste had shifted from relief to colour. The talented Moser mastered the art of enamelling and his first work in the medium retained the rococo cartouche. This style is represented by a watch with an enamelled scene of Apollo with the Four Seasons, with the London hallmark for 1766–7, and another owned by Queen Charlotte depicting the nine-year-old Hannibal swearing enmity to the Romans, after an engraving by H. F. Gravelot.[223] Another of Queen Charlotte's commissions, which represents her two eldest sons when they were very young, is mentioned by Edward Edwards in his *Anecdotes of Painters* (1808), p. 92; according to the *Dictionary of National Biography*, Moser received 'a hatful of guineas' for it. This must be the double portrait of the Prince of Wales and his brother, Prince Frederick, in the manner of Zoffany, in Van Dyck dress, the elder with the ribbon of the Garter, the younger with that of the Bath, reproduced by Moser on the case of a watch in the Grimsthorpe collection (Plate XXXVI).

Lord Harcourt's correspondence with William Whitehead (1715–85), Poet Laureate, illustrates how much care was taken over the iconography of watch cases. The first letter, dated 24 December 1773, set out the problem:

> I want your Lordship very much in London to consult about an enamel'd case for Miss Sanderson's watch. Their own design was an Apollo, a Minerva, & God knows who, but the enamel was ruined by the fire. They now desire I would superintend it, & propose what alterations I chuse. A finely-executed naked Venus was proposed by the painter, but rejected with disdain; the artificer is Parker, in Panton-street, but I have not yet called, nor shall I be able now till I return from the Grove. The Minerva, I apprehend, must be there, but I shall judge better when I have seen the design: I am determined to admit of no nudities. What think you of *Old Time* presenting a wreath of flowers to *Youth*, whilst she is taking him by the forelock? It is for a watch, you know, & for a young lady.

Later he writes:

> Miss Sanderson's watch is still in debate; the pictures are too small for telling an allegorical story. I have taken the liberty, however, of adding an olive branch to Minerva, alluding to the old story:–
>
> 'Thus Pallas with her javelin smote the ground,
> And peaceful olives flourish'd from the wound.'
>
> I could not find a Hebe to my fancy, & have therefore given them a Herculaneum figure for the middle compartment.[224]

The fully developed neo-classical style closely associated with engraved gems is represented by the fine chatelaine and watch case back enamelled by William Hopkins Craft with a sacrificial scene, a swan and the profiles of Hercules, Medusa, George III and Queen Charlotte all standing out like onyx cameos *en grisaille* on the dark-brown ground. It was commissioned by Sir James Napier in 1777[225] (Plate XXXVII). G. M. Moser also responded to the severe influence of neo-classicism by eliminating the gold cartouches and interpreting in grisaille subjects taken from engravings of classical cameos and intaglios, framing them in sober-coloured ovals and circles. Queen Charlotte owned a watch case of this kind, 'beautifully enamelled with figures sacrificing and medallions in chiaroscuro'.[226]

Such watches were extremely expensive; in 1777 Lord Monson paid Jeffreys and Jones £330 for a 'rich gold watch and chain ornamented with diamonds and paintings'.[227] In the 1780s thinner, flatter cases came into fashion, with plain translucent enamels in royal blue or pinkish purple, ornamented with stars or ciphers and rimmed in pearls or diamonds.

Men wore their watches hanging from the fob on a black ribbon threaded through metal slides. The delicate enamelled or embossed cases were protected by a pair case of horn, filigree or shagreen decoratively studded with gold. In the late 1770s two watches might be worn; in 1777 Mrs Lybbe Powys noticed the ultra-fashionable Lords Villiers and Malden wearing two watches. The second was usually a dummy or *fausse-montre*, with imitation dial, enclosing a miniature or vinaigrette instead of a movement.[228] The Prince of Wales bought one such dummy for his equerry, Captain Payne, in 1788, and another of steel with a matching chain.[229]

Most ladies' watches hung from chatelaines of precious metal, pinchbeck or steel. The shield-shaped hook plate with hanging plaques flanked by chains for trinkets, watch key and seals might be richly jewelled, cast, enamelled and set with hardstones or mother-of-pearl. Designs were published by Thomas Flach (1736), S.H. Dinglinger (1751) and T.D. Saint (1761), and some are shown on trade cards. Allegorical figures such as Britannia, scenes from classical history, such as Cleopatra and the pearl and Alexander the Great and the family of Darius, or chinoiseries were embossed on the hook plate, framed in rococo scroll-work.[230] Enamelling is exemplified in a chatelaine by Moser *c.* 1766 with putti personifying the Four Elements,[231] and by others with baskets of flowers or medallions painted in grisaille simulating engraved gems.[232] A superb jewelled chatelaine was given by George III and Queen Charlotte to Lady Harcourt. The small hook plate is enamelled in translucent royal blue studded with stars like the night sky, with a large star in the centre. The motif is repeated in other sections, two of which are navette-shaped and the third similar to the hook plate; all are linked by pierced enamelled gold chains with two tiers of accessories: a seal and watch key, a quiver and eggs, flanked by pairs of tassels. Either a miniature of George III in an engine-turned enamelled gold case with stars and a crowned royal cipher could be hung from it, or a watch in a similar case.[233]

The final development came with the hookless chatelaine, which passed through the close-fitting waistband so that the two ends hung down, one terminating in a watch, the other in seals, keys and tassels.[234]

Etuis as well as watches and miniatures might hang from the chatelaine, and were equally well decorated. They were usually tapering cylindrical or oval cases, of finely chased gold, silver-gilt, painted enamel or shagreen, sometimes ornamented with sprays of rose diamond flowers.[235] G.M. Moser's style *c.* 1760 is represented by an etui with six enamelled plaques: three at the front representing Medicine, Literature and Painting, three at the back representing Music, Architecture and Sculpture, and the side panels chased with scrolls, foliage and flowers. It contains two ivory tablets riveted with gold, a combined tooth and ear pick in gold, a pair of scissors, a pair of tweezers, a steel nail-file, a gold bodkin, a gold pencil-holder and a gold penknife with steel blade.[236] Less expensive etuis were made of Staffordshire enamels, with plaques of flowers or pastoral scenes in beautiful shades of turquoise, green, rose pink and royal blue. Similar plaques could be set in chatelaines, and others were made *c.* 1750–75 at the Battersea enamel works.[237] The etui balanced the watch when worn at the waist, a fashion illustrated by Francis Hayman in his portrait of Mrs Pritchard on stage in the play, *The Suspicious Husband.*[238]

SNUFF BOXES

The taking of snuff continued to be popular with both sexes throughout the early Georgian period. In 1743 Horace Walpole wrote to Horace Mann at Florence about a 'snuff-box from Naples' which the Duke of Newcastle's secretary, Andrew Stone, wanted for his wife.[239] Paris was a major centre for choice boxes, and on his visits Walpole would be asked by friends, who could rely on his excellent taste, to buy snuff boxes for them. In 1771, however, he wrote to Lady Ossory: 'As to snuff-boxes and tooth-pick cases, the vintage has entirely failed this year.'[240] The Meissen manufactory also produced fine snuff boxes and in 1748 Henry Fox commissioned boxes with the portrait of his wife through Sir Charles Hanbury Williams, minister at the Saxon court. Apart from the ones with his wife's picture – for himself and his mother-in-law, the Duchess of Richmond – he also wanted plain ones, 'one Man's and two Women's.' The boxes with a portrait cost £20 each, the 'Box and Picture' coming to £11 and the setting to £9. The plain boxes worked out as: 'The Box for a Man 13£: One of the small ones with Angels – 10£. The other small one with flowers 8£'.[241]

Snuff boxes were increasingly used as suitable gifts for diplomats and courtiers. In 1742 Lord Forrester, who had delivered money to Vienna for Maria Theresa, was given 'a crystal snuff-box very rich with jewels', and in 1764 Cardinal Albani presented the Duke of York with 'Une tabatière d'or, dans laquelle il est enchassée un cameo de la dernière beauté, et par son antiquité d'un prix inestimable', depicting Alexander the Great.[242] A gold snuff box which belonged to the Duke of Kent (1767–1820) had an onyx cameo of his parents, George III and Queen Charlotte, mounted in the lid.[243]

Not all snuff boxes were so costly. In 1755 Horace Walpole wrote to his old friend, Bentley: 'I shall send you a trifling snuff-box, only as a sample of the new manufacture at Battersea, which is done with copper-plates', and in 1776 he ordered others made from cannel-coal (a soft coal like jet) for Mme de Guerchy, one of his friends in Paris.[244] A Battersea box of the type Walpole mentions was included in an exhibition of snuff boxes at the Royal Archaeological Institute with 'flowers in Chelsea style on the lid and sides; on the bottom is a representation of Daphne transforming into a laurel, this last is a transfer from copper plate printed in light red'.[245] Silver snuff boxes could be engraved with the arms of the owner, and some were made with two compartments for different blends, or with other accessories, like a folding reading-glass.[246]

More rarely, snuff boxes were ordered from Japan through the Dutch East India Company. Decorated with carved chinoiseries in the lustrous dark Shakudo alloy on a gilt ground, they have a particular splendour.[247]

SMALL-SWORDS

The hilt of the small-sword continued to be highly ornamented, and the decoration favoured varied almost from decade to decade. Figural subjects were rare, although nymphs and heroes occur *c.* 1730–45 and military or naval figures *c.* 1745–60. The hilt was commonly faceted or enamelled but could also be set with paste or diamonds, especially on the swords made for presentation by civic authorities and others.[248] A small number of swords have hilts made in Japan, of the dark copper alloy Shakudo, a material also favoured by Japanese sword-smiths for fittings.[249]

9

The social context of later Georgian jewellery 1790 – 1837

George Fox, historian of the famous jewellers Rundell, Bridge and Rundell, and a former employee of the firm, dated their rise from 1803 when the war with France was resumed; with

> the consequent advance of Rents generally, the Nobility and Gentry seemed anxious to vie with each other in every species of Luxury and Extravagance and such orders were given by them for Splendid Services of Plate and costly suits of Jewels as had not been before thought of.[1]

Arriving in London in 1817, the new American ambassador, Richard Rush, was astonished by the wealth, the miles and miles of shops, and the signs of national energy and opulence everywhere, 'much of it as if bursting just out'.[2] Among the abundance of luxury goods available were gem-stones, whose high prices, resulting from their rarity, added to their desirability.

ROYALTY

The lead came from the court, and in particular from the Prince of Wales, who was appointed Regent in 1811 and succeeded as George IV in 1820. His expenditure on jewellery as a young man led to huge debts, which a Memorandum of 1792, perhaps drafted as an appeal to George III, attempted to justify:

> The importance of the monarchy to the civil order of this country is inestimable, the necessity of attaching splendour to the person and family indispensable. By the most ancient custom of England the blood royal formed a separate and preeminent class of subjects. They were provided with suitable appanages.[3]

After 1815 the Prince Regent could add to the pride of rank the glory of the national triumph over Napoleon, and he esteemed himself the greatest ruler on earth.

He invariably cut a magnificent figure, whether presiding over a Carlton House ball, resplendent in field-marshal's uniform with his Garter star on his breast and diamonds in his hat, or at his mother's funeral with the collars of the four Orders gleaming over his dark cloak. His interest in jewels transcended their value for prestige; they appealed to his love of beauty, and the prodigious commissions to the leading jewellers were an important aspect of his patronage of the arts. These purchases were most numerous at

Christmas and New Year, for he was generous and from an early age enjoyed giving jewels to the women in his life: his mother, his governesses, his sisters and sisters-in-law, as well as the many who attracted him. Mrs Maria Fitzherbert, with whom he made an illegal marriage, was splendidly installed in a house in Park Lane and loaded with expensive love tokens and diamonds.[4] He spent hours looking at jewels with his last love, the Marchioness of Conyngham; his presents to her exhausted the Privy Purse, and she was allowed to borrow the historic Stuart sapphire, sometimes wearing it as a clasp to her diamond belt or, alternatively, in the centre of her tiara.[5] In Brighton for Christmas in 1823 Lady Granville saw Lady Conyngham's Christmas gifts:

> A magnificent cross . . . An almanack, gold with flowers embossed on it of precious stones. A gold melon, which upon being touched by a spring falls into compartments like the quarters of an orange, each containing different perfumes . . . [6]

The Prince ordered over £54,000 worth of jewellery for Princess Caroline of Brunswick-Wolfenbuttel on their marriage in 1795, but he took a great dislike to her, refused to pay the bills, and Nathaniel Jeffreys, the unfortunate jeweller, was bankrupted.[7] Although estranged from her husband, who gave her best pearl bracelets to his current mistress, Lady Jersey,[8] Princess Caroline retained a good collection of jewels thanks to the kindness of George III. The king was seldom on good terms with his eldest son and disapproved of his treatment of his wife; a correspondent wrote of the king that 'His mind is ever employed for her comfort and pleasure; the presents he has made her in gold plate and jewels are of immense value.'[9] Some of her jewels were sold to Prince Torlonia in Rome, but the remainder were returned to the Crown at her death in 1822.[10] The only child of this marriage, Princess Charlotte, received a succession of charming gifts from her father – among them a small enamelled watch for her fourth birthday, gold bracelets with cameo clasps, and a brilliant and ruby Maltese cross.[11] Parliament voted £10,000 to be spent on jewellery for her wedding in 1816; part of this was spent on a diamond necklace and bracelets chosen by her grandmother, Queen Charlotte.[12] After her death in childbirth, her father ordered memorial jewellery for those closest to her (Plate XLIII).[13]

Few years passed without the prince giving Queen Charlotte his portrait, miniature, enamel or silhouette, elegantly mounted in a jewelled frame; and his well-chosen birthday gifts to his sisters gave much pleasure. To Princess Sophia, whom he always thought of as a fluttering sprite, he sent jewelled insects like butterflies. Thanking him for a ring with a bee, she wrote: 'your beautiful present is the admiration of everyone who sees it. It is the prettiest ornament I ever saw, and arrived in time for me to put it on for dinner.'[14] His taste never failed to please, as Princess Amelia acknowledged in 1802 when she thanked him for 'the most beautiful bracelets I ever saw . . . no-one but my dear angelic brother could have given me anything half so pretty'.[15] She died young, in

1810, and her brother took steps to ensure that her jewels, which she had bequeathed to General Fitzroy, went instead to her sister, Mary, later Duchess of Gloucester, while a few minor pieces were given to close friends.[16] When his brothers married, he chose superb jewels for their wives, and many years later the Duchess of Cambridge showed to her daughter, Princess Mary Adelaide of Teck, the beautiful necklace of pear-shaped emeralds and the diamond sprig of roses for her hair which had been her wedding present from the Prince Regent.[17]

According to the *Lady's Magazine*, Queen Charlotte always dressed very plainly at the Drawing-Room for her birthday on 18 January, but wore 'a profusion of diamonds both about her dress and in her hair with diamond necklace, earrings and stomacher' on 4 June to celebrate the king's birthday.[18] In the course of her long life she had acquired many jewels, including the diamonds from the Nawab of Arcot, and when she died in 1818 these were left to her four youngest surviving daughters, who sold the Arcot diamonds to Rundell, Bridge and Rundell (Fig. 34) and the remainder at auction.[19]

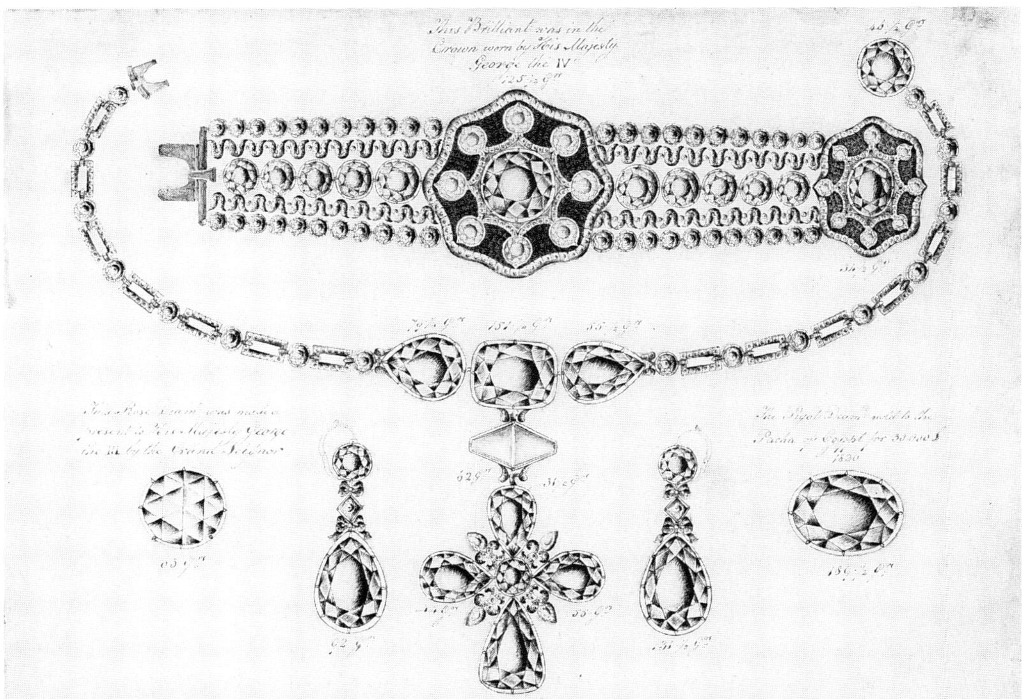

Fig. 34 Suite of diamonds sold by Rundell, Bridge and Rundell in 1837. The three stones in the centre of the necklace were given to Queen Charlotte by the Nawab of Arcot, and that in the centre of the bracelet clasp was set in the coronation crown of George IV. Victoria and Albert Museum.

The two almond-shaped Arcot diamonds were eventually bought by the Marquess of Westminster at Willis's auction rooms on 20 July 1837, together with a fine circular diamond, perhaps Warren Hastings's brilliant which Rundell's had lent to George IV for the centrepiece of his coronation crown.[20]

The king had resisted the temptation to buy new stones for a crown and hired them instead for a fee of £6,525, the interest on their estimated value. They were set in a magnificent crown with the customary fleurs-de-lis and crosses on the rim and arches of oak leaves and acorns supporting the orb. His velvet cap of estate was encircled by a jewelled band with crosses pattées alternating with sprigs of roses, thistles and shamrocks all in fine brilliants, and trimmed with heron's feathers.[21] This was a new design, perhaps influenced by the recent Act of Union with Ireland. Commemorative jewellery was also ordered with these motifs: earrings and brooch with globes hanging from crosses pattées, collars with the emblems of the three kingdoms, and large numbers of rings and lockets with the royal portrait framed in brilliants and the cipher and motto.[22] After this great manifestation of royal pomp, which was followed by a visit to Scotland, the declining health of the king led to his withdrawing from many of the court ceremonies.[23]

His brother, who succeeded him in 1830 as William IV, preferred a more retired life, as did his queen, Adelaide, who was of a quiet disposition (Plate 113). Though they spent less on jewels, the brilliant parures were still worn at court and new items were commissioned by them.[24]

ARISTOCRACY

Byron's Don Juan (1823) was impressed by the brilliance of London life, where the visitor at a ball

> Must steer with care through all that glittering sea
> Of gems and plumes and pearls and silks . . . [25]

Guests attended court receptions covered with jewels, gold and silver. Mr Rush described the Queen's Drawing-Room in 1818:

> No lady was without her plume. The whole was a waving field of feathers. Some were blue like the sky, some were tinged with red, here you saw violet and yellow, there shades of green. But most were like tufts of snow. The diamonds encircling them caught the sun through the windows and threw dazzling beams around . . . it seemed as if the curtain had risen to show a pageant in another sphere.[26]

It was the same in the palatial homes of the nobility. Sir George Beaumont, the connoisseur of paintings, compared the scene at Lord Grosvenor's in October 1812, when the rooms were filled with company, to a canvas by a Venetian master.[27] Balls were held during the season, and at some of them the guests dressed up in period

113 Queen Adelaide. Portrait by Sir William Beechey. National Portrait Gallery.

costume, impersonating historical characters resplendent in jewels. Out of London, the great houses, such as Belvoir, Burghley, Longleat and Chatsworth, were the setting for noble and enjoyable hospitality, where the guests dressed as formally as for public receptions in the capital. This English custom surprised foreigners like the Countess de Boigne who, invited to dine quietly in the country with the Countess of Liverpool in a small party of eight, which included five members of the family, found her hostess wearing a gem-studded diadem over her veil and Lady Mulgrave, another guest, in white satin with jewels and flowers in her hair.[28]

In these circumstances the bride's jewel-casket continued to have an important role in the ritual of marriage, and the acquisition of a diamond necklace was just as much part of a good match as a town mansion, a country estate and a box at the opera. The grander the wedding, the more splendid the jewellery (Plate LII). Certain families were noted for the importance of their collections. In 1795 the Duke of Bedford's appearance at court 'was by far the most magnificent and the splendour of it did credit to his Grace's princely fortune'.[29] Hugh, third Duke of Northumberland (1785–1847), who went as ambassador extraordinary to the coronation of Charles X of France in 1825 and then served as Lord Lieutenant in Ireland in 1829, always appeared in great state, as did his wife, Charlotte Florentia (Plate 114), granddaughter of Robert, Lord Clive of Plassey. The most important of the Northumberland jewels were listed in a schedule annexed to the duke's will in 1836:

B

List of Family Jewels 1836

A A Brilliant Necklace of 36 Collets very large and fine the center stone weighing Eighty Grains taken from the Crown with which King George the Fourth was Crowned.
B A large Brilliant Scroll Bandeau.
C A Diamond Cross with large Brilliants.
D Diamond Bands for the Head in three divisions.
E A large Brilliant Comb with Gold teeth.
F A Pair of Brilliant Ear Rings.
G A Pair of Brilliant Bracelets three rows each.
H A Pearl Necklace of two rows.
J Pearls with a drop for a Head ornament.
K A Grand Pearl Necklace of three rows with three Rosettes and a large Tassel.
L Pair of large Peal [*sic*] top and drop Ear Rings.
M A gold chain Necklace with a large Emerald and Brilliant Center.
N An Emerald and Brilliant Cross to the above.
O A Pair of Emerald Drops of a remarkble size and curiously engraved.
P Emerald Brooch antique engraved with a Drop set in Brilliants.
Q Emerald Brooch with a drop set in gold with Brilliants.
R A Sapphire and Brilliant Broach.
S Sapphire Ear Rings to Match.

114 Charlotte Florentia, Duchess of Northumberland.
Engraved portrait. Hulton Picture Library.

T A large Garnet and Gold Necklace the twelve Caesars engraved in Cameo.
U A Garnet Cameo Girdle Clasp 3 Cameos.
V Pair of D° top and drop Ear Rings.
W Pair of gold chain Bracelets with Carbuncle Clasps.
X A Carbuncle set in Diamonds
Y A large Amethyst set round with Pearls in filigree gold for a Waist Buckle.
Z Cameo of Queen Elizabeth engraved by Valerio Vincentino with its original setting.
Diamond Loop and Button belonging to the Garter Jewels.

RINGS

a A large Pink Brilliant Ring set round with small Brilliants belonged to Mad. du Barre [*sic*]
b A smaller Pink Brilliant Ring.
c A Yellow Brilliant Heart shaped ring.
d An Onyx Cameo Ring set round with Brilliants.
e A garnet D° D°
f A Moonstone D° D°
All the above named Articles are in the Duchess's possession.

August 1836
Northumberland

List of [ ] *Jewels* [ ] *to the Order of the Garter.*[30]

1 A large Diamond Star.
2 Blue Velvet Garter the letters in Brilliants.
3 D° D° Pearls.
4 Brilliant Loop and Button for the Hat.
5 Pair of Brilliant Buckles.
6 Pair D° Knee Buckles.
7 Brilliant Loop for the Shoulder.
8 A very curious old George studded with rose diamonds to wear with the Collar.
9 An Onyx George set round with large Diamonds to wear with the Blue Ribbon.
10 A beautiful Old Gold George for D°
11 A Magnificent Heron's Feather.
12 A magnificent Diamond Sword presented by King George the Fourth on my attending the Coronation of Charles X as Ambassador Extraordinary.

Northumberland[30]

Eclipsing all other women in brilliance was Frances Anne Vane-Tempest-Stewart (1800–62), whose husband became third Marquess of Londonderry in 1822. She was a great heiress, with emeralds and rubies inherited from her mother, the Countess of Antrim, and the Down diamonds acquired by the Stewarts through a marriage with the niece of a former Governor of Bombay, Sir Robert Cowan. Her wealth made it possible for her to buy a beautiful suite of pear-shaped pearls from the widow of the Viennese banker, de Fries, and another of turquoises which the Hungarian Count Palffy had spent a lifetime collecting. She took her jewels everywhere, including Russia in 1837, where she showed them to the empress, who gave her as a souvenir a portrait bracelet set in turquoises. She was also proud of a set of Siberian amethysts, a gift from the Emperor Alexander I at the Congress of Vienna, which she mounted in gold clasps[32] (Plate XXXVIII).

According to Captain Gronow, a well-informed man about town, some of the greatest fortunes in England were undermined by extravagant purchases of jewellery made, not only for wives and daughters but also for mistresses, in the years after Waterloo.[33] This is confirmed by Fox's account of the attention Philip Rundell paid to these ladies, who had succeeded in 'inducing the noblemen or gentlemen under whose protection they were living to spend enormous sums of money for their use'.[34] He cited the example of the Marquess of Wellesley, who got into financial difficulties through grandiose purchases not only for himself but also for a lady on whom he spent £10,000 on brilliants, emeralds and sapphires.[35]

NOUVEAUX RICHES

One of Rundell's best customers was not a member of the aristocracy at all. George Watson Taylor was a Commissioner of Excise who inherited a large property in Jamaica in 1815. His transition from modest circumstances to great wealth came at the time when the allied monarchs, statesmen and soldiers were being feted in London after Waterloo. He collected art, and ordered huge quantities of plate and new parures for his wife. George Fox described how

> the necklace and earrings tho' always considered very handsome were now broken up and considerable additions made to them of very large and fine brilliants. The brilliant ornament for the headdress consisting of a handsome sprig with large flowers was altered and enriched. A very magnificent Brilliant wreath composed of the flowers and leaves of the Hydrangea was furnished besides splendid bracelets, brooch, waist clasps &c. Some of the choicest pearls of considerable size and value were also furnished consisting of a beautiful necklace, bracelets, Earrings, pendant for the necklace, brooches etc. The different suits of rubies, emeralds, sapphires and turquoises all enriched with the finest diamonds were all of the most costly description.[36]

Richard Rush was impressed by the fortunes acquired by business men – haberdashers who cleared thirty thousand a year, brewers, silversmiths worth half a million – and said that anyone attending a Lord Mayor's dinner would be told of the sums owned by those around him, not inherited but self-acquired.[37] Their favourite summer coastal retreat was Margate; Elizabeth Grant recalled a ball there in 1811: 'Velvets and satins, feathers and jewels! such jewels as would have graced the Queen's Drawing Room were in profusion there. Large, fat, Dowager *Aldermanesses*, with a fortune in Mechlin and diamonds on them, sat playing cards with tumblers of brandy and water beside them.'[38]

Notwithstanding revolutions abroad and the clamour for Parliamentary reform at home, the life of the court and of society during the 1830s gave constant opportunity still for occasions of great splendour. At the end of the Duchess of Kent's costume ball at Windsor in 1836, Princess Elizabeth concluded: 'I think the luxury at present is tremendous, more jewels and more extravagance than ever, everything is so lovely one longs to have it.'[39] But the old pre-eminence of the court was now paralleled and threatened by the display of the newly enriched businessmen and industrialists, whose wealth alone could not buy them the entrée to the inner circle.

GENTRY

Joseph Farington observed in 1802 that 'in England everyone aims at an appearance of substantial prosperity that brings them nearer to an equality'.[40] All who could afford to do so followed the fashions set by London society.

The inventory of Miss Anderson (†1798) listed: one pair of brilliant top earrings valued at £36, seven pearl pins and a necklace valued at £20, six modest rings, an inexpensive garnet and turquoise necklace with earrings, a butterfly set with glass simulating rubies, and a locket with a pearl device and a hair ring.[41] Mrs Sampson of Dorchester, who died in 1803, left diamond stars and pins, a pair of bracelets, a pearl necklace and pin, a gold watch and chain with egg, miniatures, sixteen rings and a buckle commemorating deceased members of her family.[42] A similar collection was bequeathed by Mrs Bradshaw of Evercreech, Somerset, in 1817: a diamond suite of necklace, pin, hair sprig and cross (valued at £265 10*s*), garnet suite, amber necklace and bracelets, a coral necklace and a cat's-eye ring with many other bracelets, lockets, brooches and rings.[43]

Some women preferred variety to splendour. In 1814 Mrs Higgins wrote from Turvey Abbey, on the Bedfordshire–Buckinghamshire border, to her husband, John, who was staying in London:

> if you find the blue ornaments will be expensive I would not wish them on any account but if you see anything in blue that is not more than three guineas, necklace and bracelets together I think that would not be too much but really expensive ornaments are not at all worth while as variety is better.[44]

Emma, the beautiful blacksmith's daughter who had married Sir William Hamilton, the British Minister at Naples, was not, according to Charles Greville, her former lover, ambitious for valuable jewels and expensive clothes but rather for 'that little such as sensible and genteel people wear'. When she and her husband returned to London after the French occupation of Naples in 1800, she had to sell the diamonds she had worn at the Neapolitan court, and made modest purchases of jewellery from John Salter in the Strand. A bill listing these provides information about what was both fashionable and inexpensive, decorative as well as useful, mixing classical motifs and personal sentiment. For her hair she bought gilt combs, an antique ornament and a pearl bandeau, pairs of ear pendants of gold, mother-of-pearl and cornelian. She had a variety of necklaces of artificial pearls, imitation cornelian, coral, amethysts and aquamarines, mounted in showy filigree setting for evenings. Her purchases also included gold Maltese and Venetian chains, with mother-of-pearl sautoirs from which she hung her seals and lockets. These were designed as a classical lyre and crescent moon with the sentimental padlock and key. There were crosses of imitation topaz and jet, and a whole parure for mourning. Her most expensive brooch was a large amethyst; her cheapest was mother-of-pearl. She had many buckles, and the rings were either hoops of brilliants or pearls, with one heart-shaped bezel set with a topaz, and a cornelian intaglio engraved with her name EMMA as a signet. Her surviving jewels are all sentimental in character: a bracelet made of Sir William's plaited hair, the clasp set with his portrait engraved on chalcedony by Filippo Rega; his miniature painted in 1794 set in a locket with his hair; and *fede* rings and more lockets which were mementoes of her love affair with Lord Nelson.[45]

The letters and novels of Jane Austen (1775–1817) confirm the taste for sentimental jewellery among the gentry, and she writes of purchases of lockets and brooches for hair, 'neat and plain and set in gold'.[46] In chapter 19 of *Sense and Sensibility* (1811–13) a ring with hair, conspicuously worn, is the cause of misunderstanding between Edward Ferrars and the girl who loves him, Elinor Dashwood. In 1801 Charles Austen, then serving in the Navy, won his first prize-money, and bought topaz crosses with gold chains for his sisters, Jane and Cassandra; these are now in the museum at the Austens' last home in Chawton, near Alton.[47] This inspired the gift of an amber cross from her brother in the Navy to the heroine of *Mansfield Park* (1814), Fanny Price (chapter 26). The importance of pearls is alluded to by Mrs Elton in *Emma* (1816) when she observes, with satisfaction, that there were 'very few pearls in the room except mine' (chapter 37); and in *Northanger Abbey* (written in 1799) Miss Tilney has inherited a beautiful string of pearls from her mother (chapter 9).

GEM-STONES AND OTHER MATERIALS

PRECIOUS STONES

Vast fortunes could be worn in jewels; Farington estimated those belonging to a Mrs Dupré at £70,000.[48] In 1802 the *Lady's Magazine* commented that 'the use of diamonds is of late considerably extended: diamond collars, earrings and bracelets are not rare, they are also worn upon almost all the turbans'.[49] Twenty years later, according to the *Lady's Monthly Museum*, 'diamonds are worn in profusion by the rich and all endeavour to have a ring or brooch of the same costly gem'.[50]

Jewellery and precious stones were brought to London by the émigrés fleeing from the French Revolution. Some were sold by James Christie at auction as the property of a 'Foreigner of Rank' or an 'Emigrant of Fashion', and on 19 February 1795 there was a sale of the jewels of Madame Du Barry, formerly mistress of Louis XV. Those who needed money more quickly went directly to jewellers, and Philip Rundell took advantage of their predicament to acquire a splendid stock at very low prices. According to Fox, while other jewellers thought they would never be able to dispose of such quantities of jewellery and did not buy, Rundell predicted that 'the distress of one country would tend to the advantage of a certain class in another' – and acted accordingly.[51] The sudden influx depressed prices; speculators like Robert Gregson in Paris and his partner, Thomas Eccleston Scarisbrick, in Lancashire regretted their investments in diamonds, which not only lost them money but caused endless trouble and anxiety.[52]

There was much interest in the 187½ grain (48.63 metric carats) Pigot diamond, named after George Pigot (1719–77), sometime Governor of Madras, which was disposed of by lottery in 1801. It was subsequently owned by Rundell, Bridge and Rundell in partnership with Parker and Birkett of Princes Street, Soho, and it was eventually sold to Mohammed Ali, Pasha of Egypt.[53] Models of this celebrated stone were made in crystal and mounted in gold for brooches.

Those who worked in India continued to repatriate their wealth in diamonds and coloured stones; among those sold at Christie's was a group of Mughal jewels, set with 'lask' (lasque) diamonds, emeralds and pearls, with richly enamelled backs.[54] Not all the gem-stones from India were recut in Europe, and the 'India cut curious brilliants' and 'India emerald drops' so frequently mentioned in inventories add an exotic note to the jewels of the period.

SEMI-PRECIOUS AND HARD STONES

From Brazil came large quantities of coloured stones, as well as diamonds: chrysoberyls, aquamarines and topazes. They widened the range of semi-precious stones available and were sold at reasonable prices, so that parures of coloured stones could be worn to match the colour of the dress. Pink topazes mounted in coloured gold were considered particularly pretty, and the rich burnt-yellow stones were admired, too. Siberian amethysts were also set in gold and might be combined with diamonds; rich red carbuncles (garnets) could be obtained of such quality that they were mounted *à jour*. In 1822 the *Lady's Magazine* observed that turquoises were much worn, combined either with diamonds or pearls, and also 'mingled with topazes in gold work for rings'.[55]

Sardonyx, moss agate, chrysoprase, bloodstone, lapis lazuli, cornelian, garnets and opals are frequently reported in jewels of this period, with green malachite from Russia.[56] Since a vase or table-top of this stone was a status symbol, it was also regarded as suitable for jewellery. Other inexpensive jewels were set with rock crystals, which were available in large quantities; a sale in 1807 included 'beautiful clear cut crystals upwards of thirty one thousands for bandeau, comb ornaments, necklaces and other ornaments'.[57] Crosses set with cairngorms found on the hills of their Highland home were worn on gold chains by the three daughters of Mrs Grant of Rothiemurchus when they met the Persian ambassador in 1810. Elizabeth, who wrote her memoirs in the mid nineteenth century, recalled how he 'took a great deal of notice of us and our sparkling crosses'.[58]

PEARLS

Oriental pearls were as much in demand as ever, and in 1830 a lady might wear with evening dress 'a bandeau of pearls brought low on the forehead, necklace and earrings of pearls'.[59] Pear pearls were worn as earrings, sometimes with topaz studs. The quality of imitations improved; in 1793 Christie's sold a number of 'bunches of Roman pearls' and in 1799 Lady Bagot had a pair of Roman pearl bracelets.[60] In 1805 Mrs Dillon wore a dress to the Queen's Birthday Drawing-Room 'ornamented with fringes of Roman pearls and festooned with chains and tassels of the same', while in 1818 a diadem of them could be worn with full dress.[61]

SUBSTITUTES

The range of paste imitations of precious and semi-precious stones is illustrated by the sale of the stock of Mr Constable in 1804: a 'mock brilliant girdle clasp . . . imitative diamond necklace set in gold and silver . . . imitative turquoise earrings . . . mock topaz gold brooch . . . suite of elegant necklace, bracelets, and earrings formed of amethyst paste set in gold'.[62] This jewellery was made in Birmingham, and Lady Lonsdale observed after her visit there in 1806 that 'the imitations of precious metals and stones are in a perfection greatly beyond what is to be seen in London at about half the price'.[63]

AMBER, ELK CLAWS, WOOD

In April 1817 the *Lady's Magazine* reported that 'amber and gold ornaments seem to claim the preeminence',[64] and elk 'claws', from the Baltic states, were mounted in chains and bracelets.[65] For the literary-minded there were chips of Shakespeare's mulberry tree at Stratford-upon-Avon or of Alexander Pope's willow from the garden of his villa at Twickenham. Necklaces and earrings made from 'Pope's willow', one set with a cross, were auctioned in 1804.[66]

IVORY

According to Mrs Lybbe Powys, only two artists, G. Stephany and J. Dresch of St James's Street, could do good work in ivory.[67] It was carved into bracelets, brooches, lockets and rings, with depictions of landscapes, including seaport scenes; figures;[68] and portraits of George III, Queen Charlotte and the Prince of Wales.[69]

BOG OAK

Another organic material used for jewellery was bog oak, found either when digging for peat or in civil engineering works. In July 1837 Garrards altered a Mrs J. J. Donn's 'bog oak necklaces into a pair of bracelets' and at the same time she bought a bog oak brooch which was sketched in the ledger.[70]

CUT STEEL

Because of its brilliance by candlelight cut steel continued in use for sword-hilts and tassels, buttons and buckles and a wide variety of other ornaments.[71] Polished cut steel was made up into tiaras with pendant enrichments, bandeaux and wreaths for the head, combs, and festoon-style necklaces with imitation garnets or sapphires.[72] In 1822 the *Lady's Monthly Museum* reported that 'some ladies wear at their waist a steel button cut diamond fashion instead of the oblong buckle formerly in use';[73] during the court mourning the previous year, a lady had worn cut-steel ornaments at a Drawing-Room with her mourning clothes.[74]

PLATINA (PLATINUM)

A Spanish diminutive of *plata* – silver – given to a heavy silver-coloured metal first discovered in Latin America, platina was identified as a substance new to science, in 1750 by Sir William Watson, who had been given some grains of it in 1741. Although it fuses at a much higher temperature, it has the same qualities of malleability and ductility as gold and silver but, unlike the latter, it does not tarnish. Major sources of the metal were discovered in Russia in 1822 and Borneo in 1831; this led to an increased use of the metal for scientific apparatus and for jewellery.[75]

Rarity and the high temperature needed to melt the metal meant that it only slowly came into use for jewellery. Among the first applications of platina are those to be found in purchases by the Prince of Wales: 'A platina watch chain' in 1805 and a platina guard neck chain, etc., in 1829.[76]

LONDON JEWELLERS

While on holiday at Weymouth, Queen Charlotte and King George III met Mr Bridge, a farmer, who warmly recommended to them his nephew, John, a partner of Philip Rundell; thus began the royal patronage of the celebrated firm of Rundell, Bridge and Rundell[77] (Plate 133).

Philip Rundell (1747–1827) arrived in London in 1767 as an apprentice from Bath; he was employed by a jeweller, whom he was later able to buy out. He engaged John Bridge (1754–1834), another Bath apprentice, and made him a partner. George Fox, who worked for the firm for many years, attributed its immense success to Rundell's shrewd purchases of jewellery from the French émigrés, which he was able to sell at profits of 200 or 300% on his outlay. Besides knowing how to drive a hard bargain, Rundell had a good eye for gems and could immediately detect the smallest flaw, so that the firm won the reputation of having the best stones. Their taste in the design of both plate and jewellery, which they made in their own workshop at Greenwich, was considered excellent. They served numerous members of the royal family but their most important commissions came from the Prince of Wales, culminating in the grandiose jewels made for his coronation in 1821.[78] The Empress of Russia was a client, as was the Queen of Haiti. The firm also exported jewels to Istanbul, which was an important market for expensive jewellery.[79]

The huge capital built up by astute dealing and careful management enabled them to execute the most expensive orders, offer credit, and lend stones to those who wished to hire jewels for a special occasion. Crowds flocked in when a fashionable wedding led to a particularly important casket of jewels or service of plate being put on show, but almost every day after 5 o'clock the shop was full of the nobility, and Ludgate Hill was blocked by the number of carriages waiting outside. It was one of the sights of London. In 1810 the Persian ambassador called, and recorded in his journal the impression it made on him:

> Gold and silver dishes were neatly arranged on shelves which reached the ceiling: expensive ropes of diamonds, rubies, emeralds, corals and pearls outshone the stars! I was told that the firm's partners send their representatives to buy stones from mines all over the world. They are then made up into the styles currently popular in London. These jewellers have no equal in Europe: they are famous for mounting stones so that they are visible from all sides and any flaw may be easily detected. I have heard that the reputation of this shop is so great that the French Emperor has promised it to one of his generals as a reward for victory.[80]

Fox described Bridge's daily routine for calls:

> At this time [1806] he might have been seen every Morning about 11. O'Clock leaving the shop with his blue bag well fitted with Jewels, Jewellery &c. for the West End of the town and it is worthy of remark how much ground he passed over every day . . . Whenever the King & Royal Family were in Town the Palace and Carlton House were sure to be places where he duly called but the Houses of all the Leading Nobility and Gentry shared constantly in his attention and he would ever be (to use one of his own favourite sentiments) beating the Bush out of doors to drive the Game to Ludgate Hill and well did he succeed in his efforts.[81]

After Philip Rundell's death the firm declined, leading to its closure in 1842, and the sale of the remaining stock at Christie's.

The mantle of royal jeweller fell next on Robert Garrard, who had gone into partnership with Wickes and Wakelin in 1792 and gained complete control of the firm in 1802; he attracted the patronage of Queen Charlotte and George IV. Among the important early customers were the Marquesses of Anglesey, Wellesley and Abercorn and the Earls of Dudley, Haddington, Brownlow and Kilmorey, who were joined from the mid 1830s by members of the Rothschild family.[82]

Apart from the great firms, there were many lesser jewellers. An amusing story concerns one Forster who, at the time of the Princess Royal's wedding to the Duke of Wurtemberg in 1796, was making her ring, set with thirty brilliants. While it was being made, a chicken got into the workshop and managed to peck out all the stones; it was caught in the act of consuming the last one. They were recovered from the gizzard and the ring finished[83] – an example of the happy-go-lucky way in which even royal commissions were executed at the time.

Another of the leading London jewellers was Nathaniel Jeffreys of Pall Mall, who became the unfortunate victim of the Prince of Wales's extravagance. When the prince took an instantaneous dislike to his wife, Princess Caroline, he refused to pay for the jewels he had bought her from Jeffreys. Jeffreys appealed to his friend, Charles James Fox, to intercede for him with the prince, but the appeal was in vain, and Jeffreys had to abandon his trade as a jeweller. He later became a Member of Parliament.[84] Another jeweller, who was driven to bankruptcy by one of the royal dukes, was Thomas Hamlet, at one time accounted the richest of the West End tradesmen. He was believed to be an illegitimate son of Sir John Dashwood,[85] and his attractive shop near Leicester Square was described by Mrs Gore in her novel *Stokeshill Place* in 1837. He had sold jewels to the Prince Regent, and continued to do so after his accession – as well as to the Princesses Augusta, Elizabeth, Mary and Sophia.[86] The banker, Thomas Coutts, was a good customer, and when Hamlet called on him at dinner to show him a wonderful diamond cross worn the previous day by the Duke of York at the coronation, Coutts's wife admired it so much that a cheque for £15,000 was made out for it immediately.[87] Hamlet's financial crisis came later, when he accepted from the Duke of York securities that proved to be worthless.

Thomas Gray of Sackville Street, whose shop is mentioned by Jane Austen in *Sense and Sensibility* (chapter 33) and by Maria Edgeworth in *Tales of Fashionable Life*, was more circumspect. His letterhead stated firmly that he declined orders on credit, and dealt only for ready money. He too was patronised by George IV, both as regent and as king. Other jewellers who received this patronage are named in the accounts in the Royal Archives at Windsor; they include Edmund Smith, J. Lauriere, J. Kitching, E. and W. Smith, J. Steffenoni, F. Benois, F. Burzio and S. Sheppard. William IV gave the royal appointment to Green and Ward in Cockspur Street. The firm of Storr and Mortimer, founded in New Bond Street in 1823 by Paul Storr and John Mortimer, also had a great reputation, and visits to their shop are described in Mrs Gore's novel.[88]

The names of many others are recorded by their trade cards (Fig. 35), and by the catalogues of the sales held on their retirement or bankruptcy. One of the largest of these sales was held when W. Constable of Sackville Street, formerly a partner of

Fig. 35 Front of Hawley's shop in the Strand. British Museum.

Thomas Gray, sold his stock over eighteen days in April 1804 at Phillips's. Among the important sales held by Christie's were those of Charles Lacey (25 April 1792), 'an eminent jeweller of Ludgate Street' (21 January 1793), William Thompson of the Strand (20 October 1796), George Jeffrey (14 March 1797), Mr Innocent of Little Newport Street (6 June 1807), Mr Sevestre (19 February and 19 April 1819) and Thomas Gray (16 and 17 March 1825).

A few shops specialised in certain lines: for mourning rings and hair work, there was Weatherley of Poultry in the City, Thomas Ayres in Fenchurch Street, and Hill of Ball Alley, Lombard Street.[89] Lapidaries, like John Sowerby of Broadway, Blackfriars, sold the crystals to cover locks of hair, etc., in bracelets or rings, as well as supplying cornelians and cutting seals;[90] others dealt in diamonds, both rough and cut, and coloured stones.[91]

PROVINCIAL JEWELLERS

Most towns outside London had jewellers, and their trade cards show how they combined a limited range of jewels and trinkets, watches, seals, silver or Sheffield plate with other things, such as umbrellas and parasols. Some specialised: David Jacobs of Silver Street, Cambridge, was a necklace-maker who also dealt in cutlery.[92] Working goldsmiths and lapidaries, like Stewart of Nicholas Street, Bristol, became rarer with the advance of the Birmingham manufacturers.[93] Thomas Turner of New Parade, High Street, Oxford, a jeweller and silversmith, advertised his shop as a warehouse for the products of Birmingham, Sheffield and Staffordshire,[94] and the diaries of Henry Ellis of Exeter (1790–1857) describe the pressure put on provincial shopkeepers by the manufacturers' salesmen. Dinner and theatre invitations accompanied offers of goods of the very latest design, on terms so easy 'that one could have fancied that the goods were never expected to be paid for, indeed the parties would be much obliged by having them taken off their hands'.[95] Drink was a problem, and Ellis found it impossible to keep craftsmen, so all bespoke orders were executed in workshops at Clerkenwell; even seals were engraved there, not locally.

It was also the practice for licensed hawkers to deal in jewels. In 1812 Mordecai Simmons from Liverpool stayed for five nights at the Gunn Inn in Maryport, Cumberland, and advertised his wares: gold rings, earrings, chains, seals and keys.[96] Other salesmen called at houses, and in 1827 the Marchioness of Salisbury 'bought some gold beads of a man who came with things'.[97] The circulating libraries were another source; they are twice alluded to by Jane Austen in her novels. Writing from Brighton, Lydia Bennet, in *Pride and Prejudice*, told her mother how she had been to the library 'where she had seen such beautiful ornaments as made her quite wild' (chapter 42). In Jane Austen's last, unfinished book, *Sanditon*, Charlotte Heywood concluded her first visit to the library by reflecting that she should not spend all her money on the first evening and 'so, she turned from the drawers of rings and brooches repressed further solicitation and paid for what she bought' (chapter 6).

BIRMINGHAM

When Mrs Lybbe Powys visited Birmingham in 1800 she thought it an immense place.[98] Output continued to expand, drawing on the pool of skilled labour formerly engaged in the shoe buckle trade. Buttons and wedding rings were specialities, as was the medium class of jewellery set with garnets, amethysts and aquamarines, and the cheaper items of gilt metal and paste which could be made by machine. There were workshops for drawing wire, making beads and stamping sheet-metal settings, and all these activities might be co-ordinated by a factor who supplied the materials. The trade card of M. Kettle illustrates the range available: 'Jewellery in gold, gold-plate or gilt, gilt toys, silver Jet and black ornaments, Medals and Medallions, Toy watches, filigree buttons, cloak and shoe clasps and every description of Birmingham Fancy goods for the Home trade and foreign markets'.[99] Only a few pieces from this period have been identified: a silver-gilt hair ornament with the maker's mark of Henry Adcock (1807), and a pair of silver-gilt bracelets made by Ledsam, Vale and Wheeler (1830).[100]

PURCHASES BY THE ENGLISH ABROAD

People at home relied on travellers to buy them regional specialities. In 1814 Lord Castlereagh, a devoted husband, apologised to his wife because he could not find her anything pretty in Switzerland, having passed through Basle only.[101] Had he been in Geneva, he would have found enamelled watch cases, brooches and bracelets of linked plaques of girls in picturesque local costume, as well as portraits of William Tell and Rousseau, which were popular with the many foreign visitors.[102]

Iron jewellery was made in the foundries of Berlin, and Lady Jackson, whose husband was minister there during the war with France, bought a necklace with medallions mounted in gold recording the dates of Napoleon's victories.[103] Iron was also worked into long chains and Maltese crosses of delicate filigree.[104] In 1825 the Earl of Clanwilliam, the then minister, sent Sir William Knighton, George IV's secretary, two pairs of bracelets which he had bought direct from the foundry.[105]

After the defeat of Napoleon in 1815, travel was once more easy and many took advantage of it. The watering-places of Europe had shops where all types of 'national bijouterie' might be bought: crosses of rock crystal from Mont Blanc, carved ivory bracelets and brooches representing stags at bay, coral ornaments, Venetian chains and Swiss watches.[106] Those who went further afield found temptations in Russia, where Lady Elizabeth Belgrave bought a fine set of chrysoprases in 1828,[107] and the Marchioness of Londonderry, on the advice of Madame Nesselrode, had some of her jewels reset by a St Petersburg jeweller.[108] The English who bought jewels in Paris during the truce of 1802–3 did so in large numbers after 1815, led by Countess Granville, wife of the ambassador, a client of J. B. Fossin.[109]

ITALY

The Italian cities remained the goal of many travellers, and there were several local specialities. In 1830 the Earl of Munster sent Minney Seymour, the adopted daughter of Mrs Fitzherbert, three rosaries blessed by the Pope, and a bracelet containing pieces of stone which he had picked up in Egypt – from the Pyramids, Pompey's Pillar and Cleopatra's Needle.[110] Mrs Gore, in *Mothers and Daughters* (1831), describes travellers returning and giving a cousin a set of Roman mosaic and Neapolitan corals.[111]

Roman pearl might be bought far more cheaply in Rome than in London, and in 1823 Sir Watkin Williams Wynn wrote that 'the pearls are to be bought for nothing here . . . and as they are of alabaster will not break'.[112] Coral might be purchased at Naples or Leghorn, hardstone mosaics in Florence and glass mosaics or cameos in Rome; all of these were imported and could be found in London shops as well.

MOSAICS

Both Roman and Florentine mosaics were auctioned in London and stocked by jewellers, who bought them from wholesalers such as P. Nappi of Newman Street.[113] A ring set with a mosaic dove, attributed to Giacomo Raffaelli (1753–1836) who revived the art of miniature mosaics, was sold at Christie's on 23 January 1793. The stock of Henry Heuland included fifty mosaics for brooches and boxes.[114] Apart from birds, the subjects included Italian peasants, Roman antiquities and landscapes with coral- or lapis-lazuli-coloured borders; they were mounted in filigree and joined by gold chains, pearls or turquoises, to make parures of necklaces, earrings, combs, pairs of bracelets, belt clasps and buckles.[115] A gold wire bracelet with a mosaic of a spaniel in the Roman Campagna was one of George IV's purchases in 1824.[116] Already in 1786, after visiting St Mark's in Venice, Goethe deplored this fashion: 'the art of mosaic which gave the ancients their paved floors and the Christians the vaulted heaven of their churches has now been degraded to snuff boxes and bracelets. Our times are worse than we think.'[117]

CORAL

In 1821 the *Lady's Monthly Museum* announced that 'coral seems preferred to other articles of jewellery', especially for half dress (semi-formal) and for young persons at balls.[118] Coral was imported on a large scale, some of it worked as beads and other pieces carved. 'A set of seed coral in necklace, earrings and brooch mounted in gold' was among the royal purchases in 1811,[119] and Lady Bagot's inventory included a pair of bracelets with fifty-three coral beads.[120] Larger pieces might be carved with rosettes or acorns or cherub's heads,[121] or engraved with clasped hands.[122]

THE EAST

The colourful creations of the Muslim and Hindu jewellers brought back from India by officials and merchants were worn with European dress and appear in auctions.[123] In 1835 Mrs Backhouse appeared at the Queen's Birthday Drawing-Room wearing a suite of Indian jewels with her diamonds and white satin dress,[124] and Mrs Honeyman in Thackeray's novel, *The Newcomes*, pinned her cashmere shawl with a brooch depicting the Taj Mahal, and wore bracelets her brother, Colonel Newcome, had sent home from India.[125] The Prince Regent bought an 'elegant gold enamelled and pearl bracelet' imported from Persia in 1813 and, as king in 1824, a Cantonese enamel necklace and earrings.[126]

REMODELLING

As soon as an engagement was announced, the family diamonds were taken to be reset, for the eighteenth-century style was no longer fashionable. Elinor Maitland in Mrs Gore's novel, *The Débutante*, shows Lord Mortayne her noble casket of family diamonds and insists: 'We must get them reset before the season, in their present state they are heavy and tasteless as an old épergne, but the brilliants themselves are of great beauty.'[127] The pleasure women took in their remodelled jewellery was described in her journal by Mrs Calvert, a great beauty of the Regency, who spent a whole morning dressing for a Birthday Drawing-Room and was thrilled with her 'new-set diamonds', which looked so much more brilliant in their new mounts.[128] In Jane Austen's *Sense and Sensibility* (chapter 33), the ladies look forward to their visits to London so that they can take their jewels to be brought up to date by the fashionable jewellers, such as Thomas Gray.

Literary allusions are borne out by a number of documents. In 1793, for instance, the Marchioness de Grey sent John Duval two flowers and a pair of tops to be remodelled into a feather,[129] and in 1805 Lord Gage paid Rundell and Bridge £142 16*s* 6*d* for new-setting his wife's diamonds.[130] Similarly, Lady Walsingham sent them in 1819 two pins, a Maltese cross and a pair of earrings to break up and reset the stones in a new pair of earrings and a 'fancy pattern comb'.[131] Thus perished most of the creations of the eighteenth-century English jewellers.

MOTIFS

Jewellery made between 1789 and 1837 is characterised by a wide range of motifs: neo-classical, Gothic, sentimental, patriotic, naturalistic, literary and heraldic. Many are illustrated in the set of designs published by Jacob Petit in London in 1824 (Fig. 36).

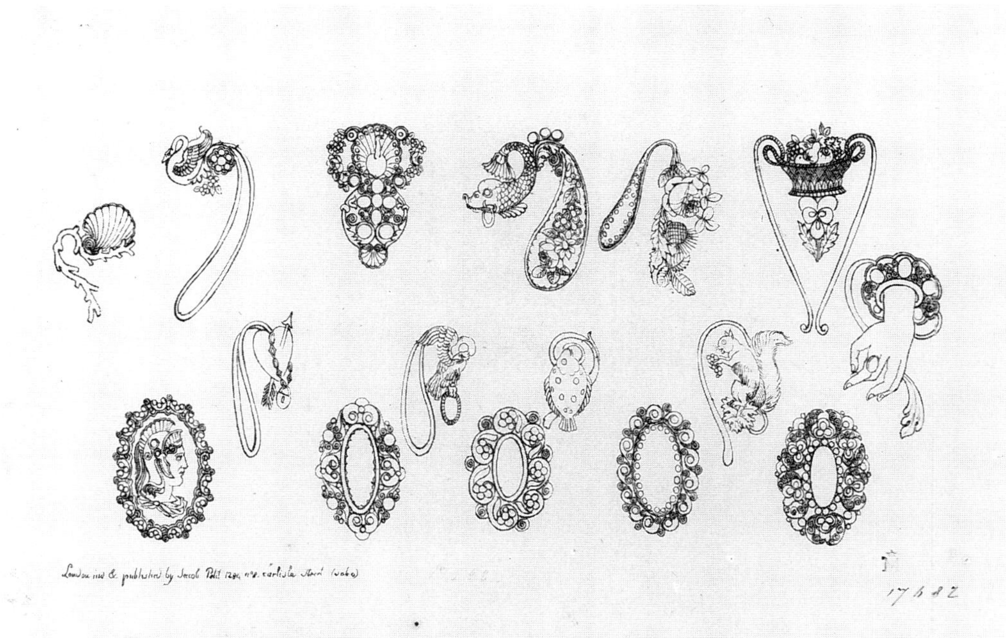

Fig. 36 Designs by Jacob Petit for watch guards and brooches, showing naturalistic and classical motifs: 1824. Victoria and Albert Museum.

With the rise of Romanticism in literature, the neo-classical Greek key fret, honeysuckle and laurel wreaths were joined by medieval motifs. In 1812, for instance, the Prince Regent bought a Gothic-style necklace with matching bracelets,[132] the first of many such jewels ornamented with tracery, trefoils, quatrefoils and 'rosaces' (Plate XXXIX). A cruciform ring set with four rubies and a brilliant sold by Rundell, Bridge and Rundell in 1821 was named after Bishop William of Wykeham, and a cross in the centre of an emerald and ruby medallion was called after Joan of Navarre, wife of Henry IV.[133] Bracelets were made like miniature Gothic crowns, and one was copied from the Lombardic 'Iron Crown of Monza', which contained a circle of iron said to have been made from one of the nails used at the Crucifixion.[134]

Early examples of archaeological jewellery were the 'necklace of marcasites and garnets connected by gold wire with chased gold clasp and pendant filigree drop strictly copied [*sic*] from an antique Roman necklace dug up in Great Britain' sold by Christie's in 1812, and an Etruscan girdle clasp altered by Garrard's for the Earl Cadogan in 1835.[135] Such jewellery was to become more popular, and more accurate in the designs used, later in the century.

Naturalistic motifs included flowers; sprigs of roses and fuchsia, trailing vines with grapes, and geraniums are found.[136] There were birds of paradise, feathers (the peacock in particular), or butterflies and insects, their wings vibrating on tremblers. A gold giraffe bracelet and brooch is an exotic among the horses, stags, dogs and foxes made for sporting enthusiasts.[137]

For those with musical tastes there were lyre and harp brooches and bracelet snaps, and for the literary minded book-shaped lockets and vinaigrettes. Ciphers or mottoes in 'Old English' (Gothic or black letter) script were worked in gold, enamelled or studded with stones. The initials of the stones used could spell out a message – *A*methyst, *M*ina Nova, *J*asper, *T*urquoise, *J*acinth and *E*merald making up the word AMITIE.

More obvious expressions of sentiment were conveyed by Cupid's bow and arrows, padlocks with keys, hearts, butterflies and hands clasped together with ruffles at the wrists and rings on the fingers. The anchor, emblem of Christian Hope, was set with stones to wear as a pendant, or engraved on lockets.[138] Snakes were made into necklaces, bracelets and earrings, and encircled (as a symbol of eternity) to frame rings, brooches and lockets. A suite composed of emblems of the Seven Ages of Man, inspired by Jaques' speech in Shakespeare's *As You Like It* (Act 2, Scene 7), was purchased by George IV in 1820.[139]

The interest in the Middle Ages inspired by the novels of Sir Walter Scott led to a revival of heraldic ornament in jewellery. At the time of the Reform Bill in 1832 the *Lady's Magazine* observed that 'notwithstanding the abolition of rank [*sic*], ladies of high family contrive to establish their claims by wearing the family crests and ciphers linked together on each side by a rich jewelled ornament on which is enamelled armorial bearings. Bracelets of great massiveness are worn to match.'[140] The choice of words reflects the rather hysterical reaction to a very limited extension of male franchise, which had nothing to do with the 'abolition of rank'. The influence of Scott and a desire to distinguish themselves from the *nouveaux riches* who were increasingly prominent on the social scene are more likely explanations.

Late-eighteenth-century styles were brought up to date by the increasing use of larger, brighter stones: violet amethysts, deep red garnets, olive green peridots, celadon chrysoprases, tawny gold and pink topazes, with striking contrasts of colour and texture. Settings *à l'antique* in massy gold – bright, dead and varicoloured – with cheaper versions in filigree, or plaques stamped with patterns of leaves, shells and scrolls, were decorative, colourful and showy. The morning attire of Lady Birmingham in the novel *Almack's* (1827) was what was most admired: 'rich in the extreme, her watch chain, her bracelets, her rings were all outrageously fine and massive'.[141]

ROYAL AND PATRIOTIC MOTIFS

The long struggle against the French which ended in the victory at Waterloo fostered patriotism, centred on the monarchy. Paste portraits of the royal family were mass-produced by James Tassie for setting in jewellery, and expensive versions in hardstones or enamelled gold were worn by the rich and those with court connexions. At the Birthday Drawing-Room on 4 June 1803, the Marchioness of Salisbury declared her loyalty by pinning a large ruby cameo head of George III to her blue and silver dress.[142] The fiftieth anniversary of his accession was marked by brooches with his portrait and an inscription.[143]

Although the badge of the Prince of Wales was the theme for bracelets, earrings and brooches,[144] his portrait appeared frequently after his appointment as Prince Regent in 1811 (Plate 115). The Viscountess Castlereagh purchased 'a Red Cornelian signet Ring Intaglio of His Royal Highness The Prince Regent with motto' from Rundell, Bridge and Rundell in 1816.[145] These intaglios were set in signets of severe Roman style or heavily chased.[146] Cameo portraits of the prince might also be set in diamonds or framed by the Garter with its motto.[147] Regency cameo brooches, too, were framed by Garters, as well as by plain blue enamelled borders or wreaths of oak and laurel, and crowned.[148] Lockets hanging from gold chains might be 'chased all over and with turquoises to open with a spring to contain a picture inside with cipher and crown'.[149] Portrait miniatures, set with diamonds, were ordered for the princesses in 1815, and also given to those like the Dowager Countess of Ilchester who were closely connected with the royal family.[150]

George IV marked his accession to the throne and his coronation in 1821 with more gifts of this character, rings being the most numerous category. His portrait was mounted in gold *à l'antique*, crowned and framed in diamonds, or flanked with gem-studded shoulders.[151] A ring in the British Museum, inscribed at the back of the

115 Sardonyx cameo portrait of George IV wreathed like a Roman emperor in laurel border (damaged). Trustees of the Chatsworth Settlement.

bezel GEORGIUS IV DEI GRATIA BRITT REX MD CCCXXI,[152] corresponds to the 'large cornelian signet set strong with turquoises and brilliants each side with the head of His Majesty finely engraved in intaglio', bought from Rundell, Bridge and Rundell on 26 April 1821.[153] Another ring in the same collection is set with a fine sardonyx cameo portrait of the king, and the back has an identical inscription.[154] Broad hoop rings inscribed VIVE LE ROI in blue enamel with a small hardstone portrait in the centre were also distributed;[155] there is one in the collection at Chatsworth (Plate XL). Cheaper versions were neatly made with gold medallic heads, and the British lion at the back.[156] Most valuable of the series were the enamelled miniatures on gold by Henry Bone, depicting the king in contemporary dress with his Orders – a contrast with the gem engravings, which depict him wreathed, with a cloak held by a brooch, like a Roman emperor.[157] Some miniatures were hidden in square diamond locket bezels, and others were covered with picture diamonds instead of crystal, the hoop set with brilliants and turquoises.[158] In the next reign, William IV's miniature was mounted in a ring of this type, with diamond frame and foliate shoulders[159] (Plate 116).

The white rose of York and the Garter, both rich in historical associations, were combined in the 'very elegant gold enamelled ring with rose of York and coronet on Garter with forget-me-not on the shank',[160] and appear separately, too. There was a Garter ring of 'broad gold with diamond buckle' and an enamelled Garter ring with the crowned GR cipher in diamonds,[161] and a locket bezel with the white rose.[162] In 1824

116 Miniature of William IV by William Essex, framed in diamonds and set beneath a portrait diamond. Private collection.

117 Garter bracelet with coronation portrait medallion of William IV. Christie's.

118 Coronation bracelet with medals of William IV and Queen Adelaide. Christie's.

119 Tudor rose chain bracelet, the roses set with diamonds and rubies. David Lavender, London.

George IV ordered a bracelet designed as an enamelled Garter, and in 1826 another, set with his cameo portrait.[163] Garter bracelets were also set with William IV's 1831 coronation medal and inscribed with the motto NEC TIMERE NEC TIMIDE in black letter[164] (Plates 117 and 118). Cameo portraits could be framed by a diamond-set Garter or a laurel wreath;[165] less expensive versions, such as Tassie's pastes, bloodstones or even gold appliqué heads on lapis lazuli, were set in crowned laurel wreaths of gold.[166] The Tudor rose appeared on bracelets (Plate 119) during the reigns of both George IV and William IV, the broad bands enamelled with the roses and leaves, and diamond ciphers in the midst of open flowers on the clasp.[167] The royal cipher GR, set with rubies and brilliants with a ruby and pearl drop, might be worn from a gold chain.[168]

Lockets were made with similar designs using the cipher and portrait, like the 'heart locket with appliqué of the king and Protecting Deity set with pearls'.[169] Portraits of the king were also set in bracelet clasps under picture diamonds and crowns set with sapphires and brilliants, rubies and turquoises, or opals.[170]

The most ambitious of all the portrait jewels was an armlet described in an invoice from Rundell, Bridge and Rundell: 'a very fine remarkably large sardonyx cameo with the device of His Majesty's bust in front with a dove, figure of Britannia and Neptune in

120 Miniature of George IV, framed in diamond thistles and roses, surmounted by a crown. Fitzwilliam Museum, Cambridge.

front, Aurora and her horses and chariot and the sign Leo surrounded with laurel the reverse, all in cameo of the finest workmanship'. It was mounted with 'very fine large brilliants and with richly chased gold compartments set with rubies brilliants and sapphires emeralds etc in devices of Roses, thistles harps and with brilliant collets on the border', and cost £1,336.[171]

These badges of the three kingdoms were also worn by supporters of the 1801 Act of Union between Ireland and Great Britain in belt clasps and brooches (the latter set with diamonds and coloured stones), and rings of bloodstone and gold or of diamonds and turquoises.[172] More elaborate was an 'elegant locket with rose, thistle and shamrock enamelled painting of His Majesty and brilliant Protecting Deity over',[173] or the miniature hanging from a crown and framed by the floral badges of the kingdoms[174] (Plate 120). The individual badges were also used: shamrock rings and emerald-set brooches, crowned or paved with diamonds, and gold and enamel harps.[175] Thistles were made of coloured stones and gold,[176] and the visit of George IV to Scotland was commemorated by medallions with his portrait engraved in quartz, a view of Edinburgh Castle and an inscription.[177]

In 1821 Rundell, Bridge and Rundell made several necklaces inspired by the Garter collar, with gold tasselled knots alternating with shamrocks, roses and thistles, with a Maltese cross in the centre with a pendant orb, with brooch and earrings *en suite*[178]

(Plate XLI). One of the sets was given to Lady Willoughby de Eresɔy, whose husband officiated as Deputy Lord Great Chamberlain.

National victories were frequently commemorated by jewelled tributes. After Admiral Earl Howe defeated the French on the 'Glorious 1st of June' in 1794, he received from George III a gold chain with medal and a ceremonial sword. His wife Mary was given a pair of diamond bracelets with centrepieces bearing the royal cipher and a maritime trophy executed in rose diamonds on blue enamel (Flate XXXV). These national heroes – Earl Howe, Viscount Nelson and the Prime Minister, William Pitt – were venerated by the public, too. Among the jewels left by Emily Marchioness of Londonderry, at the time of her death in 1829 was 'a bloodstone Locket with Motto with Hair of the late Mr. Pitt', worn in memory of her husband's colleague.[179] The Earl of Minto, after seeing Nelson 'in a mob in Piccadilly', observed that 'it is really quite affecting to see the wonder and admiration and love and respect of the whole world – and the genuine expression of all those sentiments at once from the gentle and simple the moment he is seen. It is beyond anything represented in a play oı poets of fame.'[180] Such admirers might wear pyramid brooches and lockets, alluding tɔ his victory at the Nile in 1798, or lockets of his ship, the *Victory* (Plate XLII). Nelson's bust was carved in ivory; it was worn enamelled in brooches, medallions and lockets, or engraved in intaglio for seals and signets; and after his death at Trafalgar in 1805, gold rings were inscribed with his message to the fleet: ENGLAND EXPECTS EVERY MAN TO DO HIS DUTY[181] (Plate 121). At the time of the Congress of Vienna in 1815, armlets were on sale ornamented with the arms of the victorious allies and set with seven coloured stones.[182] The hero of the Peninsula and Waterloo, the Duke of Wellington, inspired similar jewels and trinkets, and there was a large sale of rings with his portrait stamped in gold under glass. His chestnut charger, Copenhagen, shared in the glory, and the Countess of Jersey wore a jewelled bracelet with hair from the horse's tail surreptitiously obtained from a groom.[183]

121 Gold ring wiith red jasper intaglio portrait of Admiral Lord Nelson with the inscription ENGLAND EXPECTS EVERY MAN TO DO HIS DUTY; twisted anchor chain on the shoulders. S. J. Phillips.

122 Hair ornament with three shell cameos of nymphs in filigree mounts.
Collection of a Scottish nobleman.

ENGRAVED GEMS

By the turn of the century cameos and intaglios were not only collected by connoisseurs, including the Prince of Wales, who bought ancient gems from Rundell, Bridge and Rundell between 1802 and 1805;[184] they were widely worn by fashionable women, such as Emily, Viscountess Castlereagh. In 1817 Rundell, Bridge and Rundell charged her for 'Setting the Antique head of Dr. Mead's Socrates in chas'd flower and scroll Ring, Roman setting & inscription'.[185] Ancient, Renaissance and contemporary gems carved in hardstones were expensive, and not everyone could aspire to the gold necklace and bracelets set with cornelian intaglios which had belonged to Queen Charlotte.[186] Sicilian shell with figures in relief (Plate 122) was cut not only at Trapani and Rome but also in London; it was an attractive and cheap alternative. A parure set in filigree was also in the queen's collection, with a bandeau of five large and eight small cameos, the mounts linked by two rows of gold chains.[187]

Such ornaments were perhaps influenced by the cameo jewellery, based on ancient Roman designs, fashionable at the Napoleonic court. Several other head ornaments are recorded; a tiara set with an intaglio bought by the Prince of Wales in 1800 depicted Hercules resting,[188] and in 1823 Lord Charles Murray bought a shell version of the famous Aldobrandini Marriage fresco in Rome for his mother, the Duchess of Atholl. It was set in a tiara with Greek key fret pattern and crowned with acanthus[189] (Plate 123). The fashion continued to be popular, and in 1837 a Miss Stanley ordered from Garrard 'a cameo bandeau with gold chain'.[190]

Cameos for earrings were matched iconographically: Socrates with his pupil Plato, an owl with a vulture,[191] and so on. The upswept hair styles which revealed the ears were fashionable throughout the period, and in 1830 the *Lady's Magazine* noted the number of women wearing gold cameo-set earrings.

Whenever possible the gems in necklaces and parures were linked by a common theme. In 1808 the Prince of Wales bought a necklace composed of Labrador spar cameos of monkeys' heads mounted in gold.[192] More conventional was the Duchess of Northumberland's garnet cameo parure with the Twelve Caesars; and when the sixty-year-old heiress, Miss Heathcote, wore a similar necklace with her wedding dress, it inspired the lines:

> No longer at thy virgin state repine,
> Twelve Caesars now upon thy breast recline
> O happy she![193]

123 Gold hair ornament set with shell cameo of the Aldobrandini Marriage and belt clasps set with shell cameos of Thorwaldsen's reliefs, Night and Morning. Bought by Lord Charles Murray in Rome, 1823. Collection of the Duke of Atholl.

Designs varied from sets of gem-stones uniform in size and colour – nicolo intaglios or turquoise cameos – to mixtures,[194] such as 'A matchless necklace, formed of seven antique gems, viz. a *cameo head* of OMPHALE, an *intaglio* of Julia Pia, an *intaglio* on *cornelian*, a Bacchanalian Dance, a fine *cameo* of Marcus Aurelius on *lapis lazuli*, an *intaglio* of Minerva in *amethyst*, a *head* of Brutus in *sardonyx*, and a *cameo head* of Jupiter de Donicus, superbly set in *gold*, with *Venetian chain* and *clasp*, set with *turquoise, rubies, sapphires*, and *amethysts*', which was sold for £63 at auction in 1817.[195] Alternatively, cameos might be mixed with plaques of cornelian or moss agate, or shell cameos could be combined with coral rosette spacers in a necklace.[196]

Cameo medallions hung from necklaces or gold chains in lockets, often 'designed from the antique'.[197] They might be portraits of illustrious contemporaries, classical heroes like Achilles, or divinities like Bacchus; they might depict amorous themes – Mars and Venus, Cupid taming the lion – and the more expensive could be framed in diamonds or pearls, though chased and coloured gold was also made into appropriate designs.

Smaller stones were set in pins. Queen Charlotte owned a 'fine intaglio, two imperial heads engraved on cornelian, the reverse of which is a Persian inscription very tastefully executed the stone is set with small brilliants mounted in a gold shirt pin'.[198] An onyx cameo head of a Negress wearing a diamond necklace, mounted in a pin, was sold at the Sevestre sale.[199] Many brooches were expensively mounted. A cameo portrait of Mary, Queen of Scots, was mounted in an enamel border set with nineteen fine white brilliants; a 'noble large cameo of a Medusa in party coloured amethyst finely sculptured' was framed by twenty-seven large pearls; and a head of Serapis was the centre of a brilliant caduceus.[200] Cameos might be grouped according to their place of origin, as in the 'Girdle clasp, formed of three beautiful antique Egyptian cameos, of *Cleopatra*, *Omphale*, and a *Stork*, with rich massive gold venetian chain'; or they might be matched iconographically for paired brooches, as in the 'pair of matchless antique cameos, in high relief of *most beautiful workmanship*, (subjects from Homer) set as broaches, with large and fine brilliants' and said to be unique.[201]

Calling on the Duchess of Wellington on St Patrick's day, 1818, the novelist Maria Edgeworth was present when a jeweller arrived with some bracelets, one of which had the clasp set with a shell cameo portrait of the duke – which the jeweller then corrected on the advice of the duchess.[202] Besides modern portraits, other popular themes for bracelets were pairs of famous women, such as Lucretia and Cleopatra, or dancing figures from the frescoes at Herculaneum, set in chased or filigree gold clasps.[203]

According to the *Lady's Monthly Museum* for July 1801, the fashion was for yellow and white muslin dresses clasped with antique gems in filigree settings on the shoulders and belted with one gem in front and two behind.[204] In 1825 the jeweller Thomas Gray had a 'Girdle clasp of bloodstones beautifully mounted in gold'.[205] Some of these gems had a personal significance. A pair of cameo heads of the poetess Sappho in the belt clasp

124 Lady Morgan (1783–1859) with two cameo heads of Sappho set in the clasp of her girdle. Portrait by René Berthon. National Gallery of Ireland.

worn by Lady Morgan (1783–1859), as depicted at her desk in a portrait (Plate 124), allude to her successful career as a novelist and author of travel books. The Dowager Marchioness of Exeter had a belt clasp with a shell cameo of three Cupids[206] in an enamelled setting studded with thirty-eight brilliants. Lord Charles Murray bought a pair of shell cameos copying Thorwaldsen's reliefs of Night and Day to be set in a double clasp for his mother to wear with the cameo tiara[207] (Plate 125).

More engraved gems were set in rings than any other type of jewel. Signets might be set with ancient or modern intaglios, some by celebrated contemporary artists such as Pichler, Rega and Berini. Ornamental rings were set with emblematic cameos signifying Peace and Plenty, or Love, Wisdom and Affection, or else with a wide range illustrating events from classical history and mythology, either simply set in gold or framed by brilliants.

One of the principal tasks of the gem-engravers in England was carving the cameos or intaglios for the Lesser George. Royal portraits worn in jewels depicted not just the contemporary monarchs but also their Hanoverian ancestors. In 1811 the Prince Regent had a sardonyx cameo head of George I set in gold for a pin.[208] When the Duke of York died in 1827, brooches and rings set with his cameo portrait were commissioned by the king for distribution to those closest to him.[209] The engravers responsible for these have never been identified; apart from Benedetto Pistrucci and Henry Weigall, gem-engravers rarely signed their work.[210]

Paste versions of hardstone gems could be bought from James Tassie, and his catalogue, published in 1791 with the text written by Raspe, lists nearly 16,000. Composition reliefs could be applied to a hardstone ground, usually lapis lazuli or bloodstone.[211] Seals, whether armorial or classical, were used by both men and women, set in wrought gold or gilt mounts which hung from chains (Fig. 37).

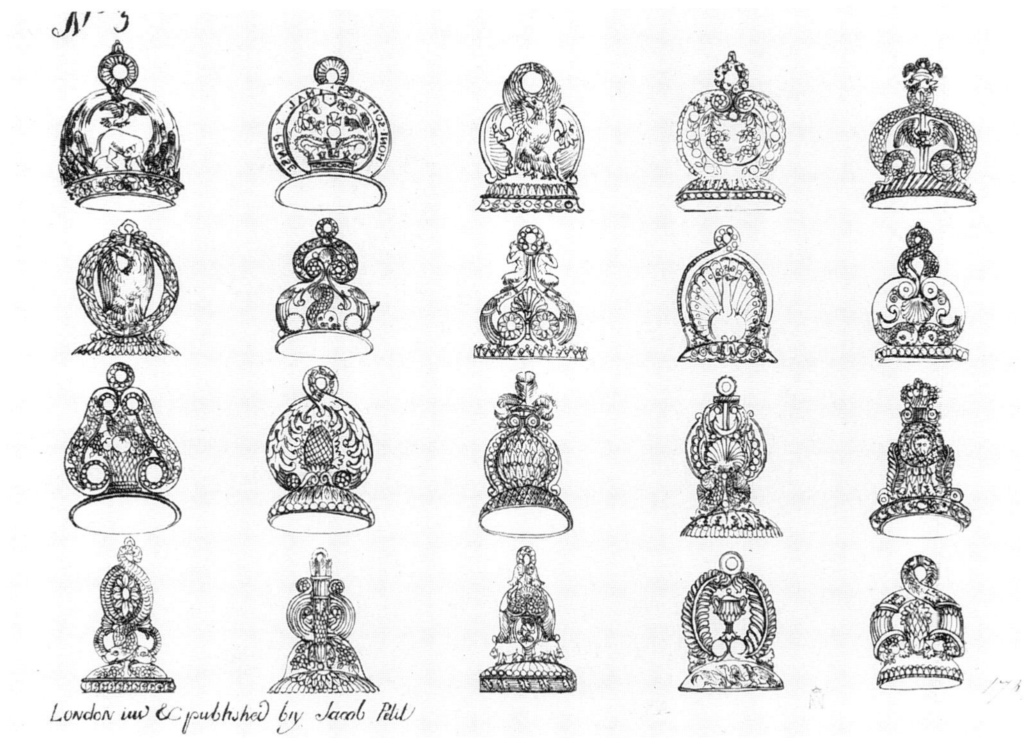

Fig. 37 Designs for seal mounts by Jacob Petit. Victoria and Albert Museum.

ORDERS AND DECORATIONS

The insignia of the British Orders of Knighthood were a source of profit to those jewellers specialising in them: Thomas Hamlet, Thomas Gray, and above all Rundell, Bridge and Rundell. The twenty-five years of war ending in 1815 led to an increase in the numbers needing to be honoured for their services to the country, to a major change in the system, and to the creation of two new Orders.

The Order of the Garter was not affected, although the custom of appointing supernumerary knights in order to accommodate the sons of George III and to honour foreign princes, became firmly established. George IV, as Prince of Wales, as regent and as king, the royal dukes and other knights all spent large sums of money on jewelled insignia, which remained the property of their heirs. The Marquess of Wellesley, who was very vain, had a collection of diamonds reset in his Garter insignia, including two Lesser Georges with onyx cameos, one of which was said to have been given by Charles I to Bishop Juxon on the scaffold and had cost £1100.[212] The greater part of the diamonds employed were taken out of the different jewels belonging to the Order of the Bath given to him by the army in India after the defeat of Tippoo Sultan, but many others were added by Rundell, Bridge and Rundell. In 1812 they refused to deliver a new diamond Garter star until their bill was settled.[213] Viscount Castlereagh was another good client, for the many fine diamonds set in snuff boxes or framing miniatures which he had been given by foreign sovereigns were reset in jewels for his wife, Emily, and in his own splendid sword, Garter insignia, epaulettes, hat button and loop. These he designated family heirlooms[214] The Duke of Wellington also had some splendid insignia, and in 1828 Rundell, Bridge and Rundell supplied the king with 'a very handsome gold and enamelled diamond George like the Duke of Wellington's', at a cost of £630.[215] The Garter insignia still at Lennoxlove, made by the same firm for the eighth Duke of Hamilton, includes a Lesser George set with a white and grey onyx cameo inscribed in Roman capitals on the Garter, and another with a sardonyx cameo with the Garter inscribed in black letter and crowned with enamelled roses and thistles. The Lesser George cameo cut by Nathaniel Marchant for the Earl of Carlisle in 1798 is still at Castle Howard, but he never completed the commission for another, using a superb oriental onyx from the collection of the Emperor of Russia, for Earl Spencer: it was eventually offered to Benedetto Pistrucci.[216] The intaglio with the motto set with diamonds was less usual.[217] Apart from the members of the royal family, only a few peers were allowed to hold two of the British Orders at the same time. Since the statutes required the wearing of the Lesser George daily, double-sided jewels were made. In 1801 Wakelin charged the Duke of Roxburghe £11 for 'setting an Onyx of the order of St. Andrew and Garter in Gold engrav[ed] on one Side Enam[elle]d on the other', and an example of such a jewel is in the collection of H.M. The Queen.[218] The letters of the motto on the Garter might be set with diamonds, but more usually gold thread, pearls or enamelled letters were used; the Garter star was made with rays of cut steel or set with diamonds to produce a shimmering effect.

At the end of the Napoleonic wars, the Order of the Bath, to which it had been necessary to appoint extra knights to reward military and naval services,[219] was reorganised. Following the example of continental Orders of Merit, it was divided into three classes with military and civil Knights Grand Cross. There was considerable opposition to this at the time, and one consequence was that there were no longer enough stalls for even the Grand Crosses, who had to wait for vacancies to occur and, until installed, needed a dispensation to wear the collar.[220] The insignia was redesigned and it was no longer necessary to resign from the Order on receiving the Garter.

The acquisition of the Ionian Islands during the war led to the creation of a new Order of Saint Michael and Saint George, with the High Commissioner as Grand Master, and three classes. The headquarters were established at Corfu and most of the early members were local Corfiote or Maltese nobles, with the principal English officials serving in the Mediterranean.[221]

George IV also instituted the Hanoverian or Guelphic Order, primarily to reward the inhabitants of his continental territory, which was elevated into a kingdom at the Congress of Vienna. It had been considered earlier by George III but nothing had been done about the idea. Like the other two new Orders, it was divided into classes with provision for civilians to be appointed according to their equivalence with military ranks. His own and his brothers' insignia were richly jewelled and a 'very elegant white and yellow brilliant Badge, the Grand Cross of the Royal Guelphic Order with yellow diamond lions and diamond horse in emerald wreath of oak' was supplied in 1820 at a cost of £324.[222]

Both as regent and as king, George IV had distributed miniatures framed in diamonds to the princesses and to ladies who had long served the court. In 1816 the Dowager Countess of Ilchester recorded her pride at receiving such a jewel: 'a magnificent present from the Regent – his own picture superbly set with diamonds. He gave it to me on Princess Mary's birthday, saying I feel myself much obliged to you.'[223] The rare miniatures of Henry Bone were used for this, set within crowned diamond frames, with the royal cipher on the back similarly set.[224] This was the beginning of the Royal Family Order, which was and is limited to the ladies of the royal family and personal attendants of the highest rank, like the Mistress of the Robes. It was also given to Lady Conyngham, and Lord Melbourne recalled only two other non-royal ladies having received the honour: Lady Cowper and Lady Aboyne.[225]

In 1816 Princess Caroline (1768–1821), the estranged wife of the Prince Regent, instituted her own Order of St Caroline of Jerusalem, with Colonel Bartholomew Pergami as Grand Master. The badge was a red cross with the royal motto, HONI SOIT QUI MAL Y PENSE, hanging from a lilac and silver ribbon. Just before she died, another cross with a different design was sent to her loyal friend, Lady Anne Hamilton. It is a

Maltese cross with her cipher in gold on black in a foliate border, inscribed in black on white enamel: BESTOWED IN HEAVEN DENIED ON EARTH CAROLINE OF BRUNSWICK ENGLAND'S INJURED QUEEN. It has rays in the angles, set with a diamond between amethysts, and three of the arms end in royal crowns, the circlets studded with small rubies. The central medallion is engraved at the back with a cross and C B TO A H, with the surround inscribed 'I DIE IN PEACE WITH ALL THE WORLD GOODBYE'. The four arms are inscribed with her message to her friend:

> [i] The doctors have done their best for me but they do not know my malady it is here [a heart] but shall never come out of my lips I did tell you this coronation [ii] would end in tragedy. I am quite ready to die I have no wish to live remember me to my good friend Lady Perceval. [iii] Thank you my dr. Lady Anne for all your kindness to me. I cannot repay you. Do not regret me. My true friends ought not to weep for me. I shall be much [iv] happier in anōr world. I could only have known misery and persecution in this they have destroyed me at last but their injured Queen forgives them.[226]

The Napoleonic wars also saw the rise of the campaign medals; a gold medal with bars is worn by the Duke of Wellington with his other Orders in the portrait by Goya in the National Gallery, London. The Prince Regent also received Orders from the allied sovereigns, sharing with Wellington the distinction of being one of the small number of Protestants to be given the Golden Fleece by the King of Spain. Later, Queen Victoria recorded her delight when, in 1834 as a young princess, she had received her first foreign Order, of Maria Luisa, from Queen Isabella of Spain.[227]

MINIATURES AND SILHOUETTES

Both men and women remained attached to miniatures worn on the finger, on the wrist or in lockets. Some were tokens of royal favour, like the Royal Family Order or like that of the King of Naples, framed in diamonds, that Viscount Castlereagh sent to his wife, Emily, commenting: 'Dearest Em, I send you an ugly face and some pretty diamonds which will become yours rather than his Sicilian majesties.'[228] She took the hint and replaced the picture with one of her own handsome husband, which she wore on her breast on all great occasions.[229]

Miniatures were treasured reminders of loved ones, and were often concealed in lockets, such as that made by Rundell, Bridge and Rundell for George IV in 1823: 'a gold engine turned locket for enamelled picture to open with a secret spring'.[230] The salesman at a fashionable jeweller's in Lady Blessington's novel, *Confessions of an Elderly Gentleman* (1836) while showing a client the diamonds and sapphires at the centre of one of the bracelets in a parure, touched the secret spring and 'the gold plate at the back flying open, discovered a small enamel miniature of Mr. Vernon'.[231] The Countess of Oxford was less discreet, and scandalised the Italian ladies at Naples in 1815 by parading with Lord Byron's miniature in the front of her girdle.[232]

Men wore miniatures in rings, in studs, and in lockets hung round the neck. The 1799 will of the Prince of Wales shows that he followed this custom, asking that 'my constant companion the picture of my beloved wife Mrs. Fitzherbert may be interred with me suspended round my neck by a ribbon as I used to wear it when I lived, placed right upon my heart'.[233] Some gentlemen set miniatures in their *fausse montres*, and in 1791 Thomas Eccleston was sent alternative designs to choose from:

we have sketched on the other side designs of setting your picture round with brilliants for a fausse montre. No. 1 represents a circle of large brilliants set transparent with blue and white enamelled borders each side of the diamonds – £120, No. 2 is a brilliant circle of smaller diamonds and may be set with or without enamel borders – £90, or with smaller diamonds 35 or 40 guineas. At the back of the fausse montre we usually introduce a blue composition and in the centre of that a medallion with a hair plait or knot and sometimes a cipher on the hair of diamonds.[234]

A variant of the miniature was the eye, painted on plaques of round, oval or heart-shaped ivory. The Prince of Wales and Mrs Fitzherbert exchanged eye miniatures set in octagonal rings,[235] and in 1799 he sent her a gold bracelet with locket containing a painting of his right eye, said to be by Richard Cosway, with the inscription on the bracelet, REJOINDRE OU MOURIR.[236] Eye miniatures might be set in lockets and also in smaller medallions to hang from a bracelet, and whole families might be commemorated in this way.[237] Settings might be enamelled, chased with gold serpents or neo-classical honeysuckle in dead gold, or framed in diamonds and pearls.[238]

From 1808 John Field, the most successful profilist of his time, was in business with John Miers; he remained in the firm after Miers died in 1821 and finally set up on his own by 1830. He received the royal appointment to William IV, Queen Adelaide and Princess Augusta. He advertised sittings of no more than five minutes, and supplied his silhouettes for bracelets and brooches, lockets and rings.[239] Unlike miniature painting, the drawing or cutting of profiles was engaged in by amateurs, whose products would be set in similar fashion by the members of their families.

JEWELLERY WITH HAIR

The hair of loved ones continued to be plaited into chains or set as curls in jewels of friendship or mourning. Thoughtful elderly people put aside a sufficient quantity of hair before they died; in 1793 Lady Bute told the maid who was cutting her hair to 'Keep this for my daughters, they will be glad of it, and very good hair it is for a woman of near seventy seven.'[240] In 1796 Viscount Castlereagh sent a locket to his future wife, Emily Hobart, followed by some of his hair to put in it; he begged her to 'wear it and be assured that it is not given with a less ardent feeling than that which you now wear as the first present I ever made to you'.[241] The love of Damon and Anna was celebrated in a set of anonymous verses in 1798 in terms of the hair treasured in a locket by Anna, whose lover exclaims:

Blest as th'immortal gods the youth
Whose hair my Anna wears;
Whose image she preserves with truth,
And views with falling tears.

The smiling girl is able at last to make Damon happy:

Hear why I prize this glittering toy:
Know, then, this hair is – yours.

And Damon is enraptured.[242]

Hair was most often enclosed in rings, either concealed and only visible when the cover was opened by its secret spring, or openly under crystal, framed by a chased gold serpent, a row of brilliants or coloured stones, and with name or cipher inscribed at the back of the bezel or inside the hoop. At Princess Mary's wedding to the Duke of Gloucester in 1816, when her arms and fingers were already laden with the sentimental jewellery given by her mother, brothers and sisters, the princess put on a ring with the hair of her mad father, George III, declaring: 'This I would not for the world omit. I have a superstitious dread of misfortune if I did.'[243]

Plain, oval, heart- or padlock-shaped lockets and brooches, sometimes embellished with pearls and gem-stones, were popular, as were diamond pins.[244] Princess Victoria was given by her mother, the Duchess of Kent, 'a lovely brooch made of her own hair'.[245] While most designs reflected current fashion, others were specially commissioned. After the death of John Keats, his friend, the artist Joseph Severn, designed a memorial brooch (now in the museum at Keats House, Hampstead) for Fanny Brawne. It is a gold Greek lyre, reproducing that carved on the poet's tomb in the Protestant cemetery at Rome, with the eight strings made from his hair, mounted under glass on an opaline base with a gold border. The poet's name is inscribed on the sound box (Plate 125). The opaline base which gives a radiant effect to the hair placed over it was generally used in memorial lockets – as in another for John Keats in the same collection, with the hair arranged in a wreath and the cipher JK in seed pearls (Plate 126). When Princess Charlotte, only child of the Prince Regent, died in childbirth in 1817, her hair was set in various memorial jewels. One of the most important was given to her uncle, the Duke of Cambridge; it is a pendant with a crowned miniature on the front and her coat-of-arms at the back. A gold and crystal urn with her hair arranged as the Prince of Wales's plumes hangs below from two chains (Plate XLIV).

Hair could also be braided into necklaces, clasped in the centre with a heart and with a cross pendant, or into chains for bracelets[246] (Plate 127). As sleeves became fuller in the 1820s, wide bracelets confined them at the wrists, with correspondingly large clasps, serpent-shaped, enamelled, and set with coloured stones or cameos. Sometimes

125 Memorial brooch to John Keats, the strings of the Greek lyre made from his hair, mounted on opaline under glass in a gold frame. Designed by Joseph Severn. Keats House, Hampstead.

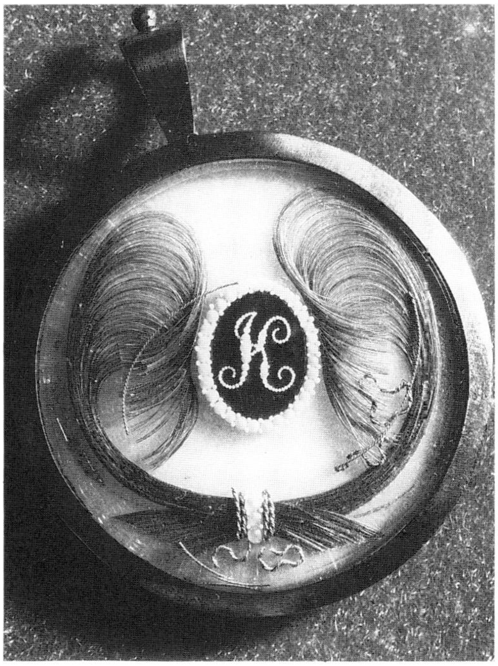

126 John Keats memorial locket, his hair arranged as a wreath and cipher JK in seed pearls. Keats House, Hampstead.

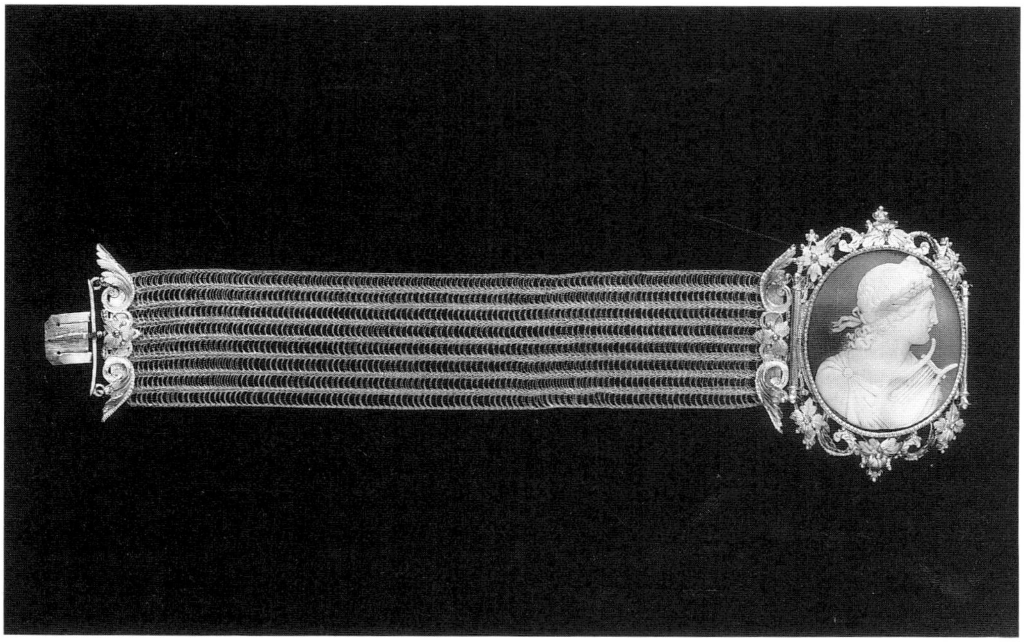

127 Bracelet with band of woven hair, clasp set with shell cameo bust of Apollo. Collection of a Scottish nobleman.

the lockets were hung from gold or pearl chains. In 1814 Lady Monson ordered from the jeweller, Robert Spilsbury, a design with six crystals enclosing hair alternating with turquoise and pearl rosettes.[247] The seven children of the seventh Earl of Denbigh gave their mother, in bed for her eighth confinement, a birthday present of a bracelet clasp with 'seven little compartments instead of gem-stones with a lock of each of their hair and one vacant for the expected little stranger'.[248]

The emotional and sentimental associations of hair jewellery were dramatised by Lady Caroline Lamb in her novel, *Glenarvon*. To mitigate the sorrow of parting from Calatha, and to bind them more closely together, Buchanan fastens round her wrist a bracelet of his braided hair with a diamond clasp inscribed with their initials and the motto STESSA SANGUE STESSA SORTE, and commands her to wear it for ever, for his sake.[249]

MOURNING JEWELLERY

The deeply rooted custom of mourning was observed with a more than usual degree of feeling when Princess Charlotte died. Henry Ellis, the Exeter jeweller, recorded the event in his journal, and its effect on his business:

> Being considered a promising scion of Royalty brighter days for England were looked forward to when she should become the occupant of the throne instead of her profligate and licentious father . . . articles of mourning were in such demand that all the stock of black in the kingdom came into request . . . my stock of black jewellery was not at this time very extensive, nor to say the truth were the patterns of the newest kind . . . this gave the first impetus to that particular part of my business after which I always continued to keep up a good stock of those articles.[250]

Richard Rush, the American ambassador, who arrived in London on Christmas Eve 1817, observed that everyone was in black, and was struck by the solemn effect created by the universal expression of national bereavement.[251]

Women wore whole parures of jet beads or black-enamelled jewellery – long jet earrings reaching half-way down the throat, and brooches in the form of reversed crescents.[252] For men there were rings, buckles and buttons enamelled black and white. The traditional symbols of butterflies, torches, crosses, ciphers and inscriptions such as MEMORIAM AETERNAM, the forget-me-not, the rosebud, the snake and the celestial crown were applied to lockets, bracelet clasps, rings, brooches and medallions worn from a black velvet ribbon round the neck.[253]

DRESS

New fashions in dress followed the French Revolution. The brocades and silks stiff with gold and silver embroidery were discarded in favour of lighter, softer fabrics made up into tunics 'à la Vestale' or 'à la Diane' inspired by classical sculpture. The waist was placed high on the bosom and emphasised by belts with ornamental clasps, with the drapery falling in loose folds to the ground, as in classical statues. Pairs of brooches would be pinned on the shoulders of the dress, the low neckline was filled with gold chains or necklaces, and the arms, left bare by short sleeves, adorned with bracelets and armlets. The hair was swept high 'à la Sappho', and kept in place by bandeaux or combs, leaving the ears showing.

Changes in style became more rapid. In 1797 the *Lady's Magazine* reported that simplicity was the criterion of good taste and diamonds wholly out of fashion except at court. Two years later Beau Nash observed the growing taste for Eastern magnificence, with dress becoming more brilliant every day.[254] The picturesque clothing of far-away places was adopted for its exotic and literary associations, and Turkish velvet and crimson turbans trimmed with aigrettes evoked the splendour of oriental court life.

Past fashions depicted in family portraits were revived for fancy-dress balls, such as that held at Carlton House in 1819 when the American ambassador, Rush, was impressed by the care taken to avoid anachronisms.[255] Lady Trevilion, in the novel *Almack's*, was 'always trying for effect, so today she dresses after a Murillo, tomorrow perhaps she will be Rembrandt's wife. In the morning she is Mary Queen of Scots, or the Lady of the Lake, in the evening Raphael's Madonna or Titian's mistress.'[256] Soon these historical costumes were worn at Court (Plate XLIV); the Duchess of Sutherland's dress for the Birthday Drawing-Room in 1831 was admired as 'the most Queen Elizabeth effect possible'.[257]

Around 1830 the fully developed Romantic style came into its own: bell-shaped skirts meeting the bodice at the natural waist, balloon sleeves, and bâteau neckline revealing the shoulders, which were covered by a deep collar or lace fichu during the day. A distinction between informal and formal wear for day and evening continued to apply to both dress and jewellery. Diamonds, pearls and precious stones were reserved for court or full dress, and gold beads, strings of coral, amber, cornelian and garnet beads, long gold chains with eye-glass, watch or vinaigrette, and sentimental jewels were kept for informal morning and afternoon dress.

Men's dress, too, changed, although court dress clung to older modes. At the time of Waterloo, the well-dressed Englishman wore a

> coat of light blue or snuff colour with brass buttons, the tail reaching nearly to the heels, a gigantic bunch of seals dangled from his fob, while his pantaloons were short and tight at the knees. His toilette was completed by a spacious waistcoat with voluminous muslin cravat and frilled shirt.[258]

Hats were either encircled by a velvet band with a buckle, or cocked with jewelled button and loop, while dandified men loaded their waistcoats with glittering and elaborately worked chains. Beau Brummel copied the chain hung as a warning outside

Newgate Prison for the guard chain on his watch, but only allowed two links to show between the waistcoat button and fob pocket. The quality of the jewels on his cravat and cuffs was another sign of the taste of a man of fashion. One colonel in a Guards regiment paid £25 a year to Storr and Mortimer for the loan of a new set of studs every Saturday night during the London season.[259] The young Disraeli, well-known for his elegance, contrasted the jewels worn by characters in his novel *Henrietta Temple*. Mr Bond Sharpe, a model of fashion, dressed entirely in black; his studs, made from huge turquoises, were his only ornament. The money-lender and coal-merchant, Mr Leveson, with a green velvet waistcoat guarded by a gold chain 'which would have been the envy of a new town council', wore an immense opal on his shirt front, and covered his fingers with very fine rings. Count Alcibiades de Mirabel was proud of 'his wrist bands turned up with compact precision and fastened by jewelled studs'.[260]

Rings were as much in evidence as seals, and were worn on several fingers; the Duke of Myrtlegrove in *Glenarvon* is described as 'more enamoured of his diamond ring and broach than of the brightest eyes that ever gazed on him'.[261] Men also wore memorial rings, signets and emblematic snake rings as well as miniatures depicting politicians, such as Charles James Fox, or national heroes like Nelson.

When Emily Ann Strutt was born in 1790, her father ordered himself a very fine suit with large buttons, an inch or more in diameter, painted with landscapes.[262] In the

Fig. 38 Designs for stickpins for men by Jacob Petit.
Victoria and Albert Museum.

nineteenth century, designs were less individual; they might be worked in silver or gold filigree, but were rarely enamelled or jewelled. The English fashion seems to have been for rather larger buttons than on the continent, to judge from portraits by the Swiss artist, Agasse (1767–1849), who worked in both countries.[263] Sets of silver buttons with different animals of the chase, struck in relief or incised on mother-of-pearl, were sewn on the jackets worn by English sportsmen in the country.[264] Lord Ossulston's stag dies were used by Garrard in 1835 to make forty-eight gilt coat buttons and twenty-eight for the waistcoat, and in 1837 a further twenty waistcoat buttons were ordered.[265] The sportsman might choose a fist-fight, a hound or a fox's mask enamelled or carved from Labrador spar for his shirt pin (one of Petit's designs is of pugilists fighting – see Fig. 38), but after 1840, according to Surtees's character, Jorrocks, no gentleman would be seen with such things.[266]

Typical jewellery for a gentleman was supplied by Garrard in 1836 to the Revd E. J. Daniell: gold chain, onyx ring engraved with arms and on the shank for hair, a chain with 'rings for Briquet and keys', an opal and diamond ring set in fine gold and an engine-turned gold watch. They repaired his gold eye-glass at the same time.[267]

10

The categories of later Georgian jewellery 1790 – 1837

PARURES

The hero of Lady Blessington's novel *Confessions of an Elderly Gentleman* (1836) recounts a visit to Rundell and Bridge which ends in the purchase of 'a necklace of rubies, set in diamonds, *requiring* [my italics] ear-rings, brooches, head ornaments, and bracelets, *en suite*'.[1] Such matching parures were *de rigueur* with court dress (Plate XLV): Mrs Benckendorff and the ladies attending Princess Charlotte at her marriage in 1816 wore matching sets of amethysts, chrysolites and topazes provided by the Prince Regent.[2] Smaller sets, demi-parures, could consist of various combinations: earrings with matching Sévigné brooch or Maltese cross, or a necklace with bracelets or earrings, or, like that supplied to Thomas Fitzgerald by Garrard in 1837, a pair of earrings with a brooch with a drop in the centre, set with pink topazes.[3] In addition to the main jewels for head, neck and wrists, various accessories – smelling-bottles, belt clasps and heart-shaped lockets – were also designed to match the main items.

JEWELLERY FOR THE HEAD

In London as in Paris, head jewellery was inspired by the pomp of Imperial Rome. Tiaras, diadems, coronets, bandeaux and wreaths, crowning unpowdered hair dressed in curls or braids, gave an air of magnificence to formal occasions. Richly studded with brilliants or coloured stones, or hung with pear pearls or drops swinging from jewelled circles, they were placed over foil-spangled veils or worn with plumes. According to the *Lady's Magazine*, Jane, Duchess of Gordon, appeared at Queen Charlotte's Drawing-Room in 1806 wearing 'wreaths and rosettes of diamonds and a large plume of ostrich feathers'.[4] These plumes, white or coloured, were held in steel or brilliant 'porte-plumes' and made the wearer seem taller.[5] Other severely classical designs were wrought from 'dead'[6] or bright-coloured gold; wearing one of these in 1816, Viscountess Castlereagh was compared to a Priestess of the Sun.[7] Her diamond bandeau, which could be divided into brooches, was of a scroll pattern.[8]

Motifs from antiquity predominated: honeysuckle, Greek key fret, ears of corn, wreaths of noble laurel and the festive vine, in coloured gold with bunches of cabochon amethysts or garnet grapes – and the olive, symbol of peace.[9] Such wreaths were usually constructed in two parts, with branches or festoons meeting at a central motif with an important stone, as in the 'brilliant tiara consisting of a double olive sprig meeting at the centre where it is divided by a plant with leaves and buds the latter formed of a single spread brilliant of pure water and an umbellated flower in the centre on a spring wire', sold at Christie's in 1829.[10] Princess Elizabeth ordered a bandeau of formal scroll and leaf pattern from Rundell, Bridge and Rundell in 1818,[11] and a tiara in the Newcastle collection was of this design, with the optional fitting of a large peacock's feather which could be inserted behind the central scroll.[12]

Naturalistic wreaths of roses, jessamine and pinks never went out of fashion (Fig. 39), with the blooms mounted on tremblers for extra sparkle.[13]

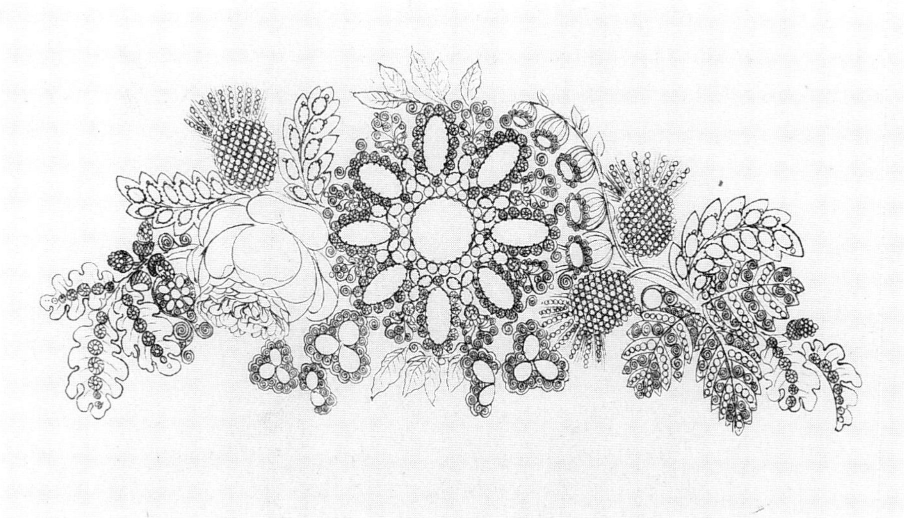

Fig. 39 Design for a naturalistic head ornament by Jacob Petit. Victoria and Albert Museum.

The tiara of Henrietta, wife of the fourth Duke of Portland, was of this kind, being composed of wild roses, all paved with diamonds.[14] Worn by married women only, tiaras were appropriate wedding presents. Lord Seymour, heir to the Duke of Somerset, ordered a tiara of diamonds and emeralds for his bride, Jane Georgiana, to wear over her veil when they married in 1830.[15]

The tops of the gilt or tortoiseshell combs worn either at the front or back of the head were similarly decorated with either formal neo-classical or naturalistic motifs. The fashion is described by Mrs Calvert, who went to Queen Charlotte's Drawing-Room in 1805 with her 'hair without powder, turned up in a bunch behind with a diamond comb low on the forehead in little curls, a wreath of diamonds with some purple velvet and seven flat white feathers'.[16] These ornaments could be costly, like the arrow set with a large diamond surmounting a comb ordered for Princess Charlotte in 1818, or Lady

Walsingham's brilliant comb valued at £360 by Rundell, Bridge and Rundell in 1819.[17] Some were designed to be used in other ways as well, like the 'brilliant comb composed of three brilliant brooches to be worn separately' ordered by the Prince Regent in 1818.[18] Contrast of material and colour appealed to Lady Monson, who bought a comb embellished with pearls and amethyst drops from her jeweller, Fletcher, in 1814.[19] Cheapest of all were gilt combs; their price was determined by size.

Feather jewels were royal favourites. The Duchess of York wore one to a court reception in 1791, and the Prince of Wales gave them to his sisters, Princess Amelia and Princess Sophia.[20] In a portrait by Peltro Tomkins, Princess Charlotte Augusta (1766–1828) wore her diamond feather just above the forehead, with the tall ostrich plumes towering behind.[21] The 'peacock's tail ornament set with amethysts, rubies, turquoises and emeralds' which George IV bought from Rundell, Bridge and Rundell in 1821 may have been for Lady Conyngham, who was observed by the Hon. Henry Edward Fox in 1822 'with a profusion on jewels and a peacock's tail in jewels on her head'.[22]

Other designs used included formal scrolls and clusters, rosettes [23] 'ears of corn in brilliants'[24] and sprigs of flowers (Fig. 40):

Fig. 40 Designs for floral sprays for the head by Jacob Petit.
Victoria and Albert Museum.

roses in full bloom, fuchsia, honeysuckle and pansies, hydrangeas and lilies.[25] They might be composed of pearls as well as brilliants and coloured stones, as in the 'rose sprig showing blossom, flower and leaf composed of rubies, emeralds and rose diamonds' sold in 1825.[26] The Duchess of Kingston wore a dove in her hair, and a bird of paradise, 'the body composed of a very fine opal with emeralds, the wings of rubies

128 The Countess of Blessington wearing a jewelled comb and ferronière, holding a vinaigrette. Engraved portrait after A. E. Chalon, National Gallery of Ireland.

and brilliants', was made for George IV in 1827.[27] For her birthday in 1809, the Princess Sophia asked him to give her a butterfly similar to the one her sister, Princess Amelia, wore in her hair.[28] It could have been either alone or combined with crescent moon or sprigs of orange flowers.[29] The crescent moon, symbol of the chaste goddess Diana might be set inexpensively with pearls and topazes, or more grandly, as for Lady Grenville in 1806 who wore a 'magnificent crescent of diamonds out of which from behind issued a beautiful turret of white ostrich feathers the whole encircled with a magnificent diamond bandeau'.[30] Stars were also effective, worn either singly or in a set.[31] Other classical motifs were Cupid's arrow (sometimes with his bow), Apollo's lyre and Mercury's caduceus.[32] All these ornaments looked well set against rich dark hair, or pinned to turbans, caps or hats of black velvet turned up in front and backed by white ostrich plumes or bird of Paradise feathers.

Peeresses wore a new fashion at the coronation of William IV the ferronière, so called from the portrait by Leonardo da Vinci of the blacksmith's wife beloved by Francis I. The ferronière was twice defined, in 1831 as a 'narrow plait of hair with a small gold or jewelled ornament', and in 1832 as 'a delicate gold chain and lozenge cross[ing] the brow à la Ferronière'[33] (Plate 128). The centre ornament could be worn as a drop over the brow, or it might be a cameo or large cabochon stone surrounded by smaller stones matching the necklace.[34] On her fourteenth birthday the future queen, Princess Victoria, was given two ferronières, one of pink topazes, the other of turquoises.[35] In 1837 Garrard strung Miss de Rothschild's pearls as a ferronière and made up centres from two head ornaments: one of diamonds and emeralds, the other of diamonds and pearls.[36] At the other extreme, a cheap version was supplied in the same year, made from imitation pearls and emeralds on a gilt chain, price 11 shillings.[37]

EARRINGS

Earrings were designed for both dress and undress occasions, and the distinction seems to have been based on the materials used rather than on style. Amber, coloured beads and wrought gold were worn in the morning and afternoon, and the more valuable pearls and precious gems were reserved for evening dress. Ear-piercing was advertised by jewellers, and although the operation was dreaded, there was still no satisfactory alternative to hooks passed through the ear-lobes.[38]

Since they framed the face, the best stones were often set in earrings, but colour was also an important consideration. Bright stones – aquamarines, chrysoprases, golden and pink topazes, coral, malachite and bloodstone – were mounted in chased and enamelled gold, scroll-work or filigree. Sometimes strong tints were contrasted with others: opals with emeralds, turquoises with amethysts and topazes, brilliants with turquoise or sardonyx, garnets with pearls.[39] Pearls might be set with rich purple amethysts, and worn as star-like studs or as single or girandole drops hanging from brilliant tops, or strung into loops and tassels.[40]

At the King's Birthday Drawing-Room of 1790, according to the *Lady's Magazine*, 'the earrings most in fashion were clump earrings in the shape of a button of gold. This fashion was lately brought over from Paris by Lady Duncannon. Others which were likewise much worn were long earrings of filigree work.'[41] The emphasis on length continued, and in 1828 the same magazine reported that 'the length of ear pendants is indeed remarkable'. Very long earrings were worn *en suite* with an amethyst and burnished gold ferronière and necklace at dinner in 1833.[42]

Top and drop pendants predominate, with single or girandole drops, a smaller stone sometimes set between the two elements and also a bow. In 1818 Rundell, Bridge and Rundell sold 'a pair of brilliant cluster new pattern long drop earrings'.[43] Coloured drops – emeralds, sapphires and amethysts – might also be enclosed in brilliant loops or festoons of laurel.[44] Hoops set with brilliants were always in fashion for full dress wear, and set with turquoises in gold for undress.[45] Drops hung from serpents, with coils worked in chased and enamelled gold, and heads studded with turquoises, or rubies and sapphires.[46] Floral designs – turquoise sprig, flower baskets, forget-me-nots, roses and lilies – were smaller versions of those worn as aigrettes or brooches[47] (Fig. 41).

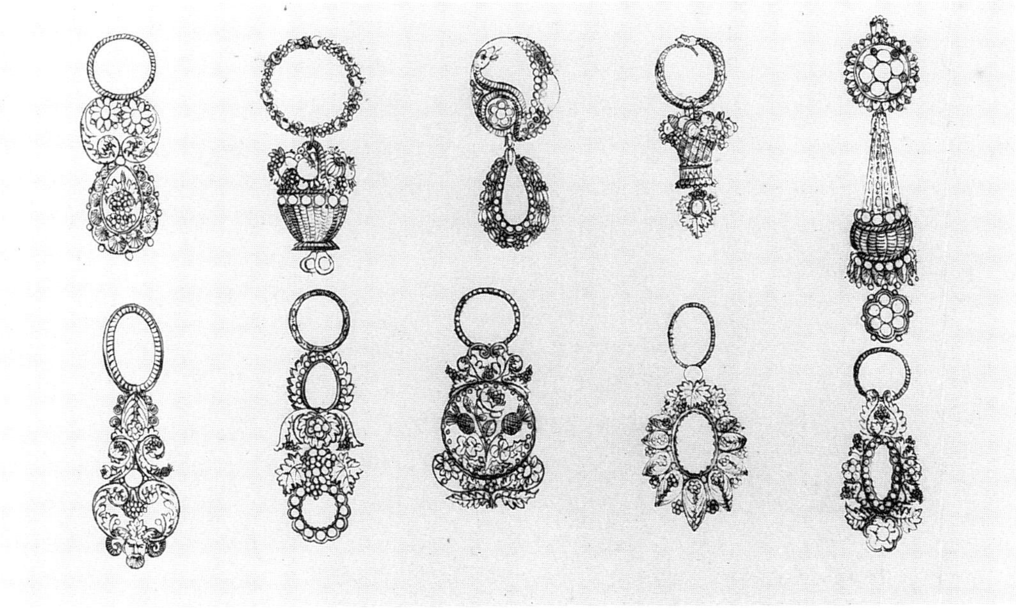

Fig. 41 Designs for earrings by Jacob Petit. Victoria and Albert Museum.

Egyptian motifs became popular in 1823, as the *Lady's Monthly Museum* reported: 'the favourite earring is the Isis pendant formed of pure gold and ornamented with small Egyptian hieroglyphs exquisitely wrought'.[48]

NECKLACES

Necklaces looked particularly well with the low necklines of early-nineteenth-century dresses. Designs vary: there were short chokers (Plate XLVI), single and multiple rows of stones strung in festoons, and Arabian-style negligées ending in a pair of tassels thrown over the shoulders. The London market could offer a wider range of stones than ever before, but the diamond, rose- and brilliant-cut, reigned supreme (Plate 133).

The largest and finest brilliants in silver collets were linked in rivières, such as that worn by the Duchess of Northumberland when she accompanied her husband to Paris in 1825, when he represented George IV at the coronation of Charles X. The stones were graduated in size to each side of a large brilliant, which had been lent by Rundell, Bridge and Rundell to George IV for his coronation crown in 1821, and which was subsequently bought by the duke.[49] Multiple strands of smaller stones might be joined by rosettes with an ornamental medallion or plaque in the middle, or the very smallest stones could be composed into round clusters or chains of openwork links. In 1816 Princess Mary bought a fringe pattern consisting of 'separate pieces to hang', and in 1823 George IV acquired another more elaborate variation of the fringe style, 4 feet 10 inches long, set with 3175 brilliants and roses in 371 separate sections.[50]

The rich colours of sapphires, rubies, and emeralds might be set off by the white diamonds framing them (Plate XLVII), set as spacers between them, or strung in festoons linking them together.[51] Diamonds also enhanced the less expensive but equally decorative amethysts, turquoises and topazes[52] (Plate XLVII). Coloured stones might also be mixed together: amethysts with chrysolites, or turquoises with rubies and pearls, in rainbow-like splendour.[53] As an alternative to diamonds, pearls might be used to encircle rubies, turquoises and opals. In 1829 a necklace of Ceylon rubies was 'set round with pearls à l'antique'.[54] Those with more severe tastes preferred the uniform character of a single colour richly set in filigree worked into patterns of scrolls and rosettes called cannetille (after embroidery in gold or silver thread) and linked by strong chains, or mounted in chased gold leaves, either matt or brightly burnished.[55] Garnets were still popular; they were cut into conventional flower heads, carved into beads, and strung in festoons, 'worn in rows twisted and finished in front with an elegantly wrought gold ornament on each side of which depends a tassel à la negligée', or 'richly set in a Gothic pattern'.[56] Quality was good and garnets and other coloured stones might be set transparent, matching in size and colour.

Amber, transparent as well as opaque, and hardstones, in the form of beads or plaques set in openwork gold mounts or chased gold leaves, could be linked by gold chains or strung together with pearl spacers.[57] While some were uniform in colour, others were composed of a variety of stones 'in gold filigree enchained together'.[58] Striped agates and sardonyxes were faceted to reveal the contrasting layers, and others, like cat's-eyes and cornelians, were polished smooth and rounded so as to show the rich colour and lustre to advantage.[59] Occasionally, hardstone beads might be fluted or grooved, like the basalt necklace 'cut in the form of a melon with gold chains and mounts', or carved into acorns.[60] Hardstones could also be strung in elegant neo-classical designs, like the 'gold wreath necklace with beautiful cornelian medallions' sold at auction in 1804.[61]

Pearls were knotted into necklaces of festoons, or in single, double or multiple rows. To find a specimen of the best pearls – round, large and white – one would have to choose the wedding present the Prince Regent gave his daughter in 1816: 'a fine large pearl necklace containing fifty four pieces with a single stone brilliant clasp', which cost £861.[62] The Duchess of Northumberland in 1836 had a small necklace of two rows, and also a grander one with three rows, rosettes and a tassel.[63] A design later associated with Queen Alexandra and the Edwardian era was already in fashion in 1832; it consisted of six or seven rows of large pearls, 'fastened on the top of the chemisette and forming what is called a collier de chien round the throat'.[64] In 1836 Garrard mounted Mrs St John Leger's chrysolites and pearls 'in a handsome gold necklace'.[65] Pearls were also enlivened by sparkling brilliants, with the centre emphasised by a drop or plaque set with a gem-stone of contrasting colour such as an amethyst, an emerald or a sardonyx cameo.[66] The small seed pearls were strung into wreaths, linked together by amethysts or pink topaz pansies, or else they could be massed into bunches of grapes amidst chased gold vine leaves, made into flowers and foliage like hop blossom, and joined by triple chains of gold and pearls.[67]

Contrasting gold, of different colours, matt or burnished, chased or enamelled, was also an important element in necklace design. There were wrought gold carcanets 'in the antique style', cannetille settings, and woven or corded gold wire, which was made into snakes with pearl heads and tails.[68] Some designs were figurative, like the 'gold matt necklace of large links the clasps set with small turquoises, the plates richly chased in gold in three colours with boys in relief and butterflies set with small coloured stones'.[69]

Necklaces could be clasped, either in the front or at the back, by a snap set with a gem: a diamond, or a large coloured stone such as a ruby, or a cameo.[70]

CHAINS AND SAUTOIRS

Worn round the neck in single or multiple rows, sometimes in festoons, chains looked well with the Grecian style of dress fashionable at the turn of the century. Mr Vernon, squire of Sudbury in Derbyshire, gave his daughter, Georgiana, a gold chain for her fifteenth birthday, and in 1800 Viscount Castlereagh wrote to his wife from the Foreign Office apologising for the delay in obtaining gold chains both strong and long.[71] They were useful as well as decorative: watches, crosses, cameos, hearts, padlocks, eye-glasses, vinaigrettes and other trinkets could be hung from them, falling down to the waist. Mrs Benson, the mother of a rich banker, is introduced to the reader by Lady Charlotte Bury in her novel *Marriage in High Life* (1828), 'nervously twisting the gold chain round her neck to which was suspended her daughter's portrait'.[72] By the 1830s chains were considered too florid by those of refined taste, such as the elegant Lady Bellair in Disraeli's novel *Henrietta Temple*, who lives in a house decorated in the classical style of Thomas Hope, and is prejudiced against the worthy but unsmart Mrs Twoshoes because of her gold chains.[73]

Whether light or massive, wrought in vari-coloured golds, chains came in different patterns: curb, cable, Maltese, Damascus, Lisbon, Brazilian, Trinchinopoly, Manila and Venetian are all mentioned in this period.[74] Others were made from links of square plates, beads, globes, scales and oak levaes.[75] The same patterns were repeated for earrings and bracelets.[76] In 1832 the *Lady's Magazine* reported that 'enamelled chains of massive gold lozenges and roses placed alternately are much worn: they hang to the belt and are very becoming'; the lozenges might be filled with seed pearl.[77] Garrard sold silver chains as well. In 1836 Viscount Sidney purchased 'a silver muff chain, gilt inside'.[78] They might be fastened with Gothic-style clasps embellished with bright turquoises, with hands (single or clasped together), or set with cameos, coloured stones and pearls.[79]

LOCKETS

Mrs Grant of Rothiemurchus went to a rout at the Duchess of Gordon's in 1804 dressed in 'a gown of white satin trimmed with white velvet cut in a formal pattern, then quite the rage, a copy of the Grecian borders in Mr. Hope's book . . . She had feathers in her hair and a row of pearls on her neck from which depended a large diamond locket.'[80] These lockets enclosed hair or miniatures covered by glass, crystal or picture diamonds.[81] The less expensive cases were made of filigree, or engine-turned, and set with clusters of small coloured stones and seed pearls, with the loops always part of the design[82] (Plate XLIX).

The hair devices – classical urns, allegorical female figures, ciphers and pastorals – of the late eighteenth century were succeeded by straightforward symbols of sentiment. Gold hearts were left plain or studded with brilliants and coloured stones: turquoises, opals, rubies, jasper and amethysts.[83] They might be inscribed; they might bear the symbol of eternity, the snake biting its tail, or the butterfly emblem of Psyche; or they might be guarded by padlocks and framed in laurel.[84]

The symbolism of the snake was popular and it could be the dominant motif, as in a 'beautiful brilliant locket consisting of an extremely fine and coiled serpent formed of beautiful yellow brilliants and holding from its mouth a large pendant pink topaz with smaller brilliant drop'.[85] Alternatively it could be combined with the butterfly, as in 'an elegant circular brilliant locket with diamond serpent round and diamond butterfly in blue enamel'.[86] The padlock was another favourite motif, sometimes expensively set with diamonds, with a diamond key and gold chains.[87] Other lockets were designed with pansies, forget-me-nots and books, all of which might have miniature padlocks and keys or hearts hanging from them.[88] The enclosed hair was sometimes visible through a glass window.

CROSSES

Describing the London fashions in 1801, the *Lady's Magazine* noted that 'crosses of white cornelian edged with gold are universal and bestow even to a modern belle a certain nun-like air'.[89] They were part of parures and demi-parures, and were worn as brooches, or as pendants hanging from the necklace, chain or black velvet ribband.

There was a plain gold convent cross worn at home over a lace frill, and jewelled Latin, Greek and Maltese crosses. These last were the choice of the Prince of Wales, who bought them, set with brilliants, for his sisters, Princess Amelia and Princess Mary, in 1806 and 1807, and for his daughter, Princess Charlotte, in 1811.[90] It was a design which showed off good stones admirably, the best being open-set and enclosed by pavé borders.[91] In 1822 the *Lady's Magazine* commented on a new fashion for 'Mary Stuart's chaplets with a St. Andrew's cross of brilliants round the neck', with different diamond crosses: St Augustine's, Maltese and St Andrew's, of which 'we must say at present the St. Andrew's is the favourite'.[92] Some were combined with hearts – for instance, the 'Jeannette cross and heart of pearls suspended from a braid of dark hair',[93] and the gold cross and heart hung from a black velvet ribbon.[94]

The plain shape of the cross could be ornamented in different ways. Upright and arms might be adorned with sprigs of leaves and flowers, which could be set with gemstones, or the entire cross might be composed of brilliants alternating with turquoise rosettes.[95] Bright contrasts of colour also enlivened designs – brilliants with rubies, pink topazes with turquoises, emeralds with rubies and pearls.[96] Some crosses were plain arrangements of semi-precious stones such as topazes, either set open or close-set and foiled like that given by John Keats to Fanny Brawne's sister Margaret[97] (Plate 129). Jacob Petit's designs were more elaborate, with decorative motifs of shells and flowers, the symbolic snake, the anchor, the ardent heart and the Holy Dove, as well as a knight in armour and St George battling with the dragon (Fig. 42).

129 Amethyst cross in a gold mount, given by John Keats to Margaret Brawne. Keats House, Hampstead.

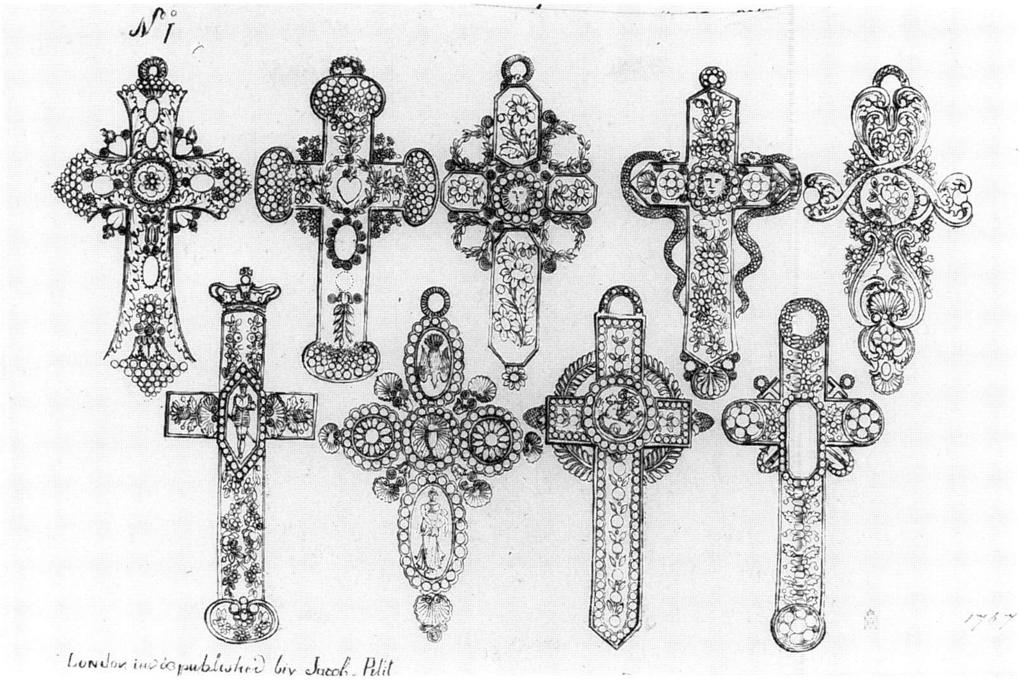

Fig. 42 Designs for crosses by Jacob Petit. Victoria and Albert Museum.

Enamel was also used, and the Duke of York owned a cross 'enamelled to imitate lapis lazuli and cornelians the extremities embellished with gold filigree and set with turquoises'.[98]

In 1819 the Prince Regent bought 'a fine antique cross composed of oriental coloured stones, enamel etc' from Rundell, Bridge and Rundell, and this may be the one given to the Marchioness of Londonderry.[99] It is an interesting example of early Gothic Revival jewellery (Plate XXXIX). The 'Holyrood or Mary Stuart's cross' hanging from a weighty gold chain, fashionable in 1822 and must also have been derived from medieval or Renaissance crosses.[100] Other examples of such historically inspired jewels were the medallion with a ruby cross in the middle after the 'pattern of Joan of Navarre' and two crosses 'in fine Gothic pattern' all bought by George IV.[101] His sister, Princess Sophia, also owned a cross of this style, with tracery and crockets on the arms and upright.[102]

BROOCHES

Brooches could be worn pinned to turbans or to the feathers in the up-turned brims of hats, fastening shawls and capes, looping back folds, confining lace at the throat, attaching drapery, worn à la Sévigné at the front of the neckline, or mounted in the centre of tiaras and necklaces. Although they sometimes contained hair or miniatures, most were decorative clusters of gem-stones (Plate 130) or simple geometric shapes:

130 Baroness Dufferin and Clandeboye with jewelled clasps on her sleeves, two large brooch pendants on her bodice and a snake bracelet on her wrist. After the portrait by J. H. Robinson. National Gallery of Ireland.

rectangles, circles, ovals and lozenges set with a variety of stones, of which the grandest were diamonds. Large emeralds, sapphires or rubies and turquoises might be framed with pearls, or white or coloured brilliants, and with attached drops, either pear pearls or stones. Typical was the 'large lozenge shape brilliant brooch with a very fine emerald in the centre and ditto India cut solid emerald drop to suspend to ditto with brilliant frame around' bought by George IV in 1820.[103] Mrs Toree had Garrard mount her garnets as a Sévigné in coloured gold in 1837.[104] Other cheaper stones – jacinths, chrysolites, peridots, aquamarines, amethysts and topazes – were similarly set in filigree or chased gold foliate mounts, sometimes studded with smaller stones of contrasting colours like the 'beautiful brooch composed of a large square amethyst in filigree border set with pearls and turquoises and with a pendant heart' sold at auction in 1816.[105] Hardstones – jasper, sardonyx and moss agate, prized on account of their unusual markings – were also mounted in brooches, as were *lusus naturae* such as a baroque pearl of grotesque shape resembling a tortoise.[106]

Brooches in the form of insects, flies and butterflies (Plate L), fluttering on trembler springs, might be made of gold filigree and pearls, or set with coloured stones and brilliants – like the brilliant fly with an emerald back sold to the Prince of Wales by Rundell, Bridge and Rundell in 1805.[107] A butterfly might perch on an orange-flower sprig, but most flowers were presented on their own: pearl hop blossoms, roses of wrought gold and rose- or brilliant-cut diamonds, turquoise forget-me-nots, amethyst violets, and emerald and diamond bouquets of lilies of the valley.[108] In 1823 the *Lady's Monthly Museum* described the latest elegant novelty: a chaplet brooch formed of pink topazes, the foliage representing oak leaves, 'wrought in the most exquisite manner'.[109]

In the novel *Glenarvon*, Alice entreats Lord Glenarvon to wear a pansy brooch in memory of one who loved him, inscribed HEART'S EASE TO YOU BUT TRISTE PENSÉE POUR MOI, and she wore one herself.[110] Such brooches were wrought in gold and set with a variety of stones, principally amethysts and yellow topazes with a sprinkling of brilliants.[111] Vine leaf brooches were associated with Bacchus and happiness; sometimes they had bunches of grapes attached, and were worn in pairs.[112] Lady Monson bought a pair in 1814, set with turquoises and pearl centres.[113] Vine leaves were also entwined round lyre brooches (Plate LI), and Mrs Planta, daughter of Queen Charlotte's Assistant Wardrobe-Keeper, who was a musician of professional standard, wore one fastening the drapery at her neck in the 1804 portrait by Sir Thomas Lawrence.[114] Bought at a cost of £787 10*s*, the 'fine large brilliant arrow with brilliant festoons and drapery, diamond motto, large sapphire brooch in the centre set with brilliants', which the Prince of Wales gave to Queen Charlotte on her birthday in 1805, was one of the most important jewels on the theme of Cupid.[115] In the same sentimental vein were brooches designed as keys and snakes, such as the 'small gold snake brooch and heart drop' which Sir Richard Hussey bought from Garrard in 1837.[116]

The largest brooches adorned the centre of the bosom, and during the Christmas season of 1828 George IV bought no less than four: a very elegant ruby and brilliant stomacher (£295), another with emeralds and brilliants (£278), a third with brilliants (£400), and the fourth a 'fine ruby stomacher with fuchsia sprig' (£360).[117]

BUCKLES AND CLASPS FOR THE GIRDLE

Very rich women, such as the Duchess of Rutland, the Duchess of Buccleuch and the Marchioness of Londonderry, who owned quantities of diamonds, had some of them set in belts which emphasised the waistline, which was now raised high to just below the bosom.[118] As a cheaper alternative, garnets might be similarly set in bands ending in tassels;[119] pearls too were worked into ropes for the waist, called cordeliers.[120] Such jewelled belts were exceptional, and most were of leather or velvet fastened by a single or double buckle.

According to the *Lady's Monthly Museum* in 1820, the 'cestus à la Grecque was fastened by two brilliant clasps', and the stones used were generally of uniform colour: aquamarines, topazes, pairs of oval sardonyxes, bloodstones or cornelians, mounted in chased gold or filigree.[121] A round clasp enamelled blue and set round with pearls was sold in 1819.[122] The two parts could be joined by a snake: 'a girdle clasp of two noble amethysts very pure and fine set in delicately chased gold openwork wreath and connected by a double serpent with brilliants' was sold by Christie's in 1812.[123] The

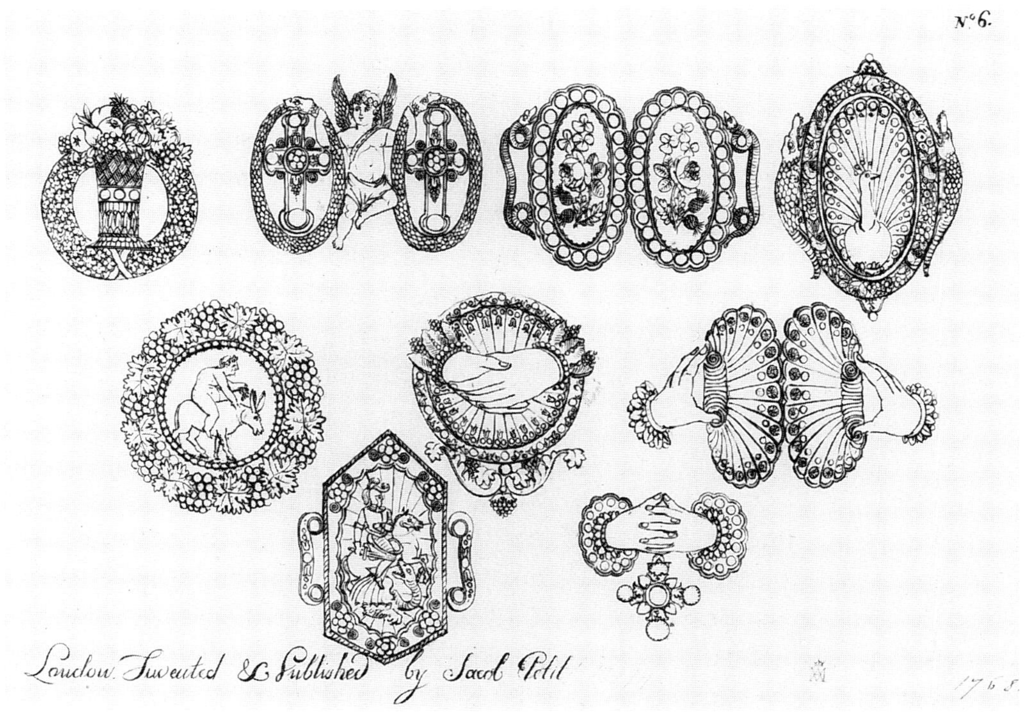

Fig. 43 Designs for belt clasps by Jacob Petit. Victoria and Albert Museum.

Lady's Magazine in 1823 described a duke's daughter receiving guests at home with her waist encircled by a black velvet band clasped with fine brilliants,[124] while the Duchess of Northumberland had a large amethyst mounted in a gold filigree buckle and set round with pearls.[125]

Cheaper versions might be set with coq-de-perle or Egyptian pebble. Gold buckles were made with the Union Wreath – entwined roses, thistles and shamrocks – at the time of the Act of Union in 1801, or with hands, beringed and with ruffles at the wrists.[126] At Christmas 1836 Princess Victoria's mother gave her a belt buckle of massive gold with two snakes[127] – not unlike the snake designs shown in Fig. 43.

In 1830 it was announced that the 'ceinture must be very broad and it is *de rigueur* that the buckle which fastens it must be of massive gold and of the Gothic form'.[128]

SHOULDER CLASPS

In 1798 the *Lady's Monthly Museum* recommended pairs of clasps to fasten the newly fashionable muslin robes at the shoulders.[129] These might be cornelian with pink, or pearls with lilac. Other pairs were set with brilliants, brilliants and sapphires, turquoises and topazes, and amethysts, topazes and brilliants in pansies.[130]

BRACELETS AND ARMLETS

Bracelets could be worn from wrist to elbow by heiresses, according to Charlotte M. Yonge in *Heartsease* (Chapter 5) and by older women like Mrs Major Ponto in Thackeray's *Book of Snobs*, who wore 'about nine bracelets and bangles consisting of chains and padlocks, the Major's miniature and a variety of brass serpents with fiery ruby or tender turquoise eyes writhing up to her elbow in the most profuse contortions'.[131]

Since no one could have too many bracelets, they made ideal presents. When twenty ladies of London society subscribed to give a jewel to Princess Lieven, wife of the retiring Russian ambassador, as a token of their regard on her leaving England, they chose a bracelet. It was a large pearl bracelet inscribed with all their names and the words TESTIMONY OF REGARD, REGRET AND AFFECTION PRESENTED TO THE PRINCESS LIEVEN ON HER DEPARTURE, BY SOME ENGLISH LADIES OF HER PARTICULAR ACQUAINTANCE, JULY 1834.[132]

As sleeves grew fuller, the bracelets confining them at the wrist grew broader (Plate 131). Although they were often made in matching pairs, it was observed in 1828 that 'the fashion of odd bracelets still prevails. On one wrist is a superb cameo head clasping a band of dark braided hair while the other wrist is distinguished by fine oval pieces of onyx or agate distinctly set in wrought gold.'[133] Pearls could be worn strung in rows or trellis patterns, sometimes mixed with turquoises. For formal occasions chains of

131 The Duchess of Rutland wearing bracelets on full sleeves and holding a lorgnette attached to a long chain. Portrait by M. Archer Shee. P. and D. Colnaghi.

precious stones, like the Duchess of Northumberland's triple rows of diamonds (see above, p. 307), would be preferred. Brilliants, in collets or clusters, might also be set with sapphires, opals, emeralds, rubies and even elk's 'claws'.[134] For her fifteenth birthday, Miss Georgiana Vernon was given a pair of garnet bracelets by her aunt, and these and other coloured stones were mounted in gold collets joined by chains or chased gold leaves.[135] Bloodstone bracelets were enlivened by brilliants set in the centre of each plaque, which were joined by gold chains.[136] Pearls and turquoises, with either emeralds or rubies, might be set in the petals of chased gold roses joined together in bands.[137]

Other bracelets might be enamelled to represent the Iron Crown of Monza, the Seven Ages of Man, shamrocks, heart's-ease and butterflies.[138] Some were inscribed with messages or mottoes, such as SOUVENIR, or with the giver's name: 'She gave me a lovely bracelet with her name in diamonds.'[139]

132 Chased gold snake bracelet inscribed with the date of gift, 28 October 1834. Christie's.

Lizards and serpents were well adapted to make bracelets (Plate 132), like the 'elastic gold serpent with diamond eyes' mentioned in 1800.[140] Variations on the theme used two serpents biting a globe, a panther and serpent, a snake held by two hands, and four snakes in rows clasped by hands with hearts.[141] As an alternative, the hands terminating the gold bands might hold a flower, like the symbolic pansy.[142]

Bracelets were also made of bands of chased gold, oak leaves being a favourite pattern. After a catastrophic robbery in 1835, Elizabeth Duchess of Gordon was left with nothing but her jet, and a little curb bracelet which she wore at home every day.[143] There were different chain patterns: globe, lily, Jazeroon, Maltese, round elastic and pillar.[144]

Chain bracelets might be of single or multiple rows, and the clasp, like those of the Duchess of Northumberland set with carbuncles (see above, p. 309), was a prominent feature. One bracelet had the jewels in the clasp selected to spell the word REGARD: Ruby, Emerald, Garnet, Amethyst, Ruby and Diamond.[145] Others had clasps set with jewels or cameos.[146] Gold clasps in symbolic designs were common. They represented serpents, clasped hands, padlocks, hearts held by hands, flowers, butterflies, the classical lyre and the peacock.[147] Velvet bands round the wrists were similarly fastened, and in 1828 the *Lady's Magazine* described the wearing of 'bracelets of black velvet clasped with a large turquoise stone, set in filigree gold à l'antique' with carriage dress.[148]

When Queen Charlotte died in 1819 and the Prince Regent was sharing out some of her jewels between his sisters, Princess Sophia asked for a diamond and ruby bracelet to wear on the upper part of her arm, explaining that she was 'compelled from necessity to wear such an ornament'.[149] Besides hiding scars, armlets were part of fashionable dress, and were worn with both short and long sleeves.

Although they were narrower than the bracelets worn at the wrist, the design of armlets was similar. In 1836 Garrard altered two of Lady Wenman's 'Armlets to act as bracelets and armlets'.[150] They were made of gold chains or of bands of chased and enamelled gold, some with the emblems of the Seven Ages of Man.[151] More expensive designs were jewelled, with the stones set in naturalistic motifs such as grapes and vine leaves,[152] or 'open at the back with three rows of brilliant collets round the arms and large scroll pattern centre one sapphire and two emerald drops added to the centre brooch and small extra sprigs'.[153] As with the bracelets, the clasp was the main decorative feature, enriched with gem-stones in clusters, or with snaps of amethyst and chrysolite grapes.[154]

RINGS

William Taylor, a footman in service with Mrs Prinsep, widow of a City businessman, described some of her friends playing cards at a party in 1837, 'dressed up monsterous fine with their jewelrey. I took notice whow many rings there were on the fingers of four of these old cats, as I call them, and there were no less than thirty one, some wedding, some mourning and others set with diamonds and precious stones of great value'.[155] The elongated octagons and marquise shapes of the late eighteenth century, with neatly enamelled, bright-cut or beaded edges, were followed by broader, more compact squares and ovals with wide shoulders and substantial hoops worked with flowers and leaves or studded with gem-stones. White or fancy-coloured brilliants were set as solitaires, or flanked by clusters of smaller stones, often grouped in three collets. Pearls and white brilliants set in silver might be mounted beside a large coloured stone set in gold. Alternatively, they could encircle it, the frame thus enhancing the colour or exotic character of the central stone, like a ring of diamonds round a large striped cat's-eye. Other striking juxtapositions included moss agate with chrysoprase, and bloodstone with opals. The new style, emphasising width rather than length, meant that more than one ring could be worn on the finger, and hoops, enamelled or set with stones or pearls round half or the entire circumference, were very popular. In Lady Charlotte Bury's novel, *A Marriage in High Life* (1828), the bride, Lady Fitzhenry, wore above her wedding ring 'circles of diamonds, rubies, – presents of doting parents and perhaps envious friends'.[156] The stones might be of uniform colour, or else a harlequin mixture of groups of two to four stones: alternate pearls with sapphires, rubies and brilliants, or diamond, ruby, emerald and sapphire together. Hoops might be doubled or tripled, with a different-coloured, larger stone set across the middle between the rows.[157]

Other rings might be worked with the Gordian knot, sometimes studded with turquoises.[158] Multiple hoop rings called puzzle rings, made to take apart but difficult to fit together again, were also made.[159] Multiple hoop rings might also be joined by a bar set with small stones spelling REGARD or a similar message.[160]

George IV wears a snake ring in his portrait by Lawrence and it was believed to be his favourite ring.[161] Serpent rings, symbolising eternity, took many forms – single and twinned, or winged[162] – and were set with diamond or turquoise heads and ruby eyes; the coils could be encrusted with brilliants.[163] There were also rings with bezels of flies or butterflies in diamonds, or set with coloured stones in chased gold or filigree mounts.[164] Butterflies were also combined with snakes or with heart's-ease, each petal being set with a different-coloured stone – turquoise and either amethyst or topaz.[165] Other rings suitable for gifts were the 'ingenious kind of rings, given as remembrance from one friend to another, where the little blue flower "Forget-me-not" is in the centre, and is formed of turquoise stones with a diminutive diamond or topaz in the centre of the flower, to imitate the natural appearance'[166] (Plate LII).

Gem-set rings were love-tokens, and in Mrs Gore's novel, *The Débutante* (1846), the heroine looks down with pleasure at 'a small ruby ring that sparkled on her finger, the first pledge of love from Lord Mortayne which brought back all the pride of conquest to her heart'.[167] Some were more explicit in their design: single or double hearts, which could be combined with butterflies, snakes, lovers' knots and hands.[168] The clasped hands motif might be worked in gold and set with turquoises and rubies.[169] All these rings might have messages, dates and initials engraved within the hoop and at the back of the bezel. The fashion for mottoes worked in seed pearl continued, with inscriptions such as GAGE D'AMOUR or DE FIDELITATE on a blue enamel ground.[170] These were the successors to the posy rings of earlier ages. A gold hoop romantically inscribed SANS PEUR, alluding to the ideals of the knights in the age of chivalry, was given by Miss Milbanke to Lord Byron in 1815.[171]

ACCESSORIES

WATCHES

Men's watches were kept in the pocket of the waistcoat or breeches, hanging from strong chains of gold or platina.[172] Women wore watches attached to hooks at the waist, with various pretty trinkets – seals, finely wrought keys and tassels – or to a chain round the neck which linked up with the belt. On her fourteenth birthday, Princess Victoria was given an enamelled watch chain and blue topaz hook for her watch by her aunt, the Princess Sophia Matilda.[173] Watches were considered suitable presents for children: on 7 April 1805 the Prince of Wales bought a small gold hunting watch and key for Princess Charlotte,[174] and Viscount Nelson promised his infant daughter, Horatia, that he would send her one.[175]

The cases, now much smaller and flatter than before, might be chased, engine-turned or enamelled with arabesques, flowers, Cupids, and mottoes on contrasting green, coquelicot or blue grounds.[176] Some were shaped as snails, oysters, tulips or strawberries.[177] The snake motif might ornament both the case and the runner attached to the watch chain, as in 'the Elegant Engine turned gold chased Lady's Watch, set both sides with Circles of Brilliants, and ditto Elegant gold Maltese chain to ditto to suit with diamond Serpent Runner and a bunch of seals and key set with

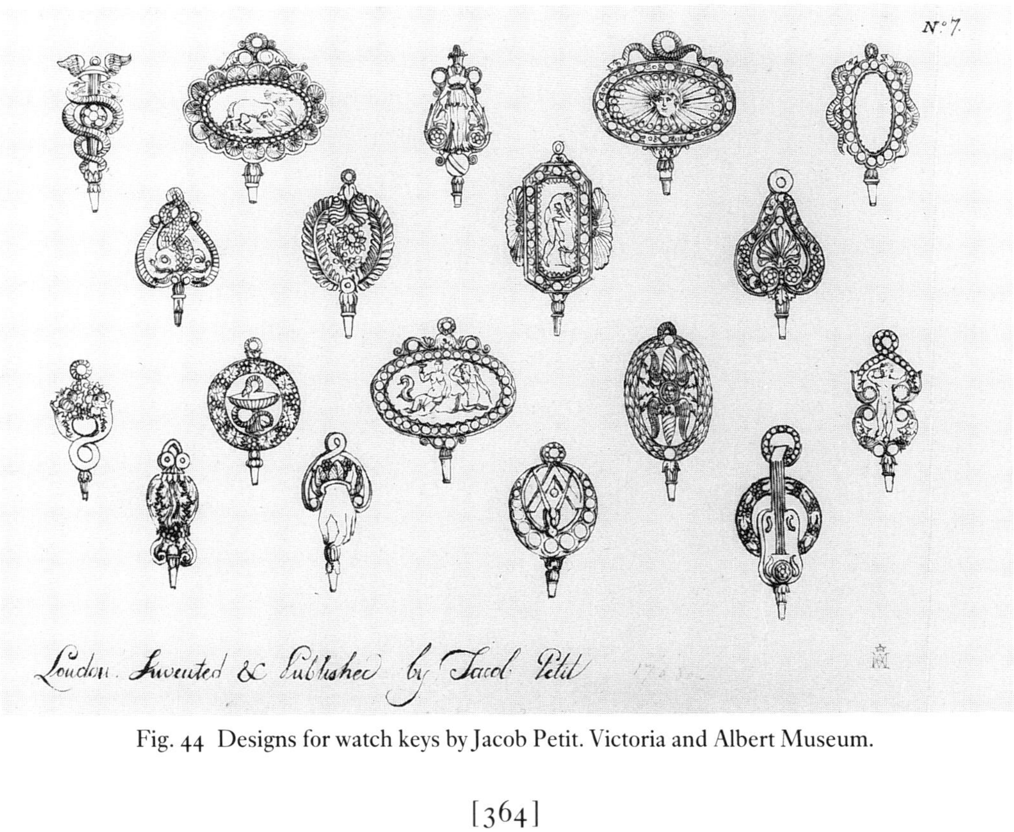

Fig. 44 Designs for watch keys by Jacob Petit. Victoria and Albert Museum.

brilliants', bought in 1807.[178] Turquoises and pearls were also set in concentric circles, diminishing towards the centre, on brightly coloured green or blue grounds.[179]

The watch bracelet was an innovation, and in 1828 E. and W. Smith sold George IV a snake bracelet 'containing a watch set with pearls and turquoises' for £80.[180] Jacob Petit's designs for keys show a variety of classical, sporting and emblematic motifs, including Masonic symbols (Fig. 44).

VINAIGRETTES

Vinaigrettes or smelling-bottles were successors to the pomander. The small sponge, hidden beneath a perforated inner lid, was soaked in aromatic essences (mint, rosemary, juniper, sage, mace, cinnamon, lavender, lemon and cloves with a base of acetic acid and alcohol) and was believed to give protection against cholera. Some were designed as small boxes for the pocket, others as lockets to hang round the neck or from a long chain caught in the belt beside the watch. Many were silver-gilt, but the most valuable were made of vari-coloured golds, engine-turned or chased, and set with turquoises or coloured stones, sometimes in the petals of a pansy or spelling out I REGARD. The cases were often in the shape of thin rectangular boxes, but could be made like a book, an urn, a bugle, a vase of flowers, a thimble, a heart or a purse. Some covers were inlaid with mosaics from Italy, panels of bloodstone, mother-of-pearl, cornelian and agate; others were engraved with vine leaves and grapes on a matt ground. Such ornament became more elaborate in the 1820s, with rich chasing and embossing. Views of famous places – Kenilworth Castle and Abbotsford (the home of Sir Walter Scott) – were a speciality of Nathaniel Mills of Birmingham. Other makers whose marks appear on vinaigrettes are A. J. Strachan and Charles Rawlings. To complete the decoration, the thumb-piece was usually set with a gem-stone, or ornamented with acanthus or flowers, and the grid covering the aromatic sponge decoratively pierced with roses, foliage or even sheets of music with a lute. The inside of the lid could be inscribed with a message: TO HARRIOTT FROM MAMA AND PAPA, a gold heart or a poem. Some verses entitled 'Musings of a slip of paper enclosed in the vinaigrette of a pretty woman', dated from *c.* 1820, express the longing of the lover (in the guise of a piece of paper) for the lid to open and for the sparkling eyes and lovely smile of the owner to gaze down in his direction as she enjoys the scent of the vinaigrette.[181]

SNUFF BOXES AND OTHERS

Lorgnettes, or spy-glasses which hung from chains, followed the same fashions in techniques and motifs as vinaigrettes (Fig. 45).

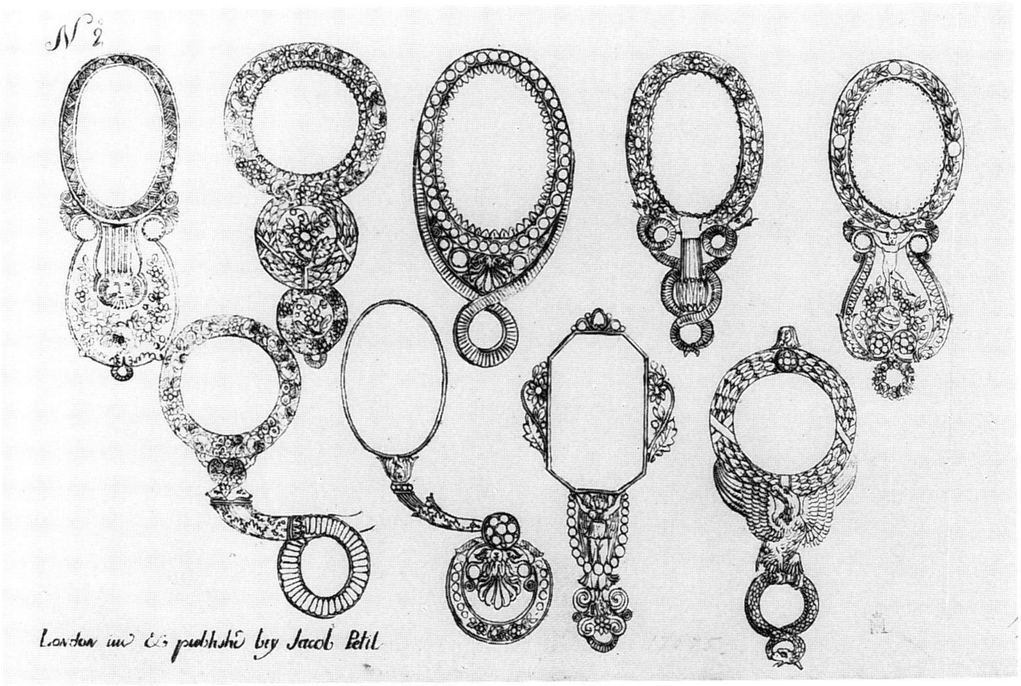

Fig. 45 Designs for lorgnettes by Jacob Petit. Victoria and Albert Museum.

Boxes for snuff were made from a wide range of materials: gold and silver predominated, but 'lava from Mount Vesuvius', hardstones, petrified wood and tortoiseshell were also used.[182] They could be octagonal or oval, round or square, and they varied in size. Most prized were those presented by sovereigns, usually with the donor's portrait on the outside or inside of the lid. A collection sold in 1817 included examples with 'an elegant enamelled portrait' of George III and 'an exquisitely chased medallion of the Prince Regent, surrounded by emblems'.[183] A coloured gold box with a miniature of George IV, and his cipher on the underside, was made about 1821 by John Northam and given to Richard Cavell, Treasurer of the Levant Company.[184]

Classical scenes were also used. A late-eighteenth-century tortoiseshell and gold snuff box, perhaps for a doctor, has a Wedgwood plaque of Aesculapius and Hygeia mounted in it.[185] Renaissance copies after the antique also served as models, as in the 'massy and richly chased *large gold snuff box*, with *medallion* from *the antique, representing the Judgment of Paris, Jupiter, Mars, &c.* of the fine taste of the fifteenth century'.[186]

Other elaborate gold boxes, chased and enamelled, were made for the grant of the freedom of a city given to generals and admirals who had distinguished themselves in the Napoleonic wars. The boxes presented by the City of London which can be documented from the Common Council Books and the City Cash Accounts cost 100 guineas apiece. Those given to Admiral Jervis and Admiral Howe were decorated with their and the City's coats-of-arms; that given to Captain Berry of Nelson's flagship, *Vanguard*, at the Battle of the Nile had a scene of a naval battle.[187]

SMALL-SWORDS

George IV's diamond-set sword has already been mentioned (p. 309), and the Napoleonic wars saw the preparation of many splendidly decorated swords of honour presented to naval and military heroes. The highly decorated hilts were made by the same goldsmiths who created the gold and enamel boxes. Such presentation swords are documented from earlier in the century, but most date from 1793 to 1816. Some were paid for by the 'subscribers for encouraging the capture of French privateers' or by the beneficiaries of the action commemorated.[188] Many were presented by the City of London, and are mentioned in the same sources as the freedom boxes. The average price was 200 guineas, and the decoration included enamelling and brilliants.[189] Others, of equal value, were made of two-colour gold and elaborately chased with armorial and other devices.[190] Viscount Castlereagh was rich enough to pay Rundell, Bridge and Rundell £2306 15*s* in 1818 for 'Setting his Lordship's Brilliants in a most elegant Gold Sword with Devices of the Order of the Garter & addition of Brilliants, Rubies'.[191] With so many diamonds flashing out from this sword, his hat band George and Garter star he stood out at the coronation of George IV in 1821: 'the people echoed his name from one to the other the whole length of the platform and received him with repeated cheers. It was unanimously voted that he was the handsomest man in the procession.'[192]

133 Diamond necklace composed of flowerheads graduated in size between foliate spacers; together with pair of George III diamond girandole earrings. Made by Rundell, Bridge and Rundell for Lady Clonbrock, 1806. Christie's.

Source Notes

1 *The social context of medieval jewellery, 1066–1509*

1 Langland 1954, B text, Passus II, lines 7–17. *Pelure* means fur; *fetislich*, neatly; *ewages*, beryl or aquamarine; and *engreyned*, dyed.
2 37 Edward III, Statut' de victu et vestitu (1363), c.3–15
3 3 Edward IV, c.5.
4 PRS, 36 (1914), 197.
5 Stothard 1817, pls 6–7 and 16; for the dating see JBAA, 3 ser. 34 (1971), 9; Hope 1907B, pp. 523 and 529.
6 *Rot. chart.*, I.i, p. 134; *Rot. litt. pat.*, I.i, pp. 54–5
7 Jenkinson 1923, p. 162.
8 Matthew Paris 1871, III, p. 319.
9 Roger of Wendover 1889, III, p. 109; BL, Royal MS. 14 C.vii, f. 123b; in Lewis 1987, fig. 163.
10 EETS, 246, p. 4, lines 122–3.
22 Kendall 1962, p. 161.
12 *CSP Milan*, p. 322.
13 Collins 1955, p. 84, no. 1.
14 *C. Cl. R. 1323–27*, p. 631; Berkeley 1883, I, p. 240.
15 HMC 69, p. 465.
16 Baildon 1909, p. 164.
17 Palgrave 1836, III, pp. 364–5.
18 EETS, O.S. 78, pp. 117–18.
19 McKisack 1959, p. 4; Rymer 1816–39, II.i, p. 203–4.
20 PRO, E403/472 m.5, 21 May 1379.
21 CLRO, Court of Hustings 42/15.
22 *Ibid.*, 89/192.
23 EETS, O.S. 212, p. 9.
24 *Paston Letters* 1900–1, I, p. 254.
25 Ibid., III, p. 215.
26 PRO, Prob. 2/3.
27 Surtees Soc., 2, p. 3.
28 *C. Lib. R., 1226–40*, p. 321.
29 Rock 1903, I, pp. 302–6.
30 Soc. of Ant., Drawings of monuments.
31 PRO, E101/397/4, f. 4b.
32 London 1984A. no. 324 a and b (not illus.); Stratford 1982, p. 87, fig. 1D.
33 Soc. of Ant., Drawings of monuments.
34 BL, Add. Ch. 57334.
35 London 1987, nos. 606–9, 620; Hope 1907A, pp. 466–85.
36 PRO, C1/12/250.
37 Soc. of Ant., MS. 120, p. 180.
38 Chaucer 1957, p. 18, *Canterbury Tales*, Prologue, lines 158–62.
39 Wright 1859, I, p. 334.
40 London 1976; Reddaway and Walker 1975, *passim*.
41 See n. 5 above; Rymer 1816–39, I.i, p. 410.
42 Palgrave 1836, II, pp. 142–6, 163–7, 170–2, 175–7, 183–6.
43 *Paston Letters* 1900–1, I, p. 249.
44 PRO, E101/349/11–13, 393/10.
45 Cannon 1918, p. 128; Safford 1928, p. 116.
46 Barker 1986, p. 108.
47 BL, Cotton MS. Nero D i, ff. 146b–147; in Lewis 1987, pp. 45–8, figs 23–4; London 1984A, no. 318.
48 Hartshorne 1909, pp. 98–9.
49 Hakluyt Soc., 2 ser. 168, p. 43.
50 Fellowes 1939, pp. 58ff.
51 Ashmole 1672, p. 220.
52 Barker 1986, Appx II; *Col. top et gen.*, IV (1837), 63–72.
53 *Register of the Black Prince*, IV p. 73.
54 Ehingen 1929, p. 40; Letts 1926, pp. 215, 221.
55 London 1987, fig. 101.
56 Goodall 1959–61.
57 Goodall 1977; Johnson 1964, *passim.*
58 Rymer 1816–39, I.i, p. 93
59 BL, Add. Ch. 57334.
60 Evans 1922; Albertus Magnus 1967, Bk II and Appx B.
61 Chaucer 1957, p. 295, *House of Fame*, lines 1350–2.
62 Babelon 1897, I, pp. lxiv–lxv.
63 *Ibid.*, p. lxviii; Paris 1981, p. 205.
64 Wright 1844, pp. 439–46.
65 Albertus Magnus 1967, pp. 134–5.
66 Evans 1922, pp. 119–20.
67 London 1984A, no. 314; Henig 1983, p. 59.
68 London 1984A, no. 324C; Henig 1983, pp. 57–8, pl. 1A; Stratford 1982, p. 87.
69 Wright 1844, pp. 449–57.
70 *Ibid.*, p. 448.
71 *CPR, Henry III, 1266–72*, pp. 136–40.
72 Kagan 1973, nos. 6, 7 and 1.
73 *CPR, Henry III, 1266–72*, p. 137.

74 Palgrave 1836, III, p. 141.
75 Rymer 1816–39, II.i, pp. 203–4.
76 PRO, E101/393/4, f. 9.
77 *C. Lib. R., 1226–40*, p. 278.
78 PRO, E101/386/3, f. 2.
79 Soc. of Ant., MS. 120, p. 182.
80 Oman 1974, pl. IIG.
81 Ward 1981, no. 122.
82 *Ibid.*, no. 123.
83 *Ibid.*, no. 134.
84 *PSA*, 2 ser. VII (1876–8), 368.
85 Nichols 1780, p. 115.
86 Ward 1981, no. 143.
87 *Ibid.*, no. 140.
88 Reddaway and Walker 1975, pp. 110–11, 218 and 246.
89 Palgrave 1836, III, p. 139.
90 Hakluyt Soc., 2 ser. 37, pp. 157–8, 168.
91 Safford 1928, pp. 137–9.
92 Poole 1955, p. 89.
93 PRS, n.s. 28 (1951–2), p. 112; PRO, E101/350/28; *C. Lib. R., 1240–5*, p. 83.
94 Parsons 1977, pp. 11, 84–5, 102 and 130.
95 Origo 1963, p. 85.
96 *Ibid.*, p. 300, n. 7.
97 *Ibid.*, p. 86.
98 Ruddock 1951, p. 74.
99 Reddaway and Walker 1975, p. xix.
100 *Ibid.*, p. xxiv; 28 Edward I, c.20, and London 1978, p. 14.
101 37 Edward III, c.7.
102 Reddaway and Walker 1975, p. 252; cf. Surtees Soc., 120, p. 75 and YAS, RS, 120, p. 10.
103 2 Henry VI, C.14; London 1978, pp. 25–30.
104 Hartopp 1927, pp. 4, 7, 11, 15, 18, 31, 40–1 and 56–7.
105 Analysis based on Surtees Soc., 96, *passim*.
106 Sutherland 1969, p. 119.
107 Reddaway and Walker 1975, pp. 227–8.
108 Surtees Soc., 96, pp. 63 and 84.
109 Reddaway and Walker 1975, p. 223.
110 5 Henry IV, c.13.
111 Reddaway and Walker 1975, p. 195.
112 Barker 1957, p. 6.
113 *Ibid.*, p. 7.
114 London 1984A, no. 310; Sutherland 1969, pls 44–5, 46 and 48.
115 London 1984A, no. 228.
116 London 1987, nos. 580, 586.
117 London 1984A, no. 256; London 1987, no. 641.
118 London 1987, nos. 647 and 643; cf. Parker 1850, II.i, pls 121, 123.
119 London 1987, no. 651; cf. Evans 1933B and Gardner 1927.
120 *Rot. parl.*, IV, p. 215.
121 Dodwell 1961.
122 London 1987, nos. 448–9.
123 *Ibid.*, no. 450.
124 Reddaway and Walker 1975, p. 259.
125 Campbell 1983.
126 London 1984A, no. 311 and 312; cf. nos. 314–17.
127 PRO, E101/411/9, m.3.
128 *Ibid.*, m.1.
129 Goldsmiths' Co., Wardens Min. A, pp. 108, 123 (1466–7).
130 Johnson 1964, chapter iv.
131 Ruddock 1951, p. 80.
132 Soc. of Ant., MS. 541/41; Goldsmiths' Co., Wardens Min. A, p. 212 (1480–1).
133 Goldsmiths' Co., Wardens Min. A, pp. 128, 218, 272.
134 London 1984B, no. 62; Hamel 1986, pls 45, 51, 56; Stothard 1817, pls 11–12.
135 Stothard 1817, pls 2, 4, 8 and 11; London 1978, no. 1.
136 Stothard 1817, pls 6, 13, 16; Hollis 1840–2, pt 2, pl. 5.
137 Stothard 1817, pls 105, 128, 136.
138 *Ibid.*, pls 8, 16; Hollis 1840–2, pt 3, pl. 1.
139 Nevinson 1973 and Urešová 1980; Stothard 1817, pl. 169.
140 Newton 1980; Stothard 1817, pl. 79.
141 London 1987, fig. 104, no. 720; Stothard 1817, pl. 101.
142 Stothard 1817, pls 103–4, 105, 137.
143 Scott 1980.

2 *The categories of medieval jewellery, 1066–1509.*

1 Twining 1960, 1967.
2 PRO, E101/411/9, m.1.
3 Twining 1960, p. 349; Sutherland 1969, pl. 45.
4 London 1987, no. 13.
5 Palgrave 1836, III, pp. 287–8; PRO, E101/411/9, m.1.
6 Urešová 1980.
7 EETS, O.S. 199, pp. 4–5, lines 33–48.
8 Palgrave 1836, III, pp. 267–8.
9 Stothard 1817, pls 102–4.
10 Twining 1960, p. 350, pl. 107c.
11 Edinburgh, National Museum of Antiquities, no. Hx36.
12 *Arch.*, XXI (1827), pl. 22.
13 Courtauld Institute, Conway Library.
14 Chaucer 1957, p. 570, *Romaunt of the Rose*, lines 562–6.
15 Palgrave 1836, III, p. 183, no. 151.
16 *Birmingham Arch. Soc.*, 47 (1921), 82–3, pl. 17.2–3.
17 Stothard 1817, pl. 100.
18 Hollis 1840–2, pt 2, pl. 9.
19 Palgrave 1836, II p. 171, no. 10.
20 Stothard 1817, pls 105–6.
21 Hollis 1840–2, pt 6, pl. 7;
22 Stothard 1817, pls 119–20; Scott 1980, pl. 139.
23 Stothard 1817, pls 112–13; Courtauld Institute, Conway Library.
24 Courtauld Institute, Conway Library.
25 *Ibid.*
26 Hollis 1840–2, pt 6, pls 3–4.
27 Chaucer 1957, p. 487, *Legend of Good Women*,

lines 147–54.
28 Stothard 1817, pls 89–92.
29 Courtauld Institute, Conway Library.
30 National Gallery of Scotland.
31 Stothard 1817, pls 55–6.
32 Courtauld Institute, Conway Library
33 *Ibid.*
34 PRO, E101/411/9, m.3.
35 Froissart 1901, I, p. 341
36 Humphery-Smith 1984, pp. 230–1.
37 See above, chap. 1, n. 2.
38 EETS, O.S. 199, p. 16, lines 138–9.
39 Stange 1934–61, 4 Taf. 141, 144; 11 Taf. 101.
40 Camden Soc., n.s. 52, p. 101.
41 PRO, E101/411/9, m.4.
42 Chaucer 1957, p. 193 *Monk's Tale*, line 3554.
43 Hope 1915, p. 382.
44 Stothard 1817, pls 105–6.
45 *Ibid.*, pl. 100.
46 Courtauld Institute, Conway Library; National Gallery, London no. 245; Thyssen-Bornemisza colln, no. 401.
47 *Paston Letters* 1900–1, I, p. 69.
48 *Ibid.*, IV, p. 104.
49 EETS, O.S. 78, p. 34.
50 Cherry 1973, pp. 311–12, pl. 87b.
51 London 1976, nos. 360 and 268; Tait 1986, nos. 524 and 310.
52 Palgrave 1836, II p. 246, no. 39.
53 Hartshorne 1909, p. 101,
54 Nicholas 1830, p. 61.
55 *Paston Letters* 1900–1, IV, p. 111.
56 *Ibid.*, IV, p. 110.
57 HMC 24.1, p. 6.
58 Scott 1980, pls 121, 119 respectively.
59 Caviness 1981, pp. 261–3, figs 442–64; the glass is much restored.
60 Hepburn 1986, pls 25, 38, 54.
61 *Ibid.*, pl. 55.
62 Courtauld Institute, Conway Library.
63 PRO, E101/411/9, mm.3–4.
64 London 1987, fig. 104, and no. 61.
65 Clarke 1937, p. 281, no. i.
66 Bongi 1871, p. 68.
67 Courtauld Institute, Conway Library.
68 Paris, Bib. Nat., MS. latin 1158, f. 27 verso.
69 Palgrave 1836, II, p. 143, no. 14.
70 Clarke 1937, p. 283, citing *Rot. parl.*, III, p. 313.
71 Hope 1913, pp. 297–9.
72 *Ibid.*, p. 300.
73 PRO, E403/589, m.4 3 Nov. 1406.
74 Blair and Delamer 1988, pp. 115–22, pls 13 and 14.
75 Camden Soc., n.s. 52, pp. 280, 283, 286.
76 PRO, E403/658, m.24 23 February. 1419.
77 PRO, E403/715, m.1 1434; Lind 1894, Taf. 25.2, 45.2, 51.2.
78 London 1981B, pp. 1–2 and no. 6.
79 Courtauld Institute, Conway Library; Hollis 1840–2, pt 1, pls 7–8.
80 Stothard 1817, pls 102–4.
81 Rymer 1704–26, X, p. 387.
82 Hollis 1840–2, pt 2, pl. 9.
83 Stothard 1817, pls 105–6.
84 Palgrave 1836, III, p. 321, no. 49.
85 Hepburn 1986, pp. 43–8, pl. 35.
86 *Ibid.*, pl. 35.
87 Spencer 1985.
88 Hepburn 1986, pl. 34.
89 Stothard 1817, pls 129–30.
90 Hollis 1840–2, pt 2, pl. 9.
91 Hakluyt Soc., 2 ser. 108, p. 45.
92 Hollis 1840–2, pt 5, pl. 10.
93 *Birmingham Arch. Soc.*, XLVII (1921), pls 13.2 and 14.
94 National Gallery, London, no. 6275.
95 Stothard 1817, pls 136–7; *Paston Letters* 1900–1, IV, p. 110.
96 Stothard 1817, pls 134–5.
97 Hepburn 1986, pl. 29.
98 Palgrave 1836, III, p. 395, no. 6.
99 Hope 1913, p. 313.
100 *Register of the Black Prince* IV, p. 142.
101 Palgrave 1836, III, p. 357, no. 333.
102 PRO, E403/805, m.2 22 Oct. 1455.
103 Twining 1961 pl. 48a.
104 Stothard 1817, pls 122–6.
105 *Ibid.*, pls 127–8; Hollis 1840–2, pt 5, pl. 10.
106 Hollis 1840–2, pt 6, pl. 7
107 PRO, PCC 36 Milles.
108 *Ibid.*, 2 Ayloffe.
109 London 1984A, no. 34; Lewis 1987, fig. 24; BL, Cotton MS. Nero D.vii, f. 100b.
110 Palgrave 1836, III, p. 185, no. 177.
111 Soc. of Ant., MS. 545/45.
112 *Ibid.*, MS. 120, p. 185.
113 Hepburn 1986, pls 47–9, 53.
114 Cherry 1973, pp. 312–13, pl. 86d; Tait 1986, no. 328c.
115 *Paston Letters* 1900–1, IV, p. 111.
116 *Birmingham Arch. Soc.*, XLVII (1921), 82–3, pl. 17.2–3.
117 Cherry 1983–4.
118 Chaucer 1957, p. 478, *Troilus and Cressida*, V, lines 1688–91.
119 London 1984A, no. 303.
120 *Ibid.*, no. 310.
121 BL, Cotton MS. Nero D.vii, f. 110.
122 London 1976, no. 366.
123 Baildon 1909, p. 173.
124 Norfolk RO, Norwich Consistory wills, Jekkys, f. 50b.
125 Evans 1921, pl. 15, p. 8; *PSA*, 2 ser. 6 (1876), 510.
126 London 1976, no. 367.
127 Fitch 1852.
128 Sotheby's, London, Works of Art, 11 Dec. 1988, no. 196.
129 Nichols 1780, pp. 181–2.
130 Williams 1979, fig. 107.8.
131 Nichols 1780, p. 37.

132 *Rot. parl.* IV, p. 220.
133 Hartshorne 1909, p. 99.
134 Cherry 1973, pp. 313–14, pl. 86c.
135 PRO, PCC 13 Bennett.
136 PRO, Prob 2/3.
137 Baildon 1909, p. 170.
138 *PSA Scot.*, 58 (1923–4), 163, fig. 2.
139 *Ibid.*, p. 160, fig. 1.
140 Hartshorne 1909, p. 99.
141 Camden Soc., 83, p. 2.
142 Lewer 1933, p. 12.
143 PRO PCC 25 Godyn.
144 Maclagan and Oman 1936, p. 18, pl. 6.3.
145 Cunliffe 1979.
146 Sotheby's, 5 July 1990, no. 9.
147 *Arch J.*, II (1846), 348.
148 London 1987, no. 880.
149 PRO, E403/556, m.4 22 Oct. 1397.
150 London 1976, no. 372; V & A 250–1874, M.544–5–1910.
151 Rymer 1704–26, XI, p. 76.
152 Rushforth 1927, pp. 22–6.
153 Palgrave 1836, III, p. 190, no. 227.
154 PRO, E101/393/40.
155 PRO, PCC 2 Adeane.
156 *Ibid.*, 12 Milles.
157 *Ibid.*, 25 Godyn.
158 *Ibid.*, 23 Horne.
159 Goldsmiths' Co., Wardens Minutes A, pp. 136, 283, 442.
160 Thordeman 1939, pp. 117–18, figs 117–18, 120.
161 Wright 1909, p. 93.
162 *Arch. Cant.*, VI (1866), 209.
163 Cherry 1983.
164 *Paston Letters* 1900–1, IV, p. 17, in BL, Add. MS. 34889, f. 143; cf. Humphery-Smith 1984, pp. 222–3.
165 Brewis 1927, Callander 1933–4, and London Museum 1940, pp. 273–6.
166 *The Times*, London, 8 Jan. 1983, p. 8; London 1990, no. 305.
167 London 1987, nos. 650–1.
168 Biddle 1990, II, Inv. nos. 2025, 2027, the latter hexagonal.
169 Inv. 286–983 and 151.940 (4), communicated by J. A. Goodall, FSA.
170 Lewis 1985.
171 Gai 1984, figs 96–7.
172 Heidelberg 1988, Abb. 8.
173 Goodall 1991, *Ant. J.*
174 Evans 1931, p. 2.
175 Struthers 1868–70, pp. 330–3.
176 *Visio* 1869, p. 54.
177 Nichols 1780, p. 157.
178 Callander 1933–4, p. 170, no. 10.
179 Spencer 1974–6, p. 309.
180 Callander 1933–4, pp. 183–4.
181 *Arch.*, XIV (1808), 275, pl. 48.2–4.
182 London 1984A, no. 320f.
183 Brewis 1930.
184 Fritz 1982, pls 310–12, the latter with a shield in the middle.
185 BM, MLA 49, 3–1, 33; Norwich 76–94 (666).
186 Nichols 1780, p. 100.
187 London 1976, no. 369a.
188 Baildon 1909, p. 170.
189 Cherry 1973, pp. 314–15, pl. 86a, c.
190 London 1987, no. 642.
191 London 1987, no. 644.
192 London 1990, no. 303.
193 Chaucer 1957, p. 18, *Canterbury Tales*, Prologue, lines 160–2.
194 Smith 1854, p. 152, no. 748.
195 London 1987, no. 641.
196 Soc. of Ant., Minute Book I (1718–32), p. 96.
197 Baltimore 1979, no. 371.
198 London 1987, no. 640.
199 RCHM, *Oxford*, 1939, p. 43a.
200 Paris, St Denis, inv.
201 BL, Cotton MS. Nero D.vii, ff. 7 and 110; Surtees Soc., 4, p. 267.
202 London 1984A, no. 468; the 'p' in Gotpine is a mistake for the Anglo-Saxon letter 'wyn'.
203 *Arch.*, IV (1786), 839, pl. 21.F.I.II.
204 *PSA*, 2 ser. 24 (1911–12), 127–31; Evans 1933, p. 197, fig. 4.
205 Callander 1933–4, p. 184.
206 Rymer 1816–39, II.i, p. 203.
207 *Register of the Black Prince*, IV p. 142.
208 Hollis 1840–2, pt 2, pl. 5.
209 PRO, E101/393/4.
210 *Arch. J.*, XV (1858), 270.
211 Hollis 1840–2, pt 1, pl. 9; pt 2, pl. 8.
212 Guildhall Library, London, Commissary of London wills, 9, f. 36.
213 London Museum 1940, pp. 255–6.
214 Wharton 1691, 2, p. 481.
215 Spencer 1990, *passim.*
216 London 1987, nos. 54–65; Tait 1986, nos. 518–19.
217 London 1987, nos. 71–4, 78–80, 82.
218 Baildon 1909, p. 164.
219 Chaucer 1957, p. 115, *Canterbury Tales*, Prologue, line 115.
220 V & A. 2280–1855.
221 HMC 24.1, p. 6.
222 *C. Lib. R., 1240–5*, p. 213; Rhodes 1897, p. 528; PRO, E101/411/9.
223 Goodall and Cherry 1985.
224 EETS, ES. 33, p. 57.
225 Ashmolean Museum, Oxford, loan 306 (1981).
226 London 1987, no. 659; Tait 1986, nos. 310–11.
227 Chaucer 1957, p. 49, *Miller's Tale*, lines 3265–6.
228 Rickert 1948, p. 110; Courtauld Institute, Conway Library.
229 Hope 1913, p. 311, fig. 186; Surtees Soc., 30, p. 13.
230 Horrox and Hammond 1979–83, II, p. 42.
231 Hepburn 1986, pl. 35.
232 Stothard 1817, pl. 31.

233 *Ibid.*, pls 127, 134, 139.
234 *Ibid.*, pls 69, 79.
235 *Arch. J.*, II (1846), 348.
236 Hollis 1840–2, pt 1, pl. 6.
237 Stothard 1817, pls 79–81.
238 Soc. of Ant., Drawings of monuments.
239 Gardner 1951, pl. 107b.
240 Stothard 1817, pls 102–4.
241 *Ibid.*, pls 105–6.
242 Courtauld Institute, Conway Library.
243 *Ibid.*; *Trans. of the Anglesey Antiq. Soc.* (1921), 52.
244 Stothard 1817, pl. 78.
245 *Ibid.*, pls 112–13; Courtauld Institute, Conway Library.
246 Hollis 1840–2, pt 3, pl. 3; pt 4, pls 3–4.
247 Surtees Soc., 4, p. 267.
248 Palgrave 1836, II, p. 143, no. 14.
249 Soc. of Ant., MS. 120, p. 180.
250 Rymer 1816–39, II.i, p. 203.
251 Soc. of Ant., MS. 120
252 PRO, E101/390/4.
253 *Register of the Black Prince*, IV, p. 66.
254 Rymer 1704–26, XI, pp. 76–7.
255 PRO, PCC 36 Milles.
256 *Arch. J.*, II (1846), 348.
257 PRO, E101/393/10.
258 PRO, E101/411/9.
259 Palgrave 1839, III, p. 314, nos. 4–5.
260 Stothard 1817, pls 112–13.
261 Hope 1916, p. 310.
262 PRO, E101/411/9.
263 *Paston Letters* 1900–1, I, p. 249.
264 Palgrave 1836, III, p. 223, no. 33.
265 PRO, E101/390/4.
266 Palgrave 1836, III, p. 348, no. 246, p. 349, no. 257.
267 *Ibid.*, III, p. 365, no. 6.
268 Rymer 1704–26, XI, pp. 76–7.
269 *Paston Letters* 1900–1, I, p. 249.
270 PRO, E101/390/4.
271 *Rot. chart.*, I.i, p. 134; *Rot. litt. pat.*, I.i, pp. 54–5.
272 Surtees Soc., 2, pp. 8–9.
273 Palgrave 1836, III, p. 142, nos. 142, 185 and 184.
274 Fingerlin 1971, p. 288, no. 3.
275 BHRS, 58, nos. 4, 16 (p.24), 34 (p.48).
276 Stothard 1817, pls 44–5.
277 *Ibid.*, pl. 58.
278 *Ibid.*, pls 55–6.
279 *Ibid.*, pls 85–6.
280 Courtauld Institute, Conway Library.
281 *Ibid.*
282 *Register of the Black Prince*, 4, p. 252.
283 Stothard 1817, pls 85–6.
284 John Cray, Chinnor, Oxon, †1392 (MS VII); Stothard 1817, pl. 77; Sir Robert Goushill, Hoveringham, Notts., †1403 and Sir William Wilcote, Northleigh, Oxon., †1410, both in the Courtauld Institute, Conway Library.
285 Hollis 1840–2, pt 5, pl. 8.
286 Stothard 1817, pls 129–30.
287 Courtauld Institute, Conway Library.
288 *Ibid.*
289 Stothard 1817, pls 6–7 and 16.
290 Riley 1868, p. 470.
291 PRO, E101/354/16.
292 Safford 1928, p. 118.
293 PRO, E101/393/10.
294 Hollis 1840–2, pt 1, pl. 9; pt 2, pl. 8.
295 Stothard 1817, pls 102–4.
296 *Ibid.*, pls 69–70.
297 *Ibid.*, pls 79–81.
298 Fingerlin 1971, fig. 517.
299 Hollis 1840–2, pt 3, pl. 1
300 Soc. of Ant., Drawings of monuments.
301 Lincolnshire Rec. Soc., 5, p. 15.
302 London 1987, no. 609.
303 Stothard 1817, pl. 101.
304 EETS, O.S. 78, p. 48.
305 Palgrave 1836, III, p. 184, no. 164.
306 CLRO, Court of Hustings 80/1 James de Holegh, 1349.
307 Hartshorne 1909, p. 100.
308 Fingerlin 1971, p. 392, no. 256, p. 394, no. 271.
309 BL, Cotton MS. Nero D.vii, f. 142b.
310 Surtees Soc., 4, p. 417.
311 Soc. of Ant., Drawings of monuments.
312 Camden Soc., 83, pp.5–6
313 Palgrave 1836, III, p. 337, nos. 158–9.
314 Hope 1914–15, p. 331.
315 Courtauld Institute, Conway Library.
316 Caviness 1981, figs 458, 460; much restored.
317 Safford 1928, p. 137.
318 Chaucer 1957, p. 49, *Miller's Tale*, lines 3250–1.
319 Lewer 1933, p. 14.
320 EETS, O.S. 210, p. 76, lines 2038–9.
321 Rickert 1948, p. 342; cf. BL, Cotton MS. Nero D.vii f. 146b.
322 *Arch. J.*, II (1846), 348.
323 EETS, O.S. 78, p. 58.
324 Rickert 1948, p. 343.
325 Surtees Soc., 4, p. 417.
326 *Paston Letters* 1900–1, IV, p. 111.
327 Courtauld Institute, Conway Library.
328 Surtees Soc., 4, p. 417.
329 Chaucer 1957, p. 18, *Canterbury Tales*, Prologue, lines 158–60.
330 PRO, E101/411/9, m.16.
331 Soc. of Ant., Drawings of monuments.
332 PRO, PCC 36 Horne, and Lewer 1933, p. 12.
333 PRO, PCC 4 Holgrave.
334 Riley 1868, p. 455.
335 Rickert 1948, p. 346.
336 PRO, E101/411/9, m.16.
337 EETS, O.S. 149, pp. 49–5[illegible].
338 Surtees Soc., 53, p. 153.
339 Maclagan and Oman 1936.
340 Soc. of Ant., Drawings of monuments.
341 *Register of the Black Prince*, IV, pp. 402, 427.
342 London 1972, no. 98.
343 PRO, E403/502, m.16 Easter 1384.

344 Hollis 1840–2, pt I, pl. 5, and pt 3, pls 5–6.
345 Stothard 1817, pls 69–70.
346 *Ibid.*, pl. 101.
347 Planché 1878–9, I, p. 67.
348 EETS, O.S. 221, p. 42, lines 649–50.
349 Stothard 1817, pl. 100.
350 Hollis 1840–2, pt 2, pls 3–7.
351 Stothard 1817, pls 87–8.
352 HMC 69, p. 465.
353 *Arch. J.*, XV (1858), 270.
354 Biddle 1990, II, p. 352.
355 *Ibid.*, pp. 581–3.
356 Murphy 1971, p. 55.
357 PRO, E101/411/9, m.7.
358 *Ibid.*, m.6.
359 *Rot. parl.*, IV, p. 215.
360 PRO, E101/409/14.
361 Palgrave 1836, III, p. 369, no. 11.
362 *Ibid.*, II, pp. 128–9.
363 *Ibid.*
364 Jacob and Johnson 1937, p. 88.
365 EETS, O.S. 78, p. 10.
366 PRO, PCC 2 Ayloffe.
367 Ward 1981, p. 53, pl. 154.
368 Evans 1922.
369 EETS, O.S. 149, p. 51.
370 London 1987, no. 636; Ward 1981, no. 126.
371 Ward 1981, nos. 120–1.
372 London 1987, no. 637.
373 London 1984A, nos. 311, 313.
374 *Ibid.*, no. 320a-c.
375 *Ibid.*, no. 317.
376 *Ibid.*, no. 318.
377 Ward 1981, no. 130.
378 Ward 1981, no. 129, pl. 154, pp. 74–5.
379 London 1987, no. 635; Ward 1981, no. 127.
380 BL, Add. MS. 57334.
381 PRS, n.s. 44, p. 36.
382 *C. Lib. R., 1240–5*, p. 83.
383 Ward 1981, no. 133.
384 CLRO, Hustings rolls 89/134.
385 *Rot. litt. pat.*, I.i, p. 55.
386 *Register of the Black Prince*, IV, p. 70, etc.
387 PRO, PCC 23 Horne.
388 Nichols 1780, p. 100.
389 Ward 1981, no. 148.
390 Camden Soc., 3 ser. 30, p. 15.
391 *Ibid.*, n.s. 52, p. 34.
392 Ward 1981, nos. 164–5; London 1978, no. 350.
393 Ward 1981, nos. 174 and 171.
394 *Ibid.*, no. 170.
395 *Ibid.*, nos. 173 and 177.
396 PRO, PCC 25 Godyn.
397 PRO, PCC 36 Wattys.
398 *PSA*, 2 ser. 17 (1899), 165–6.
399 PRO, PCC 2 Moore.
400 Cherry 1973, pp. 310–11, fig. 3 and pl. 87.2; Ward 1981, no. 163.
401 Ward 1981, no. 172.
402 PRO, PCC 13 Horne; Ward 1981, no. 187.
403 London 1987, no. 638.
404 PRO, E101/400/7.
405 BHRS, 58, no. 18.
406 *Paston Letters* 1900–1, III, p. 215.
407 Ward 1981, no. 174.
408 Oman 1974, p. 64, no. 15.
409 Ward 1981, no. 152; London 1987, no. 657.
410 PRO, PCC 12 Milles, Ward 1981, no. 189.
411 *Paston Letters* 1900–1, IV, p. 111.
412 PRO, PCC 11 Bennett.
413 Ward 1981, no. 184.
414 PRO, PCC 23 Horne.
415 *Arch. J.*, XV (1858), 270.
416 *King Horn* 1901, line 1038, no. 153.
417 Södergärd 1956, pp. 310–11.
418 PRO, E101/393/10.
419 PRO, E101/411/9.
420 PRO, PCC 19 Wattys.
421 Ward 1981, no. 114.
422 *Ibid.*, no. 195.
423 *Ibid.*, no. 125.
424 *Ibid.*, nos. 160 and 196.
425 PRO, PCC 13 Bennett.

3 *The social context of Renaissance jewellery, 1509–1625.*

1 6 Henry VIII, c.1.
2 24 Henry VIII, c.13.
3 Stubbes 1585, p. 70.
4 *L & P Henry VIII*, I, no. 1113.
5 Nicolas 1827, p. xxix.
6 *L & P Henry VIII*, I, nos. 44, 11.
7 *Ibid.*, XXI.i, no. 127; London 1981A, G48, illus. p. 4.
8 Steingräber 1957, fig. 98; Twining 1960, p. 146, pl. 48b.
9 Soc. of Ant., MS. 129A, f. 229; BL, Harl. MS. 611, f. 20b; Royal MS. Appx 68, f. 2
10 *L & P Henry VIII*, VI, no. 32; VII, no. 9.
11 *Ibid.*, III.i, no. 403; BL, Royal MS. Appx 89, f. 20.
12 *L & P Henry VIII*, X, no. 619.
13 *IBid.*, V, no. 1377.
14 *Ibid.*, X, no. 351.
15 Strickland 1857, II, pp. 594–5.
16 Ridley 1988, p. 35.
17 *L & P Henry VIII*, V, nos. 276, 1299, 1376.
18 *Ibid.*, no. 1485.
19 BL, Royal MS. Appx 89, ff. 36b, and 34b respectively; *L & P Henry VIII*, XII.ii, no. 1315.
20 Vertue IV, p. 54.
21 BL, Royal MS. 7C.xvi, ff. 18–32; *L & P Henry VIII*, XII.ii, no. 973.
22 Rowlands 1985, no. 62.
23 Strickland 1857, iii, p. 94.
24 *L & P Henry VIII*, XV, no. 925.
25 *Ibid.*, XVI, no. 1389.
26 Strickland 1857, III, p. 210.
27 *Ibid.*, p. 206.
28 *L & P Henry VIII*, XIII.i, no. 1290
29 *Ibid.*, XX.i, no. 686.

30 BL, Harl. MS. 611, f. 2b.
31 *Ibid.*, f. 3.
32 *Ibid.*, ff. 20b and 21b.
33 Soc. of Ant., MS. 129A, ff. 150–220; another copy in BL, Harl. MS. 1419.
34 His 1866, pl. xxxiv. 4.
35 *L & P Henry VIII*, XVIII.i, no. 44.
36 Madden 1831, pp. 178, 194, 197–8.
37 *CSP Ven.*, V, p. 533.
38 Babelon 1922, pp. 25–7.
39 Anne of Denmark, f. 44. no. 406; Scarisbrick 1986A, p. 233.
40 *CSP Span., Eliz.*, I, p. 10.
41 Wedel 1895, p. 234.
42 *CSP Ven.*, VII, no. 77, p. 92.
43 Nichols 1788–1805, II, E. Bohun, 'The Character of Queen Elizabeth (1693)', p. 47.
44 Nichols 1788–1805, II and III; BL, Royal MS. Appx 68.
45 Arnold 1988, pp. 251 ff.; HMC 9, Salisbury MSS., X, pp. 356–9.
46 Neale 1934, p. 326.
47 Labanoff 1844, VII, pp. 132–3.
48 *CSP Span., Eliz.*, III, no. 279.
49 Strong 1987, *passim*; Arnold 1988, chapter IV, pp. 70 ff.
50 Collins 1955, p. 3.
51 Scarisbrick 1986A, pp. 228–9.
52 *CSP Ven.*, XI, no. 154.
53 *CSP Dom., James I*, IX, p. 171.
54 Nichols 1828, II, pp. 45–7.
55 Anne of Denmark's inventory, NLS, Ad. MS. 31.1.iv, ed. Scarisbrick, 'Anne of Denmark's jewellery inventory', *Arch.*, 109 (1991).
56 Heriot 1822, pp. 195–227; PRO, LR 2/122.
57 Lemon 1827, pp. 148–57; Nichols 1828, IV, pp. 849–54 note.
58 Lewer 1933, pp. 12–15; Chatsworth MS., 21 Aug. 1537.
59 *Lisle Letters*, V, nos. 1523–4.
60 *Ibid.*, III, nos. 758–9.
61 *Ibid.*, II, no. 466.
62 *Ibid.*, III, no. 759.
63 *L & P Henry VIII*, IV.iii, no. 6748, pp. 3041 §7, 3042 §9 and 3064 §11.
64 Rowlands 1985, no. 27; Collins 1955, p. 26.
65 NPG, no. 535.
66 V & A, loan.
67 Shirley 1873, pp. 398–9.
68 *CSP Ven.*, VII, no. 10 p. 12.
69 V & A, MS. L.30–1982.
70 Essex RO, D/DP/F240/1.
71 BL, Harley Roll D35, i–xi, ff. 67–70; Scarisbrick 1987B, pp. 324, 326.
72 Chambers 1936, pp. 309–10; PRO, C24/418 no. 53.
73 *Gent. Mag.*, CXV.i (1845), 374–7.
74 Scarisbrick 1983, I, pp. 1542–4.
75 *The Reliquary*, I (1860–1), 118.
76 Montagu 1864, p. 398.
77 Prestwich 1966, pp. 374, 405, 472.
78 Shirley 1869, p. 375.
79 *Ibid.*, p. 349.
80 HMC 58, Seymour Papers, IV, p. 202.
81 Cammel 1939, p. 255.
82 BL, Add. MS. 4176, f. 164, undated.
83 Grose 1807, I, p. 281.
84 *Lisle Letters*, V, no. 1406, p. 407.
85 Surtees Soc., 106, p. 228.
86 Cumbria RO, P1574.
87 Fairholt 1856, p. 337.
88 BHRS 58, pp. 162–3.
89 *Ibid.*, pp. 170–82.
90 Surtees Soc., 2, p. 109.
91 Moryson 1907–8, IV pp. 232–4.
92 Dowell 1888, III, p. 31.
93 Shakespeare 1951, *Winter's Tale*, IV.iii, 224.
94 Jonson 1981–2, *Eastward Ho*, III.iii.
95 Oxfordshire R S, 44, pp. 62, 81.
96 Emmison 1987, IV, p. 72.
97 London R S, 3, p. 100.
98 *Ibid.*, pp. 107–8.
99 Guildhall Lib., MS. 9171/20, f. 118.
100 *Ibid.*, f. 23.
101 *L & P Henry VIII*, XXI *passim*.
102 Collins 1955, p. 93.
103 Rymer 1704–26, XIII, pp. 239–42.
104 London 1981A, p. 5.
105 *CSP Dom., James I*, IX, p. 275.
106 Nicolas 1827, p. 88.
107 HMC 9, Salisbury MSS., XIX, p. 141.
108 *CSP DOM., James I*, X, p. 585.
109 BL, Royal MS. Appx 89, f. 36.
110 HMC 9, Salisbury MSS., V, pp. 445–6.
111 *DNB*, Sir Henry Wotton.
112 Essex RO, D/DD/M1, Box 19, 1–35.
113 Devon 1836, p. 16.
114 HMC 58, Seymour Papers, IV, p. 201.
115 *CSP Ven.*, XI, no. 763.
116 Sjögren 1980, p. 699, no. 14.
117 Essex RO, D/BPF/240/1.
118 Ellis 1825–6, 1st ser. 3, pp. 145–8.
119 Chambers 1936, p. 267.
120 HMC 58, Seymour Papers, IV, p. 185.
121 Ellis 1825–7, 2 ser. 3, p. 192.
122 Wilson 1986, pp. 318, 325.
123 Nichols 1788–1805, III, p. 112.
124 BL, Harley Roll D35.i–xi, f 68.
125 HMC 9, Salisbury MSS., V, p. 206; *CSP Dom., Eliz.*, VI, p. 65.
126 *L & P Henry VIII*, XIV.i, no. 37, p. 18.
127 V & A MS., L.30–1982, f. 34b.
128 Bodleian Lib., MS. Ashmole 1148.
129 Tait 1986A, pp. 197–200.
130 HMC 55, Various IV, p. 323; Tait 1986A, cat. 33.
131 EETS, O.S. 243, pp. 120–1.
132. *Lisle Letters*, VI, pp. 183–4.
133 *Ibid.*, IV, p. 165.
134 Wynn 1926, p. 183.
135 *L & P Henry VIII*, IV.iii, no. 5789 p. 3071.

136 Madden 1831, p. 177.
137 *CSP Span.*, XIII, p. 441.
138 BL, Royal MS. Appx 68, f. 33.
139 Cammell 1939, p. 113.
140 Drayton 1932, II, pp. 248–9.
141 London 1981A, pp. 12–19.
142 Fitch 1811, p. 409.
143 London 1981A, pp. 12–19.
144 Leicester RO, DG9/2409.
145 Fitch 1811, p. 407.
146 Jenkins 1958, p. 232.
147 *L & P Henry VIII*, XIV.i, no. 910.
148 V & A, 846–1890.
149 *DNB*, Sir Paul Pindar.
150 HMC 9, Salisbury MSS., V, p. 457; XIX, p. 109.
151 Moryson 1907–8, IV, p. 233.
152 BL, Stowe MS, 559, f. 64.
153 Thomson 1815, p. 88.
154 V & A, MS. L. 30–1982, f. 31; Anne of Denmark, f. 34, no. 326.
155 Nichols 1788–1805, III, 'Lady Jane Gray', p. 11.
156 Kidd, p. 32.
157 *Ibid.*, p. 48.
158 CLRO, MCI/78/103, 21 Oct. 1603; Rowse 1962, p. 191; Heriot 1822, p. 216.
159 Maddison 1888, no. 22.
160 Stowe 1615, p. 575.
161 Collins 1955, p. 275.
162 *Ibid.*, p. 274.
163 *L & P Henry VIII*, XV, no. 809; XIII.i, no. 1193.
164 Huguenot Soc., 10.i, pp. 270, 415, 436, 438–9, 441, 452; 57, nos. 115, 152, 253, 546, 604, 611, 702, 906, 1040, 1069, 1103.
165 Kagan 1980, pp. 29–20.
166 *Ibid.*, no. 78, pp. 33–4; *L & P Henry VIII*, VII, no. 9; VI, no. 566; Vertue II, p. 91.
167 EETS, O.S. 243, pp. 120·1.
168 London 1981A, no. 17; Oman 1974, p. 31.
169 Kagan 1980, p. 30, nos. 15–16; Ilchester 1922, p. 71.
170 London 1976, no. 391; V & A, 889–1894.
171 HMC 24, Rutland MSS., IV, p. 388.
172 Kagan 1980, p. 32.
173 *Ibid.*, pp. 33–4.
174 *Ibid.*, p. 32.
175 SNPG, no. 156; cameos at Windsor and Museo degli Argenti, Florence.
176 Soc. of Ant., MS. 129A, ff. 191, 197b.
177 Essex RO, D/DP F/240/1; Shirley 1869, p. 350
178 Shakespeare 1951, *Romeo and Juliet*, I.iv. 55–6.
179 Soc. of Ant., MS. 129A, f. 222b.
180 London 1981A, no. 30.
181 Soc. of Ant., MS. 129A, f. 205; London 1981A, no. 45.
182 London 1981A, no. 45.
183 Soc. of Ant., MS. 129A, f. 205.
184 Rowlands 1985, no. 55.
185 Scarisbrick 1987B, figs 8–9.
186 Rowlands 1985, pl. 90; Strong 1969, no. 75.
187 *Art at Auction 1982*, pp. 190–1, fig. 1; Washington 1985, no. 206; London 1976, no. 550.
188 Leicester RO, DG9/2409; Chatsworth, no. 287.
189 Rymer 1704–26, XV, p. 757.
190 NPG, no. 4451.
191 Nichols 1788–1805, II, 'New Year's Gifts', p. 12.
192 *Ibid.*, pp. 12, 14, 25, 101.
193 Essex RO, D/DP F/240/1.
194 HMC 9, Salisbury MSS., II, p. 131.
195 Valeriano Bolzano 1614, p. 382.
196 Soc. of Ant., MS. 129A, ff. 221b, 179, 222; BL, Harl. MS. 611, f. 3.
197 Nichols 1788–1805, III, 'Lady Jane Gray', p. 11; PRO, E36/85, f. 5b.
198 Rymer 1704–26, XV, p. 758.
199 Soc. of Ant., MS. 129A, f. 222.
200 London 1981A, no. 46; V & A, MS. L30–1982, f. 75b.
201 London 1981A, no. 40.
202 Rymer 1704–26, XV, pp. 758–9.
203 London 1981A, no. 39; Scarisbrick 1989, pl. 5.
204 London 1978, nos. 25, 30 and 27 respectively.
205 1 Henry VIII, c.13; *L & P Henry VIII*, II.i, no. 1675; XXI.ii, nos. 331.50, 332.48, 476.51, 90, 94, etc.
206 Halle 1547–50, I, p. 168.
207 Collins 1955, p. 92, no. 1.
208 London 1981A, p. 4, G48.
209 *Ibid.*, p. 40.
210 Collins 1955, p. 94; London 1981A, p. 40.
211 HMC 9, Salisbury MSS., XVI, p. 441.
212 London 1981A, G10; London 1988, nos. 206–9.
213 Huguenot Soc., 4to ser. 8, 10,i and 57.
214 J. Goodall, unpublished research into the history of London and provincial alien goldsmiths.
215 Cust 1905–6.
216 Tait 1985, pp. 39–45, figs 11–17.
217 Shaw 1906, II, p. 138.
218 Hayward 1986.
219 Shaw 1906, II, p. 178.
220 Scarisbrick 1986A and Anne of Denmark.
221 Glanville 1984.
222 Rymer 1704–26, XV, pp. 756–9.
223 Leicester RO, DG9/2409.
224 Auerbach 1961.
225 Heriot 1822.
226 Thirsk and Cooper 1972, pp. 716–17.
227 *CSP Span., Eliz.*, I, p. 213.
228 Fitch 1811, p. 410.
229 BL, Royal MS. Appx 89, f. 31.
230 Marlow 1910, *Jew of Malta*, II.816, p. 262.
231 O'Dell-Franke, 1977, Taf. 122–9 and 130–53.
232 Drayton 1932, II, p. 248, lines 28–32.
233 Hayward 1986.
234 BL, Royal MS, Appx 68, f. 15.
235 Steingräber 1957, pp. 85 ff. 98–9; London 1988, nos. 206–9.
236 Ward-Jackson 1967, pp. 90–9; His 1866, pl.xxxiv, 10–12.
237 Camden Soc., 83, p. 18; Madden 1831, pp. 189, 194.

238 Massinger and Field 1632, *The Fatal Dowrie*, II.ii.
239 Nicolas 1827, p. 415.
240 Anne of Denmark, f. 21, no. 196.
241 *Ibid.*, f. 24, no. 231.
242 *Ibid.*, f. 37, no. 352; BL, Sloane MS. 814, f. 27.
243 Scarisbrick 1986A, p. 233, fig. 6.
244 London 1981A, nos. 116, 119.
245 BL, Royal MS. Appx 89, f. 29b; Anne of Denmark, f. 32, no. 314/3.
246 BL, Royal MS. Appx 68, f. 3b.
247 BL, Royal MS. Appx 68, f. 9; Anne of Denmark, f. 37, no. 350.
248 Washington 1985, no. 206.
249 Seton 1882, p. 158.
250 Scarisbrick 1987B, p. 328, fig. 17.
251 *L & P Henry VIII*, IV.iii, no. 6789; III.i, no. 463.
252 *Ibid.*, V, no. 276.
253 Strong 1987, p. 156; BL, Royal MS. Appx 68, f. 8.
254 Whitney 1586; Wither 1635.
255 Arnold 1988, p. 61 (anchor); BL, Royal MS. Appx 68, f. 31b. (arrow); Anne of Denmark, f. 9, no. 80 (crossbow).
256 BL, Royal MS. Appx 68, ff. 14b, 25b, 27, 19b and 30.
257 *Ibid.*, ff. 3b–4b, 25b, 30b, 32b, 33, 34, 35.
258 Rowlands 1985, no. 61; NPG, no. 668.
259 His 1866, pl.xxxix.1–12; London 1981A, no. 37; SNPG, no. 156.
260 *L & P Henry VIII*, XVI, no. 1389.
261 BL, Harl. MS. 611, f. 24.
262 BL, Royal MS. Appx 68, f. 23.
263 *Ibid.*, f. 15b, 16b; NLS, MS. 360.
264 Scarisbrick 1986A, p. 234.
265 London 1981A, no. 41; Hayward 1986, pl. lxxxiii.d.
266 V & A, MS. L.30–1982, f. 35b; BL, Royal MS. Appx 68, f. 12.
267 BL, Harley Roll D35.i–xi, f. 69.
268 Nichols 1788–1805, III, 'New Year's Gifts', p. 135.
269 BL, Stowe MS. 557, f. 97; London 1981A, no. 45.
270 Hayward 1986, pl. lxxxiv.b, d; Strong 1986, figs 133, 137, 156.
271 *L & P Henry VIII*, VII, no. 9; viii, no. 907.
272 *Ibid.*, XVI, no. 1389.
273 BL, Royal MS. Appx 68, f. 2b.
274 Spenser 1912, *Faerie Queene*, II.iii.27.
275 Washington 1962–3, no. 107a, c, e.
276 BL, Royal MS. Appx 89, f. 30b; *L & P Henry VIII*, VII, no. 9.
277 BL, Royal MS. Appx 68, ff. 4, 5b, 7; Nichols 1788–1805, II, 'New Year's Gifts', p. 29.
278 Anne of Denmark, f. 29, no. 283.
279 13 Elizabeth I, c.2.
280 3 James I, c.5.
281 *Lisle Letters*, II, p. 390.
282 BL, Stowe MS. 559, ff. 55 ff.
283 Camden Soc., 83, p. 19.
284 BL, Royal MS. 7C.xvi, f. 18b.
285 *Ibid.*, f. 69.
286 Madden 1831, pp. 189, 197.
287 White 1935, p. 163.
288 Anstruther 1953, p. 253.
289 Oman 1974, p. 57.
290 Christie's, 13 December 1989, no. 430.
291 PRO, PCC 22 Thrower.
292 *CSP Ven.*, VII. no. 452, pp. 403–4; *CSP Foreign 1553–8*, p. 225.
293 *CSP Ven.*, III, no. 91; EETS, O.S. 243, p. 103.
294 *L & P Henry VIII*, X, no. 351, p. 154.
295 Camden Soc., 83, p. 19; Lewer 1933, p. 12.
296 Tait 1986B, figs 56–7.
297 Hackenbroch 1977, pp. 43–4, fig. 1.
298 West Sussex RO, BA74.
299 Madden 1831, pp. 177, 182–3, 186–7.
300 BL, Stowe MS. 559, f. 68.
301 Nichols 1788–1805, II, 'New Year's Gifts', p. 19.
302 Strong 1987; pelican, p. 83, figs 64, 90, 154; phoenix, p. 82, figs 65–7, 90, 154.
303 *Ibid.*, fig. 172; NPG, no. 2651; Reading Museum.
304 Strong 1987, p. 139.
305 Millar 1963, no. 80.
306 *L & P Henry VIII*, V, no. 686; Nichols 1788–1805, II, 'New Year's Gifts', p. 9; Rymer 1704–26, XV, p. 757.
307 Somers Cocks 1985, no. 29; London 1981A, no. 18; Heriot 1822, p. 177.
308 Washington 1962–3, no. 107b; BM, Sloane no. 5308–25; Rowlands 1985, no. 69.
309 Madden 1831, pp. 177, 182–3, 186–7.
310 BL, Royal MS. Appx 68, f 12; London 1981A, no. 38.
311 His 1866, pl. xl.10–11; Washington 1962–3, no. 107c.
312 BL, Harl MS. 611, f. 2b; Madden 1831, p. 177; London 1981A, no. 9.
313 BL, Royal MS. Appx 89, f. 30b; *L & P Henry VIII*, V, no. 276.
314 *Lisle Letters*, III, no. 759, p. 477.
315 Soc. of Ant. collection.
316 Anne of Denmark, f. 29, no. 287, f. 23, no. 321.
317 Shirley 1869, p. 350; Seton 1882, p. 58.
318 Rowlands 1985, no. 62; Soc. of Ant., MS. 129A, f. 178b; BL, Royal MS. Appx 68, f. 6; Anne of Denmark, f. 17, no. 163; etc.
319 Scarisbrick 1986A, pl. 1; Nichols 1828, III, p. 845.
320 Ingestre B/54/1014; Washington 1985, no. 50; Duke of Norfolk.
321 Hayward 1986, pl. lxxxi.a.
322 *L & P Henry VIII*, IV, no. 6789; II, no. 5114; V, no. 1712.
323 PRO, PCC 7 Thrower.
324 *L & P Henry VIII*, V, no. 1712.
325 *Ibid.*, XII.i, no. 5.
326 BL, Add. MS. 5498, f. 27b
327 National Gallery of Wales; Ashmolean Museum, Fortnum Colln, no. 280.
328 Bedford RO, Wills, ABP/W 622/60.
329 BL, Harl. MS. 39, f. 380.
330 London 1981A, no. 13.
331 Rymer 1704–26, XV, p. 756 Essex RO, D/DP F/

211.
332 Newdigate-Newdegate 1898, p. 157.
333 Information for this section is drawn from Hansen 1977.
334 *L & P Henry VIII*, XVII, no. 124, p. 54.
335 Thomson 1815, p. 246.
336 Hansen 1977, p. 44.
337 London 1981A, no. 8.
338 Hansen 1977, p. 10.
339 *Ibid.*, p. 12.
340 Browne 1646, CX.xiii, p. 3.
341 G. Chapman, *Bussy D'Ambois* (1607), II.i.117–23.
342 *Lisle Letters*, III, no. 604.
343 V & A, M97–1917; Leicester RO, DG9/2409.
344 BL, Royal MS. Appx 68, ff. 7, 7b.
345 *Ibid.*, f. 32b.
346 Jonson 1981–2, *Volpone*, II.v.12.
347 Bedford RO, ABP/W1622/60; Ashmolean Museum, Fortnum Colln, no. 299.
348 London 1981A, no. 58.
349 Reynolds 1951, p. 7.
350 Norris 1977, *Memorials*, II, pl. 238.
351 *Ibid.*, pls 254 and 267–8.
352 Reynolds 1951, pl. 18.
353 *Ibid.*, p. 9.
354 *Ibid.*, pls 25, 28 and 30; Norris 1977, *Memorials*, II, pl. 274.
355 Reynolds 1951, pl. 27.

4 *The categories of Renaissance jewellery, 1509–1625.*

1 *CSP Span.*, XI, p. 262.
2 Soc. of Ant., MS. 129A, f. 7a-b.
3 White 1935, p. 219.
4 Strong 1969, II, pl. 185; Strong 1987, pl. II, and fig. 137, etc.
5 Jenkins 1958, p. 233.
6 Palgrave 1836, II, p. 300.
7 *CSP Ven.*, VII, p. 17.
8 HMC 9, Salisbury MSS., II, p. 129.
9 Collection of Lord Leigh at Stoneleigh Abbey.
10 *CSP Ven.* II, no. 219, p. 90.
11 HMC 9, Salisbury MSS., I, p. 129.
12 Tait 1962.
13 BL, Royal MS. Appx 68, f. 31b.
14 London 1981A, no. 15.
15 HMC 9, Salisbury MSS., VII, p. 356.
16 London 1981A, P20.
17 HMC 3, 4th Rept, pt i, Earl de la Warr, p. 286.
18 Strong 1966, p. 151.
19 Cammell 1939, p. 203.
20 Scarisbrick 1986A, p. 233.
21 Hayward 1986, pl. lxxxviii.b.
22 London 1981A, P22.
23 Strong 1986, pl. 42.
24 NPG, no. 4515; National Portrait Gallery 1969, p. 162.
25 *Loseley MSS.*, p. 410.
26 Moryson 1907–8, IV, p. 235.
27 *Lisle Letters*, V, no. 1136a, p. 93.
28 Strong 1969, no. 117.
29 V & A, MS. L.30–1982, ff. 31V, 32.
30 BL, Royal MS. Appx 68, ff. 18–19.
31 Nichols 1788–1805, II, 'New Year's Gifts', p. 29.
32 Scarisbrick 1986A, pl. I; Weinstein 1989, pp. 323–40.
33 Scarisbrick, 1986D, figs 2 and 5.
34 BL, Royal MS. Appx 68, ff. 28b–32.
35 Scarisbrick 1986A, p. 232, pl. I.
36 *Ibid.*, p. 232.
37 *Ibid.*, fig. 3.
38 *CSP Ven.* XII, p. 498.
39 Scarisbrick 1986A, pl. i, fig. 7.
40 *Ibid.*, pl. 2.
41 Hayward 1986, pls lxxxvi.b, lxxxvii.a, b.
42 Scarisbrick 1987B, figs 17–18, pp. 331–2.
43 EETS, E.S. 10, p. 199.
44 Nichols 1788–1805, II, 'New Year's Gifts', p. 11.
45 Strong 1987, figs 141, 172.
46 Jonson 1981–2, 3, p. 382, *Cataline*, II.i.
47 Anne of Denmark, f. 25, no. 236.
48 Anne of Denmark, ff. 4–8, nos. 25–68; f. 10, nos. 85–8.
49 Scarisbrick 1986A, p. 233.
50 Anne of Denmark, f. 25, no. 236.
51 Hayward 1986, pl. lxxxv.b, d (with caduceus).
52 Scarisbrick 1987B, fig. 17.
53 Stubbes 1585, p. 63; and Wilson 1956, p. 53.
54 NPG, no. 7.
55 Collection of Archibald Stirling of Keir.
56 *L & P Henry VIII*, V, no. 1298.
57 BL, Royal MS. 7C.xvi, f. 31.
58 Rowlands 1985, pl. 199.
59 V & A, MS. L.30–1982, f. 32; Essex RO, D/DP F240/1.
60 Edwards 1869, pp. 353–4.
61 Anne of Denmark, f. 36, no. 346, f. 37, nos. 349–50, f. 38, no. 360.
62 Scarisbrick 1986A, p. 233.
63 *Ibid.*
64 BL, Royal MS. Appx 68, f. 29b.
65 Anne of Denmark, f. 39, no. 364; Nichols 1788–1805, II, 'New Year's Gifts', p. 13.
66 Strong 1987, fig. 65.
67 BL, Royal MS. Appx 68, f. 29b.
68 Nichols 1788–1805, II, 'New Year's Gifts', pp. 13, 93.
69 Anne of Denmark, f. 37, no. 354.
70 Heriot 1822, p. 217.
71 Scarisbrick 1986A, fig. 5, p. 232; *Arch. Cant.*, XI (1877), 236.
72 *L & P Henry VIII*, XVI, no. 1389.
73 Leicester RO, DG9/2409.
74 HMC 69, Middleton MSS., p. 604.
75 Friedman 1989, pl. 3.
76 London 1981A, P16.
77 *Gent. Mag.*, CXV. i (1845), 376.
78 Madden 1832, p. 179.
79 *L & P Henry VIII*, I, no. 463, IV.iii, no. 6879.
80 Nichols 1788–1805, II, 'New Year's Gifts',

pp. 26, 30.
81 *Ibid.*, p. 15.
82 *Ibid.*, p. 18.
83 *Ibid.*, III, 'New Year's Gifts', p. 129.
84 *Ibid.*, p. 130; II, 'New Year's Gifts', p. 35.
85 Strong 1987, pp. 125–8.
86 Scarisbrick 1986A, p. 235.
87 *Ibid.*, p. 234.
88 Williamson 1933, p. 42.
89 *CSP Ven.*, III, no. 67, p. 50.
90 *Ibid.*, II, no. 918.
91 BL, Royal MS. Appx 89, f. 29b.
92 Gutch 1781, II, p. 290.
93 PRO, PCC 9 Manwaring.
94 HMC 77, De L'Isle and Dudley, I, p. 244.
95 *CSP Ven.*, VII, no. 79.
96 Collins 1955, p. 251.
97 Moryson 1907–8, IV, p. 233; PRO, LC 5 *passim*.
98 Leicester RO, DG9/2409.
99 C. Oman, 'Flagon chains', *Society of Jewellery Historians Newsletter*, 8 (1979), 4.
100 Collection at Hagley, Worcs.
101 *Gent. Mag.*, CXV.i (1845), 376; BL, Royal MS. Appx 68, f. 12b.
102 London 1976, no. 291; BL, Royal MS. Appx 68, f. 14b.
103 PRO, PCC 7 Ayloffe, Sir Robert Peyton.
104 BL, Royal MS. Appx 60, f. 29b.
105 BL, Royal MS. Appx 68, ff. 12b, 14.
106 Nichols 1788–1805, II, 'New Year's Gifts', p. 28; BL, Royal MS. Appx 68, f. 12b.
107 BL, Royal MS. Appx 68, ff. 13, 13b and 12 respectively.
108 *Ibid.*, f. 13b; Nichols 1788–1805, II, 'New Year's Gifts', p. 28.
109 London 1981A, no. 119.
110 Anne of Denmark, f. 21, no. 195.
111 Rymer 1704–26, XV, p. 757.
112 BL, Royal MS. Appx 68, f. 14.
113 *Gent. Mag.*, CXV.i (1845), 375–6.
114 Anne of Denmark, f. 10, no. 89.
115 Nichols 1828, IV, p. 1123, no. 1.
116 Moryson 1907–8, IV, p. 233.
117 *Gent. Mag.*, CXV.i (1845), 377.
118 Nichols 1788–1805, III, 'New Year's Gifts', p. 138.
119 Anne of Denmark, f. 3, no. 23.
120 *Ibid.*, f. 18, no. 166.
121 *Ibid.*, f. 9, no. 77.
122 *CSP Dom., James I*, IX, p. 121.
123 Anne of Denmark, f. 29, no. 288, f. 9, no. 77.
124 *Ibid.*, ff. 4–8, nos. 25–68.
125 *Ibid.*, f. 42, nos. 357–8.
126 *Ibid.*, f. 29, no. 289, f. 32, no. 308.
127 *CSP Ven.* III, no. 50, p. 16.
128 *L & P Henry VIII*, I, no. 463.
129 Strong 1987, fig. 28.
130 Soc. of Ant. 1951, pl. XV.
131 Surtees Soc., I, p. 227.
132 *L & P Henry VIII*, III.i, no. 463.
133 Rowlands 1985, no. 64; Stapylton 1892, p. 38.
134 Rowlands 1985, no. 190
135 *Lisle Letters*, VI, p. 274.
136 BL, Royal MS. Appx 68, f. 6; cf. Soc. of Ant., MS. 129A, f. 178b.
137 Nichols 1788–1805, II, 'New Year's Gifts', p. 15.
138 Strong 1969, no. 299; Rymer 1704–26, XV, p. 757.
139 Scarisbrick 1986A, fig. 7
140 Anne of Denmark, f. 27, no. 267.
141 Scarisbrick 1986A, p. 234.
142 Ashmole 1672, Statutes c.38.
143 *L & P Henry VIII*, IV.iii, no. 6789.
144 *Ibid.*, no. 5114.
145 *CSP Span., Eliz.*, I, p. 10.
146 *Complete Peerage*, X, p. 146, note d.
147 BL, Add. MS. 5702, f. 67; Essex RO, D/DP F240/1.
148 BL. Harley Roll D35, i–xi, f. 68.
149 BL, Royal MS. Appx 68, ff. 11b, 27.
150 London 1981A, P20.
151 Bray 1806, pp. 18–20.
152 Portrait of Prince Henry by Robert Peake, Palazzo Chiablese, Turin.
153 Christian IV, no. 565–7.
154 Rowlands 1985, no. 55.
155 London 1981A, no. 2.
156 Camden Soc., O.S. 54, p. 359 no. 3.
157 BL, Royal MS. Appx 68, ff. 2–5b; Anne of Denmark, f. 9, no. 84.
158 BL, Royal MS. Appx 68, f. 2; National Portrait Gallery 1969, no. 202.
159 Anne of Denmark, f. 17, no. 156.
160 Nichols 1788–1805, III. 'New Year's Gifts', p. 137.
161 London 1981A, G48.
162 Rymer 1704–26, XV, p. 758.
163 *CSP Dom., Eliz*, IV, p. 277.
164 London 1981A, P16.
165 Nichols 1788–1805, II, 'New Year's Gifts', p. 28.
166 Rymer 1704–26, XV, pp. 757–8.
167 BL, Royal MS. Appx 68, f. 4b; Nichols 1788–1805, II, 'New Year's Gifts', p. 16.
168 Nichols 1788–1805, II, 'New Year's Gifts', pp. 15–16.
169 Wilson 1983, p. 133, no. 20.
170 Nichols 1788–1805, II, 'New Year's Gifts', pp. 23, 27, 33, 34.
171 Whitney 1586, p. 29; Wither 1635, p. 40.
172 London 1981A, P6; Valeriano Bolzano 1614, p. 569.
173 Heriot 1822, p. 215.
174 Nichols 1788–1805, II, 'New Year's Gifts', pp. 4, 17.
175 BL, Royal MS. Appx 68, f. 5b.
176 Nichols 1788–1805, II, 'New Year's Gifts', pp. 27, 97.
177 *L & P Henry VIII*, II, nos. 3746, 5144.
178 Rymer 1704–26, XV, p. 758.
179 BL, Royal MS. Appx 68, f. 5b.
180 Nichols 1788–1805, II, 'New Year's Gifts', pp. 12,

63.
181 Westminster City Library, orig. will.
182 Anne of Denmark, f. 18, no. 174.
183 Devon 1836, p. 162; Heriot 1822, pp. 217–18.
184 Nichols 1788–1805, II, 'New Year's Gifts', pp. 6, 15, 37 and 27 respectively; BL, Royal MS. Appx 68, f. 4.
185 Westminster City Library, orig. will.
186 Heriot 1822, p. 220.
187 Nichols 1788–1805, II, 'New Year's Gifts', pp. 9–12, 25–9, 63.
188 *Ibid.*, p. 10; BL, Royal MS. Appx 68, f. 5.
189 *L & P Henry VIII*, IV.iii, no. 6349; Scarisbrick 1986A, p. 234.
190 Nichols 1788–1805, II, 'New Year's Gifts', p. 24; Anne of Denmark, f. 27, no. 268.
191 BL, Royal MS. Appx 68, ff. 3b, 4, 5b.
192 Anne of Denmark, f. 16, no. 154.
193 *Lisle Letters*, V, no. 1126, p. 71.
194 Soc. of Ant., MS. 129A, ff. 152b, 155, 185b, 221; Lewer 1933, p. 12.
195 BL, Royal MS. Appx 68, ff. 7–8b; Rymer 1704–26, XV, p. 759.
196 BL, Royal MS. 7C.xvi, f. 22.
197 BL, Royal MS. Appx 68, f. 8b.
198 *Gent. Mag.*, CXV.i (1845), 377.
199 V & A, MS. L30–1982; BL, Royal MS. Appx 68, f. 7; Jonson 1981–2, I, p. 171 (V.12. 124–30).
200 London 1981A. no. 31.
201 Soc. of Ant., MS. 129A, f. 180; Camden Soc., O.S. 83, p. 18.
202 Strong 1983, pp. 53, 64.
203 London 1981A, no. 46; Hackenbroch 1979, p. 296, fig. 292.
204 London 1981A, no. 40.
205 *Ibid.*, nos. 35, 37, 39.
206 *Ibid.*, no. 36.
207 Scarisbrick 1986A, pl. IV; Anne of Denmark, f. 24, no. 230.
208 Anne of Denmark, f. 28, no. 281.
209 Shirley 1869, p. 349.
210 Scarisbrick 1986A, p. 234.
211 *Ibid.*, p. 236, fig. 8, pl. III.
212 London 1981A, no. 22; Tait 1986A, p. 189.
213 London 1981A, no. 117.
214 Tait 1986A, pp. 187–8.
215 Backhouse 1989, pp. 13–16.
216 Madden 1831, p. 178.
217 Durrant 1977, p. 19.
218 Soc. of Ant., MS. 129A, f. 185b; BL, Royal MS. Appx 68, f. 10b.
219 Soc. of Ant., MS. 129A, f. 187b.
220 Lyly 1580, p. 443.
221 Tait 1986A.
222 Brasses of: Isabel Uvedale (†1572), Crichel More, Dorset (MS I); Kath. Throckmorton (*c.* 1573). Haseley, Warwickshire (MS I); Tait 1985, figs 5, 7; pp. 32–6.
223 HMC 9, Salisbury MSS., xvi, p. 402.
224 Tait 1985, pp. 36–8, figs 8–10.
225 *Ibid.*, figs 19–20.
226 *Ibid.*, fig. 25; Scarisbrick 1989, pl. 5.
227 Tait 1985, pp. 46–52, figs 21–3.
228 *Ibid.*, fig. 11, pp. 39–45.
229 V & A, MS. L.30–1982, f. 34b; BL, Royal MS. Appx 68, f. 10b.
230 Soc. of Ant., MS. 129A, ff. 154b, 155b, 161–61b, 168–68b, 178–8b, 185b, 187b, 209, 217, 221, 222.
231 BL, Royal MS. Appx 89, f. 36.
232 Rymere 1704–26, XV, p. 759; BL, Royal MS. Appx 68, f. 6b.
233 BL, Royal MS. Appx 68, f. 20.
234 V & A, MS. I.30–1982, f. 31b.
235 BL, Harl. MS. 611, f. 5b.
236 BL, Royal MS. Appx 68, f. 20.
237 National Portrait Gallery 1969, no. 650.
238 London 1976, no. 292; Tait 1962A, pp. 112–13.
239 Anne of Denmark, f. 37, no. 348, f. 38, no. 361.
240 Scarisbrick 1986A, fig. 5, p. 320.
241 Soc. of Ant., MS. 129A, ff. 154, 159b, etc.
242 *Ibid.*, ff. 204–5b, 207–8b, 219, 225b.
243 Rymer 1704–26, XV, p. 759.
244 Soc. of Ant., MS. 129A, f. 217; *L & P Henry VIII*, IV.iii, no. 6789, p. 307.
245 Essex RO, D/DP F240/1.
246 V & A, MS. L.30–1982, ff. 72b, 36b.
247 BL, Stowe MS. 557, f. 102b, no. 8, f. 96b, no. 34, f. 102, no. 5; BL, Add. MS. 5971A, f. 98, no. 58; Nichols 1788–1805, II, 'New Year's Gifts', p. 14; BL, Add. MS. 5971A, f. 99, nos. 72, 76, f. 101, no. 19; BL, Stowe MS. 557, f. 102, no. 3, f. 96b, no. 33.
248 Reynolds 1951, pl. 2; Soc. of Ant., MS. 129A, ff. 207–9, 228.
249 Camden Soc., O.S. 61, p. 3.
250 *Lisle Letters*, VI, p. 192.
251 HMC 9, Salisbury MSS., I, p. 129.
252 BL, Royal MS. Appx 68, f. 25b.
253 BL, Stowe MS. 557, f. 95b, no. 10.
254 Anne of Denmark, f. 15, no. 245, f. 24, no. 227.
255 *Ibid.*, f. 43, no. 396.
256 Spenser 1912, *Faerie Queene*, II.iii.26.
257 BL, Add. MS. 5498, f. 25.
258 Benger 1821, p. 270.
259 Nichols 1788–1805, III, 'A lottery, presented before the Queenes Maiestie at the Lord Chancellor's House, 1601', p. 36.
260 Camden Soc., O.S. 83, p. 19.
261 *Gent. Mag.*, CXV.i (1845), 377.
262 Soc. of Ant., MS. 129A, f. 150.
263 *Ibid.*, ff. 150–1, 168, 178, 189b.
264 Nichols 1788–1805, II, 'New Year's Gifts', p. 34.
265 BL, Royal MS. Appx 68, f. 16.
266 *Ibid.*, ff. 15b–16.
267 *Ibid.*, f. 15b; Arnold 1988, pp. 76–7.
268 BL, Royal MS. Appx 68, f. 16b; Scarisbrick 1989, pl. 3.
269 *L & P Henry VIII*, VIII, no. 907.
270 Soc. of Ant., MS. 129A, ff. 150, 150b.
271 BL, Royal MS. Appx 68, ff. 15b, 16b, 17.

272 London 1981A, P17.
273 Scarisbrick 1987B, fig. 12.
274 Anne of Denmark, f. 29, no. 293–4, f. 38, no. 357.
275 Scarisbrick 1986A, fig. 7.
276 *Gent. Mag.*, CXV.i (1845). 377; BL, Harl. MS. 6853, f. 187; V & A, MS. L.30–1982, f. 33b; Leicester RO, DG9/2409.
277 Marston 1606, IV.i.177–9.
278 Rowlands 1985, no. 62.
279 *L & P Henry VIII*, XVI, no. 1389.
280 BL, Royal MS. 7C.xvi, f. 25; Camden Soc., O.S. 83, p. 19; *Lisle Letters*, IV, no. 859.
281 Rymer 1704–26, XV, p. 759.
282 Leicester RO, DG9/2409.
283 Ellis 1846, 3 ser., I, p. 221.
284 *L & P Henry VIII*, I, no. 1193.
285 Rymer 1704–26, XV, p. 759.
286 Lewer 1933, p. 14; Tait 1986B, no. 353; Scarisbrick 1989, pl. 16; Nichols 1788–1805, II, 'New Year's Gifts', p. 11.
287 BL, Royal MS. Appx 68, ff. 13, 13b, 14b–15.
288 BL, Harley Roll D35i–xi, f. 67.
289 BL, Stowe MS. 557, f. 196b, no. 32.
290 Scarisbrick 1986A, p. 233.
291 Tait 1987, p. 16, figs 8–9.
292 BL, Royal MS. Appx 68, ff. 9, 10; Nichols 1788–1805, II, 'New Year's Gifts', p. 3.
293 BL, Royal MS. Appx 68, ff. 9–10.
294 London 1981A, G50.
295 Scarisbrick 1986A, p. 236.
296 Jagger 1988, pl. 18 (p. 31), pl. 16 (p. 29).
297 Soc. of Ant., MS. 129A, ff. 151, 209; Anne of Denmark, f. 27, no. 275; National Portrait Gallery 1969, no. 164.
298 BL, Royal MS. Appx 68, f. 39b; V & A, M160–1922.
299 Hayward 1982, pp. 10–11.
300 *CSP Ven.* I, no. 570; Scarisbrick 1986A, p. 236.
301 BL, Royal MS. Appx 68, f. 19b.
302 *EHD*, V, p. 388.
303 Oman 1974, p. 133.
304 BL, Royal MS. Appx 68, ff. 21b, 23b.
305 Moryson 1907–8, IV, p. 233.
306 Rymer 1704–26, XV, p. 759; Oman 1974, p. 131; BL, Royal MS. Appx 68, ff. 22b, 23.
307 BL, Royal MS. Appx 68, f. 22b.
308 Heriot 1822, p. 201.
309 Nichols 1788–1805, II, 'New Year's Gifts', p. 4; Rymer 1704–26, XV, p. 759.
310 Lewer 1933, p. 12; BL, Royal MS. Appx 68, f. 22b; Anne of Denmark, f. 9. no. 81.
311 London 1981A, no. 37.
312 *L & P Henry VIII*, XI, no. 148.
313 Scarisbrick 1986A, p. 235.
314 Oman 1974, p. 131.
315 Rymer 1704–26, XV, p. 759.
316 BL, Royal MS. Appx 89, f. 32.
317 Nichols 1788–1805, II, 'New Year's Gifts', p. 7; BL, Royal MS. Appx 68, ff. 22b–4; Scarisbrick 1986A, p. 235.
318 Oman 1974, p. 131; BL, Royal MS, Appx 68, f. 23.
319 *Ibid.*, Rymer 1704–26, XV, p. 759.
320 Lewer 1933, p. 112; BL, Royal MS. Appx 68, f. 22.
321 Rowlands 1985, no. 40; Oman 1974, p. 131.
322 Westminster City Library, orig. will.
323 National Portrait Gallery 1969, nos. 535, 164.
324 Scarisbrick 1989, pl. 25.
325 London 1981A, no. 30.
326 Oman 1974, p. 133; *CSP Dom., James I*, X, p. 215.
327 Oman 1974, pl. 52A; PRO, Prob. ii/68, f. 21; Westminster City Library, orig. will of John Cotton.
328 Oman 1974, pl. 45A and D.
329 Reading Museum and Art Gallery, acquired 1970.
330 Harari 1977, no. 130; Oman 1974, p. 135.
331 BL, Harl. MS. 6910, cited in Evans 1931, p. xvii.
332 Essex RO, D/ABW10/15.
333 Dalton 1912, no. 952.
334 Bedford RO, ABP/W/1622/60.
335 Soc. of Ant., MS. 129A, f 218.
336 V & A, 920–1871.
337 Oman 1974, p. 62.
338 *CSP Ven.* VI.i, no. 473.
339 BL, Harl. MS. 611, ff. 27b, 28.
340 *CSP Span.* XII, pp. 177, 195.
341 Oman 1974, pp. 62–3.
342 *Lisle Letters*, II, pp. 117, 127, 139; IV, p. 48.
343 *Ibid.*, IV, p. 348.

5 *The social context of Stuart and Commonwealth jewellery, 1625–1714*

1 Lemon 1827, p. 148.
2 Twining 1960, pp. 148–9; Collins 1955, pp. 168–95.
3 *CSP Dom., Charles I*, I, pp. 77, 79, 97, 141, 571; VIII, p. 122.
4 BL, King's MS. 136, ff. 430–31b.
5 *CSP Ven.* XXIV, p. 365.
6 Green 1857, p. 365.
7 Twining 1960, pp. 148–9.
8 Camden Soc., n.s. 31, p. 23.
9 PRO, S.P.78/128/19, Scarisbrick 1990b.
10 Collins 1955, p. 191.
11 HMC 6, 7th Rept, House of Lords, p. 88, note 9 May 1660.
12 *CSP Dom., Charles II*, III, p. 189.
13 *Ibid.*, II, p. 60.
14 PRO, L.C.5/107, ff. 62, 65.
15 Jesse 1840, III, p. 284.
16 *CSP Dom., Charles II*, III p. 438.
17 Pepys 1971–83, IV, p. 57.
18 *CSP Ven.*, XXXIII, no. 233, p. 180.
19 *Ibid.*, no. 238, p. 183.
20 Wheatley 1964, p. 8; Jusserand 1892, p. 92.
21 Pepys 1971–83, IX, p. 38.
22 Oman 1962, pp. 3, 22, 27.
23 NPG, no. 214.
24 Dangeau 1854–60, vi, p. 267.

25 Ferrers 1817, p. 237.
26 *Ibid.*, p. 236.
27 Misson 1698, p. 19.
28 BL, Add. MS. 5751A.
29 BL, Add. MS. 44825, f. 67.
30 BL, Stowe MS. 560, ff. 68b–73.
31 Coke 1719, II, p. 533.
32 Marlborough 1930, p. 74.
33 Green 1967, p. 134.
34 Lamport Hall, Northants.
35 *Arch. Cant.*, XI, (1877), 236.
36 PRO, Prob. 10, probate 10 June 1675.
37 HMC 27, Duke of Beaufort, p. 55.
38 PRO, Prob. 10, probate 7 and 24 Nov. 1642.
39 Verney 1925, I, p. 155.
40 Marshall 1973, pp. 23, 85, pl. facing p. 64.
41 HMC 43, 15th Rept, Appx VII, p. 159.
42 Verney 1925, II, p. 134.
43 PRO, Prob. 10, probate 10 June 1675.
44 Burghley House Archives, MS. Ex41/82.
45 Grammont 1908, I, p. 216; II, p. 134.
46 Pepys 1971–83, VII, p. 372.
47 HMC 27, Duke of Beaufort, p. 55.
48 Evelyn 1959, p. 606.
49 NLS, MS. 14548.
50 La Mothe 1913, p. 317.
51 Rochester 1699, pt 2, p. 57.
52 Gay 1974, I, p. 83.
53 Cartwright 1883, pp. 262–3.
54 BL, Add. MS. 9125, ff. 1b–4, specifications of diamonds with valuations, and ff. 9–11, inventory *c.* 1715–18; BL, Add. MS. 61472, ff. 206–7b, two lists of jewels; BL, Add. MS. 61644, ff. 46–8, list of jewels of Charles, Earl of Sunderland, *c.* 1723; also BL, Add. MS. 61472, ff. 52, 53, 127–30b, and BL, Add. MS. 61655, ff. 172–4.
55 BL, Add. MS. 33462, f. 112.
56 Camden Soc., O.S. 83, pp. 92–7.
57 Oxinden 1937, pp. xxxiii, 182.
58 Marshall 1973, p. 94, no. 10.
59 Hutchinson 1806, II, p. 171.
60 Butler 1967, p. 242 (Canto II, lines 303–6).
61 *EHR*, XXXVI (1921), 624.
62 Sidney 1843, I, p. 301.
63 Pepys 1971–83, IX, pp. 88–9.
64 Stapylton 1892, p. 171.
65 Behn 1915, I, p. 54.
66 Wynn 1926, p. 266.
67 *CSP Ven.*, XXII, p. 154.
68 *Ibid.*, p. 302.
69 *Ibid.*, p. 576.
70 *CSP Dom., Commonwealth*, XII, p. 168.
71 Whitelocke 1855, II, pp. 200 ff.
72 *Ibid.*, I, p. 86.
73 *Ibid.*, II, p. 273.
74 Noble 1787, p. 307.
75 PRO, L.C.5/107, f. 62; L.C.5/112, pp. 4, 10–12, 15–18; L.C.5/114, 11 Oct. 1698.
76 Camden Soc., O.S. 71, p. 111.
77 *Ibid.*, p. 32.
78 Essex RO, D/D Rg 2/120.
79 BL, Add. MS. 36243, f. 2.
80 Smith 1901, p. 31.
81 Ashmole 1966, pp. 196–7, pl. xix
82 *CSP Dom., Commonwealth*, XI, p. 127.
83 Fanshawe 1907, p. 147.
84 Goodall, forthcoming.
85 *CSP Dom, James I*, VIII, p. 244.
86 Finett 1656.
87 HMC 1, 2nd Rept, p. 83.
88 By John Riley, at Rousham.
89 PRO, L.C.5/108, f. 17.
90 PRO, L.C.5/109, pp. 101, 424; L.C.5/110, p. 305; L.C.5/111, p. 227.
91 PRO, L.C.5/109, p. 28.
92 Scarisbrick 1985A, fig. 8, p. 736.
93 Fraser 1859, p. 318.
94 Pepys 1971–83, IX, p. 67.
95 *Ibid.*
96 Cartwright 1883, p. 109.
97 *CSP Ven.*, XXIV, p. 589.
98 Pepys 1971–83, VI, pp. 190–1.
99 Seymour 1940, pp. 17–18.
100 *CSP Dom., Charles I*, VII, p. 27.
101 *CSP Ven.*, XXXII, p. 308.
102 *CSP Dom., Charles I*, p. viii, p. 122.
103 *Ibid.*, VI, p. 195.
104 HMC 29, Portland, II, p. 260.
105 Pepys 1971–83, VI, pp. 299–300.
106 Yogev 1978, p. 83.
107 Ellis 1825–46, 2nd ser., IV, 1827, p. 20.
108 Yogev 1978, p. 67.
109 *Ibid.*, p. 140.
110 Berquen 1669, p. 134.
111 Yogev 1978, pp. 150–1.
112 Cartwright 1883, p. 164.
113 PRO, Prob. 10, probate 10 June 1675.
114 CLRO, Orphans Inv. 1744.
115 Pro, Prob. 10, probate 10 June 1675.
116 London Museum 1928.
117 Burnaby 1701, II.ii.
118 Vaughan 1674, p. 240.
119 Kidd 1979, p. 49.
120 *CSP Dom., Charles I*, IX, p. 323; Larkin 1983, no. 217, p. 508.
121 Massinger 1639, *The Unnaturall Combat*, III.ii.
122 Nicols 1652, p. 147.
123 Evelyn 1959, p. 244.
124 Butler 1967, p. 312.
125 CLRO, MCI/94.18.
126 Nicols 1652, p. 76.
127 Kidd 1979, p. 49.
128 *Ibid.*, p. 37.
129 CLRO, MCI/78.7.
130 CLRO, Orphans Inv. 1744.
131 *Ibid.*, 2411.
132 PRO, L.C.5/108, f. 28b.
133 Behn 1915, III, pp. 205–6.
134 Library of Congress, Halliwell Papers.
135 BL, Add. MS. 9125, *passim*.

136 *Spectator* 1965, III, p. 183.
137 Burnaby 1701, p. 26.
138 Boyle 1672, p. 37.
139 CLRO, Orphans Inv. 1744.
140 *Ibid.*, 711, 2245.
141 Surtees Soc., 168, p. 189; Evelyn 1959, p. 338.
142 Fiennes 1949, p. 267.
143 Hawkins 1633, p. 188.
144 Wynn 1926, p. 337.
145 Magalotti 1821, p. 400.
146 Pepys 1971–83, VII, pp. 108, 111, 113, 412; Jourdain 1924, p. 922, fig. 4
147 CLRO, Orphans Inv. 1744.
148 Smith 1901, p. 35.
149 Vaughan 1675, pp. 241–2.
150 CLRO, Orphans Inv. 1138.
151 *Ibid.*, 520.
152 *Ibid.*, 2856.
153 Gwynn 1985, p. 181.
154 CLRO, Orphans Inventories 1662–1725, index s.v. Jewellers.
155 PRO, L.C.5 *passim.*
156 *CSP Dom., Charles I*, I, p. 391.
157 *Ibid.*, II, p. 465; IV, p. 543; IX, p. 7; and I, p. 571.
158 PRO, S.P.76/107/17, f. 33b.
159 Huguenot Soc., 4to ser., 57, nos. 36, 47, 343, 461, 487, 683, 752, 980, 1125, 1275, 1355, 1431–2, 1435, 1510, 1579, 1714, 1722, 1812, 1821, 1855, 1947, 2003, 2084, 2256, 2281, 2301, 2415, 2515, 2538, 2716.
160 Osborne 1928, p. 142.
161 *CSP Dom., Charles I*, I, pp. 52, 56, 66, 97; X, p. 80.
162 Millard, unpaginated.
163 NLS, MS. 14636.
164 *CSP Dom., Commonwealth*, II, pp. 34, 115, 127.
165 PRO, L.C.5/107, f. 54b; Mayo 1897, p. 15.
166 *CSP Dom., Commonwealth*, VIII, pp. 8, 594.
167 *Ibid.*, II, p. 416; HMC 24, Rutland, IV, p. 541; PRO, Prob. 10, probate 10 June 1675.
168 *CSP Dom., Charles II*, II, pp. 22, 466; III, p. 250.
169 *Ibid.*, III, p. 128; V, pp. 25, 38, 591.
170 *Ibid.*, I, p. 77.
171 Pepys 1971–83, VI, p. 215; *DNB*, Sir Robert Vyner.
172 Wynn 1926; p. 407.
173 *CSP Dom., Commonwealth*, XIII, p. 425; *CSP Dom., Charles II*, I, p. 583.
174 Wheatley 1964.
175 *DNB*, Sir John Chardin.
176 *London Gazette*, 6 Oct. 1683.
177 Twining 1960, p. 157; BL, Add. MS. 5751, f. 126.
178 Price 1902, pp. 161–4.
179 BL, Add. MS. 9125, f. 26, n. 13.
180 PRO, Prob. 10, probate 10 June 1675; HMC 24, Rutland, IV, p. 541.
181 NLS, MS. 14548.
182 Grammont 1908, I, p. 106.
183 CLRO, Orphans Inv. 363, 491, 690, 1744, etc.
184 PRO, Prob. 10, probate 10 June 1675.
185 NLS, MS. 14548.
186 Suffolk RO, IC 500/3/c and 7/31(57).
187 London Museum 1928, no. A14159, pl. vi.
188 *Ibid.*, nos. A14172, A14072, pl. i.
189 *Ibid.*, nos. A14064, A14112, pl. vii.
190 *Ibid.*, no. A14124, pl. vii no. A14125, pl. vi.
191 *Ibid.*, no. A14100, pl. iv.
192 Price 1902, pl. xxvii.
193 BL, Add. MS. 9125, f. 11, nos. 41, 45.
194 London Museum 1928, pl. v.2 (no. A14082).
195 Price 1902, pl. xxvii; Curie 1906, p. 58.
196 Wright 1982, nos. 18–19.
197 London Museum 1928, p. 30 (no. A14259).
198 Syon House, Duke of Northumberland's collection; London 1982, no. 31, pl. VII.
199 Millar 1963, no. 159, pl. 84.
200 HMC 10, Appx I, Eglinton, p. 35.
201 Burghley House Archives, MS. Ex41/82.
202 Wharton 1844, p. 174.
203 Price 1902, pl. XXVII.
204 V & A, M3–1958, maker's mark R A.
205 Massinger 1629, *The Roman Actor*, III.ii.178.
206 Formerly Hay family. Collection of Mr Richard Falkiner.
207 Behn 1915, VI, pp. 15, 80–9.
208 *Spectator* 1965, II, p. 453.
209 Christie's, London, 19 Dec. 1989, no. 474; Scarisbrick 1990A, p. 59.
210 Rhodes 1723.
211 Herbst 1710.
212 Scarisbrick 1985A, figs 3, 4, 6.
213 *Tatler* 1898, III, p. 194.
214 *Ibid.*, IV, p. 249.
215 Curle 1906, p. 58; Christie's, 20 Feb. 1973, nos. 189, 192; Evans 1921, p. 135; Evans 1970, pl. 125c.
216 Somers Cocks 1985, nos. 53–7.
217 Behn 1915, VI, p. 91.
218 Lightbown 1968, p. 84.
219 Massinger 1655, *The Guardian*, I.ii.
220 London Museum 1928, pp. 27–31.
221 NRA, 7829, p. 37, no. 23.
222 CLRO, Orphans Inv. 1744.
223 London Museum 1928, no. A14243, X5, p. 28.
224 HMC 10, Eglinton, p. 35.
225 Dalton 1925, no. 1106; Kagan 1981, pl. iii.2–4.
226 Fortnum 1883 and 1887.
227 Buckley 1932, unpaginated.
228 Verney 1925, I, p. 483.
229 Kagan 1981, p. 182.
230 Scarisbrick 1986B, pl. xc (b); Dalton 1915, no. 388.
231 Kagan 1981, pp. 182–3.
232 Scarisbrick 1989, pl. 45.
233 Kagan 1981, p. 182, no. 35; Evelyn 1697, p. 239.
234 Gori 1767, II, p. 287.
235 Kagan 1981, pl. i (2, 3, 5, 6).
236 Wright 1982, no. 3.
237 Kagan 1981, p. 192, pl. iii, p. 195, no. 56, and p. 186, nos. 59–60.
238 Sutherland 1955, pp. 187–8; Kagan 1981, p. 186,

nos. 39, 61.
239 Kagan 1981, p. 186; *CSP Dom., William III*, I, p. 4.
240 Kagan 1981, pl. i, no. 9.
241 Burghley House Archives, MS. Ex41/82.
242 BL, Add. MS. 61420, f. 116, no. 25.
243 Fraser 1859, p. 317.
244 Berkshire RO, D/EBy F 16; Christie's, Fountaine colln, 6 July 1894, no. 82.
245 Osborne 1928, p. 135.
246 Fraser 1888, p. 241.
247 London Museum 1928, no. A14011, pl. xii; Jagger 1988, col. pl. 13, p. 125.
248 London 1981, no. 127.
249 Cartwright 1894, p. 30.
250 Nicolas 1841–2, I, pp. 225–6; Ashmole 1672, p. 216.
251 Ashmole 1715, p. 182.
252 London 1982–3, no. 25.
253 Wellington 1953, p. 159.
254 Ashmole 1672, p. 202.
255 Nicolas 1841–2, I. p. 247.
256 Pepys 1971–83, II, p. 49.
257 PRO, L.C.9/41.
258 Scarisbrick 1989, pl. 267.
259 Kagan 1981, pl. ii, nos. 1–3; Ashmole 1672, p. 226.
260 Wellington 1953, pl. xix.a.
261 Sotheby's, London, 16 Nov. 1988, no. 27.
262 London 1978, nos. 251–2; Washington 1985, no. 110.
263 Smith 1902–3, p. 242.
264 Christie's, 20 Feb. 1973, no. 187.
265 PRO, L.C.9/41.
266 London 1872, no. 568.
267 Kagan 1981, pl. ii, nos. 4a-b, 5a-b.
268 Babelon 1897, no. 622.
269 BL, Add. MS. 61420, f. 116.
270 CLRO, Orphans Inv. 1744; Marshall 1973, p. 159.
271 *CSP Dom., Charles II*, III, p. 813.
272 Evelyn 1959, p. 813; Scarisbrick 1989, pls 55–6.
273 Nicolas 1841–2, III, pt 1, pp. 26–7.
274 *Ibid.*, III, pt 2, p. 37.
275 Nevinson 1954, p. 157; Nicolas 1841–2, III, pt 2, p. 36.
276 Oxinden 1933, p. 108.
277 Oman 1930, p. 144.
278 Christie's, 25 Nov. 1975, no. 56.
279 V & A, 92–1866; Burghley House, Exeter colln.
280 Oman 1974, 80A.
281 Sharp 1922–3, p. 232.
282 Christie's, 20 Feb. 1973, nos. 151, 162; *Gent. Mag.*, LVIII.ii (1788), 769.
283 V & A, M145–1962; Oman 1974, 79A.
284 Sharp 19222–3, pp. 233–5, fig. 7; Christie's 27 Nov. 1991, no. 271.
285 Jesse 1846, II, p. 192; SNPG, L208, on loan from the Earl of Rosebery.
286 Evelyn 1959, p. 823.
287 Christie's, 20 Feb. 1973, no. 169.
288 London 1889, no. 611.
289 V & A, 827A–1864; *Gent. Mag.*, LXI i (1791), 401; LXI ii (1791), 814.
290 V & A, M811–1926.
291 Christie's, 20 Feb. 1973, no. 166.
292 NMS, M/1828.
293 NMS, M/1831.
294 Chiddingstone Castle colln.
295 Oman 1974, 79E; V & A, M251–1975.
296 Wotton 1741, IV, pp. 363–80 for list, and p. 363, n. b.
297 Christie's, 13 Nov. 1890, no. 305.
298 V & A, M898–1904.
299 Colln of the Duke of St Albans, dated 1684. O.S. calendar; Scarisbrick 1989, pls 49–50.
300 V & A, M9–1960; Oman 1974, 88B.
301 Dalton 1912, no. 1415.
302 London 1889, no. 662.
303 Dalton 1912, nos. 1376–7; V & A, M10–1948, MM107–1962 and M289–1962.
304 Collection of Her Majesty The Queen, Windsor; bt Christie's 6 Aug. 1913, no. 53.
305 Delany 1861, VI, p. 202.
306 Christie's, 13 Nov. 1890, no. 339.
307 V & A, M109–1962.
308 Mayo 1897, pl. 6, pp. 15–17.
309 PRO, L.C.5/107, f. 54b.
310 Christie's, 20 Apr. 1784, Lady Frankland, relics of Oliver Cromwell.
311 Dalton 1912, no. 1106.
312 V & A, M114–15–1962.
313 Jesse 1846, II, p. 220.
314 *CSP Ven.*, XXIV, p. 69.
315 Millar 1963, no. 148, pl. 68.
316 Norfolk 1857, p. 272.
317 *Ibid.*, pp. 302–3.
318 HMC 1, 1 Rutland MSS., p. 526.
319 Berkeley 1971, p. 87.
320 Christie's, 13 Nov. 1890, no. 315.
321 London Museum 1928, p. 33, pl. xv; p. 20, no. A14105, pl. iv; nos. A14157 and A14095, pl. vi; p. 19, no. A14011, pl. xii, nos. A14093, A14095, pl. vi.
322 CLRO, MCI/72.11.
323 Wither 1635, p. 39.
324 CLRO, Orphans Inv. 711, MCI/131b.64.
325 NLS, MS. 14548.
326 Burghley House Archives, MS. Ex41/82.
327 BL, Add. MS. 61472, f. 52.
328 Dangeau 1854–60, II, p. 100.
329 CLRO, Orphans Inv. 2856.
330 Pope 1941, Canto I, line 23.
331 BL, Add. MS. 9125, f. 10, no. 12.
332 BL, Add. MS. 61472, f. 53.
333 Oman 1974, p. 57, pl. 73A-C.
334 Evans 1931, p. 64.
335 Butler 1967, II, Canto 3, lines 1098–1102.
336 Green 1857, p. 15; cf. Christie's, 13 Nov. 1890, no. 307.
337 Jesse 1840, IV, p. 47.

338 Nicols 1652, p. 32.
339 Boyle 1672, p. 177.
340 Fraser 1888, p. 232.
341 Nicols 1652, p. 159.
342 CLRO, Orphans Inv. 1744.
343 Evans 1922, p. 178.
344 *Holy Dying* (1651 edn), p. vii, in Dedication.
345 NPG loan.
346 Smith 1901, p. 154.
347 Beaumont and Fletcher 1905–12, *The Chances*, I.v.
348 Oman 1974, p. 72.
349 Camden Soc., O.S. 49, p. 201; Guildhall, MS. 9171/31.i, ff. 13b, 30.
350 Berkshire RO, EBY F16; Bedford RO, ABP/W/1683/58.
351 CLRO, Orphans Inv. 2856.
352 Dalton 1912, no. 1451; Oman 1974, 86A.
353 Lindsay 1868, p. 84.
354 Verney 1925, I, p. 219.
355 V & A, M156–1962.
356 V & A, 1639–1903.
357 Oman 1974, 87D-E.
358 Blair 1985, p. 73.
359 Oman 1974, 87H.
360 Burghley House Archives, MS. Ex41/82.
361 Weber 1914, pp. 438–9.
362 Christie's, 30 July 1952 (Old English silver), no. 119.
363 V & A, M14–1960.
364 Sharp 1922–3, pp. 236–7, fig. 9.
365 Weber 1914, p. 439.
366 Wither 1635, p. 94.
367 Sharp 1922–3, p. 230, fig. 2; V & A, M50–1967.
368 Christie's, 12 Dec. 1989, no. 474.
369 BL, Add. MS. 61472, f. 10b, no. 26.
370 *Tatler* 1898, IV, p. 249.
371 Osborne 1928, p. 240.
372 Isham 1971, p. 109.
373 Grammont 1908, II, p. 3.
374 A. Daly Briscoe, *A Stuart Benefactress: Sarah Duchess of Somerset* (1973), p. 214.
375 Fitzwilliam Museum, PER326.
376 Christie's, 12 Dec. 1989, no. 474; Scarisbrick 1990A, p. 59.
377 Malcolm 1806, II, p. 315.
378 *Spectator* 1965, II, p. 453.
379 BL, Add. MS. 61655, f. 174.
380 Pope 1941, Canto IV, lines 113–16, p. 193.
381 London 1982.
382 Howarth 1985, p. 154; Hollar 1977.
383 Somerset 1984, p. 138.
384 Millar 1963, nos. 257–66, pp. 124–6 (text vol.).
385 BL, Add. MS. 61420, f. 117; Add. MS. 9125, f. 10b.
386 James, Duke of Richmond, by Van Dyck, Iveagh Bequest, Kenwood, London.
387 Pepys 1971–83, I, p. 26.
388 Beer 1938.
389 Sir Jeremy Smith, by Lely *c.* 1685, National Maritime Museum, Greenwich.

6 *The categories of Stuart and Commonwealth jewellery, 1625–1714.*

1 Twining 1960, pp. 150–1.
2 *Ibid.*, p. 15.
3 *Ibid.*, p. 157; Blair, forthcoming.
4 Sandford 1687, p. 208.
5 PRO, Prob. 11/174, f. 170.
6 London Museum 1928, no. A14164; Fraser 1888, II, p. 241.
7 London Museum 1928 A 14124: p. 34 no. 95.
8 Courtauld Institute, Witt Library.
9 Somers Cocks 1985, no. 57.
10 BL, Add. MS. 61472, f. 206, no. 9.
11 Evelyn 1974, p. 4.
12 *Ibid.*, p. 18.
13 Library of Congress, Wrottesley Inv.
14 BL, Add. MS. 61472, f. 206, no. 10.
15 Scarisbrick 1985A, fig. 1
16 Fiennes 1949, p. 338.
17 *ILN*, 25 Nov. 1933, p. 835; Gay 1974, I, p. 83.
18 Welbeck Abbey 1897, p. 30; the pearl is seen in Van Dyck's portrait in the National Gallery.
19 MS. in author's collection.
20 NLS, MS. 5158, f. 33.
21 Russell 1853, I, p. 244; cf. Pepys 1971–83, VII, p. 358.
22 Sedley 1702, p. 6.
23 PRO, Prob. 10, probate 10 June 1675.
24 NLS, MS. 14548.
25 *ILN*, 25 Nov. 1933, p. 837.
26 BL, Add. MS. 9125, f. 10, no. 2.
27 *Ibid.*, no. 23.
28 *Ibid.*, f. 4, no. 26.
29 *Ibid.*, f. 10, nos. 9, 45 and 46.
30 Scarisbrick 1985A, fig. 2.
31 Verney 1904, II, p. 374.
32 London Museum 1928, no. A14071.
33 PRO, Prob. 11/174, f. 70.
34 Wharton 1844, p. 379.
35 BL, Add. MS. 9125, f. 10 no. 5.
36 PRO, Prob. 10, probate 24 Nov. 1642.
37 *Ibid.*, probate 10 June 1675.
38 London Museum 1928, nos. A14069, A14202, pp. 33 and 35.
39 *ILN*, 25 Nov. 1933, p. 837.
40 BL, Add. MS. 9125, f. 10b, no. 33.
41 London Museum 1928, nos. A14195, A14108, A14251–2.
42 PRO, Prob. 10, probate 7 and 24 Nov. 1642.
43 NLS, MS. 14548.
44 PRO, Prob. 10, probate 10 June 1675. BL, Add. MS. 9125, f. 11, no. 54; f. 10, no. 11; Add. MS. 61472, f. 207, no. 18.
45 CLRO, MCI/62B.129.
46 Sedley 1702, p. 6.
47 CLRO, Orphans Inv. 1526, 1634, 1744.
48 London Museum 1928, p. 33, no. 18, X2.
49 NLS, MS. 5158, f. 33.
50 Hamilton Archives, RH 13/11/9.

51 Verney 1925, II, p. 134.
52 Duns Castle archives, EDNC 837; Christie's, 3 March 1971, no. 104.
53 CLRO, MCI/60A.28
54 Fraser 1859, p. 318.
55 CLRO, Orphans Inv. 1634.
56 PRO, Prob. 10, probate 13 Nov. 1690.
57 NLS, MS. 14487.
58 CLRO, MCI/232.52; Surtees Soc., 62, p. 338.
59 London Museum 1928, no. A14100.
60 Verney 1925, II, p. 134; Collins 1734, p. 364.
61 CLRO, Orphans Inv. 711.
62 NLS, MS. 14548.
63 Cartwright 1883, p. 307.
64 PRO, Prob. 10, probate 10 June 1675.
65 NLS, MS. 14548; Curle 1906, p. 58.
66 *ILN*, 25 Nov. 1933, p. 837.
67 Scarisbrick 1985A, fig. 3, p. 734.
68 Fiennes 1949, p. 338.
69 Oxinden 1933, p. 226.
70 PRO, Prob. 11/174, f. 70.
71 Tait 1986A, no. 35, pp. 192–6.
72 V & A, M67–1975, attributed and dated by Tait 1986A, p. 195.
73 PRO, Prob. 10, probate 10 June 1675.
74 Bristol 1894, pp. 67–9, 133.
75 Scarisbrick 1983, II, p. 1696, figs 4 and 5.
76 Green 1967, p. 190.
77 BL, Add, MS. 9125, f. 10, no. 6.
78 *Ibid.*, no. 16.
79 *Ibid.*, nos. 14 and 32; Add. MS. 61472, f. 206, no. 13.
80 Curle 1906, p. 58; CLRO, MCI/57C.23; and Fiennes 1949, p. 73.
81 PRO, Prob. 10, probate 7 and 24 Nov. 1642.
82 BL, Add. MS. 9125, f. 3b.
83 *Ibid.*
84 *Ibid.*
85 Evelyn 1974, pp. 3, 4.
86 BL, Add. MS. 9125, f. 10b.
87 NLS, MS. 14548.
88 BL, Add. MS. 9125, f. 10b.
89 Verney 1925, I, p. 224.
90 CLRO, Orphans Inv. 1744.
91 Bedford RO, ABP/W/1683/58.
92 CLRO, Orphans Inv. 2602.
93 Fraser 1859, p. 317.
94 NLS, MS. 5158, f. 33.
95 Fraser 1859, p. 318.
96 Fraser 1888, p. 241.
97 London Museum 1928, nos. A14074, A14202–4.
98 Behn 1915, I p. 54.
99 Fraser 1859, p. 317.
100 Behn 1915, V, p. 380.
101 PRO, Prob. 10, probate 10 June 1675.
102 NLS, MS. 14548.
103 NLS, MS. 14487, 2 Dec. 1694.
104 NLS, MS. 14548.
105 BL, Add. MS. 9125, f. 10.
106 CLRO, Orphans Inv. 1744; Fraser 1859, p. 288; PRO, Prob. 11/499, f. 41, Dorothy Pickering; CLRO, MCI/131B.64.
107 Cripps 1975, p. 96.
108 Fraser 1888, II, p. 253.
109 CLRO, MCI/83.312.
110 Pepys 1971–83, IX, p. 7.
111 CLRO, MCI/229.76.
112 Bedford RO, ABP/W/1683/58.
113 Camden Soc., O.S. 83, p. 117.
114 Hartmann 1934, pp. 392–3.
115 CLRO, MCI/182.76.
116 Behn 1915, V, pp. 14, 20.
117 PRO, Prob. 11/381, f. 108.
118 *Ibid.*, f. 112.
119 NLS, MS. 5158, f. 33.
120 Fraser 1859, pp. 317–18.
121 Pepys 1971–83, VII, pp. 25–9.
122 *Spectator* 1965, IV, p. 413; Gay 1974, II, p. 461.
123 NLS, MS. 14548.
124 Curle 1906,. p. 58.
125 Burghley House Archives, MS. Ex41/82.
126 Oman 1974, 63C.
127 BL, Add. MS. 36243, f. 2.
128 East Sussex RO, ASH 2759; Fraser 1888, II, p. 241.
129 Oman 1974, 51B.
130 Ashmole 1672, p. 208.
131 Oman 1974, 86A.
132 *Ibid.*, 60A.
133 CLRO, Orphans Inv. 1744.
134 V & A, M86–1960.
135 Oman 1974, 60F.
136 CLRO, Orphans Inv. 1744.
137 Pepys 1971–83, I, p. 39.
138 Evans 1931, p. xxv.
139 *Ibid.*, p. xxvii.
140 Hutton 1891, p. 188.
141 Scarisbrick 1981, I, p. 322, fig. 8.
142 Curle 1906, p. 58.
143 Fitzwilliam Museum, Cambridge, M3 1966; Oman 1974, 94C,
144 Camden Soc., O.S. 58, p. 27.
145 Guildhall, MS. 9171/25, f. 267.
146 Camden Soc., O.S. 83, p. 118.
147 Jagger 1988, pl. 58, p. 70.
148 *Ibid.*, pl. 27, p. 40.
149 *Ibid.*, p. 29, p. 41.
150 *Ibid.*, p. 40.
151 *Ibid.*, col. pl. 6, facing p. 55.
152 *Ibid.*, pl. 28, p. 41.
153 *Ibid.*, col. pl. 7, facing p. 70.
154 London Museum 1928, no. A14162.
155 NLS, MS. 14548.
156 Castle Howard, J8/23.
157 Jagger 1988, col. pl. 13, facing p. 124.
158 CLRO, MCI/94.51.
159 *Ibid.*, Orphans Inv. 1526.
160 Misson 1698, p. 239.
161 Massinger 1658, *The City Madam*, I.i, p. 30.
162 London Museum 1928, p. 23.

163 PRO, Prob. 11/74, f. 70; *Tatler* 1898, IV, p. 247.
164 V & A, M108–1939; London Museum 1928, no. A14156.
165 Evelyn 1974, p. 11.
166 *Tatler* 1898, IV, pp. 247–9.
167 Fitzwilliam Museum, Cambridge, Smart watches, 64; Cumhaill 1970, p. 54.
168 CLRO, Orphans Inv. 1744.
169 PRO, Prob. 11/726, f. 259.
170 London 1971, p. 45.
171 Pepys 1971–83, II, p. 29; cf. VII, p. 353.
172 Aylward 1960, pp. 88 ff., and 104; CLRO, Orphans Inv. 2941.

7 *The social context of early Georgian jewellery, 1714–89*

1 Walpole 1818, p. 23; Twining 1960, p. 159.
2 Delany 1861, I, p. 140.
3 *Ibid.*, p. 437.
4 *Ibid.*, p. 432.
5 Marlborough 1838, II, p. 168; Victoria 1844, Appx, pp. 14–15.
6 Delany 1861, I, p. 437; Piper 1984, no. 116.
7 Walpole 1937–83, XX, p. 112.
8 *Ibid.*, pp. 111–12.
9 *Ibid.*, p. 112.
10 Victoria 1844, p. 3.
11 *Ibid.*, p. 6.
12 Walpole 1937–83, XVII, p. 343.
13 Victoria 1844, p. 39.
14 Northumberland 1926, p. 28.
15 Fitzgerald 1899, p. 40.
16 Victoria 1844, pp. 22, 59.
17 Twining 1960, p. 162.
18 *Ibid.*
19 HMC 43, Ailesbury MSS., p. 787.
20 Victoria 1844, p. 67.
21 Coke 1889–96, III, p. 83.
22 Levey 1977, pl. 10.
23 Coke 1889–96, III, p. 83.
24 Powys 1899, p. 117.
25 HMC 43, Ailesbury MSS., p. 272.
26 Victoria 1844, p. 49.
27 HMC 43, Ailesbury MSS., p. 285.
28 Fitzgerald 1899, p. 60.
29 Piper 1984, no. 121.
30 *Lady's Mag.*, X (1779), 575.
31 *A Royal Miscellany* (1990), nos. 36 and 39.
32 Leinster 1949–54, III, p. 2.
33 Mahoney 1873, II, p. 275.
34 Milner 1904, p. 226.
35 Seymour 1805, II, p. 259.
36 Delany 1861, I, p. 191.
37 Coke 1899, p. 123.
38 T. W. Pritchard, *The Wynns at Wynnstay* (1982), p. 88.
39 Powys 1899, p. 209.
40 Clark 1895–6, I, p. 81.
41 Northumberland 1926, p. 147.
42 Clark 1895–8, II, p. 135.
43 Foote 1799, II, p. 296.
44 Macaulay 1921, p. 621.
45 Goldsmith 1968, II.440.
46 Walpole 1937–83, XXII, p. 293; Yogev 1978, p. 149;; BL, India Office Library and Records, Eur. MSS., Clive Papers, G 37, Box 46, ff. 33, 41, 59, 77, 86b, 94, 105, 122, 143, 179 and 182.
47 BL, India Office Library and Records, Eur. MSS., Clive Papers, G 37, Box 26, ff. 86, 88; Box 36, no. 15.
48 Delany 1861, II, p. 171.
49 Murray 1938, p. 106.
50 Richardson 1932, I, p. 207.
51 Goldsmith 1981, p. 78.
52 Bleackley 1923, p. 143.
53 Lichtenberg 1938, p. 68.
54 Richardson 1972, I, p. 320.
55 *Lady's Mag.*, IV (1773), 140.
56 Berkeley 1971, p. 122.
57 Personal communication from the archivist at Mapledurham.
58 Stapylton 1892, p. 51.
59 Richardson 1932, IV, p. 219.
60 Bedford RO, AD980.
61 *Ibid.*, X216/13.
62 Stapylton 1892, p. 240.
63 Thomson 1847, I, p. 116
64 V & A, M34–1951; Fitzwilliam Museum, Cambridge, PER281.
65 Raspe 1791, nos. 15071–2.
66 Clark 1895–8, II, p. 139.
67 Yogev 1978, p. 68.
68 Montagu 1970, II, pp. 19 43.
69 Raspe 1791, p. vi.
70 Jeffries 1751.
71 Yogev 1978, p. 142.
72 *Ibid.*, pp. 141–2.
73 Jeffries 1751, p. 30.
74 Goldsmith 1968, III.116.
75 Christie's, 3 May 1773, no. 27.
76 Rouquet 1755, p. 90.
77 *Ibid.*, p. 136.
78 Lewis 1957.
79 Sheffield City Library, Rockingham Papers, WWM R 168/3.
80 Christie's, 13 June 1782, p. 18, no. 136.
81 Ashmolean Museum, Oxford, Fortnum colln 366.
82 Christie's, 18 Feb. 1772, no. 55.
83 Delany 1861, II, p. 82.
84 Coke 1899, p. 44.
85 NLS, MS. 14527, f. 105.
86 *Lady's Mag.*, III (1772), 295.
87 Berkshire RO, D/EEg F14.
88 Christie's, 17 Aug. 1772, p. 11, mos. 12, 20.
89 Purefoy 1931, II, p. 235.
90 Lewis 1953, p. 40.
91 Goldsmith 1968, III.150–4.
92 Walpole 1937–83, XXVIII, pp. 253–4.
93 Fontanieu 1787, sig. A2 Advertisement.
94 Pearce 1911, p. 296.

95 Lewis 1953, pls 16, 17 and 23.
96 Wickes's Accts.
97 Christie's, 1 July 1772, no. 76.
98 Falke 1911, p. 335.
99 Christie's, 19 May 1768, p. 13, no. 10; 3 May 1778, no. 91.
100 Falke 1911, pl. B, facing p. 335; Christie's, 27 Jan. 1784, no. 2.
101 Evans 1921, po. xxix, nos. 1, 4.
102 Wedgwood 1906, p. 54; Ginsburg 1977, p. 65, fig. 7.
103 Meteyard 1866, II, p. 397.
104 *Ibid.*, II, pp. 398, 520.
105 Christie's, 30 April 1935, no. 26.
106 *Ibid.*, 3 Dec. 1781 ff.
107 Wedgwood 1906, p. 277.
108 *Ibid.*, p. 370.
109 Meteyard 1866, II, p. 565.
110 *Ibid.*, II, p. 523.
111 Fort Worth 1982, no. 28.
112 London 1948, no. 285.
113 V & A, Schreiber I.249.
114 Hughes 1956, fig. 8.
115 V & A, C492–1914; C1669–1871.
116 Lumas and Cox 1981; Leamington Spa 1967; V & A, E7279–1903.
117 Muralt 1933, p. 109.
118 La Roche 1933, p. 221.
119 Bodleian Library, MS. North d 27, f. 218r.
120 Walpole 1937–83, XVII, p. 413.
121 Hughes 1954, pp. 86–7.
122 Frenilly 1908, p. 80.
123 *Lady's Mag.*, II (1771), 248.
124 Powys 1899, p. 200.
125 Neville 1950, p. 282.
126 Lichtenberg 1933, p. 97.
127 Robinson 1963, p. 59.
128 Clifford 1971; Rawlings 1978; Gill 1959–61.
129 Clark 1895–8, III, p. 156.
130 Rouquet 1755, p. 90.
131 BL, Althorp Papers, E12.
132 Heal 1935, pl. xl.
133 BM, Banks colln, P & D 67.155.
134 Heal 1935, pl. lxii; cf. lxiii.
135 Bodleian Library, John Johnson colln, Jewellery and Silver, no. 2.
136 BM, Banks colln, P & D 67.227.
137 Heal 1935, pl. I; Grimwade 1976, p. 240.
138 BM, Banks colln, P & D 67.205, 226.
139 Chatsworth Archives, bill for purchases of Mrs Garrick, 10 May 1755; Heal 1935, pl. lxv.
140 Heal 1935, pl. lxx; Grimwade 1976, p. 449.
141 Le Corbeiller 1970.
142 Neville 1950, p. 24.
143 Northumberland RO, 2DE 31/10/20–6.
144 Jekyll 1894, p. 17.
145 Neville 1950, p. 24.
146 Lumas and Cox 1981.
147 Lincoln RO, Mon 11/31, 22 April 1767; Edwards 1974, p. 133.
148 Christie's, 26–31 Jan., 2–3 and 26–7 Feb. 1784; 26 Feb. 1788.
149 Sheffield City Library, VWM 156/5, 9–10, 13, 15, 26.
150 Norfolk RO, 50/23/1; 50/24/9.
151 La Roche 1933, p. 221.
152 Rohan 1786.
153 Scarisbrick 1989, pp. 64, 66, pl. 264.
154 RAW, no. 25651.
155 *Ibid.*, nos 25640, 25644, 25659–60.
156 *Ibid.*, nos. 25647, 25677–80.
157 *Ibid.*, no. 25645.
158 Bedford Archives.
159 Kroll 1970, p. 127.
160 Muralt 1933, p. 109.
161 Barr 1980, p. 156; Lincoln RO, Mon 11/31; Sheffield City Library, WWM A1089, 1089A, 1098.
162 London 1985, no. 381; Chatsworth Archives, bills 27 May, 2 June 1731; Dec. 1740; 6 Jan. 1741; 28 Jan., 7 March, 27 April, 15 Oct. 1743; 5 Feb. 1748, etc.
163 London 1985, no. 381.
164 *Ibid.*, no. 382.
165 Leinster 1949–54, I, p. 244; Sheffield City Library, WWM R 168/3; Coke 1899, p. 105.
166 Milner 1904, p. 226; see p. 000 above.
167 London 1985, no. 387.
168 Chatsworth Archives.
169 Leinster 1949–54, I, p. 50.
170 Lincoln RO, Mon 11/31.
171 London 1985, no. 380.
172 Grimwade 1976, p. 524; Heal 1935, pl. xxxii.
173 West Sussex RO, PHA 6613, 8046, 8049; Clwyd RO, DD/WY/6659.
174 RAW, no. 25641; Victoria 1844, p. 67.
175 Personal communication from the archivist at Uppark.
176 Grimwade 1976, p. 708.
177 London 1984C, 11 note.
178 Heal 1935, p. 233.
179 BM, Banks colln, P & D 67.196.
180 Sketchley 1767, pp. 37–8.
181 Bodleian Library, John Johnson colln, Jewellery and Silver, no. 2.
182 BM, Banks colln, P & D 67.232.
183 Grimwade 1976, p. 536.
184 Le Corbeiller 1970, p. 355.
185 Lincoln RO, MC5/3/2.
186 Meteyard 1866, II, p. 398.
187 Piozzi 1789, I, p. 192.
188 V & A, E1651–1907.
189 Clwyd RO, DD/WY/6659.
190 Bristol 1953, p. 96.
191 Angelo 1828–30, II, p. 91.
192 Leinster 1949–54, I, pp. 383, 516.
193 Christie's, 22 Feb. 1772, p. 15, no. 52.
194 Neville 1950, p. 24.
195 Muller 1972, pp. 148–9.
196 RAW, no. 25652.
197 Leinster 1949–54, I, pp. 49–50.

198 *Ibid.*, II, p. 83.
199 *Ibid.*, III, p. 193.
200 Delany 1861, II, p. 94.
201 Anjou 1956, pp. 57–8, p. 51; Scarisbrick 1985A, fig. 7.
202 London 1984C, H16; V & A, E2041–1914.
203 Colman and Garrick 1766, *The Clandestine Marriage*, I.ii.
204 Cox 1773.
205 Guilmard 1880, Bibliography, under Pattern Books.
206 MS. 'Dictionary of engravers in London to 1800', by J. A. Goodall, F.S.A., 1969.
207 *Ibid.*
208 Soc. of Ant., MS. 420; Sheila O'Connell, MS., BM, Dept. of Prints and Drawings.
209 Rouquet 1755, p. 86.
210 Kagan and Neverov 1984; Nau 1966.
211 Soc. of Ant., MS. 420; Sheila O'Connell, MS., BM, Dept. of Prints and Drawings.
212 Neville 1950, p. 48.
213 RAW, no. 25648.
214 Herbert 1939, p. 486.
215 Scarisbrick 1983, II, p. 1696, figs 1–2.
216 Christie's, 13–14 March 1778, p. 23, no. 48; 27 April 1769, p. 5, no. 55.
217 *Ibid.*, 14 April 1740, p. 7, no. 92; London 1984D, p. 114.
218 RAW, no. 25606. cf. V & A M 153 – 1962.
219 Herbert 1939, p. 414.
220 Argyll 1910, II, p. 414.
221 Leinster 1949–54, I, p. 522.
222 Christie's, 9 April 1789, no. 14.
223 *Ibid.*, 30 Jan. 1772, nos. 74–5.
224 RAW, no. 25661.
225 Raspe 1791, p. xliv.
226 Scarisbrick 1983, II, figs 6–7.
227 V & A, E5664–1904; London 1984C, II.
228 Scarisbrick 1983 II, fig. 9.
229 Kagan 1973, no. 40; and Kagan 1981, p. 191, no. 99.
230 Christie's 14 March 1778, p. 29, no. 41; 1–2 July 1772, no. 89.
231 RAW, no. 25780.
232 *Ibid.*, nos. 2560–3, 25666.
233 Nicolas 1841–2, III.
234 Anjou 1956, p. 59, no. 71; BM, MLA 1978, 1–4, 1.
235 Powys 1899, p. 91.
236 BL, India Office Library and Records, Eur. MSS., Clive Papers, G37, Box 37, no. 15.
237 Manuel 1902, p. 155.
238 *Ibid.*, p. 156.
239 *Ibid.*, pp. 157–8.
240 Christie's, 1 May 1788, no. 9.
241 BM, Heal colln, P & D.
242 Tait 1984, no. 335.
243 Frick 1968, pp. 68–72, pl. 21.
244 Coke 1899, pp. 99–100.
245 Frick, 1968 p. 21. Cross on bowknot.
246 Victoria 1844, p. 39.
247 West Sussex RO, PHA 8046.
248 NLS, MS. 14527, f. 105; Lincoln RO, LD 9711/3.
249 Christie's, 14 April 1770, p. 7, no. 90.
250 *Ibid.*, 28 April 1768, nos. 1–2.
251 Guien 1762.
252 Mahoney 1873, II, p. 246.
253 Christie's, 9 April 1767, p. 26, no. 71.
254 V & A, M6a–1957.
255 Broughton 1887, p. 212.
256 Coke 1899, p. 44.
257 Leinster 1949–54, I, p. 259.
258 Robinson 1963, p. 47.
259 Delany 1861, I, p. 96.
260 Scarisbrick 1977.
261 Richardson 1932, IV, p. 373.
262 Wickes's Accts, II, f. 130v.
263 Oman 1974, 89D, E.
264 Hone 1826, I, p. 1083, 9 August.
265 White 1950, pp. 25, 242–3.
266 Christie's, 9 Oct. 1956 (Objects of Art), no. 145.
267 *Ibid.*, 11 Dec. 1902, no. 53.
268 Bury 1985, p. 25.
269 Graham 1927, p. 231.
270 Bury 1985, pl. 27c.
271 Richardson 1932, IV, p. 373.
272 Hickey 1913, II, p. 264.
273 Bury 1985, pl. 25b.
274 Thomson 1847, I, p. 331.
275 Althorp Papers F1–22.
276 Delany 1861, I, p. 190.
277 Bristol 1953, p. 111.
278 Hamilton 1925, p. 159.
279 Broughton 1887, p. 12.
280 Lennox 1901, p. 300.
281 Coke 1889–96, IV, p. 90, illus. opp. p. 91.
282 Delany 1861, II, p. 574; London 1873, no. 357.
283 Hotham 1919, p. 160.
284 Hamilton 1925, p. 159.
285 RAW, no. 25640.
286 BM, Banks colln, P & D 67.60.
287 Boswell 1951, p. 199.
288 Raspe 1791, no. 13996.
289 Dalton 1912, no. 1372; Scarisbrick 1989, pl. 91.
290 Shelley 1912, p. 4.
291 Scarisbrick unpbld, no. 7; cf. *Arch. J.*, XXX (1873), 284.
292 Scarisbrick 1989, pls 87–90.
293 *Ibid.*
294 Ryder 1939, pp. 314–15.
295 Scarisbrick 1988, p. 128, and unpbld, no. 1.
296 Lang 1897, p. 100; Raspe 1791, nos. 14024–28.
297 Ashmolean Museum, Oxford, with the Fortnum rings, the gift of Mrs Calcott; Christie's, 27 Oct. 1959, no. 176.
298 Stevenson 1945–6, p. 128; Fort William Museum, L2669, from Mrs Ruthven.
299 BL, Add. MS. 33050, f. 126b.
300 *Ibid.*
301 *Ibid.*, f. 429.
302 Lang 1897, p. 119.

303 Stevenson 1945–6, p. 127.
304 *Ibid.*, p. 129.
305 Chiddingstone Castle colln.
306 Raspe 1791, nos. 14029–33.
307 Scarisbrick unpbld, no. 3.
308 Highland Museum, Inverness.
309 Scarisbrick unpbld, no. 5.
310 *Ibid.*, no. 6; Oman 1974, p. 68.
311 See p. 271 below.
312 Christie's, 9 July 1935, no. 103.
313 Scarisbrick 1988, p. 129.
314 Fort William Museum.
315 Stevenson 1945–6, p. 128.
316 London 1889, no. 614.
317 National Museum of Scotland NJ84.
318 London 1889, nos. 527, 558.
319 *Ibid.*, no. 1100.
320 Chiddingstone Castle colln.
321 Scarisbrick 1988, p. 128; Stevenson 1945–6, p. 129.
322 Stevenson 1945–6, p. 127.
323 *Ibid.*, p. 128.
324 Chambers 1896, III, p. 136.
325 Sheffield City Library, VWM 158/35, 158/14.
326 Fürstenhaus, Herrenhausen, Hanover FDR; Sotheby's, 17 March 1971, no. 81.
327 Bedford RO, will of Letitia Pattison 1788.
328 La Roche 1933, p. 246.
329 Richardson 1932, IV, p. 419.
330 Bishop 1951, p. 33.
331 T. E. Carpenter in *CL*, CXIX (1956), p. 811.
332 RAW, no. 25668.
333 Oman 1974, 84A.
334 Mahony 1873, I, p. 329.
335 Northumberland RO, 2 DE 31/10/20.
336 Bedford RO, Wrest Park Papers, L30/13/9 (75).
337 Seaby 1955, p. 26, pl. 10.
338 Scarisbrick 1989, pl. 73.
339 Sotheby's, 22 Feb. 1985 (Leonard Morgan May colln of silhouettes); Lister 1953.
340 Leonardus 1750, pp. ix–x.
341 Wickes's Accts, II, f. 56v., Delany, 1861 I, p. 132.
342 Malcolm 1810, p. 175.
343 *Ibid.*, p. 414.
344 Ribeiro 1977, p. 834.
345 Richardson 1932, I, p. 512.
346 Bedford RO, Wrest Park Papers, L30/9a/8.

8 *The categories of early Georgian jewellery, 1714–89.*

1 Clwyd RO, DD/WY/6659.
2 Christie's, 22 Feb. 1769, p. 35, no. 70.
3 Scarisbrick 1985A, p. 735, fig. 1.
4 Malcolm 1810, p. 176.
5 Christie's, 11 March 1778, p. 28, no. 36.
6 Coke 1899, p. 123.
7 Milner 1904, p. 226.
8 Christie's, 3 May 1778, p. 34, and 5 Feb. 1789, no. 22.
9 Lennox 1901, I, p. 178.
10 Bedford RO, Wrest Park Papers.
11 Seaby 1955, p. 24.
12 *Lady's Mag.*, V (1774), 379.
13 Leinster 1949–54, I, p. 186.
14 Graham 1927, p. 94.
15 Burgoyne 1786, *The Heiress*, III.iii.
16 Christie's, 1 July 1772, no. 57.
17 *Ibid.*, 29 Oct. 1787, no. 63.
18 Milner 1904, p. 226.
19 Seaby 1955, p. 22.
20 NLS, MS. 14527, f. 106.
21 Christie's, 18 April 1771, no. 47.
22 Osborn 1890, p. 161.
23 *Lady's Mag.*, XIII (1782), 156.
24 Leinster 1949–54, I, p. 49.
25 *Ibid.*, II, pp. 77–8.
26 Plumb 1974, p. 77.
27 *Ibid.*, p. 157.
28 Blundell 1952, p. 257.
29 North Riding RO, 2 DG (A) V 1/25.
30 Milner 1904, p. 226.
31 Clwyd RO, DD/WY/6659.
32 Langford & Son, 7 March 1770, no. 75.
33 Christie's 18 Feb. 1772, no. 62.
34 Guien 1762.
35 Wickes's Accts, Iff. lv, 79v, 100v.
36 RAW, nos. 25661, 25663, 25666, 25678–9.
37 BL, Althorp Papers, E12.
38 Delany 1861, I, p. 100.
39 Colman and Garrick, 1766, *The Clandestine Marriage*, I.ii.
40 Bedford RO, Wrest Park papers, 10 Feb. 1769.
41 Delany 1861, II, p. 462.
42 Clwyd RO, D/PT/899 (1769); West Sussex RO, PHA 8046 (1773).
43 Clwyd RO, DD/WY/6659.
44 Christie's, 1–3 Feb. 1773, no. 28.
45 Seaby 1955, p. 24.
46 Christie's, 2 Feb. 1776, no. 97.
47 Leinster 1949–54, I, p. 244.
48 Sheffield City Library, VWM 158/26.
49 Coke 1899, p. 44.
50 Christie's, 12 June 1782 and 27 Jan. 1784.
51 Courtauld Institute, Witt Library.
52 Colman and Garrick 1766, *The Clandestine Marriage*, I.ii.
53 Clwyd RO, DD/WY/6659.
54 Christie's, 2 March 1774, no. 100.
55 *Ibid.*, 1 Feb. 1773, no. 83.
56 Malcolm 1810, pp. 175–6.
57 Smith 1920, p. 16.
58 Christie's, 1–3 Feb. 1773, nos. 21, 74, 80.
59 *Ibid.*, 12 June 1780, no. 135.
60 Essex RO, D/DE: B24.
61 Christie's, 19 March 1778, no. 7.
62 Wickes's Accts, II, f. 162v.
63 Christie's, 14 April 1770, p. 7, no. 88.
64 *Ibid.*, 1–3 Feb. 1773, no. 27.
65 R. Murray, *Dulwich Picture Gallery, A Catalogue* (1980), p. 72, no. 606.

66 Ribeiro 1977.
67 *Lady's Mag.*, IV (1773), 152.
68 Christie's, 2 March 1774, no. 105.
69 Seaby 1955, p. 24.
70 Delany 1861, III, p. 400.
71 Clwyd RO, DD/WY/6659.
72 Essex RO, D/DE: B24.
73 Colman and Garrick 1766, *The Clandestine Marriage*, I.ii.
74 West Sussex RO, PHA 8049.
75 Leinster 1949–54, III, p. 193.
76 RAW, no. 25663.
77 Langford & Son, 7 March 1770, p. 6, no. 35.
78 Christie's, 3 April 1786, no. 11.
79 Wickes's Accts, I f. 146v.
80 Christie's, 3 Feb. 1784, nos. 132–3.
81 NLS, MS. 14527, 123/1, f. 105.
82 Christie's, 14 April 1770, no. 14.
83 *Ibid.*, 25 April 1769, no. 37.
84 *Ibid.*, 7–8 June 1773, p. 12, no. 22; 26 Jan. 1784, no. 1004.
85 Blundell 1952, p. 59.
86 V & A, E3666–1910.
87 *Gent. Mag.*, VI (1736), 221.
88 BL, Althorp Papers, E12.
89 Wickes's Accts, 1738.
90 Lincoln RO, Mon 11/31.
91 Suffolk RO, 312/21, Will of Lady Ann Hervey 1757.
92 Christie's, 2 Feb. 1773, no. 74.
93 Christie's, 7 March 1785, no. 102; 9 Dec. 1776, no. 57.
94 Lincoln RO, Mon 11/31.
95 Christie's, 15 Feb. 1785, no. 2.
96 Wickes's Accts, II, f. 155v; I, f. 186v.
97 *Ibid.*, I, f. 107v.
98 Christie's, 9 Oct. 1782, no. 3.
99 *Ibid.*, 8 Dec. 1784, no. 69.
100 *Ibid.*, 10 April 1783, no. 68.
101 Malcolm 1810, p. 437.
102 *Ibid.*, p. 175.
103 Wickes's Accts, 1737.
104 *Ibid.*, I, f. 178v.
105 Somerset RO, DD/MKG 4.
106 Christie's, 19 May 1768, no. 13.
107 *Ibid.*, 20 Jan. 1768, no. 62.
108 *Ibid.*, 11 July 1769, no. 7.
109 Bedford RO, Wrest Park Papers.
110 Wickes's Accts, I, f. 107v.
111 Christie's, 17 June 1782, no. 126.
112 Welbeck Abbey 1897, p. 31, no. 148.
113 Scarisbrick 1985A, fig. 3.
114 Christie's, 2 July 1772, nos. 62, 68.
115 Wickes's Accts, I, f. 19v; Somerset RO, DD/MKG 4.
116 Northumberland 1926, p. 50.
117 Christie's, 17 May 1819, no. 83.
118 Northumberland 1926, p. 28.
119 Clwyd RO, DD/WY/6659.
120 Northumberland RO, 2 DE 31/10/6.
121 West Sussex RO, PHA 8046.
122 Powys 1899, p. 183.
123 Christie's, 2 March 1774 no. 95.
124 Clwyd RO, DD/WY/6659.
125 North Riding RO, 2 DG (A) V 1/17; RAW, no. 25644.
126 Walpole 1937–83, XVII, p. 413.
127 Swan 1981, pls 45, 52.
128 Allen 1987, no. 39.
129 *Lady's Mag.*, XIV (1783), 121.
130 Southerne 1774, III, p. 101.
131 Seaby 1955, p. 24.
132 *Lady's Mag.*, XV (1784), 154.
133 Richardson 1932, I, p. 152; Allen 1987, no. 40.
134 Smith 1920, p. 16.
135 Swan 1981, pl. 50a and section on 1760–90; V & A, M2–1969.
136 RAW, no. 25671.
137 Christie's, 8 July 1774, no 13; RAW, no. 25661.
138 West Sussex RO, PHA 6613.
139 Swan 1981, unpaginated.
140 Powys 1899, p. 132.
141 RAW, no. 25673.
142 Sheridan 1975, *A Trip to Scarborough*, I.ii.
143 Swan 1981.
144 Delany 1861, III, p. 400.
145 Seaby 1955, p. 24.
146 Bedford RO, Wrest Park Papers, acct of Philip Hardel, 1762.
147 Lennox 1901, p. 189.
148 Bedford RO, Wrest Park Papers, acct of Thomas Harrache, 1756; Clwyd RO, DD/WY/6659.
149 Clwyd RO, D/AN/828.
150 Christie's, 20 Feb. 1771, p. 11, no. 81; 3 May 1776, no. 97; Clwyd RO, DD/WY/6659.
151 Christie's, 1 Feb. 1773, nos. 25, 88, 95; Evans 1921, pl. 146a.
152 RAW, nos. 25652, 25661, 25668, 25671.
153 Colman and Garrick 1766, *The Clandestine Marriage*, I.ii.
154 Isle of Wight RO, JER/WA/35321.
155 *Idler* 1761, 13 Jan. 1759, no. 39.
156 Evans 1921, p. 163, no. 4.
157 V & A, M79 and a-1962; Evans 1970, p. 163.
158 V & A, M42–1962 and M42a–1962; *SJH Newsletter*. IX (1980), 3; Christie's, 12 June 1782, no. 69.
159 Christie's, 23 May 1776, no. 20; 16 Jan. 1784, no. 23.
160 Raspe 1791, no. 14059.
161 Forrer 1977, under Tassie.
162 Christie's, 2 Feb. 1784, no. 42; RAW, nos. 25661–74.
163 Christie's, 29 Oct. 1789, no. 55.
164 *Ibid.*, 17 June 1782, no. 79. Northampton RO, YZ0091.
165 Christie's, 19 July 1776, no 33.
166 Clwyd RO, DD/WY/6659.
167 BL, Add. MS. 61472, f. 203; Langford & Son, 7–10 March 1770, p. 7, no. 73.
168 Wickes's Accts, II, f. 20v.

169 West Sussex RO, PHA 8046.
170 Ginsburg 1977, p. 62.
171 West Sussex RO, PHA 8949; Russell-Smith 1957; Ginsburg 1977, fig. 9.
172 Ginsburg 1977, p. 66, no. 8.
173 Oglander 1940, p. 58.
174 Broughton 1887, p. 212.
175 Russell-Smith 1961, p. 63.
176 *Ibid.*, p. 64, fig. 5.
177 Christie's, 3 May 1778, p. 8, no. 26.
178 *Ibid.*, 26 March 1917 (Red Cross Sale), no. 798.
179 Wickes's Accts, II, f. 34v.
180 Christie's, 14 April 1770, p. 7, no. 40; 4 Dec. 1770, p. 19, no. 45; Wickes's Accts, I, f. 165v, II, f. 34v; Christie's, 3 April 1786, no. 21; 27 Jan. 1784, no. 60; Ginsburg 1977, p. 64; *Lady's Mag.*, X (1779), 575.
181 Powys 1899, p. 189.
182 RAW, nos. 25661, 25663–4, 25668–9.
183 *Ibid.*, nos. 25668–9.
184 *Ibid.*, no. 25646.
185 *Ibid.*, no. 25664.
186 *Ibid.*, no. 25673.
187 Mahony 1873, I, p. 168.
188 *Ibid.*, I, p. 291.
189 Christie's 17 June 1782, no. 62.
190 *Ibid.*, 13 June 1778, no. 79; 21 May 1787, no. 20; 9 Oct. 1782, no. 65; 7 March 1787, no. 102.
191 Wickes's Accts, I, f. 9v.
192 RAW, no. 25671.
193 Bedford RO, Wrest Park Papers, accts Philip Hardel, 1762.
194 Isle of Wight RO, JER/WA/35/23; Clwyd RO, DD/WY/6659.
195 Bedford RO, Wrest Park Papers, accts Peter Romilly, 1762.
196 Clwyd RO, DD/WY/6659.
197 Christie's, 19 July 1776, no. 38.
198 RAW, no. 25669.
199 Christie's, 1–3 Feb. 1773, p. 3, no. 28; Berkshire RO, D/EEg F14.
200 Lincoln RO, Lind. Dep. 97/1/3.
201 RAW, no. 25647.
202 Christie's, 13–14 March 1778, no. 35; 1–3 Feb. 1773, p. 3, no. 26; Berkshire RO, D/EEg F14.
203 Clwyd RO, DD/WY/6659.
204 Christie's, 13–14 March 1778, p. 5, no. 48.
205 *Ibid.*, p. 29, no. 5.
206 *Ibid.*, 2 May 1953, no. 45.
207 Clwyd RO, DD/WY/6659.
208 Christie's, 1–3 Feb. 1773, p. 3, no. 25.
209 RAW, nos. 25650, 25664.
210 *Ibid.*, no. 25644.
211 *Ibid.*, nos. 25661, 25677, 25650.
212 *Ibid.*, nos. 25650, 25663–5, 25669, 25671.
213 Scarisbrick 1987A, p. 92.
214 Berkeley 1971, p. 122.
215 Leinster 1949–54, I, p. 61.
216 London 1984C, I, I14.
217 Rouquet 1755, p. 85.
218 London 1984C, H6, H8, H9.
219 *Ibid.*, H25.
220 *Ibid.*
221 *Ibid.*, H3, H7.
222 West Sussex RO, PHA 6613.
223 London 1984C, I11, I12; Christie's, 18 May 1819, day 2, no. 6.
224 Harcourt 1880–1905, VII, pp. 305–6.
225 Tait 1983, pp. 73–5.
226 Christie's 18 May 1819, day 2, no. 11.
227 Lincoln RO, MON 11/31.
228 Powys 1899, p. 189.
229 RAW, nos. 25668, 25673.
230 Evans 1921, pl. B.5; Dukelskaya 1979, pp. 66–7.
231 London 1984C, I10.
232 V & A, M261b–1975; Bury 1982, 6.I.62.
233 Scarisbrick 1989, pl. 82.
234 At Fitzwilliam Museum, Cambridge; illustrated Evans 1921, pl. C2. See also Evans 1921, pl. XXX, nos. 1 and 3.
235 Seaby 1955, p. 25.
236 London 1984C, no. 17, pl. xi.
237 Benton 1967, no. 138.
238 Allen 1987, no. 39.
239 Walpole 1937–83, XVIII, p. 30.
240 *Ibid.*, III, p. 44.
241 Clarke 1985, p. 715.
242 Walpole 1937–83, XXII, p. 234 and no. 14.
243 Boulton 1909, fig. 11, pp. 94–5.
244 Walpole 1937–83, XXXV, p. 252; XXXI, p. 105.
245 *Arch. J.*, XIX (1862), 297.
246 Wenham 1936, p. 72.
247 B. Beet collection, London.
248 Aylward 1960, p. 104.
249 Blair 1974, p. 136.

9 *The social context of later Georgian jewellery, 1790–1837*

1 Fox 1846, p. 6.
2 Rush 1873, p. 6.
3 George IV 1963–71, II, no. 674.
4 *Ibid.*, IV, no. 1467; Scarisbrick 1989, pp. 75–6, pl. 99.
5 Creevey 1912, p. 385; Holland 1854, I, p. 351; Palmerston 1957, p. 79; Greville 1963, p. 120.
6 Surtees 1990, p. 178.
7 George IV 1963–71, IV, pp. 243–4.
8 Bury 1908, II, pp. 23, 160.
9 George IV 1963–71, V, p. 168 n.
10 *Ibid.*
11 RAW, nos. 25713, 25742, 25761, 25820, 25831.
12 George IV 1963–71, III, pp. 243–4.
13 RAW, no. 25920.
14 George IV 1963–71, VI, no. 2656.
15 *Ibid.*, IV, no. 1859.
16 Wynn 1864, p. 227; Pemberton 1910, pp. 268–9; George IV 1963–71, nos. 2764, 2765, 2775.
17 Cooke 1900, I, p. 52.
18 *Lady's Mag.*, XXI (1790), 40; XXVII (1796), 7.
19 Christie's, 17 May 1819; Balfour 1987, p. 94.

20 Twining 1960, p. 162, no. 5, pl. 68a-c.
21 *Ibid.*, pp. 160–1, pl. 60a.
22 Scarisbrick 1987A, pl. 101; RAW, no. 26021.
23 Fox 1846, p. 82.
24 Field 1987, pp. 71, 80.
25 Byron, *Don Juan*, Canto XI, stanza 70, lines 555–6.
26 Rush 1873, p. 103.
27 Farington 1978–84, XI, p. 4426.
28 Le Borgne 1907, II, p. 167.
29 *Lady's Mag.*, XXVI (1795), 44.
30 Part of this line is illegible.
31 PRO, Prob. 11/20059, f. 378 (new foliation).
32 Scarisbrick 1989, pp. 73–75.
33 Gronow 1892, I, p. 170.
34 Fox 1846, p. 21.
35 *Ibid.*, p. 22.
36 *Ibid.*, p. 44.
37 Rush 1873, p. 49.
38 Grant 1988, I, p. 191.
39 Elizabeth 1898, p. 290.
40 Farington 1978–84, V, p. 1849.
41 BL, Egerton MS. 1973, f. 129.
42 Somerset RO, DD/HLM Box 3.
43 *Ibid.*, DD/X MLH C/2088 Box 105.
44 Bedford RO, HG 12/4/78.
45 Scarisbrick 1985B.
46 Austen 1953, p. 310.
47 *Ibid.*, p. 137.
48 Farington 1978–84, VII, p. 2723.
49 *Lady's Mag.*, XXXIII (1802), 207.
50 *Lady's Mon. Mus.*, XIII (1821) 292.
51 Fox 1846, p. 8.
52 Lancashire RO, DD Sc 9/34–39.
53 Bury 1981.
54 Christie's, 12 Feb. and 12 June 1829; Mughal jewellery, 19 April 1809.
55 *Lady's Mag.*, LIII (1822), 388, 575.
56 Christie's, 19 May 1808, no. 6.
57 Christie's, 2 June 1807, no. 6.
58 Grant 1988, I, p. 146.
59 *Lady's Mon. Mus.*, XXXII (1830), 175.
60 Staffordshire RO, D 3259/13/25; Demay and Page, Christie's, 1793, nos. 97, 101.
61 *Lady's Mag.*, XXXVI (1805), 39; XLIX (1818), 41.
62 Phillips's, 9 April 1804.
63 Clark 1895–8, III, p. 156.
64 *Lady's Mag.*, XLVII (1817), p. 137.
65 RAW, no. 25755.
66 Angelo 1829, p. 45; Phillips's, 9 April 1804, nos. 110, 246.
67 Powys 1899, p. 298.
68 Tait 1984, no. 187 n.; Christie's, 11 June 1799, no. 76.
69 Powys 1899, p. 298; Christie's, 2 Feb. 1910, no. 117.
70 V & A, GL 10, f. 134.
71 *Lady's Mag.*, XXXI (1800), 301.
72 Phillips's, 9 April 1804, nos. 263, 818–19, 2130; Christie's, 14 April 1813, no. 59.
73 *Lady's Mon. Mus.*, imp. ser. XV (1822), 291.
74 *Ibid.*, imp. ser. XIV (1821), 112.
75 *Encyclopaedia Britannica*, 11th edn, s.v. Platinum.
76 RAW, nos. 25757 and 26320.
77 Fox 1846, pp. 5–6.
78 *Ibid.*, p. 2 ff.
79 Wynn 1920, p. 238.
80 Khan 1989, p. 240.
81 Fox 1846, pp. 26–7.
82 Garrard 1912, p. 100; V & A, GL 10, ff. 93, 110, 117.
83 Fitzgerald 1899, p. 22, no. 1.
84 George IV 1963–71, IV, pp. 243–4.
85 Gronow 1892, I, p. 135.
86 Goldsmiths' Company, C.I, 3ii.
87 Gronow 1892, I, p. 170.
88 Gore 1850, p. 76.
89 BM, Banks colln, P & D, 67.229, 67.8.
90 *Ibid.*, 67.199.
91 Christie's, 8 June 1808.
92 Bodleian Library, John Johnson colln, Trade cards, 10.
93 BM, Banks colln, P & D, 67.201.
94 *Ibid.*, 67.223.
95 Scarisbrick 1985C.
96 Cumbria RO, D/Sen, Sebhouse of Netherhall, Maryport, colln of printed notices.
97 Oman 1968, p. 64.
98 Powys 1899, p. 333.
99 See n. 92 above.
100 Birmingham 1973, B112.
101 Londonderry Family Archives, Castlereagh Papers, Letter xxxiii.
102 Chatsworth Archives, purchases by sixth Duke of Devonshire; RAW, no. 26098.
103 Christie's, 21 July 1942, no. 201.
104 Clifford 1971, pl. 40.
105 George IV 1938, III, pp. 108–9.
106 Disraeli 1837, pp. 278, 282.
107 Huxley 1965, p. 366.
108 Londonderry 1973, pp. 52, 83.
109 Surtees 1990, pp. 198 and 200.
110 Fitzherbert 1940, p. 229.
111 Gore 1831, I, p. 104.
112 Wynn 1920, p. 295.
113 RAW, no. 26095.
114 Christie's, 1 May 1812.
115 *Ibid.*, 16 March 1825, p. 5, no. 20; RAW, no. 26254.
116 RAW, no. 26058.
117 J.W. von Goethe, *Italian Journey*, trans. W. H. Auden and E. Meyer (1970), p. 94.
118 *Lady's Mon. Mus.*, XIII (182), 112, 174, 343.
119 RAW, no. 26256.
120 Staffordshire RO, D3259/13/25.
121 Christie's, 16 March 1825, no. 7.
122 RAW, nos. 26114–17.
123 Christie's, 19 April 1809, nos. 1–29.
124 *Lady's Mag.*, enl. imp. ser., VI (1835), 237.
125 Thackeray 1869, p. 199.
126 RAW, nos. 25856, 26098.

127 Gore 1846, III, p. 147.
128 Calvert 1911, p. 152.
129 Bedford RO, Wrest Park Papers, 22 July 1793.
130 East Sussex RO, SAS 6 ACC 74/.
131 Norfolk RO, WLS LII/25 427x6.
132 RAW, no. 25842.
133 *Ibid.*, nos. 26028, 26161.
134 *Ibid.*, nos. 26107, 26327.
135 Christie's, 22 April 1812, no. 27; V & A, GL 10, f. 4.
136 V & A, GL 10, f. 11.
137 RAW, no. 26200.
138 Christie's, 25 April 1792, nos. 20, 50.
139 RAW, no. 26001.
140 *Lady's Mag.*, enl. imp. ser., I (1832), 60.
141 Stanhope 1827, II, p. 265.
142 *Lady's Mag.*, XXXIV, (1803), 313.
143 Grant 1988, I, p. 113.
144 Christie's, 17 March 1825, p. 18, no. 78.
145 Durham RO, D/LO/F 667 [4] (14).
146 RAW, nos. 26256, 25871.
147 *Ibid.*, nos. 25975, 25860.
148 *Ibid.*, nos. 26256, 25860.
149 *Ibid.*, no. 25979.
150 *Ibid.*, no. 2586; see p. 000 below, Orders and Decorations.
151 RAW, nos. 26043, 26162.
152 Tait 1984, no. 845.
153 RAW, no. 26021.
154 Tait 1984, no. 899.
155 RAW, no. 26190.
156 *Ibid.*, no. 26004.
157 Chatsworth colln.
158 RAW, no. 26027.
159 Author's colln.
160 RAW, no. 26114.
161 RAW, nos. 26043, 25990.
162 *Ibid.*, no. 26013.
163 *Ibid.*, nos. 26098, 26114.
164 Christie's, 22 Oct. 1974, no. 119.
165 RAW, nos. 25990, 26161.
166 *Ibid.*, no. 26003.
167 Scarisbrick 1989, pl. 105.
168 RAW, no. 26316.
169 *Ibid.*, nos. 26161, 26041.
170 *Ibid.*, nos. 26117, 26027.
171 *Ibid.*, no. 26161.
172 *Lady's Mon. Mus.*, VI (1801), 72; Phillips's, 9 April 1804, no. 1391; RAW, no. 25999.
173 RAW, no. 26161.
174 Fitzwilliam Museum, M4 1962.
175 RAW, nos. 26073, 26026, 25990; Christie's, 1 July 1964, no. 161.
176 Christie's, 13 June 1816, p. 4, no. 35.
177 *Ibid.*, 23 June 1947, no. 47a.
178 RAW, no. 26026.
179 Durham RO, D/LO/F 667 (1).
180 Minto 1874, III, p. 266.
181 RAW, nos. 25771; London 1978B, no. 158.
182 Christie's, 24 May 1819, no. 24.
183 Oman 1968, p. 109.
184 RAW, nos. 25657, 26271, 25776, 25757, 25779.
185 Durham RO, D/LO/F 667 [4] (15).
186 Christie's, 17 May 1819, no. 94.
187 *Ibid.*, no. 105; B.M., Banks colln, P & D 67.131, trade card of P. Nappi, 31 Newman Street.
188 RAW, no. 25698.
189 Washington 1985, no. 531.
190 V & A, GL 10, f. 207.
191 RAW, no. 26053; Phillips's, 9 April 1804, no. 1326.
192 RAW, no. 25789.
193 PRO, Prob. 11/2059, f. 378 (new foliation); Powys 1899, pp. 352–3.
194 Christie's, 11 June 1799, nos. 85, 87.
195 Farebrother, 21 April 1817, no. 297.
196 Phillips's, 9 April 1804, nos. 287, 531; Christie's, 17 March 1825, no. 11.
197 Phillips's, 9 April 1804, no. 1092.
198 Christie's, 17 May 1819, no. 87.
199 *Ibid.*, 19 Feb. 1819, no. 71.
200 *Ibid.*, 10 June 1830, no. 73; 13 March 1811, no. 91; 19 May 1819, no. 59.
201 Farebrother, 21 April 1817, p. 18, no. 296, p. 13, no. 170.
202 Hare 1894, I, p. 266.
203 RAW, no. 25752.
204 *Lady's Mon. Mus.*, VI (1801), 61.
205 Christie's, 16 May 1825, no. 12.
206 *Ibid.*, 6 April 1837, no. 13.
207 Washington 1985, no. 531.
208 RAW, no. 25824.
209 *Ibid.*, no. 26154.
210 Henig *et al.*, forthcoming, no. 786a; Christie's, 28 June 1843, no. 411.
211 Phillips's, 9 April 1804, nos. 1088, 1097, 1304–5, etc.
212 Wellington 1953, pp. 163–7; Fox 1846, p. 40.
213 Farington 1978–84, XI, 11 Jan. 1812, no. 3950.
214 Fox 1846, p. 40.
215 RAW, no. 26324.
216 G. Seidmann, *Nathaniel Marchant Gem Engraver*, Walpole Society, 53 (1989), p. 720.
217 RAW, no. 25776.
218 V & A, Wakelin accts, 24, 25 June 1801; *Conn.*, CIV (1939), 301.
219 Nicolas 1841–2, III, Bath, pp. 111–20;.
220 *Ibid.*, pp. 124–30.
221 *Ibid.*, IV, St Michael and St George.
222 RAW, no. 26001.
223 Frampton 1885, p. 279.
224 RAW, no. 26001.
225 Victoria 1912, II, p. 91; James 1951.
226 Scarisbrick 1989, pl. 104.
227 Victoria 1912, II, p. 92.
228 Londonderry Family Archives, Castlereagh Papers, Letter xxiii.
229 Fox 1846, p. 41.
230 RAW, no. 26054.
231 Blessington 1836, p. 55.

232 Broughton 1909–11, I, p. 231.
233 George IV 1963–71, III, no. 1067.
234 Lancashire RO, DDSc9/32.
235 Williamson 1933, p. 188.
236 George IV 1963–71, IV, p. 3.
237 Williamson, 1933, p. 193.
238 RAW, no. 25905.
239 Jackson 1931.
240 Clark 1895–8, II, p. 221.
241 Londonderry Family Archives, Castlereagh Papers, Letter xxiii.
242 'The Locket', *Lady's Mag.*, XXIX (1798), 375.
243 Stuart 1939, p. 238.
244 Somerset RO, DD/HLM Box 3, Mrs Sampson valuation.
245 Victoria 1912, I, p. 117.
246 *Lady's Mag.*, imp. ser. I (1832), 129.
247 Lincoln RO, Mon 11/31, Inv. 18 Aug. 1814.
248 Elwes 1890, p. 35.
249 Lamb 1816, I p. 67.
250 Exeter RO, Henry Ellis Papers, III, pp. 113–14.
251 Rush 1873, p. 27.
252 *Lady's Mag.*, XLVII (1817), 569.
253 RAW, no. 25920; V & A, M82–1969.
254 *Lady's Mag.*, XXVII (1797), 274; XXX (1799), 214.
255 Rush 1873, p. 115.
256 Stanhope 1827, II, p. 122.
257 Wyndham 1955, p. 202.
258 Gronow 1892, II, p. 83.
259 *Ibid.*, p. 84.
260 Disraeli 1871, p. 372.
261 Lamb 1816, I, p. 234.
262 Strutt 1939, p. 95.
263 *SJH Bulletin*, III (1989), 5.
264 Russell-Smith 1961.
265 V & A, GL 10, f. 39.
266 Russell-Smith 1961.
267 V & A, GL 10, f. 51.

10 *The categories of later Georgian jewellery, 1790–1837*

1 Blessington 1836, p. 29.
2 RAW, no. 25917.
3 V & A, GL 10, f. 75.
4 *Lady's Mag.*, XXXVIII (1806), 28–9.
5 *Ibid.*, XXI (1790), 314.
6 *Ibid.*, XLI (1810), 277.
7 Fox 1923, p. 64.
8 Durham RO, D/LO/F 667 [4] (14).
9 Christie's, 23 March 1822, no.31; RAW, no. 25697; *Lady's Mon. Mus.*, XIII (1821), 174; *Lady's Mag.*, XXXIII (1802), 305; RAW, no. 25757.
10 Christie's, 12 June 1829, no. 71.
11 RAW, no. 25940.
12 Scarisbrick 1989, pls 246–7.
13 *Lady's Mag.*, XXXI (1802), 305; Christie's, 17 March 1825, p. 17, no. 75.
14 Scarisbrick 1989, pl. 248.
15 W. H. Mallock and Lady Guendolen Ramsden (ed.), *Letters, Remains, and Memoirs of Edward Adolphus Seymour Twelfth Duke of Somerset* (1893), p. 26.
16 Calvert 1911, p. 33.
17 Norfolk RO, WLS LIV/5/4 427–9.
18 RAW, no. 25944.
19 Lincoln RO, Mon 11/31.
20 Bamford 1936, p. 116; George IV 1963–71, IV, no. 1719.
21 BM, P & D 1890.5–17.141.
22 Fox 1923, p. 105; RAW, no. 26026.
23 RAW, nos. 25940, 26026.
24 *Lady's Mag.*, imp. ser. III (1833), 48; *Lady's Mus.*, I (1829), 10–12, 60.
25 RAW, nos. 25886, 26301; Christie's, 17 March 1825, p. 18, no. 82; *Lady's Mag.*, n.s. VIII (1836), 236.
26 Christie's, 16 March 1825, p. 9, no. 85; 17 March 1825, no. 61; RAW, no. 25937.
27 Christie's, 2 Feb. 1791, no. 17; RAW, no. 26324.
28 George IV 1963–71, VI, no. 2651.
29 RAW, nos. 25769, 26324.
30 *Lady's Mag.*, XXXVII (1806), 308.
31 Christie's, 2 Feb. 1791, no. 10; Somerset RO, DD/HLM Box 3.
32 RAW, nos. 25741; 26271 Christie's, 17 Dec. 1812, no. 34.
33 *Lady's Mus.*, II (1831), 145; *Lady's Mag.*, imp. ser. III (1832), 129.
34 *Lady's Mag.*, imp. ser. II (1833), 183.
35 Victoria 1912, I, p. 75.
36 V & A, GL 10, f. 117.
37 *Ibid.*, f. 63.
38 Davies 1872, II, p. 134.
39 Christie's, 16 March 1825, no. 46; 19 April 1819, no. 82; 19 Feb. 1819, no. 104.
40 *Lady's Mag.*, n.s. IV (1823), 607; Christie's, 16 March 1825, nos. 62, 77.
41 *Lady's Mag.*, XXI (1790), 315.
42 *Ibid.*, n.s. IX (1828), 447; imp. ser. III (1833), 47.
43 RAW, no. 25940.
44 Christie's, 16 March 1825, no. 88; 28 April 1825, no. 79.
45 Phillips's, 9 April 1804, nos. 314–15.
46 Christie's, 16 June 1816, no. 124; RAW, nos. 25991, 26017; Phillips's, 9 April 1804, no. 2772.
47 RAW, no. 25788; Phillips's, 9 April 1809, no. 1098.
48 *Lady's Mon. Mus.*, imp. ser. XVIII (1823), 344.
49 See p. 247 above; Holland 1946, p. 39.
50 RAW, nos. 25917, 26054.
51 Christie's, 17 March 1825, no. 76; RAW, no. 26005.
52 Christie's, 26 March 1825, no. 69; RAW, nos. 25860, 26073.
53 Christie's, 16 June 1816, no. 91; 16 March 1825, no. 45.
54 *Lady's Mag.*, n.s. X (1829), 10.
55 Christie's, 17 March 1825, no. 35; RAW, no. 25975.

56 Phillips's, 9 April 1804, no. 1496; *Lady's Mag.*, n.s. IV (1823), 247; RAW, no. 26054.
57 Phillips's, 9 April 1804, no. 1435; Christie's, 19 Feb. 1819, day 5, p. 7, no. 68; RAW, no. 26054.
58 Christie's, 16 March 1825, p. 10, no. 90.
59 Phillips's, 9 April 1804, no. 1478.
60 RAW, no. 25806; *Lady's Mag.*, XXVII, (1796), 8.
61 Phillips's, 9 April 1804, no. 990.
62 RAW, no. 25911.
63 See p. 350 above.
64 *Lady's Mag.*, imp. ser. I (1832). 278.
65 V & A, GL 10, f. 50.
66 RAW, nos. 26149, 25786.
67 Christie's, 14 April 1825, p. 10, no. 98; 13 June 1816, nos. 45, 103; 10 June 1830, no. 34.
68 *Lady's Mag.*, imp. ser. I (1832), 80; RAW, nos. 26027, 25697, 25806.
69 Christie's, 27 March 1827, no. 37.
70 *Lady's Mus.*, I (1829), 176; RAW, no. 26021.
71 Sudbury Hall, Vernon Archives, Diary of Georgiana Vernon, *sub die* 9 Jan. 1803; Londonderry Family Archives, Castlereagh Papers, Letters xcii, cviii.
72 Bury 1828, p. 5.
73 Disraeli 1837, p. 221.
74 RAW, nos. 25936, 26261, 25829, 25755; Christie's, 22 April 1812, no. 23; 13 June 1816, no. 95.
75 *Lady's Mon. Mus.*, II (1799), 228; RAW, nos. 25773, 26024; Phillips's 9 April 1804, nos. 2010, 1118.
76 RAW, no. 26324.
77 *Lady's Mag.*, imp. ser. I (1832), 128.
78 V & A, GL 10, f. 45.
79 RAW, nos. 26058, 26013.
80 Grant 1988, I, p. 52.
81 RAW, no. 25698.
82 *Ibid.*, nos. 25788, 26054.
83 Christie's, 17 March 1825, p. 13, no. 9; 13 March 1811, nos. 2–3; RAW, nos. 26085, 25999, 26255, 25755; Phillips's 9 April 1804, no. 270.
84 RAW, nos. 25975, 26060, 25836; Christie's, 17 March 1825, p. 17, no. 62.
85 Christie's, 17 March 1825, no. 85.
86 RAW, no. 26060.
87 *Ibid.*, no. 26072.
88 *Ibid.*, nos. 26082, 26316, 26036, 25925; Phillips's, 9 April 1804, no. 870.
89 *Lady's Mag.*, XXXII (1801), 39.
90 RAW, nos. 25778, 25786, 25831.
91 Christie's, 15 Feb. 1810, no. 46.
92 *Lady's Mag.*, n.s. III (1822), 442.
93 *Lady's Mus.*, I (1830), 55.
94 *Lady's Mag.*, imp. ser. IX (1836), 193.
95 Christie's, 16 March 1825, no. 79.
96 *Ibid.*, 13 March 1811, p. 153.
97 Keats House, Hampstead.
98 Christie's, 27 March 1827, p. 38, no. 44.
99 RAW, no. 25982; Scarisbrick 1989, p. 75.
100 *Lady's Mag.*, n.s. III (1822), 441.
101 RAW, nos. 26261, 26306.
102 Christie's, 7 Oct. 1987, no. 17.
103 RAW, no. 25995.
104 V & A, GL 10, f. 311.
105 Christie's, 13 June 1816, p. 5, no. 43.
106 *Ibid.*, 19 Feb. 1819, p. 15, no. 47.
107 RAW, no. 25757.
108 *Lady's Mon. Mus.*, imp. ser. XXVI (1827), 294; *Lady's Mag.*, n.s. IV (1823), 487; RAW, no. 26200.
109 *Lady's Mon. Mus.*, imp. ser. XVIII (1823), 344.
110 Lamb 1816, II, p. 332.
111 Christie's, 24 May 1819, no. 11.
112 RAW, no. 26183.
113 Lincoln RO, Mon 11/31, Fletcher accts.
114 Scarisbrick 1986C, fig. 5, p. 33.
115 RAW, no. 25756.
116 V & A, GL 10, f. 61.
117 RAW, no. 26301.
118 *Lady's Mag.*, XLV (1831), 292; V & A, GL 10, f. 90; Scarisbrick 1989, pl. 258.
119 Christie's, 24 May 1819, no. 2.
120 *Lady's Mag.*, imp. ser. VII, VIII (1836), 440.
121 *Lady's Monthly Mus.*, imp. ser. XI (1820), 111–12.
122 Christie's, 24 May 1819, no. 9.
123 *Ibid.*, 22 April 1812, no. 14.
124 *Lady's Mag.*, n.s. IV (1823), 63.
125 See p. 350 above.
126 *Lady's Mon. Mus.*, VI (1801), 72; RAW, no. 26304.
127 Victoria 1912, I p. 179.
128 *Lady's Mus.*, I (1830), 178.
129 *Lady's Mon. Mus.*, I (1798), 480.
130 RAW, no. 25755; Christie's, 22 April 1812, no. 17; 13 March 1811, no. 30; 16 March 1825, no. 22; 17 March 1825, no. 41.
131 C. M. Yonge, *Heartsease* (1854); Thackeray 1869, p. 110.
132 Dino 1909–10, II p. 256.
133 *Lady's Mag.* n.s. IX (1828), 165.
134 RAW, no. 25774.
135 Sudbury Hall, Vernon Archives, Diary of Georgiana Vernon, 9 Jan. 1803; Sotheby's, 8 May 1986, no. 142.
136 Christie's, 24 May 1819, no. 27.
137 RAW, no. 25975.
138 *Ibid.*, nos. 26327, 26001, 26095, 26098, 26140.
139 *Ibid.*, no. 26093; Ponsonby 1958, p. 49.
140 *Lady's Mon. Mus.*, V (1800), 72.
141 RAW, nos. 25858, 26187, 26306, 25779.
142 RAW, no. 26187; Sotheby's, 25 Oct. 1985 (Sheldon sale), no. 285.
143 Stuart 1865, p. 168.
144 Phillips's, 9 April 1804, nos. 1253, 992; Christie's, 13 June 1816, no. 121; RAW, nos. 25757, 26011; V & A, GL 10, f. 39.
145 RAW, no. 26011.
146 *Lady's Mus.*, II (1829), 288; RAW, no. 26024.
147 RAW, nos. 26011, 26024, 26081, 26089, 25779, 26093, 26001, 26114; Christie's, 17 May 1825, p. 16, no. 49.
148 *Lady's Mag.*, n.s. IX (1828), 445.
149 Stuart 1939, p. 294.

150 V & A, GL 10, f. 44.
151 Christie's, 24 May 1819, no. 22; RAW, no. 26001.
152 RAW, no. 25858.
153 *Ibid.*
154 Christie's, 27 March 1827, p. 37, no. 39.
155 Tayler 1987, pp. 59–60.
156 Bury 1828, p. 28.
157 RAW, no. 25752.
158 *Ibid.*, nos. 26028, 25959.
159 Phillips's, 9 April 1804, no. 140.
160 BM, MLA F.2172.
161 Wallace Colln, portrait 559; Oman 1930, no. 958.
162 RAW, nos. 26001, 26058, 25779.
163 *Ibid.*, no. 25785; Christie's, 16 March 1825, p. 8, no. 61.
164 RAW, nos. 26044, 25848.
165 *Ibid.*, nos. 26089, 25848, 25823; Christie's, 22 April 1812, p. 6, no. 30.
166 *Lady's Mag.*, n.s. III (1822) 388.
167 Gore 1846, II, p. 110.
168 RAW, nos. 25794, 26060, 26044, 26327.
169 *Ibid.*, no. 25991.
170 *Ibid.*, no. 26030; Christie's, 27 Feb. 1795, p. 4, no. 22.
171 Evans 1931, p. 91.
172 RAW, nos. 25884, 26082.
173 Victoria 1912, I p. 76.
174 RAW, no. 25770.
175 G. Callender (ed.), *Loan Collection of Nelson Relics, Exhibition at Spink and Son* (1928), no. 54.
176 RAW, nos. 26023, 26031, 26262; Christie's, 13 March 1811, nos. 42, 63, 39.
177 *Lady's Mag.*, XXXVII (1806), 206; RAW, nos. 26271, 25732.
178 RAW, no. 25780.
179 Christie's, 13 March 1811, no. 61.
180 RAW, no. 26135.
181 Collection of Jonathan Norton, London.
182 Farebrother, 21 April 1817, p. 14, nos. 189, 194, 198, 200.
183 *Ibid.*, p. 14, nos. 200–1.
184 Bury 1982, p. 39, no. 72.
185 *Ibid.*, no. 70.
186 Farebrother, 21 April 1817, p. 15, no. 208.
187 Blair 1972, p. 46, nos. 7–8, p. 48, no. 21.
188 *Ibid.*, p. 46, nos. 6, 9–10, etc.
189 *Ibid.*, p. 48, no. 22, p. 53, no. 42.
190 *Ibid.*, p. 52, no. 38, pls 2c, 26.
191 Durham RO, D/LO/F 667 [4] (14).
192 Scarisbrick 1989, p. 173.

Bibliography and abbreviated references

Books and other sources are entered under the abbreviations or short references used for them in the source notes. For convenience two groups of important source material – exhibition catalogues and pattern books – have been collected together and listed under these general headings, using the short form by which they are identified in full elsewhere in the Bibliography.

ALBERTUS MAGNUS 1967: Albertus Magnus (tr. D Wyckoff): *Book of Minerals*.

ALLEN 1987: B. Allen: *Francis Hayman*.

ALTHORP PAPERS: British Library.

ANGELO 1828–30: H. C. W. Angelo: *Reminiscences of Henry Angelo, with Memoirs of His Father and Friends*, 2 vols.

ANJOU 1956: S. Anjou: 'Marc Gunther's designs for jewellers 1684 to 1713', *Röhsska Konstlöjdmuseet Göteborg* (1956), pp. 43–60.

ANNE OF DENMARK: D. Scarisbrick: 'Anne of Denmark's jewellery inventory', *Arch.*, 109 (1991), 193–237.

ANSTRUTHER 1953: G. Anstruther: *Vaux of Harrowden: A Recusant Family*.

Ant. J: *The Antiquaries Journal*, 1 (1921), in progress.

Arch.: *Archaeologia*, 1 (1770), in progress.

Arch. Ael.: *Archaeologia Aeliana*, 1 (1816), in progress.

Arch. Cant.: *Archaeologia Cantiana*, 1 (1858), in progress.

Arch. J.: *Archaeological Journal*, 1 (1845), in progress.

ARGYLL 1910: J. D. S. Campbell, Duke of Argyll: *Intimate Society Letters of the Eighteenth Century*, 2 vols.

ARNOLD 1988: J. Arnold: *Queen Elizabeth's Wardrobe Unlock'd*.

ASHMOLE 1672: E. Ashmole: *The Institutions, Laws and Ceremonies of the Most Noble Order of the Garter*.

ASHMOLE 1715: E. Ashmole: *The History of the Most Noble Order of the Garter*.

ASHMOLE 1966: E. Ashmole (ed. C. H. Josten): *Elias Ashmole, 1617–1692. His Autobiographical and Historical Notes, His Correspondence*, 5 vols.

AUERBACH 1961: E. Auerbach: *Nicholas Hilliard*.

AUSTEN 1953: J. Austen (ed. R. W. Chapman): *Jane Austen's Letters to Her Sister Cassandra and Others*. *N.B.* Jane Austen's novels are cited by title and chapter.

AYLOFFE 1775: J. Ayloffe: 'An account of the body of king Edward the First, as it appeared on opening his tomb in the year 1774', *Arch.*, 3 (1775), 376–413.

AYLWARD 1960: J. D. Aylward: *The Small-sword in England Its History, Its Forms, Its Makers, and Its Masters*.

BABELON 1897: E. Babelon: *Catalogue des camées antiques et modernes*.

BABELON 1922: J. Babelon: *Jacopo da Trezzo et la construction de l'Escorial. Essai sur les arts à la cour de Philippe II 1519–1589*.

BACKHOUSE 1989: J. Backhouse: 'Illuminated MSS. and the early development of the portrait miniature', in *Early Tudor England (The 1987 Harlaxton Symposium)*, pp. 1–17.

BAILDON 1909: W. O. Baildon: 'Three inventories: (1) The Earl of Huntingdon, 1377; (2) Brother John Randolf, 1419; (3) Sir John de Boys, 1426', *Arch.*, 61 (1909), 163–76.

BALFOUR 1987: I. Balfour: *Famous Diamonds*.

BALTIMORE 1979: Walters Art Gallery (ed. A. Garside): *Jewelry Ancient to Modern*.

BAMFORD 1936: F. Bamford: *Dear Miss Heber. An Eighteenth Century Correspondence*.

BARKER 1957: T. C. Barker: *The Girdlers' Company, A Second History*.

BARKER 1986: J. R. V. Barker: *The Tournament in England, 1100–1400*.

BARR 1980: E. Barr: *George Wickes: Royal Goldsmith, 1698–1761*.

BEAUMONT & FLETCHER 1905–12: F. Beaumont and J. Fletcher (ed. A. Glover and A. R. Walker): *The Works of Francis Beaumont and John Fletcher*, 10 vols, cited by title.

BEDFORD ARCHIVES: Bedford Estate Office, Bloomsbury.

BEDFORD RO: County Hall, Bedford:
Wills; Wrest Park Papers.

BEER 1938: E. S. de Beer: 'King Charles II's own fashion: an episode in English–French relations 1666–1670's, *JWCI*, 2 (1938–9), 105–15.

BEHN 1915: A. Behn (ed. M. Summers): *The Works*, 6 vols.

BENGER 1821: E. O. Benger: *Memoirs of the Life of Anne Boleyn, Queen of Henry VIII*, 2 vols.

BERKELEY 1883: Berkeley Manuscripts (ed. J. Maclean): *The Lives of the Berkeleys*, 2 vols.

BERKELEY 1971: J. Berkeley: *Lulworth and the Welds*.

BERKSHIRE RO: Shire Hall, Reading:

D/EBy/F16; D/ED F12; D/EEg F14.

BERQUEN 1669: R. de Berquen: *Les merveilles des Indes orientales et occidentales, ou nouveau traité des pierres précieuses et perles. Avec augmentation.*

BHRS: Bedfordshire Historical Record Society:
58. M. McGregor: *Bedfordshire Wills Proved in the Prerogative Court of Canterbury 1383–1548*, 1979 [abstracts only].

BIDDLE 1990: M. Biddle: *Artefacts from Medieval Winchester. Object and Economy in Medieval Winchester* [Winchester Studies 7.i–ii].

BIRMINGHAM 1960: City Museum and Art Gallery: *Gemstones and Jewellery.*

BIRMINGHAM 1973: City Museum and Art Gallery: *Birmingham Gold and Silver, 1773–1973.*

BIRMINGHAM ARCH. SOC: Transactions and Proceedings of Birmingham Archaeological Society, 47 (1921).

BISHOP 1951: M. Bishop: *Blake's Hayley. The Life, Works and Friendships of William Hayley.*

BL: The British Library.
Additional MSS.: 1498, 5751A, 9125, 17019, 33050, 33462, 36243, 44825, 46348, 61420, 61472, 61644, 61655; Additional charter 57334;
Cotton MSS.: Appx B.1, Nero D.i, D.vii;
Egerton MS.: 1973, 2983;
Harleian MSS.: 39, 611, 1419, 6853; Harley Roll D35.i–xi.
King's MS.: 126;
Royal MSS.: 7 C.xvi, 14 B.xlii, C.vii; Appx 68;
Sloane MS.: 814;
Stowe MSS.: 557, 559, 560.

BLAIR 1972: C. Blair: *Three Presentation Swords in the Victoria and Albert Museum, and a Group of English Enamels.*

BLAIR 1974: C. Blair: *Arms, Armour and Base Metalwork.* [The James A. de Rothschild Collection at Waddesdon Manor].

BLAIR 1985: C. Blair: 'A mourning ring of 1690', *JS.* 2 (1985), 73.

BLAIR AND DELAMER 1988: C. Blair and I. Delamer: 'The Dublin civic swords', *Proceedings of the Royal Irish Academy*, 88C n. 5 (1988), 5–142.

BLEACKLEY 1923; H. W. Bleackley: *Casanova in England: being an Account of the Visit to London in 1763–4 of Giacomo Casanova.*

BLESSINGTON 1836: M. Gardiner, Countess of Blessington: *Confessions of an Elderly Gentleman.*

BLUNDELL 1952: N. Blundell (ed. M. Blundell): *Blundell's Diary and Letter Book, 1702–1728.*

BM: The British Museum, with Departmental references.

BM: The Burlington Magazine, 1 (1903), in progress.

BMS: W. de G. Birch: *Catalogue of Seals in the Department of Manuscripts in the British Museum*, 6 vols: cited by piece number.

BODLEIAN LIBRARY, Oxford:
Ashmole MS. 1148; John Johnson collection, trade cards; MS. North d.27.

BONGI 1871: E. Bongi: *Di Paolo Guinigi e le sue richezze.*

BOSWELL 1951: J. Boswell (ed. F. A. Pottle): *Boswell's London Journal, 1762–3.*

BOULTON 1909: E. B. Boulton: 'Some royal snuff-boxes', *Conn.*, 25 (1909) 93–5.

BOYLE 1672: R. Boyle: *An essay on the origins and Virtues of Gems.*

BRAUN 1980: P. Braun: *Sir Hugh Middleton, Practical Idealist.*

BRAY 1806: W. Bray: 'An account of the revenue, the expences, the jewels, &c. of Prince Henry', *Arch.* 15 (1806), 18–26.

BREWIS 1927: P. Brewis: 'Six silver ring brooches of the fourteenth century from Northumberland', *Arch. Ael.*, 4 ser. 4 (1927), 104–8.

BREWIS 1930: P. Brewis: 'A gold fede-ring brooch, English of the fifteenth century', *Arch. Ael.*, 4 ser. 7 (1930), 184–5.

BRISTOL 1894: J. Hervey, Earl of Bristol (ed. S. H. A. H[ervey]): *Letter-books of John Hervey, first Earl of Bristol*, 3 vols [Suffolk Green Books, 1].

BRISTOL 1953: A. J. (Hervey), Earl of Bristol (ed. D. Erskine): *Augustus Hervey's Journal. Being the Intimate Life of a Captain in the Royal Navy Ashore and Afloat, 1746–1759.*

BROUGHTON 1887: F. D. [i.e. A. M. A.] Broughton: *Court and Private Life in the Time of Queen Charlotte: being the Journals of Mrs Papendiek.*

BROUGHTON 1909–11: J. C. Hobhouse, Lord Broughton (ed. Lady Dorchester): *Recollections of a Long Life*, 6 vols.

BROWNE 1646: T. Browne: *Pseudodoxia Epidemica: or, Enquiries into Very Many Received Tenents and Commonly Presumed Truths*, in (ed. G. Keynes): *The Works of Sir Thomas Browne*, 6 vols., 1928–31.

BUCKLEY 1932: F. Buckley: *Fob Seals in the Seventeenth Century.*

BURGHLEY HOUSE ARCHIVES: MS. Ex 41/82.

BURGOYNE 1786: J. Burgoyne: *The Heiress; A Comedy.*

BURNABY 1701: W. Burnaby: *The Ladies Visiting Day; A Comedy.*

BURY 1828: see under Campbell.

BURY 1908: C. Bury (ed. F. Stuart): *The Diary of a Lady in Waiting Lady Charlotte Bury.*

BURY 1981: S. Bury: 'The Pigot diamond 2 – The growth of a legend'. *SJH Newsletter*, 2.1 (1981), 2–4.

BURY 1982: S. Bury: *Jewellery Gallery Summary Catalogue.*

BURY 1985: S. Bury: *Introduction to Sentimental Jewellery.*

BUTLER 1967: S. Butler (ed. J. S. Wilders): Hudibras.

CALLANDER 1923–4: J. G. Callander: Fourteenth-century brooches and other ornaments in the National Museum of Antiquities of Scotland', *PSA Scot.*, 58 (1923–4), 160–84.

CALVERT 1911: F. Calvert (ed. W. Blake): *An Irish Beauty of the Regency. Compiled from "Mes Souvenirs" the Unpublished journals of the Hon. Mrs Calvert, 1789–1822.*

CAMDEN SOC.: The Camden Society, O.S. (Original

series):

24, 54, 89 (ed. A. Way): *Promptorium parvulorum . . . lexicon Anglo-latinum princeps, auctore fratre Galfrido Grammatico . . . A.D. circa MCCCCXL*, 3 vols, 1843–65.

37 (tr. C. A. Sneyd): *A Relation or Rather a True Account of the Island of England . . . about the Year 1500 . . . from the Italian*, 1847.

49 (ed. S. Tymms): *Wills and Inventories from the Registers of the Commissary of Bury St Edmunds and the Archdeaconry of Sudbury*, 1850.

56 (ed. J. Bruce): *Letters and Papers of the Verney Family down to . . . 1679*, 1859.

58 (ed. T. T. Lewis): *Letters of Lady Brilliana Harley, Wife of Sir Robert Harley, of Brampton Bryan, Knight of the Bath*, 1854.

61 (ed. J. G. Nichols): *Inventories of the Wardrobe, Plate, Chapel Stuff, etc., of Henry Fitzroy, Duke of Richmond, and of the Wardrobe Stuff at Baynard's Castle of Katherine, Princess Dowager*, 1855.

71 (ed. W. D. Cooper): *Savile Correspondence. Letters to and from Henry Savile . . . Vice-Chamberlain to Charles II and James II . . .* , 1858.

83 (ed. J. G. Nichols and J. Bruce): *Wills from Doctor's Commons. A Selection of Wills of Eminent Persons proved in the Prerogative Court of Canterbury*, 1883.

n.s. (New series):

31 (ed. M. G. Hanotaux): *Memoir by Madame de Motteville on the Life of Henrietta Maria*, in *Camden Miscellany*, vol. 8, 1883.

53 (ed. L. T. Smith): *Expeditions to Prussia and the Holy Land made by Henry, Earl of Derby . . . in the Years 1390–1 and 1392–3*, 1894.

3.s. (Third series):

29–30 (ed. C. L. Kingsford): *The Stonor Letters and Papers 1290–1483*, 1919.

CAMMELL 1939: C. R. Cammell: *The Great Duke of Buckingham*.

CAMPBELL 1828: C. S. M. Campbell, afterwards Bury: *Marriage in High Life*, 1826.

CAMPBELL 1983: M. L. Campbell: *An Introduction to Medieval Enamels*.

CANNON 1918: H. L. Cannon ed.: *The Great Rolls of the Pipe for . . . A.D. 1241–1242*.

CARTWRIGHT 1883: J. J. Cartwright: *The Wentworth Papers 1705–1739. Selected from the . . . Correspondence of Thomas Wentworth*.

CARTWRIGHT 1894: J. Cartwright: *Madame. A Life of Henrietta, Daughter of Charles I. and Duchess of Orleans*.

CASTLE HOWARD ARCHIVES.

CAVINESS 1981: M. H. Caviness: *The Windows of Christ Church Cathedral Canterbury*. [Corpus vitrearium medii aevi, Great Britain, 2].

C. CL. R: PRO: *Calendar of Close Rolls, Henry III* to *Richard III*. Cited by reign and volume.

CHAMBERS 1896: R. Chambers: *The Life and Works of Robert Burns*.

CHAMBERS 1936: E. K. Chambers: *Sir Henry Lee*.

CHARDIN 1686: J. Chardin: *The Travels of Sir John Chardin into Persia and the East-Indies. The first volume*.

CHATSWORTH ARCHIVES: Will of George, Earl of Shrewsbury 1537; Bill to Lady Burlington, 17 Nov. 1736; Bill for purchases of Mrs Garrick, 10 May 1775; Valuation of rings, etc.

CHAUCER 1957: G. Chaucer (ed. F. N. Robinson): *The Works of Geoffrey Chaucer*. Cited by titles of works.

CHERRY 1973: J. Cherry: 'The medieval jewellery from the Fishpool Nottinghamshire hoard', *Arch.*, 104 (1973), 307–21.

CHERRY 1983: J. Cherry, 'Medieval gold brooch found in Manchester', in M. Morris, *Medieval Manchester*. pp. 77–8 [Archaeology of Greater Manchester 1].

CHERRY 1983–4: J. Cherry: 'A late medieval love jewel', *JS*, 1 (1983–4), 45–7.

CHRISTIAN IV: Foundation for Christian IV year 1988: *Christian IV and Europe. The 19th Art Exhibition of the Council of Europe Denmark*.

CHRISTIE'S: cited by date of sale, subject if not jewellery, with page or lot number.

CL: *Country Life*.

CLARK 1895–8: A. Clark: *Gleanings from an Old Portfolio, containing Correspondence between lady Louisa Stuart and her Sister Caroline, Countess of Portarlington*, 3 vols.

CLARKE 1937: M. V. Clarke (ed. L. S. Sutherland and M. McKisack): *Fourteenth Century Studies*.

CLARKE 1985: T. H. Clarke: 'A Meissen snuff box with a portrait of Lady Caroline Fox', *BM*, 127 (1985), 713.

CLERICI 1907: G. P. Clerici: *A Queen of Indiscretions. The Tragedy of Caroline of Brunswick, Queen of England*.

C. LIB. R.: PRO: *Calendar of Liberate Rolls*, 6 vols.

CLIFFORD 1971: A. Clifford: *Cut-steel and Berlin Iron jewellery*.

CLRO: Corporation of the City of London RO: Hustings court rolls, selected wills; Mayor's Court, original bills MC1; Orphans' inventories *c*, 1629–1723.

CLWYD RO: D/AN/828, DD/WY/6659, D/PT/899.

COKE 1719: R. Coke: *A Detection of the Court and State of England during the Reigns of K. James I. . . . The Fourth Edition continued thro' the Reigns of King William . . . to the Death of Queen Anne*.

COKE 1889–96: M. Coke (ed. A. J. Home): *The Letters and Journals of Lady Mary Coke*, 4 vols.

COKE 1899: J. Coke (ed. A. Rathbone): *Letters from Lady Jane Coke to her friend Mrs Eyre at Derby, 1747–58*.

COLL. TOP. ET GEN.: *Collectanea topographica et genealogica, 1–8, 1834–43*.

COLLINS 1734: *A. Collins: Proceedings . . . on Claims and Controversies concerning Baronies by Writ, and Other Honours*.

COLLINS 1955: A. J. Collins ed.: *Jewels and Plate of Queen Elizabeth I. The Inventory of 1574*.

COLMAN & GARRICK 1766: G. Colman and D. Garrick: *The Clandestine Marriage, A Comedy*.

COMPLETE PEERAGE: G. E. C[ockayne] *et al.* (eds.): *The Complete Peerage*, 13 vols in 14.

CONN.: *The Connoisseur*, 1 (1901), in progress.

COOKE 1900: *C. K. Cooke: A Memoir of her Royal Highness Princess Mary Adelaide, Duchess of Teck*, 2 vols.

COWPER 1864: M. Countess Cowper (ed. C. S. Cowper): *Diary of Mary, Countess Cowper, Lady of the Bedchamber to the Princess of Wales, 1714–1720.*

COX 1773: J. Cox: *A Descriptive Inventory of the . . . Pieces of Mechanism and Jewellery, comprised in a Schedule annexed to an Act of Parliament . . . enabling Mr. James Cox to dispose of his Museum by . . . Lottery.*

CPR: PRO: *Calendar of Patent Rolls, Henry III* – in progress. Cited by reign and volume.

CREEVEY 1912: H. Maxwell: *A Selection from the Correspondence and Diaries of the late Thomas Creevey M.P.*, 2 vols.

CRIPPS 1975: D. Cripps: *Elizabeth of the Sealed Knot: Elizabeth, Countess of Dysart.*

CSP DOM.: PRO: *Calendar of State Papers Domestic, Edward VI – in progress. Cited by reign and volume.*

CSP FOREIGN: *Calendar of State Papers, Foreign Series, of the Reign of Mary 1553–1558.*

CSP MILAN: PRO: *State Papers and Manuscripts relating to English Affairs in the Archives and Collections of Milan*, vol. 1, all publd.

CSP SPAN.: PRO: *Letters, Despatches and State Papers relating to the Negotiations between England and Spain*, 13 vols.

CSP VEN.: PRO: *State Papers and Manuscripts relating to English Affairs, existing in the Archives and Collections of Venice*, 38 vols.

CUMBRIA RO: D/SEN, P1574.

CUMHAILL 1970: P. W. Cumhaill: *Investing in Clocks and Watches.*

CUNLIFFE 1979: B. Cunliffe: *Excavations in Bath, 1950–1975.* [Committee for Rescue Archaeology in Avon, Gloucestershire and Somerset, Excavation Report, 1).

CURLE 1906: A. O. Curle: 'Notes on some inventories of the house of Rossie, near Montrose, dating from the year 1693–1740', *PSA Scot.*, 40 (1906), 53–9.

CUST 1905–6: L. Cust: 'John of Antwerp, goldsmith, and Hans Holbein', *BM*, 8 (1905–6), 356–60.

DALTON 1912: O. M. Dalton: *Catalogue of Finger Rings in the British Museum.*

DALTON 1915: O. M. Dalton: *Catalogue of Engraved Gems of the Post-Classical Periods in the British Museum.*

DANGEAU 1854–60: P. de Coucillon, Marquis de Dangeau (ed. MM. Soulie, Dissieux *et al.*): *Journal du marquis de Dangeau*, 19 vols.

DAVIES 1872: L. C. Davies: *Recollections of Society in France and England*, 2 vols.

DE BOIGNE 1907: Clea de Boigne (ed. M. C. Nicoullaud) Mémoires de la Comtesse de Boigne.

DE LA COUR 1747: W. De la Cour: *Eighth Book of Ornaments.*

DELANY 1861: M. Delany (ed. Lady Llanover): *The Autobiography and Correspondence of Mary Granville, Mrs Delany*, 3 vols.

DEVON 1836: F. Devon: *Issues of the Exchequer, James I, from the Pell Records.*

DINGLINGER 1751: S. H. Dinglinger: *A New Book of Designs for Jewellers Work.*

DINO 1909–10: D. Talleyrand-Périgord, Duchesse de Dino (ed. Princess Radziwill): *Memoirs of the Duchesse de Dino*, 3 ser.

DISRAELI 1871: B. Disraeli (afterwards Earl of eaconsfield): *Henrietta Temple, A Love Story*, first published 1837.

DNB: S. Lee (ed.): *The Dictionary of National Biography*, 69 vols.

DODWELL 1961: C. R. Dodwell (ed. and tr.): *Theophilus: De diversis artibus.*

DOWELL 1888: S. Dowell: *History of Taxation and Taxes in England*, 4 vols.

DRAYTON 1932: M. Drayton (ed. W. Hebel): *The Works.*

DUKELSKAYA 1979: [L. Dukelskaya]: *The Hermitage. English Art Sixteenth to Nineteenth Century.*

DURANT 1977: D. N. Durant: *Bess of Hardwick.*

DURHAM RO: D/LO/F/667 [1] (Inventory of jewels of Emily, Marchioness Dowager of Londonderry, 16 July 1829); D/LO/F 667 [2] 5 (x–xxv) (Agreement between Viscount Castlereagh and Marquess of Lothian 1830 regarding property of Emily Marchioness Dowager of Londonderry inherited from her mother, the Countess Dowager of Buckinghamshire); D/LO/F 667 [4] 13, 14, 15 (Account of purchases by Viscount and Viscountess Castleeagh from Rundell, Bridge and Rundell, 1813–19).

DUTENS 1776: L. Dutens: *Des pierres précieuses et des pierres fines avec les moyens de les connoître et de les évaluer.*

EAST SUSSEX RO: ASH 2759, SAS 6 ACC 74/[*sic*].

EDGECUMBE 1980: E. R. P. Edgecumbe: 'The embossed watchcase in England, *c.* 1700–*c.* 1770' [Unpbld D. Phil. thesis, Oxford University].

EDWARDS 1869: G. O. Edwards: 'Notes on the Howard monument in the south aisle of Framlingham church', *Proc. Suff. Inst. of Arch.*, 3 (1869), 352–7.

EDWARDS 1974: A. C. Edwards (ed.): *The Account Books of Benjamin Mildmay Earl of Fitzwalter.*

EETS: Early English Text Society, O.S. (original series):

4 (ed. R. Morris): *Sir Gawayne and the Green Knight*, 1864.

78 (ed. J. Heritage): *Catholicon Anglicum, and English–Latin Word-Book*, 1881.

81 (ed. F. J. Furnivall): *The Fifty Earliest English Wills in the Court of Probate, London, A.D. 1383–1439* [The wills are taken from the Prerogative Court of Canterbury] 1885.

149 (ed. A. Clark): *Lincoln Diocesan Documents 1450–1544*, 1914.

190 (ed. J. Evans and M. Serjeantson): *English*

Medieval Lapidaries, 1933.
199 (ed. M. Day and R. Steele): *Mum and the Sothsegger*, 1936 [also called *Richard the Redeless*].
212 (ed. S. B. Meech and H. E. Allen): *The Book of Margery Kempe*, 1940.
221 (ed. L. F. Carson): *The Romance of Sir Degrevant*, 1949.
243 G. Cavendish (ed. R. S. Sylvester): *The Life and Death of Cardinal Wolsey*, 1959.
246 (ed. M. Y. Offord): *The Parlement of the Thre Ages*, 1959.
E.S. (extra series):
10 A. Boorde (ed. F. J. Furnivall): *The Fyrst Boke of the Introduction to Knowledge*, 1870.
33 (ed. S. J. H. Herrtage): *The Early English Versions of the Gesta Romanorum*, 1879.

EHINGEN 1929: J. von Ehingen (tr. M. Letts): *The Diary of Jörg von Ehingen*.

EHD: (D. C. Douglas ed.): *English Historical Documents, vols. 1, 5*.

EHR: *English Historical Review*, 1 (1886), in progress.

ELIZABETH 1898: Elizabeth [of England], Consort of Frederick V, Landgrave of Hesse-Hamburg (ed. P. C. Yorke): *Letters of Princess Elizabeth of England written for the Most Part to Miss Louisa Swinburne*.

ELLIS 1825–46: H. Ellis (ed.): *Original Letters Illustrative of English History*. 3 vols; 2 ser., 4 vols; 3 ser., 4 vols.

ELWES 1890: W. M. E. Elwes: *The Feilding Album*.

EMMISON 1987: F. G. Emmison (ed.): *Essex Wills, The Archdeaconry Courts 1577–84*, [abstracts only].

ENCYCLOPAEDIA BRITANNICA, 11th edn.

ESSEX RO: D/ABW/5/7 and 10/15; D/DE: B24; D/DP F240/1, 211, L 84; D/D Rg 2/120; DD/MI Box 19, 1–35.

EVANS 1921: J. Evans: *English Jewellery from the Fifth Century A.D. to 1900*.

EVANS 1922: J. Evans: *Magical Jewels of the Middle Ages and the Renaissance*.

EVANS 1931: J. Evans: *English Posies and Posy Rings*.

EVANS 1933A: J. Evans: 'Medieval wheel-shaped brooches', *Art Bulletin*, 15 (1933), 197–210.

EVANS 1933B: J. Evans: *Nature in Design A Study of Naturalism in Decorative Art from the Bronze Age to the Renaissance*.

EVANS 1970: J. Evans: *A History of Jewellery 1100–1870*.

EVELYN 1697: J. Evelyn: *Numismata. A Discourse on Medals Antient and Modern*.

EVELYN 1959: J. Evelyn (ed. E. S. de Beer): *The Diary of John Evelyn*.

EVELYN 1974: M. Evelyn: *Mundus Mulieribus: or, The Ladies Dressing Room Unlock'd . . . with the Fop-dictionary . . . Second edition* [1690] [Costume Soc., E.S. 5].

EXETER RO: Henry Ellis Papers.

EXHIBITIONS: *see under*: Allen 1987; Birmingham 1960, 1973; Christian IV; Fort Worth 1982; Heidelberg 1988; Leamington Spa 1967; London 1873, 1889, 1928, 1948, 1972, 1976, 1978, 1978B, 1981A, 1981B, 1982, 1982–3, 1984A, 1984B, 1984C, 1984D, 1985, 1987, 1988; Marks and Payne 1978; Paris 1981; Washington 1962–3, 1985.

FAIRHOLT 1856: F. W. Fairholt: 'On an inventory of the household goods of Sir Thomas Ramsey, Lord Mayor of London, 1577', *Arch.*, 40 (1856), 311–42.

FALKE 1911: D. Falke: 'Old marcasite jewellery', *BM*, 18 (1911), 335–7.

FALKINER 1968: R. Falkiner: *Investing in Antique Jewellery*.

FANSHAWE 1907: A. Fanshawe (ed. H. C. Fanshawe): *The Memoirs of Anne Lady Fanshawe, Wife of the Right Honble Sir Richard Fanshawe, Bart., 1600–1672*.

FAREBROTHER, 21 April 1817: Farebrother & Son (auctioneers).

FARINGTON 1978–84: J. Farington (ed. K. Garlick and A. MacIntyre): *The Diary of Joseph Farington*, 16 vols.

FELLOWES 1939: E. H. Fellowes: *The Knights of the Garter 1348–1939* [Hist. Monogr. Rel. to St Geroge's Chapel, Windsor Castle].

FERRERS 1817: E. Ferrers: 'A letter . . . accompanying an authenticated copy of the will of King James II, with an inventory', *Arch.*, 18 (1817), 223–39.

FIELD 1987: L. Field: *The Queen's Jewels: The Personal Collection of Elizabeth II*.

FIENNES 1949: C. Fiennes (ed. C. Morris): *The Journeys of Celia Fiennes*.

FINETT 1656: J. Finett: *Finetti Philoxenis: Som Choice Observations . . . touching the Reception and Precedence, the Treatment and Audiences . . . of Forren Ambassadors in England*.

FINGERLIN 1971: I. Fingerlin: *Gürtel des hohen und späatern Mittelalters*.

FITCH 1811: R. Fitch: 'The voyage of Mr. Ralph Fitch, to . . . the East India . . . ', in J. Pinkerton (ed.): *A General Collection of the Best and Most Interesting Voyages and Travels*, vol. 9.

FITCH 1852: R. Fitch: 'On a gold niello, found at Matlask, Norfolk', *Norfolk Archaeology*, 3 (1852), 97–104.

FITZGERALD 1899: P. Fitzgerald: *The Good Queen Charlotte*.

FITZHERBERT 1940: M. A. Fitzherbert (ed. S. Leslie): *The Letters of Mrs Fitzherbert and connected Papers*.

FLACH 1736: T. Flach: *A Book of Jewellers Work Design'd by Thomas Flach in London*.

FONTANIEU 1787: M. Fontanieu (tr. and augmented by W. Drew): *The Art of Making Coloured Crystals, to Imitate Precious Stones*.

FOOTE 1799: S. Foote: *The Works*, 2 vols.

FORRER 1977: L. Forrer: *Biographical Dictionary of Medallists, Coin-, Gem-, and Seal-engravers, Mint-masters, &c.*, 8 vols, 1904, rev. edn.

FORTNUM 1883: C. D. Fortnum: 'The diamond signet of Henrietta Maria, Queen of England', *Arch.*, 47 (1883), 393–401.

FORTNUM 1887: C. D. Fortnum: 'Some further notice of the diamond signet of Henrietta Maria, Queen of Charles I; of the king's diamond; and of the sapphire signet believed to be that of Mary Queen of William III', *Arch.*, 50 (1887), 104–17.

FORT WORTH 1982: Kimball Art Museum (ed. J. Ballio): *Elizabeth Louise Vigée le Brun 1755–1848.*

FOX 1846: G. Fox: Typescript copy of an unpubld MS. on the history of the firm of Rundell, Bridge and Rundell, in the Baker Library, Harvard University; V. & A Library, 276, E.3.

FOX 1923: H. E. Fox (ed. G. S. Strangways, Earl of Ilchester); *The Journal of the Hon. Henry Edward Fox 1818–1830.*

FRAMPTON 1885: M. Frampton (ed. H. G. Mundy): *The Journal of M. Frampton from 1779; until 1846.*

FRASER 1859: W. Fraser: *Memorials of the Montgomeries Earls of Eglinton.*

FRASER 1888: W. Fraser: *Memorials of the Family of Wemyss*, 3 vols.

FRENILLY 1908: A. F. F. de Frenilly (ed. A. Chuquet): *Souvenirs de Baron de Frenilly, pair de France (1768–1808).*

FRICK 1968: H. G. Frick: *The Frick Collection: An Illustrated Catalogue*: 1–2, *Paintings.*

FRIEDMAN 1989: A. T. Friedman: *House and Household in Elizabethan England: Wollaton Hall and the Willoughby Family.*

FRITZ 1982: J. M. Fritz: *Goldschmiedekunst der Gotik in Mitteleuropa.*

FROISSART 1901: J. Froissart (tr. Lord Berners, ed. W. P. Ker): *The Chronicle of Froissart*, 6 vols [W. E. Henley ed., The Tudor Translations XXVII–XXXII].

FRYDE 1902: E. B. Fryde (ed.): *Book of Prests of the King's Wardrobe for 1294–5.*

GAI 1984: L. Gai: *L'altare argenteo de san Jacopo nel duomo di Pistoia.*

GANS 1961: M. H. Gans: *Juwelen in mensen. De geschiednis van het bijou van 1400 tot 1900, voor namelijk naar Nederlandse bronnen.*

GARDNER 1927: S. Gardner: *English Gothic Foliage Sculpture.*

GARDNER 1951: A. Gardner: *English Medieval Sculpture.*

GARRARD 1912: Garrard & Co.; *Garrard's, 1721–1911, Crown Jewellers and Goldsmiths during Six Reigns and in Three Centuries.*

GAY 1974: J. Gay (ed. V. A. Dearing and C. E. Beckwith): *Poetry and Prose of John Gay.*

GEMINUS 1548: T. Geminus: *Moryes and Damsashin Renewed and Encreased Very Profitable for Goldsmythes and Embroderers.*

GENT. MAG.: *The Gentleman's Magazine*, 1731–1868.

GEORGE IV 1938: George IV of Great Britain (ed. A. Aspinall): *Letters of George IV, 1812–1830*, 3 vols.

GEORGE IV 1963–71: George IV, Prince of Wales (ed. A. Aspinall): *Correspondence of George, Prince of Wales, 1770–1812*, 8 vols.

GILL 1959–61: T. Gill: 'On fine and delicate steel work', *Journal of the Arms and Armour Society*, 3 (1959–61), 298–311.

GINSBURG 1977: M. Ginsburg: 'Buttons: art and industry', *Apollo*, 105 (1977), 462–7.

GLANVILLE 1984: P. Glanville: 'Robert Amadas, goldsmith to Henry VIII'. *Proceedings of the Silver Society*, 3.5 (1986), 106–13.

GOLDSMITH 1968: O. Goldsmith (ed. A. Friedman): *She Stoops to Conquer.*

GOLDSMITH 1981: O. Goldsmith (ed. A. Friedman): *The Vicar of Wakefield.*

GOLDSMITHS' COMPANY, LONDON: Warden's accounts and court minutes, A 1444–1516; C II 3.ii.

GOODALL 1959–61: J. A. Goodall: 'The use of armorial bearings by London Aldermen in the Middle Ages', *Transactions of the London and Middlesex Archaeological Society*, 20 (1959–61), 17–21.

GOODALL 177: J. A. Goodall 'On the choice of a gem', *SJH Newsletter*, 1.1 (1977), 5–6.

GOODALL 1991: J. A. Goodall: 'Medieval Brooches', *Ant. J.*, 'Ballot exhibits 1991'.

GOODALL MS.: J. A. Goodall 'Dictionary of Engravers in London to 1800', 1969. Address c/o the Society of Antiquaries.

GOODALL AND CHERRY 1985: J. A. Goodall and J. Cherry: 'A twelfth century gold brooch from Folkingham Castle, Lincs', *Ant. J.*, 65 (1985), 471–2.

GORE 1831: C. G. F. Gore: *Mothers and Daughters, A Tale of the Year 1830.*

GORE 1846: C. G. F. Gore: *The Débutante, or, The London Season*, 3 vols.

GORE 1850: C. G. F. Gore: *The Hamiltons; or, Official Life in 1830.*

GORI 1767: A. F. Gori: *DactyLotheca Smithiana.*

GRAHAM 1927: E. M. Graham: *The Beautiful Mrs Graham, and the Cathcart Circle.*

GRAMMONT 1908: A. Hamilton (ed. G. Goodwin): *Memoirs of the Comte de Grammont.*

GRANT 1988: E. Grant of Rothiemurchus: *Memoirs of a Highland Lady*, 2 vols.

GREEN 1967: D. S. Green: *Sarah Duchess of Marlborough.*

GREENSTREET: *Genealogical Tracts: Wills relating to Cobham Hall.*

GREVILLE 1963: C. C. F. Greville (ed. R. Fulford): *The Greville Memoirs* [1814–1860].

GRIMWADE 1976: A. Grimwade: *The London Goldsmiths, 1697–1837, Their Marks and Lives.*

GRONOW 1892: R. H. Gronow: *The Reminiscences and Recollections . . . 1810–1860*, 2 vols.

GROSE 1807: T. Grose: 'An account of the expenses of Robert Sidney Earl of Leicester printed from a fair ms written in the times of Chas. I by Mr. Crittenden, his Lordship s steward', *Antiquarian Repertory*, 1 (1807), 274–95.

GUARDIAN (1713): R. Steele, J. Addison *et al.*: *The Guardian.*

GUIEN 1762: J. Guien [*sic*, for Quien]: *Livre d'ouvrage de juaillerie inventé et gravé par Jean Quien . . . A Book of Ornaments for Jewellers, &c. by the late John Guien.*

GUILDHALL LIBRARY, London: Commissary of London Wills, MS. 19171 selected volumes.

GUILMARD 1880: D. Guilmard: *Les maîtres ornemanistes dessinateurs, peintres, architectes, sculpteurs et graveurs.*

GUTCH 1781: J. Gutch: 'An account of plate . . . made for Cardinal Wolsey, from the ninth year of Henry VIII, unto the nineteenth year', *Collectanea curiosa*, 2 (1781), 283–333.

GWYNN 1985: R. D. Gwynn: *Huguenot Heritage: The History and Contribution of the Huguenots in Britain.*

HACKENBROCH 1977: Y. Hackenbroch: 'Two relics of Sir Thomas More', *Conn.*, 194 (1977), 43–4.

HACKENBROCH 1979: Y. Hackenbroch: *Renaissance Jewellery.*

HAKLUYT SOC.: The Hakluyt Society, 2 ser.:

37 F. B. Peglotti; 'Notices of the land route to Cathay', in H. Yule (ed.): *Cathay and the Way Thither*, III (1914), 137–73.

108 (M. Letts, ed. and tr.): *The Travels of Leo of Rozmital through Germany, Flanders, England . . . 1465–1467, 1957.*

HALLE 1547–50: E. Halle: *Chronicle* [Henry IV – Henry VIII].

HALLE 1548: E. Halle: *The Union of the Two Noble and Illustre Famelies of Lancastre and York.*

HAMEL 1986: C. de Hamel: *A History of Illuminated Manuscripts.*

HAMILTON ARCHIVES: RH 13/11/9.

HAMILTON 1925: M. Hamilton (ed. E. and F. Anson): *Mary Hamilton, afterwards Mrs John Dickenson, at Court and Home. From Letters and Diaries, 1756 to 1816.*

HANCARVILLE 1766: P. F. Hugues, styled Baron d'Hancarville: *Collection of Etruscan, Greek and Roman Antiquities, from the Cabinet of the Honble Wm Hamilton*, 4 vols.

HANSEN 1977: A. Hansen: 'Sermons in Stones, The Symbolism of Gems in English Renaissance Literature' [Unpubld thesis, Harvard University].

HARARI 1977: J. Boardman and D. Scarisbrick: *The Ralph Harari Collection of Finger Rings.*

HARCOURT 1880–1905: E. W. Harcourt: *The Harcourt Papers*, 11 vols.

HARE 1894: A. J. C. Hare: *The Life and Letters of Maria Edgeworth*, 2 vols.

HARTMANN 1934: C. H. Hartmann: *Charles II and Madame* [i.e. Henrietta Anna, Duchess of Orléans].

HARTOPP 1927: A. Hartopp: *Register of Freemen of Leicester*, vol. 1 – there is a hiatus 1381–1464.

HARTSHORNE 1909: A. Hartshorne: 'The gold chains, the pendants, the paternosters and the zones of the Middle Ages, the Renaissance and later times', *Arch. J.*, 66 (1909), 77–102.

HAUDICQUER DE BLANCOURT 1699: F. Haudicquer de Blancourt: *The Art of [Making] Glass; to which is added the Method of Painting in Glass and Enamelling.*

HAWKINS 1633: H. A. [i.e. Henry Hawkins]: *Partheneia Sacra. Or, The Mysterious and Delicious Garden of the Sacred Parthenes* [Rouen]. STC 12958.

HAYWARD 1983: H. Hayward: 'Portrait jewels', *SJH Newsletter*, 2.3 (1983), 10.

HAYWARD 1986: J. Hayward: 'The Arnold Lulls book of jewels and the court jewellers of Queen Anne', *Arch.*, 108 (1986), 227–37.

HEAL 1935: A. Heal: *The London Goldsmiths 1200–1800.*

HEIDELBERG 1988: Universitätsbibliothek Heidelberg: *Codex Manesse Katalog zur Austellung* (ed. E. Mittler and W. Werner).

HENIG 1983: M. Henig: 'Archbishop Hubert Walter's gems', *JBAA*, 136 (1983), 56–61.

HENIG forthcoming: M. Henig *et al.*: *Classical Gems. Ancient and Modern Intaglios and Cameos in the Fitzwilliam Museum.*

HENRIETTA MARIA 1857: Henrietta Maria, Queen of England (ed. M. A. E. Green, formerly Wood): *Letters of Queen Henrietta Maria, including her Private Correspondence with Charles the First.*

HEPBURN 1986: P. Hepburn: *Portraits of the Later Plantagenets.*

HERBERT 1939: G. C. Herbert: *Henry, Elizabeth and George (1734–1780); Letters and Diaries of Henry tenth Earl of Pembroke and His Circle.*

HERBST 1710: J. B. Herbst: *A Book of Several Jewelers Work, Made by J. B. Herbst A° 1710.*

HERIOT 1822: G. Heriot: *Memoir of George Heriot, Jeweller to King James VI* [of Scotland, I of England].

HICKEY 1913: W. Hickey (ed. A. Spencer): *Memoirs of William Hickey*, 4 vols.

HIS 1866: E. His: *Dessins d'ornements de Hans Holbein.*

HMC: Historical Manuscripts Commission:

The numbering follows that adopted by the HMSO *Sectional list*, 17: *Publications of the Royal Commission on Historical Manuscripts*, 1985.

1 Cottrell-Dormer MSS., second report, 1871.

3 Earl De la Warr, fourth report, part I, 1874.

6 House of Lords, seventh report, part II, 1879.

8 A. Morrison, ninth report, part II, Appx, 1884.

9 Salisbury (Cecil) MSS., at Hatfield, 24 vols, 1883–1976.

10 Earl of Eglinton, 1865.

24 Duke of Rutland at Belvoir Castle, 4 vols, 1888–1905.

27 Duke of Beaufort, twelfth report, Appx IX, 1891.

29 Duke of Portland, 2 vols, 1891–3.

43 Marquess of Ailesbury, 1898.

55 Various collections, IV, 1907.

58 Marquess of Bath at Longleat, 4, Seymour Papers 1532–1686, 1968.

69 Middleton MSS., 1911.

77 Lord De L'Isle and Dudley MSS., 6 vols, 1925–66.

HOLLAND 1854: S. Holland and Mrs Austin: *A Memoir of the Reverend Sydney Smith . . . with a Selection from His Letters . . .*, 2 parts.

HOLLAND 1946: E. Vassall, Baroness Holland (ed. G. S. Strangways, Earl of Ilchester): *Elizabeth, Lady Holland to Her Son, 1824–1843.*

HOLLAR 1977: W. Hollar: *Ornatus muliebris Anglicana: or the Severall Habits of Englishwomen from the Noble Born to the Country Women* [Costume Soc., E.S. 5].

HOLLIS 1840–2: T. and G. Hollis: *Monumental Effigies of Great Britain.*

HONE 1826: W. Hone: *The Everyday Book*, 2 vols.

HOPE 1907A: W. H. St J. Hope: 'The episcopal ornaments of William of Wykeham and William Waynfleet, sometime bishops of Winchester, and certain bishops of St Davids', *Arch.*, 60 (1907), 465–72.

HOPE 1907B: W. H. St J. Hope: 'On the funeral effigies of the kings and queens of England, with special reference to those in the abbey church of Westminster', *Arch.*, 60 (1907), 517–70.

HOPE 1913: W. H. St J. Hope: *Heraldry for Craftsmen and Designers.*

HOPE 1914–15: W. H. St J. Hope: 'The last testament and inventory of John de Veer, thirteenth Earl of Oxford', *Arch.*, 66 (1914–15), 275–348.

HORROX AND HAMMOND 1979–83: R. Horrox and P. W. Hammond (ed.): *British Library Harleian Manuscript 433*, 4 vols.

HOTHAM 1919: W. Hotham (ed. A. M. W. Stirling): *Pages and Portraits from the Past: being the Private Papers of Sir W[illiam] Hotham*, 2 vols.

HOWARTH 1985: D. Howarth: *Lord Arundel and His Circle.*

HUGHES 1954: G. B. Hughes: 'English steel jewellery', *CL*, 115 (1954) 85–7.

HUGHES 1956: G. B. Hughes: 'Georgian and Victorian chatelaines', *CL.*, 120 (1956), 727–31.

HUGUENOT SOC.: The Huguenot Society, 4to ser.:

3 (ed. W. Page): *Letters of Denization and Acts of Naturalization for Aliens in England 1509–1603*, 1893.

10.i *Returns of Aliens Dwelling in the City and Suburbs of London from the Reign of Henry VIII to That of James I*, 1900.

57 (ed. I. Scouloudi): *Returns of Strangers in the Metropolis 1593, 1627, 1635, 1639 A Study of an Active Minority*, 1985.

HUMPHERY-SMITH 1984: C. R. Humphery-Smith: *Anglo-Norman Armory Two.*

HUTCHINSON 1810: L. Hutchinson: *Memoirs of the Life of Colonel Hutchinson, Governor of Nottingham Castle, . . . to which is prefixed the Life of Mrs Hutchinson Written by Herself*, 2 vols.

HUTTON 1891: C. Hutton (ed. C. H. Beale): *Reminiscences of a Gentlewoman of the Last Century: Letters of Lady Catherine Hutton.*

HUXLEY 1965: G. Huxley: *Lady Elizabeth and the Grosvenors.*

IDLER 1761: S. Johnson *et al. The Idler.*

ILCHESTER 1922: R. Ilchester: 'Cameos of Queen Elizabeth and their reproduction in contemporary portraits', *Conn.*, 63 (1922), 65–72.

ILN: *The Illustrated London News.*

INDIA OFFICE LIBRARY: MS. Eur. G.37 Boxes 37, 46.

ISHAM 1971: T. Isham (ed. G. Isham): *Diary of Thomas Isham of Lamport . . . Kept by Him in Latin from 1671–1673.*

ISLE OF WIGHT RO: JER/WA/35/23.

JACKSON 1931: N. Jackson: 'John Field profilist', *Conn.*, 88 (1931), 316–21.

JACOB AND JOHNSON 1937: E. F. Jacob and H. C. Johnson (ed.): *The Register of Henry Chichele Archbishop of Canterbury 1414–1443*, vol. II: *Wills Proved before the Archbishop or His Commissaries.*

JAGGER 1988: C. Jagger: *The Artistry of the English Watch.*

JAMES 1951: G. P. L. James: *The Royal Family Orders, Badges of Office.*

JBAA: *Journal of the British Archaeological Association*, 1 (1846), in progress.

JEFFRIES 1751: D. Jeffries: *Treatise on Diamonds and Pearls . . . and the True Method of Manufacturing Diamonds.*

JEKYLL 1894: J. Jekyll (ed. A. Bourke): *The Correspondence of Mr Joseph Jekyll with His Sister-in-law Lady Gertrude Sloane-Stanley, 1818–38.*

JENKINS 1958: E. Jenkins: *Elizabeth the Great.*

JENKINSON 1923: 'The jewels lost in the Wash', *History*, n.s. 8 (1923–4), 161–8.

JESSE 1840: J. H. Jesse: *Memoirs of the Court of England during the Reign of the Stuarts, including the Protectorate*, 4 vols.

JESSE 1843: J. H. Jesse: *Memoirs of the Court of England, from the Revolution in 1688, to the Death of George II*, 3 vols.

JOHNSON 1964: J. R. Johnson: *The Radiance of Chartres; Studies in the Early Stained Glass of the Cathedral* [Columbia University Studies in Art History and Archaeology, 4].

JONSON 1981–2: B. Jonson (ed. G. A. Wilkes): *The Complete Plays of Ben Jonson*, 4 vols.

JOURDAIN 1924: M. Jourdain: 'The Pepys Cockerell collection of relics of Samuel Pepys', *CL*, 61 (1924), 921–4.

JS: *Jewellery Studies*, 1 (1983–4), in progress.

JUSSERAND 1892: J. H. A. J Jusserand: *A French Ambassador at the Court of Charles the Second, le Comte de Cominges, from His Unpublished Correspondence.*

JWCI: *Journal of the Warburg and Courtauld Institute.*

KAGAN 1973: J. Kagan: *Western European Cameos in the Hermitage Collection.*

KAGAN 1980: J. Kagan: 'Portreti'ie kamei epokhi Tyodorov: problem'i interpretatsii, datiprovki, atributs'i, *Muzeum*, 1 [Portrait cameos of the Tudor age: problems of interpretation, dating and attribution].

KAGAN 1981: J. Kagan: *K istorii gliptiki v Anglii, xvii vek. Zapolno-evropiiskoe iskustsvo xvii veka* [On the History of Seventeenth Century Glyptics in England, Western Art of the Seventeenth Century, Publications and Studies].

KAGAN AND NEVEROV 1984: J. Kagan and O. Neverov: 'Lorenz Natter's Museum Britannicum: gem collecting in eighteenth-century England', Apollo, 120 (1984), 114–21, 162–9.

KENDALL 1962: P. M. Kendall: *The Yorkist Age. Daily Life during the Wars of the Roses.*

KHAN 1989: M. A. H. Khan (ed. M. M. Cloake): *A Persian at the Court of King George 1809–10. The Journal of Mirza Abul Hassan Khan.*

KIDD 1979: K. E. Kidd: *La fabrication des perles de verre, du Moyen Age au dbut du XIXe siècle* [Histoire et archéologie, 30].

KING 1865: C. W. King: 'On the use of antique gems in the Middle Ages', *Arch. J.*, 22 (1865), 118–33.

KING HORN 1901: J. Hall (ed.): *King Horn.*

KNIGHT 1818: *Knight's Modern and Antique Gems.*

KROLL 1970: M. Kroll: *Letters from Liselotte Elizabeth Charlotte, Princess Palatine and Duchess of Orléans 'Madame' 1655–1722.*

LABANOFF 1844: A. Labanoff (ed.): *Lettres, instructions et mémoires de Marie Stuart reine d'Écosse*, 7 vols.

LADY'S MAG.: *The Lady's Magazine*, 1770–1818, n.s. 1820–9, improved ser. 1830–2.

LADY'S MON. MUS.: *The Lady's Monthly Museum*, 1798–1806, n.s. 1807–11, improved ser. ?–1828; contd as: *The Lady's Museum*, 1829–30, new and impr. ser. 1831–2.

LAMB 1816: C. Lamb: *Glenarvon*, 3 vols.

LA MOTHE 1913: M.-C. de la Mothe, Comtesse d'Aulnoy (tr. Mrs W. H. Arthur): *Memoirs of the Court of England in 1675.*

LANCASHIRE RO: DD SC 9/32, 34–9.

L AND P HENRY VIII: PRO: *Letters and Papers, Foreign and Domestic, of Henry VIII*, 21 vols in 37.

LANG 1897: A. Lang: *Pickle the Spy; or, The Incognito of Prince Charles.*

LANGFORD & SON, 7 March 1770: *A Catalogue of the Noble Collection of the Right Honourable Lady Elizabeth Germain.*

LANGLAND 1954: W. Langland (ed. W. W. Skeat): *The Vision and Creed of Piers Ploughman*, 2 vols.

LARKIN 1983: J. F. Larkin (ed.): *Stuart Royal Proclamations*, II: *Royal Proclamations of King Charles I 1625–1646.*

LA ROCHE 1933: S. von La Roche: *Sophie in London 1786 being the Diary of Sophie von La Roche.*

LEAMINGTON SPA 1967: Public Library, Art Gallery and Museum: *Exhibition of Gilt-metal and Enamel Work of the Eighteenth Century. An Exhibition of Georgian 'Toys' chosen to Illustrate the Use Made of Gilt-metal, Pinchbeck, Painted Enamel, Silver and Silver-plated Copper.*

LEICESTER RO: DG/2409.

LEINSTER 1949–54: E. M. Fitzgerald, Duchess of Leinster (ed. B. Fitzgerald): *Correspondence of Emily, Duchess of Leinster, 1731–1814*, 3 vols.

LEMON 1827: R. Lemon: 'Warrant of indemnity and discharge to Lionel Earl of Middlesex, Lord High Treasurer, . . . for having delivered certain jewels to King James the First, which were sent by his Majesty into Spain, to the Prince of Wales and Duke of Buckingham', *Arch.*, 21 (1827), 148–57.

LENNOX 1901: S. Lennox (ed. Earl of Ilchester and Lord Stavordale): *The life and letters of Lady Sarah Lennox, 1745–1826.*

LEONARDUS 1750: C. Leonardus: *Mirror of Stones* [tr. of: *Speculum lapidum*, 1502].

LETTS 1926: M. Letts (ed. and tr.): *Pero Tafur Travels and Adventures 1435–1439.*

LEVEY 1977: M. Levey: *A Royal Subject: Portraits of Queen Charlotte.*

LEWER 1933: H. W. Lewer: 'The testament and last will of Elizabeth, widow of John de Veer, 13th Earl of Oxford', *Transactions of the Essex Archaeological Society*, n.s. 20 (1933), 7–16.

LEWIS 1953: M. D. S. Lewis: 'Antique paste jewellery', *Connoisseur Year Book*, pp. 103–12.

LEWIS 1957: M. D. S. Lewis: 'Antique garnet jewellery', *Connoisseur Year Book*, pp. 96–9.

LEWIS 1987: J. Lewis: 'The Oxwich brooch', *JS*, 2 (1985), 23–8.

LEWIS 1987: S. Lewis: *The Art of Matthew Paris in the Chronica Majora.*

LIBRARY OF CONGRESS, Washington DC: J. O. Halliwell Phillips, Archer accounts; Wrottesley papers.

LICHTENBERG 1938: G. C. Lichtenberg (tr. M. L. Mare and W. H. Quarrell): *Lichtenberg's Visits to England, as Described in his Letters and Diaries.*

LIGHTBOWN 1968: 'Jean Petitot and Jacques Bordier at the English court', *Conn.*, 168 (1968), 82–91.

LINCOLN RO: LD 97/1/3, MG 5/3/2, Monson Papers, Mon 11/31.

LINCOLNSHIRE REC. SOC.:
5 (ed. C. W. Foster): *Lincoln Wills registered in the District Probate Registry at Lincoln, i: A.D. 1271 to A.D. 1526*, 1914.

LIND 1894: K. Lind: *Kunsthistorischer Atlas herausgegeben von K. K. Central-Commision zur Erforschung und Erhaltung der Kunst- und historischen Denkmale, X Abtheilung. Sammlung von Abbildung mittelalterlicher Grabdenkmale.*

LINDSAY 1868: A. W. C. Lindsay, Earl of Crawford: *A Memoir of Lady Anna Mackenzie, Countess of Balcarres and afterwards of Argyll, 1621–1706.*

LISLE LETTERS 1981: M. St. C. Byrne: *The Lisle Letters*, 6 vols.

LISTER 1953: R. Lister: *Silhouettes.*

LONDON 1873: Victoria & Albert Museum, ed. R. H. Soden-Smith: *Catalogue of an Exhibition of Ancient and Modern Jewellery.*

LONDON 1889: New Gallery, Regent St: *Exhibition of the Royal House of Stuart.*

LONDON 1928: Spink & Sons (ed. G. Callendar): *Loan Exhibition of Nelson Relics.*

LONDON 1948: English Ceramic Circle: *English Pottery and Porcelain. Commemorative Catalogue of an Exhibition held at the Victoria and Albert Museum.*

LONDON 1956: Christie's: *The Ageless Diamond.*

LONDON 1972: London Museum: *Chaucer's London.*

LONDON 1976: British Museum (ed. H. Tait): *Jewellery through 7000 years* [For a later edn with new pictures, see below, Tait 1986B].

LONDON 1978: Goldsmiths' Hall (ed. S. Hare): *Touching Gold and Silver 500 Years of Hallmarks.*

LONDON 1978B: S. J. Phillips (ed. D. Scarisbrick): *Further Wellington Gems and Historic Rings.*

LONDON 1981A: Victoria & Albert Museum (ed. A. Somers Cocks): *Princely Magnificence, Court Jewels of the Renaissance, 1500–1630.*

LONDON 1981B: Victoria & Albert Museum (ed. D. Chambers and J. Martineau): *Splendours of the Gonzaga.*

LONDON 1982: National Portrait Gallery: *Van Dyck in England.*

LONDON 1982–3: The Queen's Gallery, Buckingham Palace: *Kings and Queens.*

LONDON 1984A: Arts Council of Great Britain: *English Romanesque Art 1066–1200.*

LONDON 1984B: British Museum (ed. J. Backhouse *et al.*): *The Golden Age of Anglo-Saxon Art 966–1066.*

LONDON 1984C: Victoria & Albert Museum (ed. M. Snodin): *Rococo Art and Design in Hogarth's England.*

LONDON 1984D: Colnaghi, Bond St: *Art, Commerce, Scholarship. A Window in the Art World, Colnaghi: 1760 to 1984.*

LONDON 1985: Museum of London: *The Quiet Conquest, the Huguenots 1685 to 1985.*

LONDON 1987: Royal Academy of Arts (ed. J. G. Alexander and P. Binski): *Age of Chivalry, Art in Plantagenet England 1200–1400.*

LONDON 1988: British Museum (ed. J. Rowlands): *The Age of Dürer and Holbein, German Drawings 1400–1500.*

LONDON 1990: Museum of London (compiled by T. Murdoch): *Treasures and Trinkets: Jewellery in London from Pre-Roman Times to the 1930s.*

LONDONDERRY FAMILY ARCHIVES: Letters of Lord Castlereagh.

LONDONDERRY 1973: E. H. V. Tempest Stewart, Marchioness of Londonderry, and J. R. Sewell (eds.): *Russian Journal of Lady Londonderry 1836–7.*

LONDON GAZETTE: 1665, in progress.

LONDON MUSEUM 1928: London Museum catalogues: *The Cheapside Hoard of Elizabethan and Jacobean Jewellery.*

1940: *Medieval Catalogue* [reptd 1954, 1967].

LONDON REC. SOC.: London Record Society:

3 (ed. I. Darlington): *London Consistory Court Wills 1492–1547.*

LOSELEY MSS.: (ed. A. J. Kempe): *The Loseley Manuscripts . . . illustrative of . . . English History*, 1835.

LUMAS AND COX 1981: S. Lumas and J. Cox: 'False gold in Fleet Street', *CL*, 170 (1981), 1049–50.

LYLY 1580: J. Lyly: *Euphues and his England.*

MACAULAY 1921: T. B. Macaulay (ed. A. D. Innes): *Lord Clive.*

MACLAGAN & OMAN 1935: E. Maclagan and C. Oman: 'An English gold rosary of about 1500', *Arch.*, 85 (1935), 1–22.

MCKISACK 1959: M. McKisack: *The Fourteenth Century, 1307–1399.*

MADDEN 1831: F. Madden: *Privy Purse Expenses of Princess Mary Daughter of King Henry the Eighth.*

MADDISON 1883: A. R. Maddison: *Domestic Life in the Sixteenth and Seventeenth Centuries, Illustrated by Wills in the Registry at Lincoln.* In *Associated Architectural Societies' Reports and Papers*, 17.i. (1883).

MADDISON 1888: A. R. Maddison: *Lincolnshire Wills First Series A.D. 1500–1600.*

MAGALOTTI 1821: L. Magalotti: *Travels of Cosimo the Third through England during the Reign of Charles the Second in 1669.*

MAHONY 1873: M. F. Mahony: *A Chronicle of the Fermors: Horace Walpole in Love.*

MALCOLM 1810: J. P. Malcolm: *Anecdotes of the Manners and Customs of London during the Eighteenth Century.*

MANUEL 1902: R. Manuel: 'Craft Masonic jewels', *Conn.*, 4 (1902), 155–8, 263–6.

MARKS & PAYNE 1978: R. Marks and A. Payne: *British Heraldry from its Origins to c. 1800.*

MARLBOROUGH 1838: A. Churchill, Duchess of Marlborough: *Private Correspondence of Sarah Duchess of Marlborough*, 2 vols.

MARLBOROUGH 1930: S. Churchill, Duchess of Marlborough (ed. W. King): *The Opinions of Sarah, Duchess of Marlborough.*

MARLOWE 1966: C. Marlowe (ed. T. W. Craik): *The Jew of Malta.*

MARSHALL 1973: R. C. Marshall: *The Days of Duchess Anne, Life in the Household of the Duchess of Hamilton, 1656–1716.*

MARSTON 1606: J. Marston: *Parasitaster, or, The Fawne.*

MASSINGER 1629: P. Massinger: *The Roman Actor.*

MASSINGER 1639: P. Massinger: *The Unnaturall Combat.*

MASSINGER 1655: P. Massinger: *The Guardian.*

MASSINGER 1658: P. Massinger: *The City Madam.*

MASSINGER & FIELD 1632: P. Massinger and J. F[ield]: *The Fatall Dowrie.*

MATTHEW PARIS 1871: Matthew Paris (tr. J. A. Giles): *English History*, 3 vols.

MAY 1938: L. M. May: *A Master of the Silhouette: John Miers: Portrait Artist, 1757–1821.*

MAYO 1897: J. H. Mayo: *Medals and Decorations of the British Army and Navy.*

METEYARD 1866: G. Meteyard: *The Life of Josiah Wedgwood from his Correspondence and Family Papers*, 2 vols.

MILLAR 1963: O. Millar: *The Tudor, Stuart and Early Georgian Pictures in the Collection of H.M. The Queen*, 2 vols.

MILLARD: A. M. Millard: 'List of goods imported into London from Port Books 1560–1640' [Unpubld TS., PRO].

MILNER 1904: E. Milner: *Records of the Lumleys of Lumley Castle.*

MINTO 1874: G. Elliot, Earl of Minto (ed. E. E. E. Elliot-Murray-Kynynmound, Countess of Minto): *Life and Letters of Sir Gilbert Elliot, first Earl of Minto, from 1751 to 1806*, 3 vols.

MISSON 1698: M. M[isson]: *Mémoires et observations faites par un voyageur en Angleterre*.

MITCHINER 1986: M. Mitchiner: *Medieval Pilgrim and Secular Badges*.

MONTAGU 1864: W. D. Montagu, Duke of Manchester: *Court and Society from Elizabeth to Anne . . . from the Papers at Kimbolton*.

MONTAGU 1970: M.W. Montagu (ed. R. Halsband): *The Selected Letters of Lady Mary Wortley Montagu*.

MORYSON 1907–8: F. Moryson: *An Itinerary*, 4 vols.

MS: Mill Stephenson: *A List of Monumental Brasses in the British Isles*, 1926; with *Appendix*, 1938, reptd 1964.

MULLER 1972: P. E. Muller: *Jewels in Spain*.

MURALT 1933: B. L. de Muralt (ed. G. Gould and C. Oldham): *Lettres sur les Anglois et les François et sur les voiages 1728*. [Bibl. de la Revue de litt. comparée].

MURPHY 1971: J. J. Murphy (ed.): *Three Medieval Rhetorical Arts*.

MURRAY 1938: K. C. Murray: *Beloved Marian. The Social History of Mr and Mrs Warren Hastings*.

NATIONAL PORTRAIT GALLERY 1969: (ed. R. Strong): *Tudor and Jacobean Portraits*, 2 vols.

NAU 1966: Elisabeth Nau: *Lorenz Natter*.

NEALE 1934: J. E. Neale: *Queen Elizabeth*.

NEVILLE 1950: S. Neville (ed. B. Cozens-Hardy): *The Diary of Sylas Neville, 1713–1788*.

NEVINSON 1954: J. L. Nevinson: 'The robes of the Order of the Bath', *Conn.*, 134 (1954), 153–7.

NEVINSON 1973: J. L. Nevinson: 'Buttons and buttonholes in the fourteenth century', *Costume*, 11 (1977), 38–44.

NEWDIGATE-NEWDEGATE 1898: A. E. Newdigate-Newdegate: *Gossip from a Muniment Room: Passages in the Lives of Anne and Mary Fitton*.

NEWTON 1980: S. M. Newton: *Fashion in the Age of the Black Prince. A Study of the Years 1340–1365*.

NICHOLS 1780: J. Nichols: *A Collection of All the Wills . . . of the Kings and Queens of England*.

NICHOLS 1788–1805: J. Nichols: *The progresses, and Public Processions of Queen Elizabeth*, 3 vols, each section being separately paginated: II, F29–32, 'An inventory of the mony and jewels of Anne Dutches of Somerset: . . . 1587'; F2, p. 38, 'Gifts by Gilbert Earl of Shrewsbury on a Garter Mission 1596'; B2, pp. 3–40, 'New Year's gifts' (1571–94), from BL, Sloane MS. 814; K, p. 63, and L, pp. 65–80 and 93–106, 'Various lists of jewels, New Year gifts' (1577–8, 1588–9 and 1600): III, A, pp. 12–23, *03–*15, pp. *93–*117, S42, pp. 129–51, 'New Year gifts' (1561, 1578–9, 1599–1600).

NICHOLS 1828: J. Nichols: *The Progresses . . . of King James the First*, 4 vols.

NICOLAS 1826: N. H. Nicolas: *Testamenta vetusta*, 2 vols.

NICOLAS 1827: N. H. Nicolas: *Privy Purse Expenses of King Henry the Eighth*.

NICOLAS 1830: N. H. Nicolas: *Privy Purse Expenses of Elizabeth of York*.

NICOLAS 1841–2: N.H. Nicolas: *History of the Orders of Knighthood of the British Empire*, 4 vols; each of the sections on the orders is individually paginated.

NICOLS 1652: T. Nicols: *A Lapidary: or, The History of Pretious Stones*.

NLS: National Library of Scotland: Adv. MS. 31.1.10; MSS. 360, 1694, 5158, 14269, 14487, 14527, 14548, 14618, 14636, 14648.

NMS: National Museum of Scotland.

NOBLE 1787: M. Noble: *Memoirs of the Protectoral-House of Cromwell*, 2 vols.

NORFOLK 1857: H.G. F. Howard, Duke of Norfolk: *The Lives of Philip Howard, Earl of Arundel and of Anne Dacre, His Wife*.

NORFOLK AND NORWICH RO: Consistory court and other wills.

NORRIS 1977: M. Norris: *Monumental Brasses: The Memorials*, 2 vols.

NORTHAMPTON RO: YZ 0091.

NORTH RIDING RO: 2 DG (A) V 1/25.

NORTHUMBERLAND RO: 2 DE 31/10, 6, 20–26.

NORTHUMBERLAND 1926: E. Percy, Duchess of Northumberland (ed. J. Grieg): *The Diaries of a Duchess. Extracts from the Diary of the first Duchess of Northumberland*.

NPB: National Portrait Gallery: *Complete Illustrated Catalogue 1856–1979*, compiled by K. K. Kung, 1981.

NRA: National Register of Archives, with report number.

O'CONNELL: S. O'Connell, 'Wray, Robert Bateman 1715:1779 *Gem Engraver*', Ts. in the writer's possession.

O'DELL-FRANKE 1777: I. O'Dell-Franke: *Kupferstiche und Radierungen aus der Werkstatt des Virgil Solis*.

OGDEN 1981: J. Ogden: 'The Pigot diamond 1 – the lottery', *SJH Newsletter*, 12 (1981), 6–7.

OGLANDER 1940: C. A. Oglander: *Admiral's Wife. Being the Life and Letters of the Hon. Mrs Edward Boscawen from 1719 to 1761*.

OMAN 1930: C. Oman: *Catalogue of Rings in the Victoria and Albert Museum*.

OMAN 1968: C. M. A. Oman: *The Gascoyne Heiress: The Life and Diaries of Frances Mary Gascoyne-Cecil, 1802–1839*.

OMAN 1974: C. Oman: *British Rings, 800–1914*.

ORIGO 1963: *The Merchant of Prato* [Peregrine Books 433].

OSBORN 1890: S. Osborn (ed. E. Osborn): *Political and Social Letters of a Lady of the Eighteenth Century (the Hon. Mrs Osborn) 1721–1771*.

OSBORNE 1928: D. Osborne (ed. G. C. M Smith): *The Letters from Dorothy Osborne to William Temple*.

OXFORDSHIRE RS:

44 (ed. M. A. Havinden): *Household and Farm In-*

ventories in Oxfordshire, 1550–1590, 1965.

OXINDEN 1933: (ed. D. Gardiner): *The Oxinden Letters 1607–42*.

OXINDEN 1937: (ed. D. Gardiner): *The Oxinden and Peyton Letters, 1642–1670*

PALGRAVE 1836: F. Palgrave (ed.): *Antient Kalendars and Inventories of H.M. Exchequer*, 3 vols [Record Commissioners, Publns 22].

PALMERSTON 1957: A. M. Temple, Lady Palmerston (ed. T. Lever): *The Letters of Lady Palmerston*.

PARIS 1981: Galeries nationales du Grand Palais: *Les fastes du gothique le siècle de Charles V*.

PARIS BIB. NAT.: Bibliothèque Nationale, Paris: MS. latin 1158.

PARKER 1850: J. H. Parker: *A glossary of terms used in Grecian, Roman, Italian and Gothic Architecture*, 2 vols in 3.

PARSONS 1977: J. C. Parsons: *The Court and Household of Eleanor of Castile in 1290*.

PASTON LETTERS 1900–1: J. Gairdner (ed.): *The Paston Letters 1423–1509*, 4 vols.

PATTERN BOOKS: *see under* De la Cour 1747, Dinglinger 1751, Flach 1736, Geminus 1548, Guien 1762, Herbst 1710, Knight 1828, Petit 1824, Rhodes 1723, Saint 1770, Taute 1750, Terry *c.* 1770.

PEARCE 1911: C. E. Pearce: *The Amazing Duchess; being the Romantic History of Elizabeth Chudleigh . . . The Hon. Mrs Hervey, Duchess of Kingston, and Countess of Bristol*, 2 vols.

PEMBERTON 1910: W. S. C. Pemberton: *The Romance of Princess Amelia, Daughter of George III (1783–1810)*.

PEPYS 1971–83: S. Pepys (ed. R. Latham and W. Matthews): *The Diary of Samuel Pepys*, 11 vols.

PETIT 1824: J. Petit: *No. 2 [correctly 3] of a Series of Ornamental Books Devoted to Artists in General*.

PHILLIPS's, 9 April 1804 (Constable sale).

PIOZZI 1789: H. L. Salusbury, afterwards Piozzi: *Observations and Reflections made in the Course of a Journey through France, Italy and Germany*, 2 vols.

PIPER 1984: D. Piper: *Kings and Queens of England and Scotland*.

PLANCHÉ 1878–9: J. R. Planché: *Cyclopedia of Costume*, 2 vols.

PLUMB 1974: J. H. Plumb: *The First Four Georges*.

PONSONBY 1958: D. A. Ponsonby: *The Last Duchess. The Story of the Prince Consort's Mother*.

POOLE 1955: A. L. Poole: *From Domesday Book to Magna Carta, 1087–1216*.

POPE 1941: A. Pope (ed. G. Tillotson): *The Rape of the Lock*.

POWYS 1899: E. J. Climenson (ed.): *Passages from the Diaries of Mrs Philip Lybbe Powys, of Hardwick House, Oxon., A.D. 1756 to 1808*.

PRESTWICH 1966: M. Prestwich: *Cranfield: Politics and Profits under the Early Stuarts*.

PRICE 1902: F. G. H. Price: *The Marygold by Temple Bar*.

PRO: Public Record Office:
C1/12/250, 24/418 n. 53.
E36/85; 101/350/28, 353/4, 354/16, 372/11, 386/3, 390/4, 393/4, 10, 40, 397/4, 400/3, 409/14, 410/2, 411/9, 403/396, 415, 472, 490, 502, 556, 576, 589, 638, 653, 715, 805;
LC5/107–8, 111–12, 114; 9/41;
LR2/122;

PCC [Prerogative Court of Canterbury], now Prob.;
Prob. 2, selected inventories; 10 selected original wills; 11 registered wills cited either by name or volume number, with the quire number;
S.P. Dom. 58/5/15; 16/107/17; 143 n.20.

PRS: The Pipe Roll Society, in progress.

PSA: *Proceedings of the Society of Antiquaries*, 1–4 (1843–59), n.s. 1–32 (1859–1920); continued as *Ant. J.*

PSA SCOT.: *Proceedings of the Society of Antiquaries of Scotland*, 1 (1851), in progress.

PUREFOY 1931: E. Purefoy (ed. G. Eland): *The Purefoy Letters, 1735–1753*, vols. 2.

QUIEN, *see under* Guien.

RASPE 1791: R. E. Raspe: *A Descriptive Catalogue of . . . Engraved Gems . . . Cast by J. Tassie*, 2 vols.

RAW: Royal Archives, Windsor Castle:
Annotated Queen Charlotte record;
Accounts, cited by piece number, 25640–26329.

RAWLINGS 1978: R. D. Rawlings: 'The manufacture of cut steel and beads', *Journal of the Historical Metallurgy Society* (12/2/78), 88–97.

RCHM OXFORD 1939: Royal Commission on Historical Monuments: *City of Oxford*.

REDDAWAY AND WALKER 1975: T. F. Reddaway and C. M. Walker: *The Early History of the Goldsmiths' Company, 1327–1509*.

REGISTER OF THE BLACK PRINCE: PRO: *The Register of Edward the Black Prince*, 4 vols.

RELIQUARY, 1 (1860–1).

REYNOLDS 1951: G. Reynolds: *Elizabethan and Jacobean* [Costume of the Western World].

RHODES 1723: B. Rhodes: *A New Book of Cyphers Containing in General All Names Interwoven and Reversed*.

RHODES 1897: W. Rhodes: 'Inventory of the jewels and wardrobe of Queen Isabella (1307–8)', *EHR*, 12 (1897), 517–21.

RIBEIRO 1977: A. Ribeiro: 'Some evidence of the influence of the dress of the seventeenth century on costume in eighteenth century female portraiture', *BM*, 119 (1977), 834–40.

RICHARDSON 1932: S. Richardson: *Clarissa. Or, The History of a Young Lady*, 4 vols [Everymans Library 882].

RICHARDSON 1972: S. Richardson (ed. J. Harris): *The History of Sir Charles Grandison*, 3 vols.

RICKERT 1948: E. Rickert: *Chaucer's World*.

RIDLEY 1988: Jasper Ridley (ed.): *The Love Letters of Henry VIII*.

RILEY 1868: H. T. Riley (ed.): *Memorials of London, and London Life in the XIIIth XIVth and XVth Centuries.*

ROBINSON 1963: E. Robinson: 'Eighteenth century commerce and fashion, Matthew Boulton's marketing techniques', *Economic History Review*, 2 ser. 16 (1963), 39–60.

ROCHE 1927: J. C. Roche: *The History, Development and Organisation of Birmingham Jewellery and Allied Trades.*

ROCHESTER 1699: J. Wilmot, Earl of Rochester (ed. T. Brown): *Familiar Letters*, 2 parts in 1.

ROCK 1903: D. Rock (ed. G. H. Hart and W. H. Frere): *The Church of Our Fathers*, 4 vols.

ROGER OF WENDOVER 1889: Roger of Wendover (tr. J. A. Giles): *The Flowers of History*, 3 vols.

ROHAN 1786?: L. R. E. Cardinal de Rohan: *Pièces justificatives pour M. le Cardinal de Rohan, accusée. Declarations authentiques selon la forme Anglaise*, app. to: *Sommaire pour la comtesse de Valois-La Motte, accusée; contre M. le procureur-général, accusateur; en présence de M. le Cardinal de Rohan, & autres co-accusés.*

ROT. CHART.: *Rotuli chartarum in Turri Londinensi asservat, 1199–1216*, 1837 [Record Commissioners, Publns 25].

ROT. LITT. PAT.: *Rotuli litterarum patentium in Turri Londinensi asservat, 1201–1216*, 1835 [Record Commissioners, Publns 17].

ROT. PARL.: *Rotuli parliamentorum*, 6 vols, n.d., index vol., 1832.

ROUQUET 1755: J. A. Rouquet: *The Present State of the Arts in England.*

ROWLANDS 1985: J. Rowlands: *Holbein: The Paintings of Hans Holbein the Younger.*

ROWSE 1962: A. L. Rowse: *Ralegh and the Throckmortons.*

RUDDOCK 1951: A. R. Ruddock: *Italian Merchants and Shipping in Southampton 1270–1600* [Southampton Record Soc., n.s. 1].

RUSH 1873: R. Rush: *The Court of London from 1819 to 1825.*

RUSHFORTH 1927: G. McN. Rushforth: 'The Kirkham monument in Paignton church, a study in medieval iconography, and in particular of the Mass of St Gregory', *Transactions of the Exeter Diocesan Architectural Society*, 15, pt. i.

RUSSELL 1853: R. Russell (ed. A. R. (Earl Russell) and J. Martin): *Letters of Lady Rachel Russell*, 2 vols.

RUSSELL-SMITH 1957: F. Russell-Smith: 'Sleeve-buttons of the seventeenth and eighteenth centuries'. *Conn.*, 139 (1957), 36–40.

RUSSELL-SMITH 1961: F. Russell-Smith: 'English sporting buttons of the eighteenth and nineteenth centuries', *Connoisseur Year Book*, pp. 62–7.

RYDER 1939: D. Ryder (ed. W. Matthews): *The Diary of Dudley Ryder, 1715–16.*

RYMER 1704–26: T. Rymer (ed.): *Foedera, conventiones, literas . . . inter reges Angliae . . . 1101–[1654]*, 20 vols.

RYMER 1816–37: T. Rymer and Record Commissioners: *Foedera [1066–1383]*, 4 vols in 7.

SAFFORD 1928: E. W. Safford: 'An account of the expenses of Eleanor, sister of Edward III, on the occasion of her marriage to Raymond, count of Guelders', *Arch.*, 77 (1928), 111–90.

SAINT 1770: T. D. Saint: *New Book of Designs for Jewellers Work.*

SAINT-DENIS 1973: B. de Montesquiou-Fezensac and D. Gaborit-Chopin (eds): *Le trésor de St Denis: inventaire de 1634.*

SANDFORD 1687: F. Sandford: *The History of the Coronation of . . . James II . . . and of His Royal Consort Queen Mary.*

SCARISBRICK: MS. inventory of Mrs Mary Brett, n.d., 17th century hand.

SCARISBRICK 1977: D. Scarisbrick: 'The Harley memorial ring', *Art at Auction, the Year at Sotheby Parke Bernet*, pp. 483–4.

SCARISBRICK 1980: D. Scarisbrick: 'The Ramsden jewels', *SJH Newsletter*, 9 (1980), 3.

SCARISBRICK 1981 I, II: D. Scarisbrick: 'With heart and hand, royal wedding jewellery I', '"Wear it for my sake", royal wedding jewellery II', *CL*, 170 (1981), 321–3, 508–9.

SCARISBRICK 1982 I, II: D. Scarisbrick: 'Mirror of tragedy: the jewels of Mary Stuart I', 'Treasured in adversity, the jewels of Mary Stuart II', *CL*, 171 (1982) 1632–34, 1740–2.

SCARISBRICK 1983 I–III: Scarisbrick: 'Precious chain of history, the Cavendish family jewellery I', 'Deaths and sentiments, the Cavendish family jewellery II', 'The crowning glory, the Cavendish family jewellery III', *CL*, 173 (1983), 1542–4, 1696–8; 174 (1983), 28–30.

SCARISBRICK 1984A: D. Scarisbrick: 'Blazing like the sun: the Marchioness of Londonderry's jewellery', *CL*, 175 (1984), 1728–31.

SCARISBRICK 1984B: D. Scarisbrick: *Il valore dei gioelli e degli orologi da collezione* (Turin).

SCARISBRICK 1985A: D. Scarisbrick: 'Alchemist with the golden touch, Marcus Gunter's designs for jewellery', *CL*, 177 (1985), 734–6.

SCARISBRICK 1985B: D. Scarisbrick: 'Emma Hamilton and her jewellery', *International Silver and Jewellery Fair and Seminar*, pp. 19–25.

SCARISBRICK 1985C: D. Scarisbrick: 'Henry Ellis, a 19th century Exeter goldsmith', *Antique Dealer and Collector's Guide* (July 1985), pp. 55–7.

SCARISBRICK 1986A: D. Scarisbrick: 'Anne of Denmark's jewellery, the old and the new', *Apollo*, 123 (1986), 228–36.

SCARISBRICK 1986B: D. Scarisbrick: 'The Devonshire parure', *Arch.*, 108 (1986), 239–54.

SCARISBRICK 1986C: D. Scarisbrick: 'Musical themes in jewellery', *Handbook of the British Antique Dealers' Association*, pp. 30–5.

SCARISBRICK 1986D: D. Scarisbrick: 'Symbols of rank and riches, jewellery in the portraits at Woburn', *CL*, 179 (1986), 254–6.

SCARISBRICK 1987A: D. Scarisbrick: 'Gem connoisseurship – the 4th Earl of Carlisle's correspondence with Francesco de Ficoroni and Antonio Maria Zanetti', *BM*, 129 (1989), 90–104.
SCARISBRICK 1987B: D. Scarisbrick: 'Jewellery in Tudor and Jacobean portraits at Newhaven', *Apollo*, 127 (1987), 323–33.
SCARISBRICK 1988: D. Scarisbrick: 'The jewellery of treason', *CL*, 182 (1988), 128–9.
SCARISBRICK 1989: D. Scarisbrick: *Ancestral Jewels*.
SCARISBRICK 1990A: D. Scarisbrick: 'A becoming mourning', *CL*, 184 (1990), 58–60.
SCARISBRICK 1990B: D. Scarisbrick: 'For richer for poorer', *CL*, 184 (1990), 136–8.
SCARISBRICK unpubld: D. Scarisbrick: Drumlanrig Castle, Handlist of Jacobite jewellery.
See also under Anne of Denmark.
SCOTT 1980: M. Scott: *Late Gothic Europe, 1400–1500* [History of Dress series].
SCOTT 1986: M. Scott: *A Visual History of Costume. The Fourteenth and Fifteenth Centuries*.
SEABY 1955: W. A. Seaby: 'Objects of vertu in the Bentinck Beresford collection', *Conn.*, 136 (1955), 22–6.
SEDLEY 1702: C. Sedley: *The Happy Pair: or, A Poem on Matrimony*.
SETON 1882: G. Seton: *Memoir of Alexander Seton, Earl of Dunfermline*.
SEYMOUR 1805: F. Seymour, Duchess of Somerset: *Correspondence between Frances, Countess of Hertford (afterwards Duchess of Somerset) and Henrietta Louisa, Countess of Pomfret, between the Years 1738 and 1741*, 3 vols.
SHAKESPEARE 1951: W. Shakespeare (ed. P. Alexander): *The Complete Works*.
SHARP 1922–3: A. Sharp: 'Notes on Stuart jewellery', *PSA Scot.*, 57 (1922–30), 226–41.
SHEFFIELD CITY LIBRARY: VWM 158/5, 9, 10, 13–15, 26, 35, A1089 and A1098; WWM R168/7.
SHELLEY 1912: F. Shelley (ed. R. Edgecumbe): *The Diary of Frances Lady Shelley*.
SHERIDAN 1975: R. B. Sheridan (ed. C. Price): *Plays*.
SHIRLEY 1869: E. P. Shirley: 'An inventory of the effects of Henry Howard, K.G., Earl of Northampton, taken on his death in 1614, together with a transcript of his will', *Arch.*, 42 (1869), 347–78.
SHIRLEY 1873: E. P. Shirley: 'The will, inventories and funeral expenses of James Montagu, Bishop of Norwich, anno 1610', *Arch.*, 44 (1873), 393–421.
SIDNEY 1843: H. Sidney (ed. R. W. Blencoe): *Diary of the Times of Charles the Second, by the Honourable Henry Sidney, afterwards Earl of Derby*, 2 vols.
SJH BULLETIN: *Society of Jewellery Historians Bulletin*, 1 (1988), in progress; *Newsletter*, 1.1–12, 2.1–3 (1977–81).
SJÖGREN 1980: C. Sjögren: 'Portrait of a young lady, 1569', *BM*, 122 (1980), 696–700.
SKETCHLEY 1767: *Sketchley's Birmingham and District Directory*.
SMITH 1854: C. R. Smith: *Catalogue of the Museum of London Antiquities*.
SMITH 1901: C. F. Smith: *Mary Rich, Countess of Warwick, 1625–1678, Her Family and Friends*.
SMITH 1902–3: H. C. Smith: 'The king's gems and jewels at Windsor Castle', *Conn.*, 4 (1902), 221–6; 5 (1903), 77–83 and 233–44.
SMITH 1920: J. T. Smith: *Nollekens and His Times*.
SMITH 1972: C. B. W. Smith: *Queen Victoria: Her Life and Times*.
SMOLLETT 1748: T. G. Smollett: *The Adventures of Roderick Random*, 3 vols.
SNPG: Scottish National Portrait Gallery.
SOC. OF ANT.: Society of Antiquaries:
Drawings of monuments;
MSS, 120, 129A, 420, 541/41, 545/45.
SOC. OF ANT. 1787: *Liber quotidianus contrarotulatoris garderobae, A.D. 1299 and 1300*.
— 1951: *The Society of Antiquaries. Notes on its History and Possessions*.
SÖDERGÅRD 1956: O. Södergård: 'Un art d'aimer Anglo-Normand', *Romania*, 77 (1956), 289–330.
SOMERS COCKS 1985: A. Somers Cocks: *The Countess' gems, An Exhibition of 16th- and 17th- century Jewels and Artefacts as Recorded in a Schedule of 1690 from the Collection at Burghley House*.
SOMERSET RO: DD/HLM Box 3, Box 105; DD/MKG/4.
SOMERSET 1984: A. Somerset: *Ladies-in-waiting from the Tudors to the Present Day*.
SOTHEBY'S: sales cited by date, subject where appropriate, and number.
SOTHEBY PARKE BERNET, New York: sales cited in same manner.
SOUTHERNE 1774: T. Southerne: *Plays . . . Now First Collected*, vol. 3: *Money the Mistress*.
SPECTATOR 1965: R. Steele and J. Addison (ed. D. F. Bond): *The Spectator*, 5 vo s.
SPENCER 1980: B. Spencer: *Medieval Pilgrim Badges from Norfolk*. [Norfolk Museums Service].
SPENCER 1982: B. Spencer: 'Pilgrim souvenirs from the medieval waterfront. Excavations at Trig Lane, London, 1974–6', *Transactions of the London and Middlesex Archaeological Society*, 33 (1982), 304–20.
SPENCER 1985: B. Spencer: 'A fifteenth-century collar of SS. and hoard of false dice with their container, from the Museum of London', *Ant. J.*, 65 (1985), 449–51.
SPENCER 1990: B. Spencer: *Pilgrim Souvenirs and Secular Badges*, Medieval Catalogue Part II, Salisbury and South Wiltshire Museum (1990), pp. 95–106.
SPENSER 1912: E. Spenser (ed. J. C. Smith and E. de Selincourt): *The Poetical Works*.
STAFFORDSHIRE RO: D 3259/13/25.
STANGE 1934–61: A. Stange: *Deutsche Malerei der Gotik*, 11 vols.
STANHOPE 1827: [M. S. Stanhope, *sic* London Library, but M. S. Hudson in BL catalogues]: *Almack's, A Novel*.
STAPYLTON 1892: H. E. C. Stapylton: *The Chetwynds of Ingestre*.

STATUTES OF THE REALM, 11 vols, 1810–28: cited by regnal year and chapter or title in the usual form.

STEINGRÄBER 1957: E. Steingräber: *Antique Jewellery: Its History in Europe from 800 to 1900.*

STEVENSON 1945–6: R. B. K. Stevenson: 'Jacobite rings', *PSA Scot.*, 80–1 (1945–7), 127–31.

STEVENSON & THOMPSON 1982: S. Stevenson and D. Thompson: *John Michael Wright: The King's Portrait Painter.*

STOTHARD 1817: C. A. Stothard: *The Monumental Effigies of Great Britain* [the first edition and best for the plates].

STOW 1615: J. Stow: *The Annales, or Generall Chronicle of England . . . continued . . . by E. Howes.*

STRATFORD 1982: N. Stratford: 'Archbishop Walter's tomb and its furnishings, notes on the metalwork', in *Medieval Art and Architecture at Canterbury before 1220* [British Archaeological Association, Transactions for 1979, no. 5], pp. 87–90.

STRICKLAND 1857: A. Strickland: *Lives of the Queens of England*, 6 vols [Bohn's Historical Library].

STRONG 1966: R. Strong: 'Three royal jewels: the Three Brothers, the Mirror of Great Britain and the Feather', *BM*, 108 (1966), 350–2.

STRONG 1969: R. Strong: *The English Icon: Elizabethan and Jacobean Portraiture.*

STRONG 1983: R. Strong: *Artists of the Tudor Court: The Portrait Miniature Rediscovered.*

STRONG 1986: R. Strong: *Henry Prince of Wales and England's Lost Renaissance.*

STRONG 1987: R. Strong: *Gloriana: Portraits of Queen Elizabeth I.*

STRUTHERS 1868–70: J. Struthers: 'Note of a gold brooch of the 13th or 14th century, found in the Water of Ardoch near Doune Castle', *PSA Scot.*, 8 (1868–70), 330–3.

STRUTT 1939: C. Strutt: *The Strutt Family of Terling.*

STUART 1865: A. M. Stuart: *Life and Letters of Elizabeth, Last Duchess of Gordon*, 3d edn.

STUART 1939: D. M. Stuart: *The Daughters of George III.*

STUBBES 1585: P. Stubbes: *The Anatomie of Abuses . . . Now . . . Augmented the Third Time.*

SUDBURY HALL: Vernon papers, diary of Georgiana Vernon.

SUFFOLK RO, Bury St Edmunds: IC 500/3/4; Will of Ann Hervey.

SUTHERLAND 1955: C. H. V. Sutherland: *Art in Coinage.*

SUTHERLAND 1969: C. H. V. Sutherland: *Gold its Beauty, Power and Allure.*

SURTEES 1990: V. Surtees (ed.): *A Second Self. The Letters of Harriet Granville 1810–1845.*

SURTEES SOC.: Surtees Society:

- 2 (ed. J. Raine): *Wills and Inventories . . . of the Northern Counties of England.*
- 4 *Testamenta Eboracensia*, pts 1–5, 1836–1902; continued in vols 30, 45, 53, 106.
- 62 (ed. C. Jackson): *The Autobiography of Mrs Alice Thornton, of East Newton, co. York*, 1875.
- 68 (ed. G. Ormsby): *Selections from the Household Books of Lord William Howard of Naworth Castle*, 1878.
- 96 (ed. F. Collins): *Register of the Freemen of the City of York, I. 1272–1558*, 1897.
- 106 (ed. F. Collins): *Register of the Freemen of the City of York, II. 1559–1779*, 1900.
- 120 (ed. M. Sellers): *York Memorandum Book, pt i 1376–1419*, 1912.
- 168 (ed. C. R. Hudleston): *Naworth Estate and Household Accounts 1648–1660*, 1958.

SWAN 1981: J. Swan: *Catalogue of Shoe and Other Buckles in the Northampton Museum.*

TAIT 1955: H. Tait: 'Pilgrim signs and Thomas, Earl of Lancaster', *British Museum Quarterly*, 20 (1955), 39–46.

TAIT 1962: H. Tait: 'Historiated Tudor jewellery', *Ant. J.*, 42 (1962), 226–46.

TAIT 1962A: H. Tait: 'A Tudor gold-enamelled buckle', *British Museum Quarterly*, 26 (1962–3), 112–13.

TAIT 1963: H. Tait: 'An anonymous loan to the British Museum, 1: Renaissance jewellery', *Conn.*, 54 (1963), 147–53.

TAIT 1983: H. Tait: 'Sir James Napier's Watch', *Antique Collector*, XII (1983), 73–5.

TAIT 1984: H. Tait (ed.), with C. Gere, J. Rudoe and T. Wilson: *The Art of the Jeweller, A Catalogue of the Hull Grundy Gift to the British Museum: Jewellery, Engraved Gems and Goldsmith's Work*, 2 vols.

TAIT 1985: H. Tait: 'The girdle-prayerbook or "tablett": an important class of Renaissance jewellery at the court of Henry VIII', *JS*, 2 (1985), 29–58.

TAIT 1986A: H. Tait: *The Waddesdon Bequest: I, The Jewels.*

TAIT 1986B: H. Tait: *Jewellery through 7000 Years.*

TAIT & COOLE: H. Tait and P. G. Coole: *Catalogue of Watches in the British Museum*, vol. 1.

TATLER 1898: G. A. Aitken (ed.): *The Tatler*, 4 vols.

TAUTE 1750: C. Taute: *A Book of Ornaments Useful for Jewellers.*

TAYLER 1987: William Tayler (ed. D. Wise & A. Saunders), *Diary of William Tayler*, Footman 1837.

TAYLOR 1869: J. Taylor, the Water poet: *Works . . . comprised in the Folio Edition of 1630*, 3 vols [Spenser Society].

TAYLOR & SCARISBRICK: G. Taylor and D. Scarisbrick: *Finger Rings from Ancient Egypt to the Present Day.*

TERRY 1770: G. Terry (engraver): *a Complete Round of Cyphers for the Use of . . . Jewellers, Hair Workers . . .* [A note at the foot of the titlepage adds: 'Just published Terrys allegorical hair devices containing 200 elegant subjects'].

THACKERAY 1864: W. M. Thackeray: *The Newcomes.*

THACKERAY 1869: W. M. Thackeray: *The Book of Snobs.*

THIRSK & COOPER 1972: J. Thirsk and S. P. Cooper:

Seventeenth-century Economic Documents.

THOMPSON 1940: G. S. Thompson: *The Russells in Bloomsbury, 1669–1771*.

THOMSON 1815: T. Thomson (ed.): *A Collection of Inventories and Other Records of the Royal Wardrobe and Jewelhouse . . . m.cccc.lxxxviii. – m.dc.vi.*

THOMSON 1847: K. M. Thomson: *Memoirs of Viscountess [sic, recte Baroness] Sundon, Mistress of the Robes to Queen Caroline, Consort of George II*, 2 vols.

THORDEMAN 1939: B. Thordeman *et al.*: *Armour from the battle of Wisby 1361*, 2 vols [Kungl. Vitterhets Historie och Antikuitate Akademien].

TROLLOPE 1883: E. Trollope, Bishop of Nottingham: 'King Henry VIII's jewel book', *Associated Architectural Societies Reports*, 17 (1883), 155–229.

TWINING 1960: [E.F.] Lord Twining: *A History of the Crown Jewels of Europe*.

TWINING 1967: [E. F.] Lord Twining: *European Regalia*.

UREŠOVÁ 1980: L. Urešová: 'Stříbrný poklad z Vrcholného Středověku', *Sborník Statína počest 60, výročí narození Ph Dr Dagmar Hejdové, CSS; Acta UPM* [Umĕleckopru°myslové Muzeum] *XCV: Comentationes 2*, pp. 10–29 [on a 14th century hoard].

V & A: Victoria and Albert Museum, Library: MS. L30–1982; GL 10, Garrard's ledgers; Wickes's accounts.

VALERIANO BOLZANO 1614: G. P. Valeriano Bolzano: *J. P. Valeriani Bellunensis hieroglyphicam sive de sacris Aegyptiorum aliarumque gentium literis commentariorum libri LVIII*, 3 parts.

VAUGHAN 1675: R. Vaughan: *A Discourse of Coin . . . as also Tables of the Value of . . . Pearls, Diamonds, Gold, Silver, &c.*

VERNEY 1925: F. P. Verney: *Memoirs of the Verney Family during the Seventeenth Century*, 2 vols.

VERTUE 1930–55: G. Vertue: Vertue Notebooks I – VI, *Walpole Society*, 18, 20, 22, 24, 26, 29, and 30.

VICTORIA 1844: Victoria, Queen of Great Britain: *Statement on behalf of Her Majesty in Answer to the Claims made on behalf of His Majesty the King of Hanover to Certain Jewels*.

VICTORIA 1912: [R. A. Brett] Viscount Esher (ed.): *The girlhood of Queen Victoria. A Selection from Her Majesty's Diaries between the Years 1832 and 1842*.

VISIO 1869: *Visio monachi de Eynsham* [written by Adam, chaplain of St Hugh of Lincoln]; *The Revelation of the Monk of Evesham, 1196* [E. Arber (ed.): English Reprints, 18].

WALPOLE 1818: H. Walpole afterwards Lord Orford: Lord Orford's Reminiscences.

WALPOLE 1937–83: H. Walpole (ed. W. E. Lewis): *The Yale Edition of Horace Walpole's Correspondence*, 48 vols.

WARD 1981: A. Ward, J. Cherry, C. Gere and B. Cartlidge: *The Ring*.

WARD-JACKSON 1967: P. Ward-Jackson: 'Some mainstreams and tributaries in European ornament 1500–1750: Part 2'. *Victoria & Albert Bulletin*, 3 (1967), 90–104.

WASHINGTON 1962–3: Smithsonian Institution (ed. A. E. Popham and F. Stampfle): *Old Master Drawings from Chatsworth*.

WASHINGTON 1985: National Gallery of Art (ed. G. Jackson-Stops): *The Treasure Houses of Britain, Five Hundred Years of Private Patronage and Art Collecting*.

WEBER 1914: F. G. Weber: *Aspects of Death in Art and Epigram*.

WEDEL 1895: L. von Wedel (tr. G. von Bülow): 'Journey through England and Scotland 1584 and 1585', *Transactions of the Royal Historical Society*, n.s. 9 (1895), 233–70.

WEDGWOOD 1906: J. Wedgwood (ed. K. E. Farrer): *Correspondence of Josiah Wedgwood 1781–1794*.

WEINSTEIN 1989: R. Weinstein: 'An early seventeenth-century head-dress fragment – a further remarkable chance find from the Thames foreshore', *Ant. J.*, 69 (1989), 323–4.

WELBECK ABBEY 1897: [G R. & H. W. Harding]: *Catalogue of the Ornamental Furniture, Works of Art and Porcelain at Welbeck Abbey*.

WELLINGTON 1953: [G. Wellesley] Duke of Wellington: 'The scaffold George of Charles I', *Ant. J.*, 33 (1953), 159–68.

WENHAM 1936: E. Wenham: 'Snuff-boxes by English goldsmiths', *Conn.*, 97 (1936), 72–5.

WESTMINSTER PUBLIC LIBRARY, ARCHIVES DEPT: original wills, formerly in the Phillips Collection.

WEST SUSSEX RO: BA 74, PHA 6613, 8046, 8049; IC 500/3/4 and 7/31(57).

WHARTON 1691: H. Wharton (ed.): *Anglia sacra*, 2 vols.

WHARTON 1844: House of Lords, Committee of Privileges: *Minutes of Evidence . . . Petition of Charles Kemeys Kemeys Tynte . . . to be Baron Wharton*.

WHEATLEY 1964: W. Wheatley: 'Isaac le Gooch the king's jeweller and Latymer benefactor', *Hammersmith Local History Group*.

WHITE 1935: B. M. I. White: *Mary Tudor*.

WHITE 1950: G. White (ed. W. S. Scott): *The Antiquities of Selborne*.

WHITELOCKE 1855: B. Whitelocke (ed. H. Reeve): *A Journal of the Swedish Embassy in the Years 1653 and 1654*, 2 vols.

WHITNEY 1586: G. Whitney: *A Choice of Emblemes*.

WICKES'S ACCOUNTS: *see under* V & A.

WILLIAMS 1979: J. H. Williams: *St Peter's Street Northampton. Excavations 1973–1976*.

WILLIAMSON 1933: G. C. Williamson: *Memoirs in Miniature. A Volume of Random Reminiscences*.

WILSON 1956: D. H. Wilson: *King James VI and I*.

WILSON 1983: C. C. Wilson: *Renaissance Small Bronze Sculpture and Associated Decorative Arts at the National Gallery of Art* [Washington DC].

WILSON 1986: J. Wilson: 'The Harefield entertainment and the cult of Elizabeth I', *Ant. J.*, 66 (1986), 315–28.

WITHER 1635: G. Wither: *A Collection of Emblems*.

WOTTON 1741: T. Wotton: *The Baronetage*, 4 vols.

WRIGHT 1844: T. Wright: 'On antiquarian excavations and researches in the Middle Ages', *Arch.*, 30 (1844), 438–57.

WRIGHT 1859: T. Wright (ed.): *Political Poems and Songs Relating to English History*, 2 vols [Rolls series 14].

WRIGHT 1909: W. A. Wright (ed).: *Femina. Printed from a MS in the library of Trinity College, Cambridge* [Roxburghe Club, 154].

WRIGHT 1982: J. M. Wright: *The King's Painter: Catalogue of an Exhibition*, SNPG.

WYNDHAM 1955: M. M. Wyndham, Lady Leconfield, and J. Gore: *Three Howard Sisters. Selection from the Writings of Lady Caroline Lascelles, Lady Dover and Countess Gower, 1825–1833*.

WYNN 1864: F. W. Wynn (ed. A. Hayward): *Diaries of a Lady of Quality from 1797 to 1844*.

WYNN 1920: C. W. Wynn (ed. R. A. Leighton): *Correspondence of Charlotte Grenville, Lady Williams Wynn*.

WYNN 1926: *Calendar of Wynn (of Gwydir) Papers 1515–1690*, National Library of Wales.

YAS, RS: Yorkshire Archaeological Society, Records Series.

YOGEV 1978: G. Yogev: *Diamonds and Coral: Anglo-Dutch Jews and Eighteenth Century Trade*.

Index

The colour plates are in Roman and the monochrome in italic Arabic numerals